Lehrerrolle

SCHREIBER, MAGISTER, LEHRER

SCHRIFTENREIHE ZUM BAYERISCHEN SCHULMUSEUM
ICHENHAUSEN
Zweigmuseum des Bayerischen Nationalmuseums
Herausgegeben vom
Bayerischen Nationalmuseum

Band 8

Dieser Band enthält die Vorträge des Symposions, das die Erziehungswissenschaftliche Fakultät der Universität Erlangen-Nürnberg und das Bayerische Nationalmuseum München in Ichenhausen vom 1. bis 4. Oktober 1987 unter Leitung von Herrn Prof. Dr. Max Liedtke durchführten.

SCHREIBER, MAGISTER, LEHRER

Zur Geschichte und Funktion
eines Berufsstandes

Herausgegeben von
Johann Georg Prinz von Hohenzollern
und
Max Liedtke

KLINKHARDT

1989

VERLAG JULIUS KLINKHARDT · BAD HEILBRUNN/OBB.

CIP-Titelaufnahme der Deutschen Bibliothek

Schreiber, Magister, Lehrer : zur Geschichte und Funktion eines Berufsstandes ; [Vorträge des Symposiums, das die Erziehungswissenschaftliche Fakultät der Universität Erlangen-Nürnberg und das Bayerische Nationalmuseum München in Ichenhausen vom 1. bis 4. Oktober 1987 unter Leitung von Max Liedtke durchführten] / hrsg. von Johann Georg Prinz von Hohenzollern u. Max Liedtke. – Bad Heilbrunn/Obb. : Klinkhardt, 1989
(Schriftenreihe zum Bayerischen Schulmuseum Ichenhausen, Zweigmuseum des Bayerischen Nationalmuseums ; Bd. 8)
ISBN 3–7815–0620–7
NE: Hohenzollern, Johann Georg Prinz von [Hrsg.]; Universität <Erlangen; Nürnberg> / Erziehungswissenschaftliche Fakultät

<Nürnberg>; Bayerisches Schulmuseum <Ichenhausen>: Schriftenreihe zum Bayerischen ...

Redaktion: Dr. Hans-Uwe Rump

Das Bayerische Schulmuseum Ichenhausen wird gefördert von den bayerischen Sparkassen.

Gesamtherstellung: Graphischer Großbetrieb Friedrich Pustet, Regensburg
Printed in Germany 1989
ISBN 3-7815-0620-7

Inhalt

VI. *Der internationale Vergleich*

VII. *Gegenwart und Zukunft der Lehrerbildung*

Vorwort

Die Geschichte des Lehrerstandes ist außerordentlich wechselvoll. Sie hat extreme Höhen und extreme Tiefen.

Diese Geschichte begann vor etwa 5000 Jahren in Mesopotamien und Ägypten, als mit Erfindung der Schrift der Schreib- und Leseunterricht der Kinder institutionalisiert wurde. Die Institutionalisierung bestand darin, daß bestimmte Personen, die schriftkundig waren, beauftragt wurden, die Kinder in dieser neuen Kulturtechnik zu unterweisen. In den frühen Hochkulturen zählten die Lehrer zu den ranghöchsten Beamten, denn sie verfügten über die neueste wissenschaftliche Errungenschaft, nämlich das gesprochene Wort schriftlich zu fixieren und es nach Bedarf wieder lebendig werden zu lassen. Sie konnten sich so allen Wissens bemächtigen, sofern es nur aufgezeichnet war.

Als in der griechischen Antike Lesen und Schreiben längst zu verbreiteten und nahezu selbstverständlich beherrschten Kulturtechniken geworden waren, war der Elementarunterricht vielfach bereits Aufgabe der Sklaven. Mindestens der Elementarlehrer hatte seinen hohen gesellschaftlichen Rang völlig verloren.

Das änderte sich erneut im christlichen Mittelalter, als der Lehrer, der nunmehr fast ausschließlich angehende Geistliche zu unterrichten hatte, als Nachfolger des Christus magister, des göttlichen Lehrmeisters, angesehen wurde. Die Schrift, die gelehrt wurde, galt als das irdische Instrument, mit dem die göttliche Offenbarung in der Heiligen Schrift faßbar gemacht worden war.

Als die Schule aber in nachreformatorischer Zeit nicht mehr vornehmlich den zukünftigen Klerikern vorbehalten blieb, sondern sich stärker auch dem Laien öffnete, verlor der Elementarlehrer im Gegensatz zu den Lehrern der höheren Schulen wie auch im Gegensatz zu den städtischen Schreib- und Rechenmeistern erneut an gesellschaftlichem Ansehen. Die folgenden Jahrhunderte waren bis weit ins 19. Jahrhundert hinein die Zeit des armen Dorfschulmeisterleins. Es gab in diesen Jahrhunderten kaum einen Lehrer, der finanziell nicht darauf angewiesen war, seine Schultätigkeit durch Nebentätigkeiten als Bauer, Schreiber, Meßner, Organist, Leichen- oder Hochzeitsbitter usw. zu ergänzen. Oft war das Unterrichten die Nebentätigkeit. Gerade die »sitzenden« Berufe wie Schuster und Schneider findet man häufiger mit dem Amt des Lehrers verbunden.

Ein neuer Abschnitt der Geschichte des Lehrerstandes begann mit der Einführung der Schul- (genauer: Unterrichts-) pflicht. Nach mehrfachen Proklamationen hatte Preußen 1796 die Schule zu einer Staatsangelegenheit erklärt und die Schulpflicht durchgesetzt. Bayern folgte 1802. Die Schulpflicht, formuliert aus aufklärerisch-pädagogischem Impetus wie aber auch in Kenntnis der wirtschaftlichen und machtpolitischen Bedeutung der Schule, veränderte auch Stellung und Selbstbewußtsein der Lehrer. Es wurden wesentlich mehr Lehrer benötigt, ihre Ausbildung wurde vereinheitlicht und verbindlich geregelt, ihre unterrichtlichen Aufgaben und ihre gesellschaftlichen Funktionen neu überdacht.

Das 6. Schulgeschichtliche Symposion am Bayerischen Schulmuseum Ichenhausen (01.–04. 10. 1987) hat sich unter dem Titel »Schreiber, Magister, Lehrer« nicht nur darum bemüht, die Tiefen und Höhen der Geschichte des Lehrerstandes nachzuzeichnen. Es ging, wie bei allen bisherigen Ichenhausener Symposien, zugleich um systematische Fragen. In der historischen Analyse war immer auch zu fragen, was bewirkt der Lehrer, welche anthropologische und gesellschaftliche Funktion hat er, was macht seine Qualifikation aus, wie müßte er ausgebildet sein. Die Ergebnisse dieses 6. Ichenhausener Symposions, das wiederum von einer durch Michael Schneider, Schulmuseum der Universität Erlangen-Nürnberg, gestalteten Sonderausstellung begleitet war, werden in diesem Band vorgelegt.

Der Deutschen Forschungsgemeinschaft, dem Bayerischen Nationalmuseum, der Universität Erlangen-Nürnberg, dem Landkreis Günzburg und der Stadt Ichenhausen gebührt Dank, daß sie es durch ideelle und finanzielle Unterstützung ermöglicht haben, das Symposion durchzuführen bzw. die Ergebnisse des Symposions in dieser Form zu veröffentlichen.

Für die freundliche Hilfe bei der redaktionellen Überarbeitung der deutschen und englischen Texte danken wir Frau Birgit Albersdörfer, Frau Barbara Brehm, Frau Ute Riedl, Frau Mary Waegner, Herrn Dr. Uwe Krebs und Herrn Gerd Müller.

Johann Georg Prinz von Hohenzollern — Max Liedtke

J. G. Prinz von Hohenzollern/Max Liedtke
Writers, masters, teachers –
About the history and function of a profession

Contents and Summaries

I. Anthropological requirements

II. Middle Eastern advanced civilizations

III. The classic antiquity

IV. The christian teacher of the Middle Ages and of the modern era

V. The teacher of the lower and higher schoolsystem in the Germany of the 18th to the 20th Century

VI. An international comparison

VII. Present and future of teachertraining

I. Anthropological requirements

O. Koenig

The anthropological Function of Teaching

The contribution deals with phylogenetical, ecological, ethological and comparative aspects of the ability to learn and to teach:
Animals do not learn only by own experience but also in several species by imitation of high-ranking individuals. This imitation learning was seen as a first step to learning by instruction or teaching, which became dominant form in men. Based on the ability of handing down experiences, which was forced by culturally generated fixing techniques (e.g. the alphabeth und printing), human knowledge cumulated in a lot of cultures. In industrial societies this degree of cumulated knowledge grew faster and faster as an indirectly effect of the establishing of educational institutions (e.g. school and university) too.
Today the – in the beginning ecologically caused – learning and teaching abilities of men do no longer serve as survive techniques but as lethal factors; nevertheless the correction of the industrial society to an environment-compatible one is only thinkable with intensive teaching and learning too.

II. Middle Eastern advanced civilizations

Hartmut Waetzoldt

The writer as a teacher in Mesopotamia

Since the invention of the cuneiform script around 3000 B. C. scribes themselves trained their successors – usually their own sons. However, they could also take on other children for instruction. It was only at the end of the third millennium, and at the instigation of the kings, that there developed schools. The teachers active in these schools – as far as is known – required no more specialized training than their colleagues in the private sphere.
The heads of the schools were expected to have competence in the whole knowledge of that time, as well as in Sumerian literature and in music. Their activities also included the composition of Sumerian songs and inscriptions in the honour of kings.
The subject matter used in instruction was extremely varied in nature and arranged according to particular educational objectives. At any rate, it is not possible to reconstruct a full curriculum for either elementary instruction or more advanced studies.
In spite of the considerable prestige enjoyed by scribes and teachers, their pay was by no means excessive.

Gunther Wanke

The teacher of the old Israel

Evidences from the Old Testament, Palestinan Inscriptions, and the comparison of Egyptian and Mesopotamian schools with the Palestinian situation in pre-exilic time during the reign of the Judaean and Israelite kings do not permit the supposition there were schools in ancient Israel. The texts points to the existence of literate persons, but it remains unclear, where literacy was acquired.

Hans-Werner Fischer-Elfert

The writer as a teacher in the early Egyptian advanced civilization

Ancient Egyptian Scribes enjoyed the privilege of belonging to the highest couche sociale which by virtue of its literacy represented the leading class of the society. Scribal training began at the age of five and lasted for some four years. After reaching competence in reading and writing, the apprentices received further education by already experienced and distinguished officials, to whom they were entrusted individually. The profession of scribe was regarded superior to all other occupations, especially to craftsmanship. Competition in school as well as after having taken over a position in the bureaucracy seems to have been extensive, being fostered by the teachers incessantly. The main intention of the so-called "Satirical Letter", a much copied schooltext of the Ramesside period (13.–11. century B. C.), is to put forward general critics as to the degree of knowledge a contemporary scribe was expected to possess. Another point of discussion in this letter is the right way of how to teach such subjects as mathematics, geography and literature in schools.

III. The classic antiquity

Egert Pöhlmann

The writer as a teacher in the classical period of Greece

In his "Histoire de l'éducation dans l'antiquité" (1957) H. I. Marrou has coined a formula for the ancient education, which he considered to represent the "transition from a culture of Knights to a culture of scribes" (p. 5). But trying the chronological setting of this transition he brought forward only guesswork (p. 70).

Greek literature (except Comedy) is not very interested in daily life. Therefore the testimony of literature concerning reading, writing and teaching of both in the 5th century B. C. is far from being repraesentative. However we can see, that the art of alphabetic writing, which Greece had acquired in the early 8th century B. C., was wide spread in the second half of the 5th century B. C.

On the other side, Greek Vase Painting from the beginnings of the read figured style is open to scenes of daily life. F. A. Beck's "Album of Greek Education" (1975) now facilitates an overall view over the vast material. We find the first illustrations of boys learning to read and write in the second half of the 6th century B. C. In the early 5th century follow testimonies for girls reading or going to school. Teaching of writing in school-houses by professional teachers is attested for 496 B. C.; it seems to be a necessity for the late 6th century too.

Gerhard Wirth

Teacher, Church and Emperor – about the literary picture at the end of the antiquity

Teachers, professors and education can only be understood if seen from their historical and social environment. In the Roman empire school and a certain curriculum were a necessity not only in the respect of romanization, but of pure survival when the imminent catastrophe became inevitable. And we know very well, how Romans did everything possible to save institutions and people although public possibilities seem more and more overstressed this time. There is a strong preference of the artes liberales as the most effective way to a common form of education and to an available surplus of trained hands for the various ranks of higher administrazion and public service: New ways of special training and education, promoted to the same level, may therefore be seen as a first step of dissolution. Not to be overseen is an always existing clientela between teacher and pupil, in later antiquity not only used as a surrogate für modern ways of qualification, but now more than before as a form of mutual support for both and during their whole life. Christian education has its special forms according to the aims of christian ethics, and also the functions of people, whose concern it is, to teach the forms of christian life and thinking, can hardly be compared with teachers in any period of ancient society. The emperor had to yield to this demands. But until Justinian he tries to do his best not to subdue the rest of this higher education, and he obviously even refrains from fighting too severe against the paganism of philosophic schooles and their most important representatives.

Alfons Rösger

Teacher and Teacher-Instruction in the Roman Empire

In early Rome, children were educated within families, by their mothers until their 7th year of age, henceforward by their fathers. To them were due education and instruction of sons especially, they were originally regarded as proper instructors. In the conquest of the Hellenic world Rome was confronted with the Greek style of education, practised outside of the family by professional teachers. As the result of an evolutionary process this system was adopted by the Romans. In the beginning, Greeks were employed as private teachers within Roman families, but soon ran schools of their own. This antagonism of the Greek (public) and the early Roman (private) styles of education was a major item in the discussion on ideal education until early principate. In this controversy of principles, *Quintilianus* (ca. 35–100), the most important Roman writer on education, took a position of compromise. On the one hand, he pleaded for school-instruction in the Greek way, on the other he regarded as indispensable a personal style of education by teachers as was practised in early times by the *pater familias*.

IV. The christian teacher of the Middle Ages and the modern era

Hans-Uwe Rump

Schoolmaster and scholar: the new prestige of the teacher in Christian times

On the grounds of primary sources, the teacher in the Middle Ages can only be seen in connection with the history of schools and culture in Christian western civilisation at that time. Above all, it is the monastic school, cathedral school, convent school and parish school which today can no longer simply be seen as a continuous development of schools from ancient to modern times. On the other hand, the ancient traditions of the school in the Middle Ages should not be overlooked. The training, function and personality of the teacher in the Middle Ages stand at the centre between two poles: between the continuity of ancient thinking and the new Christian orientation.

The latter consisted mainly of the idea that knowledge and education were no longer to be acquired primarily in order to survive on earth, but mainly in order to prepare oneself during this life for eternal salvation after death. From this there resulted a tension between the two poles, between mastering one's existence on earth and striving for eternal salvation. The school of Christianity becomes a school of exegesis, the teacher becomes an interpreter of the Holy Scripture, of handed-down knowledge, and of the practical mastery of one's life.

The foundation-stone for the development of the medieval school was laid at the end of the 8th century, when the Church and also the Franconian King pressed for the improvement of the education of priests in monastic schools, cathedral schools and convents; soon after that, however, there was a demand for proper parish schools for the pious laymen. Right up to their gradual decline at a later date, the monastic schools were first of all considered to be models. It was their teachers, who were priests as a rule, but here and there also private teachers, who for the first time in the history of education tried to understand and to form the individual as a unit in his entire being.

From the 9th and 10th centuries onwards, the cathedral schools and convents were to steal a march on the monastic schools. The bishop appointed a scholar as their headmaster, who was usually a member of the cathedral chapter. The headmaster then looked for a suitable master who was responsible for the actual teaching and education of the pupils. According to the number of pupils, he was allowed to employ one or several assistants. Generally he also had a choirmaster to help him as a singing teacher. Renowned cathedral schools in the 11th and 12th centuries with recognized and in some cases famous masters are, among others, Lüttich, Bamberg, Würzburg, Magdeburg, Hildesheim, Freising, Bremen and Salzburg. While the main emphasis of their teaching within the seven free arts was placed on grammar at first, it shifted in the period of scholasticism to dialectics.

As the towns in Germany in the Middle Ages grew in importance, they very soon competed with the Church for the monopoly of the schools. From the 13th century onwards, more and more town schools and council schools for well-to-do citizens came into being. At the same time, primary schools, the German schools, in contrast to the Latin schools, came into existence, as well as masters for writing and arithmetic, organised in guilds. The German schoolmaster was no longer in the service of the Church, but was under the protection of the town. In the late Middle Ages he began to compete with the Latin schoolmaster by trying with all possible means to entice the pupils away from him. In so doing, it often happened that a certain amount of encroaching and blending in the teaching matter occurred.

As a result of such a development, teachers were divided up into two groups right up to the beginning of modern times: the Latin school teachers with a humanist, academic education, and the German schoolmasters, whose work was looked upon as a trade, and to start with was even carried out as an extra job. This distinction has continued to have an effect right up to the present, as can be seen from the varying assessments of teaching positions in different types of schools.

Rudolf Endres

Training and social position of the writing and adding masters in the Franconian free cities

In the capital cities of Franconia it is proved that there existed since the early 14th century besides the Latin- und Theological schools also "teutsche" teachers for writing and mathematic, who instructed boys and girls in reading, writing, counting and later also in book-keeping for which they were paid privately.

In Nuremberg there lived finally in 16th century 75 teachers for writing and counting, which was an extremely high number. The council of the city issued school regulations for them to give an exact controll about training the teachers of writing and mathematics. After 6 years of education an examination for teaching had to be done, however the candidate had mostly to wait some more time until there was an open position for him at school.

Most of the teachers descended from generations of craftsman and later on this developped to "Dynasties of schoolmasters". The schoolmaster was seen as a craftsman in the social hierarchy of the capital city. Some of the outstanding modists and masters of mathematic however reached a high level of prestige and were therefore upgraded to the "Genannten-Stand". But most of them had to struggle hard for their existance and were suffering of great poverty.

Alfred Fickel

The Status of the Teacher at Municipal Schools from the Early Beginnings up to the 19th Century, shown by the example of the Mühldorf School Situation

As from the 11th and 12th century it was the clergy who took care of their parishioners' education and their endeavours and influence increased in the 13th century, which was due to Pope Gregory IX's decree dating from the year 1234.
In the city of Mühldorf there was a schoolmaster mentioned for the first time in the year 1294. Around 1400 the school of Mühldorf consisted of a Latin grammar school, run by the town's clergy and a non Latin institution of learning in the care of the Mühldorf community. In 1480 the city built a schoolhouse of their own. Since that time the sources have discerned between teachers of Latin and German schoolmasters.
While up to Luther's reformation of the Catholic church Mühldorf's schoolmasters had been men of education and political experience, who on their city's behalf would negotiate with the then Holy Roman Empire of German Nationality's emperor and the bishops of the curia schoolmasters working during the period from Luther's reformation up to the Thirty-Year's-War were men who had received their qualification by serving as clerks of the magistrate, as supernumeraries at schools and organists and choir leaders in the service of a parish church. At that time scholars who had received their education at a university would often be given a living at a Latin school.
The decline of the teachers' status and standard of living commenced during the Thirty-Years'-War. The mommon man's craving for a learned erudition decreased rapidly during the 17th and 18th century. Now teachers had to restrict their activities to the mere tradition of a basic knowledge in the three "r"s (reading, writing and reckoning), plus some knowledge in ethics and theology and they ruled out when it came to filling a more sophisticated and better paid job in the government.
More and more schoolmasters were led by the tight strings of severe regulations laid on them by the state, the cities, and the country's church potentates.
At the beginning of the 19th century both the church and the government saw their aim in turning ordinary scholars and pupils into teachers and students both of whom had been brought up in the spirit of true subordination. At the same time they claimed that the end of illiteracy had begun in their age; and false idolaters of culture, pedagogy, and pseudo-masters of the didactic science controlled the scene and overstocked the market with trivial and irrelevant literature referring to the subject.

V. The teacher of the lower and higher schoolsystem in the Germany of the 18th to the 20th century

Rudolf Keck

The development of teachertraining in Germany in the 18th and 19th centuries

On the one hand this contribution provides a survey of the development of Teacher Education in Germany from a social history viewpoint and, on the other, of the history of professionalisation in the teaching profession.
Teacher Education in Germany should basically be considered as a dichotomous development:

1. In the case of Secondary School teachers (11–18 yrs) qualification was by way of *specialist university training*. This had a philological and academic subject base and lacked the training of the independent vocational science of pedagogy. Only when the practical vocational training period (Referendariat) was tacked on to the end of the initial university education period, did pedagogy enter the lists as a necessary vocational discipline. However, it must be noted that, until well into the 1970s, the latter led a wallflower existence being heavily practice-oriented (concentration on methods), so the term *quasi-professionalisation* best summarises the whole development.
2. In the case of Lower School teachers (6–16 yrs) the model of the *all subjects teacher* already existed at the end of the 18th century in the framework of that specially created institute, the "Lehrerseminar". It wasn't until 1872 (General Regulations in Prussia) that this seminar type of training found its final six-year form. The preparatory ('Präparanden') institution had been compulsorily added to the former and the seminar training had taken on a clear profile in the direction of the vocational science of pedagogy, including educational psychology. From the point of view that there was a lack of academic qualification for specialist subject teaching we may, however, speak of a *semi-professionalisation*. The academic accentuation of the seminar-type of training in the guise of the "Pädagogische Akademie" (1925–1936) and the "Pädagogische Hochschule" (1949 till approx. 1975) came to fruition in the *institutional integration* of the latter *into the universities*. This integration was the expression of a full professionalisation.

Thus both specialist subject academic training and educational training for both levels of teacher education were installed at the universities.
This contribution will attempt to make clear the beginning of both directions of development in their *different phases*.

Franz Hauzenberger

Kaspar Buchner – A Lower-Bavarian teacher in the 19th century

Kaspar Buchner (1804–1875) taught at elementary schools in Lower Bavaria for exactly 50 years. He spent 40 years of his professional life solely in the little parish village of Thurmansbang, in the lower part of the "Bavarian Forest", where he worked at different times as a probationary teacher, then as a fully-qualified schoolteacher, as organist, choir-master, parish clerk, tithe collector (when he collected payment in kind from the local farmers for ringing the church-bells) and grocer. Over and above teaching the general subjects on the school curriculum, Buchner attached great importance to educating the young pupils placed in his charge in the arts (music, drawing, women's handwork).

Kaspar Buchner had achieved excellent results with his pupils on the occasion of the annual school inspections. The government of Lower Bavaria paid tribute to Buchner's achievements both in the form of written praise, and by appointing him at various times as a teacher-training instructor, responsible for educating and preparing student-teachers for their examinations. Buchner's immediate superiors unfailingly awarded him good or very good marks for his efforts and successes, both in and out of school.

Gerhard Silberer

Position and training of the elementary school teachers in Baden during the 18th and 19th centuries

Within the area of the later grandduchy of Baden, primary school teachers were first trained in a kind of pedagogic apprenticeship, similar to the training in all German-speaking countries. Towards the end of the 18th century school regulations used to regulate details about qualifications and employment. In 1768 a schooltraining college was founded in Karlsruhe, which did not impart basic training, however, but additional qualifications. A similar scheme applies to the normal school in Freiburg i. Br., founded in 1773. Basic teacher training has been taught at the Catholic training college in Rastatt since 1809, at first still dependent on lyceums, and at the reestablished Protestant teachers' training college in Karlsruhe. Up to the beginning of the 19th century, new training colleges were founded whenever needed, and they are legally and organizationally secured by pre-training colleges and decisions on the school curriculum. Education for female teachers has been imparted at the public training college for female teachers, the "Prinzessin-Willhelm-Stift" since 1878, and also increasingly in the tutorial classes of certain selected grammar school for girls.

The pedagogic philosophy in the training colleges corresponds to the usual conceptions of the respective eras. Independent theories can be found with W. A. Lay, who works at the training college II in Karlsruhe and is one of the founders of an empiric theory of education.

Hubert Buchinger

The education of teachers of secondary schools in Bavaria from its beginning to the end of the 19th century

The history of education of secondary schools' teachers is as varied as the history of secondary schools itself. In the beginnings of Bavarian secondary schools (end of the 18th century) they didn't pay much attention on the education of teachers for secondary schools. The teachers at the secondary schools first were drawn from the circle of the grammar school teachers or under Heinrich Braun also from the circle of the best pupils who had completed the secondary school. Georg Friedrich Baron of Zentner's (1752–1835) suggestion of creating an own training system for the futural "teachers for citizens" (teachers of secondary schools) was rejected. Though the Bavarian examregulations of 1809 also initiated a scientifically based, specific education for teachers of secondary schools. From 1818 on this door to the examregulations too was open for specially qualified teachers of elementary schools. With the change of the secondary schools into trade schools in 1833 finally a regulated course of studies for teachers was introduced as well. The examregulations of 1873 strengthened this tendency and 1873 can be counted among the central historical dates of the development of the secondary school teachers' status.

Albert Reble
Education for elementary school teachers in the Weimar period

After pointing out the specific difficulties of the subject (the time-limited development of the new primary school teacher education and the multitude of institutions), the first paragraph shows basic and background information categorized into five points: the postulate of the constitution of the German Reich, the primary school teacher movement, the reformatory theory of education, the development of science and the needs of the democratic fundamental order. The second paragraph deals with the multitude of institutions relating to teacher training in the Weimar epoch, using the federal states of the Reich as examples. Finally, the third paragraph compares the two main types ("University-solution" and "College of Education-solution") with each other, relating to some of the various duties of the former elementary teacher education.

Hans-Jürgen Apel
The training for grammar school teachers in the 19th century – A comparison of Bavaria and Prussia

There is a need for studies of German school history which trace and compare developments in different states. Such a method can be expected to afford deeper insights into the formation and evolution of the educational systems, to place one-sided accounts of them in a wider perspective and to provide a sounder basis for assessing actual developments. The present contribution attempts to identify congruencies, similarities and differences in the development process.
If one compares the founding and further evolution of institutionalized grammar-school teacher training in the two great 19th-century German states, Bavaria and Prussia, one can discern paralleis and similarities as well as differences. In both of these states, the professionalization of grammar-school teaching was initiated in the

early 19th century through the introduction of a compulsory examination within the context of an overall educational reform, albeit in different political situations. In the further course of development, too, some problems can be seen to have been solved in similar ways, cases in point being the introduction of the probationary year and, later on, the setting up of trainee seminars. On the other hand, distinct differences are noticeable in the effects of oversupply and scarcity crises: they made themselves felt at different times in the two states.

Heinrich Kanz

Politicization of teachertraining during the NS-regime

In this essay the question is asked, if between 1933 and 1945 there is to be shown a so far unknown image of teachers and a corresponding teacher training. The following aspects are discussed:

1. The terms of "politics, political, talk politics" are to be seen in an historical context. The historical interpretation of political power, force an terror of states has to consider this context.
2. It is asked considering the political conditions, by some well-known german scientists of history called "the thesis of singularity" if today the namely facts could happen again.
3. The historical development of teachers from the ancient "writer" to the "magister" and betely the teacher has to be completed with "political leader" (political soldier), in so far history is not yet finished.

The fashion of teacher is, under the time of Naziregime, getting known by a further aspect which is singular in history. (Hildegard Macha)

VI. An international comparison

Jürgen Zwernemann

Teachers in traditional West African Societies

In some West African secret societies certain functionaries may be considered as teachers. The Poro Society of the Mano in Liberia and three societies (N'domo, Komo, Kore) of the Bambara in Mali are quoted as examples. In the N'domo, the society of uncircumcised boys, children get their knowledge from children. The other societies have special teachers, but old men as well impart their knowledge to novices. The teachers of the Poro receive a special education. In the Komo elders and high ranking officials are teachers, but able young men get an additional training to serve as teachers. Members of the 5th initiation degree of the Kore teach the novices although they have not the last knowledge reserved to the members of the 8th degree. In Liberia and Mali teachers and elders consider the individual abilities of novices and young initiates for their education.

Tomiji Nagao
The development of teachertraining in Japan in the 19th and 20th centuries

The history of teacher education in Japan began in the early years of Meiji-era, under the strong influence from the U.S.A., where the Pestalozzianism was at the best days. But at the middle years of Meiji-era the life and discipline in the normal schools became militarized and suppressive. These tendencies became at the end of Meiji-era to some extent milder and more liberal. Since the beginning of Shouwa-era some of the liberal educators insisted on eagerly teacher education in college or university. During the war (1943) they have realized the wish. And after the Second World War they have acquired even the Open-system of teacher licence. There are many advantages in this system, but there are some defects too. Man points out, for instance, the quality of teachers has dropped evidently, in spite of the increase of candidates. Needless to say there are antagonistic arguments. But the Ministry of Education has begun reexamination of this Open-system.

VII. Present and future of teachertraining

Max Liedtke
Timeindependent and timedependent qualifications of a teacher

There are a canon of attitudes and personality-characteristics which are basic qualification-characteristics of a teacher, independent on the historical situation. These are so-called general human characteristics, but which are – as contactability, patience, humor, and the preparedness to offer oneself to the health of the following generation – in their specific appearance basic qualification-characteristics of a teacher.
Among the timedependent qualifications count independent on science-cumulatives changing topics and methodical knowledge to develope these topics in their cognitive, emotional, and ethic aspects appropriately. It corresponds to relevant compulsions even as to historical demands of teachers' associations that prospective teachers can only get topical and methodical knowledge, which is qualifying, at institutions like universities. At the same time it shows that under this way of teachertraining the conveying of appropriate professional ethics of teachers in the sense of the timeindependent qualifications neither has to suffer nor provably has suffered.

I. ANTHROPOLOGISCHE VORAUSSETZUNGEN

Otto Koenig

Die anthropologische Funktion des Lehrens

Die Lernfähigkeit der einzelnen Individuen bildet die plastische Wachstumsspitze der Phylogenie. Ohne Lernen gibt es keine biologische Entwicklung, keine Differenzierung. Lernen setzt Empfindungsfähigkeit und Bewußtsein voraus. Es zählt zu jenen entscheidenden Faktoren, die Leben überhaupt möglich machen. Alle Tiere können lernen, dies allerdings nur im Leistungsbereich ihrer Sinnesorgane und im Rahmen ihrer existenznotwendigen ökologisch adaptierten Fähigkeiten. Ein jagendes Tier lernt andere Dinge als ein äsendes, eines aus strukturiertem Gelände weicht auffassungsmäßig völlig ab von Bewohnern freier offener Steppenlandschaften. Lernen ist eine ökologisch notwendige Anpassungsmöglichkeit, es nützt die Erfahrungen aus Gegenwart und Vergangenheit für die Zukunft. Dementsprechend müßte die gesamte biologische Entwicklungs- und Wandlungsgeschichte ein Prozeß der genetischen Weitervermittlung von Lernerfahrung sein. Da sich die gesamte Phylogenie nur auf Individuen aufbaut, die im Lebensbereich das einzige konkret Vorhandene sowie Lern- und Anpassungsfähige darstellen, kann die unabdingbare Beziehung zwischen Individuum und Stammesgeschichte nur über die bewußte oder unbewußte Erfahrung des Einzelwesens führen. Die Individuen sind die einzigen Umweltsensoren der durch Werden und Vergehen charakterisierten Entwicklung (*Koenig* 1987).

Erlerntes dient aber nicht unbedingt nur den Lernenden, den Trägern des neu erworbenen Wissens, sondern kann, selbstverständlich auch bei Tieren, durch Vorbildwirkung weitergegeben werden. Hier stellt sich allerdings die Frage, ob dies etwa bei brutpflegenden, ihren Nachwuchs betreuenden Lebewesen gezielt oder ungezielt geschieht. Bei Menschenaffenmüttern gewinnt man den Eindruck, daß sie mitunter ihre Kinder bei Aktionen absichtlich unterweisen, doch geschieht dies immer in augenblicksbezogener, praktizierender Art (vgl. *Lawick-Goodall* 1971, *Linden* 1980, *Schaller* 1965, *Waal* 1983). Nachahmend gelernt wird in der Regel von ranghohen, kaum jemals von sozial niedriger stehenden Artgenossen. Ohne Zweifel wird von den Eltern als den Ranghohen sehr viel übernommen, was zur Tradierung von Erfahrungen und Gewohnheiten führen kann. Bei Tieren besteht nur kein Zwang, dies zu tun. Selbst wenn Eltern gewisse Dinge gezielt vormachen sollten, sind die Kinder in keiner Weise zum Nachmachen, also zum Lernen genötigt. Sie können das Vorbild der Eltern ohne Bestrafung ignorieren. Komplizierter liegen die Dinge beim Menschen. Er nützt die Lernfähigkeit anderer aus, um sie bestimmte Dinge zu »lehren«. Er zwingt seine Kinder auch dort zu lernen, wo kein sichtbares Vorbild auf sie einwirkt, das Lerngut kann rein theoretisch übermittelt werden. Die menschliche Gruppe gibt ihr Wissensinventar gezielt weiter und setzt Sanktionen gegenüber dem, der nicht lernen will.

Daß der Mensch über das Lernen hinaus zu einem lehrenden Lebewesen wurde, hängt auf das engste mit seinem Werkzeuggebrauch und der hohen kulturellen

Differenzierung zusammen (*Koenig* 1983). Wer Geräte zurichtet und sie zum täglichen Leben gebraucht, muß alles, was damit zusammenhängt, seinen Kindern beibringen und sie notfalls auch mit Strenge zum Lernen anhalten. Dies einfach darum, weil es sich um sehr vielschichtige, oft von Vorfahren überlieferte Kenntnisse handelt, die sich der einzelne nicht selbst erwerben kann, ohne die er aber weder innerhalb der Gruppe noch gegenüber der Außenwelt zu bestehen vermag. Das Nichtbeherrschen von Überlebenstechniken wie etwa Jagd- oder Ackerbaumethoden ist für das Mitglied einer Urhorde letal. Mit dem Werkzeuggebrauch muß zwangsläufig auch das Lehren und Belehren aufgekommen sein. Der nächste Schritt führt zur organisierten Schulung und damit letztendlich zur Institution der Schule, wo der eigens bestellte Lehrer bereits mit speziell ausgearbeiteten pädagogischen Methoden die Jugend zu motivieren und eventuelle Lernunlust zu überwinden sucht (*Liedtke* 1983, 1986). Dies mag auf den ersten Blick positiv und daher begrüßenswert erscheinen, bringt aber doch eine große Zahl von Problemen mit sich.

Solange nämlich beim urtümlichen Menschen das persönliche Lernen nur in bezug zu sich selbst respektive der eigenen Körperfähigkeit steht und weder durch nennenswerten Werkzeuggebrauch noch durch intensives Belehrtwerden gesteigert wird, entsteht keine Gefahr für das biologische Gesamtsystem, weil jedes einzelne Individuum mitfunktionierender Teil des Ganzen bleibt und es in der Gruppe wohl einfachste kulturelle Lokalanpassungen, aber keine bewußt angestrebte Leistungssteigerung gibt. Erst das gezielte Lehren bringt die immer rascher werdende Vorwärtsentwicklung, weil jede individuelle neue Erkenntnis, jedwede lernbedingte Verhaltensverbesserung gezielt in die Sozietät eingebracht und weiter tradiert werden kann, wodurch sich die fortschreitende Perfektionierung ständig beschleunigt (*Koenig* 1986).

Das Wort »lehren« ist in seiner historischen Entwicklung wohl mit »lernen« und »List« verwandt, geht aber auf »leisten« zurück und bedeutet ursprünglich so viel wie »Wissen machen« (*Kluge* 1975). Genau darinnen aber liegt seine ureigenste Funktion. Wer lehrt, »macht Wissen«, und wer dadurch zulernt und selbst wiederum lehrt, vergrößert das Wissen, steigert die Leistung. In allen Kulturen ist es die Sprache, die sich als zentrales Hilfsmittel des Lehrens erweist und alles fördert, was Gebrauchstechnik ist. Die entwicklungsgeschichtlich nachfolgende bildliche Darstellung, die Bilderschrift und letztlich die Buchstabenschrift ermöglichen dann eine Tradierung über beliebig viele Generationen, die infolge zeitlicher und auch örtlicher Trennung niemals persönlichen Kontakt miteinander haben könnten (*Brunner* 1986, *Waetzoldt* 1986).

Es ist ethologisch erklärlich, wieso der Mensch zu seiner phylogenetischen Spitzenposition gelangen konnte. In der Evolution ist er bereits durch den aufrechten Gang, das Freiwerden der Vorderextremitäten zu verbessertem Greifen und Tasten befähigt. Die damit in engstem Zusammenhang stehende Hirnschädelvergrößerung geht mit einer Zunahme an Intelligenz einher, die sensomotorischen Kreisprozesse und mit ihnen die Lernvorgänge werden intensiver (*Rensch* 1965, *Smolla* 1967). Das soziale Zusammenwirken in der Gruppe, die für den belauernden, verfolgenden, überlistenden Jäger typische Befähigung zu raschen Problemlösungen, erweitern das

Lernpotential und zwingen dadurch zu einer Verlängerung der Nachwuchsbetreuung, die ihrerseits die soziale Weitergabe des Wissens, also das Lehren, unerläßlich macht. Der Mensch ist ganz einfach aufgrund seiner stammesgeschichtlichen Entwicklungshöhe, der ökologischen Einpassung und der sozialen Struktur einschließlich seiner Fortpflanzungs- beziehungsweise Kinderaufzuchtsmethode zu gesteigertem Lernen und damit auch zum Lehren nicht nur prädestiniert, sondern auch gezwungen.

Dieser permanente Leistungszwang wird dort am vielfältigsten sein, wo die Umweltvariabilität am größten ist. Das gilt für die gemäßigte Zone mit den klimatisch stark differierenden Jahreszeiten, die im Grunde genommen periodisch »Warmzeit« und »Eiszeit« präsentieren. Hier muß der Mensch jeweils vorbereiten und vorsorgen, muß umgestalten, dem Wetter anpassen und neu ordnen. Klimatisch weitgehend gleichbleibende Regionen, seien sie heiß oder kalt, bringen beim Menschen genetisch wie kulturell äußerst statische Extremanpassungen mit sehr geringer Variabilität hervor. Auch der Sozialbereich wie Paarbildung, Kinderaufzucht und Verkehr innerhalb der Gruppe sind bei diesen Menschenformen klar in Richtung Einfachheit prädisponiert. Man kommt weitgehend mit Mimik, Gestik und Stimmungslauten aus. In den mitmenschlichen Beziehungen genügt die Lernerfahrung, weil hier die angeborenen Verhaltenselemente stark tragend wirken. Die Sprache als Verständigungswerkzeug und Mittel des Lehrens konzentriert sich primär auf die Bewältigung der Umwelt, auf das Gerät, auf die kulturellen Bezeichnungen. Unter extremen Klimabedingungen und schwerstem Umweltdruck kann eine luxurierende Vorwärtsentwicklung nicht stattfinden. Es ist kein Zufall, daß die Wiegen unserer Hochkulturen in gemäßigten Zonen liegen (*Koenig* 1962, 1971).

Die kulturelle Leistungspalette des Menschen ist also zweifelsfrei ökologisch bedingt und genetisch verankert. Sie zwingt ihn, vom individuellen Lernen zum sozial ausgerichteten Lehren fortzuschreiten. Das Lehren kumuliert Wissen, dieses wird durch die Schrift fixiert, gelangt dadurch zu breiterer Anwendung und wird folglich in höhere Potenzen überführt. Das wiederum nötigt zu intensiverem Lernen und gesteigertem Lehren, wodurch abermals Wissen vermehrt und in noch höhere Potenzen gesteigert wird. Die Kettenreaktion ist in vollem Gang. Der Weg von der Werkzeuglosigkeit zum Faustkeil war sehr lang, doch vom Faustkeil bis zur modernen Elektronik überstürzte sich das Tempo infolge der zentralen, in Wechselwirkung sich steigernden Kombination von Lehre und Schrift. Hier, im sogenannten »Intellektuellen«, liegt die ökologisch bedingte Spezialisation des Menschen. Wie jede Spezialisation birgt sie in sich den Weg zur Übertreibung und damit auch den Schritt über alle Toleranzgrenzen hinweg in den Letalbereich. Das ist die eigentliche und unbewältigte Problematik unseres Kommunikations- und Lehrsystems.

Die individuelle Einpassung des Einzelwesens ist der zellulare Mikroansatz zum gigantischen Urwald der Phylogenie. Dieser plastische Vorfühlbereich steht in einer sinnvollen, funktionsgerechten Geschwindigkeitsrelation zum Weiterwachsen des phylogenetischen Astes. Sinkt die Plastizität der betroffenen Art, so stirbt sie ab und wird zu totem Holz. Beginnt sie aber in restloser Selbstverwirklichung über das tragbare, lebensfähige Maß hinaus zu wuchern, so entweicht sie dem Schutz des

stammesgeschichtlichen Geästes und gibt sich preis. Genau das aber ist die heutige Position der Art Homo sapiens. Dank hochentwickelter Sprache und Schrift, dank intensiven Lehrens mittels raffinierter elektronischer Mitteilungs- und Merksysteme können wir Menschen heute weit mehr, als wir auf dieser Welt tatsächlich tun dürfen. Unser hochtechnisiertes Zivilisationssystem steht in keinem Sinnbezug mehr zur genetischen Basis. Wir fällen bereits den Stammwald, der uns erhält, indem wir Biotope zerstören und Arten ausrotten. Wir vernichten letztendlich uns selbst, weil auch unser zu hoch entwickeltes, zu Vieles erschließendes Lernen und Lehren seine Ursprungsfunktion gesprengt und seine Zielsetzung verändert hat. Wir bauen Geräte, die sich Sachverhalte für uns merken, die für uns denken und rechnen, die autonom Maschinen steuern, die weitaus zahlreichere und kompliziertere Arbeiten bedeutend rascher verrichten, als dies ein Mensch je vermochte. Wir müssen eigentlich garnichts mehr lernen, als jene Maschinen, Geräte und Apparate zu bedienen, denen wir die Elementarfunktion von Hirn und Hand überantwortet haben (*Koenig* 1976).
Wahrscheinlich ist es zur Umkehr bereits zu spät, ist unsere technisch total überbaute Gesellschaftsstruktur nicht mehr in die Ausgewogenheit des irdischen Kräftepotentials rückführbar. Denn eines ist klar: Wenn die Stammesgeschichte eine Folge des Umweltkontaktes, der Umwelterfahrung des Einzelwesens ist, wenn die Gesetze des Lernens und auf höherer Stufe auch des Lehrens die Triebkräfte der Stammesgeschichte sind, dann muß ihre Übergabe an Maschinen einen tiefgreifenden Einfluß auf die genetische Dynamik ausüben. Die sensomotorischen Kreisprozesse zwischen Hirn und Hand haben den Homo sapiens geformt, die Fülle des auf Erden vorhandenen, sich zur Bearbeitung und Gestaltung anbietenden Materials, die Vielfalt der Umweltanforderungen waren seine entscheidenden, ihn zum Lernen zwingenden Lehrer. Wenn die Gegenwartsmenschen sich davon distanzieren, die auf unendlich langem Erfahrungsweg gewonnene Intelligenz in Maschinen verlegen, werden sie zu Knöpfchendrückern rudimentieren. Die Technik hat sich zwar der physikalischen und chemischen Gesetze bedient, wird aber die biologische, durch natürliche Hemmungsmechanismen gesteuerte Integration niemals erreichen. Sie muß, angetrieben von den zivilisatorisch ausufernden Vermehrungs- und Optimierungstendenzen des durch und durch biologischen »Wesens Mensch«, letztendlich zu dessen Zerstörung führen.
Wollen wir das uns erhaltende System in letzter Minute retten, dann müssen wir in raschen mutigen Vorwärtsschritten die alte systemgerechte Spur wieder erreichen, die wir hätten niemals verlassen dürfen. Mit dem Gewicht angeborener Dispositionen hat uns die extrem hemmungslose Hochzüchtung des Prinzips »Lernen und Lehren« in die größte Gefahr gelockt, in der sich die Menschheit jemals befand. Jetzt gilt es, dieses anthropologische Urprinzip mit ökologiegerechten Zielsetzungen neu zu beleben. Mit Hilfe kulturell erworbener Erkenntnisse, unter Mobilisierung ethischer Verantwortung müssen wir der Zügellosigkeit steuern, die gesamte pädagogische Potenz in den Dienst des uns gerade noch tragenden Gesamtökosystems stellen und die Jugend das Wichtigste lehren, das es heute für uns gibt: Verzicht auf den Überfluß und Einschränkung auf das Notwendigste (*Liedtke* 1985). Vielleicht könnte es uns damit gelingen, eine noch mögliche Gesundung unserer Lebensbasis einzuleiten.

Literaturverzeichnis

Brunner, H. (1986): Schrift und Unterrichtsmethoden im alten Ägypten. In: Lenz Kriss-Rettenbeck/Max Liedtke (Hrsg.): Erziehungs- und Unterrichtsmethoden im historischen Wandel. Bad Heilbrunn (Schriftenreihe zum Bayerischen Schulmuseum Ichenhausen, 4), S. 27–35

Kluge, F. (1975): Etymologisches Wörterbuch der deutschen Sprache. Berlin–New York

Koenig, O. (1962): Kif Kif. Menschliches und Tierisches zwischen Sahara und Wilhelminenberg. Wien

Koenig, O. (1971): Das Paradies vor unserer Tür. Wien–München–Zürich

Koenig, O. (1976): Arbeitsteilung. In: Menschliches Verhalten. 1. Kolloquium der Schweiz. Geisteswiss. Gesellschaft 1983. Freiburg/Schweiz

Koenig, O. (1983): Kulturelle Bedeutung von Lernen und Lehren. In: Lenz Kriss-Rettenbeck/Max Liedtke (Hrsg.): Schulgeschichte im Zusammenhang der Kulturentwicklung. Bad Heilbrunn (Schriftenreihe zum Bayerischen Schulmuseum Ichenhausen, 1), S. 33–39

Koenig, O. (1986): Das Problem lernabhängiger Methodenverbesserung unter ethologischem Aspekt. In: Lenz Kriss-Rettenbeck/Max Liedtke (Hrsg.): Erziehungs- und Unterrichtsmethoden im historischen Wandel. Bad Heilbrunn (Schriftenreihe zum Bayerischen Schulmuseum Ichenhausen, 4), S. 20–26

Koenig, O. (1988): Das Problem der Trennung zwischen den sogenannten Geistes- und Naturwissenschaften. In: Johann Georg Prinz von Hohenzollern/Max Liedtke (Hrsg.): Naturwissenschaftlicher Unterricht und Wissenskumulation. Bad Heilbrunn (Schriftenreihe zum Bayerischen Schulmuseum Ichenhausen, 7), S. 189–197

Lawick-Goodall, J. van (1971): Wilde Schimpansen. Reinbek b. Hamburg

Liedtke, M. (1983): Die Kultur des Menschen als Faktor und Produkt von Erziehung und Schule. In: Lenz Kriss-Rettenbeck/Max Liedtke (Hrsg.): Schulgeschichte im Zusammenhang der Kulturentwicklung. Bad Heilbrunn (Schriftenreihe zum Bayerischen Schulmuseum Ichenhausen, 1), S. 40–52

Liedtke, M. (1985): Technik – Erlösung oder Sündenfall des Menschen. Zum Problem der Humanität in der technischen Entwicklung. Schriftenreihe Verein für Ökologie und Umweltforschung, 2. Wien

Liedtke, M. (1986): Die geschichtliche Bedeutung der Verbesserung von Unterrichts- und Erziehungsmethoden. In: Lenz Kriss-Rettenbeck/Max Liedtke (Hrsg.): Erziehungs- und Unterrichtsmethoden im historischen Wandel. Bad Heilbrunn (Schriftenreihe zum Bayerischen Schulmuseum Ichenhausen, 4) S. 11–19

Linden, E. (1980): Die Kolonie der sprechenden Schimpansen. Wien-München

Schaller, G. B. (1965): Unsere nächsten Verwandten. Bern-München-Wien

Smolla, G. (1967): Epochen der menschlichen Frühzeit. Studium Universale. Freiburg-München

Waal, F. de (1983): Unsere haarigen Vettern. München

Waetzoldt, H. (1986): Keilschrift und Schulen in Mesopotamien und Ebla. In: Lenz Kriss-Rettenbeck/Max Liedtke (Hrsg.): Erziehungs- und Unterrichtsmethoden im historischen Wandel. Bad Heilbrunn (Schriftenreihe zum Bayerischen Schulmuseum Ichenhausen, 4), S. 36–50

Rensch, B. (1965): Homo sapiens. Vom Tier zum Halbgott. Göttingen

II. ORIENTALISCHE HOCHKULTUREN

Hartmut Waetzoldt

Der Schreiber als Lehrer in Mesopotamien*

1. Zur Einführung

Für Mesopotamien fehlt eine zusammenfassende Untersuchung über Schule und Erziehung, wie sie Helmut Brunner bereits 1957 für Ägypten mit seinem Buch »Altägyptische Erziehung« vorgelegt hat. Die vorhandenen Arbeiten basieren fast ausschließlich auf den Schulerzählungen, einigen Streitgesprächen und den Examenstexten.[1] Die Wirtschaftstexte und abertausend Schulübungen bleiben meist unberücksichtigt. Da der größte Teil dieses Textmaterials noch unpubliziert und unbearbeitet in den Museen liegt, wird es noch viele Jahre dauern, bis dieser unbefriedigende Zustand beendet werden kann.
Vorliegende Ausführungen stützen sich hauptsächlich auf Texte aus der Zeit um 1800 und 1700 v. Chr., ergänzt durch Material aus der 2. Hälfte des 3. Jahrtausends.
Die Schule heißt é-dub-ba, wörtlich ›Tafelhaus‹. Von ihr hören wir allerdings erst um 2050 v. Chr.[2] Ähnlich wie in Ägypten[3] dürfte das Herausbilden von Schulen auf den damaligen großen Bedarf an gut ausgebildeten Beamten zurückzuführen sein. Er entstand in Mesopotamien durch die starke Ausdehnung des Reiches und die Zuweisung neuer Aufgaben an die Verwaltung unter König Schulgi.
Lehrer muß es seit der Erfindung der Schrift gegeben haben (um 3000 v. Chr.). Eine eigene Bezeichnung für sie hatte man allerdings m. W. nicht, sie hießen einfach Schreiber (dub-sar). Dies ist verständlich, denn jeder erfahrene Schreiber konnte als Lehrer tätig werden. Auch Schulgi nennt seinen Lehrer offenbar noch so.[4] Dub-sar bedeutet einfach ›Tafelschreiber‹ und jeder Funktionär oder Beamte, der die Schreiberausbildung hinter sich brachte, durfte sich so nennen. Die Ausbildung zum dub-sar fand normalerweise im Rahmen der Familie statt. Der Vater unterrichtete seinen Sohn selbst oder nahm ein Kind bei sich auf. Er zog sich so seinen Nachfolger selbst heran, wie dies im Handwerk – wozu auch der Beruf des Schreibers gehörte – üblich war. War der Vater dazu aus irgendeinem Grund nicht in der Lage, bat er einen ihm bekannten Schreiber, seinen Sohn auszubilden. Ob dazu Lehrverträge abgeschlossen wurden, wie etwa für die Ausbildung zum Koch oder Sänger[5], muß wegen fehlender Quellen offen bleiben. Allerdings ist auch aus jüngerer Zeit kein solcher Vertrag bekannt.[6]
Mit der Einführung von Schulen kurz vor der Wende des 3. zum 2. Jahrtausend benötigte man auch besondere Bezeichnungen für die Lehrkräfte. Den »(Schul)meister« nannte man um-mi-a – ebenso wie den Handwerksmeister – oder auch ad-da-é-dub-ba ›Schulvater‹ (wörtlich »Vater des Tafelhauses«). In größeren Schulen hieß so der Schulleiter, während man den Lehrer ugula (wörtlich »Aufseher«) und den Hilfslehrer šeš-gal (wörtlich »großer Bruder«) nannte. Die Bezeichnungen

»Vater des Tafelhauses«, »großer Bruder« und »Sohn des Tafelhauses« für Schüler (dumu-é-dub-ba) weisen übrigens deutlich auf den Ursprung der Schule im familiären Bereich.
Was einen Mann zum Lehrer befähigte, verraten die Texte uns nicht. Die Bezeichnungen ›Meister‹ und ›Vater‹ weisen wohl – ähnlich wie in Ägypten[7] – auf ein gewisses Alter. Langjährige Erfahrung als Schreiber in der Verwaltung dürfte eine der Voraussetzungen sein, möglicherweise auch erfolgreiche Tätigkeit als Privatlehrer. Eine besondere Ausbildung gab es mit größter Wahrscheinlichkeit nicht.
Alle Fähigkeiten und Kenntnisse, die einen guten Schreiber ausmachten, sollte in noch größerem Maße der Lehrer besitzen: Beherrschung aller sumerischen Vokabulare, der Verwaltungssprache, der juristischen Phraseologie, des Briefschreibens, Erstellens von Abrechnungen und der Landvermessung. Hinzu kommen das Spielen mehrerer Musikinstrumente, Gesang und die Kenntnis der literarischen und religiösen Texte und der Königsinschriften.[8]
Ein guter ›Meister‹ (um-mi-a) sollte demnach alles damalige Wissen in sich vereinigen, ein Universalgelehrter sein. Der König übertrug diesen Meistern das Abfassen von Götterhymnen, Steleninschriften und Preisliedern auf den König ebenso wie die Ausbildung seiner Kinder.[9]
Mehrere Könige rühmen sich ihrer besonderen Fähigkeiten und Kenntnisse als Richter, Musiker, Sänger und Schreiber, doch behauptet keiner von sich, ein ›Meister‹ (um-mi-a) zu sein. Nur König Schulgi vergleicht seinen Nachruhm mit dem eines Meisters.[10]
Wie weit es in der Zeit um 1800/1700 v. Chr. schon Fachlehrer gab, läßt sich wegen des schlechten Erhaltungszustands einer Textpassage nicht abschließend beurteilen. Der Text nennt unter anderen einen »Mann der Zeichnung / des Planes« und einen »Mann des Sumerischen«. Sollte es sich um die Lehrer für ›technisches Zeichnen‹ und für Sumerisch handeln?[11] (Sumerisch war in dieser Zeit bereits ausgestorben, bildete aber die Basis des gesamten Unterrichts).
Wieviel ein Lehrer verdiente (als Naturalleistung oder an Silber), verraten uns die Texte nicht. Auf jeden Fall war ein Lehrer nach der Erzählung über den Schulalltag sehr froh, von den Eltern eines Schülers zum Essen eingeladen und anschließend noch reich beschenkt zu werden.[12] Die normale Getreidezuteilung eines Schreibers lag auf derselben Höhe wie die eines Handwerkers. Zu den Handwerken wurde – wie erwähnt – auch die Schreibkunst gezählt.[13] Ein Lehrer hat sicher mehr bekommen als ein Schreiber, doch üppig leben konnte er davon wohl kaum.

2. Disziplin

Die Lehrer achteten sehr auf Disziplin. Einem Schüler drohten für Zuspätkommen, schlecht gemachte Aufgaben oder sonstige Vergehen Schläge.[14] Ein Hilfslehrer (šeš-gal) würde am liebsten einem Schüler folgende Strafen auferlegen: 60 Stockschläge,

Fußfesseln aus Kupfer und Verbot, für 2 Monate die Schule zu verlassen.[15] Selbst zu Hause konnte der Schüler vor Prügeln nicht sicher sein, wenn er in der Schule faul war oder sich nach Meinung des Vaters nicht richtig verhalten hatte.[16]
Respekt, wenn nicht sogar Unterwürfigkeit, wurde von den Schülern verlangt. Ein Vater rät seinem Sohn ausdrücklich: »Sei doch bescheiden, zeige deinem ›Aufseher‹ Respekt; wenn du ihm immer wieder Respekt zeigst, wird er dich sehr gerne haben.«[17]
Tadel und Kritik wegen ihres Verhaltens und ihrer Leistungen hörten die Schüler wohl am häufigsten, Lob scheint nach den Schulerzählungen und Streitgesprächen weit seltener.[18] Ärger und Frustration konnten daher nicht ausbleiben. Die Schüler zerbrachen, zerkratzten oder zerdrückten ihre Schreibtafeln (aus weichem Ton), schlugen sie auf den Ecken auf oder schrieben sie einfach nicht fertig (Abb. 1). Schülertafeln mit derartigen Merkmalen findet man in allen Museen mit entsprechenden Sammlungen, in Istanbul konnte ich zahlreiche ansehen.[19]
Einige Schüler hielten auch damals nichts von Schönschrift und schluderten die Texte nur so hin. Einen Fall habe ich in Istanbul gefunden, bei dem die Schüler eine Liste von 123 Zeilen wohl auswendig zu schreiben hatten. Ein Schüler schaffte es, alles sauber auf die Tafel zu bringen. Einen anderen mußte der Lehrer bereits nach 72 Zeilen unterbrechen, da dessen Schriftzeichen wie Kraut und Rüben durcheinander gingen. Zur Disziplinierung ließ er ihn die letzten 8 Zeilen in Schönschrift auf der Rückseite der Tafel wiederholen.[20]
Einen völlig anderen Eindruck machen die 700 oder 800 Jahre älteren Schülerarbeiten. Sie weisen neben oder nach dem Text Zeichnungen mit Tieren, Pflanzen oder geometrischen Mustern auf (Abb. 2–5).[21] Nach der Häufigkeit und Sorgfalt der Ausführung zu urteilen, geschah dies mit Billigung der Lehrer. Auf den oben erwähnten altbabylonischen Schülertafeln – obwohl weitaus zahlreicher – konnte ich nichts derartiges finden.[22] Die Lehrer erlaubten den Schülern offenbar nicht, Zeichnungen auf ihren Übungstafeln anzubringen.
Den Kindern wurde andererseits immer wieder vor Augen geführt, daß diese Strenge und die Höhe der Anforderungen nur zu ihrem Besten seien. Denn wenn sie im Wettbewerb mit ihren Kameraden gut abschnitten und die Schule erfolgreich beendeten, erwartete sie eine sorgenfreie Zukunft und hohes Ansehen in der Gesellschaft.[23]

3. Didaktik

Das Schreibmaterial, feuchter Ton, war überall leicht zu gewinnen und äußerst billig. Die Schüler mußten nicht damit sparen, die Lehrer konnten die Übungen mehrfach wiederholen lassen.
Für den Elementarunterricht verwendeten die Lehrer linsenförmige Tafeln, die der kindlichen Hand gut angepaßt waren. Die etwas älteren Schüler, aber gelegentlich auch Anfänger, bekamen große, ungewöhnlich dicke rechteckige Tafeln. Der Lehrer

oder sein Gehilfe schrieben auf derartige runde oder rechteckige Tafeln die jeweilige Übung, die der Schüler darunter, daneben oder auf der Rückseite, je nach seinem Kenntnisstand, wiederholen mußte (Abb. 6–8).
Der Lehrstoff war – soweit man dies bisher beurteilen kann – recht systematisch aufgebaut. Zuerst schrieben die Schüler nur senkrechte, waagrechte und schräge Keile (bzw. Winkelhaken)[24], aus denen jedes Keilschriftzeichen zusammengesetzt ist (Abb. 9). Dann begann man mit dem Üben von Silbenzeichen, anschließend wurden 2 oder 3 Zeichen kombiniert. Später folgten Personennamen- und Wortlisten. Um die verschiedenen ›Aussprachen‹ der Keilschriftzeichen (Sumerogramme) und wohl auch ihre akkadische Entsprechung zu lernen, gab es wieder eigene Listen. In ihrer Anordnung der Zeichen folgen sie meist einfachen pädagogischen Prinzipien (Abb. 10), z. B. Beginn und Abschluß mit einem senkrechten Keil (a), Kombination eines senkrechten mit einem waagrechten (b) oder zwei zusammenlaufende Keile (c).[25]
Bei der Beschäftigung mit der altbabylonischen Schule und ihrem Lehrstoff fällt sofort auf, daß die Lehrer schon den Anfängerunterricht auf rein sumerischem Textmaterial aufbauten. Sumerisch war damals bereits ausgestorben. Als Muttersprache hatten die Kinder und Lehrer einen babylonischen Dialekt des Akkadischen. Von den rund 400 Schultexten, die man in einem Privathaus in Ur fand, sind rund 80% sumerisch und nur 20% akkadisch, darunter meist Briefe, Verwaltungstexte und Rechtsurkunden, aber nur wenige literarische Texte.[26] In diesem Archiv fehlten alle Anfängertexte; kämen diese noch hinzu, so wäre der Prozentsatz der akkadischen Texte noch weitaus geringer. Die Frage, warum die Lehrer dem Sumerischen eine derart zentrale Rolle einräumten, läßt sich nicht eindeutig beantworten. Wahrscheinlich handelten sie gemäß einer Jahrhunderte alten Tradition. Erst gegen Ende dieser Epoche ergaben sich offenbar immer größere Schwierigkeiten mit diesem rein sumerischen Lehrstoff. Daher fügten die Lehrer zu den Listen und manchen literarischen Texten akkadische Übersetzungen hinzu.
Eine weitere ungeklärte Frage ist, warum die Lehrer im Unterricht relativ früh die so schwierigen sumerischen Sprichwörter einsetzten.[27]
Die wichtigsten pädagogischen Mittel im Unterricht waren einerseits Abschreiben, Wiederholung und Diktat und andererseits Auswendiglernen. Ersteres läßt sich an den Tausenden von Übungstexten ablesen. Vom vielen Auswendiglernen erfahren wir aus den Schulerzählungen. Ein Schüler rühmt sich einmal, er könne 600 Zeilen einer Wortliste auswendig[28], und wenn ihm jemand einige Eintragungen sage, könne er sie an die richtige Stelle einordnen. Auch literarische Texte mußten völlig beherrscht werden.
Auf eine Tontafel in Postkartengröße hatte ein Schreiber 5 literarische Kompositionen mit insgesamt 639 Zeilen aufgeschrieben. Aus Platzmangel konnte er von längeren Zeilen nur den Anfang notieren. Daraus muß man schließen, daß er die Zeilenenden auswendig wußte. Der Text kann folglich nur jemandem – gleichgültig, ob es sich dabei um einen Lehrer oder einen Schüler handelte – als Gedächtnisstütze gedient haben.[29] Vielleicht war es der ›Spickzettel‹ eines fortgeschritteneren Schülers, den er sich vor einer Prüfung anfertigte.

Den Kenntnisstand der Schüler dürften die Lehrer schon mittels ›Klassenarbeiten‹ geprüft haben. Dies kann man wenigstens für das Fach ›Mathematik‹ wahrscheinlich machen. In einem Text – offenbar die Aufgaben für eine solche Arbeit oder Prüfung – waren Quadratzahlen, Multiplikationen mit 2 und 12 und wieder Quadratzahlen sorgfältig gemischt. Am Ende des Textes stehen noch Zahlen, deren Sinn bisher nicht rekonstruierbar ist.[30]

4. Examen

Abschlußprüfungen bei der Beendigung der Schule hat es in der Zeit der 3. Dynastie von Ur wohl ebensowenig gegeben wie zu Beginn der altbabylonischen Zeit. In seinem Selbstpreis-Lied hätte es König Schulgi mit Sicherheit nicht versäumt, auf das Bestehen einer Prüfung hinzuweisen. Auch in den Schülererzählungen hören wir nichts von Prüfungen. Die zukünftigen Schreiber haben ihre Stellen als Famulus, bzw. später als Schreiber m. E. auf Empfehlung ihrer Lehrer bekommen.
Ein ganz anderes Bild zeigen die sogenannten Examenstexte, von denen wir meist nur neuassyrische oder noch jüngere Abschriften besitzen.[31] Diese Texte dürften jedoch einen älteren Kern haben, der wohl zum Teil bis in die altbabylonische Zeit zurückreicht. Nach dem Examenstext A fand die Prüfung vor der Versammlung der Schulmeister (um-mi-a) statt. Der Text beginnt mit folgenden Worten: »Der Schreiber prüft seinen Schüler (wörtlich: Sohn) (und sagt): ›In der Versammlung der Meister im Hof des Tafelhauses, setze dich, mein Sohn, zu meinen Füßen nieder; ich will dich fragen und du wirst mir Auskunft geben! Von Kindheit an bis ins Mannesalter verbrachtest du in der Schule ...‹« usw. Es folgt eine lange Liste von Fragen, zu deren Beantwortung der Prüfling viele Stunden benötigt hätte. Seine Antworten sind nicht notiert, sondern am Ende beschimpft ihn der Prüfer. Er sei wie ein alter Ochse nicht mehr belehrbar, wie verdorrtes Getreide habe er die rechte Zeit verpaßt. Der Prüfer erweist sich hier als schlechter Pädagoge. Er schüchtert den Prüfling ein, statt ihn zu ermutigen.[32]
Wann derartige Abschlußprüfungen eingeführt wurden, entzieht sich unserer Kenntnis. Wegen des verwendeten Vokabulars halte ich es jedoch für wahrscheinlich, daß die Examenstexte zum Teil in der 2. Hälfte der altbabylonischen Zeit entstanden sind und damals bereits derartige Prüfungen abgehalten wurden.[33] Die Schulerzählungen spiegeln ganz offensichtlich eine ältere Tradition.

5. Schüler und Schuldauer

Das Alter der Schüler bei Schuleintritt wird ebensowenig angegeben wie das Alter der fertig ausgebildeten Schreiber. Rückschlüsse erlauben allerdings Texte, die die Länge der Schulzeit z. B. mit folgenden Worten umschreiben: »von der Kindheit bis zum ›Mannwerden‹ saßest du in der Schule«.[34] Demnach hätte die Schulzeit etwa vom 5. oder 6. Lebensjahr bis zum 14./15. gedauert, also 8–10 Jahre. Recht junge Schüler muß auch folgendes Sprichwort charakterisieren: »Der Schüler ist allzusehr mit (seinem) Brot (und) seiner Nahrung beschäftigt, auf die Schreibkunst kann er sich nicht konzentrieren«.[35] Einige Schüler waren sicher auch älter als 15 Jahre. So beklagt sich der Vater in der Erzählung »Der Vater und sein mißratener Sohn« über seinen Sohn mit den Worten (Z. 79ff.):

> »Mein Feld zu pflügen, habe ich dir nie als Arbeit zugewiesen,
> Mein Feld zu hacken, habe ich dir nie als Arbeit zugewiesen,
> Oder auch sonst irgendeine Arbeit auszuführen:
> ›Geh, arbeite, versorge mich!‹
> habe ich nie in meinem Leben dir gesagt;
> Leute wie du arbeiten sonst (und)
> versorgen ihre Eltern.«[36]

Dieser Sohn war nach den Klagen des Vaters bereits so alt, daß er hätte einen Pflug führen und für den Lebensunterhalt seiner Eltern sorgen können. Trotz seines Alters von wohl 18 oder 20 Jahren besuchte er noch die Schule.
Der Schulunterricht dauerte von morgens bis in den Nachmittag hinein. In der Schule nahmen die Kinder eine Mahlzeit ein, die sie sich mitgebracht hatten.[37] Heute würden wir eine solche Schule als ›Ganztagsschule‹ bezeichnen. Die Arbeitszeit der Lehrer war entsprechend lang. Lehrer und Schüler hatten im Monat 3 Tage frei, hinzu kamen noch 3 religiöse Feste, so daß der Unterricht an 24 Tagen stattfand. Auch Arbeiter hatten in der Regel 3 Tage im Monat frei, bei Frauen waren es sogar bis zu 6 Tage.[38]

6. Gliederung der Schreiberausbildung

Aus diesen Schulerzählungen aus altbabylonischer Zeit geht eindeutig hervor, daß die Kinder und Jugendlichen die Schule bis zum Ende ihrer Ausbildung besuchten. Dies mag für die Kinder der Oberschicht und der wohlhabenderen Leute gelten. Die Kinder der kleineren Verwaltungsbeamten mußten früher mitverdienen. Ich bin der Überzeugung, daß uns die Wirtschaftstexte genügend Argumente an die Hand geben, um von einer Zweiteilung der Schreiberausbildung in eine Elementarausbildung und eine berufsorientierte Ausbildung in Form einer Famulatur auszugehen.

6.1 Elementarunterricht

Der Elementarunterricht erfolgte in sehr kleinen Gruppen (man kann diese kaum als Klasse bezeichnen). Bei der Durcharbeit verschiedener Archive mit Schultexten stellte ich fest, daß genau dasselbe Textstück höchstens 2 oder 3 mal in dem Archiv vorhanden ist. Dies gilt für Archive aus der Zeit nach 2250 v. Chr. ebenso wie für altbabylonische, ungefähr 500 Jahre jüngere Archive. Man muß folglich davon ausgehen, daß in der Regel nur 2, seltener 3 oder gar 4 Schüler gleichzeitig unterrichtet wurden.[39] Das ist bei Anfängern wie auch bei Fortgeschrittenen der Fall.[40]
Die geringe Zahl an Schülern in einer Altersstufe mag überraschen, läßt sich aber aufgrund folgender Berechnungen stützen. Die publizierten Texte aus der Hauptstadt Ur nennen insgesamt 202 Schreiber aus der Zeit von 2070 bis 2003 v. Chr. (3. Dynastie von Ur).[41] Nimmt man wegen der Zufälligkeiten der Ausgrabungen und der Veröffentlichungen an, daß wir nur ⅕ der tatsächlichen Gesamtzahl kennen, so können wir eine Zahl von 1000 voll ausgebildeten Schreibern zugrunde legen. Bei einer durchschnittlichen Lebensarbeitszeit von 10 Jahren, die wir wegen der damals noch sehr geringen Lebenserwartung nicht höher ansetzen können[42], mußten jährlich nur etwa 15 bis 16 fertig ausgebildete Schreiber aus den Schulen und von den Privatlehrern entlassen werden.
In der Provinzhauptstadt Girsu versorgte der dortige Stadtfürst 12 Schüler mit Lebensmitteln.[43] Die Schulen dürften daher recht klein gewesen sein.
Der Lehrstoff wurde bereits kurz in dem Abschnitt »Didaktik« beschrieben. Das Studium der lexikalischen Listen begann man sicher mit der Holzliste. Wir kennen noch zahlreiche Listen, die ebenfalls im Natur- und Realienkunde-Unterricht durchgenommen und gelernt wurden. Ein Curriculum können wir allerdings derzeit nicht zusammenstellen[44], dazu sind erst noch umfangreiche Untersuchungen notwendig. Aufgrund von Unsicherheiten bei der Text-Datierung und der Wahrscheinlichkeit von mindestens einer, wenn nicht sogar von zwei ›Schulreformen‹[45] ergeben sich diesbezüglich allerdings Schwierigkeiten.
Nach der Schulerzählung D (*Civil* (1985) S. 71 f., Z. 4 ff.) berichtet ein junger Schreiber, was er alles in der Schule (im Elementarunterricht) gelernt hat: Sumerisch in Wort und Schrift, die sumerischen und akkadischen Wörter des Syllabars a-a me-me, die Personennamenliste Inanna-téš, die Serie lú-*šu* (Berufe, Personenbezeichnungen). Aus diesen Texten kennt er die Schreibung und Lesung der Keilschriftzeichen und kann bei der Serie lú-*šu* jede einzelne Zeile richtig einordnen. Multiplikationen, Erstellen von Abrechnungen, Beherrschung der Hohlmaße bis 600 Kor (ca. 180 000 Liter) und der Gewichte bis 20 Minen (ca. 10 kg) Silber sowie die Kenntnis der folgenden Rechtsurkunden-Typen zählten zu seiner Ausbildung: Ehe- und Gesellschaftsvertrag, Haus-, Feld- und Sklavenkauf, Silberdarlehen, Feldpacht, Palmgartenpacht, Adoption, ... (mehrere Zeilen abgebrochen). Am Ende rühmt sich der Schüler, er kenne bestens verschiedene Sammlungen von Sprichwörtern und Berufsbezeichnungen. Nebenbei verweist er zudem auf seine Fähigkeit, jede Beleidigung mit einer Beleidigung beantworten zu können.

6.2 ›*Oberstufe*‹

Wie erwähnt, mußten m. E. nicht alle Schüler diese ›Oberstufe‹ besuchen. Sie war wohl hauptsächlich den Kindern wohlhabenderer Eltern vorbehalten. Von diesen handeln auch die verschiedenen Schulerzählungen.
Runde Schultafeln wurden in der ›Oberstufe‹ in Nippur wahrscheinlich nicht mehr verwendet, denn diese enthalten nur Auszüge aus einfachen literarischen Texten.[46] In Ur fanden sich in dem Haus 1 Broad Street hauptsächlich noch Sprichwörter, Rätsel und Exzerpte aus Steitgesprächen auf derartigen Tafeln, aber keine schwierigen Textgattungen.[47] Möglicherweise gehörten all diese noch zum Lehrstoff der Elementarstufe.
In der ›Oberstufe‹ behandelten die Lehrer vor allen Dingen einerseits sumerische literarische Texte und Briefe sowie andererseits altbabylonische Briefe, Rechts- und Verwaltungsurkunden. Akkadische literarische Kompositionen kommen dagegen nur selten vor. Zu den sumerischen literarischen Texten gehörten z. B. mythologische Texte, Epen, Streitgespräche, Hymnen an Götter und Könige, Gebete, Klagen, Weisheitstexte, historische Briefe und Texte. Insgesamt sind 48 sumerische, aber nur 6 akkadische Kompositionen vertreten.[48] Die Gesamtzahl der altbabylonischen Briefe, Rechts- und Verwaltungsurkunden und Wirtschaftstexte beträgt 90. Welchen Teil der Texte man als Schulübungen und welchen als reale Briefe und Dokumente einzuordnen hat, läßt sich nicht immer klären.[49]
Wie bereits von *M. Civil* vermutet, nahmen die Lehrer die verschiedenen sumerischen Werke in einer bestimmten Reihenfolge nach didaktischen Gesichtspunkten durch.[50] Diese These wurde durch neue Textfunde aus Isin glänzend bestätigt.[51] Das Curriculum für den sumerischen Literatur-Unterricht galt in mehreren Städten. Um es festzulegen, hatten die (Schul-)›meister‹ irgendwann einmal ein Treffen veranstalten müssen. Diese enge Zusammenarbeit der Schulmeister klappte auch in Zeiten der Kleinstaaterei und der politischen Trennung, denn z. B. auch in Susa (in Elam, heute im Iran gelegen) verwendete man wenigstens im Elementarunterricht weitestgehend dieselben Texte wie in Mesopotamien.[52]
Sehr wahrscheinlich waren nicht alle Lehrer in der Lage, die vielen schwierigen sumerischen Kompositionen zu unterrichten. Sumerisch mußten jedoch alle können. Andere Fremdsprachen gehörten nicht zum Lehrplan. König Schulgi rühmt sich, er könne Amoritisch und Elamisch so gut wie Sumerisch sprechen, selbst einen Dolmetscher könne er korrigieren. Wo er diese Sprachen lernte, verrät er allerdings nicht.[53]
Nach dem Besuch der ›Oberstufe‹ durften sich die Jugendlichen möglicherweise schon Schreiber nennen. Es könnte aber auch sein, daß ihnen dies erst nach der Famulatur erlaubt wurde. Eine Famulatur war m. E. auch für diese ehemaligen ›Oberstufen‹schüler erforderlich, bevor sie die erste richtige Stelle übernehmen konnten.

6.3 Famulatur

Hatte ein Schreiberschüler bei seinem Vater, einem Privatlehrer oder in der Schule alle notwendigen Elementarkenntnisse erworben, kam er als Famulus zu einem Schreiber in die Verwaltung. Auch ›Oberstufen‹schüler mußten m. E. vor Antritt der ersten Stelle noch eine Famulatur machen. Der Lehrherr konnte der Vater oder ein anderer Funktionsträger sein.

Eine Famulatur müssen wir m. E. wenigstens für die Zeit der 3. Dynastie von Ur und wohl auch für die altbabylonische Zeit postulieren. Zu den Gründen:

1. Die Verwaltungen des Staates, der Tempel und der Wirtschaftsbetriebe benötigten Schreiber mit ganz verschiedenen Qualifikationen. Das Spezialwissen konnte erst in der Praxis erworben und keinesfalls in der Schule vermittelt werden.
2. Die Wirtschaftstexte geben genügend Hinweise auf eine derartige Famulatur.

Eltern mit geringem Einkommen konnten wohl kaum 8 bis 10 Jahre einen Privatlehrer bezahlen oder ihre Söhne in die Schule schicken, wodurch diese als Mitverdiener ausfielen (über ›Schulgeld‹ steht in den Texten nichts). Ein Schreiber, dessen Aufgabe das Anfertigen von Kopien war, mußte nur Lesen und ›Schönschrift‹ beherrschen. Ein anderer, der bei der Tieranlieferung eines Viehhofes arbeitete, sollte alle Tiere genau klassifizieren und die entsprechenden Zahlen und sonstigen Angaben notieren können, mehr nicht. Die Abrechnungen besorgten andere. In der höheren Verwaltung, z. B. als Rechnungsführer, Verwalter der Getreidemagazine oder Leiter eines Tempels bedurfte es eines sehr viel breiteren Wissens und der völligen Beherrschung aller Rechenarten. Entsprechend dem Berufsziel und den dafür notwendigen Voraussetzungen konnte m. E. eine Famulatur in ganz verschiedenem Alter beginnen und kürzer oder länger, d. h. viele Jahre dauern.

Die Bezeichnung für Famulus ist šeš-tab-ba, was man wörtlich mit »Bruder, der ›dabei‹ ist« übersetzen kann. Der Famulus erhielt für seine Arbeit eine Gersteration in der gleichen Höhe wie sie bei Kindern zwischen etwa 10 und 15 Jahren üblich war. Gelegentlich bekam er auch mehr, was für ein höheres Alter spricht.[54] Während der mehrjährigen Famulatur erwarb der Jugendliche alle Spezialkenntnisse, z. B. der verschiedenen Techniken und Fachausdrücke, die ihn befähigten, später eine Stelle in einer Weberei, einem metallverarbeitenden Betrieb oder in der Tempel- oder Staatsverwaltung einzunehmen. Nach der Beendigung der Famulatur konnte er die erste selbständige Stelle übernehmen. Ein junger Schreiber, der an seinem bisherigen Ausbildungsplatz, einer Weberei, noch die Ration für Jugendliche (20 Liter Gerste) bekam, erhielt als neue Stelle das Amt des »Schreibers der Aufseher über die Weberinnen«. Hierbei wird er erstmalig als »Mann« (guruš) bezeichnet[55], folglich wird er in Zukunft als Mann bezahlt (mit 50 oder 60 ›Liter‹ Gerste).

Aufgrund von anderen Wirtschaftstexten läßt sich das Alter beim Antritt der ersten Stelle mit etwa 18 Jahren bestimmen. Bei Stellen in der höheren Verwaltung dürfte das Alter ähnlich wie in Ägypten wenigstens 20 Jahre oder mehr betragen haben, denn eine solche Position wird nicht gleich mit dem Ende der Ausbildung frei gewesen sein.[56] Wir können häufig beobachten, daß der Sohn die Stelle seines Vaters übernahm.[57] Gelegentlich arbeitete der Sohn aber auch in einem ganz anderen Bereich der Verwaltung als der Vater.

7. Schlußbemerkung

Wie bereits erwähnt, gab es – soweit dies aus den Texten hervorgeht – keine besondere Ausbildung für Lehrer. Möglich wäre, daß ältere Schreiber bei erfahrenen Lehrern hospitierten oder unter deren Aufsicht unterrichteten. Auf jeden Fall wurden nach den Schulerzählungen und den Schulübungen sehr viele Fähigkeiten und ein großes Wissen von ihnen verlangt.

Die damaligen Lehrer hatten bereits vielfältiges Lehrmaterial entwickelt und folgten von Anfang an pädagogischen Gesichtspunkten. Sie wußten auch schon, daß kleine Kinder besser schreiben lernen, wenn sie große Schriftzeichen machen dürfen. So war bei den Anfängerübungen eine Schrifthöhe von ca. 1 cm mit großen Zeilenabständen üblich. Fortgeschrittenere Schüler schrieben meist 5–6 mm hoch, während gut ausgebildete Schreiber mit 4–5 mm auskamen. Den Anfängern gab man runde Tafeln, die gut in der Hand lagen, oder große, dicke Tontafeln, bei denen sie nichts kaputt machen konnten, sondern ein Auswischen mit dem Finger jederzeit möglich war. Je besser die Schüler schreiben lernten, desto kleinere und dünnere Tafeln erhielten sie von den Lehrern.

Für den Sprachunterricht in Sumerisch hatten die Lehrer bereits Paradigmen zusammengestellt. Im Unterricht behandelten sie die Singular- und Pluralformen häufig zusammen, z. B. Abb. 8 Zeile 1f. ì-ba-e, ì-ba-e-meš »er/sie/es teilt zu«, »sie teilen zu«.[58] Später wurden derartige Verbalformen zu großen Paradigmentafeln zusammengefaßt und mit akkadischen Übersetzungen versehen. Die Anordnung weicht aber von der uns gewohnten ab. So gab es z. B. bei der Nennung der 1., 2. und 3. Person keine feststehende Regel: 3., 2. und 1., worauf 2., 1. und 3. folgt oder 3., 1. und 2. Person[59]:

Sumerisch	Akkadisch	Übersetzung
ba-gar	*ittaškan*	er/sie/es ist hingestellt worden
ba-gar-re-en	*attaškan*	ich bin hingestellt worden
ba-gar-re-en	*tattaškan*	du bist hingestellt worden.

Oder auf den Imperativ folgten Prekativ/Kohortativformen[60]:

gar-ra	*šukun*	stelle hin
ga-gar	*luškun*	ich will hinstellen
bé-gar	*liškun*	er/sie/es möge hinstellen.

Negierte und nicht negierte Formen stehen nacheinander[61]:

ì-zi-gi-en	*etbi*	ich stand auf
nu-zi-gi-en	*ul etbi*	ich stand nicht auf
ì-zi-gi-en	*tetbi*	du standest auf
nu-zi-gi-en	*ul tetbi*	du standest nicht auf.

Die Lehrer hatten sich schon ein sehr differenziertes Unterrichtsmaterial geschaffen und paßten es den jeweiligen Erfordernissen an. Um die Schüler ›bei der Stange‹ zu halten, verwendeten sie etwa im Sumerisch-Unterricht abwechslungsreichen Stoff, z. B. Rätsel, Sprichwörter, Königsinschriften, Götterlieder und Beschwörungen.[62] Gleichzeitig hatten diese Texte einen hohen Bildungswert.
Die damaligen Schreiber und Lehrer vollbrachten vor mehr als 3700 Jahren Leistungen, über die wir heute nur staunen können. Sie verdienten ohne Zweifel die Hochschätzung, die man ihnen und den von ihnen geleiteten Schulen entgegenbrachte. Ohne diese besondere Achtung wäre ein Rätsel wie das folgende undenkbar[63]:

»Ein Haus, das auf ein Fundament wie der Himmel gegründet ist,
ein Haus, das man wie eine Schatzkiste mit einem Leintuch verhüllt,
ein Haus, das auf einer Basis steht wie eine ›Gans‹, –
man betritt es blind,
man verläßt es sehend!
(Des Rätsels) Lösung ist: die Schule.«

Abbildungen[64]

Vorderseite, vom Lehrer beschrieben | Rückseite, vom Schüler begonnen

1

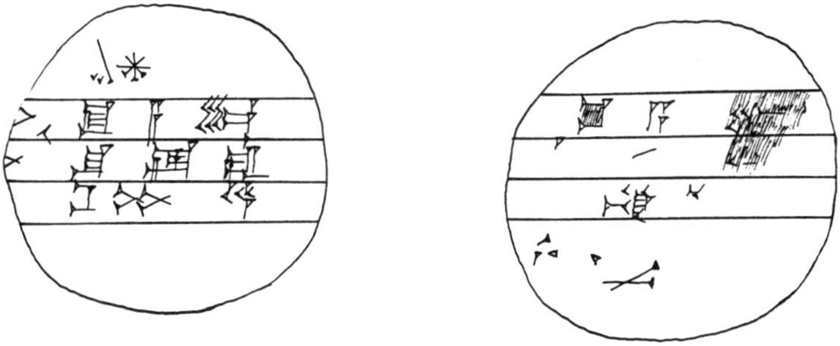

Zeichnungen auf Tafeln aus der Zeit kurz nach 2600 v. Chr.:

2

3

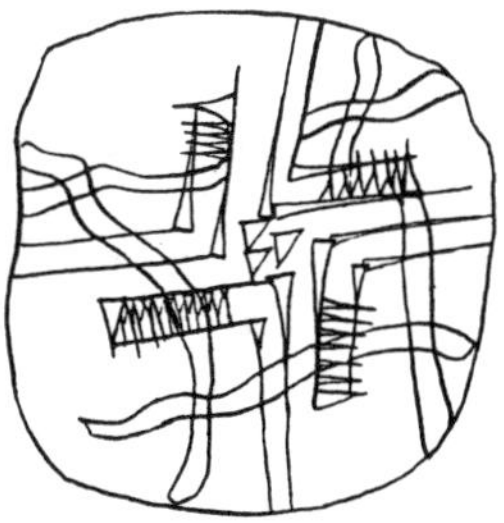

4

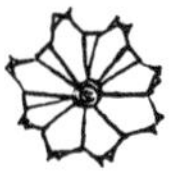

5

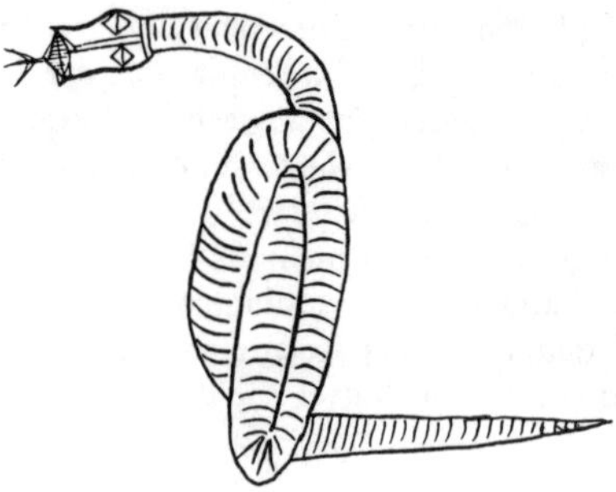

Übungstafeln mit Personennamen. Die oberen beiden Zeilen schrieb der Lehrer vor, darunter wiederholte sie der Schüler:

6 7

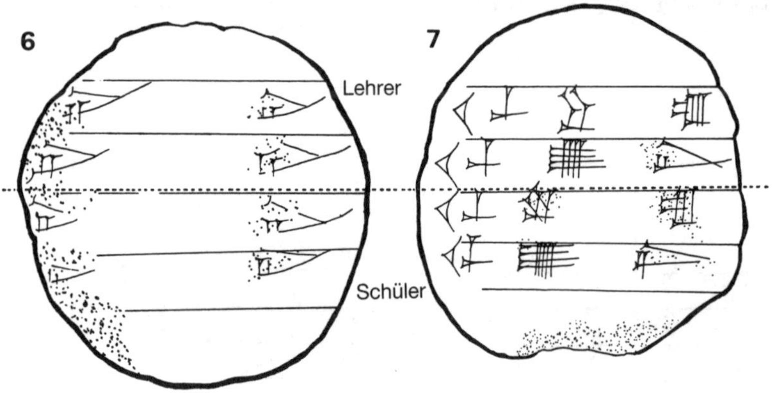

Übungstafel mit Verbalformen. Die Vorderseite schrieb der Lehrer und die Rückseite der Schüler:

8

Vs.

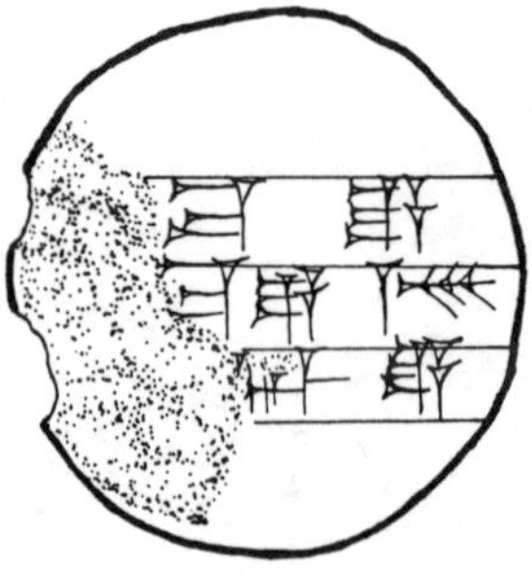

Rs.

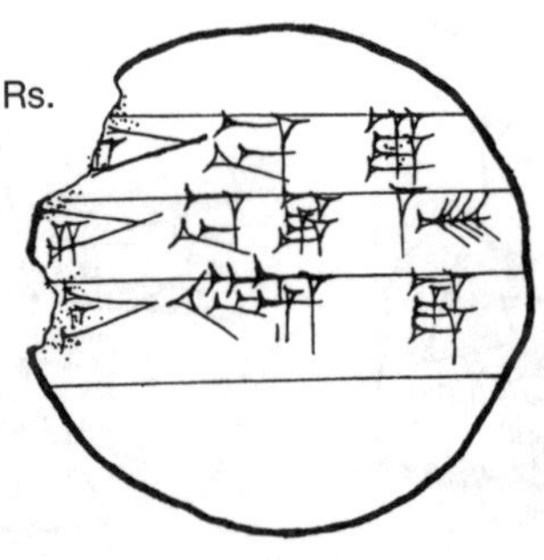

Anfängerübungen mit den 3 Elementen, aus denen alle Keilschriftzeichen zusammengesetzt sind:

9

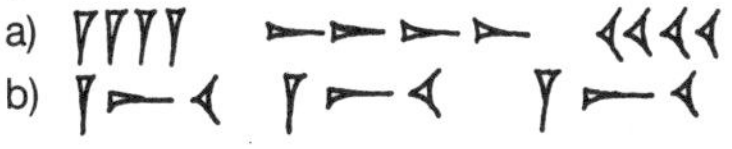

Anordnung der Keilschriftzeichen nach pädagogischen Kriterien in den Listen:

10

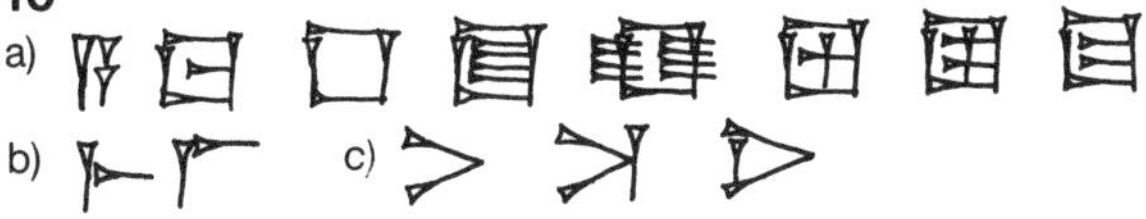

Anmerkungen

* Dank des Entgegenkommens und der vielfältigen Hilfe von Frau *F. Yıldız* konnte ich im September 1987 zahlreiche Schultexte aus Nippur und Sippar in den Istanbul Arkeoloji Müzeleri durchsehen. Sie gestattete mir auch, das einschlägige Material hier zu zitieren. Herr *C. Wilcke* stellte mir dankenswerterweise seinen Artikel über die neuen Texte aus Isin (*Wilcke* 1987) lange vor dessen Erscheinen zur Verfügung. [Aussprache von Š wie Deutsch sch].

[1] Z. B. *Falkenstein* (1953), *Gadd* (1956), *Sjöberg* (1975), *Römer* (1977).

[2] *Castellino* (1972), S. 30f., Z. 13 und S. 62f., Z. 314.

[3] *Brunner* (1957), S. 14.

[4] *Castellino* (1972), S. 32f., Z. 20, anders *Sjöberg* (1975), S. 173, der dub-sar auf Schulgi bezieht; vgl., daß in Schulgi B, Z. 312 der dub-sar die Königshymne schrieb – wie sonst der um-mi-a – (so nach der Interpretation von *Sjöberg* (1975), S. 174).

[5] *Wilcke* (1987), S. 92 zu IB 1515 + 1534.

[6] *Petschow* (1983), S. 558.

[7] *Brunner* (1957), S. 37.

[8] Vgl. *Sjöberg* (1975), S. 161–176.

[9] *Sjöberg* (1975), S. 166, 172, 174 = *Castellino* (1972), S. 62, Z. 312, hier allerdings dub-sar genannt; *Ludwig* (1987), S. 54, 68 mit Anm. 123 (Verweis auf *Sjöberg* 1972, S. 129, Komm. zu Z. 15), 177 + 182, Z. 18. *Ludwig* nimmt an, die um-mi-a hätten die Lieder auch komponiert. Dies halte ich für sehr unwahrscheinlich, da dies die Möglichkeit der Fixierung von Tonfolgen, Höhen und Rhythmen voraussetzte. Meiner Ansicht nach schrieben die um-mi-a die Liedtexte und die Sänger trugen diese nach bestimmten Regeln vor. – *B. Lafont* und *F. Yıldız* werden in Kürze den Text L. 896 veröffentlichen; auf Rs. V 1 f. findet man die Eintragung lú-^{d}nanna um-mi-a dumu-lugal »Lunanna ist der (Schul-)Meister des Prinzen«.

[10] Könige als Schreiber: Schulgi, Lipiteschtar, Ischmedagan s. *Sjöberg* (1975), S. 172ff.; *Römer* (1965), S. 26; *Ludwig* (1987), S. 177 und 182; Vergleich mit um-mi-a *Ludwig* (1987), S. 50 und 52, anders *Castellino* (1972), S. 61f., Z. 306.

[11] *Kramer* (1949), S. 202, Z. 35–40, aber *B. Landsberger,* ibid. S. 214, zu Z. 34 »giš-hur probably means ›good conduct‹ rather than ›drawing‹«; mir sind keine Texte bekannt, die die

sichere Lesung der ersten Zeichen in Z. 35f. ermöglichen. Es handelt sich wohl meist um Aufsichtspersonal (z. B. lú-usan-na »Mann der Peitsche«, Z. 39, bereits Z. 31 »Mann der Hof(aufsicht)«.

[12] *Kramer* (1949), S. 203, Z. 47ff.

[13] *Falkenstein* (1953), S. 127; *Waetzoldt* (1986), S. 42 mit Anm. 29f.; vgl. die Übersetzung von *Sjöberg* (1973), S. 112, Z. 109.

[14] Z. B. *Kramer* (1949), S. 205, Z. 17, 26, 29, 35–41.

[15] *Gadd* (1956), S. 35 = *Römer* (1982), S. 110.

[16] *Sjöberg* (1973), S. 111 + 116, Z. 62.

[17] *Sjöberg* (1973), S. 115, Z. 32f. = *Hörner* (1986), S. 109; vgl. *Römer* (1982), S. 110.

[18] *Sjöberg* (1973), S. 114ff. = *Hörner* (1986); *Sjöberg* (1975), S. 163, 165, 168f.; *Römer* (1982), S. 108ff. Vgl. Examenstext A, Z. 32ff. = *Sjöberg* (1975a), S. 145ff.

[19] *Falkowitz* (1983/84), S. 21; s. auch *Falkenstein* (1953), S. 131.

[20] Beide Texte (Sippar 203 und 204) sind unpubliziert und werden hier mit freundlicher Genehmigung von Frau *F. Yıldız* zitiert.

[21] *Deimel* (1922), S. 73; *Deimel* (1923), S. 31. 37, 63, 71, Tf. 8. *Biggs* (1974), S. 30f. und Text Nr. 47, 60, 282.

[22] Nur flüchtige Zeichnung auf sonst unbeschriebener runder Tafel, s. *Falkowitz* (1983/84), S. 29 CBS 11600 mit Photographie.

[23] *Sjöberg* (1972), S. 127; *Sjöberg* (1973), S. 117, Z. 102ff., S. 119, Z. 178ff.

[24] In Istanbul sah ich eine größere rechteckige Tafel (Ni 3253), die ausschließlich mit Senkrechten, Waagrechten und Winkelhaken gefüllt ist.

[25] *Michalowski* (1983), S. 151f. und D. O. *Edzard*, Der Aufbau des Syllabars »Proto-EA«, in: Societies and Languages of the Ancient Near East. Studies in Honor of I. M. Diakonoff (ed. M. A. Dandamayev e. a). Warminster 1982, S. 42–61, besonders S. 55ff.

[26] *Charpin* (1986), S. 439ff., 448ff., zu den akkadischen Texten S. 459ff.

[27] Vgl. *Waetzoldt* (1988a), S. 43 mit Anm. 49.

[28] *Sjöberg* (1975), S. 163 (Dialogue 1), S. 171, Anm. 41; *Civil* (1985), S. 72, Z. 18f., 34f.

[29] *Wilcke* (1987), S. 85ff.

[30] Nach freundlicher Mitteilung von *J. Friberg* (Brief vom 5. 5. 87) zu JCS 36, 243–251 2N-T 585 = A 30016.

[31] Examenstext A = *Sjöberg* (1975a); Examenstext B = *Langdon* (1931), S. 135 Sm 947; *Gadd* (1957), S. 263ff. K. 4815, 11856; Examenstext D = *Sjöberg* (1972).

[32] *Sjöberg* (1975a), S. 140ff., Z. 1ff., die Fragen beginnen Z. 12ff., Beschimpfung durch den Lehrer 32ff. = *Hörner* (1986).

[33] Vgl. *Sjöberg* (1975), S. 160.

[34] *Sjöberg* (1975a), S. 141 Examenstext A, Z. 4, zum Alter des Prüflings Z. 33 (S. 145) »Du bist schon ein reifer Mann, schon fast in vorgerücktem Alter«. Vgl. Schulgi, s. *Sjöberg* (1975), S. 172f. »Since I was a child (I was in) the eduba«.

[35] *Gordon* (1959), S. 210, Z. 53.

[36] *Sjöberg* (1973), S. 116f.

[37] *Kramer* (1949), S. 201, Z. 1–15.

[38] *Civil* (1985), S. 71, Z. 10, S. 72, Z. 22ff. Ausfallzeiten und Freizeit nach den Texten aus der Zeit der 3. Dynastie von Ur, s. *Waetzoldt* (1988), S. 36ff.

[39] In archivmäßigem Zusammenhang wurden bisher nur jeweils 2 Texte mit identischem Lehrstoff gefunden/publiziert. Daher ist anzunehmen, daß auch nicht mehr Kinder diesen Lehrstoff gleichzeitig durchnahmen. (Die Texte beginnen und enden stets mit derselben Zeile): altakkadische Schultexte aus Lagasch: *Genouillac* (1921), Nr. 9201 = 9208, 9202 = 9207

(Anfang und Ende, Kolumneneinteilung jeweils übereinstimmend); altbabylonische Texte aus Nippur: *Al-Fouadi* (1979) Nr. 46 + 83, 50 + 52, 74 + 88, 136 + 143, vgl. 17 + 26, 145 + 152; *Falkowitz* (1983/84) S. 32 UM 29-16-337 = S. 33 UM 29-16-400, S. 33 N 5080 = S. 34 N 5524, S. 32 UM 19-15-850 = S. 41 2 NT 520; und aus Sippar Si. 203 + 204 (unpubl.).

40 Für Dialogue 1 (Streitgespräch zwischen 2 Schreibern), Z. 76–97 gibt es aus Nippur drei Exemplare, (*Heimerdinger* (1979), pl. 56 : 3 N-T 919, 461 (= A); 3 N-T 923, 503 (= B); pl. 59 3 N-T 903, 104 (= C)). Eventuell ist 3 N-T 908, 296 (ibid. pl. 57 (= D)) ein weiteres Exemplar. Die erstgenannten Texte stimmen in der Unterteilung der Zeilen in Halbzeilen (Z. 79f.) überein, während die anderen Paralleltexte aus Nippur (ibid. pl. 57 3 N-T 903, 106 (= E), SEM 65 Rs. (= F), SLT Ni 113 Rs. (= G)) keine Halbzeilen machen. In Z. 79 haben A + C i-ni-kal-kal (B ist abgebrochen), E i-ni-⌜kal⌝, F in-kal, G i-ni-kal-e. Die Texte A–C wurden wegen dieser formalen Übereinstimmungen ganz offensichtlich gleichzeitig von drei Schülern geschrieben (für D gibt es zu wenige Vergleichspunkte, um sicher zu gehen). – Selbstverständlich ist nicht völlig auszuschließen, daß ein oder zwei Schüler die Aufgabe bekamen, einen Text von einer vorhandenen Vorlage möglichst genau zu kopieren.

41 *Legrain* (1937/1947); *Waetzoldt* (1974), S. 5.

42 *Waetzoldt* (1974), S. 18, die durchschnittliche Lebensarbeitszeit beträgt je nach Provinz zwischen 8,9 und 12,4 Jahren.

43 *Waetzoldt* (1974), S. 12.

44 Vgl. *Hallo* (1982), S. 85ff.; *Cavigneaux* (1983), S. 610ff.; *Waetzoldt* (1988a), S. 42f., s. auch S. 32ff.

45 *Falkowitz* (1983/84), S. 19 mit Anm. 4 und die Einführung von Prüfungen wohl in der spätaltbabylonischen Zeit (s. oben Abschnitt »Examen«).

46 Vgl. *Falkowitz* (1983/84), S. 21f.

47 *Charpin* (1986), S. 443f.

48 *Charpin* (1986), S. 449ff. – Für die hier diskutierten Fragen ist es nicht unmittelbar von Belang, ob die in Broad Street Nr. 1 gefundenen Texte einem Lehrer oder einem ›Oberstufen‹-Schüler gehörten. Da fast keine der größeren Kompositionen vollständig ist, neige ich zur zweiten Möglichkeit. Die beiden dort gefundenen ›Literaturlisten‹ (ibid. S. 453ff.) könnten entweder Curriculum (der ›Oberstufe‹) oder Bibliothekskataloge/-inventare sein. In letzterem Fall würde man allerdings erwarten, daß ein weit größerer Prozentsatz der Texte auch tatsächlich gefunden worden wäre.

49 *Charpin* (1986), S. 460ff. Die juristische Sprache wurde anhand umfangreicher Sammlungen mit Modellverträgen, Prozeßurkunden und sonstigen juristischen Texten geübt, wie die reichen Funde bei den Ausgrabungen von Isin zeigen (*Wilcke* (1987), S. 92f.).

50 *Civil* (1975), S. 145 Anm. 36, vgl. *Hallo* (1982), S. 81ff.

51 *Wilcke* (1987), S. 85f.

52 *Tanret* (1986), S. 141ff. Vgl. dazu die Beziehungen Mesopotamien-Ebla (Syrien) kurz nach der Mitte des 3. Jahrtausends, s. *Waetzoldt* (1986), S. 43ff.

53 Civil (1985), S. 73 Komm. zu Z. 3 und *Sjöberg* (1975), S. 167 Anm. 32.

54 In dem unpublizierten Text FM 1 des Altorientalischen Seminars, Berlin, wird Kol. I 1f. ein Jugendlicher als Sohn eines Schreibers, in der Summierung VI 6' aber als »Famulus« bezeichnet; *Schneider* (1930) 324 : 31 + 32 = 172f., *Genouillac* (1912) 5270 : 6f. Auch andere ›Beamte‹ mit Schreiberausbildung haben einen Famulus, z. B. Rechnungsführer, Aufseher über die Getreidemagazine, Katasterleiter, Inspektoren, Aufseher über Weberinnen und ›Meister‹ (um-mi-a): FM 1 I 5–10 + IV 7'f., *Schneider* (1930) 324 : 1–7 = 147 (ugula-uš-bar!) –148; 34–37, 81–85 = 176f.; *Genouillac* (1910) 865 : 2f., 3536 : 4–7, 4192 : 5f.; *Genouillac* (1912) 5270 : 2–9. Ein Famulus erhält 30 Liter Gerste, *Legrain* (1937) 1391 II 12.

[55] Obwohl er noch die Ration eines Jugendlichen erhält, wird er bereits als »Schreiber« bezeichnet: *Reisner* (1901) 159 V 19ff. »ausgeschieden, 20 ›Liter‹ (Gersteration) Urbaba, der Schreiber, Sohn der Geme-Šulpae« und XII 15ff.

[56] *Brunner* (1957) 39f.; *Feucht* (1986), S. 248f., für Mesopotamien s. *Waetzoldt* (1974), S. 16f.

[57] *Waetzoldt* (1974), S. 105ff.

[58] Die Pluralform ist kein korrektes Sumerisch (richtig wäre ì-ba-e-ne), diese Bildungsweise ist aber in altbabylonischen Wirtschafts- und Rechtsurkunden sehr häufig anzutreffen. Ferner z. B. *Al-Fouadi* (1979) Nr. 112: 2f. in-sum, in-sum-e-eš »er/sie/es gab, sie gaben«.

[59] *Landsberger* (1956), S. 68, Z. 2–7, bzw. S. 82, Z. 85–87, S. 84, Z. 160–162.

[60] *Landsberger* (1956) S. 79 Zeile 1–3.

[61] *Landsberger* (1956) S. 76 I 3ff.

[62] Einige sumerische literarische Texte dienten – nach bisherigem Kenntnisstand – dazu, den Gebrauch der verschiedenen Verbformen im Kontext zu üben. So verwendete man m. E. den Anfang von Edubba B = Der Vater und sein mißratener Sohn (*Sjöberg* 1973) unter anderem zur Übung von Imperativen und Prekativ/Kohortativ-Formen, s. z. B. S. 109f. Zeile 8–22, aber auch Formen mit Prospektiv-Präformativ sind besonders häufig. Dazu s. *Hallo* (1982) S. 91 mit weiterführender Literatur.

[63] *Civil* (1987) S. 19f.

[64] Abb. 1: Dieser Text wurde in einer bereinigten Kopie (ohne die Rückseite und die Kritzeleien) von *D. O. Edzard* in »Texts in the Iraq Museum« Vol. 7. Wiesbaden 1971 als Nr. 246 publiziert. Vorliegende ältere Kopie von *D. O. Edzard* fand sich im Nachlaß von *H. Lenzen* und ich erhielt sie dank der Vermittlung von *R. M. Boehmer.* Mit Schreiben vom 2. 11. 1987 erlaubte mir *D. O. Edzard* dankenswerterweise, sie hier zu publizieren.
Abb. 2–5: nach *Deimel* (1923) S. 63 VAT 12526 (Mann mit Becher); S. 71 VAT 12772 (Keilschriftzeichen für Feld viermal in einer fast symmetrischen Zeichnung verwendet); S. 37 VAT 12606 (Rosette); *Deimel* (1922) S. 73 auf der Rückseite von VAT 9130 (Schlange).
Abb. 6–8: nach *Al-Fouadi* (1979) Nr. 167, Nr. 125 und Nr. 8.
Abb. 9a: vgl. *Falkowitz* (1983/84) S. 35 N 5928, Abb. 9b: nach Ni 3253 (vgl. Anm. 24).
Abb. 10a–c: vgl. *Michalowski* (1983) S. 152.

Literaturverzeichnis

Al-Fouadi, A.-H. (1979): Lenticular Exercise School Texts, Part 1 = Texts in the Iraq Museum Vol. X, Baghdad

Biggs, R. D. (1974): Inscriptions from Tell Abū Ṣalābīkh = Oriental Institute Publications Vol. XCIX, Chicago

Brunner, H. (1957): Altägyptische Erziehung, Wiesbaden

Castellino, G. R. (1972): Two Šulgi Hymns (BC) = Studi Semitici 42, Roma

Cavigneaux, A. (1983): Lexikalische Listen. In: Reallexikon der Assyriologie, Bd. 6. Berlin, S. 609–641

Charpin, D. (1986): Le clergé d'Ur au siècle d'Hammurabi (XIXe–XVIIIe siècles av. J.-C.) = École Pratique des Hautes Études, IVe Section, Sciences historiques et philologiques II, Hautes Études Orientales 22. Genève/Paris

Civil, M. (1975): Lexicography. In: Assyriological Studies, No. 20. Chicago, S. 123–157

Civil, M. (1985): Sur les »Livres d'écolier« à l'époque paléo-babylonienne. In: Miscellanea Babyloniaca, Mélanges offerts à Maurice Birot (ed. J.-M. Durand, J.-R. Kupper). Paris, S. 67–78
Civil, M. (1987): Sumerian Riddles: A Corpus. In: Aula Orientalis Vol. 5. Barcelona, S. 17–35
Deimel, A. (1922): Die Inschriften von Fara I = Liste der Archaischen Keilschriftzeichen. Wissensch. Veröffentl. der Deutschen Orient-Gesellschaft, Bd. 40. Leipzig
Deimel, A. (1923): Die Inschriften von Fara II = Schultexte aus Fara, Wissensch. Veröffentlichung der Deutschen Orient-Gesellschaft, Bd. 43. Leipzig
Falkenstein, A. (1953): Die babylonische Schule. In: Saeculum 4, S. 125–137
Falkowitz, R. S. (1983/84): Round Old Babylonian School Tablets. In: Archiv für Orientforschung 29/30, S. 18–45
Feucht, E. (1986): Geburt, Kindheit, Jugend und Ausbildung im Alten Ägypten. In: Zur Sozialgeschichte der Kindheit. J. Martin/A. Nitschke (Hrsg.): Freiburg/München, S. 225–265
Gadd, C. J. (1956): Teachers and Students in the oldest Schools. London
Gadd, C. J. (1957): Fragments of Assyrian Scholastic Literature. In: Bulletin of the Schools of Oriental and African Studies 20. London, S. 255–265
Genouillac, H. de (1910): Inventaire des Tablettes de Tello conservées au Musée Impérial Ottoman, Tome II. Paris
Genouillac, H. de (1912): Inventaire des Tablettes de Tello conservées au Musée Impérial Ottoman, Tome III. Paris
Genouillac, H. de (1921): Inventaire des Tablettes de Tello conservées au Musée Impérial Ottoman, Tome V. Paris
Gordon, E. I. (1959): Sumerian Proverbs. Glimpses of Everyday Life in Ancient Mesopotamia. Philadelphia
Hallo, W. W. (1982): Notes from the Babylonian Collection II. In: Journal of Cuneiform Studies, 34. Philadelphia, S. 81–93
Heimerdinger, J. W. (1979): Sumerian Literary Fragments from Nippur = Occasional Publications of the Babylonian Fund 4. Philadelphia
Hörner, H. (1986): Der Vater und sein mißratener Sohn. In: G.-B. Reinert (Hrsg.): Kindgemäße Erziehung, Festschrift für Hans Gieding zum 65. Geburtstag = Erziehungskonzeptionen und Praxis, Bd. 7. Frankfurt, S. 107–121; identisch mit Sjöberg (1973)
Kramer, S. N. (1949): Schooldays: A Sumerian Composition Relating to the Education of a Scribe. In: Journal of the American Oriental Society 69. New Haven, S. 199–215
Landsberger, B. (1956): Materialien zum Sumerischen Lexikon Bd. 4. Roma
Langdon, S. (1931): Assyrian Syllabaries and other Texts. In: Revue d'Assyriologie 28. Paris, S. 117–141
Legrain, L. (1937/1947): Ur Excavations Texts, Vol. III/1. Plates; Vol. III/2 (1947) Indexes, Vocabulary, Catalogue, Lists. London
Ludwig, M.-Ch. (1987): Untersuchungen zu den Hymnen des Išme-Dagān von Isin (unpubl. Diss., Münster)
Michalowski, P. (1983): Book Review »Materials for the Sumerian Lexicon« Vol. 14 (ed. M. Civil). In: Journal of Near Eastern Studies 42. Chicago, S. 151–152
Petschow, H. P. H. (1983): Artikel »Lehrverträge«. In: Reallexikon der Assyriologie, Bd. 6. Berlin, S. 556–570
Reisner, G. (1901): Tempelurkunden aus Telloh. Berlin
Römer, W. H. Ph. (1965): Sumerische ›Königshymnen‹ der Isin-Zeit. Leiden
Römer, W. H. Ph. (1977): Iets over School en Schoolonderricht in het Oude Mesopotamië.

Rede uitgesproken bij de aanvaarding ... de katholieke Universiteit te Nijmegen op donderdag 3 Nov. 1977. Assen/Amsterdam

Römer, W. H. Ph. (1982): Critical Review zu J. Heimerdinger, Sumerian Literary Fragments from Nippur. In: Journal of Cuneiform Studies 34. Philadelphia, S. 104–111

Schneider, N. (1930): Die Geschäftsurkunden aus Drehem und Djoha in den Staatlichen Museen zu Berlin. In: Orientalia Band 47–49. Roma

Sjöberg, Å. (1972): In Praise of the Scribal Art. In: Journal of Cuneiform Studies 24. Philadelphia, S. 126–131

Sjöberg, Å. (1973): Der Vater und sein mißratener Sohn. In: Journal of Cuneiform Studies 25. Philadelphia, S. 105–169 = Hörner 1986

Sjöberg, Å. (1975): The Old Babylonian Eduba. In: Assyriological Studies 20. Chicago, S. 159–179

Sjöberg, Å. (1975a): Der Examenstext A. In: Zeitschrift für Assyriologie 64. Berlin, S. 137–176

Tanret, M. (1986): Fragments de Tablettes pour des fragments d'histoire. In: Fragmenta Historiae Elamicae, Mélanges offerts à M. J. Steve (ed. L. de Meyer, H. Gasche, F. Vallet). Paris S. 139–150

Waetzoldt, H. (1974): Das Schreiberwesen in Mesopotamien (unpubl. Habilitationsschrift). Heidelberg

Waetzoldt, H. (1986): Keilschrift und Schulen in Mesopotamien und Ebla. In: Lenz Kriss-Rettenbeck/Max Liedtke (Hrsg.): Erziehungs- und Unterrichtsmethoden im historischen Wandel. Bad Heilbrunn. (Schriftenreihe zum Bayerischen Schulmuseum Ichenhausen, Bd. 4), S. 36–50

Waetzoldt, H. (1988): Die Situation der Frauen und Kinder anhand ihrer Einkommensverhältnisse zur Zeit der III. Dynastie von Ur. In: Altorientalische Forschungen 15. Berlin, S. 30–44

Waetzoldt, H. (1988 a): Die Entwicklung der Naturwissenschaften und des Naturwissenschaftlichen Unterrichts in Mesopotamien. In: J. G. Prinz v. Hohenzollern/Max Liedtke (Hrsg.): Naturwissenschaftlicher Unterricht und Wissenskumulation. Bad Heilbrunn. (Schriftenreihe zum Bayerischen Schulmuseum Ichenhausen, Bd. 7), S. 31–49

Wilcke, C. (1987): Die Inschriftenfunde der 7. und 8. Kampagnen. In: B. Hrouda (Hrsg.): Isin–Išān-Baḥrīyāt, Bd. III. Die Ergebnisse der Ausgrabungen 1983–84. München, S. 83–120

Gunther Wanke

Der Lehrer im alten Israel

I. Schulen im alten Israel?

Neuere Untersuchungen, das Erziehungswesen im alten Israel betreffend, konfrontieren mit einer auffälligen Aporie. Wird auf der einen Seite zwar einhellig zugestanden, daß das gesamte Alte Testament so gut wie nichts über Schulen zu berichten weiß, so scheut man sich auf der anderen Seite keineswegs, die Existenz von Schulen im alten Israel zu postulieren[1]; und obwohl der erste direkte Beleg für die Existenz von Schulen (Sir 51,23) aus der hellenistischen Zeit des alten Israel stammt, halten es nicht wenige für erforderlich, eine solche auch für die vorexilische Epoche, also für die judäische und israelitische Königszeit anzunehmen[2]; dabei wird für die Entstehung eines Schulwesens dem davidisch-salomonischen Staat zentrale Bedeutung zugemessen. Es wird darauf hingewiesen, daß die hochstehende Literatur der vorexilischen Zeit, die Verwaltung des davidisch-salomonischen Staates, die Organisation des Kultus und die fast durchgehende orthographische Korrektheit der ca. 250 bekannten hebräischen Ostraka ohne einen ausgebildeten Schreiberstand nicht vorstellbar sei und darum Schulen verschiedener Art in Israel vorausgesetzt werden müßten. Man denkt an Beamten-, Priester- und Levitenschulen[3], gelegentlich auch an Prophetenschulen[4]. *André Lemaire*[5], der sich in jüngster Zeit intensiv mit der Problematik auseinandergesetzt hat, möchte das israelitische Schulsystem sogar nach regionalen Gesichtspunkten und nach dem Ausbildungsniveau differenzieren. Er unterscheidet zwischen Schulen der Hauptstadt, Schulen der Provinzmetropolen und lokalen Schulen. Ihr Unterrichtsangebot habe sich an den jeweiligen lokalen bzw. überregionalen Bedürfnissen sowie an berufsspezifischen Anforderungen orientiert. Beschränkte sich der Elementarunterricht im wesentlichen auf die Unterweisung im Lesen und Schreiben, so sollen in den Regionalschulen, die der Ausbildung von kleinen und mittleren Beamten dienten, die Schüler darüber hinaus in der Abfassung von Verträgen und anderen Rechts- oder Verwaltungsdokumenten oder im Umgang mit Waffen unterrichtet worden sein. In den verschiedenen Schulen der Hauptstadt schließlich wäre den Schülern eine gehobene Bildung vermittelt worden. In diesem Zusammenhang sollen Texte verwendet worden sein, die später in den Kanon des Alten Testaments Eingang gefunden haben; in den Beamtenschulen etwa das Proverbienbuch, in den Prophetenschulen entsprechende prophetische Überlieferungen und in den Priesterschulen Priesterwissen, wie es heute in Lev gesammelt vorliegt.
Zur Begründung dieser These werden im wesentlichen drei Beweisgänge angeboten[6]:

1. Auswertung von alttestamentlichen Hinweisen auf außerfamiliäre Erziehung, auf Lehrer und auf Schüler, sowie auf die Verbreitung der Lese- und Schreibfähigkeit;

2. die Charakterisierung von bestimmten hebräischen Ostraka der Königszeit als Schülertexte; und
3. der Analogieschluß von den Schulverhältnissen in Ägypten, Mesopotamien und in den phönikisch-kanaanäischen Stadtstaaten auf die Verhältnisse der judäisch-israelitischen Monarchien.

Geht man die angebotenen Belege und Argumentationsketten im einzelnen durch, dann ergibt sich, daß mit ihnen die Existenz eines institutionalisierten Schulwesens wenigstens im vorexilischen Israel nicht zwingend nachweisbar ist. Alle Belege und Tatbestände erklären sich ausreichend auch bei der Annahme von Famulaturen oder von Unterweisung in der Familie. Das sei an einer Reihe von Beispielen verdeutlicht.

ad 1) *August Klostermann,* der sich als erster in unserem Jahrhundert ausführlicher mit der Frage nach dem Schulwesen im alten Israel beschäftigt hat[7], führt drei Texte als Belege an. Jes 28,7–13 bietet eine Auseinandersetzung Jesajas mit betrunkenen Priestern und Propheten, in deren Zusammenhang er einen an ihn gerichteten Vorwurf zitiert: »Wen will er Wissen lehren und wem die Kunde deuten, – den von der Milch Entwöhnten, den von der Mutterbrust Abgesetzten? Denn: (so sagt er) ›*ṣaw lāṣāw, ṣaw lāṣāw, qaw lāqāw, qaw lāqāw.* Kleiner, paß auf, Kleiner, paß auf‹« (v. 9–10)? Diese sehr umstrittene Passage soll nach *Klostermann* eine Unterrichtssituation widerspiegeln, in welcher ein Lehrer seine Schüler auffordert, die Buchstaben Ṣade und Qoph zu schreiben. Selbst wenn diese Deutung zutreffend sein sollte, reicht sie als Beleg nicht zu, denn der Kontext bezieht das Lehrerzitat auf gerade Entwöhnte, die den Familienverband kaum verlassen haben werden. In Jes 50,4–9 findet *Klostermann* das Bild des prinzipalen Lehrers gegenüber dem zungensicheren Eliteschüler verwendet, dem diejenigen anvertraut werden, deren Sprechen noch ein hilfloses Stammeln ist. Doch Jes 50,4–9 spricht von der Schülerschaft bzw. Jüngerschaft des Propheten, ganz abgesehen davon, daß Klostermann nicht ohne Textkonjekturen auskommt. Und selbst wenn der Ausdruck *limmûd* in v. 4 ›Schüler, Jünger‹ und nicht ›geübt‹ bedeuten sollte, genügt auch hier die Annahme der Famulatur für die Beschreibung des Verhältnisses ›Jahwe-Prophet‹: »Der Herr, Jahwe, hat mir die Zunge eines Jüngers gegeben, damit ich verstehe, die Müden zu stärken durch ein aufmunterndes Wort. Jeden Morgen weckt er mein Ohr, damit ich auf ihn höre wie ein Jünger.« Schließlich interpretiert *Klostermann* Prov 22,17–21 als Abschiedsworte eines Lehrers an seinen ausgereiften Schüler, welche belegen, daß »in den altisraelitischen Schulen auf den höheren Stufen der Lehrer diktierte, was der Schüler schreiben sollte, und daß ebenso der Schüler in Schrift zu reproduzieren hatte, was ihm von den mündlichen Vorträgen des Lehrers im Gedächtnis geblieben war«.[9] Auch dieser letzte Text leistet nicht das, was er leisten soll. Unabhängig davon, daß er von der ägyptischen Lehre des Amen-em-ope abhängig ist – was *Klostermann* noch nicht wissen konnte – und daß *Klostermann* auch hier zu gravierenden Textänderungen greifen mußte, mag er zwar einiges über das Verhältnis von Lehrer und Schüler aussagen, liefert aber keinen Beleg für die Existenz von Schulen.

Als indirekte Hinweise auf das Vorhandensein von Schulen werden ferner diejenigen Texte angesehen, welche die weite *Verbreitung der Lese- und Schreibfähigkeit* im alten Israel belegen sollen; eine Verbreitung, die trotz der Einfachheit des hebräischen Alphabets im Vergleich mit den Schriftsystemen der umliegenden Hochkulturen ohne schulische Ausbildung nur schwer erklärbar sei.[10] Dazu einige Beispiele: Nach Ri 8,13–17 soll Gideon einen jungen Mann aus der Stadt Sukkot festgenommen haben, der in der Lage war, ihm die Namen der 77 Honoratioren der Stadt aufzuschreiben. Dtn 6,9 gebietet, daß jeder Israelit die Worte, auf welche er durch Mose verpflichtet wird, an die Türpfosten seines Hauses schreiben soll. Dtn 24,1–3 soll voraussetzen, daß jeder Ehemann in der Lage sei, einen Scheidebrief abzufassen. Jer 32,12 berichtet, daß eine vom Propheten abgefaßte Kaufurkunde von Zeugen unterschrieben worden ist. Nach Hab 2,2 erhält der Prophet den Auftrag, eine Vision schriftlich so festzuhalten, daß sie mühelos wieder gelesen werden kann. Diese Beispiele, die mühelos um weitere vermehrt werden könnten, lassen zwar erkennen, daß es im vorexilischen Israel eine Schicht Gebildeter gegeben hat, die des Lesens und Schreibens kundig war, liefern aber keinerlei Hinweise dafür, *wie* diese Fähigkeiten erworben wurden. Auch können sie nicht als Beleg für die Verbreitung des Schreibens im Volk herangezogen werden, denn die Anweisungen aus Dtn 6,9 und 24,1–3 lassen sich mühelos auch ohne eine solche Voraussetzung verstehen (bildliche Redeweise; Erledigung des Auftrags durch Schreibkundige), was für die übrigen Belege erst recht gilt.

Einige Texte weisen darauf hin, daß *Königssöhne* eine *besondere Erziehung* genossen. So berichtet 2. Kön 10,1–6 von Erziehern *('omᵉnîm)* der Prinzen Ahabs, die offensichtlich der Oberschicht der Stadt Samaria angehörten. 1. Chr 27,32 nennt unter den Beamten Davids einen Beamten, der bei den Söhnen des Königs war, also doch offensichtlich für ihre Erziehung zuständig war. Vielleicht kann noch die Erwähnung von jungen Leuten, die mit dem König Rehabeam groß geworden sind (1. Kön 12,8) als Hinweis dafür verstanden werden, daß die Königssöhne gemeinsam mit den Söhnen der Großen des Landes erzogen worden sind. Damit sind die Belege auch schon erschöpft. Für die Annahme einer Hofschule etwa bieten aber auch sie keine ausreichende Basis.

Schließlich hat man darauf hingewiesen, daß von den *Weisen (ḥᵃkāmîn)* gesagt wird, sie erteilten Unterweisung *(tôrāh)* (Prov 13,14) und vermittelten Erkenntnis *(daʿat)* (Prov 15,2.7). Und in Prov 5,13 bekennt einer, er habe nicht auf die Stimme seiner Unterweiser *(môrîm)* und seiner Lehrer *(mᵉlammᵉdîm)* gehört. Wie in Ägypten begegnet auch in den Proverbien die Anrede »Vater« bzw. »Sohn« für Lehrer und Schüler (Prov 4,1; 5,7; 7,24; 8,32), wobei auch die Erwähnung einer Mehrzahl von Schülern/Söhnen als Indiz dafür gewertet wird, daß die genannten Stellen nicht die Unterweisung in der Familie, sondern die schulische Unterweisung im Blick haben[11].

Am Rande sei noch vermerkt, daß *Ausdrücke für Lehrer (môrāh, mᵉlammed, mebîn) und für Schüler (limmûd, talmîd)* im Alten Testament nur ganz selten vorkommen[12]; ein Tatbestand, der auch nicht gerade für die Existenz von Schulen spricht, zumal an keiner Stelle erkennbar ist, daß die Ausdrücke sich auf einen Berufsstand beziehen.

Das zur Verfügung stehende alttestamentliche Quellenmaterial liefert also kein überzeugendes Bild. Klare Zeugnisse für ein Schulwesen im alten Israel mit berufsmäßigen Lehrern und einem geregelten Unterricht fehlen[13]. Das gilt vor allem für die vorexilische Zeit, wohl aber auch für die nachexilische Zeit während der Perserherrschaft. Erst in hellenistischer Zeit ist es, wie Sir 51,23 belegt, im Zusammenhang mit der Integration von Weisheitslehre und Torahfrömmigkeit zur Ausbildung eines mit der Lehre befaßten Berufsstandes und zur Einrichtung von Schulen gekommen[14].

ad 2) Angesichts der schlechten Quellenlage verwundert es nicht, daß man sich bei den *hebräischen Inschriften*, die in den letzten Jahrzehnten in Palästina bei Ausgrabungen zutage getreten sind, nach Belegmaterial umgesehen hat. Die in Frage kommenden Inschriften wurden von *André Lemaire*[15] zusammengestellt, ausführlich beschrieben und als Schülertexte qualifiziert. Das einschlägige Material wird schließlich nach bestimmten Merkmalen klassifiziert, die Hinweise auf das Schulwesen liefern sollen. Im einzelnen handelt es sich um folgende Textsorten:

1. Alphabettexte (Lachisch, Kadesch-Barnea, Kuntillet ʿAğrūd, vll. Aroër ʿIzbet Ṣartah); 2. Texte mit isolierten Buchstaben oder Buchstabengruppen (vll. Arad und ʿIzbet Ṣartah); 3. Texte mit Buchstaben, die entsprechend ihrer Ähnlichkeit gruppiert sind (vll. Lachisch); 4. Texte, auf denen einzelne Wörter mehrmals geschrieben wurden (Arad, Kadesch-Barnea, vll. Kuntillet ʿAğrūd); 5. Texte mit Eigennamen (Arad, Aroër); 6. Briefeingangsformulare (Kuntillet ʿAğrūd); 7. Monatsliste (Geser); 8. Ostraka mit Zahlensymbolen (Kadesch-Barnea, vll. Lachisch und Arad); 9. Ostrakon mit einer Zahlenfolge (Einer, Zehner, Hunderter) verbunden mit einer Maßangabe (Kadesch-Barnea); 10. Zeichnungen (Kuntillet ʿAğrūd; wahrscheinlich Lachisch); 11. Schülerübung beim Erlernen einer Fremdsprache (Phönizisch) (Kuntillet ʿAğrūd).

Sieht man einmal davon ab, daß einzelne der von *Lemaire* vorgelegten Textbeispiele auch anderen institutionellen Kontexten zugeordnet werden können[16], sieht man ferner davon ab, daß *Lemaire* selbst das Belegmaterial »très pauvre et très fragmentaire« nennt[17], und setzt man demgegenüber voraus, daß die vorgeschlagene Klassifikation und Qualifizierung der Texte korrekt ist, dann belegen sie zwar wie zahlreiche alttestamentliche Beispiele auch, daß es im vorexilischen Israel Gebildete gegeben hat, die des Schreibens und Lesens mächtig waren, sie sagen aber nichts darüber aus, *wie* diese Fähigkeiten erworben wurden. Die Spärlichkeit des Materials spricht auch hier nicht gerade für die Annahme eines differenzierten und über das Land verbreiteten Schulwesens. Der gegenwärtige Stand der Ausgrabungen in Palästina läßt mehr und den umliegenden Kulturen entsprechendes erwarten, als bislang zutage getreten ist. Demgegenüber genügt es auch hier vorauszusetzen, daß Kenntnisse und Bildung über die Famulatur vermittelt worden sind.

ad 3) Schließlich ist der Versuch zu erwähnen, *von den Schulverhältnissen* in *den Hochkulturen Mesopotamiens und vor allem Ägyptens auf die Situation in Palästina* zur Zeit der judäischen und israelitischen Könige *zurückzuschließen*[18]. Dieses Verfahren hat einiges für sich. Zum einen ist unbestritten, daß sich der neu konstituierende Staat Davids und Salomos in Ermangelung eigener Traditionen auf dem Gebiet der Verwaltung an den benachbarten Großreichen, im besonderen an Ägypten orientierte. Die grundlegende innere Organisation des Staates wurde vor allem zur Zeit Salomos ins Werk gesetzt, und man kann davon ausgehen, daß sie in den Nachfolgestaaten Juda und Israel im wesentlichen beibehalten wurde. Die ausgedehnte Finanzverwaltung (1. Kön 4), ein gut ausgebauter Innen- und Außenhandel (1. Kön 9,27f.; 10,26–30), die beeindruckenden Baumaßnahmen in der Hauptstadt Jerusalem (1. Kön 5,17–7,51), der Ausbau zahlreicher Städte zur militärischen Sicherung des Staates und die damit zusammenhängende Organisation der Fron (1. Kön 9,15–23) erforderten gewiß eine nicht geringe Zahl von Beamten. Entsprechend hoch war das Bildungsbedürfnis. Neben den elementaren Kenntnissen des Schreibens und Lesens waren für die Verwaltung sicherlich auch gewisse mathematische und juristische Kenntnisse erforderlich; für die im diplomatischen Verkehr eingesetzten Beamten darf man wohl auch die Beherrschung des Akkadischen voraussetzen, das nach Ausweis der Amarna-Texte ab der Mitte des 2. Jt. die Sprache der Diplomatie in Syrien-Palästina gewesen ist. Die Vermittlung dieser Kenntnisse traut man der Erziehung in den Familien nicht mehr zu und setzt daher voraus, daß zu diesem Zweck mindestens am Jerusalemer Hof eine Beamtenschule nach ägyptischem Vorbild – in der Sprachausbildung vielleicht auch nach mesopotamischem Vorbild – eingerichtet worden ist. Als Beweis für diese Annahme wird ins Feld geführt, daß in den Beamtenlisten Davids und Salomos (2. Sam 8,16–18; 20,23–26; 1. Kön 4,2–6) neben anderen mit *mazkîr* »Kanzler« (?) und *sôper* »Schreiber« Ämter begegnen, die ebenfalls auf ägyptische Vorbilder zurückgeführt werden müssen (ägypt. *wḥm* bzw. *sš*)[19]; ferner, daß es zahlreiche Bezüge zwischen der ägpytischen und der israelitischen Weisheitsliteratur gibt, deren Träger ja vorwiegend bei den Lehrern dieser Schulen vermutet werden. Erwähnt seien u. a. nur die Bezeichnung »Vater/Sohn« für »Lehrer/Schüler« oder die engen Beziehungen zwischen Prov 22,17–24,33 und der Lehre des Amen-em-ope[20]. Schließlich wird darauf hingewiesen, daß Salomo mit dem ägyptischen Königshaus verschwägert war, also ägyptischer Einfluß am Jerusalemer Hof zu erwarten ist (1. Kön 9,16[21]) und die Einrichtung einer Schule nach ägyptischem Vorbild sehr wahrscheinlich erscheint.

Dieser Auffassung wird nun entgegengehalten, daß es zu denken geben müsse, wenn unter den Beamten Davids und Salomos keiner erwähnt ist, der für die Hof- oder Beamtenschule verantwortlich war. Darüber hinaus sei die Rekrutierung von Beamten für den jungen, entstehenden Staat kein Problem gewesen, weil David und Salomo auf die Erfahrung derjenigen Beamten zurückgreifen konnten, die mit der Integration der kanaanäischen Stadtstaaten in das davidisch-salomonische Reich (Jerusalem!) in die israelitische Verwaltung übernommen wurden. Über diese kanaanäischen Beamten erkläre sich auch der starke ägyptische Einfluß in der israelitischen Staatsverwaltung. Schließlich sei auch in der Folgezeit eine eigenständige schulische Ausbildung der Beamten nicht nötig gewesen, da das Amt der Schreiber in den Familien erblich war[22]. Etwas weniger überzeugend ist *Friedemann Golkas* Gegenargument, man dürfe die hochentwickelte Organisation des ägyptischen Mittleren und Neuen Reichs nicht mit den in den Anfängen steckenden israelitischen Staaten vergleichen, sondern müsse zum Vergleich das ägyptische Alte Reich heranziehen, dessen Gesellschaftsstruktur schon eher dem davidischen Staat entspreche[23]. Abgesehen davon, daß die Entwicklung von Gesellschaften verschiedener Staaten nicht in jedem Fall parallel verläuft, ist nicht einzusehen, warum ein weniger entwickeltes Staatsgebilde nicht von

den Erfahrungen eines entwickelteren profitieren und lernen kann, so es die Möglichkeit dazu hat.
Trägt man alles zusammen, dann ergibt sich bei kritischer Betrachtung der Quellen nach dem gegenwärtigen Stand unserer Kenntnisse, daß ein schlüssiger Beweis für Existenz von Schulen im alten Israel nicht zur Verfügung steht. Und es ist ratsamer, angesichts dieses Tatbestands Zurückhaltung in der Konstruktion von Hypothesen zu üben, als auf nicht ausreichend begründete Annahmen weitere Hypothesen aufzubauen[24].

II. Erzieher im alten Israel

Das eher ernüchternde Ergebnis bisheriger Versuche, Licht in das Schulwesen des alten Israel zu bringen, nötigt natürlich auch zur Zurückhaltung bei der Beschreibung der Funktion des Lehrers, bescheidener ausgedrückt, bei der Beschreibung der Funktion derjeniger, die Träger von Erziehung und Unterweisung gewesen sind.
Auch wenn wir dafür keine Belege haben, kann als selbstverständlich und natürlich angenommen werden, daß der *Familie* eine zentrale Bedeutung in der Unterweisung zukam. In der Regel wird der Vater seinen Kindern diejenigen Kenntnisse vermittelt haben, die für ihr künftiges Leben von elementarer Bedeutung gewesen sind. Dabei hat gewiß der Beruf des Vaters eine dominierende Rolle gespielt, zumal man davon ausgehen kann, daß sowohl im Bereich der Landwirtschaft als auch im Bereich des Handwerks und »gehobener« Berufe die Söhne in die Fußstapfen ihrer Väter getreten sind. Von der Erblichkeit etwa des Schreiberamtes war schon die Rede. Ähnliches wird man auch für die Berufe des Priesters, des Musikers, des Töpfers und der verschiedenen Bauhandwerke annehmen dürfen.
Mit dem Zusammenbruch der staatlichen und kultischen Institutionen Judas und Israels im Kontext der babylonischen und assyrischen Eroberungen des 8.–6. Jh. gewinnt auch die *religiöse Unterweisung* im Rahmen der Familie zentrale Bedeutung. Eine Reihe von Texten, die der Gattung »Kinderbelehrung« zuzuordnen sind (Dtn 6,20–24; Ex 12,26ff.; 13,14ff.; Jos 4,6ff.; 4,21–24), lassen erkennen, daß nicht nur die Vermittlung der geschichtstheologischen Überlieferungen, sondern auch die Unterweisung in grundsätzlichen kultischen Fragen in die Kompetenz des Vaters gehörte: »Wenn euch eure Söhne fragen: Was bedeutet diese Feier?, dann sagt: Es ist das Passa-Opfer zur Ehre Jahwes, der in Ägypten an den Häusern der Israeliten vorüberging, als er die Ägypter mit Unheil schlug, unsere Häuser aber verschonte.« (Ex 12,26f.)[25].
Die Proverbien lassen erkennen, daß auch die *Mutter* wesentlichen Anteil an der Unterweisung der Kinder hatte. So ermahnen Prov 1,8 und 6,20 den Sohn, auf die Mahnung des Vaters und die Lehre der Mutter zu hören. Eine kleine Sammlung von Weisheitssprüchen trägt sogar die Überschrift: »Worte an Lemuel, den König von Massa, mit denen ihn seine Mutter ermahnt hat« (Prov 31,1).
Die zentrale Bedeutung der väterlichen Erziehung kommt auch darin zum Ausdruck,

daß in *außerfamiliärer Erziehung* die Bezeichnung ›Vater‹ bzw. ›Sohn‹ üblich gewesen ist. Auf die entsprechende Anwendung dieser Ausdrücke auf Weisheitslehrer und ihre Schüler wurde oben bereits hingewiesen. Auch Propheten scharten Schüler bzw. Jünger um sich wie etwa Elisa (2. Kön 4,1.38; 6,1) oder Jesaja (Jes 8,16). Und von Elisa ist bezeugt, daß er bei der Entrückung seines Meisters Elia diesen als »mein Vater« anrief (2. Kön 2,13). Ähnlich bezeichnet der Priester Eli den ihm anvertrauten Samuel als »mein Sohn« (1. Sam 3,6). Aus den genannten Belegen geht ferner hervor, daß Kinder und junge Männer zur Ausbildung für einen bestimmten Beruf etwa Priestern und Propheten übergeben werden konnten bzw. sich diesen anschlossen und in einem familienähnlichen Lehrer-Schülerverhältnis lebten. Daß dies jedoch nicht der Regelfall gewesen ist, zeigt die Spärlichkeit der Belege. Sie lassen auch kaum etwas davon erkennen, *wie* sich die Unterweisung im einzelnen vollzog, so daß auch die Rekonstruktion der Funktion des Lehrers im alten Israel auf Vermutungen und Analogieschlüsse angewiesen bleibt.

Das Ergebnis stellt sicherlich nicht zufrieden. Die Frage nach einem Schulwesen mit professionellen Lehrern muß letztlich offen bleiben. Die Gründe dafür sind zum einen in der Eigenart der alttestamentlichen Überlieferung zu suchen, die primär die religiösen Traditionen Israels bewahrt hat und an den gesellschaftlichen Strukturen Israels nur insoweit interessiert war, als sie theologisch relevant waren. Dazu kommt zum anderen, daß das Alte Testament nur einen ganz bestimmten Ausschnitt auch der religiösen Literatur Altisraels darstellt, also keineswegs seine gesamte literarische Überlieferung präsentiert. Schließlich sind die durch die Ausgrabungen ans Licht gekommenen schriftlichen Zeugnisse Israels mit den in Mesopotamien, Ägypten und Ugarit gefundenen Archiven weder an Umfang noch an Qualität zu vergleichen, was angesichts der intensiven Bemühungen der palästinischen Archäologie um die Erforschung der materiellen Überreste der Kultur Altisraels nicht mehr als zufällig bezeichnet werden kann.

Anmerkungen

1 G. v. Rad 1970, 31 und H.-J. Hermisson 1986, 97.
2 Neben den in Anm. 1 Genannten z. B. B. Lang 1979 und A. Lemaire 1981 (mit ausführlichen Literaturangaben).
3 G. v. Rad 1970, 31f.
4 A. Lemaire 1981, 70f.
5 A. Lemaire 1981, 49; vgl. auch B. Lang 1979, 195–199, der ebenfalls den Versuch einer Rekonstruktion eines »Lehrplans« unternimmt.
6 Siehe hierzu im einzelnen R. N. Whybray 1974, 35–38, und J. L. Crenshaw 1985, 601f.
7 A. Klostermann 1908, 193–323.
8 Zur Übersetzung siehe O. Kaiser 1983^3, 193.
9 A. Klostermann 1908, 231.

[10] B. Lang 1979, 190, gegen W. F. Albright, in: City Invincible, 1960, 122.
[11] B. Lang 1979, 192–195, und H.-J. Hermisson 1968, 121.
[12] *môrāh*: Jes 9,14; 30,20 (Gott); Hab 2,18; Hi 36,22 (Gott); Prov 5,1; 2. Chr 15,3 (Priester). – *m^elammed*: Ps 119,99; Prov 5,13. – *mebîn*: 1. Chr 25,8. – *limmûd*: Jes 8,16; 50,4; 54,13; Jer 2,24; 13,23. – *talmîd*: 1. Chr 25,8.
[13] Mit H. D. Preuß 1987, 45f., und J. L. Crenshaw 1985, 611f.
[14] Zum Schulwesen im Frühjudentum siehe L. Dürr 1934, 177–180, und Enzyklopaedia Judaica 6 (1930).
[15] Siehe A. Lemaire 1981 mit weiterer Literatur.
[16] Vgl. J. L. Crenshaw 1985, 606.
[17] A. Lemaire 1981, 84.
[18] L. Dürr 1934 u. a.
[19] H. Donner 1984, 203f., 227f., und T. N. D. Mettinger 1971.
[20] Chr. Kayatz 1966, mit weiteren Belegen.
[21] Die Identität des pharaonischen Schwiegervaters Salomos ist nicht zu ermitteln.
[22] Einzelheiten siehe bei F. W. Golka 1983, 263, und R. N. Whybray 1974, 38.
[23] F. W. Golka 1983, 264f.
[24] Vgl. A. Lemaire 1981, der der altisraelitischen Schule einen wesentlichen Anteil an der Entstehung der alttestamentlichen Überlieferung zugestehen möchte.
[25] Siehe H.-J. Fabry 1982, 754–760.

Literaturverzeichnis

Crenshaw, James L. (1981): Old Testament Wisdom. Atlanta

Crenshaw, James L. (1985): Education in Ancient Israel. In: Journal of Biblical Literature 104, S. 601–615

Donner, Herbert (1984): Geschichte des Volkes Israel und seiner Nachbarn in Grundzügen, Band I. Göttingen

Dürr, Lorenz (1934): Das Erziehungswesen im Alten Testament und im antiken Orient. In: Handbuch der Erziehungswissenschaft, V/1. München, S. 143–188

Enzyklopaedia Judaica 6 (1930): Erziehung. Berlin, Sp. 742–747

Fabry, Heinz-Josef (1982): Gott im Gespräch zwischen den Generationen. Überlegungen zur »Kinderfrage« im Alten Testament. In: Katechetische Blätter 107, S. 754–760

Golka, Friedemann W. (1983): Die israelitische Weisheitsschule oder »des Kaisers neue Kleider«. In: Vetus Testamentum 33. Leiden, S. 257–270.

Hermisson, Hans-Jürgen (1968): Studien zur israelitischen Spruchweisheit. Neukirchen-Vluyn

Kaiser, Otto (1983³): Der Prophet Jesaja Kapitel 13–39. Göttingen

Kayatz, Christa (1966): Studien zu Proverbien 1–9. Neukirchen-Vluyn

Klostermann, August (1908): Schulwesen im alten Israel. In: Theologische Studien, Festschrift Th. Zahn. Leipzig, S. 193–232

Lang, Bernhard (1975): Frau Weisheit. Düsseldorf

Lang, Bernhard (1979): Schule und Unterricht im alten Israel. In: La Sagesse de l'Ancien Testament. Löwen, S. 186–201

Lemaire, André (1981): Les écoles et la formation de la Bible dans l'ancien Israel. Fribourg–Göttingen (Mit weiterer Literatur!)

Mettinger, Trygve N. D. (1971): Solomonic State Officials. Lund
Preuß, Horst Dietrich (1987): Einführung in die alttestamentliche Weisheitsliteratur. Stuttgart-Berlin–Köln–Mainz
v. Rad, Gerhard (1970, 1982[2]): Weisheit in Israel. Neukirchen-Vluyn
Whybray, R. N. (1974): The Intellectual Tradition in the Old Testament. Berlin–New York

Hans-Werner Fischer-Elfert

Der Schreiber als Lehrer in der frühen ägyptischen Hochkultur

1. Literalität im alten Ägypten

Die Tätigkeit des Schreibens, sei es von profanen Urkunden oder religiösen und literarischen Werken, stand zu allen Epochen der pharaonischen Geschichte Ägyptens in höchstem Ansehen. Und der Beruf des Schreibers in seiner mindestens doppelten Funktion als aktenkundiger Verwalter wie als Lehrer und Ausbilder wurde über das Medium Literatur stets als der erstrebenswerteste und angenehmste aller Berufe propagiert. Im Folgenden sollen einige Äußerungen aus derartigen Werbeschriften für den Schreiberberuf zu Wort kommen. Man kann die Hochschätzung dieses Amtes um einiges besser verstehen, wenn man den ungefähren prozentualen Anteil der Schriftkundigen an der wahrscheinlichen Gesamtbevölkerung berücksichtigt. Da uns keine absoluten Zahlen über die Stärke der altägyptischen Population vorliegen, ist über grobe Schätzungen, die natürlich nur approximativen Charakter haben, nicht hinauszukommen. Nur *Diodor* spricht an einer Stelle in seinem Bericht über Ägypten (I.31.8) von angeblich 7 Millionen Menschen, eine Zahl, die aber möglicherweise auf einer Verderbnis beruht und zu hoch angesetzt ist (dazu *Baines/Eyre,* 1983, 65). Die zu dieser Frage in jüngster Zeit angestellten Überlegungen (*Baines,* 1983, 584; *Baines/Eyre,* 1983, 65ff. mit Verweisen) gelangen zu einer Zahl von etwa 1 Million Einwohnern zur Zeit des Alten Reiches, also der zweiten Hälfte des 3. vorchr. Jahrtausends, bis hin zu etwa 4 Millionen am Ende des 2. Jahrtausends. Unter Einbeziehung sämtlicher bekannten und beschrifteten Gräber der Mittel- und Oberschicht und damit des literaten Beamtenstandes beläuft sich der Grad der Literalität im Alten Reich auf gerade 1%. In späteren Zeiten dürfte er nur geringfügig höher gewesen sein.

So spekulativ diese Daten auch sind, vermögen sie uns doch eine annähernd realistische Vorstellung von dem herausragenden Stellenwert zu vermitteln, den ein Lese- und Schreibkundiger innerhalb der damaligen Gesellschaft eingenommen hat. In diesem Zusammenhang muß noch darauf hingewiesen werden, daß mit der Fähigkeit zum Schreiben auch ausnahmslos ein Amt in der Verwaltung verbunden war. Literalität unter den nicht zur Beamtenschaft gehörigen Leuten scheint nur äußerst gering und dann auch nur auf einem niedrigen Niveau verbreitet gewesen zu sein. Und wenn der Schreibertitel auch recht häufig in den Inschriften auftaucht, so besagt das nicht in jedem Falle, daß der jeweilige Träger diesen Beruf tatsächlich ausgeübt hat bzw. lesen und schreiben konnte. Denn wie noch im modernen Ägypten beschränkt sich deren Literalität bisweilen darauf, gerade den eigenen Namen niederkritzeln zu können (*Pestman,* 1982, 161 (4) und 171 n. 36).

2. Ausbildung zum Schreiber

Kommen wir nun zur Frage der Ausbildung eines ägyptischen Schreibers. Das genaue Lebensalter, in dem diese begann, ist uns nicht bekannt. Das gleiche gilt für die Dauer der Schüler- und Gehilfenzeit. Wahrscheinlich wird der Eintritt in die Schule zwischen dem fünften und zehnten Lebensjahr stattgefunden haben. Aber weniger das genaue Lebensalter, das ja zudem in wohl nicht wenigen Fällen unbekannt gewesen ist, als vielmehr das Erreichen einer bestimmten Körpergröße mag hierbei den Ausschlag gegeben haben. Bei der Rekrutierung von Soldaten war dies anscheinend der Fall, wie bestimmte Erwähnungen vermuten lassen (zur Frage des Schuleintritts s. *Brunner,* 1957, 38ff. sowie *Korostovtzev,* 1962, 34, hier zitiert nach der Rezension durch *Meeks,* 1968, 1967, 189ff.). Dieser war übrigens freiwillig, eine allgemeine Schulpflicht hat es nie gegeben. Von der Institution »Schule« hören wir zum erstenmal in der Inschrift eines Provinzfürsten namens Cheti aus der Zeit um 2100 vor Christus. In einer Ermahnung an die Besucher seines Grabes sagt er: »Jeder Schreiber, jeder Gelehrte, der ein Geschickter seines Faches ist, ein im Schreiben Perfekter, ein in der Gelehrsamkeit Perfekter, der sich den Namen eines Mannes (von Rang) erworben hat, der eine Stellung einnimmt, nachdem er in die Schule gegangen ist, ..., der eintreten sollte in dieses Grab« etc. (*Edel,* 1984, 108ff.). Was wir hier als »Schule« übersetzen, bedeutet wörtlich »Raum der Belehrung, des Unterrichts«. Was des weiteren an dieser wenn auch kurzen Passage lohnt festgehalten zu werden, ist die Tatsache, daß ein Schreiber oder »Gelehrter«, lit. »Sachkundiger«, erst dann ein Amt in der straff durchorganisierten Beamtenhierarchie bekleiden kann, wenn er vorweg die Schulbank gedrückt hat.

Unterrichtet wurden die Schüler wohl in der Regel nicht von hauptamtlichen Lehrern – von einem eigenen Berufsstand erfahren wir nur sehr wenig; dazu unten –, sondern von in der Verwaltung tätigen Beamten, die ja durchweg schreib- und lesekundig sein mußten. Es geht aus den Quellen nicht ganz eindeutig hervor, wann, d. h. zu welcher Tageszeit der Unterricht stattfand, und ob dies etwa während der regulären Dienstzeit der Beamten oder nach Feierabend geschah. Vielleicht darf aber eine Bemerkung in der noch heranzuziehenden »Lehre des Dua-Cheti«, einer ausgesprochenen Propagandaschrift zur Werbung des Beamtennachwuchses, in diesem Kontext herangezogen werden, aus der hervorgeht, daß der Schultag um die Mittagsstunde beendet war: »Wenn du aus der Schule kommst, nachdem dir der Mittag verkündet worden ist, dann gehe in die Vorhalle des Gebäudes und diskutiere« den durchgenommenen Schulstoff (*Helck,* 1970, 134). Diese Stelle spricht zumindest für feste Unterrichtszeiten, darf aber nicht gleichzeitig für die Existenz eines installierten Lehrerkollegiums mit geregelter Arbeitszeit in Anspruch genommen werden.

Dennoch hören wir gelegentlich von Beamten, deren einzige Aufgabe darin bestanden zu haben scheint, an einer Ausbildungsstätte zu lehren. Ein Herr namens Seneb führt auf seinem Siegel nur den Titel eines »Lehrers des Lebenshauses« (*Brunner,* 1957, 32 n. 82; der angebliche »Schreiber der Schule des Pharao« und »Oberste Lehrer des Palastes« Teti-anch, dessen Stele sich in Florenz befindet, ist wohl eher eine Art

»Hofastronom« gewesen, wie *Černý*, 1963, 173, wahrscheinlich gemacht hat). Dieses »Lebenshaus« als einer den örtlichen Tempeln angegliederten Institution ist aber nicht mit dem gewöhnlichen Terminus für »Unterrichtsraum« oder »Schule« zu verwechseln, auch wenn diese sich mitunter auf Tempelgelände befunden hat (*Brunner*, 1957, 18).
Auf einer Stele des Kunsthistorischen Museums in Wien ist ein »Lehrer der Schrift« zwar namentlich genannt, über seine konkrete Tätigkeit oder Karriere wird aber leider nichts mitgeteilt.
Als Verfasser einer Besucherinschrift im Pyramidenbezirk des Königs Djoser lernen wir einen ansonsten unbekannten »Schreiber der Schule« namens Sethemheb kennen (*Firth / Quibell*, 1935, 78 A).
In einer anonymen Weisheitslehre aus der Zeit um etwa 1700 v. Chr. findet sich an einer Stelle die so lapidar anmutende Bemerkung: »Der Gehilfe betrachtet (respektvoll) den Lehrer« (*Barns*, 1956, pl. 7, iii4 und p. 12). Der genaue Kontext ist bedauerlicherweise noch immer unklar, da aber in demselben Text kurz zuvor von »alten Schriften« die Rede war, werden mit dem »Gehilfen« und dem »Lehrer« ein Schreiberschüler und sein Meister gemeint sein und nicht etwa Angehörige aus dem handwerklichen Milieu, für die diese Bezeichnungen ja auch verwendet werden.
Nach den grundlegenden Untersuchungen von Hellmut *Brunner* über das altägyptische Erziehungswesen (1957) ist davon auszugehen, daß die Schüler seit ca. 2100 v. Chr., also der ersten Erwähnung eines »Unterrichtsraumes« (s. o.), zunächst klassenweise in einer Art Elementarschule mit Hilfe der Ganzwortmethode in die zeitgenössische Kursive eingeführt wurden. Für die Epoche davor, grob gesagt also das Alte Reich, wird allgemein davon ausgegangen, daß die auszubildenden Schreiberschüler nach Art der Famulatur unterrichtet wurden, von ihrem jeweiligen Lehrer Einzelunterricht erhielten.
Nach Absolvierung der Grundschule, deren Dauer wie bereits betont unbekannt ist, wurden die Eleven dann zur weiteren Ausbildung einem Beamten anvertraut und in den Beruf eingewiesen, den sie später einmal praktizieren sollten. Während dieser Zeit durften sie sich bereits »Schreiber« nennen, ebenso häufig begegnet aber auch die etwas unterwürfige Bezeichnung »Gehilfe«, was wörtlich übertragen soviel bedeutet wie »der sich unter der Aufsicht / Anleitung jmds. befindet«. Aus der Autobiographie des Hohenpriesters Bakenchons (Zeit: 13. Jhdt. v. Chr.) erfahren wir, daß dieser zunächst vier Jahre die Grundschule besucht hat, um danach in den königlichen Pferdestall überzuwechseln, bis er schließlich am Ende seiner Laufbahn und zugleich seines für ägyptische Verhältnisse langen Lebens »Hohenpriester des Amun« von Theben, der damaligen Hauptstadt, wurde. In dieser seiner letzten Stellung hat er dann auch erzieherisch gewirkt. Immerhin heißt es im Verlaufe der Aufzählung seiner zahlreichen Ämter, daß er auch »ein guter Vater (s)einer Untergebenen« gewesen sei und »deren Nachkommen aufgezogen« habe (*Plantikow-Münster*, 1969, 118ff.). Wie im Falle des Bakenchons ist auch bei allen übrigen Priestern und Beamten ein fortgeschrittenes Lebensalter Voraussetzung für die Befähigung und eventuell auch Berechtigung zum Lehrer gewesen. Der weise Ptahhotep z. B., seines Zeichens Vezier und damit oberster Staatsbeamter, schildert eindrücklich zu Beginn seiner berühmten

Lehre all seine körperlichen Gebrechen, die ihn im Alter ereilt haben. Eine gehörige Portion Lebenserfahrung und Reife war vonnöten, bevor Beamte ihren Wissensfundus und vor allem ihre moralischen und ethischen Maximen und Einsichten ihren Nachfolgern vermitteln konnten. Ihr Leben und ihre Karriere sollte dabei gleichsam als Vorbild dienen. Der Verfasser der »Lehre für Kagemni« aus dem Alten Reich reicht seine Erkenntnise erst in dem Augenblick an seine Nachkommen weiter, »nachdem«, wie der Text feststellt, »er das Wesen der Menschen erkannt hatte und ihr Charakter ihm klargeworden war« (*Gardiner,* 1946).

3. Leistungswettbewerb

In einer der zahlreichen sog. »Schülerhandschriften« (*Brunner,* 1984) aus der Ramessidenzeit (13.–11. Jahrh. v. Chr.) reflektiert der Lehrer über seine eigene Vergangenheit als nicht eben strebsamer Schüler (*Gardiner,* 1937, 65f.; Übersetzung bei *Caminos,* 1954, 250f.). Zur Strafe für seine Pflichtsäumigkeit wird er in den »Stock« gesperrt, wohl eine Art Fußfessel, und dies für die Dauer von drei vollen Monaten. Nachdem er aber die Strafe verbüßt und er die Schändlichkeit seines Treibens außerhalb der Schule erkannt hat, setzt er zu wahren Höchstleistungen im Schreiben an: »Ich übertraf den, der vor mir war, und ich war an der Spitze all meiner Kameraden. Ich überflügelte sie (im Beschriften) von Papyrusrollen.« Ein anderer »Schreiber und Lehrer der Gehilfen in der Halle der Schriften« namens Hori schmückt sich mit u. a. so hochtrabenden Epitheta wie »Erster seiner Kameraden, Vorderster in seiner Sippe, Erster in seiner Generation, dessen Ebenbild es nicht gibt«. Und bezüglich dessen, weswegen man ihm nacheifert, gibt er an: »Man handelt nach ihm gegenüber jedem Knaben, ..., dessen Hand hervorkommt, dessen Finger das Kind fördern«, lit. »großmachen« (*Fischer-Elfert,* 1983, 15f.; Übersetzung ders., 1986, 16f.).
Wie schon diese wenigen Zitate erkennen lassen, muß der Leistungsdruck in den ägyptischen Schulklassen außerordentlich hoch gewesen sein. Stets galt es, schneller und besser zu sein als der Andere (*Brunner,* 1957, 60f.). Allerdings dürfen wir darunter wohl nicht so sehr eine rasche Auffassungsgabe oder kritisches Denken und Reflektieren verstehen. Eher scheint sich der Unterricht in einem sturen Rezipieren und Reproduzieren erschöpft zu haben (zur damaligen Kritik an derartigen Zuständen s. u.).
Ob die Lehrer die Elaborate ihrer Schüler in irgendeiner Weise zensiert oder benotet haben und was mit den weniger Begabten oder Fleißigen geschah, können wir nicht sagen. Möglicherweise wurden sie einer anderen, nämlich handwerklichen Ausbildung zugeführt. Diesbezügliche Drohungen von seiten der Lehrer legen diese Vermutung jedenfalls nahe. Im übrigen berichten uns vornehmlich die biographischen Quellen nur von den Klügsten und Besten.
Gelegentlich versteigt sich aber ein Schreiber, der die Schule schon hinter sich hat,

dazu, seine Berufskollegen öffentlich der Unfähigkeit und Stümperei zu bezichtigen. Dies geschieht natürlich unter Herausstreichen der eigenen Einmaligkeit: »Der Schreiber mit fähigen Fingern kam (nämlich, um den Grabbezirk des Königs Djoser zu besichtigen), der tüchtige Schreiber ohne seinesgleichen unter den Männern von Memphis, der Schreiber Amenemhet. Ich sage: Erklärt mir diese Worte! Mein Herz ist ganz krank, wenn ich das Werk ihrer Hände betrachte (womit die übrigen Besuchergraffiti gemeint sind). Es ist wie das Werk einer Frau, die keinen Verstand hat. ... Einen Skandal habe ich gesehen; sie sind (jedenfalls) keine Schreiber, die (der Gott der Schriften) Thot erleuchtet hätte« (*Firth / Quibell*, 1935, 81 L).
Die Aufforderung zum ständigen Wettbewerb ist aber nur eines der pädagogischen Mittel, wodurch die Schüler zum eifrigen Lernen angehalten werden sollten. Neben drakonischen disziplinarischen Maßnahmen wie Arrest und Prügel war es vor allem das Inaussichtstellen einer sorgenfreien Zukunft, die den Schreiber nach Abschluß seiner Schulzeit erwartete. Am Ende des wohl meistkopierten Schulbuches »Kemyt«, zu deutsch etwa »das Vollendete«, heißt es über den in der Administration beschäftigten Schreiber: »Was den Schreiber auf jeglichem Posten des Staates betrifft, der wird in ihm keinen Mangel haben« (*Helck*, 1970, 24f.; *Barta*, 1978, 13f.). Ja sogar nach dem Tode soll das Schreiberamt noch von Nutzen sein: »Übe du diesen bedeutenden Beruf aus, dann wirst du ihn auch nach dem Alter (noch nützlich) finden« (*Gardiner*, 1937, 24; *Caminos*, 1954, 83). Gedacht ist dabei konkret an eine standesgemäße Grabausstattung und, was das Entscheidende ist, an das Weiterleben im Bewußtsein der Nachwelt. Denn nur wer des Schreibens kundig war, vermochte der Vergessenheit durch die Zukünftigen zu entgehen, indem er beispielsweise als Krönung seiner Vita durch die Komposition literarischer Werke wie Lehren für die rechte Lebensführung, Prophezeiungen, ja schlicht durch die schriftliche Fixierung der eigenen musterhaften Biographie sich ein »Denkmal« setzen konnte, dem größere Dauer zugemessen wurde als protzigen Grabanlagen (*Brunner*, 1966; *Assmann*, 1985). Nur dies hebt ihn über die ansonsten anonyme namenlose Masse des ägyptischen Volkes heraus.

4. Abgrenzung des Schreibermetiers gegenüber dem illiteraten Handwerk

Die bereits herangezogene »Lehre des Dua-Cheti« aus der Zeit um etwa 2000 v. Chr. nimmt bezüglich der Geschichte des Selbstverständnisses der ägyptischen Schreiber eine richtungweisende Position innerhalb der lehrhaften Literatur ein. In ihr wird nämlich erstmalig eine zuvor nur mündlich tradierte Sprechsitte inkorporiert, die mit ihrem Entdecker Peter *Seibert* (1967) in der Ägyptologie »Charakteristik« genannt wird. Inhalt einer solchen Charakteristik ist die mehr oder minder detaillierte Beschreibung und Bewertung handwerklicher Berufe, mit dem Ziel, diese mit all ihren abstoßenden, ja z. T. sogar lebensbedrohenden Begleiterscheinungen von der um soviel angenehmeren und eben diese Metiers überwachenden Tätigkeit des

Schreibers abzugrenzen. Nicht nur, daß der Schreiber nach Ansicht der Lehrautoritäten die einmalige Chance hat, über das irdische Dasein hinaus im Gedächtnis der Nachfahren weiterzuexistieren, der Handwerker oder gar ungelernte Tagelöhner ist bereits zu Lebzeiten infolge seiner strapaziösen und mitunter auch unreinen Geschäfte dem Tode näher als dem Leben. In einem späteren, von der »Lehre des Dua-Cheti« inspirierten Text wird über den Soldaten beispielsweise bemerkt: »Wenn der Feind herangekommen ist und ihn mit Pfeilen umzingelt, dann ist das Leben fern von ihm« (*Gardiner*, 1937, 108; *Caminos*, 1954, 400f.). In diesem und weiteren Schultexten wird von seiten der Lehrer am Ende ihrer Ausführungen häufig noch als Quintessenz hervorgehoben, daß der Schreiber weder irgendwelche Steuern zu zahlen habe wie der Bauer, noch sei er einem bzw. zumindest nicht so vielen Vorgesetzten unterstellt. Nun, für die rein administrative Arbeit des Aufsetzens und Führens von Urkunden aller Art ist er sicher nicht besteuert worden. Auch war er in erster Linie nur einem Dienstherrn, wenn auch in der Person des Veziers dem höchsten des Staates, Rechenschaft schuldig. Sobald ein Schreiber jedoch in den Genuß von Landbesitz kam, und dies scheint nicht gerade selten der Fall gewesen zu sein, unterliegt auch er der allgemeinen Steuer- und Abgabenpflicht. Und wie wir aus Akten der Agrarverwaltung wissen, genoß der Schreiber gegenüber dem Soldaten, Stallmeister oder Bauern nicht den geringsten Steuervorteil, wie es die Schultexte glauben zu machen versuchen. Aus einem umfangreichen Felderinventar der Ramessidenzeit geht hervor, daß Schreiber für die Bestellung landwirtschaftlicher Nutzflächen sogar geringfügig höher steuerlich veranlagt wurden als beispielsweise der von ihnen so vielgeschmähte Soldat (*Katary*, 1983, 78; *Černý*, 1973, 324f.; *Gardiner*, 1948, 70; 83). Dabei gehören die Lehrmeister dieser Propagandaschriften für den Schreiberberuf gerade derjenigen Gruppe von Beamten an, die tagtäglich mit der Registrierung und Archivierung von Abrechnungen und Steuererhebungen zu tun haben. Wir finden unter ihnen einen »Schreiber des Schatzhauses«, einen »Oberbuchhalter des Schatzhauses Pharaos« wie einen »Königlichen Schreiber und Rindervorsteher des Gottes Amun-Re«.

Bezüglich der Frage, in welcher Form bzw. Höhe ein gewöhnlicher Schreiber für seine Tätigkeit monatlich entlohnt wurde, ist es des weiteren aufschlußreich festzustellen, daß er nicht wie zu erwarten an oberster Stelle der Gehaltsklassen rangiert. Dieses Bild vermitteln uns jedenfalls – mit gewissen Ausnahmen – zahlreiche Rationenlisten aus der Handwerkersiedlung im Westen des antiken Theben. Den hier ansässigen Arbeitern waren zwei Schreiber und zwei Vorarbeiter vorgesetzt. Und genau diese Vorarbeiter erhalten ein höheres Salaire als die Schreiber (*Černý*, 1973, 224).

5. Schreiber und Schule in Deir el-Medineh (West-Theben)

Dennoch ist es gerade diese überwiegend von Handwerkern bewohnt gewesene kleine Siedlung, die uns eine stattliche Anzahl von Produkten des damaligen Schulunterrichts hinterlassen hat. Die dort beschäftigten Schreiber haben sich neben ihren täglichen Aufgaben besonders um die Tradierung der als klassisch geltenden Literaturwerke der Vorfahren verdient gemacht. In zahllosen, zumeist recht kurzen Abschriften auf Ostraka haben die Schüler aus dem Gedächtnis bzw. nach schriftlicher Vorlage die alten, kanonischen Texte kopiert, mit bisweilen völligem Unverständnis, wie die überdurchschnittlich hohen Fehlerquoten belegen. Der zeitliche Abstand zwischen der dem Alten und Mittleren Reich entstammenden Literatursprache und der alltäglichen Umgangssprache – derjenigen der Ramessidenzeit nämlich – war einfach zu groß (*Junge*, 1985; *Assmann*, 1985). Das mündliche Diktat scheint nach jüngeren textkritischen Untersuchungen keine wesentliche Rolle gespielt zu haben (*Burkard*, 1977). Die klassischen Texte wurden auswendig gelernt und dann im Schulunterricht laut rezitiert bzw. »gesungen«, wie es in der »Lehre für König Merikare« aus der Zeit um 2100 v. Chr. heißt (*Brunner*, 1957, 158 VIII b). Während die Schüler zum lauten Lesen angehalten wurden, sollten sie ihre Rechenaufgaben demgegenüber mit »verschlossenem Munde«, also schweigend lösen.

Die als Lehrer tätigen Schreiber haben sich nun aber nicht damit begnügt, lediglich die Vergangenheit zu reproduzieren, als kreative Autoren waren sie auch bemüht, eigenständige Kompositionen, insbesondere Lehren, zu verfassen (nähere Angaben zur literarischen Produktion in Deir el-Medineh bei *Valbelle*, 1985, 336ff.). Diese Werke gelten dann der moralischen Erziehung der ihnen zur Ausbildung anvertrauten Schüler oder »Söhne«, wobei diese nicht immer die eigenen sein müssen. Eine geistige Nachfolge galt mehr als die rein leibliche (*Brunner*, 1957, pass.). Doch ging eine starke Tendenz dahin, das Amt des Schreibers vom Vater auf den Sohn zu vererben (*Černý*, 1973, 223ff.; *Gutgesell*, 1983, 568). Wir kennen mehrere Generationen umfassende Schreiberdynastien, doch mußte der jeweilige Nachfolger vom Vezier formell in seinem Amt bestätigt werden (*Černý*, 1973, 224; 317ff.). Es sind auch Beispiele dafür bekannt, daß ein ehemals gewöhnlicher Vorzeichner und Maler, der u. a. mit der Dekoration von Grabwänden befaßt war, regelrecht zum Schreiber ernannt wurde (Černý, 1973, 193; 348). Einer von ihnen hat sich als Vorzeichner dazu bemüßigt gefühlt, seinem leiblichen Sohn und »Gehilfen« eine gehörige Standpauke zu halten. Dieser hatte sich nämlich ungebührlich betragen, indem er z. B. im Verlaufe einer langen Wanderschaft mit asiatischen Beduinen Blutsbrüderschaft geschlossen hatte (*Černý*, 1955; vollständige Übersetzung bei *Guglielmi*, 1983). Diese, nebenbei recht ausführliche Ermahnung ist gespickt mit teils nur leicht modifizierten Zitaten aus alten literarischen Werken, was zeigt, daß auch ein Maler, der bis zu einem gewissen Grad lesen können mußte, über sozusagen klassische Bildung verfügte. Allerdings scheint seine Moralpredigt bei seinem Sohn nicht gerade auf fruchtbaren Nährboden gefallen zu sein, denn aus einem Prozeßprotokoll geht hervor, daß dieser wegen mehrfachen Ehebruches mit einer frisch verheirateten Frau vor das örtliche Gericht gezogen wurde (*Allam*, 1973, 301ff.; *Janssen*, 1982, 119ff.).

6. Zeitgenössische Kritik am Schreiberstand und seinen Ausbildungsmethoden

Wenn das Metier des Schreibers in den einschlägigen Schultexten auch stets und ohne die geringsten Abstriche als das einzig Lohnenswerte dem Nachwuchs angepriesen wurde, so hat es dennoch nicht an zeitgenössischen Versuchen gefehlt, es einer grundsätzlichen Kritik zu unterziehen, die noch dazu aus den eigenen Reihen kam. Diese Kritik hat den wohl recht verbreitet gewesenen Bildungsdünkel auf der einen Seite aufs Korn genommen, und, das mutet geradezu modern an, auch nicht davor Halt gemacht, die Didaktik der Wissensvermittlung prinzipiell in Frage zu stellen. Zeuge hierfür ist die in der Ägyptologie sog. »Literarische oder Satirische Streitschrift«, deren Autor mit einem fiktiven und daher anonym gehaltenen Partner in einen Wissenstreit eintritt. Die Palette des behandelten Stoffes ist reich: die Fähigkeit, alltäglich anfallende Rechenaufgaben zu meistern wird ebenso auf die Probe gestellt wie die Kenntnis geographischer Gegebenheiten. Nicht zuletzt an der Erwähnung eines Zitates aus einer alten Weisheitslehre wird das konkrete didaktische Anliegen des Autors evident. Es scheint danach zu urteilen gang und gäbe gewesen zu sein, mit dem unreflektierten Dahersagen von Passagen aus literarischen Standardwerken zu prahlen, ohne jedoch deren textlichen Zusammenhang zu kennen. Man hat sich offenbar damit begnügt, sog. incipit-Verse zu memorieren, wie sie auf zahlreichen Ostraka überliefert sind, die als Gedächtnisstütze und Kapiteleinteilung für die vollständige Kopie des jeweils reproduzierten Textes gedient haben. Somit bestand die so viel beweihräucherte Bildung der Schreiber bzw. einiger ihrer Vertreter wohl allzu häufig aus derartigen Fragmenten. Da diese Streitschrift in den Schulen sowohl Unter- wie Oberägyptens in bis heute nahezu 100 Abschriften kopiert wurde, darf in ihr ein öffentlicher Feldzug gegen das damalige Bildungswesen gesehen werden.
Auch mit der Sozialethik ist es in den Kreisen der Gebildeten nicht zum besten bestellt gewesen. Die Neigung scheint nur allzu weit verbreitet gewesen zu sein, sich in Spott und Hohn über körperlich Behinderte zu ergehen. Sie ist für den Verfasser der Streitschrift ein weiterer Anlaß, mit der eigenen Zunft hart ins Gericht zu gehen (*Fischer-Elfert,* 1986, 95 f.; 84 ff.; 286 ff.). Das Thema wird übrigens auch im 25. Kapitel der »Lehre des Amenemope« aufgegriffen, derjenigen Lehre, die bei der Komposition einer längeren Spruchsammlung im Buche der Proverbien (22, 17 ff.) Pate gestanden hat.

7. Verhältnis Schüler – Lehrer: Kritik versus Loyalität

Abschließend soll noch ein Aspekt der Schreiberausbildung erörtert werden. Er betrifft das Verhältnis Schüler – Lehrer, denn die Kehrseite haben wir bereits kennengelernt. Ebenso wie grundsätzliche Auseinandersetzungen über den Wert der als ausreichend empfundenen Wissensmenge und die Didaktik ihrer Vermittlung geführt worden sind, hat es sich ein Lehrer auch zuweilen gefallen lassen müssen, wenn seine moralischen Ermahnungen bezüglich ihrer Umsetzbarkeit in die Praxis von seiten des Zöglings kritisch hinterfragt wurden. In dem berühmten – weil einmalig in der ägyptischen Weisheitsliteratur – Epilog der Unterweisung des Schreibers Anii kommt es zu einem regelrechten Disput zwischen »Vater« und »Sohn« über die Frage, ob es denn wirklich möglich sei, daß jeder Mensch unabhängig von seinen Naturanlagen die Chance habe und / oder dazu gezwungen sei, den Pfad der Tugend oder den »Weg Gottes« einzuschlagen. Der Schüler jedenfalls bezweifelt dies. Er fühlt sich, nicht nur aufgrund seines seiner Ansicht nach noch zu geringen Alters, vom hohen Anspruch der Lehre überfordert. Der Vater weist diese Kritik mit harschen Worten zurück, dennoch, es kommt zu keiner Einigung. Der Text endet in einer Aporie.

Ein gänzlich anderes Bild dieser Schüler–Lehrer-Beziehung wollen uns wahre Lobeshymnen auf die Qualitäten ihres Lehrmeisters vermitteln, die man wohl eher den Schülern in den Mund gelegt hat als daß sie von diesen selbst verfaßt worden wären. Irgendwelche Ansätze zu einer noch so zaghaften Kritik oder theoretischen Auseinandersetzung mit der nötigenfalls gewaltsam eingebleuten Lehre suchen wir hier vergebens. Ja, die Schüler schrecken nicht einmal vor der Beteuerung zurück, die erhaltenen Prügel als angenehm empfunden zu haben. Sie schätzen diese sogar vergleichsweise höher ein als etwa »den Duft der Lotusblume zur Sommerzeit« (*Fischer-Elfert,* 1983b, 337).

Ein ehemaliger Schüler hat seinem Lehrer selbst auf seiner privaten Familienstele noch seine Reverenz erwiesen, indem er ihn neben seinem leiblichen Vater mit aufführt und ihm gleichfalls die ehrfürchtige Bezeichnung »Vater« zulegt. Wenn auch dieser Lehrer den Schreibertitel nicht in seiner Titulatur führt, können wir ihm die Niederschrift mehrerer Schultexte zuschreiben (*Brunner*, 1959).

Die vorangegangenen Ausführungen dürften deutlich gemacht haben, daß viele Details an dem von den schriftlichen Quellen gezeichneten Bild des Schreibers und Lehrers stark idealisiert sind. Dies gilt insbesondere für die eigene Abgrenzung gegenüber den übrigen, als minderwertig betrachteten Berufen. Es darf hierbei nicht vergessen werden, daß die relevanten Texte durchweg aus der Feder von Angehörigen der eigenen Zunft stammen, die Perspektive also stets die gleiche, einseitige ist. Bildliche Quellen, so reich sie auch fließen, überwiegend in Gräbern, vermögen an diesem Bild nichts zu ändern, sie bestätigen es vielmehr in jedem Einzelfall. Text und bildliche Darstellung unterlagen ja demselben Anspruch, nämlich die göttliche Weltordnung, die Maat, wie die Ägypter sie nannten, in ihrem Idealzustand zu fixieren. Man könnte es knapp aber präzise auch so formulieren: es galt, die ewige und unwandelbare Wahrheit festzuhalten, nicht die Wirklichkeit. Und dieses sich durch die ganze pharaonische Zeit Ägyptens hindurchziehende Konzept der Maat schloß auch die einmal geschaffene soziale Hierarchie in sich ein.

Wenn hier gelegentlich auch versucht wurde, den altägyptischen Schreiber und Lehrer in etwas differenzierterem Licht zu betrachten als seine Selbstäußerungen unbesehen zu übernehmen, dann darf aber keinesfalls außer Acht gelassen werden, daß er es war, der das Erbe seiner Kultur tradiert hat und sich dieser verantwortungsvollen Aufgabe auch durchweg bewußt war. Ohne die Aktivitäten der Schreiber und damit der Gebildeten wüßten wir um Gesellschaft und Kultur im vorchristlichen Ägypten nicht mehr als über eine Steinzeitkultur. Es ging an dieser Stelle eben auch darum, den altägyptischen Literaten mit all seinen Qualitäten wie auch Schwächen zu demonstrieren. Und letztere scheinen im Bereich dessen, was wir gemeinhin als Bildung bezeichnen, nicht selten nur allzu deutlich zum Vorschein getreten zu sein.

Literaturverzeichnis

Allam, Shafik (1973): Hieratische Ostraka und Papyri der Ramessidenzeit. Tübingen

Assmann, Jan (1985): Gibt es eine »Klassik« in der Ägyptischen Literaturgeschichte? Ein Beitrag zur Geistesgeschichte der Ramessidenzeit. Leipzig und Wiesbaden. In: Zeitschrift der Deutschen Morgenländischen Gesellschaft, Supplement VI, S. 35–52

Baines, John (1983): Literacy and Ancient Egyptian Society. London. In: MAN 18, Nr. 3 (September), S. 572–599

Baines, John/Eyre, Christopher (1983): Four Notes on Literacy. Göttingen. In: Göttinger Miszellen 61, S. 65–96

Barns, John (1956): Five Ramesseum Papyri. Oxford

Barta, Winfried (1978): Das Schulbuch Kemit. Leipzig und Berlin. In: Zeitschrift für Ägyptische Sprache und Altertumskunde 105, S. 6–14

Brunner, Hellmut (1957): Altägyptische Erziehung. Wiesbaden

Brunner, Hellmut (1959): A Much Honoured Teacher of the Ramesside Period. London. In: Journal of Egpytian Archaeology 45, S. 3–5

Brunner, Hellmut (1966): Die »Weisen«, ihre »Lehren« und »Prophezeiungen« in altägyptischer Sicht. Leipzig und Berlin. In: Zeitschrift für Ägyptische Sprache und Altertumskunde 93, S. 29–35

Brunner, Hellmut (1984): Stichwort Schülerhandschriften. Wiesbaden. In: Lexikon der Ägyptologie, Bd. V, Sp. 737–739

Burkard, Günther (1977): Textkritische Untersuchungen zu ägyptischen Weisheitslehren des Alten und Mittleren Reiches. Wiesbaden (Ägyptologische Abhandlungen, Bd. 34)

Caminos, Ricardo (1954): Late Egyptian Miscellanies. Oxford

Černý, Jaroslav (1955): Reference to Blood Brotherhood among Semites in an Egyptian Text of the Ramesside Period. Chicago. In: Journal of Near Eastern Studies 14, S. 161–163

Černý, Jaroslav (1963): A possible Egyptian word for »astronomer«. London. In: Journal of Egyptian Archaeology 49, S. 173

Černý, Jaroslav (1973): A Community of Workmen at Thebes in the Ramesside Period. Cairo (Bibliothèque d'Etude, T. L)

Edel, Elmar (1984): Die Inschriften der Grabfronten der Siut-Gräber in Mittelägypten aus der Herakleopolitenzeit. Opladen (Abhandlungen der Rheinisch-Westfälischen Akademie der Wissenschaften, Bd. 71)

Firth, Cecil M./Quibell, J. E. (1935): The Step Pyramid I. Cairo

Fischer-Elfert, Hans-Werner (1983): Die Satirische Streitschrift des Papyrus Anastasi I – Testzusammenstellung. Wiesbaden (Kleine Ägyptische Texte)

Fischer-Elfert, Hans-Werner (1983b): »Ich bin das Schiff – Du bist das Ruder« – Eine Danksagung an den Lehrer. Hamburg. In: Studien zur Altägyptischen Kultur 11, S. 335–345

Fischer-Elfert, Hans-Werner (1986): Die Satirische Streitschrift des Papyrus Anastasi I – Übersetzung und Kommentar. Wiesbaden (Ägyptologische Abhandlungen, Bd. 44)

Gardiner, Alan H. (1937): Late Egyptian Miscellanies. Brüssel

Gardiner, Alan H. (1946): The Instruction Addressed to Kagemni and his Brethren. London. In: Journal of Egyptian Archaeology 32, S. 71–74

Gardiner, Alan H. (1948): Papyrus Wilbour, Commentary. Oxford

Guglielmi, Waltraud (1983): Eine »Lehre« für einen reiselustigen Sohn. Göttingen. In: Welt des Orients XIV, S. 147–166

Gutgesell, Manfred (1983): Die Datierung der Ostraka und Papyri aus Deir el-Medineh und ihre ökonomische Interpretation (2 Teile). Hildesheim (Hildesheimer Ägyptologische Beiträge, Bd. 18–19)

Helck, Wolfgang (1970): Die Lehre des Dw3-Ḫtjj (2 Teile). Wiesbaden (Kleine Ägyptische Texte)

Janssen, Jacobus J. J. (1982): Two Personalities. Leiden. In: Janssen, Jacobus J. J. / Demaree, R. J. (Hrsg.): Gleanings from Deir el-Medina (Egyptologische Uitgaven, Bd. I), S. 109–131

Junge, Friedrich (1985): Sprachstufen und Sprachgeschichte. Leipzig und Wiesbaden. In: Zeitschrift der Deutschen Morgenländischen Gesellschaft, Supplement VI, S. 17–34

Katary, Sally L. D. (1983): Cultivator, Scribe, Stablemaster, Soldier: The Late Egyptian Miscellanies in Light of P. Wilbour. Chicago. In: The Ancient World VI, Nos. 1–4, S. 71–93

Korostovcev, M. A. (1962): Pistsy Drevnevo Egipta. Moskau

Meeks, Dimitri (1968): Rezension zu Korostovcev (1962). Paris. In: Revue d'Egyptologie 19, S. 189–193

Pestman, P. W. (1982): Who were the owners in the ›Community of Workmen‹ of the Chester Beatty Papyri?. Leiden. In: Janssen, J. J. J. / Demaree, R. J., 1982, S. 155–172

Plantikow-Münster, Maria (1969): Die Inschrift des B3k-n-ḫnsw in München, Leipzig und Berlin. In: Zeitschrift für Ägyptische Sprache und Altertumskunde 95, S. 117–135

Seibert, Peter (1967): Die Charakteristik. Wiesbaden (Ägyptologische Abhandlungen, Bd. 17)

Valbelle, Dominique (1985): »Les Ouvriers de la Tombe« – Deir el-Medineh à l'époque ramesside. Cairo (Bibliothèque d'Etude, T. 96)

III. DIE KLASSISCHE ANTIKE

Egert Pöhlmann

Der Schreiber als Lehrer in der klassischen Zeit Griechenlands

Die Schreiber von Keilschrift in Mesopotamien und die Schreiber von Hieroglyphen in Ägypten waren Bedienstete von Palastherrschaften, Angehörige eines wegen seiner Spezialkenntnisse privilegierten Berufstandes und gleichzeitig die Lehrer ihres eigenen Nachwuchses. Als ihre jüngeren Kollegen darf man betrachten die Schreiber von Linear B in Kreta und im mykenischen Griechenland. Letztere dürften, in jener ersten Epoche griechischer Schriftlichkeit ab 1450, eine ähnliche Funktion gehabt haben: sie waren Bedienstete einer zentralistischen Bürokratie, für die man sich durch das mühevolle Erlernen eines wenig benutzerfreundlichen Schriftsystems qualifizieren mußte.[1]
Die Überflutung der Ägäis durch die »Seevölker«, eine Wanderungslawine aus dem Nordwesten, im 12. Jh.[2], zerstörte die mykenischen Palastherrschaften und warf Griechenland wieder in die Schriftlosigkeit zurück, in der es auch nach dem Einströmen der Dorer im 11. Jh. zunächst verharrte.[3] Erst um die Wende vom 9. zum 8. Jh. schufen Griechen im Osten eine dem Modell, einem semitischen Konsonantenalphabet, weit überlegene Alphabetschrift, die auch die Vokale bezeichnete.[4] Doch bis zur Wiedergewinnung der Schriftkultur war noch ein langer Weg. So konnte *Henri-Irénée Marrou* in seiner »Histoire de l'éducation dans l'antiquité« die Geschichte der antiken Erziehung auf eine prägnante Formel bringen: sie spiegele den »Übergang von einer Kultur adliger Krieger zu einer Kultur von Schreibern« wieder.[5]
Nun signalisieren die hellenistischen Bibliotheken in Alexandria, daß spätestens im 3. Jh. vor Christus die Herrschaft des Buches etabliert ist, daß eine Schreib- und Lesekultur besteht, die samt dem dazugehörigen Schulsystem vom Imperium Romanum bruchlos übernommen wurde. Doch ist dies nur der Endpunkt einer langen Entwicklung, die auf weite Strecken hin von der Koexistenz von Mündlichkeit und Schriftlichkeit gekennzeichnet war.
Von der Funktion, der Bewertung und der Verbreitung der Schrift in einer bestimmten historischen Situation hängt unmittelbar der Stellenwert des Schreibens und Lesens im Unterricht ab. Deshalb muß sich der Versuch, den »Schreiber als Lehrer in der klassischen Zeit Griechenlands« zu entdecken, vor allem auf die Frage konzentrieren, von welcher Zeit an die Fähigkeit des Lesens und Schreibens zum unverzichtbaren Rüstzeug eines jeden Bürgers der griechischen Polis gehörte. Von diesem Zeitpunkt an ist der »Schreiber als Lehrer« eine selbstverständliche Notwendigkeit. Ich möchte zeigen, daß man diese Situation, jedenfalls in Athen, schon im 6. Jh. vor Christus voraussetzen muß, und mich dabei nicht nur auf literarische Zeugnisse, sondern auch auf den Befund der Vasenmalerei ab 530 vor Chr. stützen.
Bekanntlich ist der Aussagewert literarischer Zeugnisse begrenzt dadurch, daß zu bestimmten Zeiten bestimmte Bereiche nicht als literaturfähig gelten. Hierher gehört noch im 5. Jh. vor Chr. in Griechenland der Elementarunterricht, der erst in dessen

letztem Drittel von der Komödie als möglicher Gegenstand entdeckt wird.[6] Dazu kommt weiter, daß das Epos und die Tragödie gar nicht die Absicht haben, ihre eigene Gegenwart darzustellen, sondern ihren Gegenstand im Mythos suchen. Daraus folgt, daß die literarischen Zeugnisse über Lesen, Schreiben und Elementarunterricht lange eher zufälliger Natur sind. Das sei an einigen Beispielen erläutert:

Ilias und Odyssee versetzen den Hörer konsequent in eine schriftlose Adelsgesellschaft. Nur an einer Stelle läßt der Iliasdichter, beinahe wider Willen, durchblicken, daß ihm das Phänomen der Schrift geläufig ist: Er läßt den Bellerophon, das Opfer einer achäischen Potiphar, der Königin Anteia von Tiryns, mit einem Uriasbrief nach Lykien ziehen und muß nun – dies der Preis für die Rezeption zweier orientalischer Erzählmotive – sprechen von einer »gefalteten Tafel«, einem Diptychon, das in »verderbenbringenden Zeichen« den Todesbefehl enthält.[7] Mit der Endredaktion der Ilias zeitgleich sind die ältesten griechischen Gefäßinschriften der Zeit von 730–700[8]: Der Ilias-Dichter denkt somit bei seinem Uriasbrief an die um 800 neuerfundene griechische Alphabetschrift.

Wie das Epos bewegt sich auch die Tragödie in der Regel in der Welt des Mythos. Doch finden sich schon bei *Aischylos* zahlreiche Hinweise auf Schreiben und Lesen, freilich zunächst nur im metaphorischen Gebrauch.[9] Dramatische Funktion erhält die Schrift bei *Euripides,* der den Brief bühnenreif macht: Im »Hippolytos« (428 vor Chr.) wird der Held von der liebeskranken Phaidra nach deren Selbstmord durch einen an der Leiche befestigten Brief bei seinem Vater Theseus verleumdet. In der »Taurischen Iphigenie« (nach 412 vor Chr.) möchte Iphigenie dem Orestes einen Brief in die Heimat mitgeben, und in der »Aulischen Iphigenie« (nach 406) schreibt Agamemnon von Aulis zwei Briefe an Klytaimnestra.[10]

Die Alte Komödie wurzelt, anders als die Tragödie, im Aktuellen. Sie bietet daher auch zahlreiche Hinweise auf Bücher und Lesen[11] und hat mehrfach auch Erziehungsprobleme thematisiert.[12] Wichtig ist der verklärende Rückblick des »Anwalts der Guten Sache« in den »Wolken« (423 vor Chr.) auf die »Alte Erziehung« der Generation der Marathonkämpfer, in der freilich nur der Elementarunterricht beim Musiklehrer (κιθαριστής) und Turnlehrer (παιδοτρίβης) ausgeführt wird (Wolken 961–1023). Bemerkenswert ist, daß dieses Bild einer Zeit vor 490 vor Chr. nicht auf Einzel-, sondern auf Klassenunterricht abzielt, und daß die Disziplin durch körperliche Züchtigung aufrechterhalten wurde.[13] Die vom »Anwalt der Schlechten Sache« vertretene Moderne Erziehung (1036–1104) ist die modische Rhetorik der Sophisten.[14] Den Schreib-Leseunterricht, der bei *Aristophanes* fehlt, hat nach 403 *Kallias* auf die Bühne gebracht in seiner aus Fragmenten rekonstruierbaren »Grammatik«.[15] Hier tritt ein Schreiblehrer auf und führt, nach der Schriftreform von 403, die ersten Übungen mit dem neuen Alphabet vor. Ein Porträt des Elementarlehrers erhalten wir erst im 3. Jh. vor Chr. im 3. Mimos des *Herodas* von Kos, dem Διδάσκαλος: Eine arme Witwe, Metrotime, bringt ihren nichtsnutzigen Sohn Kottalos, der nicht schreiben, lesen und auswendiglernen will, in die Schulklasse des Lehrers Lampriskos, der ihn durch eine ordentliche Tracht Prügel wieder bildungswillig macht. Bemerkenswert sind die realistischen Details: das Klassenzimmer ist mit den Bildern des Apollon und der neun Musen geschmückt, drei namentlich genannte Mitschüler helfen bei der Züchtigung mit, der Lehrer hat einen Riemen und ein Rohr zur Auswahl, unbotmäßige Schüler werden in die Ecke gestellt oder müssen mit Fußfesseln nachsitzen. Lampriskos war Privatlehrer und erhielt monatlich Schulgeld.[16]

Daß die Dichtung uns den Blick in die Schulstube in solcher Deutlichkeit erst im 3. Jh. vor Chr. erlaubt, erklärt sich ausreichend aus den allgemeinen Tendenzen hellenistischer Dichtung: nicht nur *Herodas,* sondern auch *Theokrit* und *Kallimachos* suchten Gattungen und Gegenstände, die in der klassischen Zeit noch nicht verbraucht worden waren. Dafür, daß der Elementarunterricht schon zu Beginn des 5. Jhs. vor Chr. in Form des Klassenunterrichts durchgeführt wurde, besitzen wir eine Hand voll Zufallsbelegen von Prosaautoren:

Herodot weiß zu erzählen, daß kurz vor der Seeschlacht bei Lade (496) nahe Milet in Chios das Dach eines Schulhauses eingefallen sei und 119 Kinder erschlagen habe, die eben im Schreiben unterrichtet wurden. Die Geschichte wird nur deswegen mitgeteilt, weil *Herodot* das Unglück als ein schlechtes Vorzeichen deutet.[17]

Plutarch und *Pausanias* teilen eine ähnliche Geschichte wegen ihres mirakulösen Charakters mit: Der Athlet Kleomedes, wegen Totschlags 496/3 disqualifiziert, verliert den Verstand, dringt in Astypaläa in ein Schulhaus ein und zertrümmert den das Dach stützenden Pfosten. Bei dem Einsturz des Daches kommen 60 Schüler ums Leben. Kleomedes wird verfolgt, aber auf wunderbare Weise entrückt.[18]

Von *Plutarch* erfahren wir auch, daß es schon vor 480 vor Chr. den Elementarlehrer als öffentlichen Angestellten gegeben hat: Vor der Schlacht bei Salamis wurde ein großer Teil der Bevölkerung von Athen auf die Peloponnes nach Troizen evakuiert und dort großzügig aufgenommen. Ein von einem Nikagoras erwirkter Volksbeschluß stellte unter anderem die Lohnfortzahlung für die Lehrer der Kinder sicher.[19]

Der nächste Beleg für die Elementarschule (διδασκαλεῖον παίδων) fällt schon in den Peloponnesischen Krieg: *Thukydides* berichtet, Thraker hätten 413 Mykalessos überfallen und alle im Schulhaus versammelten Kinder niedergemacht.[20]

Die besprochenen literarischen Zeugnisse über Schreiben, Lesen, Schreibunterricht, Schulhäuser, Elementarlehrer haben eins gemeinsam: sie stammen (mit den bezeichnenden Ausnahmen der ABC-Komödie des *Kallias* oder des Schulmimos des *Herodas*) sämtlich aus Texten, deren Gegenstand eben nicht der Schreibunterricht ist. Der erste Autor, der sich ernsthaft mit dem Elementarunterricht um seiner selbst willen auseinandersetzt, ist *Platon.* Im »Staat« greift er, im Bestreben, seine προπαιδεία zu skizzieren, zurück auf die schon von Aristophanes verklärte »Alte Erziehung« der Zeit vor 490[21] und bringt sie auf die Formel: »Für den Körper der Sport, für die Seele die Musik« (II 376e). Der Begriff der Μουσική umfaßt Dichtung, Musik und Tanz; offen bleibt, ob Schreiben und Lesen zu deren Voraussetzungen gehört. Doch verrät *Platon* später, daß ihm methodischer Schreibunterricht ganz geläufig ist (III 402a/b). In den »Gesetzen« tritt neben die Gymnastik der Schreib-Leseunterricht, dem das 10.–12. Lebensjahr zugewiesen ist, und das Leierspiel, das im 13.–15. Lebensjahr erlernt wird. Neben der Dichtung kommt jetzt auch Prosa als Lesestoff in Frage (VII 809/10). Freilich sind die Aussagen *Platons* im »Staat« und den »Gesetzen« Teile eines Erziehungsprogramms, dessen Verhältnis zur historischen Wirklichkeit der ersten Hälfte des 4. Jhs. vor Chr. problematisch bleibt. Einen kleinen Schritt nach oben führt der »Protagoras«, der zwischen 399 und 388 entstand und der die Situation in Athen um 432 abbildet: Dort beschreibt Protagoras, wie vor allem die reichen Bürger ihre Kinder erziehen: am Anfang steht der Schreibleseunterricht, dann werden Gedichte gelesen und auswendiggelernt und es folgt der Musikunterricht. Der Sportunterricht läuft ständig nebenher (325 a–326 c). Verunklärt wird die Situation freilich wieder dadurch, daß *Platon* im »Phaidros« (274 c–277 a) grundsätzlich an der Schrift Kritik übt, sie auf die Funktion eines Hilfsmittels der Erinnerung beschränken will und der schriftlichen Belehrung die mündliche Unterweisung bei weitem vorzieht. Diese Haltung hat innerhalb des platonischen Philosophierens ihren guten Sinn[22]; sie mag provoziert sein durch die Fülle von Prosatexten (vor allem von Fachbüchern und philosophischen Traktaten, aber auch von publizierten Reden und Geschichtswerken), die in der zweiten Hälfte des 5. Jhs. neben die längst eingeführten Texte von Dichtung traten.[23] *Platons* Schriftkritik ist aber nur zu gern als kulturhistorisches Zeugnis gelesen worden und hat den Anlaß gegeben, das Athen des 5. Jhs. mit wohltrainierten, hochmusikalischen, dem Schönen und Guten ergebenen Analphabeten aus gutem Hause zu bevölkern.[24] Und auch *Marrou* rechnet zwar mit drei Elementarlehrern, dem παιδοτρίβης, dem κιθαριστής und dem γραμματιστής, läßt aber den Schreib-Lese-Lehrer erst spät neben Sport- und Musiklehrer treten und gestattet sich über den Zeitpunkt allgemeiner Verbindlichkeit des Schreib-Lese-Unterrichts nur Vermutungen.[25] Das oben ausgewertete Herodotzeugnis belegt zwar für 496 in Chios Schreib-Leseunterricht, doch für ein aussagekräftiges Bild des Elementarunterrichts im ausgehenden 6. und frühen 5. Jhs. müssen wir bildliche Zeugnisse heranziehen.

Schon *Winter* (1916), *Beazley* (1948) und *Turner* (1951) hatten Vasenbilder mit Darstellungen von Papyrusrollen zur Illustration der Schrift-, Schul- und Buchgeschichte im 5. Jh. vor Chr. verwendet. Eine nahezu vollständige Sammlung der »Book Rolls on Vases« verdanken wir *Immerwahr* (1964, 1973). Doch erst *Beck* hat in seinem »Album of Greek Education« (1975) neben Musik- und Sportszenen so gut wie das ganze Material zum Thema Lesen und Schreiben auf Vasenbildern zusammengetragen.

Man sieht nun, daß die ältere, schwarzfigurige Vasenmalerei wegen ihrer engen Bindung an mythologische Gegenstände das Lesen und Schreiben nicht thematisiert hat.[26] Die rotfigurige Vasenmalerei jedoch bezieht von Beginn an den Alltag ein. So finden sich in der Zeit von 530–500 ein Fall von Buchrollen neben drei Fällen von Schreibtafeln, in der Zeit von 500–475 sechs Fälle von Buchrollen neben siebzehn Fällen von Schreibtafeln. Das Übergewicht der Schreibtafeln erklärt sich aus deren Bedeutung im Elementarunterricht, der schon um 500 ein beliebtes Motiv der Vasenmalerei ist. Dann gleichen sich die Zahlen aus: Im Zeitraum von 475–450 stehen sechzehn Fälle von Buchrollen neben siebzehn Fällen von Schreibtafeln.

Allein diese Zahlen genügen, um die Ansicht zu widerlegen, die Kenntnis der Schrift sei erst im ausgehenden 5. Jh. Allgemeingut geworden. Weiter möge eine Reihe von Beispielen führen, die überwiegend der Zeit von 530–470 angehören:

1. Die bisher älteste Schulszene findet sich auf einer Schale aus Vulci, heute in

München. Sie ist dem Euergides-Maler zugeschrieben und gehört in die Zeit um 520.[27] In der Mitte des einen Außenbildes sitzt auf einem Steinblock ein junger Mann, der einen Stab in der Rechten hält und aufmerksam nach links blickt. Dort sitzt, ihm zugewendet, auf einer Steinbank ein Knabe, der die Hände im Rednergestus vorstreckt[28] und in der Linken einen Stab hält. Am rechten Bildrand sitzt ein Knabe auf einem Klappstuhl, der aufmerksam in einer aufgeschlagenen Schreibtafel liest. Über und zwischen den Figuren liest man ΗΟ ΠΑΙΣ ΚΑΛΟΣ.ΝΑΙΧΙ (Der schöne Knabe. Ja gewiß).

Die Deutung der Szene muß von dem Stab ausgehen, den der Knabe zur Linken hält. Beim Symposion war es üblich, einen Stab rechts herum von Gast zu Gast wandern zu lassen. Wer den Stab gerade führte, mußte ein Lied oder ein Gedicht vortragen.[29] Nun ist unsere Szene kein Symposion, denn einmal fehlen die üblichen Liegesofas, außerdem befinden wir uns im Freien, wie die Steinbänke andeuten. Der Stab in der Linken des Knaben und dessen Rednergestus bedeuten aber, daß dieser zum auswendigen Vortrag an der Reihe ist. Der Knabe rechts wird als nächster drankommen, deshalb geht er sein Pensum auf der Schreibtafel noch einmal durch.

2. Nahe verwandt ist eine Schale aus Spina, heute in Ferrara, aus der Zeit um 500 vor Chr.[30] Das Innenbild zeigt frontal einen Jüngling auf einem Hocker, der in der Linken eine Lyra und in der Rechten ein Plektron hält. Ein Außenbild zeigt zwei bis über den Kopf eingehüllte Knaben, die beide in Papyrusrollen lesen. Zwischen ihnen steht ein Bücherkasten. Beide sitzen auf Felsensitzen – wir befinden uns folglich im Freien. Rechts von ihnen sitzt frontal auf einem Hocker ein Jüngling mit einem Schreibgriffel. Deutlich erkennt man dessen abgeflachtes Ende, mit dem man das Wachs der Schreibfläche glätten und so Buchstaben tilgen konnte. Auf dem Knie hält der Jüngling eine aufgeklappte Schreibtafel. An der Wand hängen zwei zusammengeklappte und verschnürte Schreibtafeln. Das andere Außenbild zeigt, von links nach rechts, zwei Jünglinge, die frontal auf Hockern sitzen und beide nach rechts blicken. Der linke hat Schreibtafel und Griffel, der in der Mitte hält mit der rechten Hand eine Lyra. Ganz rechts sitzt auf einem Stuhl ein wieder bis über den Kopf eingehüllter Knabe, der in einer Papyrusrolle liest. Die insgesamt drei Rollen tragen versprengte Zeichen, die Schrift andeuten sollen. An der Wand hängt eine verschnürte Schreibtafel. Ebensowenig wie bei der Münchener Schale wird man hier in den jungen Männern Lehrer im professionellen Sinn sehen. Vielmehr ist beidemal dargestellt, wie Kinder mit und von Heranwachsenden vielleicht desselben Familienverbands lernen.

3. Noch in das Jahr 510 gehört eine Hydria des Phintias in München, die nun professionellen Musikunterricht zeigt. Rechts, bärtig, der Musiklehrer Smikythes, der seine Lyra stimmt. In der Mitte der Jüngling Euthymides, der Leier spielt. Und zwischen beiden ein bis zum Kopf verhüllter Knabe, der singt. Links der bärtige Erzieher und Begleiter des Tlepolemos, der Παιδαγωγός, Demetrios, hinter dem der Vasenmaler mit dem naiven ΝΑΙ ΖΩΝ (wie lebendig) sein Werk qualifiziert.[31]

Die Geschichte hat noch eine Fortsetzung: Der schöne Lyraschüler Euthymides war selbst Vasenmaler[32], und sein Kollege Phintias macht ihm auf der Schulter des gleichen Gefäßes ein weiteres Kompliment: zwei lockere Hetären spielen Kottabos, und eine widmet ihren nächsten Wurf ΣΟΙ ΚΑΛΩ ΕΥΘΥΜΙΔΕ (Dir, dem schönen Euthymides).

4. Zurück zur Schule: Eine Schale im Louvre um 500[33] zeigt ebenfalls professionellen Unterricht, diesmal in Geometrie: In der Mitte sitzt, gelangweilt, der glatzköpfige Lehrer. Er hat unter seinem Gewand lässig das linke Knie hochgezogen und betrachtet wie seine beiden Schüler den Boden, auf dem man sich im Sand geometrische Figuren denken mag. An der Wand hängt eine Sandale, die zur körperlichen Züchtigung diente. Die Deutung der Szene wird gesichert durch den Schüler zur Linken, der einen Zirkel in Händen hält. Das andere Außenbild dieser Schale zeigt, wie zwei Schüler in der Schule ankommen. Einer trägt seine Siebensachen im Netz mit sich. In der Mitte sitzt, in autoritätheischender Positur, der Lehrer.

5. Sicher professionellen Schreibunterricht zeigt eine Schale von 490 in Basel: der bärtige Lehrer hat die geöffnete Schreibtafel auf den Knien und ist im Begriff, einen Buchstaben zu tilgen und zu verbessern. Der Schüler steht erwartungsvoll vor ihm. An der Wand ein Futteral für den Doppelaulos.[34]

6. Den gesamten Bereich der ΜΟΥΣΙΚΗ, nämlich Schreiben, Lesen, Vortrag, Gesang, Lyraspiel, stellt die bekannte Schale des Duris in Berlin dar, die um 485 entstanden ist.[35] Je zwei Unterrichtsszenen verteilen sich auf die beiden Außenbilder; das Innenbild zeigt einen Athleten, der die Sandalen auszieht.

Die Vorderseite zeigt von links nach rechts einen Lehrer, der eben auf der Lyra vorgespielt hat. Die rechte Hand mit dem Plektron hängt herab. Der Schüler hat beide Hände in den Saiten und spielt das Gehörte nach. In der Mitte sitzt ein Lehrer, der eine Papyrusrolle hält, die, abweichend vom Üblichen, parallel zu den Rollen einen holprigen Hexameter enthält.

> ΜΟΙΣΑ ΜΟΙ ΑΦΙ ΣΚΑΜΑΝΔΡΟΝ ΕΥΡΩΝ ΑΡΧΟΜΑΙ ΑΕΙΝΔΕΙΝ
> (Muse, für mich, über den schön dahinfließenden Skamander ... ich beginne zu singen).

Offenbar trägt der Schüler vor, und der Lehrer liest in der Buchrolle mit. Rechts wartet der Pädagoge auf das Ende des Unterrichts, um seine Schützlinge wieder mitzunehmen. An der Wand hängen der Reihe nach eine Schale, eine Lyra, ein Tragekorb, ein Aulosfutteral, eine Lyra, eine Schale.

Sind die Lehrer der Vorderseite als bärtige Erwachsene stilisiert, so sind die der Rückseite junge Männer. Einer bläst einem Knaben eine Melodie vor, die dieser sich merken soll. Und in der Mitte überprüft der Lehrer mit dem Stilus in einer Schreibtafel die Hausaufgaben des Schülers vor ihm. Rechts wartet wieder der Pädagoge. An der Wand hängen von links nach rechts eine verschnürte Papyrusrolle, eine verschnürte Schreibtafel und eine Lyra.

7. Der gleiche Vasenmaler, Duris, hat sich nicht gescheut, Herakles in eine Schulklasse zu versetzen. Das für uns leicht komische Motiv des Schülers Herakles hat Anklang gefunden, so daß wir hier eine Bildergeschichte erzählen können: Ein Skyphos aus Cervetri, jetzt in Schwerin[36], um 455 vor Chr., zeigt Herakles, wie er sich recht unwillig von seiner Amme Geropso in die Schule begleiten läßt. Die Rückseite des Gefäßes zeigt den mythischen Lehrer Linos, der dem menschlichen Halbbruder des Herakles, dem folgsamen Iphikles, Lyraunterricht erteilt. Und eine Schale des

Duris aus Vulci, jetzt in München, von 480[37], zeigt, wie Herakles mit den Trümmern seines Stuhls den Linos niederschlägt, während die vier Mitschüler entsetzt davonrennen. Eine verschnürte Schreibtafel an der Wand stellt die Deutung als Unterrichtsszene sicher.

8. Ebenfalls um 480 entstand eine panathenäische Preisamphora, heute in München[38], die auf der einen Seite einen Speerwerfer, auf der anderen aber Athena zeigt, die Schreibtafel und Griffel in Händen hält. Offenbar macht sich die Stadtgöttin Notizen über den Verlauf der zu ihren Ehren veranstalteten Wettkämpfe.

Was der Göttin recht ist, ist den Frauen billig: Eine Schale, jetzt in Amsterdam[39], stellt um 475 ein Mädchen dar, das aus einer großen, mit Andeutungen von Schriftzeichen bedeckten Rolle zwei Frauen vorliest. Beck verzeichnet für die Zeit von 475–450 vier weitere Beispiele für lesende Frauen.[40] Und ab 450 finden wir die Buchrolle, später auch die Schreibtafel, auch als Attribut der Musen.[41]

Daß auch die Mädchen zur Schule gingen und Schreibunterricht erhielten, beweist eine Schale von 460 vor Chr., jetzt in New York[42], deren Außenbilder die Frauen bei der Unterhaltung zeigen, in einem Raum, in dem Schreibtafeln an der Wand hängen. Das Innenbild zeigt ein Mädchen, das eine verschnürte Schreibtafel trägt und das sich höchst widerwillig von einer älteren Frau in die Schule führen läßt.

Um 485 tritt die Buchrolle auch im Kontext von Musikunterricht auf: Fragmente einer Schale, heute in Oxford[43], zeigen den Musiklehrer, der den Doppel-Aulos spielt, und einen Schüler, der in einer Buchrolle liest und wohl singt. Eine ähnliche Konstellation finden wir auf einer Schale von 450 vor Chr. in Berlin.[44] Zwei Jünglinge, der eine mit zusammengerollter, der andere mit entrollter Buchrolle, stehen vor einem sitzenden Lyraspieler, der sein Instrument spielt. Solche Szenen sind zwischen 450 und 400 nicht selten[45], wir wollen sie mit einem Grabrelief um 400 vor Chr., heute in München[46], beschließen. Der Tote ist dargestellt, wie er die Lyra spielt, und vor ihm steht ein Schüler, der aus einer Buchrolle singt.

Rückt man die Auswahl bildlicher Zeugnisse neben die literarischen Belege, so wird auch der Skeptiker zugeben müssen, daß der dritte Elementarlehrer, der γραμματιστής, neben dem κιθαριστής und παιδοτρίβης nicht nur im 5., sondern auch im ausgehenden 6. Jh. hinreichend belegt ist. Das heißt aber, daß der von *Marrou* postulierte »Übergang von einer Kultur adliger Krieger zu einer Kultur von Schreibern« im 6. Jh. längst vollzogen ist.[47]

Drei archaische Sitzfiguren scheinen in die gleiche Richtung zu deuten[48]: Gegen 530, gegen Ende der Herrschaft des Peisistratos (+ 528/27) wurden in geringem zeitlichen Abstand nacheinander drei Ehrenstatuen auf der Akropolis aufgestellt, die einen Schreiber zeigen. Zwei sind etwas beschädigt, sind aber wegen der Armhaltung wichtig, die dritte aber läßt klar eine Sitzfigur mit einem Schreibkasten auf den Knien erkennen, der für sich gearbeitet war und bei Nr. 1 und 2 nur weggebrochen ist. In den »Wespen« des *Aristophanes* benutzt der komische Held als Protokollant eine solche κίστη, die als Unterlage diente und Schreibtafeln aufzubewahren erlaubte (529 ff.).

Nun hatte schon die solonische Verfassung (nach 594/93) mit den Organen der Volksversammlung (Ekklesia), der Volksgerichte (Heliaia) und des Rates der 400

(Boule) einen Bedarf an Schreibern geweckt. Die Γραμματεῖς waren aber nie Angestellte, sondern ehrenamtlich tätige Bürger.[49] Drei solche »Staatssekretäre« konnten sich offenbar um 530 nach absolvierter Amtszeit auf der Akropolis ein Denkmal setzen: ein schönes Zeugnis für die hohe Einschätzung der Fähigkeit des Schreibens schon in dieser frühen Zeit. Was man sonst noch aus der ersten Hälfte des 6. Jhs. zum Thema der Schriftlichkeit beibringen kann, fügt sich ein: Solon ließ die Gesetze auf eine Reihe von hölzernen Balken, den Axones, einmeißeln und diese drehbar in Gestellen aufstellen[50]: der Schritt von der Mündlichkeit zur Schriftlichkeit in der Rechtspflege. Dazu kommt die Fülle der Inschriften auf schwarzfigurigen Vasen und auf Stein.[51] Gründe dafür, im Athen des 6. Jhs. das Schreiben zu lernen, gab es genug; der letzte Beleg dafür, daß Schreiben und Lesen in allen Schichten schon im 6. Jh. weitverbreitet waren, liefern die Graffiti von den Agora-Grabungen, die bis ins 8. Jh. vor Chr. hinaufreichen.[52] All dies aber führt mit Notwendigkeit auf Schreib-Leseunterricht, führt auf die Figur des Schreiblehrers, der möglicherweise im 6. Jh. die ersten Schritte zur Professionalisierung dieser Tätigkeit getan hat.

Anmerkungen

[1] Vgl. *Heubeck* (1966).

[2] Vgl. *Lehmann* (1985).

[3] Anders in Zypern: Vgl. *Heubeck* (1979), S. 54–73.

[4] Vgl. *Heubeck* (1979), S. 73ff.

[5] *Marrou* (1957), S. 5.

[6] Vgl. *Aristophanes* »Wolken« 961–1023, *Kallias* »ABC-Komödie«, zu dieser *Pöhlmann* (1971), S. 230–40, *Pöhlmann* (1986), S. 55–57.

[7] Ilias 6, 168–170, vgl. *Heubeck* (1979), S. 128–146.

[8] »Ischia-Becher«, »Dipylon-Kanne«: vgl. *Heubeck* (1979), S. 109ff., 116ff.

[9] *Pfeiffer* (1978), S. 44–46.

[10] *Euripides* »Hippolytos« 856ff., »Taurische Iphigenie« 584f., »Iphigenie in Aulis« 98ff., 111ff., 314ff.

[11] *Pöhlmann* (1986), S. 54, Anm. 24–27.

[12] *Aristophanes* »Daitaleis«, »Wespen«, »Wolken«.

[13] *Aristophanes* »Wolken« 964f., 971.

[14] *Aristophanes* »Wolken« 1038–1042.

[15] Vgl. Anm. 6.

[16] *Herodas*, »Didaskalos«, vgl. *Cunningham* (1971), S. 102–127.

[17] *Herodot* 6, 27.

[18] *Plutarch* Romulus 28, *Pausanias* 6, 9, 6.

[19] Plutarch Themistokles 10.

[20] *Thukydides* 7, 29.

[21] Siehe oben Anm. 13.

[22] Vgl. *Erler* (1987), S. 21–37.

[23] Vgl. *Erler* (1987), S. 38–59, *Knox* bei *Easterling* (1985), S. 1–16 (Books and Readers in the Greek World).

[24] *Havelock* (1982), S. 185–207 (The Preliteracy of the Greeks).
[25] *Marrou* (1957), S. 70.
[26] *Simon* (1981), S. 12–15.
[27] München Z 607 (J 1168) ARV² S. 104,4, Beck (1975), S. 22, Anm. 7h.
[28] *Lippold* (1950), S. 302f., Tafel 108,2.
[29] *Schmid* (1929), S. 157 Anm. 1.
[30] Ferrara T 45 C VP, ARV² S. 349,1, *Beck* (1975), S. 22, Anm. 7 l.
[31] München 2421 (J 6), ARV² S. 23,7, *Beck* (1975), S. 25, III 10, Abb. 107.
[32] Vgl. *Simon* (1981), S. 97f., Abb. 99–101.
[33] Paris Louvre G 318, ARV² S. 348,3, *Beck* (1975), S. 18, II 35, Abb. 57 und 84.
[34] Basel Antikenmuseum BS 465, *Beck* S. 22, Anm. 7m, Abb. S. 6.
[35] Berlin 2285, ARV² S. 431,48, *Beck* (1975), S. 18, II 31, Abb. 53/54 und 168.
[36] Schwerin 708, ARV² S. 862,30, *Beck* (1975), S. 13, I 37, Abb. 25 und 31.
[37] München 2646 (J 371), *Beck* (1975), S. 13, I 38, Abb. 26.
[38] München 2314 (J 1185) ARV² S. 362,14, *Beck* (1975), S. 13, I 48, Abb. 32.
[39] Amsterdam, Allard Pierson Museum 8210, ARV² S. 838,27, *Beck* (1975), S. 56, X 1, Abb. 349 und Frontispiz.
[40] *Beck* (1975), S. 56, X 2/4, 5/6.
[41] *Immerwahr* (1964), S. 28–35.
[42] New York 06.1021.167, ARV² S. 908,13, *Beck* (1975), S. 56, X 3, Abb. 350.
[43] Oxford G 138, 3, 5, 11, ARV² S. 326,93, *Beck* S. 26, III 26, Abb. 119.
[44] Berlin F 2549, *Beck* (1975), S. 19, II 47, Abb. 63, 79 und 348.
[45] *Pöhlmann* (1976), S. 55 Anm. 16 und S. 57–62.
[46] München, Glyptothek G 481, *Beck* (1975), S. 26, III 29, Abb. 122.
[47] Siehe oben Anm. 5.
[48] *Payne* (1936), S. 72, Tafel 118,1–5; *Schrader* (1939), S. 207–212, Tafeln 132/133.
[49] Vgl. *Schultheß* (1912), S. 1710–40.
[50] Vgl. *Ruschenbusch* (1966), *Havelock* (1982), S. 205f., Anm. 8.
[51] Vgl. *Kretschmer* (1894) und *Jeffery* (1961).
[52] *Lang* (1974), S. 4ff.

Literaturverzeichnis

Beazley, J. D. (1948): Hymn to Hermes. In: American Journal of Archaeology 52, 1948, S. 336–340 und Tafeln 34–38

Beck, F. A. (1964): Greek Education 450–350 B. C. London

Beck, F. A. (1975): Album of Greek Education. Sydney

Beck, F. A. (1986): Bibliography of Greek Education and Related Topics. Sydney

Cunningham, I. C. (1971): Herodas Mimiambi, edited with intr. comm. app.. Oxford

Easterling, P. E. and Knox, B. M. W. (1985): The Cambridge History of Classical Literature I. Cambridge

Erler, M. (1987): Der Sinn der Aporien in den Dialogen Platons. Berlin–New York (Untersuchungen zur antiken Literatur und Geschichte, hrsg. von W. Bühler, P. Herrmann und O. Zwierlein, Bd. 25)

Havelock, E. A. (1982): The Literate Revolution in Greece and its Cultural Consequences. Princeton

Heubeck, A. (1966): Aus der Welt der frühgriechischen Lineartafeln. Göttingen (Studienhefte zur Altertumswissenschaft 12)
Heubeck, A. (1979): Schrift. Archaeologia Homerica Band III Kapitel X, Göttingen
Immerwahr, H. R. (1964): Book Rolls on Attic Vases, in Classical, Medieval and Renaissance Studies in Honour of B. L. Ullmann, Bd. I, S. 17–48. Rom
Immerwahr, H. R. (1973): More Book Rolls on Attic Vases. In: Antike Kunst 16. 1973, S. 143–147
Jeffery, L. J. (1961): The Local Scripts of Archaic Greece. Oxford
Kretschmer, P. (1894): Die griechischen Vaseninschriften. Gütersloh
Lang, M. (1974): Graffiti in the Athenian Agora, Princeton. New Yersey (Excavations of the Athenian Agora Picture Book No. 14)
Lehmann, G. A. (1985): Die mykenisch-frühgriechische Welt und der östliche Mittelmeerraum in der Zeit der »Seevölker«-Invasionen um 1200 v. Chr. (Rheinisch-Westfälische Akademie der Wissenschaften. Vorträge. G 276. Opladen)
Lippold, G. (1950): Handbuch der Archäologie 3,1. München
Marrou, H. J. (1957): Geschichte der Erziehung im Klassischen Altertum. Freiburg–München
Payne, H. (1936): Archaic Marble Sculpture from the Acropolis. London
Pfeiffer, R. (1978): Geschichte der Klassischen Philologie. Von den Anfängen bis zum Ende des Hellenismus. München
Pöhlmann, E. (1971): Die ABC-Komödie des Kallias. In: Rheinisches Museum 114. 1971, S. 230–240
Pöhlmann, E. (1976): Die Notenschrift in der Überlieferung der griechischen Bühnenmusik. Würzburger Jahrbücher 2, S. 53–73, Tafel 1/2
Pöhlmann, E. (1986): Die Schriftreform in Athen um 403 und ihre Implikationen. In: Lenz Kriss-Rettenbeck/M. Liedtke (Hrsg.): Erziehungs- und Unterrichtsmethoden im historischen Wandel. Bad Heilbrunn 1986 (Schriftenreihe zum Bayerischen Schulmuseum Ichenhausen, Bd. 4), S. 51–64
Ruschenbusch, E. (1966): Solonos Nomoi: Die Fragmente. Wiesbaden
Schmid, W. (1929): Geschichte der Griechischen Literatur 1. Teil. München
Schrader, H. (1939): Die Archaischen Marmorbildwerke der Akropolis. Frankfurt
Schultheß, O. (1912): Γραμματεῖς, RE 7, 1912, 1710–1740
Simon, E. (1981): Die griechischen Vasen. München
Turner, E. G. (1951): Athenian Books in the Fifth and Fourth Century B. C.. London
Winter, F. (1916): Schulunterricht auf griechischen Vasenbildern. In: Bonner Jahrbücher 73. 1916, S. 275–285

Gerhard Wirth

Lehrer, Kirche und Kaiser

Zum literarischen Bild am Ende der Antike

In Erinnerung an Sinaida Udalzowa

Lehrer und Lehrerbilder haben ihre Umwelt, und diese bestimmt, was von ihnen jeweils zu halten ist. Für die späte Antike und das frühe Byzanz[1] ist die Schule[2] im weitesten Sinne des Wortes eine Existenznotwendigkeit.[3] Denn sie schafft nicht nur die Kräfte herbei[4], das Imperium zu verwalten. Sie in erster Linie ist es auch, die es ihm so ermöglicht, seine Überlegenheit gegen die von außen her drohenden, mit der Zeit immer stärker werdenden Mächte aufrechtzuerhalten[5], und nicht zuletzt so das Ende eine geraume Zeit hinauszuzögern. Von den zeitlosen Werten, die erst durch sie aus der Antike in spätere Epochen auf diesem Wege hinübergerettet wurden, ist hier nicht zu reden.

Versuche, die Bildung als Institution zur Überwindung bereits eingetretener oder sich deutlich abzeichnender Katastrophen zu benutzen, lassen sich für das 4. Jhdt. erstmals in offiziellen Zeugnissen nachweisen. War es die Schule gewesen, mit deren Hilfe man in den besseren Zeiten zugleich einen Romanisierungsprozeß in allen Teilen des Reiches eingeleitet und fortgeführt hatte, so kommt ihr demnach jetzt die Aufgabe zu, den immer deutlicher werdenden gegenteiligen Tendenzen zu wehren und so in einer Verbindung des griechischen mit dem römischen Element wenigstens eine Konsistenz im Geistigen aufrechtzuerhalten, die in anderen Lebensbereichen mehr und mehr durch Zerfallstendenzen bestimmt war.[6]

So erscheint denn die innere Geschichte der römischen Kaiserzeit und noch mehr die der entscheidenden Jahrhunderte nach der constantinischen Wende eigentlich nicht zum wenigsten als die Geschichte dessen, was die Bildung, d. h. Schule wie Lehrer, aus den Möglichkeiten machten[7], die sich für die Bewältigung ihrer stets immanenten Aufgabe boten und eigentlich von Anfang an stets auch als solche erkannt worden sind.[8] Sie stehen demnach nicht zuletzt in einem dichten, mit der Zeit sich immer mehr noch verdichtenden Gefüge von differenzierten Beziehungen und sammeln in sich auf, was an einschlägigen Erkenntnissen, selbst im Strukturellen, die Antike je entwickelt hat. Sicher, vieles bleibt dunkel. Die Pädagogik als Wissenschaft etwa läßt für diese Zeit kaum eine Entwicklung mit neuen Erkenntnisfortschritten[9] sehen: Daß es solche dennoch gab, liegt nahe, obzwar sie als das Ergebnis bloßer Empirie nach *Quintilian* offensichtlich der systematischen Darstellung oder aber auch nur der Überlieferung nicht für wert gehalten wurden. Und selbst die kaiserlichen Gesetze aus späterer Zeit, die das Bildungswesen betreffen, lassen zumindest noch einiges an äußerlichen Kriterien für einen solchen Fortschritt erkennen. Ähnlich steht es mit der Funktion des Lehrers in einem solchen Zusammenhang. Gleich danach aber, unmittelbar nach diesem Höhepunkt in der Spätantike, scheint alles zu Ende zu sein. Für Byzanz zwar gelten ähnliche Voraussetzungen[10], und bis zu gewissem Grade wahrt man auch die Tradition. Doch es kann nicht ausbleiben, daß die eigentlichen Schwerpunkte sich verschieben, auf die es bisher angekommen war. Und vollends die immer wichtigere kirchliche Unterweisung geht von vornherein von anderen Voraussetzungen aus.

Daß sich für die soziale Position des Lehrers bei all dem so viele Aspekte wie Möglichkeiten von direkter wie indirekter Wirkung aufweisen lassen, ergibt sich aus der Tradition wie aus der erwähnten Differenzierung der Funktionen und Aufgaben gleichsam von selbst. Das Ansehen des Standes paßt dazu. Den Bedürfnissen einer Gesellschaft entsprechend, die die notwendige Festigung ihrer Existenz allein noch in der ihrer geistigen Grundlagen sehen konnte, weniger aber in deren Expansion, ist das Bildungswesen längst eine öffentliche Angelegenheit und der Lehrer als gleichsam deren Verkörperung auffallend gesichert[11], dies selbst dort, wo es um bloße Äußerlichkeiten geht. Der erwähnte Wechsel von einem antiken zum christlichen Reiche ändert hier vorerst nichts. Einschlägige Postulate werden sich als Gesetz und Verordnung auch dort niederschlagen, wo die Bildungssituationen, Schulen und Hochschulen, nicht in staatlicher Regie stehen. Wenn aber, dann ist es nicht zuletzt auch diese Sicherung, selbst im Materiellen, die sich in einer zeitlosen Form als ein Gradmesser für die erkannte Wichtigkeit und die allgemeine Einschätzung versteht.[12]

Ähnlich erscheint das Schulgefüge als Ganzes[13] in einer traditionellen Stabilität und ändert sich in seinem Wesen kaum.[14] Zwar mag es eine gewisse Fluktuation und Schwerpunktsverlagerung im Laufe der Jahrhunderte geben. Sie ist dennoch minimal. So scheint etwa das Bildungswesen in Gallien[15] in der späteren Kaiserzeit besonders hoch entwickelt, ähnliches muß für Afrika gelten, und zweifellos werden für die großen Metropolen des Reiches andere Maßstäbe anzusetzen sein als für kleinere Municipien oder gar das flache Land. Soweit ersichtlich, durchläuft der jugendliche Schüler immer noch eine als auffallend unwichtig behandelte Elementarschule[16], um dann in die des Grammatikers[17] überzuwechseln. Die nächste Stufe sind der Rhetor und der Sophist[18], die wiederum auf den Unterricht des Grammatikers aufbauen, von diesem schwer zu trennen und trotz aller betonten Konkurrenz auch voneinander schwer abzuheben: Für den Lehrer gilt den einschlägigen Zeugnissen nach Entsprechendes, ohne daß dabei sich klare Kriterien für Rangabstufung oder soziales Ansehen erkennen ließen. Die Schule des Philosophen schließt sich an[18a]. Sie ist freiwillig und erweckt den Eindruck eines post-graduate-Studiums[19], ohne daß sie für die spätere Berufswahl oder die Einstellung in den öffentlichen Dienst obligatorisch wäre. In der traditionellen Weise gefördert und subventioniert, wäre die Philosophenschule demnach in erster Linie als ein Instrument der staatlichen oder kaiserlichen Selbstdarstellung zu sehen, wobei bezüglich des Ansehens[20] zwischen den altehrwürdigen Institutionen in Athen oder Alexandria und den Möglichkeiten eines entsprechenden Unterrichts an anderen Anstalten zu scheiden sein wird. Daß die Konzession an die Tradition dann im Rahmen eines christlichen Imperiums zu besonderer Spannung führen mußte, ergibt sich aus der Natur der Sache. Es fehlt an frühen Zeugnissen nicht, die nicht nur diese Endstufe, sondern den ganzen Bildungsgang in klarem Gegensatz zu einer christlichen Grundlage des politischen wie persönlichen Lebens herausarbeiten.[21] Daß sie auch mit der Kritik nicht sparen, erklärt sich aus den sozialen Gegebenheiten wie dem Unterschied im Erziehungsziel.

In der Altersstrukturierung[22] und etwa dem pädagogischen curriculum wiederum ähnelt die Institution in etwa den modernen, d. h. die schulische Erziehung beginnt um das 6. Lebensjahr, der Übergang zum Grammatiker liegt um das 10. Ein *Libanius* beginnt sein Hochschulstudium mit 15 Jahren, die Norm mag ein kleines Stück höher liegen. Die Zeugnisse über die verordnete Studiendauer passen zu diesem Bild, verständlich nicht zuletzt aus der angedeuteten Absicht, die Schicht ständig zu verbreitern, auf der letztlich das Staatswesen zu ruhen hat und ohne die auch die regionale oder municipale Verwaltung nicht auskommt.[23] Mochten für die höchsten Spitzen der Verwaltung derartige Voraussetzungen unwichtig sein, die späte Antike kennt, soweit ersichtlich, auch aus diesem Kreis kaum eine Person, die sie nicht erfüllt hätte. Die Möglichkeiten zugleich auch einer sozialen Mobilität wiederum, die sich mit all dem verbinden, sind unverkennbar und beziehen sich nicht nur auf die Kreise der curialen Oberschicht und der übrigen Reichsbevölkerung, sondern sind zweifellos ein gern gehandhabtes Mittel der Überwindung auch der Barriere von Sklavenstand[24] und Freiheit: Die zum Teil fragwürdige Provenienz[25] selbst scheinbar hocharistokratischer Familien in Rom wie anderen Teilen des Reiches erklärt sich nicht zuletzt hieraus mit.

Fixiert ist längst der Kanon der ἐγκύκλιος παιδεία[26], was immer das Wort bedeuten mag, mit dem Ziele der Beredsamkeit als der wichtigsten Grundlage aller Nutzanwendung und Problembewältigung, durchgehend auf den verschiedenen Stufen der Schule aufbauend, doch keineswegs allgemeinverbindlich, sondern an den verschiedenen Orten mit eigenen Schwerpunkten. Vieles an Fächern läßt dieser Kanon scheinbar vermissen, Geschichte, Geographie, werden nirgends erwähnt.[27] Daß sie immanent waren, ist indes unverkennbar.

Falls unsere Terminologie korrekt ist, müßte es denn die merkwürdig gering geachtete Stellung des Elementarlehrers sein, die sich mit der Zeit zu dessen Gunsten verschob, so daß er fester als zuvor in dieses Gefüge einbezogen wurde, Zeugnisse von Mobilität auch für ihn fehlen nicht: Das auffallendste scheint das des *Pamprepius*[28], der als γραμματιστής in Ägypten anfing, zum Grammatiker avancierte[29], in Athen wohl als Rhetor zu hohen Ehren gelangte, um zuletzt in Constantinopel die höchsten Stellen des Reiches einzunehmen. Sein Beispiel mag eine Ausnahme sein[30], als solche hervorgehoben aber wird sie von den Quellen nicht, ich möchte meinen, selbst die γραμματισταί des *Libanios* als bloße Funktionsbezeichnung[31] lassen bereits eine entsprechende Änderung der Perspektiven erkennen, wie sie Jahrhunderte zuvor noch undenkbar war.[32] Die Mobilität erklärt sich für die Spätantike aus einem Personalbedarf, der anhielt, ja immer noch wuchs. Bei all dem mag das Bild einer solchen oberen Schicht viel an Fragwürdigem an sich haben. Denn trotz Etablierung und Subvention eines in solcher Weise ausgeprägten Schulwesens[33], die Berichte sind voll von Konkurrenzneid der Professoren[34], von Jagd auf Schüler bis hin zu wechselseitigen Prügeleien[35] auf den Straßen zu diesem Zweck, von gegenseitigen Verleum-

dungen bis hin zur Mordanklage, die wenigstens ein *Libanius* einmal auf sich nehmen mußte. Das Bild der Studierenden scheint nicht besser.[36] Dabei ist schwer zu beantworten, ob bei all dem der Drang nach Einnahmen oder der bloße Ehrgeiz die entscheidende Rolle spielte oder aber beides zusammenkam, dies zwangsläufig besonders dort, wo die Subvention durch die öffentliche Hand nicht vorhanden war.[37]
Es hat jedoch nicht den Anschein, daß auf solche Weise der Lehrer zu einer Karikatur geworden ist[38]: Das Ansehen einzelner, freilich profilierter Vertreter und die allgemeine Einordnung des Standes in die Nomenklatur des Reiches deuten eher auf das Gegenteil[39] hin, während die literarischen Selbstzeugnisse von dem armen Pädagogen früh ihren topischen Charakter gewinnen[40] und nur allzu gern bewahren. Was auffällt, ist nicht zuletzt eine räumliche Mobilität, die lange anhielt: Gallische oder afrikanische Lehrer[41] im Osten, Fremde dafür in Gallien, ein ständiges Berufen hin und her mit den Möglichkeiten einer Verbesserung der materiellen Lage für einzelne im Hintergrunde, beide Sprachen zwischen Euphrat und Atlantik überall gelehrt[42], das ist das Kennzeichen noch des 4. Jhdts. Ein *Libanius*[43] als Redelehrer verzeichnet in seiner Laufbahn die Stationen Constantinopel, Nikaea, Nikomedia, dann wieder Constantinopel und zuletzt Antiochia, seine Heimat. Die abgelehnten Berufungen sind nicht mitgerechnet. Ein *Augustin* geht von seiner Heimatstadt nach Karthago, dann nach Rom, Mailand, um dann in Hippo seine Laufbahn zu beschließen.[44] Sicher, dies sind die spektakulärsten Namen.[45] Die Herkunftslisten aber auch anderer Personen dieses Kreises weisen die entlegensten[46] Provinzorte auf, und für die Schüler gilt das gleiche, Zeichen einer ständigen Bewegung nach gleichsam allen Dimensionen und einer Aktivität in den Randzonen des Reiches ganz im Sinne erwähnter Mobilisierung der vorhandenen geistigen Reserven. Wechsel des Studienplatzes scheint Selbstverständlichkeit. Gelegentlich schließen sich die Schüler ihren Lehrern an und ziehen mit ihnen, was etwas von den Fahrenden Scholaren des Mittelalters an sich hat.[47]. Auch eine Permeabilität solcher Art aber blieb sicher nicht ohne Folgen für die Persönlichkeitsbildung der einzelnen und selbst ihrer späteren Möglichkeiten der Verwendung. Dazu kommt noch, daß es erst die Empfehlung durch die Lehrer ist, die am Ende den Schülern die berufliche Karriere ermöglicht: Armut und geringe Herkunft werden, neben möglichen Stipendien, auch auf diese Weise durch gerne wahrgenommene Autorität auf dem Wege gerade der Lehrer-Schüler Beziehung kompensiert.[48]
Im übrigen erscheint dieser Lehrer so wie kein anderer Stand in der späten Antike als die Verkörperung von Möglichkeiten eines sozialen Aufstieges[49] und durchbricht auf dem Wege über Titel, Privilegien und Immunitäten das Kastenwesen, das die kaiserzeitliche wie die byzantinische Gesellschaft charakterisiert.[50] Auch der Übertritt in andere Laufbahnen ist nicht selten, die Familie der *Ausonier* in Gallien ist nur eines von vielen Beispielen.[51] Bestimmte Äußerlichkeiten tun wenig zur Sache, sind aber dennoch nicht zu übersehen. Im deutlichen Gegensatz zu Konkurrenzbetrieb, allzu natürlicher Gewinnsucht der Lehrer und ihren Klagen[52], man verdiene nicht genug, steht die deutliche Sicherung des Standes mittels eines gewährten Fixums von Einkünften, die durch die erwähnten sozialen Vorteile gleichsam flankiert werden. Zwar lassen die Quellen ein klares Bild nicht mehr erkennen. Kaufkraft, regionale Gegebenheiten und die allgemeinen, im Laufe der Jahrhunderte sich weitgehend

verändernden Bedingungen sind schwer auf einen gemeinsamen Nenner zu bringen, so daß entsprechende Folgerungen stets Provisorium bleiben.[53] Die Stabilität, die *Gratian* offensichtlich 376 für Gallien festlegt, mag für alle Schulen gelten, soweit diese anerkannt sind und unter einer öffentlichen Aufsicht stehen.[54] Die genannten Einkünfte erscheinen zudem als auffallend hoch[55]: Es bliebe zu fragen, ob es gerade in ihrem Fall darum geht, auf solche Weise der besonders schwerwiegenden Folge[55a] von Germaneneinfällen dadurch entgegenzuarbeiten, daß man nicht nur der Infrastruktur wieder aufhalf, sondern auch die Möglichkeiten einer geistigen Überwindung der Katastrophe verbesserte.[56] In Ägypten, wo der Schüler dem Grammatiker einen Solidus pro Jahr zu entrichten hatte[57], sind die Verhältnisse anders und waren wohl 50 Solidi Einkommen das Äquivalent des gallischen Kollegen.[58] Rhetoren erhielten mehr als die Grammatiker, hatten offensichtlich aber auch andere Ausgaben.[59] *Libanius* spricht von 1500 Solidi[60], die einmal ein Diener veruntreute; ob es sich dabei indes um ein Jahresverdienst handelte, ist nicht zu erkennen. Daß der Lehrer neben seinem staatlichen Salarium noch Schulgeld nahm, verbot *Theodosius II.* 425 zumindest für Constantinopel[61]; die Verhältnisse in der Hauptstadt mochten dafür einen besonderen Anlaß bieten. Für die Schulen in anderen Reichsteilen verlautet nichts dieser Art, und sicher fehlte es nicht an Argumenten, warum dort alles beim alten blieb.
Dies sind äußerliche Kriterien. Die inneren sind anderer Art. Man hat sie eher zu folgern, denn direkt sagen die an sich dünnflüssigen Quellen wenig aus. Genauer gesehen aber ist auch hier das Bild ebenso interessant wie aufschlußreich. Denn, mag zwischen den Möglichkeiten des Berufes und den Verhaltensweisen einzelner eine eigenartige Diskrepanz bestehen, die unmittelbaren Zeugnisse scheinen umso deutlicher, weil gar nicht beabsichtigt, man prüfe etwa das Briefwerk des *Libanius* auf solche Fragen hin, wie das gelegentlich schon geschah. Da ist neben der Mühe[62] die Liebe und Fürsorge[63], die der Lehrer, Redner, Grammatiker oder Philosoph, für seine Schüler aufwendet, die menschliche neben der fachlichen Förderung, die Sorge für das persönliche und selbst das körperliche Wohlergehen und ein Bemühen darum, daß mit der vermittelten Bildung den Anvertrauten zugleich einiges von dem zuteil werde, was das Lebensglück schlechthin ausmacht. Bloße Selbstdarstellung eigener φιλανθρωπία[64] kann dies nicht sein, und auch eine einschlägige Terminologie mit einer besonders intensiven Betonung familiarer Bande ergänzt in ihrer Weise die Zeugnisse dafür, wie ernst der Redner seine menschliche Aufgabe nahm. Die Sorge beginnt bei den einfachsten Dingen, Unterstützung[65], Unterkunft, Fürsorge bei Krankheiten und anderen, allgemeineren Problemen.[66] Dazu kommt der Kontakt mit den Eltern[67], gelegentlich das Bemühen, deren Vorbehalte gegen die Entwicklung ihrer Söhne zu beheben. Seine Verbindung mit den Schülern sucht der Redner das ganze Leben lang zu erhalten[68], und er nutzt deren Zugehörigkeit zu der sich bildenden Gemeinschaft ausgiebig, vor allem, wenn sie selbst dann Protektionen zu gewähren vermögen, die einem guten Zwecke dienen. Eine gewisse Rigorosität in finanziellen Dingen wird durch eine solche nachweisbare Großzügigkeit der Unterstützung[69], wo dies nötig ist, mehr als ausgeglichen, wobei der Lehrer sich auch für Schüler einsetzt, die das Studium abgebrochen haben. Und noch die nächste Generation wird in dieser Gemeinschaft mit vereinnahmt.[70] Lediglich Phrasen im Sinne eines

überkommenen ethischen Ideals können es allein nicht sein, was sich in den Briefen des Redners niederschlägt.[71] Entsprechende Zeugnisse gab es darüberhinaus in großer Zahl: Daß wenig davon verlautet, erklärt sich eher aus der Selbstverständlichkeit solchen Verhaltens. Allerorten entstehende Lehrerdynastien – die erwähnten *Ausonier* in Gallien sind nur ein Beispiel – werden als das geradezu natürliche Ergebnis solcher bewußten Vermenschlichung anzusehen sein. Für die bekannte, Generationen hindurch anhaltende Verbindung etwa der alexandrinischen und athenischen Philosophenschulen gelten die gleichen Voraussetzungen. *Proklos* im 5. Jhdt. rät seinen Schülern und Freunden, auf jeden Fall zu heiraten.[72] In seinem Umfeld verbinden sich Schüler, Verwandte und Freunde miteinander und übertragen so gleichsam ein geistiges Gefüge ins Biologische[73]; daß dabei auch die Gattinnen in das entsprechende Blickfeld geraten[74], ist ebenfalls bezeichnend für die Intensität geistiger Vertiefung, die diese Jahrhunderte kennzeichnet. Sicher, wie stets mag gerade hier einiges dem Zufall von persönlicher Sympathie überlassen geblieben sein und erlangten nicht alle die Förderung, die es vielleicht verdienten.[75] Auch bleibt fraglich, ob jeder Lehrer sich um jeden Schüler mit der Intensität kümmern konnte, wie dies zu wünschen gewesen wäre. Betont aber wird diese menschliche Rolle immer wieder, die über das eigentlich fachliche, pragmatische Anliegen weit hinausgeht. Sicher, bei all dem mag der zweifellos kleine Kreis der Philosophen und ihrer Schüler für all das eine besondere Prädisposition aufweisen: Kennzeichnend allein aber ist dies nicht.

Dazu kommt noch ein anderes. Wir haben, aus Ägypten stammend, für diese Zeit das Phänomen der Wanderpoeten.[76] Eine Gruppe von Grammatikern und Rhetoren, dann auch deren Schüler, meist aus der tiefsten Provinz stammend und schon deshalb wiederum ein Zeugnis für den erwähnten Mobilisierungseffekt, betätigt sich neben dem Beruf noch als Dichter, und zwar teils aus Vergnügen an der Sache, teils vielleicht, um sich das Gehalt aufzubessern.[77] Dichtung als Tätigkeit scheint dabei sich gelegentlich sogar als förderlich auf die Karriere auszuwirken. Auf jeden Fall vertieft sie neben solchem Erfolg zugleich den Eindruck einer menschlichen Intimität, die neben dem Beruflichen, gleichsam Sachlichen, einhergeht, wie es die Institution als solche ausmacht. Ein *Olympiodor, Kyros v. Panopolis, Claudian* und selbst *Pamprepius*[78] als die wichtigsten Beispiele scheinen durch eine solche Verbindung noch fester an dieses Gefüge gekettet zu sein, was im einzelnen nicht zuletzt sich allein aus ebenfalls jenem Lehrer-Schüler-Verhältnis erklärt, das man sich nicht intensiv genug wird vorstellen können.

Das Lehrerbild, dessen Einzelzüge auf diese Weise sich profilieren, nun mag nicht zum geringsten Teil mit aus der traditionellen Lehr- und Unterrichtsweise[79] herrühren. Denn diese besteht weniger in einer Verarbeitung von Stoff als in einer Methode von Dialektik, d. h. in der Unterweisung, in Gespräch, Auseinandersetzung und der Diskussion von vorgegebenen Themen, wie sie an sich nicht nur geeignet ist, sondern darauf abzielt, in der angedeuteten Weise Fähigkeiten[80] zu vermitteln und zugleich auch die menschlichen Beziehungen[81] zu vertiefen. Denn anders als in einem Bereich bloßer Wissensvermittlung steht im Mittelpunkt von Worterklärung, Redeübung und Stoffbehandlung der Mensch selbst und die Eruierung seiner Fähigkeiten, was immer sonst an Interessen der einzelne Lehrer darüberhinaus damit noch verband oder an Spezifischem entwickelt wissen wollte.[82] Die Anwendbarkeit dieser Fähigkeiten ist ein Gesichtspunkt der Beurteilung der Institution, dessen Bedeutung gewachsen sein mag. Seinem Wesen nach blieb er sekundärer Art. Es könnte nicht zuletzt auch dies sein, das eine Erklärung für die angedeutete Stagnation der Pädagogik böte. Wohl gab es Lehrbücher für alle Stufen. Ihr kanonischer Charakter indes wird nicht nur aus den antiken Publikationsmöglichkeiten zu erklären sein. Wichtiger scheint mir die natürliche Selbsteinschätzung. Diese aber legt nahe, daß man dennoch nicht zuletzt aus Erwägungen der Nützlichkeit gerade in diesem Bereiche die Tradition jedem scheinbaren Fortschritt vorzog und alles an einschlägigen Neuerkenntnissen von vornherein mit Mißtrauen betrachtete, das über ein Minimum hinausging, wie es sich ohne Mühe noch verkraften ließ. Lag doch in der Tat in der scheinbaren Erstarrung und in der Bewahrung der altüberkommenen pädagogischen wie auch strukturellen Maxime die einheitliche Stärke des Systems, das zugleich auf einer jahrhundertealten Empirie beruhte und schon deshalb eine Änderung kaum rechtfertigen ließ. Denn wenn etwas, dann brauchten beide, Bildung wie Ausbildung zugleich, eine Kontinuität, die ihnen meßbare, feste Kriterien vermittelte, und dies in einem Zusammenbruch der Wertvorstellungen, die sich auf fast alle anderen Lebensbereiche erstreckten und im Laufe des 4. und 5. Jhdts. immer weniger hinwegzuinterpretieren waren. Eine solche Kontinuität wiederum aber bestand naturgemäß gerade in der Festigkeit der einschlägigen Vorstellungen, der Möglichkeit eines ständigen Rückgriffs und zugleich in einer stofflichen Begrenzung, die allein eine Effizienz versprachen. Das Gegenteil davon, das angeordnete Sichwandeln im Ganzen wie im Detail etwa im Sinne einer Anpassung oder aber Reformen in dem von ausgedachten Verbesserungsversuchen, war hingegen schon aus Kommunikationsgründen unmöglich. In der angedeuteten Situation vollends, in der das Imperium sich befand, wie angesichts der nach wie vor notwendigen Funktion hätten sie, auch nur bekannt geworden, mit einer allgemeinen Verwirrung schnell den Zusammenbruch der Institution mit sich gebracht und dies allzu schnell, was zu erkennen weder dem kaiserlichen Hofe noch den Pädagogen selbst schwierig gewesen sein kann. Gelegentlich, schon unter Zeitgenossen, klingt gewisser Tadel an der mangelnden Beziehung dieser Art der Bildung zur Realität an, der sich auf ihre Requisiten wie ihre Methoden erstreckt. Es ist, pragmatisch gesehen, aber gerade diese scheinbare Beziehungslosigkeit, die allein in einer solchen Konzentration erst eine Effektivität erlaubt. Daß die Stärke dieser Bildung unter den damit sich abzeichnenden Bedingungen fast ausschließlich im Formalen liegen konnte, war nur natürlich. Aber allein das Beharren auf dem Prinzip des Formalen war es[83], das den so Gebildeten am Ende ihrer Schulzeit sehr wohl zu einer Bewältigung auch der Wirklichkeit um sie herum die Fähigkeiten vermittelte und sie, an welcher Stelle auch immer, ihre Aufgaben gerecht werden ließ.[84] Sicher, mit der ursprünglichen Paideia hatte sich bereits in vorrömischer Zeit diese Bildung, als Ganzes institutionalisiert, den veränderten Bedingungen angepaßt und so erst den Hellenismus ermöglicht, ohne daß sie sich in ihrem Wesen veränderte. Nun vollzieht sich eine zweite Transformation mit wieder anderen Zielen.

Eine andere Seite dieses Bildes von Schule und Lehrer in ihrem zeitgenössischem

Umfeld ist nicht zu übersehen. Es bleibt zu fragen, wie weit der Öffentlichkeit oder aber der staatlichen Leitung an der Bewahrung einer solchen Tradition und der Formung des dringend benötigten Nachwuchses mit Hilfe eines derart intensiven Lehrer-Schüler-Verhältnisses liegen konnte, die sich immer nur in einem kleinen Kreise vollzog. Denn nicht nur, daß dieses Verhältnis stets von einem Freiraum abhing, der in einem Kontrollgefüge bald als obsolet gelten mußte, das zwangsläufig sich immer mehr differenzierte und zu größerer Rigorosität entwickelte: Neben der Frage nach dem Verhältnis zwischen Schule und politischer Loyalität einzelner aus ihrem Kreise stellen sich die nach der Effizienz des Aufwandes schon angesichts der Kosten, die ja auch sonst den Staat zu ständigem Einspringen zwangen. Vom Standpunkt eines fiskalischen Nützlichkeitsdenkens her hat *Themistius* sicher recht, wenn er einmal von Ballast und Leerlauf spricht.[85] In der Tat, ignorierte man die an sich wertfreien Vorzüge der formalen Bindung, so war angesichts der erwähnten, den Betroffenen genügend bekannten Schwierigkeiten der Weg der Rhetorik[86] als die Vorbildung für Leitung und Verwaltung des Weltreiches in seiner Notlage nicht mehr adäquat. Zwar mochte bis zum 5. Jdht. hin auch das römische Reich mit einer Präferenz der Bildung gegenüber der bloßen Ausbildung gut gefahren sein[87] und hatte stets die Praxis genügt, die erworbenen Qualitäten mit dem nötigen Sachverstand zu verbinden. Nunmehr mußte eine Verselbständigung, die seit je das Verhältnis von Mittel und Zweck scheinbar auf den Kopf gestellt hatte, als eine Perversion der erwähnten Probleme wirken und der Gedanke einer technokratischen, zumindest pragmatischen Lösung sich auch an dieser Stelle aufdrängen. Die Folgen werden früh sichtbar, auch wenn es nicht grundlegende Änderungen sind, die sich anbahnen. Daß sich damit auch das Lehrerbild um einiges verschob, war nur natürlich.

Was von nun an immer mehr sichtbar wird, ist die Spezialisierung im Sinne jener anderen Art von Effektmaximierung und unter Abstoßung eben jener Bildungselemente, die man bisher für unabdingbar gehalten hatte. Sie mußte zwar nicht unbedingt zu einer Zerstörung jenes erwähnten, im eigentlichen Sinne humanistischen Potentials führen, dessen bestimmende Rolle im Grunde nicht in Frage gestellt wird, und auch nicht zum Verzicht auf jenes Prinzip des Formalen. Soweit ersichtlich, kann die Zahl von Absolventen der Spezialhochschulen nie sehr groß gewesen sein; daß man deren Nützlichkeit erkannte und die Konsequenzen zog, als dies nötig wurde, läßt sich dennoch als ein Fortschritt bezeichnen. So hatte etwa bereits ein *Constantin* die Architektenschulen mit Privilegien versehen, die sie den anderen Hochschulen gleich setzten.[88] Gleiches gilt zweifellos für die medizinischen Anstalten, die nur zum Teil den anderen Schulen angeschlossen sind, meist aber ihre Eigenständigkeit sich bewahrten. Wir kennen zwar den Typ des Iatrosophisten[89], demnach offensichtlich einen Lehrer der Medizin mit den Möglichkeiten einer philosophischen Deutung des Berufes entsprechend einer Tradition, die sich aus den vorhellenistischen Ärzteschulen herleitete. Sicher, dieser Typ von Lehrer wird die Ausnahme sein und ist sicher keineswegs an allen Schulen anzutreffen. Die handwerkliche Ausbildung vollzog sich unter anderen Kriterien.[90] Die Einschätzung des Arztes in den Gesetzen seit dem 4. Jdht. und seine Gleichsetzung weitgehend gerade mit den Lehrern und Professoren indes läßt keinen anderen Schluß zu, als den auf die vorausgegangene rechtliche

Einordnung in den Bildungsgang, was zweifellos eine Anhebung des Berufes bedeutete. Seit dem 3. Jhdt.[91] ist die Rechtsschule von Beirut ein Zentrum juristischer[92] Ausbildung. Sie wird im 6. Jdht.[93] unter *Justinian* zusammen[94] mit den beiden Hauptstädten zum Zentrum der Rechtsausbildung[95] erhoben, die Worte *Justinians*, die ihnen 529 diese Aufgabe übertragen, lassen keinen Zweifel. Sicher, der Besuch dieser Schulen kann für den Staatsdienst nicht obligatorisch gewesen sein, schon reine Kapazitätsgründe sprechen dagegen. So wird nach wie vor auch jetzt noch die Masse des Nachwuchses den herkömmlichen Bildungsgang absolviert haben.[96] Auch setzt der Besuch dieser besonderen Anstalten die übliche Vorbildung voraus und wird dem Unterricht bei Rhetor und Sophist gleichzusetzen sein. Dennoch ist nicht zu verkennen: Die hier angewendeten Lehrmethoden wie selbst die Eigenart eines derart herausgehobenen Spezialunterrichtes schalten jenes erziehende, sich auf die Persönlichkeit als Ganzes beziehende Element von vornherein aus, so daß in ihnen doch das Prinzip der Bildung durch das der in einem bestimmten, naheliegenden Bezug effektiveren Ausbildung abgelöst wurde.[97] Und wie nur natürlich, war auch die Rolle des Lehrers jetzt anderer Art.[98] Daß bereits ein *Libanios* die Abwanderung eigener Schüler zu solchen Anstalten beklagt, ist bezeichnend für die Vereinfachung des Bildungsganges, die damit verbunden war. Eine Tendenzwende, von hier aus gesehen, wiederum könnte dann die Neugründung der Hochschule in Constantinopel 425[99] bedeuten. Grammatikerstellen und Rhetoren in beiden Sprachen[100], neben einer geringen Zahl von Juristen und einem Philosophen scheinen gleichsam modellhaft auf eine den allgemeinen Bedingungen angepaßte Erneuerung des Bildungssystems abzuzielen, wie es sich solange bewährt und zugleich der alten Tradition ein Maximum an Wirksamkeit ermöglicht hatte. Ein erster Blick scheint fast den Eindruck zu erwecken, es handle sich geradezu um einen Gegenzug gegen die angedeutete Spezialisierungstendenz. Auf der anderen Seite freilich ist es eine Monopolisierung anderer Art, die, in dieser Schule damit institutionalisiert, in einer wieder anderen Weise offensichtlich das Ihre tut, jene alte Bildungswelt mit ihrer Pluralität von Wegen zum Ziel dennoch einzuschränken. Denn deren Stärke hatte nicht zuletzt darauf beruht, daß es jedem, der dazu qualifiziert war, offen stand, nach einem eigenen Unterrichtsplan innerhalb des Curriculums zu lernen und zu lehren, so daß das Ziel für den einzelnen stets unter einer Vielzahl von Bedingungen zu erreichen gewesen war.[101] Nunmehr wird für die Hauptstadt alle Bildung an einer einzigen Schule konzentriert, andere öffentliche Lehrtätigkeit hingegen untersagt. Man mag sich über die Gründe streiten. Neben Beispielen von schwer zu handhabender Kontrolle der Studierenden[102], wie sie aus anderen Gesetzen hervorgeht, steht als potentielles Ziel eine neue Form von Institutionen jetzt unter besonderer kaiserlicher Kontrolle, wobei sich die Nähe des Hofes an anderem Ort vielleicht durch die anderer staatlicher Organe ersetzen ließ. Das Neue des Gesetzes bezog sich zweifellos dann nicht nur auf den Unterricht, sondern auch auf den Lehrer: Für diesen wiederum muß das Ziel einer entsprechenden Standardisierung unter solchen Voraussetzungen dann nicht mehr nur in der fachlichen Qualifizierung, sondern mehr noch in der Gesinnung, vielleicht bereits in der religiösen Haltung liegen. *Julians* Rhetorenerlaß mehr als ein halbes Jahrhundert zuvor zwar war wirkungslos geblieben. Die pragmatischen

Erkenntnisse, die ihm zugrunde lagen, indes brauchen deshalb nicht in Vergessenheit geraten zu sein.[103]
Sicher, das Gesetz betrifft die Hauptstadt mit Voraussetzungen, die anderswo so nicht gelten konnten. Daß das Modell dennoch nicht weiter gewirkt zu haben scheint und im Lande alles blieb, wie es war, muß über solche Mutmaßungen hinaus noch andere Gründe haben. Das Programmatische des Gesetzestextes indes scheint mir unverkennbar. Dazu aber kommt ein anderes: Die neue Hochschule auf dem Capitol erhält auch einen Philosophen ... qui filosofiae arcana rimetur ... Die Naivität, mit der demnach seine Funktion umschrieben wird, muß auffallen. Sie erklärt sich nur damit, daß es sich bei einer solchen Tätigkeit weder um Philosophie im Sinne einer noch bestehenden Philosophenschule noch um einen fundierten systematischen Unterricht im Sinne einer philosophischen Disziplin handeln kann, sondern um lediglich die Vermittlung von Handbuchwissen[104], vielleicht einige naturwissenschaftliche Übungen und die Erlernung einschlägiger Elementarkenntnisse. Eine Umschreibung der herkömmlichen Sophistentätigkeit wäre an sich möglich, ist aber nicht wahrscheinlich und besagte auch nichts. Sie würde unserer Kenntnis nach auch nicht zu den im Gesetz verankerten Zahlenverhältnissen passen. Was immer aber der Kaiser beabsichtigte, es wird in den Rahmen der Tendenzen des Hofes gehören, wenn die Philosophie genau genommen als gar nicht gefragt zu gelten hat und jetzt auch die Gründung etwa einer wirklichen Schule nicht beabsichtigt ist. Alles in allem bleibt somit der Eindruck einer bloßen Ausbildungsstätte auch hier, keineswegs aber der einer Neubelebung der Tradition.[105]
Nicht zu übersehen aber wird in einem solchen Zusammenhange zugleich die Verschiebung auch der politischen Dimensionen sein. Die Einheit des Reiches hatte seit 395 bereits einiges an Krisen hinter sich, und eine allgemeine Auflösungstendenz ließ sich kaum mehr ignorieren.[106] Und mochte das Gesetz formal auch die politische Reichseinheit betonen, die Zeugnisse für die Aufhebung der geistigen zwischen Ost und West waren nicht mehr zu übersehen. Bereits damit aber verliert das Beharren bei der bisherigen Bildungstradition zum guten Teil seinen Sinn. So ist bereits ein *Libanios* stolz[107], nicht Latein zu können, und betont die Inferiorität des westlichen Kulturkreises deutlich genug. Schon 376 wiederum erhält in Gallien nach kaiserlicher Verordnung ein Lehrer des Griechischen weniger an Gehalt als der im Lateinischen. Sicher, das sind Detailaspekte. Aber von hier bis zu den Verständigungsschwierigkeiten bereits der großen Synoden des 5. Jdhts. scheint der Schritt nur noch klein. Daß man für die Hauptstadt 425 das Verhältnis beider Sprachen zueinander noch ungefähr zu halten suchte, könnte mit Aussichten auf eine Neugestaltung der politischen Lage um diese Zeit zu tun haben, die auch hier einige Verbesserungen erwarten ließen, ja solche notwendig machten. Sie waren Illusion. Gerade die Gemeinsamkeit beider Sprachen war es denn gewesen, die über eine einheimische Polyglossie hinaus nicht nur die Voraussetzung für alle soziale Mobilität einzelner ermöglichte, sondern auch die Grundlage des Romanisierungsprozesses schlechthin bedeutete, wie ihn Rom als umgestaltetes Erbe des Hellenismus übernommen hatte: Bald nach 425 mußte es wieder fraglich werden, ob es noch einen Sinn hatte, wenn die Schulen weiterhin einen Personenkreis entließen, der in beiden Teilen des Reiches gleichermaßen zu verwenden war.

Es ist aber nicht zuletzt diese Stagnation[107a], die für das Bildungswesen in einem klassischen Sinne den Zusammenbruch auf die Dauer unvermeidlich macht. Die Tatsache, daß immer noch eine große Zahl von Beamten in allen Rängen verfügbar war und auch ein *Justinian* etwa für Italien an solchen keinen Mangel hatte, widerspricht dem nicht. Dazu kommt nun eine weitere Kraft, die an der Zerstörung dieser Tradition arbeitet und genau genommen gar nicht anders kann, als ihr mit dem Sinn auch die Verwendungsmöglichkeiten zu nehmen. Dies ist das Christentum[108], d. h. die Installierung eines eigenen, christlichen Bildungsgefüges.[109] Bedeutet die christliche Lehre, hier angewendet, eine Gleichheit der Bildungsvoraussetzungen für alle, so mußte sich dies als Programm neben einer Nivellierung nach unten[110] an sich auf eine Aktivierung des geistigen Potentials vor allem bisher zu wenig beachteter unterer Schichten der Gesellschaft[111] beziehen. Und in der Tat bringt die Forderung nach einer Bemühung um den Menschen vom ersten Tage seines Lebens an[112] pädagogische Impulse mit sich, wobei die jetzt in den Vordergrund tretende Unterweisung im Rahmen der Familie den Eltern, besonders der Mutter, eine neue, bisher kaum genutzte Rolle zukommen läßt.[113] Die antike Bildung war im wesentlichen von einer Formung des Erwachsenen, zumindest des Erwachsenden ausgegangen: Die christliche füllt damit eine psychologische Lücke, die man stärker empfunden haben könnte, als dies in den Quellen sichtbar wird.[113a] Daß sie in erster Linie zugleich auch soziale Schichten einbezog, für die jene traditionellen Formen gar nicht erschwinglich waren, widerspricht dem nicht. Anderseits freilich kann die christliche Erziehung zur traditionellen auch keine Ergänzung sein, denn sie bezieht sich auf völlig andere Bereiche, und auch ihre Ziele lassen sich kaum vergleichen. Sie steht vielmehr zu ihr in einer bewußt groß gehaltenen Distanz[114], denn sie ist in dem, was sie anstrebt[115], allein auf den Heilsplan ausgerichtet[116], keineswegs aber auf eine Bewältigung dieser Welt und ihrer Fragen, so weit dies einer dienstbar gemachten Paideia möglich war. Sicher, bereits ein *Lactantius* hatte, im Gegensatz etwa zu *Tertullian*[117] wie in umgekehrtem Sinne auch zu einem *Julian*, die Bildungsziele wie auch die Methoden und die Lehrstoffe der antiken als ein nicht ganz unbrauchbares Hilfsmittel auch zu einer christlichen Unterweisung anerkannt.[118] Bei dieser Konzession[119] aber blieb es, obzwar der Übergang von da an vielleicht einen anderen Verlauf hätte nehmen können. Zwar beweisen die Kirchenväter des 4. Jhdts., ja noch die des 5.[120], in ihren Schriften wie in den Zeugnissen ihrer Rhetorik eindrucksvoll die Wirkung der heidnischen Tradition, und lassen erkennen, welch unschätzbaren Mittel diese ihnen in die Hand zu geben vermochte. Auf die Dauer war es unmöglich[121], das komplizierte Gefüge von Kompromissen beizubehalten, das damit gerade für sie entstand. Denn nicht nur, daß die Spitze der christlichen Kirche mit sich in einen Zwiespalt geriet: Ihre Vertreter wurden unweigerlich gerade damit selbst zum Objekt einer Kritik von seiten weiter Kreise der Gläubigen aus den unteren Schichten[122]. Und nicht nur, daß in der Tat im Osten deutlich die entsprechenden Emotionen zunehmen, mögen sie sich äußerlich gesehen auch mit anderen Absichten verbinden. Auch an lautstarken Äußerungen der Aversion aus dem Munde profilierter regionaler Kirchenführer und Mönchsväter gegen die in ihrer Weise als elitär empfundenen, und damit allen christlichen Grundvorstellungen widersprechenden[123] Bildungsvoraussetzungen fehlt es nicht.

Die christliche Lehre bedient sich überhaupt seit je zur Unterweisung im Glauben der Nationalsprachen. Indem sie damit ein gefährliches regionales Selbstbewußtsein fördert, tut sie auch in dieser Weise das Ihre, über die Folgen sich wohl im klaren, die gewonnenen Ansätze einer griechisch-römischen Imperiumskultur zunichte zu machen.

Dabei kommt in der Tat ohne eine gewisse Propaideusis auch diese christliche Unterweisung in Schulen und Klöstern nicht aus und hat sich trotz aller grundsätzlicher Vorbehalte im einzelnen nicht zuletzt der herkömmlichen Mittel zu bedienen. Hätten hier, wie angedeutet, Möglichkeiten einer Intensivierung des bisher vernachlässigten Elementarunterrichtes gelegen, die bei einer anderen Synthese fruchtbar werden konnten, so mochten sich die Verwendungsmöglichkeiten etwa der herkömmlichen Rhetorik überdies auch im Rahmen einer Ausbildung für Kirche und Gottesdienst abzeichnen. Grundsätzlich aber widerspricht all dem auch hier bereits die spezifisch christliche Theologie[124], die bis tief in diese unteren Stufen hineinwirkt und überdies auch die Ziele einer klassischen Bildung ablehnen muß. Selbst das vordem gültige Lehrer-Schülerverhältnis verliert damit seinen Sinn. Zwar sind christliche Schulen früh in größerer Zahl vorhanden, sei es als Waisenanstalten, sei es als Internat. Ihre Aufgabe dort, wo sie über Elementarstes hinausführen, ist die Erziehung eines in erster Linie kirchlichen Nachwuchses[125] und die Lebensgestaltung in diesem Rahmen. Und wie die erhaltenen Zeugnisse der großen östlichen Schulen zeigen, ist alles andere, insbesondere das Äußere, dabei Nebensache. Spuren eines bestimmenden Einflusses jener ἔξωθεν παιδεία[126] scheinen mit der Zeit in der einschlägigen Literatur auf. Hat aber in einem solchen Rahmen der Lehrer allein nur noch eine priesterliche Funktion[127], so ergibt sich für die christliche Ausbildung als Ganzes, daß sie schon angesichts der vermittelten Voraussetzungen als Institution zur Heranbildung eines weltlichen Nachwuchses nicht in Frage kommt. Für den Osten des ehemaligen Reiches sind denn entsprechende Absichten niemals nachzuweisen[128]. Die christliche Selbstdeutung hat in der Tat die Notwendigkeit weltlicher Bildungsanstalten einschließlich ihrer Ziele und ihrer Erziehungsmodalitäten niemals in Frage gestellt. Was sie ablehnte, waren vielmehr die Lehrinhalte[128a], und die betonte Unvereinbarkeit bezieht sich im wesentlichen auf die damit zu verbindende Grundeinstellung der Lehrenden, nicht aber deren Funktion. Soweit ersichtlich, blieb es bei der Forderung: Die Wirklichkeit sah, von einem *Origenes* angefangen, anders aus, ohne freilich, daß die Befürchtungen eines *Tertullian* oder *Lactantius* sich bewahrheiteten. Die theologische Spekulation der Kirchenväter wie der Spätantike hat eine Voraussetzung im Sinne von einer Philosophenschule nicht. Daß die Entwicklung der christlichen Kirche im Westen anders verläuft, ist bekannt, und alles in allem lassen sich bereits seit dem 4. Jhdt. die Voraussetzungen nicht mehr mit denen im Osten vergleichen; die Unterschiede beziehen sich denn auf die Stellung des Papstes, die theologische Entwicklung und wohl auch auf die soziale Rolle.[129] Die christliche Schule, die im Westen früh in das Mittelalter hinüberführt, ist an dieser Stelle nicht zu behandeln. Aber all dem braucht nicht zu widersprechen, daß alles, was an kirchengeschichtlich wichtigen Ereignissen und Bewegungen zwischen dem 4. und 6. Jhdt. nachzuweisen ist, nicht zuletzt den Verfall jener alten Paideia mit beschleunigt oder

selbst bereits eines seiner Symptome darstellt, mögen breite Schichten der hier Agierenden auch von dieser gar nicht betroffen sein.
Sicher, neben dieser Entwicklung halten sich die bisherigen Institutionen noch, so daß, genau genommen, höchstens von deren verstärkter Aushöhlung gesprochen werden kann, und gerade die Selbstdarstellung einer gebildeten Oberschicht im 6. Jhdt. läßt auch in der Nähe des Hofes die Wirkung jener alten Tradition noch einmal erkennen[130], die man unter sich ändernden Vorzeichen an manchen Stellen jetzt umso intensiver gepflegt zu haben scheint. So ist die Abhängigkeit einzelner Werke von den klassischen Vorbildern unverkennbar, und ähnliches gilt für andere literarische Tätigkeiten, mit denen man sich über die Wirklichkeit gleichsam hinwegzutrösten scheint, von handfester wie zugleich subtiler Zeitkritik zu schweigen, die sich entsprechender Mittel bedient. Daß die Epoche der Vorbilder überdies zum Teil für diese Literaten schon märchenhafte Vorzeit ist, widerspricht dem nicht.[131]
Das Ende der Tradition freilich wird demnach nicht zuletzt auf diese Weise sichtbar[132], mochte es auch bis zu *Justinian* dauern, daß man nun selbst in der Gesetzgebung die Trennung zwischen der östlichen und der westlichen Welt deklarierte und damit zugab, daß in offizieller Sicht die antike Bildungstradition sinnlos geworden war. Von einem etwa lateinischen Westen über Italien hinaus als gleichwertigem Pendant allerdings ließ sich nicht mehr sprechen.[133] Mochte an einem Fortleben dieser Tradition in Italien selbst ein *Theoderich* sich interessiert zeigen, dies nicht zuletzt aus politischen Gründen, die das eigene Volk und dessen Verhältnis zum Imperium betrafen, die Bildungsbemühungen der germanischen Reiche gehen von gänzlich anderen Voraussetzungen aus. Aber wie schon angedeutet, auch in Byzanz waren für sie die Umstände fraglich geworden und die Zeiten eines *Basilius*, der beiden *Gregorii*, eines *Johannes Chrysostomos* oder eines *Sophronios* vorbei.[134] Ein *Severus von Antiochia* wirkt merkwürdig fremd in seinem Umfeld, und nichts ist bezeichnender als die Tatsache, daß dessen Schriften nur in syrischer Übersetzung überliefert sind. So sind die Spannungen nicht zu übersehen, die die Frage der Bildung innerhalb des Staates wie innerhalb der Kirche mit sich bringt. Daß alle Versuche, sie zu beheben, letztlich zu einem Traditionsverlust führten, muß klar gewesen sein, seit das christliche Element in der Bevölkerung numerisch die Überhand gewonnen hatte. Die eigentliche Auseinandersetzung scheint sich dabei im 5. Jhdt. abgespielt zu haben. Wie angedeutet, werden die kaiserlichen Regelungen 425 und die Spuren einer Bildungspolitik, auf die sie verweisen, für die Hauptstadt gelten. Und es mochte ein Zeichen von Klugheit sein, daß man in der Provinz die Dinge ließ, wie sie waren, nicht zuletzt, um dort die noch weiter benötigten personellen Reserven zu gewinnen. Das Reich selbst war christlich geworden, und es war die christliche Form von Schule und Bildung, die um diese Zeit bereits das Verhalten der Masse der Reichsbevölkerung bestimmten. Die Folgen äußern sich in dem bekannten allgemeinen Interesse an den dogmatischen Auseinandersetzungen dieser Zeit, zugleich freilich auch in Riesendemonstrationen, Pogromen und einer Emotionalität, die in ähnlicher Breitenwirkung die Antike noch nicht gesehen hatte. Nach wie vor sind es, zumindest in der ersten Jahrhunderthälfte, die großen Kirchenführer, denen unverkennbar ihre klassische Bildung die Fähigkeiten zur Diskussion und zur logischen Durchdringung theologi-

scher Fragenkomplexe vermittelt, und auch die Art, wie sie die psychologisch erfaßten Situationen meistern, scheint zum Teil noch das Ergebnis ihrer Ausbildung in einem typisch antiken Sinne zu sein. Nicht zu verkennen freilich ist, daß in der zweiten dann, besonders in den Randgebieten, ein anderer Typ die Zügel hier in die Hand nimmt und mit dem religiösen mehr und mehr denn an Einfluß auf das allgemeine Leben gewinnt. Er kann nicht mehr griechisch und auch sein Interesse an dogmatischen Fragen ist nicht groß und beschränkt sich auf Schlagworte. Aber er beherrscht die allgemeine Emotionalität und nutzt diese aus, indem er alles an einschlägigen Gedanken und Folgerungen nach Belieben verwischt. Es werden diese Auseinandersetzungen sein, die eine fruchtbare Verbindung von antiker und christlicher Bildung verhinderten, so daß die erwähnte christliche Schule in ihren Wirkungsmöglichkeiten begrenzt blieb und trotz jener ἐγκύκλιος παιδεία auch die Hochschulen der Patriarchatssitze ihren Horizont auffallend klein hielten. Der Lehrer der kirchlichen Schulen als solche aber bleibt nach wie vor amorph.
Es könnten nicht zuletzt wiederum diese Spannungen mit sein, die bewirkten, daß der christliche Staat in Fragen von Schule und Bildung nach wie vor ein auffallendes Maß an Zurückhaltung an den Tag legt und keineswegs bereit ist, eine alte, überkommene, wenn auch heidnisch bestimmte Tradition aufzugeben. Denn wenn etwas die offizielle Haltung dieser Zeit kennzeichnet, dann ist es eine Toleranz[135], gegen die Institution wie gegen den Lehrstoff und ihre Methoden, und dies, obzwar die Gegenstimmen jetzt kaum mehr zu überhören waren. Der Lehrer selbst ist dabei einbezogen. Sicher, diese Toleranz wird sich aus der nach wie vor bestehenden Notwendigkeit einer Mobilisierung von Kräftereserven erklären, die keine Gewaltaktion vertrug: Tiefere Hintergründe werden nicht zu ignorieren sein. Sie liegen m. E. im Bereich deutlicher Erkenntnisse bezüglich des Bildungsverlustes und seiner weiteren Folgen, die sich seit dem 4. Jhdt. an verschiedenen Stellen innerhalb des Reiches abzeichneten, aber in ihren Folgen weit über den Bereich der Bildung hinausgriffen. *Justinians* Anordnung, nur ein Christ dürfe noch Lehrtätigkeit ausüben, kommt dann verhältnismäßig spät.[136] Und hatte bisher die Religionszugehörigkeit der einzelnen Lehrer keine Rolle für deren Tätigkeit gespielt, es bleibt denn auch von da an unbekannt, wie rigoros das Gebot durchgeführt wurde. Gewaltmaßnahmen werden nicht erwähnt, mag die erwähnte Konzentration des juristischen Unterrichtes auf die drei Hochschulen Rom, Constantinopel und Beirut auch, wie vermutet, darauf schließen lassen, daß man beabsichtigte, ähnlich wie 425 in Constantinopel auch die Kontrolle im Personellen künftig straffer zu handhaben als bisher. Wenn etwas, dann mochte gerade das vorausgegangene 5. Jhdt. darüber belehrt haben, wie nötig die Beibehaltung des Bisherigen war und welche Selbstzerstörung es bedeutete, mit einer Maßnahme im Sinne des julianischen Rhetorenediktes alles auf den Kopf zu stellen, was sich einfach nicht ersetzen ließ. Sicher, von klaren Grenzen ist nicht zu reden, und es mag Lehrer gegeben haben, die schon früher in ihrer Weise Beruf und Glauben verbanden und keinen Anstand nahmen, Lehr- und Missionstätigkeit zugleich auszuüben. So fand etwa ein *Severus* während seiner rhetorischen Ausbildung in Alexandria einen, der ihn mit der christlichen Lehre, insbesondere christlicher Ethik bekannt machte[137], und es war der Lehrer der Jurisprudenz in Beirut, der

ihn, wie viele andere, soweit brachte, daß er die Aussichten auf eine staatliche Karriere aufgab und sich als Mönch dem Dienst für den Glauben weihte. Auf der anderen Seite ist nicht zu verkennen, der gleiche *Severus* erlebt in Alexandria bei *Horapollon*[138], daß Kollegen, die im Unterrichtsgespräch die christlichen Argumente zu sehr strapazieren, von ihren Kommilitonen ausgepfiffen werden, und noch mehr. Beruf und religiöse Überzeugung erscheinen, wie angedeutet, als merkwürdig voneinander getrennt. Sie stellen in der Tat aber so die Norm dar. Ich möchte meinen, der Staat müsse daran interessiert gewesen sein, in einer Zeit innerkirchlicher Auseinandersetzungen und dogmatischer Kämpfe mit ihren Folgen sich gerade in diesem Bereich so neutral wie möglich zu verhalten. Nach wie vor liefert so den Grammatikern, Rednern und Dichtern die Antike neben den Methoden den Stoff, mit dem sie in jenem kanonischen Stil erfolgreich arbeiten, und wird von ihnen die Gleichgültigkeit gegenüber dem Christentum offen oder versteckt betont. Der Kaiser wiederum erlaubt Heiden mit solchen Voraussetzungen, sich zu den höchsten Staatsämtern emporzudienen[138a], während unter den Christen noch die Häretikerverfolgungen toben und die Energie verzehren.

Es läge an sich nahe, daß der Staat sein Augenmerk besonders auf die Philosophen richtete, den Kreis von Lehrern, der die antike Tradition am intensivsten pflegte und als gleichsam die Quintessenz aller Bildung den natürlichen Gegensatz zur christlichen Lehre nicht nur im eigentlichen Sinne verkörperte, sondern bis zu einem bestimmten Grade auch zu propagieren in der Lage war. Von einer zwangsweisen Beendigung der philosophischen Ausbildung aber ist nichts bekannt. Sicher, das angedeutete Beispiel Constantinopel läßt auf eine Ausdünnung schließen, die den gesamten Philosophenunterricht an den spätantiken Hochschulen betraf, und es liegt nahe, daß diese Art Hochschulphilosophie in ihrer Simplifizierung von Methode und Stoff am ehesten geeignet war, der christlichen Unterweisung Material zu liefern. Hatte diese Tatsache auch mehr innere als äußere Gründe, so war doch auch bei Verharmlosung und bloßer Information in den auf diese Weise nach wie vor sich herausbildenden Lehrer-Schülerverhältnissen eine gewisse Gefahr nicht zu verkennen. Dies umso mehr, als eine christliche Hochschulphilosophie als potentielles Äquivalent über rudimentäre Ansätze vorerst kaum hinaus kam. Losgelöst davon aber existierten nach wie vor die großen Philosophenschulen[139] in Athen und Alexandria, staatlich reich dotiert und in einer Tradition stehend, die keineswegs als beendet anzusehen war. Eher im Gegenteil. An ihnen konzentrieren sich Forschung und Spekulation, entstehen neue Systeme und wird aufgearbeitet, was die großen Lehrer zurückgelassen hatten. Gekennzeichnet ist das Philosophieren dieser Schulen bei all dem seit spätestens *Plotin* durch eine deutliche Tendenz zur Theosophie[140], das heißt, zu eben einer Verbindung von Philosophie und Religion mit einer Affinität zur Erneuerung und Vertiefung der vorchristlichen Formen von Religiosität und Religionsausübung zugleich. Die Konkurrenz zum Christentum könnte sich nicht schärfer profilieren. Auch an diesen Schulen muß das Lehrer-Schülerverhältnis in der vor Augen geführten Weise ausgeprägt gewesen sein, ja, ist ohne diese Ausprägung eine Tradition am wenigsten denkbar. Unsere Nachrichten lassen zwar auf eine Exklusivität dieser Kreise schließen. Aber neben den überlieferten Namen sind es anderseits die persönlichen, gleichsam ins Private gehenden Verbindungen untereinander und zwischen den Schulen, die in ihrer Weise eine sichtbare wechselseitige Förderung durch Austausch und Anregung bringen.[141] Die Gefahr nun, die gerade von hier aus für die noch im Entwicklungsprozeß begriffene, keineswegs schon gefestigte christliche Lehre ausging, war nicht zu übersehen.[142] Und auch nicht, was sich aus möglichen Konflikten in einem solchen Zusammenhang für den sowieso ständig strapazierten inneren Frieden des Reiches damit ergab. Indes, von einer staatlichen Kontrolle oder gar Restriktionen ist nichts bekannt. Auch diese Hochschulen behalten ihr Vermögen, und die seit *Mark Aurel* spätestens nachweisbaren Gehälter für Schulhäupter wie einzelne Lehrer werden stets gezahlt. Gewisse Ansätze einer Professorenverfolgung unter *Zeno* hängen mit dem Illusaufstand und einem vorübergehenden Auftreten des *Pamprepius* in Ägypten zusammen. Über Ägypten wirken sie nicht hinaus und haben überdies als Politicum eine Parallele in einer Absetzungswelle, die auch die christlichen Bischöfe betraf.[143] Nicht nur, daß man demnach die Sekten und Glaubensrichtungen duldete, zu deren Heimat sich gerade diese Anstalten entwickelten, und man auch die Heranbildung eines Nachwuchses an ihnen nicht beeinträchtigte. Daß Frauen mehr und mehr in diesen Kreis einbezogen wurden, gehört in den Bereich erwähnter innerer Intensivierung: Die unverkennbare Parallele zum Christentum aber kann dann nur als eine weitere gefährliche Konkurrenz empfunden worden sein.[144] Zwar wissen wir über eine Breitenwirkung dieser Schulen wenig.[144a] Doch auch wenn sie sich bewußt den Massen entzogen, der Staat hatte dennoch allen Grund, hier wachsam zu sein und mögliche Folgen zu überdenken. So betätigt sich in Athen ein *Proklos,* lange Jahre das Haupt der Akademie[145], neben seiner Lehrtätigkeit als Theurg ganz in einem neoplatonischen Sinne mit Weissagungen, Opferschauen und Ritualen der Versenkung in die Gottheit. Auch ihm geschieht nichts. Es ist dieser *Proklos,* der überdies in einem Werke von nicht weniger als 16 Büchern das Christentum widerlegt.[146] Und in den neunziger Jahren des 5. Jdhts. kann der ebenfalls heidnische *Ammonios*[147] mit dem Patriarchen zu einem spektakulären Agreement gelangen. Wir kennen den genauen Inhalt nicht, doch darf als sicher gelten, daß es dort in einer allgemeinen Aufgewühltheit unter den Nachwehen von akakianischem Schisma und monophysitischen Auseinandersetzungen[148] auf nicht weniger abzielte als die, wenn auch nur vorübergehende, gegenseitige Duldung zwischen Kirche und Philosophie.[149] Und es gibt in der Tat keine Nachricht, daß von da an die Philosophenschule etwa durch die sonst üblichen Mönchsexzesse belästigt worden wäre. Sicher, Alexandria hatte in diesen Dingen seine besondere Tradition, und daß man auf diese Weise jetzt für eine Zeitlang zur Ruhe kam, mag an sich als ein Fortschritt empfunden worden sein.[150] So hatte man zu Beginn des Jahrhunderts 415 dort die heidnische Philosophin *Hypatia*[151] gelyncht und am Beispiel einer gefeierten Lehrerpersönlichkeit gezeigt, was möglich war: Ein bloßes Politicum als Anlaß braucht dem nicht zu widersprechen.[152] Bereits im Zusammenhang mit den Kultverboten 391 aber wiederum und den sich daran anschließenden Kämpfen in Alexandria war eine Anzahl heidnischer Grammatiker und Rhetoren gezwungen worden, die Stadt zu verlassen. Einer von ihnen, der Grammatiker *Helladios,* wird später in Constantinopel mit dem höchsten Range[153] des Reiches namentlich geehrt, obwohl er

nach eigener Aussage seinerzeit in der Heimat bei den Prügeleien 9 Christen persönlich totgeschlagen hatte.[154] *Helladios* war Grammatiker.[155] Der Grund für eine solche Behandlung mag denn allein in seinen beruflichen Qualitäten und seiner Lehrerpersönlichkeit zu sehen sein, die vieles verzeihen ließ. Der Freiraum indes[156], den der Staat demnach selbst unter solchen Voraussetzungen zu gewähren bereit ist, muß trotzdem als spektakulär gelten. Und er läßt sich nur aus der Wichtigkeit der Aufgabe erklären, die die von *Helladios* verkörperte Institution immer noch besaß. Auch bei den erwähnten Literaten des 6. und 7. Jhdts. treten die Andeutungen christlicher Gläubigkeit hinter den vielfältig artikulierten Vorbehalten gegenüber der allgemeinen geistigen Entwicklung zurück.
Dazu aber scheint noch ein anderes zu kommen. Wie bekannt, schließt 529 *Justinian* die Akademie als die letzte der verbliebenen Philosophenschulen in Athen.[157] Die Hintergründe sind nicht zu ermitteln. Doch fällt in das gleiche Jahr eine Reihe einschneidender Maßnahmen und selbst militärischer Aktionen zu einer längst notwendigen, inneren Stabilisierung, so daß ein Zusammenhang nicht zu übersehen ist. Reicht aber, genau genommen, keines der möglichen Argumente für eine wirkliche Erklärung des Vorganges aus, so muß auffallen, daß auch die zeitgenössischen Quellen das Ereignis in auffallend vagen Worten berichten. Noch mehr: Die sieben Mitglieder der Schule gehen kurz danach, 531, unter Führung des *Damaskios,* eines der Nachfolger des *Proklos,* für einige Zeit nach Persien[158], um dort eine neue Heimstatt zu finden. Es hat indes den Anschein, daß man zu Unrecht dieses Ereignis als das Ende der antiken Geistesbildung bezeichnet. Und auch von hier aus wäre nach den Gründen zu fragen. Unsere Nachrichten reichen, wie angedeutet, nicht aus, um die Rolle Athens und gar der Akademie für die antike und besonders spätantike Erziehungs- und Bildungsgeschichte ganz erkennen zu lassen, so daß sich hier eine Erklärung für den Akt *Justinians* fände. Näher liegt das Gegenteil. Auch ist unklar, ob es sich bei den 529 Betroffenen ausschließlich um Philosophen handelte. Die Genannten zwar sind in ihrem Fache alle profiliert. Ihrer religiösen Überzeugung nach Heiden, verkörpern sie die erwähnte Tradition in einer Weise, die offensichtlich alle anderen Zeugnisse weit hinter sich ließ. Was freilich als wichtiger erscheint, ist für sie wie überdies auch für ihre alexandrinischen Kollegen neben der Unterweisung ihrer Schüler die Forschung, sei es im Sinne von Spekulation sei es in der Aufarbeitung der Lehre. Beides gehört enger zusammen, als es auf den ersten Blick den Anschein hat, und die Grenzen zwischen den Kategorien literarischer Tätigkeit lassen sich ebenso wenig zwischen den Stufen wie zwischen Ressorts oder Sachbereichen ziehen.[159] Bedeutet aber Forschung hier die eigentliche Aufarbeitung dessen, auf das man sich im Sinne der Tradition, in der man stand, berief, so ergibt sich von selbst, daß alle weiterführende Spekulation nur auf ihr beruhen konnte. Im übrigen waren es, und zwar auf allen Ebenen, stets die Lehrer[160], die über das Kanonische hinaus Lehrschriften und Unterrichtswerke zur Vertiefung und Verbesserung des Unterrichtes verfaßten. Kommentare, Textausgaben, Lexika, Untersuchungen und Handreichungen ähnlicher Art aber wiederum sind es, die bereits um die Zeit *Justinians* ein Fortleben der Antike allein noch zu gewährleisten scheinen und denen wir so ein Großteil der erhaltenen antiken Literatur, und zwar nicht nur der philosophischen, verdanken.

Viel war bereits verloren gegangen. Nicht zuletzt diese Art der Aufarbeitung aber wird es erklären, wenn nicht nur alle Spekulation innerhalb der Philosophenschulen in der Deutung, d. h. Analyse und Kommentierung der großen Lehrer besteht, sondern sich gerade an ihnen die Grenzen zwischen dem Grammatiker und dem eigentlichen Philosophen noch mehr verwischen als anderswo.[161] Gehören die Disziplinen der Philologie, insbesondere der Textkritik[162], denn zu den unabdingbaren Voraussetzungen allen Philosophierens wie auch des philosophischen Unterrichtes[163], so werden zwangsläufig auch die für eine Berufsbezeichnung im einzelnen üblichen Termini vieldeutig. Der Grammatiker als Haupt oder als jeweils profiliertester Vertreter selbst einer Philosophenschule[164] kann unter solchen Umständen kaum verwundern. Die Diffizilität der Aufgaben macht es im übrigen verständlich, wenn sich die Schulen ihren Nachwuchs selbst erzogen[165], und dies von möglichst frühen Stufen an, anderseits aber schon deshalb niemals zu einer großen Breitenwirkung gelangten. Was an ihnen geleistet wurde, ist an Quantität wie an Qualität ein Maximum, und die Bezeichnung einer ganzen Reihe ihrer Vertreter als *Philoponos*, dies gelegentlich auch im Superlativ[166], scheint nur allzu gerechtfertigt. Daß nicht zuletzt nun diese Qualität es war, die öffentlich Aufsehen erregte, liegt nahe.[167] Gerade sie ist denn ohne eine gesteigerte Intensität der Bemühung um die Sache und auch um die des Lehrer-Schülerverhältnisses nicht denkbar: So verwundert es kaum, wenn sich solche Wechselwirkungen zwischen beruflicher Tätigkeit und menschlicher Nähe auch in den bereits erwähnten familiären Verbindungen niederschlagen[168], die sich ihrerseits wieder erneut dann förderlich auf die Lehre wie die Forschung auswirkten und alles in allem so einen letzten Höhepunkt antiker Philosophie, ja antiker Geisteskultur ermöglichten.

Die Akademie nun hatte sich vorwiegend stets der platonischen Tradition gewidmet.[168a] Wenn aber schon ein *Proklos* gegen das Christentum polemisierte und den Lehren *Platos* ihm gegenüber den Vorzug gab, dann war es trotz des elitären Wirkungskreises und trotz der zeitgebundenen Publikationsmöglichkeiten unvermeidlich, daß auch ein kleiner Kreis von Schülern und Anhängern, in einer Zeit mühevoller christlicher Konsolidierung zu den erwähnten Befürchtungen[169] Anlaß gab. Es bleibt zu fragen, ob etwa eine Bekehrung der athenischen Lehrer[170] und Gelehrten ihnen die Einkünfte und das Fortbestehen der Schule ermöglicht hätte: Das Beispiel Alexandrias mit seinen Philosophen teilweise in der Tat christlichen Bekenntnisses und seiner offensichtlich geringeren theurgischen Ausrichtung mag einiges besagen.[171] Die Athener bekehrten sich nicht. Indes, zuleide tat man ihnen nichts, und zwischen der Schließung der Akademie und der Auswanderung liegen zumindest zwei Jahre, in denen, wie *Cameron* zuletzt nachwies, die Publikation nicht unterbrochen zu werden brauchte.[172]

Bald danach kehren die Philosophen aus Persien wieder heim, auch jetzt ungeschoren. *Simplicius*[173], jetzt der wichtigste aus ihrem Kreise, begab sich sogar zurück nach Athen, wo er ein stilles Leben führte, unter anderen großen Werken seinen Aristoteleskommentar verfaßte, sich ungestraft aber darüberhinaus in bösen Bemerkungen gegen die politische Umwelt ergehen[174] konnte, die ihm so böse mitgespielt hatte und ihm den Beweis für das bot, was schon *Epiktet* gegen Staat und Herrschaft gesagt hatte. Wir haben Anhaltspunkte, daß er sogar private Schüler weiterhin unterrichtete, ja diesen gegenüber in der Unterweisung wie im menschlichen Verhalten noch einmal das Ideal eines Lehrer darzustellen Gelegenheit hatte, wie es in einem Prozeß von nunmehr über einem Jahrtausend gleichsam gewachsen war.[175] Nach einer plausiblen Vermutung *Camerons* ist nicht einmal auszuschließen, daß man ihn auch jetzt noch aus den Fonds der Akademie dotierte.[176] Aber auch wenn nicht, um zu leben hatte er offensichtlich an Einkünften genug. Kurz, nicht einmal unter *Justinian* scheint sich im Grunde etwas zu ändern, nachdem ein scheinbar programmatischer Kraftakt gleichsam den Triumph der Theologie über die Philosophie und des Christentums über alle anderen Möglichkeiten von Religion und religiöser Deutung in derart spektakulärer Weise verkündet hatte.[177] Nach wie vor hatte die Bildung auf ihren anderen Stufen und in der herkömmlichen Form ihren Platz und wurde auch an den Kriterien des Lehrerbildes nichts geändert. Indes, eine neue Wende hat sich dennoch damit vollzogen. Zum erstenmal werden Lehrer um ihrer Religiosität willen auf Dauer aus dem Amte verwiesen, und wird der Sinn ihrer Tätigkeit von ihrem Verhältnis zur Religion aus definiert. Damit aber verschieben sich die Perspektiven entscheidend. Und was bei einem *Julian* in umgekehrtem Zusammenhang noch als Augenblicksregung zu verstehen war, ohne System und ohne Alternative, wird nun als eine nicht nur mehr äußerliche Verpflichtung gegen eine inzwischen gewachsene, wirklich herrschende und verbindlich gewordene Religion deklariert. Auch wenn in den Schulen des Reiches die Lehrinhalte formal unverändert blieben: Es ist der Lehrer, von dem man eine andere personelle Voraussetzung verlangt. Die Bildungstradition selbst aber rückt zwangsläufig auf diese Weise an den Rand. Und da ihre Inhalte von staatswegen zur Äußerlichkeit erklärt werden, ist denn auch der Lehrer als Typ zum Aussterben verdammt, der bisher die antike Tradition verkörpert hatte. Die erwähnten Zeugnisse über die Anordnungen zur juristischen Ausbildung[178] aus den gleichen Jahren lassen erkennen, daß man fortan wenigstens für diesen Zweig auf das Herkömmliche zu verzichten und sich mit dem bloßen Spezialisten zu behelfen gedachte. Kurz danach werden in Afrika die Gehälter von Grammatiker und Rhetor einander angeglichen.[179] Auch dies ist ein Programm.

Anmerkungen

[1] Die folgenden Anmerkungen können einen vollständigen Überblick über alle einschlägige Quellen- und Sekundärliteratur nicht bieten. Sie haben sich auf Notwendigstes zu beschränken. Indes enthält das Angeführte weiteres Material in Fülle und damit zugleich die Anregung zu weiterer Auseinandersetzung.

[2] Verweisen möchte ich auf einschlägige Arbeiten für den hier angesprochenen Zusammenhang: 1) Der Weg an die Grenze. Blüte und Schicksal der antiken Bildungstradition, in: Schulgeschichte im Zusammenhang der Kulturentwicklung hsg. v. L. Kriss-Rettenbeck u. M. Liedtke, Bad Heilbrunn 1983, 77ff. (zit. Schulgeschichte); 2) Die leidige Schule, in: Erziehungs- und Unterrichtsmethoden im historischen Wandel, hsg. v. L. Kriss-Rettenbeck

und M. Liedtke, Bad Heilbrunn 1986, 74ff. (zit. Wandel). Die dort zitierte Literatur ist im folgenden berücksichtigt, indes nur dort angeführt, wo es sich um notwendig ergänzende Gedankengänge handelt.

[3] S. dazu bes. CTh 14,1,1/360. Reserven müssen um diese Zeit noch vorhanden gewesen sein, ich bezweifle, daß die gleiche Forderung 100 Jahre später gestellt hätte werden können.

[4] Dazu zusammenfassend Walden, bes. S. 78ff.; S. 986ff.

[5] Siehe unten, vgl. dazu auch Wandel S. 78f.

[6] S. dazu meine Ansichten, JAC 1989. Im Gegensatz zu A. H. M. Jones (s. bes. JTS 10, 1959, 280ff.) sehe ich im Zusammenhang mit den dogmatischen Streitigkeiten mit nachweisbaren Exzessen der östlichen Reichshälfte unverkennbare Symptome regionaler Selbständigkeitstendenzen.

[7] Vgl. zu Privilegien als Zeichen dringender Notwendigkeit CJ 27,16,8,9–11. Ein Beispiel ist ILS nr. 778. Zur Expansion des Bildungsbetriebes in der Kaiserzeit siehe Walden S. 86ff.

[8] Zu der damit verbundenen auffallenden Starrheit des Bildungssystems s. u.; zur Einheit von Bildung und Kenntnisvermittlung siehe Schulgeschichte S. 88ff. Die Vielfalt der Möglichkeiten muß größer gewesen sein, als dies sich in unserer Terminologie noch erfassen läßt. Zum Verfall in der Spätantike siehe bes. H. I. Marrou, Augustin, bes. S. 25f.

[9] Einiges an Material in der Sammlung Erziehung und Bildung in der heidnischen und christlichen Antike, hsg. v. H. Th. Johann, Darmstadt 1976 (zit. Johann), s. dort bes. das Literaturverzeichnis, vgl. auch Wandel S. 74. Zu möglichen Reformen s. Rahn, Quintilian S. 810. Zeitgenössische Reflexionen ignorieren den formalen Bildungswert, der die Rhetorik zum eigentlichen Erziehungsinstrument auch im Pragmatischen macht.

[10] Zusammenfassend dazu immer noch G. Buckler, in: N. H. Baynes; H. St. L. B. Moss, Byzantium, Oxford 1948 (zit. n. dt. Übersetzung v. A. Hohlweg, München 1964), 154ff. Schwerer zugänglich ist die Behandlung einschlägiger Fragen etwa bei H. G. Beck 1977; ders. 1978, 15ff.; H. Hunger 1978, Bd. I passim, II. bes in dem Kapitel über die Philologie (s. u.). Der Informationswert genannter Werke ist dennoch unbestreitbar auch zum Vorliegenden.

[11] S. dazu im Überblick Schulgeschichte S. 90ff.; Wandel passim. Zur Immunität s. bes. Walden S. 164ff. Zu Einkünften und Gebühren für deren Festsetzung die Spätantike den einzelnen offensichtlich freie Hand ließ, s. u., vgl. E. Bolaffi S. 436. Diokletians Preisedikt wird auch in diesen Dingen wirkungslos geblieben sein (7,69–71). Die Öffentlichkeit stellt im allgemeinen die Unterrichtsräume zur Verfügung (vgl. Walden S. 266). Das Fehlen von Nachrichten über eine Besoldung etwa für Spezialisten und Lehrer der Medizin wie Jurisprudenz wird sich aus anderen Einkünften dieses Kreises erklären, ähnliches wird selbst für die Philosophielehrer des 4. Jhdts. in Thessalonike gelten (vgl. dazu O. Trafrali S. 149ff.). Ein klares Bild von Umfang und Art der Immunität ist nicht mehr zu gewinnen. Daß sie im 4. Jhdt. immer noch für das ganze Imperium als selbstverständlich galten, s. Philostratos VS 267; B272. Zu den Einkünften s. bes. Pavan S. 123.

[12] Kontrolle von öffentlicher Seite kommt selbstverständlich dazu, vgl. etwa Wandel bes. S. 81ff.; zu Byzanz s. Buckler S. 271. Ein drastisches Beispiel der Gewährung von Immunität bereits für Studierende bringt Constantins Architektengesetz (CTh 13,4,1/334, vgl. dazu Wandel S. 79f.), allgemein s. auch A. Cameron, Cah. Hist. Mond. 10, 1966 (zit. Cameron 1966), bes. 660; zum staatlichen Interesse s. auch Marrou bes. 551; das Buch wird im Folgenden mit dem Verfassernamen zitiert, s. auch St. F. Bonner, AJPh 86, 1965, bes. 130. Zur staatlichen Autorität vgl. Augustin Conf. 5,12,13, dazu Marrou, Augustin S. 1. Eine klare Grenze zwischen staatlicher und municipaler Bezahlung läßt sich offensichtlich nirgends ziehen, beide Bereiche gehen vielmehr ineinander über: Das Beispiel des Libanios (s. dazu zuletzt bes. R. A. Kaster, Chiron 13, 1983, 43) zeigt allgemeine Verfahrensweisen

auf, die sich nicht zuletzt auch aus der Übernahme der municipalen Verwaltung in die staatliche Regie mit erklären lassen. Zu den gezahlten Gehältern s. u., vgl. immer noch F. Schemmel, NJb 20, 1907, 67. Zur Titulierung s. Wandel S. 89; unklar freilich bleibt der Umfang des Kreises von Lehrern, denen ab 425 der Rang eines Comes I ordinis verliehen wurde (CTh 6,21,1/425), zu Horapollon vgl. J. Maspero, Bull. Inst. Franc. Arch. Or. 1914, 177. Zu den Kämpfen der Lehrer um ihr Prestige, auch bei öffentlicher Sicherung, s. Pavan S. 124.

13 S. dazu bes. Lib. or. 32 nach Quintilian, vgl. auch Auson. Protrept. passim, weitere Literatur bes. bei T. J. Haarhoff, bes. S. 52ff. Zur Fülle an Schulen etwa im 2. Jhdt. s. bes. Ael. Arist. 26,97, s. dazu auch R. Klein S. 113, vgl. Einführung S. 24ff. Zur Fortführung der Tradition in solchem Zusammenhang auch Buckler S. 254ff. Zum Hervortreten der Elementarbildung unter dem Einfluß christlicher Bildungsperspektiven vgl. S. 267; s. dazu u. Zu einer wirklichen Änderung der pädagogischen Methoden indes scheint es nicht gekommen zu sein.

14 Zur Mädchenbildung als Problem s. u. Wirkliche Neuansätze hier sind nicht zu verzeichnen, eine Tradition institutionalisierter Frauenbildung ist weder für die eigentlich antike noch die christliche Schule dieser Zeit nachzuweisen.

15 S. dazu Bonner passim, vgl. auch Schulgeschichte S. 93ff. Zur gallischen Tradition s. Haarhoff S. 8 zu Strabo 4,181.

16 S. dazu zuletzt V. Weber, Altertum 31, 1985, 213ff. bes. zu Cass. Dio 50,4,11,4; 50,5,2,8, dazu S. 216 mit Verweis auf pompeianische Wandmalereien. Für die Rolle und soziale Einordnung des γραμματιστής in der frühen Zeit fehlen Nachrichten so gut wie ganz, der Hinweis im diokletianischen Preisedikt (s. o.) besagt nichts. Zur allgemeinen Schriftkundigkeit s. auch J. Vogt, RhM 116, 1973, 129ff.; entsprechende Unterweisung von Sklaven auch zum Zwecke späterer Lehrtätigkeit gehört in den allgemeinen Zusammenhang von Nutzungsmaximierung, allgemein dazu auch Marrou S. 499ff.; 505. Zur normativen Bedeutung der gewonnenen Fähigkeiten s. H. Rahn, Morphologie der antiken Literatur, Darmstadt 1969, bes. 33f.

17 Die beste Darstellung des Grammatikunterrichts gibt noch immer Quintilian, ohne freilich, daß sich ein obligatorisches Bild ableiten ließe, allgemein Marrou S. 910ff. Zweifellos baute die Textbehandlung, die er betrieb, auf der der Elementarschule auf, scheint aber dem einzelnen Lehrer weitgehend freien Spielraum gelassen zu haben, was Stoffwahl, Intensivierung in den hilfswissenschaftlichen Disziplinen und wohl auch die Methode betrifft. Zur Poesie in diesem Programm s. Rahn a.a.O. S. 35. Zur Durchlässigkeit nach oben zu s. bes. Marrou, Augustin S. 9. Zur Grammatikertätigkeit in den Philosophenschulen späterer Zeit s. u., vgl. das Beispiel des Joh. Philoponos PLRE S. 615, dazu RE IX 1764ff. (Kroll), vgl. A. Cameron PCPhS 191, 1965, 26; zu Horapollon Maspero S. 166, drastisches Beispiel ist Pamprepius (s. u.). An einem vollständigen personellen Spektrum an kleineren Bildungsstätten bes. in der Provinz wird ohnehin zu zweifeln sein, so daß sich der Unterricht in mehreren Stufen und Sparten in einer Hand konzentrierte. Allg. s. dazu Hunger II 10ff.; 22ff. Zur Bedeutung bes. für die Tradition der Philosophenschulen s. u.

18 Zur Gegensätzlichkeit der beiden Fächer s. bes. Marrou S. 393; Augustin S. 148, vgl. dazu H. v. Arnim, Leben und Werk des Dion v. Prusa, Berlin 1898, passim, bes. S. 113ff. Zur Porphyriusvita Plotins 14 s. bes. J. Geffcken S. 266 (Gegensatz Philologie–Philosophie). Zur Verwischung der Bereiche wiederum s. bereits Suet. Gramm. 4,5, vgl. auch Cameron 1966, 656, s. bes. auch Marinus V. Procli 38. Zur Trennung zwischen dem Philosophieunterricht und der an den traditionellen Hochschulen im wesentlichen betriebenen Spekulation s. u.; staatliche Gehälter wurden offensichtlich für beide Gruppen bezahlt, wozu für die Akademie

in Athen noch eigene Einkünfte kamen. Für Athen mochte überdies diese Scheidung durch die Einrichtung zweier σοφιστής-Stellen unter Mark Aurel deutlich werden (vgl. Walden, S. 90), unklar bleibt, wo diese zu lokalisieren sind; ich nehme an, sie gehörten zu einer Schule mit eigenem Bildungsgang neben den bestehenden. Zu der für beide Fächer etwa gleichen Studiendauer von 4 Jahren s. Cameron a.a.O. 659 am Beispiel des Damaskios (3 Jahre als Studierender, 7 danach als Lehrender), vgl. Phot. cod. 131,126b. Zu den kanonischen Lehrwerken (Donat, Agroikos, Dorotheus für Grammatik-, Theon, Hermogenes, Aphthonios für Rhetorikunterricht) s. Haarhoff S. 60; dazu S. 71 zu Quint. 1,10,1 in diesem Zusammenhang. Das aus den Hilfswissenschaften stammende Material und dessen Behandlung unterlagen einer Normierung kaum. Auf allen Stufen verwendet, war es unvermeidlich, daß der Stoff in seiner Weise deformiert und mit Elementen von Sensationsliteratur versetzt, bzw. um der Nutzanwendung willen das Material ohne Kritik übernommen und weiterverarbeitet wurde. Das Fortwuchern von entsprechenden Traditionen ergibt sich damit von selbst. Ihr Ergebnis am Ende der Antike ist bekannt. Der Einfluß der eigentlichen Fachwissenschaften kann demnach nur mittelbarer sein. Bleibt so eine genaue Trennung der Arbeitsweisen auf den verschiedenen Stufen der Ausbildung unmöglich (zur Rhetorik s. bes. Hunger I 65ff.), so wird sich von hier aus auch die Verwischung der Termini in der Lehrerbezeichnung erklären; zu fragen bleibt, wie weit sich die Abstufung CTh 13,3,11 wirklich konsequent durchführen ließ. Ähnliches wird für das eingetriebene Schulgeld gelten, vgl. bes. Lib. ep. 80, dazu P. Petit, bes. 144.

[18a] Die Absichten Mark Aurels bei seiner Vermehrung der Philosophenlehrstühle (s. o., vgl. Walden S. 92ff.) sind schwer zu erkennen, die Maßnahmen, berichtet durch die Historia Augusta und Philostratos, beziehen sich allein auf Athen, unklar ist, wie weit sie dazu dienten, die bereits in Verfall geratenen alten 4 Schulen mit neuem Leben zu erfüllen. Näher liegt die Einrichtung von Institutionen für eine gewisse Breitenwirkung, für die Akademie, Stoa, Lykeion und Kepos sicher sowieso weniger in Frage kamen. Nichts bekannt ist von ähnlichen Gründungen an anderen Stellen. Zum σοφιστής s. H. Hunger, Aspekte der griechischen Rhetorik von Gorgias bis zum Untergang von Byzanz, Wien 1973 passim, dazu A. M. Malingrey, Philosophie. Etude d'un groupe des mots dans la litterature grecque au IV s. apres J. C., Paris 1961 passim. Auf eine gewisse Rangstufung entsprechend der jeweiligen Bildung konnten die Termini .. grammatici .. rhetores ... sophistai .. für die Funktionen im Staatsdienst hinweisen, vgl. Bréhier 1926, 92. Allgemein s. auch Marrou S. 330ff.; 391. Zur Anteilnahme des Kaisers an den Problemen der sophistischen Lehrstühle s. etwa Philostratos VS 257.

[19] Zu Themistios s. bes. G. Downey, Speculum 32, 1957, 58ff. Zur Ausdünnung des .. φιλοσοφία-Begriffes s. bes. Hunger S. 4ff.; 6. Ich halte eine Erklärung mit der Eingliederung des Faches an sich in das Bildungsgefüge für die wahrscheinlichste, die neben einem inhaltlichen Verfall (vgl. auch Downey a.a.O.) zur Verwischung in der Terminologie führte (zur Verwischung von φιλόσοφος und σοφιστής s. auch Walden S. 107); zu Themistios zusammenfassend in diesem Zusammenhang RE V A 1642 (Stegemann); zur Selbstbezeichnung als Philosoph s. or. 23; 27; 28.

[20] Zur damit verbundenen Übertragung des Postulates vom Herrscher auf dessen Dienst und der daraus erwachsenden ethischen Durchdringung des Staatswesens s. Downey, TAPhA 86, 1955, 292ff. bes. 295.

[21] S. u.

[22] S. etwa Schulgeschichte S. 89. Eine verbindliche Normierung gab es nicht, für das 4. Jhdt. legt die Studienbegrenzung mit dem 20. Lebensjahr (s. Wandel S. 84 zu CTh 14,9,1/376) indirekt eine gewisse Richtlinie fest.

[23] Zur Funktion der Beredsamkeit, d. h. der Bildung nach dem angegebenen Cursus, s. Marrou, Augustin S. 76, zu Lib. ep. 369,9.

[24] S. dazu Vogt a.a.O.; Material bei C. A. Forbes, TAPhA 86, 1955, 321 ff. mit Beispielen zum Freigelassenenstatus einer Vielzahl von Lehrern. Daß überdies die Ausbildung auch die Freilassungschancen für einzelne erhöht, liegt auf der Hand.

[25] S. dazu Marrou a.a.O. S. 80, vgl. S. 506; zur Diskussion s. auch 307. Bezeichnendes Beispiel sind die Symmachi in Rom, vgl. dazu O. Seeck, MGHAA VI, bes. XXXIX ff.

[26] Vgl. dazu Beck 1977 S. 123, grundlegend noch immer Marrou S. 335 ff.; 454 ff. Zum späteren Übergang zusammenfassend etwa V. Vavrinek, in: From Antiquity to Early Byzantium (zit. Antiquity), Prag 1985, 9f. Verschiebungen des Inhalts und die erwähnte Ausdünnung brauchen nicht in einem direkten politischen Zusammenhang zu stehen, sind als indirekte Folge aber, soweit ersichtlich, unvermeidbar. S. auch W. Richter, in: Johann S. 390 (zum Rahmencharakter des Begriffes).

[27] S. dazu Marrou, Augustin S. 96 ff. Unbekannt ist die Art und Weise, wie sie, zweifellos auf den verschiedenen Stufen, gelehrt wurden. Zu Florilegien und verkürzenden Kompendienliteratur (Aurelius Victor, Eutrop) s. Geffcken S. 173, zum verstärkten Interesse für die Geschichte im Sinne der heilsgeschichtlichen Beweisführung s. Marrou a.a.O. S. 91; 101; 352. Zur Naturkunde im Rahmen der Ausbildung in der Dialektik s. Greg. Thaumaturg., Migne PG 10,1077. Zu entsprechenden Voraussetzungen im Rahmen rhetorischer Ethopoiie s. Hunger I S. 92; die Entartung des Stoffes zur Kuriositätenschau wird durch eine solche Verwendungsweise zweifellos mit begünstigt; allgemein s. Schulgeschichte S. 90; Wandel S. 75.

[28] S. dazu Cameron 1966, 657, dazu die Hinweise PLRE 825 ff.

[29] S. o., dazu PLRE 825 ff.; RE XVIII 409 ff. (Keydell), vgl. noch immer R. Asmus, BZ 22, 1913, 320 ff., 324; 328; zusammenfassend Cameron, Historia 14, 1965, 491 ff. P. beginnt als γραμματιστής in Ägypten, ist γραμματικός in Athen und betätigt sich in Constantinopel als Philosoph. An welcher Schule dort, ist unklar, nahe liegt eine besondere Stellung von Anfang an, die Lehrtätigkeit kann nicht allzu lange gedauert haben.

[30] Zu Isidor s. R. Asmus, BZ 18, 1909, 452 ff.

[31] Zur Funktion s. Petit S. 38; 85 ff.

[32] Zur wissenschaftlichen Tätigkeit des Grammatikers s. u. für die philosophischen Schulen, allgemein auch Marrou S. 193; die Schulstufe wird auch eine Reihe anderer, im Curriculum nicht eigens erwähnter Fächer mit umschreiben, vgl. Pavan S. 21 zu Dig. 50,13,1.

[33] S. o. zu den Immunitäten selbst für Schüler, ich rechne hierher etwa CTh 11,27,1–2/315;322 mit ihrer deutlichen Begründung der Absicht, obwohl expressis verbis von Bildung nicht die Rede ist. Zu einer Sistierung der Immunität durch Caracalla s. Philostratos a.a.O. Sie erklärt sich m. E. am ehesten aus der finanziellen Situation des Reiches, ließ sich aber natürlich leicht in der üblichen Weise zu Lasten des Kaisers auslegen.

[34] Allgemein s. dazu Lib. or. 1 passim. Interessant hierzu Philostratos VS 230; B 274. Zur Rolle der Panegyrik s. B. 276. Der Streit des Herodes Atticus mit Fronto gehört in diesen Zusammenhang, vgl. RE s. v. 911 (Münscher). Allgemein s. auch Pavan S. 13 ff.; mit dem Terminus von staatlichem Mäzenatentum ist es freilich nicht getan, zum Konkurrenzneid s. S. 119.

[35] Zu Lib. or. 1,16; 85 s. Eunap. V. Soph. 483; vgl. Cameron 1966, 654 ff.; Walden S. 152 ff.

[36] CTh 14,9,1/370 ist nur von hier aus zu erklären. Zum Krawallstudententum dieser Zeit s. auch Augustin Conf. 8,14; eine andere Wurzel liegt offensichtlich früh in den innerchristlichen Auseinandersetzungen, vgl. etwa Zach. Rhet. Biogr. d. Severus, PO II 12 ff. Allgemein s. auch Schulgeschichte S. 92; vgl. Marrou S. 405 ff., drastische Beispiele bei Eunapius VS 484; 490.

[37] Bes. Marrou S. 551; der Hinweis gilt für Stipendien wie Gehälter und Immunitäten, allgemein auch Walden S. 178ff.

[38] Bezeichnend zur Kleidung Lib. ep. 304, vgl. auch Sid. Ap. 4,11,1 zur Integrationsfrage.

[39] S. dazu Wandel passim.

[40] S. u.

[41] S. o., die Tradition beginnt früh, vgl. Suet. Gramm. 3, dazu auch Haarhoff S. 50; zur Diskussion s. Marrou S. 544. Zu Arborius s. Pavan S. 70.

[42] S. allgemein Schulgeschichte S. 93ff., vgl. auch Jones, LRE 999ff. Zum instruktiven Beispiel des Prohaeresius s. Geffcken S. 170; allgemein auch G. Downey, Harv. Lib. Bull. 12, 1958, 300ff. Libanios und Augustin mochten als Lehrer profiliert sein; bezeichnend ist, daß ersterer Schüler aus Armenien aufzuweisen hatte: Es bleibt zu fragen, wie diese ihre erworbenen Fähigkeiten später in der Heimat zu verwerten gedachten, näher wird beabsichtigter Verbleib im Reich auch bereits vor 387 liegen. Der Rückgang von Zeugnissen räumlicher Mobilität erklärt sich aus dem allgemeinen Zerfall des Imperiums; der Westen bot seit dem 5. Jhdt. keine Möglichkeiten für eine Schule im herkömmlichen Sinne, während sich die Kirche auf das Regionale (s. o.) zu stützen hatte.

[43] Zusammenfassend noch immer RE XII 2465ff. (Foerster-Münscher); PLRE 505ff.

[44] Allgemein s. Marrou, Augustin passim.

[45] S. allgemein dazu M. Hopkins, CQ 11, 1961, 240ff. Zur Ablehnung ehrenvoller Berufungen s. etwa Prok. v. Gaza ep. 114; Choric. Or. funebr. 12ff., zur westlichen Seite s. Pavan S. 45.

[46] Vgl. dazu auch Beck, Jahrtausend S. 290. Für die Schule des Libanios Material bei Petit passim.

[46a] S. dazu noch immer J. H. Krause, Geschichte der Erziehung, Leipzig 1851, 381ff. Die Rhetorik wird für Symmachus, ähnlich wie Sidonius zum Ausdruck einer humanitas, die ihn über die eigene Zeit hinaushebt, im sozialen Gefüge aber bereits isoliert.

[47] Zur Tradition (Gell. 15,1) s. Haarhoff S. 35, vgl. Cameron 1966, 660; PCPhS 1965, 27.

[48] Cameron a.a.O. S. 661; Schulgeschichte S. 91; Wandel passim.

[49] Daß auch hier das Christentum im wesentlichen desinteressiert war, liegt nahe, vgl. Downey a.a.O. S. 297; 1975, 55.

[50] S. dazu Haarhoff S. 124, vgl. Hopkins bes. S. 240f. Die Chancen für einen sozialen Aufstieg werden in der Provinz besser gewesen sein als an den Zentren. Zu Ausnahmen, die auffallen müssen, s. Marrou S. 552ff.

[51] S. dazu Hopkins passim zum Aufstieg der Familie aus untersten Schichten. Der Sprung zu den höchsten Staatsämtern über die Rolle des Prinzenerziehers mag eine Mutation sein, die nicht alltäglich war (vgl. S. 246), ist aber bis zu einem gewissen Grade vorbereitet durch eine anhaltende Entwicklung nach oben bereits zuvor, d. h. möglicherweise vom Sklavenstand bis zum sozialen Rang des Grammatikers (S. 242). Zur Rolle der Heiraten in diesem Zusammenhang vgl. auch das Beispiel des Pamprepius in Athen. Dynastiebildung in den Kreisen dieser Oberschicht scheint charakteristisch.

[52] S. dazu A. Cameron, CR 15, 1965, 257 zu Palladas, AP 9,134; 169; 172; 175; vgl. auch Marrou S. 505; 522. Zur Topik s. Suet. Gramm. 9, vgl. auch noch Beck 1978 S. 31; Buckler S. 166. Zu den Verdienstmöglichkeiten im Vergleich mit anderen Berufen gleichen Ranges s. freilich Walden S. 192: Auch für einen Libanios war der Lehrerberuf anfangs offensichtlich nicht sehr attraktiv.

[53] Vgl. als Überblick Cameron a.a.O.

[54] Zu CTh 12,3,11 s. Haarhoff S. 18. Nachrichten über die Auswirkung sind nicht bekannt.

[55] Zur Tradition s. auch HA Anton. Pius 3,11, vgl. Haarhoff; ich halte für möglich, die Stelle müsse nach den Erkenntnissen im Umfeld des Gesetzes konzipiert sein.

[55a] S. dazu Bonner passim; s. dazu RE I A 380ff. (B. Kübler).

[56] Zur Tradition s. immerhin die Rede des Eumenius De instaurendis scholis (PL IX); zur Stelle vgl. auch Bonner S. 129ff. Die Höhe der Gehälter erklärt sich nicht zuletzt aus solcher Notsituation (vgl. auch S. 133). Anders Pavan S. 94ff., der in der verstärkten Institutionalisierung des Bildungsapparates und einer Ausschließlichkeit als Instrument der Nachwuchsgewinnung in der Spätantike die eigentliche Bildungskrise sieht.

[57] S. dazu Cameron a.a.O. Auszugehen ist von einem Äquivalent 1 annona = 4 Solidi (im 5. Jhdt. 5), vgl. Nov. Val. 13,3; CJ 1,27. Der Differenz 5:4 bei Juvenal (Sat. 7,217) entspricht noch die des Maximaltarifs (7,70ff.), so daß für das 4. Jhdt. demnach eine Erhöhung des Rhetoren- und Sophistenstandes gegenüber dem des Grammatikers zu folgern ist; ich nehme als Grund einen immer akuteren Mangel an Personen an, die sich dem Hochschulunterricht widmen wollten (zu Libanon s. o.).

[58] Vgl. Cameron bes. S. 258 zu Palladas a.a.O. Die Zahl ist als hoch anzusetzen und wird nur in seltenen Fällen erreicht worden sein; fraglich ist unter solchen Umständen auch die Effektivität des Unterrichtes. Nach den Berechnungen Petits (S. 70) beträgt die trotz allem zum Vergleich heranzuziehende Stärke der Schule des Libanios ebenfalls ca. 50 Studenten, die jedoch von dem Redner zusammen mit einer Reihe γραμματισταί (für die Unterstufen) unterrichtet wurden (Petit S. 93; Walden S. 272). Für den Elementarlehrer bei geringem Einkommen errechnet zuletzt Weber eine gleiche Klassenstärke als das Existenzminimum. Die Zahl der im eigentlichen Sinne privaten, weder von Immunitäten noch öffentlichen Geldern subventionierten Bildungsanstalten ist unbekannt; ich kann mir nicht vorstellen, daß sie groß war: Nicht nur den Lehrern, sondern auch deren Nachkommen gewährt (vgl. Damasc. fr. 124 ed. Zintzen hier freilich für die Mitglieder der alexandrinischen Philosophenschule), muß die Reihe der Privilegien dennoch eine gewisse Attraktion, auch im Sinne erwähnter Möglichkeit sozialer Mobilität, bedeutet haben.

[59] Zu Libanios s. o.; es scheint, daß der Redner seinen Schülern in gewisser Höhe auch Kredite gewährte. Private Liberalität muß bei der Subventionierung von Schulen stets eine Rolle gespielt haben, zu Theagenes in Athen s. etwa PLRE S. 1063 (zu Damasc. fr. 264): Zahlungsschwierigkeiten der öffentlichen Hand scheinen vorgekommen zu sein, vgl. Symm. ep. 1,79; Cassiod. Var. 5,21,1ff.

[60] Or. 1,61. Auch das offizielle Einkommen des L. muß stets über Gebühr hoch gewesen sein; zur besonderen Behandlung durch die kaiserliche Kasse bei seinem Weggang aus Constantinopel s. Kaster a.a.O. Unklar sind die Gründe für die Verlagerung des weiter gezahlten staatlichen Anteils auf die γραμματισταί. Für möglich halte ich die beabsichtigte Erhöhung der Studentenzahl. Allgemein s. auch Haarhoff S. 132.

[61] S. dazu Cameron a.a.O. mit Lit.

[62] Bezeichnend hier der von Maspero a.a.O. interpretierte Papyrus aus Aphrodisias (I 15) .. [πο]νήσαντα τὸν πάντα αὐτοῦ ἐν τοῖς Μουσείοις νέους κατὰ τὴν .. (gemeint sein kann nach Maspero in der Tat nur das Museion in Alexandria, das demnach eine Grammatikerschule enthielt). Zu den .. πόνοι .. s. auch Lib. ep. 137; vgl. auch ep. 307; 640.

[63] Material bei Petit passim. Zur Schülerzahl des Libanios (s. o.) vgl. S. 70. Bei den erwähnten, auf Staatskosten bezahlten γραμματισταί muß es sich um angehende Rhetoren handeln, die auf die erwähnte Weise im Sinne von Assistenten ihre Karriere begannen und Erfahrungen sammeln konnten. Zur menschlichen Seite s. auch Pavan S. 91.

[64] S. den erwähnten Papyrus I 20 .. τὴν ἐπιείκειαν ..

[65] So wohl das .. τρέφειν .. zu verstehen. Zur Gemeinschaft s. auch ep. 307; 643. Zu anderen Termini solcher Art s. Petit S. 18ff. Zur Tradition s. Bolaffi, S. 444.

[66] S. des weiteren auch Synes. ep. 1,16, vgl. ep. 154. Hypatia war zweifellos kein Ausnahmefall. Zu Prophairesios und Eunapios s. Walden S. 307.

[67] Vgl. Petit S. 48.

[68] Vgl. Petit S. 26; 69 vgl. auch 18; 44 zu den Bezeichnungen, die auf gemeinsame Betätigung hinweisen (s. bes. ep. 137; 640). Allgemein s. Cameron 1966, 657, zum contubernium als Studien- und Lebensgemeinschaft (Gell. 3,19) s. Haarhoff S. 112.

[69] S. o.; vgl. bes. ep. 80.

[70] Zur Sorge für Hyperechios s. Petit S. 164, vgl. dazu O. Seeck, Die Briefe des Libanius, Leipzig 1906, 182ff. allg. auch Petit S. 40; 139.

[71] Zur Verbindung über die Schulgrenzen hinaus vgl. etwa ep. 1004 (Libanios-Symmachus); Cameron, Historia 1965, 488ff. (L.-Themistios). Sie läßt die bewußte Pflege einer allgemeinen geistigen Gemeinschaft aufscheinen; die hieraus erwachsenden familiären Beziehungen (s. u.) erscheinen als lediglich stärkster Ausdruck hiervon. S. Petit S. 40.

[72] S. dazu Phot. cod. 242,351a. Anderseits ist nicht zu übersehen, daß manche gerade solcher Ehen nicht glücklich wurden, zu Damaskios s. a.a.O. 399a, zu Horapollon s. Maspero passim bes. 163ff.; 178: Die merkwürdige Art, wie der Betroffene seine Ehescheidung darlegt (Pap. I 14) muß auffallen.

[73] Zu den athenisch-alexandrinischen Beziehungen s. H. Saffery, REG 67, 1954, 396f. Zu Asklepiodotos s. Asmus 1909, 462, zu den Ausoniern s. o., vgl. auch Cameron 1966, 658.

[74] Ein Beispiel ist Aidesia, Damask. V. Isid. 76.

[75] Die Wahrnehmung der bürgerlichen Verpflichtungen (vgl. Lib. 1,106) gehört in den Zusammenhang einschlägiger Postulate eines Bemühens um Gerechtigkeit, vgl. Petit S. 69.

[76] Vgl. dazu bes. Cameron Historia 1965, 470ff. mit einer Fülle von Beispielen der Verquickung von Schuldienst und Poeterei (s. bes. Malalas S. 361B: Kyros v. Panopolis als φιλόσοφος). Mit Recht verweist Cameron auf das antikirchliche Heidentum und den immanenten Protest gegen eine christliche Überlagerung, die für das provinzielle Umfeld in Ägypten sich in einer besonders aktiven Aversion gegen die traditionelle Bildung niederschlägt, am instruktivsten dazu immer noch J. Leipoldt, bes. S. 22ff.

[77] Vgl. auch Eunap V. Soph. 493. Für die Karriere bezeichnend sind Kyros und Pamprepius. Zu Andronikos v. Hermupolis s. Lib. ep. 77; Seeck S. 70; Cameron a.a.O. S. 487; 500. Vermuteter Aufenthalt in Antiochia läßt wohl auf den Beginn einer Rhetoren-, auf jeden Fall einer Lehrerkarriere schließen. Zur Vorliebe des Libanios für Galater und Armenier (s. o.) s. Petit S. 129.

[78] Zusammenfassend zu Olympiodor PLRE S. 798ff.; Kyros S. 336ff.; Claudian S. 299; Pamprepius s. o. Eine Parallele zu den Wanderphilosophen dieser Zeit ist anzunehmen, vgl. Eunapius VS 471.

[79] S. dazu Quintilian 2,4,41; Menander S. 331 Sp.

[80] S. dazu Rawson passim, vgl. bes. auch W. Loch, in: Johann S. 448ff. bes. 449. Zu Fragen nach dem Übungsstoff s. Quintilian 2,10,1; die von der ἐγκύκλιος παιδεία ausgeklammerten Fächer scheinen von hier aus gesehen wegen ihrer Grundlagenfunktion nicht eigens erwähnt zu werden, während es sich in den überlieferten (vgl. bereits Cic. Inv. 1,35) lediglich um Sammelbezeichnungen handeln müßte.

[81] Zur stets betonten individuellen Erziehungsweise s. Loch 459; Walden S. 204; vgl. in diesem Zusammenhang Marrou S. 523; zum Philosophieunterricht S. 394.

[82] Beispiele bei Haarhoff S. 72ff. Nicht zuletzt von hier aus gesehen, muß es Zeitgenossen schwer gewesen sein, zwischen den Stufen der Bildung genau zu unterscheiden. Die Grammatikerehrung 425 (CTh 6,21,1) deutet dies offiziell an und hängt wohl mit der Neugründung der Hochschule programmatisch zusammen.

83 S. dazu Marrou a.a.O., bes. 413 mit Zitat von Julian c. Gal. 246E, der die christliche Bildung mit ihren Absichten vor Augen gehabt haben muß.

84 Die Aristokratisierung des Standes (Walden S. 146) durch die einschlägige kaiserliche Gesetzgebung ist nur von dieser Kontinuität aus zu verstehen, die ihrerseits wieder hierfür die Maßstäbe gab, vgl. in anderem Zusammenhang dazu Petit S. 64; 69 zu Lib. or. 1,103. Zum Bewußtsein von der sozialen Funktion s. das Material bei Pavan S. 84ff.

85 Dies an mehreren Stellen, direkt wie indirekt, vgl. or. 25; 27; 28, s. dazu Cameron 1966, 659; Downey 1957, bes. 59. Zu dem .. scholae non vitae discimus.. Senecas s. Haarhoff S. 250ff., allgemein auch Marrou S. 527ff.

86 Zu Fragen nach der Verselbständigung der Bildung, für die das wirkliche, auch das politische Leben nur Übungsmaterial darzustellen vermag, s. Phot. cod. 242,352a. Ich nehme an, daß nicht zuletzt hier die wirkliche Kritik der Öffentlichkeit angesichts der drängenden anderweitigen Schwierigkeiten des Reiches einsetzte.

87 Zu Justinian s. Cameron a.a.O. S. 667.

88 S. dazu Wandel S. 79ff.; vgl. auch Haarhoff S. 30 zu den Kunstschulen.

89 S. dazu Cameron a.a.O. 660; zum berufsethischen Hintergrund s. Hunger S. 287ff. Der Umfang solcher Bildungsmöglichkeiten ist unklar, auf eine staatliche Normierung weist nichts hin, mögliche Vorläufer könnte Philostratos VS 230 andeuten.

90 Medizinische Ausbildung war an den allgemeinen Hochschulen möglich, ein Basilius studierte diese Wissenschaft in Athen, vgl. Greg. Naz. or. 59,23, allgemein auch L. Bréhier, Rev. d'Hist. et de Philosophie religieuse 21, 1941, 56; Buckler S. 273, vgl. dazu bes. auch HA Alexander Sev. 44.

91 S. dazu immer noch P. Collinet, Histoire de l'école du droit de Beyrouth, Paris 1924, der ein Bestehen seit dem 2. Jhdt. annimmt. Zur Rechtsschule in Rom (vgl. Cassiod. 9,21,5) s. Haarhoff S. 82ff. Kaiserliche Regie liegt hier besonders nahe; ein Fortbestehen im 6. Jhdt. (Const. Omnem 7) erklärt sich nicht zuletzt mit den politischen Plänen dieser Zeit in Byzanz. Für Beirut nimmt Collinet ein Entstehen aus einem zentralen Archiv und der Unterweisung im Umgang mit den gesammelten Verordnungen durch die Archivar an. Zur Abwanderung der Rhetorenschüler des Libanios s. o., vgl. Walden S. 119; Collinet S. 202; Marrou S. 530.

92 Zur Betonung der Spezialkenntnisse bereits am Ende der Regelstudienzeit s. CJ 2,7,22,6/505 (..si et ipsi solito tempore legum doctrinam meruerint..), wiederholt 2,7,24,5 (517) vgl. Const. Omnem 1. Ich halte einen engen Zusammenhang mit der Stabilisierungspolitik des Anastasios für möglich, eine einschlägige Untersuchung entsprechender Wechselwirkungen steht aus. Zu Beirut s. auch Greg. Thaumaturg., PG 10,1065 ... νόμων παιδευτήριον dazu bereits Lib. ep. 652 ... νόμων μήτης ... Zum 5jährigen Studiengang s. CJ 10,50,1–3, Const. Omnem 2; dazu Collinet S. 26; das Höchstalter bei Studienabschluß betrug demnach 25 Jahre. Zum municipalen Status s. Collinet S. 197; Gründe der Bevorzugung Beiruts s. Const. Omnem 7; der Mangel an Ablenkung paßt zu dem Effektivitätsargument. Vgl. dazu auch Const. Omnem 9 mit den offenkundig zeitlosen Befürchtungen CTh 14,9,1.

93 Bezeichnend scheinen die Bemühungen des Timotheos Ailuros bei Rückkehr nach Alexandreia 475 um einen Anhang in der Schule.

94 Const. Omnem 7, vgl. auch Cassiod. 9,21,5. Die Zahl der Lehrer wurde auf 5 vermehrt, doch scheint ohne Hilfspersonal der Unterricht nicht denkbar. Das Gehalt entsprach dem der Rhetoren (vgl. CJ 10,53,6).

95 S. dazu Collinet S. 35 m. weiteren Zeugnissen. Unklar bleibt die fachliche Absicht solcher Spezialisierung. Der Bedarf lediglich an Verwaltungsbeamten für das Imperium kann durch

eine Konzentration, wie sie die Constitutio verlangt, nicht gedeckt worden sein. Zu anderen Möglichkeiten s. Jones LRE 509; Cameron a.a.O. 667. Zu einer wenigstens vorübergehenden beabsichtigten Entlastungsfunktion durch die Patriarchatshochschule s. Bréhier a.a.O. S. 40; sie wird sich aus der administrativen Funktion von Bischöfen seit Constantin mit herleiten, ist aber auf die Dauer nicht durchzuhalten.

96 Zur Vorbildung s. Collinet S. 75; ob über das Studium beim Grammatiker hinaus auch eine Zeit beim Rhetor (S. 81) obligatorisch war, ist nicht zu erkennen. Zur Verbindung von Emeritierung höherer Beamter und Lehrtätigkeit s. Plin. ep. 4,11; PLRE s. v. Eumenius.

97 Zu Unterrichtsplan und -methode s. Collinet S. 205 ff.; 220; vgl. Const. Omnem 2 ff. Die Beibehaltung der Schule unter Justinian erkläre ich mir aus der Qualifikation der an ihr wirkenden Lehrer; vgl. Collinet, Byzantion 3, 1926, 1 ff.

98 Zusammenfassend Cameron a.a.O. S. 664 ff. zur Schule von Gaza und Neubelebungstendenzen jetzt in einem veränderten allgemeinen Zusammenhang; vgl. auch bereits Lib. or. 55,33, dazu Downey 1958, 300 ff., s. immer noch auch F. Schemmel, PhWSchr. 45, 1925, 1277 ff. Abwanderung und Zuzug auf Empfehlung mögen sich die Waage halten. Gregor v. Nazianz weist Schüler dem Heiden Libanios zu.

99 Zu CTh 14,3 s. immer noch A. Fuchs, Die höheren Schulen von Konstantinopel im Mittelalter, Leipzig 1926, 1 ff.; weitere Lit. bei Bréhier a.a.O. S. 34, vgl. auch bereits 1926, 74 ff. (Anm. 18). Bezeichnenderweise wiederholt Justinian die Bestimmungen (CJ 11,19,1). Zur Verbindung mit der Lehrerehrung CTh,6,21,1 s. o., ich nehme an, auch 13,3,18 und noch 13,3,19 (vgl. Bréhier 1926 a.a.O.) gehörten noch in diesen Zusammenhang. Allgemein auch Cameron a.a.O. S. 656; eine Verbindung mit dem alexandrinischen Museion (Walden S. 49), was immer dieses 425 noch war (zur Grammatikerschule s. o.), kann m. E. kaum beabsichtigt gewesen sein; eine Verbindung der alexandrinischen Philosophenschule mit Constantinopel ist nicht zu erkennen. Sie schließt sich schon der Personalstruktur nach aus.

100 S. bes. Walden S. 116; F. Schemmel, NJ 22, 1968, 147 ff. Unklar ist, ob ein Ersatz etwa für Athen (bezeichnend Synes, ep. 136) gedacht war und Synesius sich auf einen Tiefstand der allgemeinen Ausbildung oder aber der Akademie bezieht. Zu den Einrichtungen s. Bréhier 1926 passim; die Zeugnisse für die folgenden Jahrhunderte lassen häufigen Umzug erkennen. Zur Diskussion S. Wandel S. 88.

101 Zur Tendenz einer Aristokratisierung durch die damit verbundene soziale Mobilität s. o., sie betrifft Lehrer und Studierende in gleicher Weise und hängt mit den Prinzipien der Romanisierung zusammen. S. allgemein auch Beck 1978, S. 148. Die jetzt aufgerissene Kluft zwischen Hauptstadt und übrigem Reiche läßt zwar keineswegs auf einen Abbruch dieser Entwicklung schließen, sondern legt äußerliche Gründe nahe. Doch geben die Prohibitivbestimmungen des Gesetzes zu denken. Das Zahlenverhältnis von Grammatikern zu Rhetoren scheint Dig. 27,1,6,2 (1 : 1) zu widersprechen. Ich erkläre mir dies aus dem Bedarf (s. o.) an Absolventen und vielleicht erwähntem Mangel an geeigneten Personen.

102 Zu CTh 14,9,2 s. o. Das Gesetz bezieht sich bezeichnenderweise ebenfalls auf eine Hauptstadt, vgl. auch Walden S. 139.

103 S. dazu Wandel S. 80 ff. m. weiterer Literatur, vgl. Cameron a.a.O. S. 667.

104 S. dazu Bréhier 1941, 83, der hierzu auch die Medizin rechnet. Zum Unterschied zwischen den alten Philosophenschulen und dem Philosophieunterricht an anderen Hochschulen s. o. Die Formulierung läßt vermuten, daß es sich im Vorliegenden nur um die zweite Kategorie handeln kann, dem Kaiser aber an der Gründung einer Philosophenschule in einem herkömmlichen Sinne nichts lag, auch wenn sich für deren Spekulationen ein christlicher Standpunkt verbindlich machen ließ. Zur philosophischen Unterweisung in der Hauptstadt s. Hunger I 17; Agapios als Schüler des Proklos wird Ausnahme sein: zu Pamprepius s. u. Zu

dem .. rimetur .. des Textes vgl. Arnob. Adv. mat. 2,5. Ich halte einen Einfluß zumindest auf den Formulierenden für möglich.

105 S. dazu Bréhier a.a.O. S. 84. Zum Bildungsverfall im 5. Jhdt. s. auch Marrou, Augustin XIX. Für weiter gesteckte Ziele fehlen einfach die Voraussetzungen, was sich zweifellos aus der allgemeinen, nicht zuletzt politischen Entwicklung erklärt (s. o.). Zur Weiterentwicklung der Institution s. H. G. Beck, in: Polychonia. Festschr. f. F. Dölger, München 1966, 69ff., bes. 78.

106 Marrou S. 26ff. nimmt diese Kluft schon seit Quintilian an. Der Untergrund der politischen Loslösungstendenzen, die sich sicher nicht allein auf persönliche Ambitionen einzelner zurückführen lassen, s. o.: In ihrer Gefährlichkeit sichtbar werden sie m. E. erstmals unter Mark Aurel. Allgemein s. Schulgeschichte S. 88ff.; 92ff.

107 Zu Libanios s. Walden S. 4; Geffcken S. 163, vgl. auch Beck, Jahrtausend S. 27; 246, allgemein auch Cameron a.a.O. S. 656. Zum Verlust des Griechischen im Westen s. bes. Haarhoff S. 22; 220, zusammenfassend noch immer P. Courcelle bes. S. 210ff. Literatenzeugnisse allein erlauben den Schluß auf allgemeinverbindliche Bildungsziele für die behandelte Epoche nicht mehr; das Ende auch der politischen Einheit des Reiches bahnt sich damit an, vgl. allgemein auch Marrou S. 468; zu einer versuchten Neubelebung s. S. 474. Marrou vermutet eine von vornherein stets vorhandene Affinität des Ostens für lateinische Sprache und Kultur. Zu den Griechischkenntnissen eines Augustin s. bes. Marrou, Augustin S. 455; Courcelle S. 137; 170; zu denen eines Symmachus Courcelle S. 6. Das Auseinanderfallen setzt P. Riche etwas später an (Education et cultur dans l'occident barbare, Paris 1962 passim). Zum Rückgang des Lateinischen in der Verwaltungssprache des Ostens s. Collinet S. 211 mit Bezug auf Nov. Theod. 16,8; zu Just. Nov. 7 s. bes. Bréhier a.a.O. S. 83. Collinet S. 213 stellt einen handfesten Sprachverfall bereits im 4. Jhdt. fest. Ein Lateinlehrer in Gaza noch im 6. Jhdt. besagt demgegenüber wenig (vgl. Prok. Gaz. ep. 145; vgl. G. Downey, AJA 55, 1951, 438ff.; vgl. auch PLRE S. 559 (8)).

107a S. Courcelle a.a.O.; das Vorkommen einzelner Schulen in Italien mit Vermittlung von Griechischkenntnissen widerspricht dem nicht. Ein Paulinus v. Nola verlernt bezeichnenderweise seine Griechischkenntnisse wieder (ep. 46), selbst ein Hieronymus bringt es eigener Aussage nach im Griechischen nicht weit (zu ep. 48,12; Adv. Ruf. 1,10), seine Forderung nach geeigneten Übersetzungen ist unüberhörbar und entwickelt in der Tat eine eigene Tradition. Die von Justinian für Rom eingerichtete Rechtsschule kann von vornherein nur von einer lateinischen Basis aus verstanden werden. Neubelebungsversuche (etwa Courcelle S. 221 zu PL 58,1102; s. auch 248 zu Cassiodor) bleiben nicht zuletzt deshalb ohne Wirkung. Eusebios HE 5,1–4 kennt noch eine griechisch sprechende Christengemeinde in Lyon.

108 S. dazu bes. Schulgeschichte S. 95ff.; ich verweise gerade für einschlägige Fragen auf die dort zitierte Literatur. Offiziell zu einem Soloikismus bekannte sich Papst Gregor I., vgl. aber schon Joh. Chrysostomus, De educ. lib., PG 64,298ff.

109 S. dazu immer noch W. Jaeger, Paideia Christi, zuletzt in: Johann 487ff., s. bes. 497. Zusammenfassend Marrou S. 580. Zum Versuch der Synthese s. immer noch das Material bei G. Bardy, Rev. Sc. Rel. 14, 1934, 526ff.; 15, 1935, 1ff.

110 S. dazu Haarhoff S. 176, vgl. Marrou Augustin S. 294, s. dazu immer noch bes. K. Weiß, 27; 35.

111 Zur Frauenrolle aus der Verbindung mit dem Postulat der häuslichen Erziehung zu verstehen, s. Marrou S. 602 zu Greg. Naz. PG 46,972; Basilius ep. 46; 105; 204; 6; Haarhoff S. 216; zum Problem der Kindererziehung Barclay S. 234.

112 S. dazu bes. Weiß S. 60ff. 83 zu Greg. Naz. a.a.O. S. 858.

113 Vgl. dazu Haarhoff S. XIX; 259; Marrou S. 574; Downey 1957, 55. Zur Verbindung von

Frauenbildung und christlicher Erziehung s. Clemens Al. Paed. 3,10; Hieron. ep. 22; 107. Die christliche Lehre ging spät und nicht ohne Schwierigkeiten auf diese Fragen ein. Material bei J. Stiglmayr, Kirchenväter und Klassizismus, Freiburg 1913.

114 S. bes. Weiß S. 18ff.; 29ff.

115 Instruktiv hier H. Kanz, Klemens von Alexandria. Ausgewählte Schriften zur Pädagogik, Paderborn 1966, bes. 5 zum Gegensatz scientia–sapientia; zur Auseinandersetzung um den Begriff s. Hunger I 6ff.; vgl. auch H. T. Marrou, Bull. Du Cange 9, 1934, 7ff.; allgemein Schulgeschichte S. 98ff., s. dazu E. de Fayé, Clement d'Alexandrie sur les rapport du christianisme et de la philosophie grecque au II s.[2], Paris 1906; P. Camelot, Rev. Sc. Rel. 11, 1931, 38ff.

116 S. Kanz S. 20. Zur Katechumenenschule in Alexandria s. bes. Barclay S. 209ff. Es scheint, daß es deren Bildungsansprüche waren, die die Grenze zur philosophischen Hochschule leichter verwischen ließen als anderswo. Ein Pantainos oder Didymos der Blinde wäre undenkbar.

117 S. dazu R. Scholl zuletzt in: Johann S. 507ff. Zu Tert. Id. 10 vgl. Haarhoff S. 165; Marrou S. 586; zu Lact. Inst. 2,7; 3,27 s. bes. Downey 1957, 48. Zusammenfassend G. Ellspermann, The Attitude of Early Christian Latin Writes toward Pagan Literature and Learning, Washington 1949, bes. 23ff.; Pavan 127ff.

118 Downey a.a.O. S. 51; Marrou S. 592; Augustin S. 334. Zu Origenes s. immerhin Eusebios, HE 6,12, vgl. Pavan S. 151.

119 Zur προπαίδευσις s. Bréhier a.a.O. S. 64. Sie ist es, die Tertullian und Lactantius letztlich doch wieder verbindet, vgl. auch R. Pichon, Lactance Etude sur le mouvement philosophique et religieuse sous le regne de Constantin, Paris 1901, bes. 28ff. Allgemein auch Basilius, PG 31,310; 317, dazu Weiß S. 140; Ellspermann S. 40ff.; 89. Zur christlichen Opposition gegen die klassische Bildung und die beiden Wurzeln, die religiöse und die soziale, bündig Courcelle S. 494; Stiglmayr S. 98ff. Neue Perspektiven für den einschlägigen Fragenkomplex müssen sich aus dem Auftreten des Origenes ergeben haben.

120 Auf die Studien einzelner wie des Basilius, Gregor v. Naz. und Gregors v. Nyssa braucht hier nicht eigens hingewiesen zu werden. Material bei Stiglmayr S. 16ff., vgl. auch G. Bardy Rev. Sc. Rel. 12, 1932, 1ff.; Barclay S. 219ff.; zu Augustin s. Barclay S. 252; Marrou, Augustin passim.

121 Zur Problematik s. bes. P. Stockmeier zuletzt in: Johann S. 544ff.; zu grundsätzlichen Fragen s. Bardy a.a.O. S. 12; A. H. M. Jones. in: A. Momigliano, Paganism and Christianity, Oxford 1963, 20ff.

122 S. dazu Leipoldt a.a.O.; zum Mönchtum als Protestbewegung s. Pavan S. 137.

123 Vgl. etwa Greg. Naz. ep. 4,5; Basilius ep. 94, allgemein J. Fontaine, JAC 25, 1982, 5ff., bes. 10.

124 Vgl. etwa hierzu Kanz S. 41 zu Paulus II. Kor. 11,6.

125 S. dazu Buckler S. 273ff.; Marrou S. 594ff., vgl. R. Browning, Byzantion 32, 1962, 167ff. Zur Verpflichtung ägyptischer Mönche bei Klostereintritt, das Lesen und Schreiben zu lernen s. Pachomius, Regel 139 ed. Boon, Paris 1932.

126 Vgl. dazu Greg. Nyss. PG 44,360; Greg. Naz. PG 35,1200; ep. 233; Basil. ep. 233 . . ἄσοφος σοφία . . im Zusammenhang mit dem Scientia-sapientia-Problem. Zum Gedanken der philosophia ancilla theologiae s. Hunger I 42 mit einschlägiger Literatur: Dieser Gedanke wird die Verwendung grundsätzlich aller antiken Bildung in den christlichen Schulen umreißen. Zu späteren Bezeichnungsformen von christlicher Seite s. Bréhier 1926, 86.

127 Vgl. Greg. Naz. PG 36,269; s. dazu 35,637; Greg. Thaum. PG 10,1096; Basil. PG 29,508; Euseb. HE 5,13.

128 Das Prinzip der Lehrautorität und der Lehrinhalt stehen im natürlichen Gegensatz zu den

Bildungsmethoden wie auch formalen Zielen der antiken Bildung; vgl. u. a. R. Scholl in: Johann S. 506ff., Bardy 1935, 10 zur Mädchenerziehung für den christlichen Dienst.

128a S. allgemein Marrou S. 577ff.; 586; zur kurzlebigen Idee einer allgemeinen Funktion der Mönchsschule s. S. 602f.

129 S. dazu Marrou, bes. S. 600ff. Zur Bezahlung der kirchlichen Hochschullehrer nach den Sätzen der weltlichen s. das Beispiel bei Fuchs S. 5 (Nisibis), vgl. Bréhier 1926, 84. Qualifikationskriterien und etwa Mitspracherechte des Kaisers bei Ernennung sind nicht bekannt.

130 S. dazu Schulgeschichte bes. Anm. 166a. Bréhier 1926, bes. 86 läßt an völliger Trennung von staatlicher und kirchlicher Hochschule für Constantinopel keinen Zweifel.

131 Dies hat insbesondere für das Rombild eines Johannes Lydos zu gelten.

132 Zu Courcelle s. o.; wie weit etwa die Förderung der Bildung in Rom durch Theoderich mit dessen Integrationsabsichten zusammenhängt, ist nicht klar zu erkennen. Näher liegt, er wußte um die Möglichkeiten entsprechender Überlegenheit besonders auch gegenüber den germanischen Nachbarreichen.

133 S. dazu bes. Haarhoff S. 24 zu Sid. Ap. ep. 2,5; 5,7; 8,1; Paul. Pell. 209; 290; 304.

134 Vgl. dazu als Zeugnis etwa der Stelle Joh. Chrys., PG 58,975, allgemein s. Haarhoff S. 165ff.; Downey 1958, 307; Petit S. 6: Zu Sophronios s. K. Krumbacher S. 188ff.; 671ff.; Beck 1972 S. 239ff.; Hunger II 93.
Vgl. auch S. Vailhé, Rev. Or. Chr. 7, 1902, 360; 8, 1903, 32ff., 356ff. Die antike Mythologie als Beispielrequisit beherrscht auch noch Augustin, vgl. Marrou, Augustin S. 49; in anderem Zusammenhang s. C. Fabricius, JAC 10, 1967, 187ff.

134a S. Beck a.a.O. passim, H. v. Haehling, JAC 23, 1980, 90.

135 S. dazu bes. P. Tannery RPh 42, 1896, 267ff., bes. 281. Eine innere Verbindung zwischen Berufsausübung und religiösem Bekenntnis wurde, sieht man von dem Edikt Julians ab, nicht verlangt; vgl. Hunger I 44, zu dem Freiraum s. v. Haehling S. 94.

136 CJ 1,15,18,4; 1,11,2; deutlich rangieren die Heiden verschiedener Gattung hinter den Häretikern. S. Tannery S. 282, allgemein auch E. Stein, Histoire zu Bas-empire II 327f.

137 S. dazu Zach. Rhet. a.a.O. S. 14ff. zu Paralios; zu den Verhältnissen in Beirut s. S. 54ff.

138 Zu Horapollon s. PLRE S. 569, vgl. bes. Damasc. fr. 317 ed. Zintzen. Die Ereignisse müssen noch vor der Zeit seiner Konversion stattgefunden haben. Die Stufen der Laufbahn verwischen sich auch bei ihm. Nach Zacharias lernte Severus ihn als Grammatiker kennen, an anderer Stelle begegnet er als Philosoph. Zum Glaubenswechsel s. Maspero S. 189f.

138a S. dazu bes. Courcelle S. 245ff.

139 Cameron a.a.O. S. 664f. Zu den Frauen, die jetzt auch als Philosophinnen an die Öffentlichkeit treten (Hypatia, Aidesia, wohl auch Theodora; PLRE 1085), s. u. Zur Scheidung der philosophischen Schulen s. o.; vgl. Marrou S. 108. Zur Entwicklung Alexandreias neben Athen s. S. 392ff. Material bei C. Zintzen, Damascii Vital Isidori reliquiae, Hildesheim 1967. Bezeichnenderweise dringt von den aufgezeigten Frauen keine zur philosophischen Vollendung vor, unverkennbar ist die Zurückhaltung des Damaskios selbst gegenüber Hypatia. Die Freiheit der Forschung wird für die traditionellen Schulen (Akademie, Museion) gelten, ihr steht die Ausbildung einer breiten Schicht angehender Beamter bei den σοφισταί gegenüber (vgl. Eunap. VS 487; s. auch 451; 497). Die Wahl der Bildungsstätte mochte frei sein, doch gab es für die Hochschulen mit ihrer Effektivität zweifellos besondere Voraussetzungen (Empfehlung, familiäre Beziehung).

140 S. zusammenfassend Geffcken S. 179, der für die frühe Zeit überdies einen starken Zustrom an Schülern annimmt (S. 33). Spätere Kanalisation geht zweifellos mit auf die Anforderung zurück, die die Schule an die einzelnen an Vorbildung wie Intensität des Forschens stellte.

Für Damaskios bedeutet die φιλομάθεια in den herkömmlichen Wissenschaften nur einen Weg zur προπαίδευσις. Von angegliederten Anstalten zu einer vorbereitenden Ausbildung ist nichts bekannt, auch für die erwähnte Grammatikerschule (s. o.) des Museion in Alexandria fehlt ein entsprechender Hinweis. Zur Verbindung von Philosophie, Heilkunde und Priestertum im Museion s. P. Raabe, Leben Petros' des Iberers, Leipzig 1895, 71. Zweifellos ein Qualitätskriterium bedeutet die nachgewiesene Fähigkeit zur Theurgie.

141 S. dazu Saffery a.a.O. passim, zusammenfassend auch Cameron a.a.O. passim; 1965 passim.

142 Vgl. Marrou S. 240ff.

143 Vgl. Maspero a.a.O. S. 190; zu den Bischöfen s. E. Honigmann, Evéques et évêches monophysites d'Asie anterieure au VI s., Löwen 1951, 5ff.

144 Zwar wissen wir von einer Wechselwirkung nicht. Doch ist die eheliche oder aber familiäre Rolle nicht zu übersehen, die gelegentlich hervorgehoben wird. S. dazu selbst Marinus V. Procli 9, wenngleich nur als Plan, dazu Damask. V. Isid. 47.

144a Zum Philosophiestudium des Boethius in Athen s. Courcelle S. 260.

145 S. dazu PLRE 915ff.; RE 23,186ff. (Beutler). Die Jugendzeit ist eine Ergänzung der für Libanios angedeuteten Kriterien des Lehrer-Schülerverhältnisses. Allgemein s. auch Cameron, PCPhS 1965, 9; Geffcken S. 202ff.; C. Zintzen, RhM 108, 1965, 71ff.

146 Zum möglichen Vorbild Porphyrios (vgl. Euseb. HE 6,18,2) s. Geffcken S. 63.

147 PLRE S. 15; zusammenfassend L. Westerink, Anonymus Prolegomena to Platonic Philosophy, Amsterdam 1962, Xff., älteres Material RE I 1863ff. (Freundenthal).

148 Vgl. Cameron 1966, 669; 1965, 14; vgl. auch Asmus 1909, 470; Westerink S. XI. Nicht zu übersehen ist, daß in Alexandria nach dem Tode des Petros Mongos die Tendenz zu einer allgemeinen Beruhigung stark gewesen sein muß, die ein Agreement leicht machten. Die nächsten großen Aufstände sind nicht vor 516 nachweisbar. Safferys Vermutung (S. 400 zu Damasc. fr. 316), es handle sich um den Verzicht des Ammonios, Plato zum Lehrgegenstand zu machen, hat viel für sich (vgl. Westerink S. XVff.) reicht aber zu einer Begründung m. E. nicht aus. Es hat freilich den Anschein, als habe ein Verzicht auf Platostudien der alexandrinischen Schule für die Folgezeit einen gewissen Freiraum verschafft. Als Konzession von kirchlicher Seite nimmt Tannery a.a.O. die Erlaubnis einer Aufnahme auch christlicher Studenten an, auf deren Gebühren die Schule mit angewiesen war, vgl. auch Phot. cod. 242,352a .. αἰσχροκερδής .. (Damasc. fr. 316): Die naheliegende Verleumdung wird weniger Ammonios als die Schule als Ganzes betreffen.

149 Zur Möglichkeit einer Affinität des Ammonios zu einem christlichen Standpunkt in der Weltschöpfungslehre s. Ph. Merlan, GRBS 7, 1968, 192ff.; bes. 195.

150 Die traditionellen Philosophenschulen Athen und Alexandria mochten auf jeden Fall eine Ausnahme sein, andere Schulen kannten eine Problematik solcher Art nicht. Zur Rhetorenschule von Gaza etwa s. Cameron a.a.O. S. 664; A. Chauvot, Procope de Gaza, Priscien de Cesáree, Panegyriques de l'empereur Anastase Ier, Bonn 1986, bes. 85ff.

151 S. der Einfachheit halber RE 9,242 (Praechter); PLRE 5 S. 575ff. Zum Ereignis s. M. Rist, Phoenix 12, 1964, 214ff. bes. 223, dazu Geffcken S. 201; Maspero S. 184. Unklar bleibt die Schulzugehörigkeit Hypatias, die Nachrichten über die Spezialisierung der Philosophin helfen für eine Einordnung ebensowenig weiter wie etwa die sentimentalen Briefstellen des Synesios.

152 Zu Orestes s. PLRE S. 801 (Sor. 7,14), zusammenfassend L. Cantarelli, Mem. Acc. Linc. 1913, 398ff. Die Fragen nach einem klar religiösen Charakter des Eklats ist nicht zu beantworten, doch läßt die Ermordung unter den bekannten Umständen auf ein besonderes Ansehen Hypatias in der Stadt schließen. Zu einer christlichen Bildungshierarchie s. Pavan S. 153.

[153] Zu CTh 6,21,1 s. o.; die Identität wurde ernstlich nie in Zweifel gezogen, vgl. PLRE S. 534 (2.).

[154] Socr. 5,16; vgl. Cameron, Historia 1965, bes. 476ff.; Geffcken S. 157.

[155] Zu wahrscheinlichen Vermögensverlusten des heidnischen Grammatikers Palladas in Alexandria 391, s. Cameron, JRS 55, 1965, 65ff. Einzelheiten sind nicht bekannt, auch ergibt sich ein klares Bild weder von Ereignissen und Maßnahmen noch von der staatlichen Kontrolle. Unbekannt sind auch Schicksal und Laufbahn des Helladius zwischen 391 und 425; ich halte eine Konversion nicht für möglich, wobei denn selbst die Frage nach dem Lippenbekenntnis zu stellen wäre (vgl. auch Cameron 1966, 673).

[156] Bezeichnend hier m. E. selbst noch das Vorkommen heidnischer Wanderphilosophen (zu Salustius s. PLRE S. 972 (7), vgl. Asmus, Damaskios S. 58), dies vielleicht als eine bewußt geduldete Parallele zu einem auch christlichen Phänomen, dem erst Chalkedon 451 zu steuern suchte.

[157] Agath. 2,30, CJ 1,5,18,4; 1,11,10,2, vgl. dazu Cameron, PCPhS 1965, 7ff.; Walden S. 126. Unklar bezüglich des Kreises der Betroffenen auch Malal. 449B; von Rhetoren ist bezeichnenderweise nirgends die Rede. Zu Salarium und Vermögen s. Cameron a.a.O., daß ersteres nicht mehr gezahlt wurde, liegt auf der Hand, die Einziehung des letzteren ist keineswegs einwandfrei nachzuweisen: Cameron bezweifelt sie mit Recht, vgl. dazu auch Agathias a.a.O. 69bf.; wonach von den Entlassenen jeder sein Vermögen behält. Zur Besoldung s. Walden S. 102; hatte die Zahl der besoldeten Philosophen je 2 pro Schule betragen, so halte ich für möglich, daß nach dem Aussterben der anderen drei deren Gehälter auf Mitglieder der Akademie übertragen wurden, von der nunmehr demnach 8 Philosophen ein staatliches Gehalt bezogen. Einzelheiten freilich sind unbekannt. Allgemein s. auch Asmus, Damaskios S. 110ff; allgemein auch F. Schemmel, N. Jb 24, 1909, 438ff.

[158] Die Ausreise scheint gestattet worden zu sein; sie hängt m. E. wohl mit den neuerlichen Reformversuchen zusammen, die Kavades († 531) in seiner Verbindung mit den Mazdakiten unternommen hatte und deren scheinbare Attraktivität offensichtlich im Imperium bekannt geworden war. Inzwischen hatte 529 der Großkönig wohl nach weitgehendem Erreichen seiner Ziele sich der Mazdakiten entledigt, Chosrau begann sofort nach der Regierungsübernahme eine rigorose Expansionspolitik. Sie wiederum mußte den Angekommenen, immerhin Untertanen des bekämpften byzantinischen Reiches, Schwierigkeiten bereiten. Andererseits liegt nahe, daß der Großkönig sich ihrer nur allzu gerne entledigte. S. meinen Aufsatz JAC 1989 (vgl. Anm. 6), dazu noch immer B. Rubin, Das Zeitalter Justinians, Berlin 1960, 292f.; 295.

[159] S. dazu bes. Rawson S. 267ff.

[160] Zu Haarhoff S. 165ff. s. o.

[161] Zum alexandrinischen Beispiel zusammenfassend über Methode und Beispiel s. Westerink S. 20; zur Tradition solcher Aspekte der Exegese s. Marrou S. 353.

[162] S. dazu bes. Marrou, Augustin 81ff.; 100; Hunger II S. 3ff., 10ff.

[163] Nahe liegt schon deshalb eine intensivere Grammatikerausbildung an diesen Anstalten; zum Beispiel Gazas instruktiv Downey, 1958, 272ff.; bes. 310ff.

[164] Bedeutendstes Beispiel scheint Johannes Philoponos, dazu s. RE IX 1764ff. (Kroll), vgl. Tannery S. 273; Material auch PLRE S. 615. Gerade die Intensität des Schulbetriebes verlangte, daß hier die verschiedenen Stufen der Lehrtätigkeit zwangsläufig ineinander übergehen. Ähnliche Verwischung der Bezeichnungen ist häufig, (s. o.), doch haben die großen Hochschulen des Reiches offensichtlich eine ganz spezifische einschlägige Terminologie, vgl. dazu Asmus a.a.O. S. 113; zu den Arbeiten E. Evrard, REG 78, 1965, 592.

[165] Die Diffizilität der Lehrinhalte kommt hinzu. Zwar waren die der christlichen Dogmatik

nicht leichter zu fassen. Sie hatten indes eine intensivere Verarbeitung gefunden und seit dem 4. Jhdt. spätestens eine Technik in der Verwendung von simplifizierenden Schlagworten und griffigen Formeln zu diesem Zwecke entwickelt; die berühmte Bemerkung des Gregor von Nyssa über die Teilnahme auch des Volkes auf dem Markte an den Auseinandersetzungen wird sich auf diese gründen. Die Regierung mochte nicht zuletzt wegen eines solchen Unterschiedes das Fortbestehen der Philosophenschulen dulden. S. dazu bes. Tannery S. 269, vgl. u. a. auch K. Manaphis, in: Antiquity S. 185. Ich nehme an, daß man sich überdies trotz aller Gegensätze auch auf das Christentum und seine Theologie fruchtbare Einflüsse erhoffte, wie diese die breiten Massen nicht unbedingt etwas anzugehen brauchten, s. u. a. zuletzt T. Lungi in: Antiquity S. 69ff., bes. 70.

166 Zum Beispiel des Timotheos von Gaza s. Krumbacher S. 974; 1077; Hunger II 18ff., Downey a.a.O. S. 313; zu Ammonios s. die Angaben PLRE S. 72; dazu Saffery S. 400ff. mit Bezug auf L. Vailhé, Ech. d'Orient 14, 1911, 277ff.; Stein II 370. Die Beziehung auf ein mit dem Titel verbundenes christliches Amt scheidet m. E. deshalb aus, nimmt man nicht ein bloßes Wortspiel an.

167 S. dazu Cameron 1966, 669ff.; 671 zur leichteren Rolle Alexandrias im Imperium auf Grund seiner Forschungsvorhaben gegenüber Athen, vgl. auch Saffery S. 397. Die Verbindung von Philosopie in herkömmlichem Sinne und Christentum (Johannes Philoponos; vielleicht Olympiodor) erkläre ich mir nicht zuletzt aus solchen Ansätzen. Sie sind zugleich die Übertragung dessen, was für die spätantike Schule schlechthin selbstverständlich ist (s. o.).

168 Bezeichnend in solchem Zusammenhang auch Beruf und Schicksal profilierter Forscher an der Philosophenschule, vgl. Westerink S. XXff. zu Elias. Zur Familientradition, die bes. auch die Teilnahme der Frauen erklärt, s. u. a. S. Pomeroy, Women in Hellenistic Egypt, New York 1984, 64ff.

168a S. zusammenfassend Hunger I 11ff., der mit Recht vor einer Scheidung zwischen beiden Schulen warnt.

169 Zur zeitweisen Emigration des Proklos nach Kleinasien s. Marin. V. Procli 15; vgl. Saffery, StPatr. 9, 1966, 104ff.

170 Eine ernsthafte Konfrontation hatte es zwar bisher nicht gegeben. Doch scheint es gerade die Nähe aller platonischen Philosophie (vgl. bes. Hunger I 14) zum Christentum, die eine wirkliche Flexibilität auch des persönlichen Verhaltens nur bis zu einem gewissen Grade erlaubte. Vgl. dazu bes. R. Strömberg, Eranos 1945, bes. 176. Saffery S. 396. Die Verwendung als Schullektion gehört hierher.

171 S. dazu Cameron a.a.O.

172 S. dazu Cameron, PCPhS 1965, 13; dies bes. zur Tätigkeit des Simplicius während dieser Zeit. Zur Flucht nach Persien als Verhaltensnorm s. auch R. McMullen, S. 98ff. zu Eunap V. Soph. 499.

173 Zu Simplicius s. Geffcken S. 212; Hunger S. 1,21ff.; 29, zusammenfassend auch RE III A. 204ff. (Praechter).

174 Zur .... μοχθηρὰ πολιτεία ... s. Cameron a.a.O. S. 15ff. bes. 16; 20.

175 S. bes. Cameron 1966, 663; Unterrichtsmöglichkeiten bezweifelt Tannery S. 285.

176 Vgl. Cameron, PCPhS 1965, 21f. zu den διαδοχικά. Beim Umfang des Vermögens muß der Mangel an Nachrichten über die Verwendung nach 529 auffallen. Zur Diskussion s. Westerink S. XIVff. Die Vermutung Tannerys (S. 284ff.), die Rückgabe des Akademievermögens sei eine Friedensbedingung gewesen, die Chosrau 532 stellte, hat viel für sich, nötig scheinen solche Erwägungen aber kaum.

177 Zur unverkennbaren Warnung Justinians CJ 1,5,18,4 s. o. Sie betrifft den Glauben der Lehrer, nicht aber Lehrstoff und Lehrtätigkeit.

[178] Const. Omnem passim.

[179] CJ 1,27,1,42/534; vgl. Bonner S. 126. Unklar bleibt die Doppelung (... hominibus duobus ...); ich halte den Versuch einer intensivierten Erneuerung eines Nebeneinanders von griechischem und lateinischem Unterricht für möglich.

Literaturverzeichnis

Arnim v.; H. (1898): Leben und Werk des Dion v. Prusa. Berlin

Barclay, W. (1959): Educational Ideals in the Ancient World. London

Beck, H. G. (1977): Kirche und theologische Literatur im byzantinischen Reich. München

Beck, H. (1978): Das byzantinische Jahrtausend. München

Chauvot, A. (1968): Procope de Gaza, Priscien de Cesaree, Panegyriques de l'empereur Anastase Ier. Bonn

Courcelle, P. (1948): Les lettres grecques en occident de Macrobe à Cassiodore. Paris

Fuchs, A. (1926): Die höheren Schulen von Konstantinopel im Mittelalter. Leipzig

Geffcken, J. (1929): Der Ausgang des griechisch-römischen Heidentums. Heidelberg

Haarhoff, T. J. (1958): Schools of Gaul in the Last Century of Western Empire. Johannesburg

Honigmann, E. (1951): Evéques et évêches monophysites d'Asie anterieure au VI. Löwen

Hunger, H. (1978): Die hochsprachliche Profanliteratur der Byzantiner. München

Hunger, H. (1973): Aspekte der griechischen Rhetorik von Gorgias bis zum Untergang von Byzanz. Wien

Johann, H. Th. (Hsg.) (1976): Erziehung und Bildung in der heidnischen und christlichen Antike. Darmstadt

Jones, A. H. M. (1964): The Later Roman Empire. Oxford

Kanz, H. (1966): Klemens von Alexandria. Ausgewählte Schriften zur Pädagogik. Paderborn

Klein, R. (1983): Die Romrede des Aelius Aristeides. Darmstadt

Krumbacher, K. (1898): Geschichte der byzantinischen Literatur². München

Leipoldt, J. (1903): Schenute v. Atripe und die Entstehung des nationalägyptischen Christentums. Leipzig

Marrou, H. I. (1948): Histoire d'éducation dans l'antiquite. Paris (zit. nach deutscher Übersetzung von Ch. Beumann, München 1977)

Marrou, H. I. (1938): Saint Augustin et la fin de la culture antique. Paris. (zit. nach deutscher Übersetzung von Lore Wirth-Poelchau, Paderborn 1982)

Maspero, J. (1914): Horapollon et la fin du paganisme egyptien, in: BIFAO 11, S. 165ff.

McMullen, R. (1967): Enemies of the Roman Order, Cambridge Mass.

Pavan, M. (1952): La crisi delle scuola nel VI s.d.C. Bari

Petit, P. (1965): Les etudiants de Libanius. Paris

Pichon, R. (1901): Etude sur le mouvement philosophique et religieux sous le regne de Constantin. Paris

Rahn, H. (1972:) Guintilian. Ausbildung des Redners. Lateinisch und deutsch. Darmstadt

Riche, P. (1962): Education et culture dans l'occident barbare. Paris

Rubin, B. (1960): Das Zeitalter Justinians. Berlin

Seeck, O. (1906): Die Briefe des Libanius. Leipzig

Stein, E. (1949): Histoire du Bas empire II. Brüssel

Trafrali, O. (1913): Thessalonique au IV. s. Paris

Vavrinek, V. (1985): From Antiquity to Early Byzantium. Prag
Walden, J. W. (1909): The Universities of Ancient Greece. New York
Weiß, K. (1903): Die Erziehungslehre der drei Kappadoker. Freiburg
Westerink, L. (1962): Anonymus Prolegomena to Platonic Philosophy. Amsterdam

Alfons Rösger

Lehrer und Lehrerbildung im Imperium Romanum

Roms Aufstieg vom Stadtstaat am Tiber zur italischen Großmacht und – nach Bezwingung Karthagos und der hellenistischen Großstaaten – zur Weltmacht des gesamten Mittelmeerraums war begleitet von einer tiefgreifenden Umgestaltung seiner ursprünglichen politischen, wirtschaftlichen und kulturellen Verhältnisse. Durch die Annektion des griechischen Ostens erlangte Rom die politische Herrschaft über einen Raum, der in kultureller und zivilisatorischer Hinsicht ungleich höher entwickelt war als es selbst. Rom erkannte diese Überlegenheit und akzeptierte sie.[1] Es ist Roms Verdienst, daß unter seiner Herrschaft die griechische Kultur im Osten fortbestand, seine Leistung, wenn diese darüberhinaus die künftige zivilisatorische Entwicklung im Westen entscheidend befruchten konnte. Letzteres wurde möglich, weil Rom selbst von griechischer Wissenschaft und Technik übernahm, was für die praktischen Ziele seiner Politik förderlich schien[2], vor allem aber, weil es den Römern gelang, nach dem Vorbild der griechischen Literatur ihre eigene, lateinische auszuformen und gegen Ende der Republik und zu Beginn der Kaiserzeit zu einer Höhe zu bringen, daß sie neben jener bestehen kann.

1. Erstes Auftreten griechischer Privatlehrer in Rom

Bei diesem Prozeß der Aneignung griechischen Geistes durch Rom bei gleichzeitiger Entwicklung einer durchaus eigenständigen Geistigkeit kommt nun dem römischen Erziehungswesen die entscheidende praktische Bedeutung zu. In seiner konkreten, organisatorischen Ausgestaltung als Schule ist dieses Erziehungswesen, wie es sich uns am Ende der Republik darstellt, selbst wiederum Resultat dieses Prozesses.[3]
Rom, gelegen zwischen dem etruskischen Gebiet im Norden und dem griechisch besiedelten Unteritalien im Süden, war von Anbeginn seiner Geschichte den Einwirkungen der griechischen Kultur ausgesetzt. Doch waren diese zunächst mehr indirekt.[4] Von besonderem Interesse ist aber für unseren Zusammenhang, daß Rom auf diesem Wege, wahrscheinlich durch die Vermittlung der in Campanien gelegenen griechischen Kolonie Cumae (gegründet zwischen 775 und 750 v. Chr.), seine Schrift bekam, das chalkidische Alphabet.[5] Durch die Ausdehnung seiner Herrschaft nach Unteritalien und Sizilien im 3. Jh. v. Chr. kam Rom dann in direkte und fortwährende Berührung mit den Griechen und ihrer Kultur.
Von epochaler Bedeutung für die römische Literatur und das römische Erziehungswesen erweist sich in diesem Zusammenhang das Wirken des Griechen *L. Livius Andronicus,* der nach der römischen Eroberung Tarents im Jahre 272 v. Chr. als

Gefangener nach Rom kam.[6] Er war zunächst Sklave eines *Livius,* erzog dessen Kinder und wurde von seinem Herrn wegen seiner Verdienste bald freigelassen.[7] Er blieb Schulmeister und unterrichtete in griechischer und lateinischer Sprache als Hauslehrer wie auch als Privatlehrer in seiner eigenen Schule.[8] Da es an lateinischen Schulautoren noch fehlte, übertrug *Livius Andronicus Homers* Odyssee in lateinische Saturnier und »verpflanzte (so) das (entscheidende) Schulbuch der Griechen in Übersetzung auch in die römische Schulstube«.[9] Die ›Odissia‹ des Livius ersetzte in seinem Unterricht als lateinisches Schulbuch nicht die griechischen Epen *Homers,* sondern trat ergänzend neben sie. Wir dürfen damit *Livius Andronicus* als den Begründer des für die römische Schule, solange sie bestand, charakteristischen zweisprachigen Unterrichts ansehen.[10]
Offenbar wollte sich *Livius Andronicus* nicht auf die Rolle eines Jugenderziehers beschränken, »sondern auch auf das ganze Volk als Bildner wirken«.[11] Und so brachte er anläßlich der *ludi Romani* des Jahres 240 v. Chr. griechische Dramen, eine Tragödie und eine Komödie, in lateinischer Fassung zur Aufführung. Das Jahr 240 erweist sich im Nachhinein als *das* Epochenjahr der römischen Literatur.[12] – *Livius Andronicus* ist die erste wirklich bedeutende Erzieherpersönlichkeit innerhalb der römischen Erziehungsgeschichte, die sich historisch fassen läßt und von der wir zugleich eine einigermaßen plastische Anschauung gewinnen. *Livius Andronicus,* insofern er zunächst als Hauslehrer in der Familie seines Herrn wirkte, repräsentiert einen Lehrertyp, wie er im damaligen Rom weit verbreitet war. Gebildete Griechen fanden in den adligen Familien Roms eine lernbegierige Kundschaft. Dies gilt namentlich von der 2. Hälfte des 2. Jhs. v. Chr. an, als nach dem endgültigen Sieg der Römer über das makedonische Königreich im Jahre 168 griechische Intellektuelle in großer Zahl nach Rom kamen.[13] Diese Griechen, in der Regel Sklaven vornehmer Römer, unterrichteten dabei nicht nur die Kinder ihrer eigenen Herren, sondern wurden, vermutlich gegen Entgelt, nicht selten auch an andere ›ausgeliehen‹.
Letzteres dürfen wir wohl aus einer Notiz des *Plutarch* über *Chilon,* einen Sklaven *Catos d. Ä.,* erschließen, die sich innerhalb der Cato-Biographie in einem Kontext findet, der für unser Thema auch noch in anderer Hinsicht überaus aufschlußreich ist[14]: »Als ihm (sc. *Cato*) ein Sohn geboren war, kannte er kein dringenderes Geschäft, ein öffentliches ausgenommen, als selbst zugegen zu sein, wenn seine Frau das Kind badete und wickelte. Sie nährte es nämlich selbst, legte aber oft auch die Kinder der Sklaven an ihre Brust, um ihnen durch die gemeinsame Nahrung Zuneigung zu ihrem Sohn einzuflößen. Sobald der Knabe verständig wurde, nahm ihn *Cato* selbst zu sich und lehrte ihn lesen, obwohl er einen Sklaven namens *Chilon* hatte, der ein geschickter Lehrer war und vielen Kinder Unterricht gab. Aber er wollte nicht, wie er selbst sagte, daß sein Sohn, wenn er langsamer lernte, von einem Sklaven geschimpft oder am Ohr gezupft würde; auch wollte er einem Sklaven für solchen Unterricht keinen Dank schuldig sein. Deshalb war er selbst der Elementarlehrer, der Rechtslehrer, der Turnlehrer, indem er seinen Sohn nicht nur den Speer werfen, fechten und reiten lehrte, sondern ihm auch beibrachte, mit geballter Faust zu kämpfen, Hitze und Kälte zu ertragen und über Strudel oder reißende Stellen im Tiber mit Kraft zu schwimmen. Er schrieb, wie er selbst sagt, mit eigener Hand und mit großen Buchstaben ein

Geschichtswerk, damit sein Sohn von Jugend an Gelegenheit habe, aus der Kenntnis von Taten und Sitten der Vorfahren Nutzen zu ziehen.«[15]

Livius Andronicus hatte zunächst als Sklave offenbar nur die Kinder seines Herrn erzogen. Nach seiner Freilassung wirkte er weiterhin als Hauslehrer, betrieb daneben aber auch eine eigene Schule, eine Privatschule sozusagen. Der Terminus, den *Sueton* zur Bezeichnung dieser doppelten Lehrtätigkeit verwendet, lautet: *domi forisque docere*. Eine Generation später verdiente übrigens *Q. Ennius* (239–169 v. Chr.) auf die gleiche Weise seinen Lebensunterhalt.[16]

Diese Doppelform eines freien Privatlehrertums bezeichnet die ersten Anfänge eines sich außerhalb des Kreises der Großfamilie organisierenden Schulwesens in Rom. Eine Zwischen- bzw. Übergangsform zwischen unfreiem Hauslehrer und freiem Privatlehrer stellt die Lehrtätigkeit von *Catos* Sklaven *Chilon* dar. Obwohl im Haushalt seines Herrn als Lehrer eigentlich verwendbar, erzieht der Hausvater *Cato* seinen Sohn lieber selbst und läßt seinen Sklaven, von dem es ausdrücklich heißt, daß er ein »geschickter Lehrer« war, außerhalb der Familie viele andere Kinder unterrichten. Da es *Catos* Prinzip war, seine Sklaven als Erwerbsquelle zu nutzen, dürfen wir durchaus davon ausgehen, daß er sich auch die Dienste seines *Chilon* remunerieren ließ. Ja, wir können vielleicht noch einen Schritt weiter gehen.

In dem Abschnitt seiner Cato-Biographie, in welchem sich *Plutarch* den Bereicherungspraktiken *Catos* widmet, erfahren wir u. a. auch, auf welche Weise *Cato* gewinnbringend mit den Fertigkeiten seiner Sklaven ›wirtschaftete‹: »Auch lieh er seinen Sklaven, wenn sie es wollten, Geld. Diese kauften dafür Knaben, die sie auf Kosten *Catos* ausbildeten und unterrichteten und nach einem Jahr wieder verkauften. Viele behielt auch Cato selbst und ließ sich die höchste gebotene Summe dafür anrechnen.«[17]

Über welche Fähigkeiten *Catos* geschäftstüchtige Sklaven verfügten, erwähnt Plutarch leider nicht. Aber warum sollten sich unter ihnen nicht auch Lehrer befunden haben, die ihrerseits wieder geeignete Sklaven zu Lehrern ausbildeten? Immerhin erzielten Lehrer *(grammatici)*, wie uns *Sueton* belehrt, um die Wende vom 2. bis 1. Jahrhundert v. Chr. auf dem Markt besonders hohe Preise.[18]

Ich trage diese Interpretation der zuletzt zitierten *Plutarch*-Notiz natürlich mit einem gewissen Vorbehalt vor. Sollte sie sich aber als zutreffend erweisen, hätten wir mit ihr einen Beleg für gezielte »Lehrerbildung« im Rom des 2. vorchristlichen Jahrhunderts vor uns. – Inwieweit sich *Cato* in diesem Punkte wie auch hinsichtlich seiner Verwendung *Chilons* im Kreise der römischen Aristokratie repräsentativ verhielt, ist allerdings kaum zu ermitteln.

Dagegen tritt ein anderer Sachverhalt, der in unserem Zusammenhang von Interesse ist, am Beispiel des selbsterziehenden *pater familias Cato* in wünschenswerter Deutlichkeit zutage: der Antagonismus von Familienerziehung im Sinne des römischen *mos maiorum*[19] und Fremderziehung, sei es durch nichtblutsverwandte Untergebene im Hause sei es durch Fremde außerhalb des Hauses. Dieses Problem wurde virulent, als die Römer durch die Griechen mit einem bereits öffentlich organisierten Erziehungs- und Unterrichtswesen bekannt wurden, das von der altrömischen Familienerziehung gänzlich verschieden war.

2. Der Antagonismus zwischen altrömischer Familienerziehung und Schulerziehung nach griechischem Vorbild

Nach ursprünglich römischer Anschauung war die Familie der ausschließliche Lebensraum, in welchem das Kind heranwachsen und sich bilden sollte. Man versuchte, dieser Forderung in der Realität auch nach Möglichkeit zu entsprechen. So kümmerte sich in der ersten Phase des Lebens in erster Linie die Mutter selbst um ihr Kind, nährte und erzog es. Sie bediente sich in Wahrnehmung dieser Pflichten allenfalls noch der Hilfe einer älteren vertrauenswürdigen Verwandten als Miterzieherin. Dem Kind etwa, wie in Griechenland üblich, eine Sklavin als Amme zu geben, war in den frühen republikanischen Zeiten selbst in den vornehmsten römischen Familien verpönt.

Mit dem 7. Lebensjahr trat das Kind dann aus der ausschließlich weiblichen Obhut heraus und ging in diejenige seines Vaters über. »Der Vater wurde als der eigentliche Erzieher angesehen.«[20] Er gab dem Kind die theoretische Unterweisung, bemühte sich aber vor allem, es durch sein gelebtes Beispiel zu formen und so in die künftigen Aufgaben des Lebens einzuüben. So saßen die jungen Römer beim morgendlichen Empfang der Klienten neben ihren Vätern und begleiteten sie sogar in den Senat.[21] Unterstützung erfuhr der Vater bisweilen bei seinem Erziehungswerk durch einen männlichen Verwandten, in der Regel durch den Bruder. In dieser engen Lebensgemeinschaft mit dem Vater verweilte der Sohn bis zur Anlegung der Männertoga, d. h. etwa bis zum 16. Lebensjahr. – Danach begann die – in der Regel ein Jahr dauernde – »politische Lehrzeit«, das *tirocinium fori.* Nur ausnahmsweise leitete der Vater seinen Sohn auch in dieser Phase. Normalerweise wurde der junge Römer während dieser Zeit einem bewährten älteren Freund der Familie anvertraut.[22]

In den einfachen, vor allem auch räumlich begrenzten und überschaubaren Lebensverhältnissen während der früheren Republik ließ sich eine Erziehung innerhalb des engen Kreises der Familie, wie wir sie soeben skizziert haben, mit Erfolg praktizieren. Als Rom seine politische Macht über Italien hinaus ausdehnte und schließlich die gesamte Mittelmeerwelt zu seinem unmittelbaren Herrschaftsgebiet machte, was im Gegenzug Menschen verschiedenster Herkunft nach Rom einströmen ließ, konnte die altrömische Familienerziehung den praktischen Bedürfnissen der Jugend nach Ausbildung und Information nicht mehr genügen. Um sich in der weitgewordenen und so überaus vielgestaltigen Welt des Imperium Romanum zurechtzufinden, bedurften die Römer dieser Epoche eines breitgefächerten Spezialwissens, wie es namentlich die hochzivilisierte, nun aber Rom unterworfene Welt des Hellenismus verfügbar bereithielt. Nur ein universalgebildeter Römer vom Schlage eines *Cato* mochte sich noch zutrauen, das notwendige Wissen in der gebotenen Differenziertheit seinem Sohn selbst zu vermitteln.

Dieser Sachlage war sich *Cato* allem Anschein nach bewußt. Daher lehnte nicht einmal er die Fremderziehung durch griechische Untergebene grundweg ab; sonst hätte er gewiß seinem Sklaven *Chilon* jede Lehrtätigkeit untersagt. *Cato* zählte vielleicht sogar zu den Römern, die den Wert und den praktischen Nutzen der griechischen Wissenschaften zuerst erkannten.[23] Seine bekannte Warnung vor den *litterae* der Griechen zielt expressis verbis in erster Linie auf die Medizin. Im übrigen empfiehlt *Cato* sogar, die wissenschaftliche Literatur der Griechen zur Kenntnis zu nehmen *(inspicere)*, nur solle man sie nicht ›auswendig lernen‹ *(perdiscere)*, was wohl meint: ›mechanisch und kritiklos übernehmen‹.[24] Worauf es *Cato* ankommt, ist also offenbar, die an sich als notwendig und nützlich erkannte Übernahme überlegenen griechischen Wissens bewußt und kontrolliert zu vollziehen. – Er hätte daher vermutlich auch die von seiner eigenen Praxis abweichende Erziehungsmethode seines berühmten Zeitgenossen *Aemilius Paullus* durchaus gebilligt.

Aemilius Paullus Macedonicus (229–160 v. Chr.), der Sieger von Pydna (168 v. Chr.), war von der väterlichen Erziehungspflicht gegenüber seinen Söhnen kaum weniger durchdrungen als *Cato*. Nur konnte er ihr in praxi wahrscheinlich nicht in der gleichen Art und Weise genügen. Er engagierte folglich für seine Söhne griechische Fachlehrer, war aber, wenn sie ihren Unterricht erteilten, nach Möglichkeit stets persönlich anwesend, wie wiederum *Plutarch* berichtet: »Er (sc. *Aemilius Paullus*) beschäftigte sich teils mit der Besorgung der Gottesdienste, teils mit der Erziehung seiner Söhne, die er nicht nur nach hergebrachter Landessitte, wie er selbst erzogen worden war, sondern auch mit großem Eifer in den griechischen Wissenschaften unterrichten ließ. Denn die Jünglinge waren ständig mit Sprachlehrern, Philosophen und Rednern, ja selbst mit griechischen Bildhauern, Malern, Stallmeistern und Lehrern der Jägerei umgeben; und der Vater selbst wohnte, als der größte Kinderfreund unter den Römern, wenn ihn keine öffentlichen Geschäfte abhielten, immer ihren Lehrstunden und Übungen bei.«[25]

Die angeführten Beispiele lassen erkennen, vor welches praktische Problem sich konservativ und national gesonnene vornehme Römer angesichts des wachsenden griechischen Kultureinflusses von der Mitte des 2. Jhs. v. Chr. an gestellt sahen, wenn es um die Erziehung ihrer Kinder ging. Man wollte auf der einen Seite den Kindern das als nützlich erkannte überlegene Wissen der Griechen nicht vorenthalten, mußte sich aber auf der anderen Seite eingestehen, daß man es ihnen mit den überkommenen Methoden der altrömischen Familienerziehung in der Regel nicht beibringen konnte. Die praktische Lösung des Problems, die man zunächst versuchte, bestand darin, daß man unfreie oder freie Hauslehrer engagierte, wobei der *pater familias* nach Möglichkeit an deren Unterricht mitwirkte, diesen zumindest aber beaufsichtigte. Auf diese Weise brachte er wie ehedem seine Autorität in den Unterricht ein, der nun allerdings von anderen erteilt wurde, und ließ damit zugleich erkennen, daß er für diesen letztlich die Verantwortung trug. Das schränkte natürlich auf der anderen Seite die pädagogischen Möglichkeiten des engagierten Lehrpersonals erheblich ein.

Durch die Anstellung von Hauslehrern versuchte man angesichts der veränderten Erziehungswirklichkeit von der altrömischen Familienerziehung wenigstens das Prinzip des *domi docere* zu bewahren. Doch wurde oben schon gesagt, daß bereits *Livius Andronicus* auch in einer eigenen Privatschule lehrte[26], wobei an eine Schule des höheren Unterrichts (Grammatikschule) zu denken ist.[27] *Plutarch* verknüpft allerdings die Einrichtung der ersten Schule in Rom, wohl einer Elementarschule, mit dem Namen des *Spurius Carvilius*[28], eines Freigelassenen des Consuls *Spurius Carvilius*

Maximus Ruga, der in den Jahren 234 und 228 v. Chr. das Consulat bekleidete. Nun kann aber kein Zweifel sein, daß bereits früher, wie ja auch der Fall des *Livius Andronicus* zeigt, Schulen in Rom bestanden. *Marrou* rechnet mit solchen sogar beträchtlich vor dem 4. Jh. v. Chr. Die *Plutarch*-Notiz ist also nicht ohne weiteres zu verstehen. Vielleicht bestand das Neue der Schule des *Spurius Carvilius* in ihrer Größe, ihren Unterrichtsmethoden oder in der Art ihrer geschäftsmäßigen Organisation; *Spurius Carvilius* ließ sich nämlich seine Lehrtätigkeit bezahlen.[29] Jedenfalls deuten aber all diese Zeugnisse zur Genüge an, daß sich in Rom spätestens vom 3. Jh. v. Chr. an ein öffentliches Schulwesen entwickelte. Es handelte sich dabei zunächst um Elementar- und Grammatikschulen. Erst im Jahre 93 v. Chr. gründete *L. Plotius Gallus* die erste Rhetorenschule, und zwar für lateinische Rhetorik.[30] In griechischer Rhetorik hatten sich interessierte Römer bereits ein halbes Jahrhundert früher anläßlich von Aufenthalten berühmter griechischer Rhetoren, die Rom meist in diplomatischer Mission besuchten, unterweisen lassen können.[31]

Wenn eben von einem öffentlichen Schulwesen die Rede war, das sich in Rom vom 3. Jh. an etablierte, so bedeutet das nicht, daß die erwähnten Schulen auf staatliche Initiative hin eingerichtet wurden. Es handelt sich ausnahmslos um Privatschulen, die jedoch für die Allgemeinheit – gegen Entgelt – zugänglich waren. Gezielte staatliche Förderung des Schulwesens begegnet in Rom erst erheblich später, in der Kaiserzeit. Der erste, der Lehrern der lateinischen und griechischen Rhetorik aus dem Fiskus ein hohes Jahresgehalt von 100 000 Sesterzen auswarf, war Kaiser *Vespasian.*[32] Zu diesen Lehrern gehörte auch *Quintilian.* Er ist gewissermaßen der erste ›ordentlich öffentliche Professor‹ der europäischen Bildungsgeschichte, den wir mit Namen kennen.[33]

3. Der altrömische Familienvater als Lehrerideal in der Schulkonzeption Quintilians

Das hier in großen Zügen skizzierte öffentliche Schulwesen der republikanischen Zeit trat zunehmend konkurrierend neben die überkommene Familien- und Hauserziehung, hat diese aber allem Anschein nach nicht so ganz verdrängen können. So lesen wir in einem Brief *Ciceros* an seinen Freund *Atticus,* daß er persönlich seinen Sohn und seine Neffen unterrichtete, nachdem er sich überzeugen mußte, daß der Privatlehrer *Dionysius,* der ihm von *Atticus* empfohlen worden war, pädagogisch untalentiert war.[34] Und noch Kaiser *Augustus* hielt es nicht für unter seiner Würde, die Söhne seiner Tochter *Julia* von *Agrippa* meist selbst im Lesen und Schreiben und anderen Elementarfächern zu unterweisen, wobei er sich besondere Mühe gab, daß sie lernten, seine eigene Handschrift nachzuahmen.[35] Schließlich hält gegen Ende des 1. Jhs. n. Chr. *Quintilian* es für nötig, gegen Anfang seiner Institutio oratoria der folgenden Frage eine eigene Erörterung zu widmen: »Ist es besser den Knaben beim Lernen im Hause und innerhalb der eigenen Wände zu behalten oder ihn dem Gedränge in den Schulen und gleichsam den Lehrern für jedermann auszuliefern?«[36] *Quintilian* ent-

scheidet sich in dieser Frage zugunsten der Schule. Immerhin deuten aber seine Überlegungen an, daß noch zu seiner Zeit, als sich das dreistufige und zweisprachige römische Schulsystem nach griechischem Muster bereits vollausgebildet und in speziellen Lehrinstitutionen organisiert hatte, das alte Problem ›Einzelunterricht zu Hause‹ *(domi docere)* oder ›öffentliche Schule‹ *(foris docere)* kontrovers diskutiert wurde. In der gesellschaftlichen Wirklichkeit hatte die Schule zu dieser Zeit längst den Sieg über die alte Hauserziehung davongetragen. An ein Zurückdrehen dieser Entwicklung konnte ernsthaft niemand denken.
In die Erziehungsaufgaben, die in der römischen Frühzeit der *pater familias* im Hause allein wahrgenommen hatte, teilten sich nach dem dreistufigen Schulsystem nun nacheinander der Elementar-, der Grammatik- und der Rhetoriklehrer. Durch die Zweisprachigkeit des römischen Unterrichts konnte sich die Anzahl der Lehrer, die ein römischer Schüler während seiner Schulzeit kennenlernte, in praxi noch verdoppeln. Wir haben damit in der entwickelten öffentlichen Schule Roms ein differenziertes Unterrichtssystem vor uns, daß in seinem Aufbau beinahe modern anmutet.[37] Sachlich betrachtet war es als solches der alten privaten Hauserziehung weit überlegen. Das vielfältige Wissen, das nach diesem System den Schülern von verschiedenen Fachlehrern vermittelt wurde, stand einem einzelnen Hausvater allenfalls im seltenen Ausnahmefall zur Verfügung.
Der Fortschritt, den die nach griechischem Muster differenziert organisierte Schule gegenüber der Unterweisung im Hause darstellt, wenn man beide Unterrichtsmöglichkeiten unter dem Gesichtspunkt der Vermittlung von Wissen miteinander vergleicht, liegt auf der Hand. Doch war dieser Aspekt nach römischer Anschauung nicht der entscheidende. »Denn«, so sagt z. B. *Quintilian,* »wenn es feststände, daß die Schulen zwar dem Wissen nutzen, aber den Sitten schaden, so schienen mir die Rücksichten auf ein anständiges Leben wichtiger als selbst die trefflichste Redekunst«.[38] Daß die Schule demnach Wissen vermittelte, stand außer Frage, aber man meinte, »die Sitten würden in den Schulen verdorben« – *corrumpi in scholis mores putant.*[39]
Die Kritiker der Schule und Befürworter der Hauserziehung legten einen ganzen Katalog von Gefährdungen der Kinder vor, die sich durch den Schulbesuch ergaben: sittliche Gefahren schon auf dem Wege zur Schule, in der Schule selbst schlechte Einflüsse von Mitschülern.[40] Diese Einwände nimmt *Quintilian* keineswegs leicht. »Denn«, so sagt er wieder, »es kommt bisweilen durchaus vor, daß der Charakter der Kinder« – also die *mores* – »in der Schule verdorben wird«, *sed domi quoque* – »aber das kommt zu Hause ebenfalls vor«.[41] – Ein anderer Vorbehalt der Schulkritiker betraf die Schullehrer, die *publici praeceptores,* die »Lehrer für jedermann«, wie *Rahn* übersetzt. Man argwöhnte, die Schule sei eine Stätte, wo das Kind »vernachlässigt« werde; ein Schullehrer könne sich angesichts der größeren Anzahl von zu Unterrichtenden dem einzelnen Schüler nicht mit der gleichen Intensität und Hingabe zuwenden wie der Einzellehrer in der Familie.[42]
Diesen letzten Einwand nimmt nun *Quintilian* offenbar sehr ernst. Er versucht ihn zu relativieren und zu entkräften, indem er den guten »Schullehrer« *(bonus praeceptor)* mit dem im Hause unterrichtenden Einzellehrer vergleicht. Der »gute Schullehrer«,

so meint *Quintilian* von vornherein optimistisch, »wird sich nicht mit einer größeren Schülerzahl belastet haben, als er bewältigen, ertragen, aushalten kann«.[43] Der Ausdruck *sustinere,* den *Quintilian* in diesem Zusammenhang gebraucht, ist kaum mit einem einzigen Wort im Deutschen wiederzugeben. Im übrigen stehe aber, wenn die Eltern Einzelunterricht wünschten, nichts im Wege, daß der Knabe, der in der Schule unterrichtet werde, daneben auch noch mit – wie *Quintilian* sich ausdrückt – »einem unbekannten Einzellehrer zusammensei«.[44] Die lateinische Formulierung ist noch drastischer. Man hört das Ressentiment des Schulmannes gegen die in der Familie einzeln unterrichtenden Privatlehrer geradezu heraus. Wenige Zeilen weiter charakterisiert *Quintilian* die Einzellehrer als »die Geringeren, die es im Bewußtsein ihrer Schwäche nicht für unter ihrer Würde halten, sich an Einzelschüler zu hängen und gewissermaßen die Dienste von *paedagogi* zu verrichten«.[45] Die besten Schullehrer dagegen freuen sich über zahlreichen Schulbesuch, weil sie glauben, eines größeren Publikums wert zu sein.

Es ist schwer zu unterscheiden, ob *Quintilian* hier die Erziehungsrealität seiner eigenen Gegenwart wahrheitsnah schildert, also eine bestehende Situation, in der die pädagogisch talentierten Lehrer das ihnen gemäße Wirkungsfeld nicht in der Einzelunterrichtung, sondern in der Schule erblickten, oder ob er ein Wunschbild entwirft. Bemerkenswert bleibt jedoch in jedem Falle, daß *Quintilian* die allem Anschein nach nicht ganz unberechtigten Vorbehalte der Schulkritiker und Befürworter der Einzelerziehung in der Familie vor allem dadurch zu entkräften sucht, daß er sich aufzuzeigen bemüht: die besseren Lehrer findet der Schüler in der Schule und daher gebührt dieser Unterrichtsform der Vorzug.

Wie stellt sich nun aber der »gute Schullehrer«, der *praeceptor bonus* in der Sicht *Quintilians* dar? – Da *Quintilian,* wie wir eben sahen[46], auch im Schulunterricht die sittliche Erziehung über die Wissensvermittlung stellt, steht für ihn die »Lebensführung« *(mores)* des Lehrers im Mittelpunkt des Interesses.[47] Er fordert von ihm geradezu *sanctitas,* »Makellosigkeit«, damit das zartere Alter des Schülers vor »Unbill« *(iniuria)* bewahrt werde. Weitere Lehrereigenschaften, die *Quintilian* für unerläßlich hält, sind *gravitas,* »Würde der Erscheinung«, *summa abstinentia,* »entschiedene Selbstbeherrschung«, gepaart mit *severitas disciplinae,* »Strenge der Zucht«. Durch seine *gravitas* soll der Lehrer die ungestümeren Schüler von mutwilligen Streichen *(licentia)* abschrecken, durch seine *abstinentia* und seine *severitas* ihre Sitten zügeln.[48] Doch soll seine Strenge nicht grämlich, seine Freundlichkeit nicht leichtfertig und formlos sein, damit nicht auf Seiten des Schülers Überdruß bzw. Verachtung hervorgerufen werde. Wenn der Lehrer etwas zu korrigieren hat, tue er es ohne Schimpfen und Zanken, damit nicht der Eindruck entstehe, er hasse seine Schüler. Er strafe selten und mit Umsicht, auf keinen Fall im Jähzorn.[49] Die Prügelstrafe lehnt *Quintilian* als Disziplinierungsmittel grundsätzlich ab.[50] Überhaupt soll der Lehrer seine Tätigkeit nicht in erster Linie als *officium,* als »Dienstleistung« begreifen, sondern als *affectus,* als »Ausdruck seiner Zuneigung« (zum Schüler).[51]

Es ließen sich noch weitere Eigenschaften aufzählen, die *Quintilian* für wünschenswert hält, doch würde keine noch so lange Schilderung das Lehrerideal *Quintilians* besser erschließen als ein einziger Satz von ihm selbst: »So nehme der Lehrer vor allen

Dingen gegen seine Schüler die Gesinnung eines Vaters an und fühle sich so, als trete er an die Stelle derer, die ihm die Kinder anvertrauen« – *sumat* (sc. *praeceptor*) *ante omnia parentis erga discipulos suos animum ac succedere se in eorum locum, a quibus sibi liberi tradantur, existimet.*[52]

Somit löst sich in der römischen Schule, wie *Quintilian* sie sich denkt, der alte Widerstreit zwischen griechischem Unterricht und altrömischer Familienerziehung auf, der die römische Erziehungsgeschichte seit *Cato d. Ä.* prägte. Die beiden Wege vereinigen sich. Der im Laufe der Entwicklung aus der römischen Schulwirklichkeit mehr und mehr verdrängte *pater familias,* der ursprünglich im Hause seine Kinder selbst erzog, kehrt damit in die Erziehung zurück als ideales Leitbild, an dem sich von nun an die Schullehrer orientieren konnten.

Soweit ich sehe, hat *Quintilian* dieses Lehrerideal im Römischen[53] als erster in aller Klarheit formuliert. Wirksam war es jedoch während des ganzen von uns betrachteten Zeitraums. Auf dem Hintergrund dieses Ideals wird die vielfältige Kritik, wie sie an Lehrern namentlich der ersten beiden Schulstufen immer wieder geübt wird, erst so recht verständlich. Es handelte sich bei den Schulmeistern anfangs ja in der Regel um Sklaven oder Freigelassene, um Menschen also niedriger sozialer Stellung, die man allein schon deswegen verachtete. Die vom Erzieher in erster Linie geforderte sittliche Autorität schien ihnen von vorherein zu mangeln. Insofern diese Lehrer für Geld unterrichteten, erfuhren sie überdies noch die Geringschätzung, die Handwerkern und anderen Erwerbstätigen im Altertum ganz allgemein entgegengebracht zu werden pflegte. Seinen Lebensunterhalt durch bezahlte Arbeit zu bestreiten, galt insbesondere Römern vornehmer Herkunft als eines freien Mannes unwürdig. Wie in Griechenland vor dem Auftreten der Sophisten, vertrat man auch im republikanischen Rom den Grundsatz, »daß die Schätze des Geistes nicht wie gewöhnliche Ware für Geld verkauft werden dürften«.[54] Lehrern, die für ihre Tätigkeit Honorar nahmen, wurde daher sehr häufig der Vorwurf der Gewinnsucht gemacht. Das überaus niedrige gesellschaftliche Ansehen der Lehrer wirkte sich notwendig auf das Schülerverhalten aus und führte zu Disziplinproblemen, denen die Lehrer nicht selten mit bedenklichen pädagogischen Mitteln begegneten, was dann Veranlassung zu neuer Kritik bot.

Das recht negative Lehrerbild der römischen Schulpraxis, das sich anhand der zahlreichen einschlägigen Anekdoten zeichnen ließe, mutet in seinen Hauptzügen geradezu wie ein Gegenbild des von *Quintilian* vorgestellten Ideals an. Die problematische Situation der römischen Schulwirklichkeit, was das Lehrpersonal angeht, erklärt sich nicht zum wenigsten aus dem Umstand, daß es während der Republik und der frühen Kaiserzeit eine an pädagogischen Grundsätzen orientierte Lehrerbildung noch nicht gab, die eine objektive Qualifikation der Lehrer für ihre Aufgabe einigermaßen sichergestellt hätte. Es blieb, wie z. B. Aussagen *Quintilians* und des jüngeren *Plinius* belegen, im Grunde allein den Eltern überlassen, aus dem vorhandenen Angebot an Lehrpersonal für ihre Kinder die *boni praeceptores* auszuwählen.[55]

Anmerkungen

[1] Der römische Dichter *Horaz* hat die kulturelle Überlegenheit der Griechen über die Römer auf die klassische Formel gebracht: *Graecia capta ferum victorem cepit et artis / intulit agresti Latio* (epist. 2,1, 156f.).

[2] Vgl. *Rösger* (1988), S. 93ff.

[3] Vgl. dazu vor allem *Marrou* (1957), S. 355–372.

[4] Vgl. dazu *Leo* (1913), S. 1–12.

[5] Vgl. *Leo* (1913), S. 5ff.; *Schanz / Hosius* I (1927[4]), S. 25f.

[6] Zu *L. Livius Andronicus* vgl. *Leo* (1913), S. 47–75; *Schanz / Hosius* I (1927[4]), S. 45–49.

[7] *Hier.* chron. z. J. 187 v. Chr. (p. 137 *Helm*): *Titus Livius tragoediarum scriptor clarus habetur, qui ob ingenii meritum a Livio Salinatore, cuius liberos erudiebat, libertate donatus est.* – Vgl. dazu *Schanz / Hosius* I (1927[4]), S. 46.

[8] *Suet.* gramm. 1: *Grammatica Romae ne in usu quidem olim, nedum in honore ullo erat ... initium quoque eius mediocre exstitit, siquidem antiquissimi doctorum qui idem et poetae et semigraeci erant – Livium et Ennium dico quos utraque lingua domi forisque docuisse adnotatum est – nihil amplius quam Graecos interpretabantur, aut si quid ipsi Latine conposuissent praelegebant.*

[9] Vgl. *Schanz / Hosius* I (1927[4]), S. 46.

[10] Zum zweisprachigen Unterricht in Rom vgl. *Marrou* (1957), S. 373–387.

[11] *Schanz / Hosius* I (1927[4]), S. 47.

[12] Vgl. dazu *Leo* (1913), S. 47ff.; *Schanz / Hosius* I (1927[4]), S. 47f. u. 607f.

[13] Vgl. vor allem *Polyb.* 32,10, dazu *Marrou* (1957), S. 361.

[14] *Plut.* Cato mai. 20–21.

[15] *Plut.* Cato mai. 20,4–7; Übersetzung zitiert nach: *M. Porcius Cato,* Vom Landbau – Fragmente – alle erhaltenen Schriften, lat. – dt., hrsg. von *O. Schönberger* (1980), S. 361ff. – Vgl. ferner *Krause* (1851), S. 258; *Grasberger* II (1875), S. 152f.; *Marrou* (1957), S. 342.

[16] *Suet.* gramm. 1 (vgl. oben Anm. 8).

[17] *Plut.* Cato mai. 21,7–8; zitiert nach der Übers. von *Schönberger* (s. oben Anm. 15), S. 367.

[18] Vgl. *Suet.* gramm. 3,5; dazu *Marrou* (1957), S. 361.

[19] Zur römischen Familienerziehung vgl. *Marrou* (1957), S. 337ff., bes. 341ff.

[20] *Marrou* (1957), S. 341; vgl. dazu auch *Grasberger* II (1875), S. 151–155.

[21] Vgl. dazu *Grasberger* II (1875), S. 125 u. 154.

[22] Zum *tirocinium fori* vgl. *Marrou* (1957), S. 343.

[23] Vgl. dazu *Leo* (1913), S. 268ff.

[24] Vgl. *Cato* fr. 356 der Ausgabe von *Schönberger* (s. oben Anm. 15), S. 274/75; vgl. ferner *Rösger* (1988), S. 94f.

[25] *Plut.* Aem. 6; Übersetzung zitiert nach: *Plutarch*, Lebensbeschreibungen, übers. von *F. Kaltwasser,* bearb. von *H. Loerke,* Bd. II (1964), S. 96f.

[26] s. o. S. 120

[27] *Marrou* (1957), S. 366.

[28] *Plut.* quaest. Rom. 278E; vgl. *Krause* (1851), S. 259f.

[29] Vgl. *Marrou* (1957), S. 366.

[30] *Suet.* gramm. 26; vgl. *Marrou* (1957), S. 369.

[31] Vgl. dazu *Leo* (1913), S. 261ff.; *Marrou* (1957), S. 359f.

[32] *Suet.* Vesp. 18.

[33] *Hier.* chron. z. J. 88 (p. 190 *Helm*); vgl. *Schanz / Hosius* II (1935[4]), S. 745f.

[34] *Cic.* Att. 8,4,1.
[35] *Suet.* Aug. 64,3; vgl. 64,1.
[36] *Quint.* inst. 1,2,1; Übersetzung hier und im folgenden zitiert nach: *M. Fabius Quintilianus*, Ausbildung des Redners, hrsg. u. übers. von *H. Rahn,* I (1972), S. 29.
[37] Eine gedrängte Darstellung dieses dreistufigen römischen Schulsystems bietet *Marrou* (1957), S. 389–423.
[38] *Quint.* inst. 1,2,3: *nam si studiis quidem scholas prodesse, moribus autem nocere constaret, potior mihi ratio vivendi honeste quam vel optime dicendi videretur.* – Übersetzung von *Rahn* (s. oben Anm. 36), S. 29f.
[39] *Quint.* inst. 1,2,4.
[40] Vgl. *Quint.* inst. 1,2,2.
[41] *Quint.* inst. 1,2,4; Beispiele für sittliche Gefährdungen des Kindes zu Hause nennt *Quintilian* in den folgenden Paragraphen (inst. 1,2,6–8).
[42] *Quint.* inst. 1,2,15.
[43] *Quint.* inst. 1,2,15: *sed neque praeceptor bonus maiore se turba, quam ut sustinere eam possit, oneraverit.*
[44] *Quint.* inst. 1,2,9: *ante omnia nihil prohibet esse illum nescio quem unum etiam cum eo, qui in scholis eruditur.*
[45] Mit *paedagogi* spielt *Quintilian* hier auf die Sklaven an, die die jüngeren Schüler vom Elternhaus zum Schullokal begleiteten und sie bei ihren Schularbeiten beaufsichtigten und unterstützten.
[46] s. oben S. 125
[47] *Quint.* inst. 2,2,1: *Ergo cum ad eas in studiis vires pervenerit puer, ut, quae prima esse praecepta rhetorum diximus, mente consequi possit, tradendus eius artis magistris erit. quorum in primis inspici mores oportebit.*
[48] Vgl. *Quint.* inst. 2,2,3–4: *nam et adulti fere pueri ad hos praeceptores transferuntur et apud eos iuvenes etiam facti perseverant, ideoque maior adhibenda tum cura est, ut et teneriores annos ab iniuria sanctitas docentis custodiat et ferociores a licentia gravitas deterreat. neque vero sat est summam praestare abstinentiam, nisi disciplinae severitate convenientium quoque ad se mores adstrinxerit.*
[49] Vgl. *Quint.* inst. 2,2,5–7.
[50] Zu diesem Punkt äußert sich *Quintilian* ausführlich inst. 1,3,14–17.
[51] *Quint.* inst. 1,2,15.
[52] *Quint.* inst. 2,2,7.
[53] Zum Vaterideal als Vorbild des Lehrers bei den Griechen vgl. *Grasberger* II (1975), S. 151 mit Anm. 2.
[54] Vgl. dazu *Grasberger* II (1875), S. 151.
[55] Vgl. *Quint.* inst. 1,2,1.15; 2,2,1.15; *Plin.* epist. 4,13,4–11.

Literaturverzeichnis

Grasberger, L. (1875): Erziehung und Unterricht im klassischen Altertum, Bd. II. Würzburg (Neudr. Aalen 1971)
Krause, J. H. (1851): Geschichte der Erziehung, des Unterrichts und der Bildung bei den Griechen, Etruskern und Römern. Halle (Neudr. Schaan/Liechtenstein 1982)

Leo, F. (1913): Geschichte der römischen Literatur. Berlin
Marrou, H. I. (1957): Geschichte der Erziehung im klassischen Altertum, übers. von Ch. Beumann, hrsg. von R. Harder. Freiburg/München
Rösger, A. (1988): Der naturwissenschaftliche Unterricht in der römischen Antike, in: von Hohenzollern, J. G./Liedtke, M. (Hrsg.): Naturwissenschaftlicher Unterricht und Wissenskumulation. Bad Heilbrunn (Schriftenreihe zum Bayerischen Schulmuseum Ichenhausen), S. 93–108
Schanz, M./Hosius, C. (1914ff.): Geschichte der römischen Literatur bis zum Gesetzgebungswerk des Kaisers Justinian, Bd. I (1927^{4}), Bd. II (1935^{4}). München

IV. DER CHRISTLICHE LEHRER DES MITTELALTERS UND DER NEUZEIT

Hans-Uwe Rump

Magister und Scholastikus: Das neue Ansehen des Lehrers in christlicher Zeit

Wenn vom mittelalterlichen Lehrer gehandelt wird, so kann dies aufgrund der Quellenlage weder rein biographisch noch losgelöst von der Entwicklung des mittelalterlichen Denkens geschehen. Es muß vielmehr versucht werden, seine Funktion, seine Stellung und sein Wirken im größeren Zusammenhang der christlich-abendländischen Schul- und Kulturgeschichte des Mittelalters herauszuarbeiten. Angesichts des hier vorgegebenen Rahmens soll dabei schwerpunktmäßig auf die Kloster-, Dom-, Stifts- und Pfarrschulen eingegangen werden, zumal den städtischen Schulen in diesem Band ein eigener Beitrag gewidmet ist.

Schule und Lehrer zwischen Antike und Christentum

Das mittelalterliche Schulwesen bietet ein hervorragendes Beispiel für die Wirksamkeit von Kontinuität und Diskontinuität im historischen Prozeß, in der kulturgeschichtlichen Entwicklung. Einerseits kann spätestens seit der verdienstvollen Quellenarbeit *Detlev Illmers* zu den frühmittelalterlichen Klosterschulen[1] nicht mehr ohne Widerspruch im Sinne einer diachronischen Geschichtsschreibung von einer kontinuierlichen Entwicklung der Schule von der Antike bis in die Neuzeit gesprochen werden, konnte er doch nachweisen, daß die Klosterschule des frühen Mittelalters keineswegs einfach als Verbindungsglied zwischen antiker Schule und der des Hochmittelalters angesehen werden kann. Aus Gründen, die mit der Institutionalisierung und Organisation der Kirche als Amtskirche zusammenhängen, konstatiert *Illmer* einen Bruch zwischen antiker Kultur und frühmittelalterlichem Christentum, der in den Klöstern zu einer besonderen Erziehungsform führte, für die er den Begriff »Schule« nicht ohne weiteres angewendet wissen möchte.[2]
Auf der anderen Seite sind antike Traditionen der mittelalterlichen Schule nicht zu übersehen. Dies gilt für den Unterrichtsstoff ebenso wie für die Lehrmittel, die Texte antiker Autoren. Nicht von ungefähr wurde die Qualität eines Lehrers im frühen Mittelalter noch immer daran gemessen, ob er nach »Art der Römer« unterrichten könne.[3] Darüber hinaus kann kaum bezweifelt werden, daß die ersten Schulen auf bayerischem Boden von den Römern stammten. Schließlich verweisen auch die gravierenden Einflüsse des Humanismus und des Neuhumanismus auf bereits früher vorhandene griechische und römische Traditionen.[4]
In diesem Spannungsfeld zwischen der Kontinuität des antiken Denkens und der

christlichen Neuorientierung, die durch die Institutionalisierung der Kirche als Amtskirche in feste organisatorische Formen wie Kloster-, Dom-, Stifts- und Pfarrschulen, schließlich auch in die Universitäten einmündete, stehen Ausbildung, Funktion und Persönlichkeit des Lehrers im Mittelalter, für das *Christus* der Inbegriff des Lehrers, der »unus omnium magister« ist, wie es *Bonaventura* ausdrückte[5] und wie es auf Sarkophagen des 4. Jhs. dargestellt ist.[6] Noch im 16. Jh. fand sich in den Schulen im Klassenzimmer das Bild des lehrenden Jesusknaben.
Dadurch, daß mit dem allmählichen Zerfall und der endgültigen Auflösung des weltweiten römischen Reiches der römischen Schule in der Provinz zunächst einmal die wirtschaftlichen und organisatorischen Grundlagen entzogen wurden, verfielen im Frühmittelalter in gewissem Maße auch Zielsetzung und Aufgabenbereich der antiken schulischen Erziehung. Genau betrachtet, setzte dieser Prozeß bereits in der Spätantike ein, beschränkte sich jedoch zunächst auf die damaligen Zentren christlicher Bildung. Mit dem Aufstieg des Christentums zu einem Faktor staatlicher Macht setzte sich dort auch ein neues Ideal geistiger Orientierung durch, das weiterzugeben, Aufgabe der gelehrten Theologen und der Lehrer war, wobei beides zwar nicht immer, von einem gewissen Niveau der schulischen Ausbildung an jedoch weitgehend identisch war. Die christliche Neuorientierung bestand vorwiegend darin, daß Wissen und Bildung nun nicht mehr in erster Linie dafür erworben wurden, in der irdischen Welt bestehen zu können, sondern vornehmlich dafür, sich hier im Leben auf das ewige Heil nach dem Tode vorzubereiten. Daraus ergab sich eine polare Spannung zwischen dem Meistern des irdischen Daseins und dem Streben nach ewigem Heil, für das die Welt ja zugleich Bedingung und Hindernis ist. Diese Spannung, deren Pole die Bewältigung der Natur für den Dienst am einzelnen und an der Gesellschaft sowie das Streben des Geistes nach dem ewigen Heil sind, hält im Prinzip bis zur Aufklärung an, schwächt sich jedoch im Verlauf des Mittelalters dahingehend etwas ab, daß die christliche Bildung die Natur, den Zugriff des Menschen auf sie, sein Wirtschaften in ihr und mit ihr, als einen Weg zur Gotteserkenntnis anerkennt. Nach *Bonaventura* ist sowohl in den »mechanischen Wissenschaften« als auch in den »freien Künsten« »das Licht von Gott herabgestiegen«.[7] Damit erhalten auch Handwerk, handwerkliches Wissen und seine Vermittlung einen höheren Stellenwert als nach antiker Einschätzung.
Die Schule der Christenheit wird so zu einer Schule der Exegese, der Lehrer zum Exegeten, d. h. zum sinngebenden Deuter der Hl. Schrift, des überlieferten (antiken und christlichen) Wissensgutes und der handwerklichen Bewältigung des Lebens.[8] Daraus resultiert auch die Leistung des christlichen Lehrers in der Spätantike, die darin besteht, daß er durch Weitergabe und Verkündigung der christlichen Lehre die römischen Verfolger der Christen ebenso überwinden konnte wie die germanischen Eroberer Roms. Die spezifische Leistung des frühmittelalterlichen Lehrers aber ist in der Vereinigung antiken und christlichen Denkens zu einer eigenen Kultur zu sehen. Aus dem neuen Wissen heraus treten bald Bischöfe und Priester, Kleriker und Mönche als Gelehrte und Lehrer, als Diener von Mächtigen und ab und zu selbst als Mächtige ins Licht der Geschichte.[9]
Die Entwicklung dieser neuen mittelalterlichen Kultur ging aber eben nicht kontinu-

ierlich, harmonisch vonstatten, sondern ist das Ergebnis lang andauernder und immer wieder von neuem aufflackernder geistiger Auseinandersetzung mit Antike und Christentum. *Michael Seidlmayer* hat dies so formuliert[10]: Das »Besondere und Einmalige [des Mittelalters] liegt beschlossen in den beiden bestimmenden Mächten Christentum und Antike, d. h. in jenen beiden Elementen, die den germanisch-romanischen Völkern, den Trägern des mittelalterlichen Geschehens, als ihre Formkräfte vorgegeben wurden, mehr noch: die ihnen als die von ihnen zu bewältigende Aufgabe gestellt worden sind.« Und an anderer Stelle stellt *Seidlmayer* fest[11], »daß das Abendland mit der Antike nie fertiggeworden ist, daß es sie nie wirklich bewältigen und in sich aufsaugen konnte, aber auch, daß es sie nicht auszuscheiden vermag, weil es sie nicht entbehren kann.«

Genau dies gilt auch für das mittelalterliche Schulwesen und seine Lehrer, wie es sich in den Kloster-, Dom- und Stiftsschulen sowie in den Universitäten auf unterschiedlichem Niveau manifestierte. Weniger berührt von diesen geistigen Auseinandersetzungen wurden Lehrer und Schüler der Pfarr-, Stadt- und Ratsschulen sowie der privaten und öffentlichen deutschen Schulen, die zumindest anfangs nur die elementaren Kenntnisse des Lesens, Schreibens und Rechnens vermittelten.

Das mittelalterliche Schulwesen

Versuchen wir, das mittelalterliche Schulwesen wenigstens umrißhaft nachzuzeichnen, wobei die Rolle des Lehrers im Mittelpunkt des Interesses stehen soll.

Der Grundstein für die Entfaltung der mittelalterlichen Schule wurde Ende des 8. Jhs. gelegt, als die Kirche und auch der fränkische König darauf drängten, den Bildungsstand der Priester in Kloster-, Dom- und Stiftsschulen zu verbessern, bald darauf aber auch die Forderung nach eigenen Pfarrschulen für das gläubige Volk erhoben wurde. Wichtige Impulse gingen auch von den Palastschulen an den Königshöfen aus, wenngleich diese eher den Charakter von Akademien hatten.

Auf der unter dem Vorsitz *Karls d. Gr.* tagenden Synode von Aachen 789 wurde festgelegt: »Es sollen Leseschulen für Knaben geschaffen werden. Die Priester sollen dafür sorgen, daß der Unterricht in Psalmen, im Schreiben, im Gesang, in der Kalenderkenntnis und in der Grammatik in allen Klöstern und Bistümern verbessert wird, ebenso die der heiligen Texte. Denn oft will jemand recht zu Gott beten, aber weil die Texte nicht fehlerfrei sind, betet er unzulänglich.«[12] *Alkuin* (um 730–804), Lehrer und Ratgeber *Karls,* forderte im Auftrag *Karls* die Eltern auf, »ihre Söhne in die Schule zu schicken, entweder in die Klöster oder zu den Pfarrern, damit sie den rechten katholischen Glauben und das Gebet des Herrn richtig erlernen.«[13] Und Bischof *Arn von Salzburg* verfügt in der Institutio Pastoralis aus dem 8. Jh.: »Jeder Bischof soll in seiner Stadt eine Schule errichten und einen weisen Lehrer bestellen, der nach der Überlieferung der Römer zu unterrichten vermag.«[14] Diese drei Zitate kennzeichnen die mittelalterliche Schule, genau: die frühmittelalterliche, bereits ganz wesentlich und lassen auch die Aufgaben ihrer Lehrer erkennen.

Die Klosterschulen

Die Aufnahme in die Klosterschule erfolgte mit sieben oder acht Jahren. Auf der Elementarstufe lernte man dort anhand des Psalters bis zum 10. Lebensjahr lesen, schreiben, Latein sprechen, Gesang, den Festkalender und den Glauben (mit den Hauptsünden, den Werken der Barmherzigkeit und der Beichte). In den folgenden Jahren wurden die Septem artes liberales mit Quadrivium (Arithmetik, Geometrie, Astronomie, Musik) und Trivium (Grammatik, Rhetorik, Dialektik) gelehrt, wobei das Trivium eindeutig Vorrang hatte und wiederum die Grammatik an erster Stelle stand. Mit dem Aufkommen der Scholastik mußte sie diesen Rang dann an die Dialektik als Grundlage der Philosophie und der wissenschaftlichen Bildung ganz allgemein abgeben. Der Unterricht entwickelte sich meist aus der Lektüre. Neben *Äsop, Cato, Avian* und *Tullius moralis* traten heidnische und christliche Schriftsteller der Antike, die historisch, mythologisch und geographisch erläutert wurden.[15]

An diese Allgemeinbildung sollte sich das theologische Fachstudium anschließen, das in die Bibel, die Kirchenväter, das kirchliche Recht, in Predigt und Liturgie einzuführen hatte. Die Mönchsorden richteten dafür in Hauptklöstern ein eigenes Ordensstudium ein. Außerdem sollte jede Kathedralkirche einen Theologen für den Unterricht zur Verfügung stellen.[16]

Die Schüler der Klosterschulen konnten sich mit 15 Jahren für das Mönchtum entscheiden, mit 18 die Gelübde ablegen und sich dann bis zum 24. Lebensjahr auf die Priesterweihe vorbereiten. Das Capitulare *Karls d. Gr.* über die Prüfung der Geistlichen forderte von diesen Kenntnisse in Lesen, Singen, etwas Latein, die Fähigkeit, die Feste zu berechnen und einen Gedächtnisvorrat an Gebeten, Gesängen und liturgischen Formeln.[17] Damit wird auch angesprochen, was die Lehrer den angehenden Geistlichen zu vermitteln hatten.

Allmählich jedoch entwickelten sich die Klöster mit ihren Schulen zu hervorragenden Pflanzstätten geistiger Kultur, so in Fulda, St. Gallen, Hirsau, Weißenburg, auf der Reichenau und anderswo. Von der Elementarstufe einmal abgesehen, haben die Klosterschulen bis zu ihrem späteren allmählichen Niedergang für das Mittelalter Modellcharakter. Ihre Lehrer waren es vor allem, die zum ersten Mal in der Geschichte der Erziehung die Person als Einheit in ihrem ganzen Wesen zu erfassen und zu formen versuchten. Schon der Psalter als einziger Lehrstoff auf der Elementarstufe mußte von den Schülern gelesen, geschrieben und auswendig gelernt werden, um so nicht nur Grundtechniken kennenzulernen, sondern auch vom Geist der heiligen Texte durchdrungen zu werden. Das Leben in der klösterlichen Gemeinschaft bildete für Lehrer wie Schüler den einzigen Vermittlungsrahmen. Dieser bezog sich aber im Falle des Schülers, hier wohl besser: des Zöglings, auf die gesamte Person.[18] *E. Durkheim* sieht in dieser Form der Erziehung ein qualitativ neues Moment gegenüber der Antike, das nach seiner Ausbildung im Frühmittelalter im gesamten mittelalterlichen Schulwesen bewahrt und später – allerdings in säkularisierter Form – weiter existieren wird. Im Gegensatz zu griechischen und römischen Schulen, in denen von verschiedenen Meistern ein spezielles Wissen übermittelt

wurde, zielt diese Art von Erziehung auf eine allgemeine Disposition, auf den Habitus. Der Mensch soll sich nicht nur bestimmte Kenntnisse aneignen, sondern in seinem ganzen Wesen zu einem Christen erzogen werden. Der Lehrer soll nicht nur Wissensvermittler, sondern christlicher Erzieher sein.[19]
In dieses Bild einer ganzheitlichen, christlichen Erziehung in den mittelalterlichen Schulen fügt sich harmonisch ein, daß die Lehrer in Kloster-, Dom-, Stifts- und meist auch Pfarrschulen in der Regel selbst Geistliche waren, wenngleich auch Privatlehrer nachgewiesen werden können.[20] Die Leitung der Schule wurde vom Abt oder dem Bischof einem Scholastikus übertragen. Dieser wiederum suchte sich meist einen geeigneten Magister (einen Meister, einen Lehrer), der für den eigentlichen Unterricht und die Erziehung der Schüler verantwortlich war. Er durfte je nach Schülerzahl einen oder mehrere Gehilfen, die Locati, beschäftigen. Meist stand ihm auch noch ein Kantor als Singmeister zur Seite. Der Magister taucht später in den Quellen auch als »Rector puerorum« auf. An größeren Schulen hatte dieser Rektor unterhalb des Scholastikus und über – dann meist mehreren - Magistern im Schulbetrieb aber auch bereits eine leitende Funktion inne. Die Hilfslehrer werden im späteren Mittelalter auch Scholaren genannt.
In dieser Ordnung des Schulwesens, die vor allem die Lateinschulen, die höheren Schulen, kennzeichnete, wird das hierarchische Denken des Mittelalters sichtbar. Dieses Ordo-Denken zeigt sich auch, wenn nach der standesmäßigen Einordnung, nach fremder Wertschätzung und nach der Selbsteinschätzung des mittelalterlichen Lehrers gefragt wird. Von *Christus,* dem Lehrer schlechthin einmal abgesehen, setzten im frühen Mittelalter die lateinischen Kirchenlehrer *Ambrosius, Hieronymus, Augustinus* und *Gregor* der Große den Maßstab. Sie genossen zusammen mit den griechischen Kirchenvätern als die kenntnisreichsten und bedeutendsten Lehrer der frühchristlichen Tradition besondere Wertschätzung. Die frühchristlichen Bischöfe verstanden ihren Auftrag und ihre Aufgabe ganz allgemein als »educatio prolis« als Aufziehen und mütterliche Betreuung der von der Mutter Kirche geborenen Christen. Während die »educatio«, das Aufziehen, im Gegensatz zur »instructio«, der Unterweisung und zur »docentia«, der Belehrung, bis dahin immer als Aufgabe der Mutter und anderer Frauen angesehen wurde, wird die Erziehung mit der Institutionalisierung der Kirche als Aufgabe dieser Institution und ihrer Vertreter bzw. Beamten verstanden.[21] An dieser Entwicklung hat *Benedikt von Nursia* keinen geringen Anteil. Die Intention seiner Regel ›Wo Kloster, da Schule‹ ließe sich bereits im 8./9. Jh. erweitern zu dem Satz ›Wo Kirche, da Schule, wo Priester, da Lehrer.‹[22]

Dom- und Stiftsschulen

Der Bischof war es deshalb auch, der an einem Ort, an dem neben der Domschule im Laufe der Zeit mehrere Kloster-, Stifts- oder Pfarrschulen entstanden, für sich ein Schulprivileg bzw. die Oberhoheit über das Unterrichtswesen in Anspruch nahm. Zu diesem Zweck ernannte er einen gelehrten Domherrn zum Domscholaster oder im Falle einer Stiftsschule zum Scholasticus oder Magister scholarum, der wie wir aus den Quellen wissen – die Quellenlage ist hier für das Bistum Salzburg besonders günstig – anfangs auch noch selbst unterrichtet hat. Erst im späten Mittelalter, als dieses Amt bereits mit einer gewissen Würde versehen war und seine Inhaber deshalb meist hohe geistliche Würdenträger darstellten, Doctores des kirchlichen Rechts und meist zugleich Kanzler ihres Stifts, wurde ein Rector scholarum mit der eigentlichen Schulaufsicht betraut.

Als unter Erzbischof *Arn* (785–821) die Domschule von Salzburg einen ersten Höhepunkt erreichte, wurde das Domkapitel dazu verpflichtet, für sie aus seiner Mitte »einen erprobten Lehrer aufzustellen und zu erhalten,« eben einen Magister scholarum, auch Scholaster oder Scholasticus genannt. Er hatte vor allem darüber zu wachen und dafür zu sorgen, daß die Schüler sowohl in den Wissenschaften als auch in den kirchlichen Künsten unterwiesen wurden, »vorzüglich in der Musik und in der Buchillustration«.[23] Bis ins 11. Jh. wurde mit diesem Amt ein durch Bildung herausragendes Mitglied des Salzburger Domkapitels betraut.[24]

Wie sehr der Domscholaster unter der Aufsicht des Bischofs bzw. des Domkapitels stand, wird in Bamberg sichtbar, wo das Domkapitel seinen Scholastikus das Gehalt sperrte, weil er es gewagt hatte, sich ohne dessen Erlaubnis zwei Tage zu entfernen. Dieser kam jedoch der Bestrafung zuvor, indem er von sich aus auf seine Pfründe verzichtete.[25] Aus der Frühzeit des mittelalterlichen Schulwesens läßt sich aber auch das Gegenteil belegen, die besondere Förderung von Schulvorstehern. So gestattete 976 *Willigis,* der Erzbischof von Mainz dem Scholaster der ihm unterstellten Schule von Aschaffenburg zwei bis drei Jahre »ad studium« zu reisen.[26]

Die Lehrer an den Kathedralschulen

Es fällt auf, daß Belege solcher Art meist aus dem Umkreis der Kathedralschulen, weniger aus dem der Klosterschulen stammen. Dies könnte ein Zufall der Überlieferung sein, hat aber doch wohl tiefere Gründe, die in nicht unerheblichem Maße auch mit den dort tätigen Lehrern zu tun haben. So läßt sich nicht übersehen, daß vom 9./10. Jh. an die Dom- und Kathedralschulen die Klosterschulen allmählich in den Hintergrund drängen, bis sie im 11./12. Jh. im mittelalterlichen Bildungswesen zusammen mit den Kollegiats- oder Stiftsschulen endgültig die Führung übernahmen. Dies liegt zum einen an der besonderen Förderung dieser Schulen durch *Karl d. Gr.* und seine Nachfolger und zum anderen am Aufschwung der Städte in der 2. Hälfte des 12. Jhs. Renommierte Domschulen kennen wir im 11./12. Jh. u. a. von Lüttich, Bamberg, Würzburg, Magdeburg, Hildesheim, Freising, Bremen, Salzburg und anderswo.

Betrachtet man daraufhin die Entwicklung der Kloster- und Domschulen etwas genauer, so fällt auf, daß wirkliche Bedeutung unter ihnen nur jenen Schulen zukam, die durch einen oder mehrere hervorragende Lehrer auch einen hervorragenden Ruf genossen. Gleichzeitig muß aber festgehalten werden, daß diese Lehrer ihrem Kloster, so es sich um solche an Klosterschulen handelte, meist recht treu blieben – hier wird wohl etwas von der benediktinischen »stabilitas loci« spürbar –, anders bei den Dom- und Stiftsschulen, von denen die meisten im 10. Jh. entstanden sind und deren Zweck ursprünglich die Ausbildung des Nachwuchses an Chor- und Stiftsherren war, was adelige Herkunft voraussetzte. Ihre Lehrer kann man keineswegs als seßhaft bezeichnen. Genossen sie einen guten Ruf, so ließen sie sich durch entsprechende Angebote gerne und häufig von einem Ort zum anderen weglocken. So entstand unter den Kathedralschulen ein lebhafter Austausch von Lehrkräften, was dem einzelnen nicht selten neben Ruhm auch einen gewissen Reichtum einbrachte. Dieses Werben um die jeweils besten Lehrer mag nicht zuletzt mit dazu beigetragen haben, daß sich die Dom- und Kathedralschulen im 10./11. Jh. zu neuer Blüte emporschwangen, die Klosterschulen in ihrer Entwicklung dagegen eher stehen blieben und fortan das konservative Element der Kirche repräsentierten, obwohl sich beide bis dahin auf demselben – man muß wohl sagen niederen – Niveau befunden haben, und die Grammatik hier wie dort der beinahe ausschließliche Gegenstand des Unterrichts war.

Bruno Nieser[27] sieht in der Dominanz der Domschulen im 12. Jh. geradezu den Anfang des institutionalisierten Schulwesens überhaupt. Selbst wenn man dieser Sichtweise nicht ganz folgen möchte, muß doch eingeräumt werden, daß diese Schulen zumindest einen bedeutsamen Einschnitt in der Entwicklung des mittelalterlichen Schulwesens markieren, dies nicht zuletzt deshalb, weil sie bald daran gingen, den Schulbetrieb aufzuteilen in eine innere Schule für den eigenen Nachwuchs und eine äußere Schule für Laienbrüder, arme oder uneheliche Kinder, zum Kriegsdienst untaugliche Adelige, angehende Weltpriester, eigentlich für Bürger aller Schichten.[28]

Der Zustrom der Schüler zu diesen Schulen, an denen ganz zu Anfang noch der Bischof selbst unterrichtet hatte, war bald so groß, daß ihn auch der Magister nicht mehr alleine bewältigen konnte und sich von Gehilfen unterstützen lassen mußte. Ebenso standen dem Kantor oft mehrere Subcantores zur Seite.

Der Versuch der Domschulen, in der Scholastik den Schwerpunkt des Unterrichts von der Grammatik zur Dialektik hin zu verschieben, macht das Bemühen ihrer Lehrer deutlich, neben einer verständigen Lektüre der Hl. Schrift eine Vielzahl neuer Texte philosophischer und wissenschaftlicher Natur über die Probleme der Menschen, der Welt und Gott zu befragen.

Trotzdem entwickelten sich nicht alle Dom- und Kathedralschulen zu Universitäten weiter. Viele beschränkten sich von der zweiten Hälfte des 14. Jhs. an darauf, als eine Art berufliche Schulen für den Kirchendienst mit Unterricht in Kirchengesang und Latein zu dienen oder wurden als Vorbereitungsschulen für die Universitäten betrachtet. Ihren einstigen Rang machten ihnen jetzt diese streitig. Damit sank auch das Ansehen der an ihnen verbleibenden Lehrer.

Privatlehrer

Das hier kurz angesprochene Bildungsmonopol der Kirche und ihrer geistlichen Lehrer wurde hie und da durchbrochen von Privatschulen und Privatlehrern, die uns im 9. und 10. Jh. zuerst in Italien, dann aber auch diesseits der Alpen begegnen. Über sie hat in Ichenhausen 1982 *Otto Meyer* ausführlich referiert. Der Abdruck seines Vortrages findet sich in Band 1 der Schriftenreihe zum Bayerischen Schulmuseum[29], so daß hier nur noch einige besondere Aspekte des Privatlehrertums herausgegriffen werden sollen. Der Ursprung der Privatschulen in Deutschland ist möglicherweise eine Folge des allmählichen Verfalls der Pfarrschulen. Die Einrichtung solcher, von einem Geistlichen geführten Pfarrschulen war schon von *Karl d. Gr.* angeordnet worden, und noch das 4. Laterankonzil von 1215 bestimmte, daß alle Kirchen einen Lehrer mit dem unentgeltlichen Unterricht für arme Schüler beauftragen sollten. Gelehrt wurden Lesen, kirchliche Liturgie und Gesang. Auf diese Weise wurden vor allem Chorknaben und Ministranten herangezogen. Da nun nicht überall Geistliche vorhanden waren, die einen solchen Unterricht hätten übernehmen können, könnten hier – sozusagen in einer Art Lückenbüßerfunktion – die Anfänge des Wirkens von Privatlehrern gesehen werden. Zunächst werden sie wohl nur Elementarunterricht erteilt haben, z. B. in Grammatik, um ihre Schüler auf den Besuch einer Kloster-, Dom- oder Stiftsschule vorzubereiten. Ein Schulwechsel war also gewissermaßen ›vorprogrammiert‹. Dies führte nach *Otto Meyer* dazu, daß er bald mehrfach vorgenommen wurde und die Schüler dabei auch in fremde Länder führte. *Meyer*[30]: »Das differenzierte Bildungsprogramm der Septem artes liberales überforderte eine einzige Lehrkraft, wie sie auch in Kloster- und Domschulen in der Regel nur zur Verfügung stand; sie mußte Interessenschwerpunkte bilden. Eine Allgemeinbildung bot also nur eine Mehrzahl von Lehrstätten« und – wie zu ergänzen wäre, eine Mehrzahl von Lehrern. Das gerade bot den Privatlehrern die Chance, auch auf höherem Niveau zu unterrichten.

Die Quellen berichten nur spärlich von den Privatlehrern, doch kennen wir immerhin einige mit Namen: *Benno von Osnabrück, Lanfranc, Otto von Bamberg* und noch einige mehr. Die Tätigkeit als Privatlehrer übten diese Männer oft nur in ihrer Jugend aus, während wir ihnen im späteren Leben zuweilen in hohen und höchsten Kirchenämtern wiederbegegnen.

Sowohl die Lehrer als die Schüler dieser Art von Schulen waren nach Herkunft und Zielen kein integraler Bestandteil der Kirche mehr, auch wenn sie sich vielleicht formal dem Klerus unterordneten. Ihre Autonomiebestrebungen und deren Auswirkung auf ihr Selbstverständnis veränderte Gegenstand und Methode ihres Unterrichts.

Der deutsche Schulmeister

Mit dem Aufstreben der Städte im deutschen Mittelalter machten diese sehr bald der Kirche das Schulmonopol streitig. Seit dem 13. Jh. entstanden in zunehmendem Maße Stadt- und Ratsschulen für gutsituierte bürgerliche Kreise. Daneben entwickelten sich städtische Elementarschulen, die im Gegensatz zur Lateinschule standen; die Deutsche Schule sowie zunftmäßig organisierte Schreib- und Rechenmeister, die seit dem 14. Jh. unterrichteten.
An dieser Stelle sei nur auf die große gesellschaftliche Bedeutung verwiesen, die der Tatsache zukam, daß der deutsche Schulmeister nicht mehr im Dienst der Kirche, sondern im Schutz der Stadt stand – wiederum ein Bruch mit der Tradition, ein Zeichen für Diskontinuität. Im Spätmittelalter trat er zum lateinischen Schulmeister in Konkurrenz, indem er versuchte, diesem mit allen Mitteln Schüler abspenstig zu machen. Dabei kam es nicht selten zu Übergriffen und Vermengungen im Lehrstoff. Eine solche Entwicklung führte dazu, daß der Lehrerstand, wenn man von einem solchen bereits sprechen kann, schon zu Beginn der Neuzeit deutlich in zwei Gruppen gespalten war, in die Gruppe der humanistisch, akademisch gebildeten Lehrer der Lateinschulen und die der deutschen Schulmeister, deren Tätigkeit als Gewerbe verstanden und anfänglich sogar als Nebentätigkeit ausgeübt wurde. Es ist bekannt, wie sehr solche Unterschiede bis in die Gegenwart weiter wirkten und wirken. Die unterschiedliche Bewertung verschiedener Lehrämter, der Kampf um die akademische Ausbildung des Volksschullehrers bis hin zum heute lokal wieder aufflackernden »Kampf ums Kind« – um es einmal schlagwortartig zu formulieren – wurden zu brisanten bildungspolitischen Themen und Problemen, die bis heute noch nicht alle ausdiskutiert und gelöst sind. Sollten wir etwa hier einer neuen Kontinuität auf der Spur sein?

Anmerkungen

1 *Illmer* (1971)
2 Vgl. ebenda, S. 150.
3 Siehe Anm. 14; »secundum traditionem Romanorum« wird zuweilen auch mit »nach Überlieferung der römischen Kirche« übersetzt.
4 Vgl. *Max Liedtke.* In: *Kriss-Rettenbeck / Liedtke,* Hrsg. (1983), S. 76.
5 Vgl. Bayerisches Schulmuseum (1985), S. 56.
6 Z. B. auf einem Sarkophag in S. Ambrogio, Mailand; abgebildet u. a. in: Bayerisches Schulmuseum (1985), S. 56.
7 Vgl. Bayerisches Schulmuseum (1985), S. 76.
8 Vgl. *Lenz Kriss-Rettenbeck:* Die Schule der Christen. Ein Weg zur Verkündigung des ewigen Heils. In: Bayerisches Schulmuseum (1985), S. 54f.
9 Vgl. ebenda, S. 57.

[10] *Seidlmayer* (1967), S. 10. Vgl. auch *Le Goff* (1970), S. 539ff.
[11] *Seidlmayer* (1967), S. 17.
[12] Allgemeiner Mahnerlaß (Admonitio Generalis) Karls d. Gr. vom 23. März 789, MGH Leges II/1, S. 59f.; deutsche Übersetzung u. a. in: *Engelbrecht* (1982), S. 379, Bayerisches Schulmuseum (1985), S. 61.
[13] *Wattenbach-Levison* (Hrsg.): Deutschlands Geschichtsquellen im Mittelalter. Vorzeit und Karolinger, 2. Weimar 1953, S. 227.
[14] Pastoralinstruktion (Instructio Pastoralis) Erzbischof Arns von Salzburg 798, MGH Leges III. Conc. II, 1, S. 199 (Nr. 22, can. 8); deutsche Übersetzung u. a. in: *Engelbrecht* (1982), S. 380, Bayerisches Schulmuseum (1985), S. 61.
[15] Vgl. u. a. *Nieser* (1978), S. 36; *Rosenfeld-Rosenfeld* (1978), S. 157f.; *Engelbrecht* (1982), S. 98ff.
[16] Beschluß des 3. Laterankonzils von 1179, MG Paedagogica, XLI, S. 153.
[17] Vgl. *Rosenfeld-Rosenfeld* (1978), S. 156.
[18] Vgl. *Nieser* (1978), S. 36; *Illmer* (1971), S. 150.
[19] *Durkheim* (1969), S. 35ff.
[20] Zu den Privatlehrern im Mittelalter vgl. *Meyer* (1983).
[21] Vgl. Bayerisches Schulmuseum (1985), S. 71.
[22] Vgl. *Nieser* (1978), S. 36f.; *Illmer* (1971), S. 150f.
[23] Siehe Anm. 14; vgl. *Engelbrecht* (1982), S. 103.
[24] Vgl. *Engelbrecht* (1982), S. 103.
[25] Vgl. *Reicke* (1979), S. 17.
[26] Vgl. ebenda.
[27] *Nieser* (1978), S. 37.
[28] Vgl. *Meyer* (1983), S. 119; *Rosenfeld-Rosenfeld* (1978), S. 156
[29] Siehe Anm. 20.
[30] *Meyer* (1983), S. 132.

Literaturverzeichnis

Bayerisches Schulmuseum Ichenhausen. Bildführer (1985), hrsg. vom Bayerischen Nationalmuseum München. München

Borst, A. (1979): Lebensformen im Mittelalter. Frankfurt/M.–Berlin–Wien

Borst, O. (1983): Alltagsleben im Mittelalter. Frankfurt/M.

Durkheim, E. (1969): L'évolution pédagogique en France. Paris

Engelbrecht, H. (1982): Geschichte des österreichischen Bildungswesens. Erziehung und Unterricht auf dem Boden Österreichs. Bd. 1: Von den Anfängen bis in die Zeit des Humanismus. Wien

Goetz, H.-W. (1986): Leben im Mittelalter vom 7. bis zum 13. Jh. München 2. Aufl.

Le Goff, J. (1970): Kultur des europäischen Mittelalters. München

Hesselbach, E. (1920): Die deutsche Schule im Mittelalter. In: Zeitschrift für Geschichte der Erziehung und des Unterrichts 10, S. 1–56

Illmer, D. (1971): Formen der Erziehung und Wissenvermittlung im Frühen Mittelalter. München

Limmer, R. (1928): Bildungszustände und Bildungsidee des 13. Jhs. München

Meyer, O. (1983): Der Privatlehrer des frühen Mittelalters. Eine Studie zur Entstehung und kulturellen Wirkung des Lehrerberufs. In: Kriss-Rettenbeck, L.-Liedtke, M., Hrsg. (1983): Schulgeschichte im Zusammenhang der Kulturentwicklung. Bad Heilbrunn, S. 119–142

Nieser, B. (1978): Die Entstehung der Schule als Institution bürgerlicher Gesellschaft. Vergleichende Untersuchung der institutionalisierten Erziehung und Bildung am Beispiel Frankreichs. Frankfurt/M.–New York

Reicke, E. (1979): Magister und Scholaren. Illustrierte Geschichte des Unterrichtswesens. Düsseldorf–Köln 3. Aufl., fotomechanischer Nachdruck der 1. Aufl. von 1901

Rosenfeld, H.-F. und H. Rosenfeld (1978): Deutsche Kultur im Spätmittelalter. Wiesbaden

Schmitz, K. (1980): Geschichte der Schule. Stuttgart

Seidlmayer, M. (1967): Das Mittelalter. Umrisse und Ergebnisse des Zeitalters. Unser Erbe. Göttingen 2. Aufl.

Thalhofer, F. X. (1928): Unterricht und Bildung im Mittelalter. München

Rudolf Endres

Ausbildung und gesellschaftliche Stellung der Schreib- und Rechenmeister in den fränkischen Reichsstädten

Schulwesen im Spätmittelalter

Das IV. Laterankonzil von 1215 bestimmte, daß an jeder Kirche die Errichtung einer Schule erfolgen sollte, soweit sie imstande war, einen Geistlichen für den Unterricht abzustellen. Diese Bestimmung führte dazu, daß bald in den größeren und mittleren Städten Pfarrschulen entstanden. Solche Pfarr- oder Lateinschulen gab es im Spätmittelalter in Franken in allen Reichs- und Amtsstädten, ja sogar in den meisten kleineren Marktflecken, wo sie sich zwar ebenfalls als Lateinschulen bezeichneten, in Wirklichkeit aber sog. »vermengte« oder »gemaine« Schulen waren.[1]
In den fränkischen Reichsstädten Nürnberg[2], Rothenburg[3], Schweinfurt[4], Windsheim[5] und Weißenburg[6] war mit der Erringung der Reichsstandschaft im 13./14. Jahrhundert dem Rat auch ein Teil der Kirchengewalt zugefallen und damit unter anderem die Aufsicht über das Erziehungs- und Bildungswesen. Mit den »Ratsschulen«, wie die Pfarr- und Lateinschulen jetzt auch bezeichnet wurden, war das Bildungsmonopol der Kirche durchbrochen, und der Schulmeister wurde schon vor der Reformation zu einem Bediensteten der Reichsstadt. Er wurde – meist im Einvernehmen mit dem Pfarrherrn – vom Rat bestellt, nachdem er durch eine Probelektion seine Befähigung nachgewiesen hatte, und er hatte vor dem Rat den Amtseid abzulegen. Selbst der Lehrbetrieb, also Unterrichtsstoff und Unterrichtsmethoden, sowie die Disziplin der Lehrer und Schüler standen unter der obrigkeitlichen Aufsicht des Rates, der auch eigenmächtig Schulordnungen erließ, wie etwa in Nürnberg 1485[7] und um 1510.[8] Dabei blieb die ursprüngliche Funktion der Lateinschule als Hilfsanstalt der Kirche weiter bestehen, waren Unterricht und Schulbetrieb weiterhin auf die Mitwirkung beim Kirchendienst ausgerichtet.
Mit dem schnellen Aufstieg der Städte im späten Mittelalter und mit dem Aufblühen von Handel und Gewerbe wuchs auch der Bedarf an mehr schreib- und lesekundigen Leuten, die zudem noch rechnen konnten. Diesen Bedarf aber konnten die Pfarrschulen nicht befriedigen, die außerdem kaum praxisnahe Fähigkeiten vermittelten. So entstanden in allen größeren Städten Frankens, voran in den Reichsstädten, im Spätmittelalter neben den Latein- oder Pfarrschulen auch noch die sog. »Teutschen Schulen«, die in der Literatur entweder als unbedeutende »Winkelschulen« verächtlich abgetan oder völlig übersehen werden.
Diese teutschen Schulen für Buben und Mädchen waren vor der Reformation völlig unabhängig von der Kirche. Sie konnten entweder städtische Einrichtungen sein, wie etwa in Nördlingen oder in Windsheim, oder private Unternehmungen, wie in

Rothenburg und vor allem in Nürnberg, wo die Privatinstitution der Schreib- und Rechenmeister am besten ausgebildet war. Der teutsche Schulmeister war in der Reichsstadt ein freier Geschäftsunternehmer, der aus der von ihm unterhaltenen Schule samt dem dazugehörigen Internatsbetrieb für auswärtige Schüler einen möglichst hohen Gewinn zu erzielen trachtete. Allerdings unterstanden auch die privaten teutschen Schulen und Schulmeister der Oberaufsicht des Rates, so daß sich minderwertige Winkelschulen nicht lange halten konnten.[9]

Die Anfänge der teutschen Schreib- und Rechenmeister

Seit etwa 1400 sind in den fränkischen Reichsstädten teutsche Schulmeister nachweisbar. In Rothenburg erlaubte der Rat 1403 dem Stadtschreiber Heinrich, eine teutsche Schule einzurichten, die sogleich von 18 Schülern besucht wurde und der bestehenden Lateinschule bald ernsthafte Konkurrenz machte. Daraufhin beschwerte sich der Lateinschulmeister beim Rat und erbot sich sogar, ebenfalls deutsch schreiben und lesen lehren zu wollen.[10] In Nürnberg erwarb als erster teutscher Schulmeister, auch »Stuhlmeister« oder »Guldenmeister« genannt, im Jahre 1384 ein *Conradus Vital* das Bürgerrecht.[11] Im Laufe des 15. Jahrhunderts ließen sich dann eine Vielzahl von Schreib- und Rechenmeistern in Nürnberg nieder, denen vielfach sogar das Bürgeraufnahmegeld vom Rat erlassen wurde, was zeigt, daß in der Reichsstadt ein hoher Bedarf an teutschen Schreib- und Rechenmeistern herrschte. Diese bezeichneten sich seit dem ausgehenden 15. Jahrhundert auch gerne als »Modisten«, also als Kunstschreiber.[12]

Zahl der teutschen Schulen

Im Laufe des 16. Jahrhunderts erreichte der Stand der teutschen Schulhalter offensichtlich in Nürnberg seine höchste Blüte, was aufgrund der Bevölkerungszahl und der wirtschaftlichen Leistung der Reichsstadt verständlich ist.[13] Immer mehr Schreib- und Rechenmeister ließen sich in der Reichsstadt nieder, was schließlich zu einer Überbesetzung und zu heftigen Konkurrenzkämpfen zwischen den Schullehrern führte. Daraufhin reduzierte der Rat die Zahl der teutschen Schulen von 75 auf 48 und ließ alle andern Schulen schließen.[14] Seit 1613 wurden die Lehrer auch in dem Ämterbüchlein erfaßt und festgehalten, wobei genau zwischen den »Rechenmeistern« und den »gemeinen Schulhaltern« unterschieden wurde, womit deutlich wird, daß letztere keinen Rechenunterricht erteilen durften.
In Schweinfurt, wo die Anfänge der teutschen Schulen infolge der Quellenlage nicht genau angegeben werden können, gab es nach 1560 in der Regel 4 teutsche Schulmei-

ster nebeneinander, die vom Rat mit 10 fl jährlich besoldet wurden. Darüberhinaus vergab der Rat aber noch weitere Unterrichtskonzessionen, was zeigt, daß in der Reichsstadt Bedarf an Lehrern über die 4 teutschen Schulen hinaus bestand.[15] In Windsheim besuchten um 1700 neben der Lateinschule fast 200 Kinder die städtische teutsche Schreib- und Rechenschule, so daß schließlich eine »teutsche Nebenschul« eingerichtet werden mußte, um der hohen Nachfrage genügen zu können.[16] In Rothenburg gab es neben der traditionsreichen Lateinschule stets mehrere teutsche Schulmeister, deren bekanntester *Valentin Ickelsamer* war.[17]
In Nürnberg, wo 1613 die Zahl der teutschen Schulen auf 48 festgeschrieben worden war, sank infolge der Wirren des 30jährigen Krieges die Zahl der Schulen auf 13, um bis zum Ende des Krieges wieder auf 28 anzusteigen. Die erste gedruckte Nürnberger Schulordnung von 1665 bestimmte dann: »Erstlich sollen hinfüro mehr nicht, denn 20 Rechenmeister und 8 Schulhalter, ohne der Verwittibten Schuhlen in allhiesiger Stadt seyn und mittler Zeit, bis die Schuhlen uf jetztgedachte Zahl durch absterben verringert werden; anstatt zweier abgestorbenen, nur einer eintretten, als dann über die Anzahl der 20 Rechenmeister, und 8 Schulhalter, kein Schul aufgerichtet werden.«[18]
Diese Stellenbeschränkung wurde bis 1710 eingehalten und danach die Zahl der Schulen auf 18 reduziert, da inzwischen 3 Armenschulen gestiftet worden waren. Beim Übergang Nürnbergs an Bayern 1806 erteilten nur noch 17 teutsche Schreib- und Rechenmeister Unterricht, darunter 3 Witwen.[19]

Die Schulordnungen

Für die Ausbildung und den Werdegang der Schreib- und Rechenmeister sind wir für die Frühneuzeit vor allem für Nürnberg durch die handschriftliche Ordnung der Modisten von 1614 sowie durch die gedruckte »Ordnung der Nürnberger Schreib- und Rechenschulen« von 1665 und die »Verneuerte Verordnung« von 1715 genau informiert.[20] Für die kleineren Reichsstädte in Franken war Nürnberg, wie in vielen anderen Bereichen, das große Vorbild.
Bis in das 16. Jahrhundert hinein galten Schreiben und Rechnen als freie Gewerbe und die Schreib- und Rechenmeister als private Geschäftsunternehmer, weshalb auch keine obrigkeitlichen Schulordnungen erlassen wurden. Mit der Einführung der Reformation jedoch wurde den teutschen Schulen auch die Katechese übertragen, und folgerichtig wurden die Anstalten der Schreib- und Rechenmeister entweder zu städtisch-öffentlichen Institutionen, wie in Schweinfurt und Windsheim, oder, wie in Nürnberg, der strengeren Aufsicht des Rates unterstellt. So bestimmte der Nürnberger Ratsverlaß vom 1. November 1613 nicht nur die Zahl der Schreib- und Rechenmeister, sondern auch, daß 3 oder 4 der vornehmsten Schreib- und Rechenmeister zu Vorgehern bestimmt werden sollen, welche die bestehenden Schulen visitieren und die künftigen Lehrer examinieren sollten.[21] Gegen Ende des 17. Jahrhunderts wurde

dann die Visitation und Inspektion auch der teutschen Schulen Geistlichen übertragen[22], doch unterstanden die Schreib- und Rechenmeister weiterhin einer eigenen Ratsdeputation und nicht dem Rugsamt, wie die übrigen Handwerker in Nürnberg.[23]

Die Ausbildung und der Werdegang der Schreib- und Rechenmeister

Bis zum Erlaß der Schulordnungen, in denen die Ausbildung genau vorgeschrieben wurde, konnte jeder, der glaubte, die entsprechenden Fähigkeiten und Kenntnisse zu besitzen, eine Schule eröffnen. Deshalb finden sich eine große Anzahl von Schreib- und Rechenmeistern, die zuvor ein Handwerk ausgeübt hatten. Viele Lehrer übten ihren Beruf auch nur als zusätzlichen Nebenerwerb aus, wie *Hans Kranz*, der hauptamtlich Trompeter war.[24] Der berühmte Rechenmeister *Hans Jöppel* besaß zusätzlich einen Kramladen, der ihm später zur Altersversorgung diente.[25] Viele Schreib- und Rechenmeister hatten zuvor die Lateinschule oder gar die Universität besucht, waren also gescheiterte oder abgebrochene Studenten und brachten besondere Vorkenntnisse mit. Wer Schreib- und Rechenmeister werden wollte und sich die nötigen Grundkenntnisse angeeignet hatte, ganz gleich wo und wie, ging als Lehrjunge oder »Diener« bei einem tüchtigen Schreib- und Rechenmeister in die Lehre. In der Regel begann die Lehrzeit mit 15 oder 16 Jahren und dauerte 6 Jahre, bei Lehrerssöhnen 4 Jahre. Selbstverständlich mußten die Schul-Diener auch Lehrgeld und Einschreibgebühren entrichten, wie im Handwerk.[26]

Das Lehrer-Examen

Wenn die 6 Lehrjahre vorbei waren, dann mußte der Diener sich dem Schreib- und Rechen-Examen unterziehen. Die Vorgeher mußten sich zuvor nach »des Examinandi Mores und Wissenschaften« erkundigen, und nur wenn sein Lehr-Meister ihm einen guten Leumund bestätigte, wurde er zum Examen zugelassen. Wer sich nicht dem Examen stellte, durfte nicht mehr Schule halten.[27] Aus einem Meister-Brief oder Zeugnis für den Rechenmeister *Joachim Schramm* ist ersichtlich, in welchen Fächern er geprüft worden ist, denn es heißt, daß er »wohlgeschickt seye, die liebe Jugendt in Gottesforcht, lesen, schreiben, rechnen, visiren und andern hierzugehörigen Künsten zu instituiren und zu unterweisen«.[28] Die Prüfung im Visieren war also für die Rechenmeister noch üblich, denn das Amt des Visierers oder des Ausbilders von Visierern wurde von den Rechenmeistern gerne als Nebenamt ausgeübt. Unter Visieren verstand man in Nürnberg die Berechnung des Inhaltes von Fässern oder Eimern, was die Grundlage für die Besteuerung von Wein und Bier bildete, für das sog. Ungeld.

Bevor der Schreib- und Rechen-Diener zum Examen zugelassen wurde, mußte er zu Hause einen langen Katalog von Fragen schriftlich beantworten, die ihm der älteste Vorgeher übergeben hatte. Die Fragen bezogen sich zunächst auf die Orthographie, und dann mußte das Wissen bezüglich der verschiedenen Arten der »teutschen Schrifften« unter Beweis gestellt werden. Am schwierigsten waren die Fragen aus der Rechenkunst, die sich mit Brüchen, der Regula detri, den arithmetischen und geometrischen Reihen und mit Algebra befaßten.[29]
Wenn die schriftliche Erledigung der Haus-Aufgaben die Vorgeher zufrieden gestellt hatte, dann wurde der Kandidat in das Haus des ältesten Vorgehers geladen, wo ihn nun die Vorgeher mündlich prüften. Nur wer Rechenmeister werden wollte, mußte sich auch in der Rechenkunst der Prüfung unterziehen, nicht aber der nur »gemeine Schulhalter«. Das Examen erstreckte sich über 6 Stunden, worüber genau Protokoll geführt werden mußte. Der Protokollant wurde vom Rat bestellt, damit Unterschleif nicht möglich war.[30]
Die Kosten für das Examen waren nicht gering. So mußte der Kandidat jedem Vorgeher und Prüfer einen Dukaten verehren. Außerdem mußte er den Prüfern am Abend nach der Prüfung ein opulentes Abendessen spendieren, dessen Kosten sich bis zu 50 fl belaufen konnten, so daß der Rat einschränkend eingreifen mußte, vor allem nachdem er in Erfahrung brachte, daß ein Kandidat bis zu 200 fl hatte aufwenden müssen.[31]

Die Wartezeit

Mit der langen Lehrzeit und dem schweren Examen war aber die Hoffnung des Schulkandidaten auf die Eröffnung einer eigenen Schreib- und Rechenschule noch keineswegs erfüllt. Denn die Anzahl der vorgeschriebenen Schulen durfte nicht überschritten werden, weshalb der junge Schulmeister warten mußte, bis eine Schulstelle frei wurde. Für die Expektanzzeit trat dann der junge Schreib- und Rechenmeister als Substitut oder Gehilfe in eine andere Schule ein oder er übernahm für eine Schulmeisterswitwe die Führung der Anstalt, was oftmals über mehrere Jahre sich erstrecken konnte.[32] Für viele Jung-Lehrer eröffneten sich nicht einmal diese Möglichkeiten, weshalb sie dann versuchen mußten, ihre erlernten Schreib- und Rechenkünste anderwärts an den Mann zu bringen. Viele junge Schreib- und Rechenmeister nahmen deshalb Stellen als Buchhalter bei einem Kaufmann oder als Schreiber an, und andere überbrückten die Wartezeit als Kantor oder Regimentsschreiber.[33]

Das Tafelschreiben

Wenn endlich eine Schulstelle frei geworden war, dann mußte der Kandidat im Hause des ältesten Vorgehers seine Tafel schreiben bzw. auf einem großen Bogen Papier durch das Aufzeichnen einiger Frakturbuchstaben beweisen, daß er seine Tafel schreiben konnte, was er dann zu Hause erledigen durfte. Bei der Tafel, die gewissermaßen sein Firmenschild war, wurde genau unterschieden zwischen einem »gemeinen Schulhalter« und einem Rechenmeister. Der »gemeine Schulhalter« durfte nur eine »mit Dinten auff Pergamen geschriebene Tafel« aufhängen[34], während der Rechenmeister auf den schwarzen Grund einer Tafel mit goldenen Buchstaben seinen Wahlspruch schrieb. Beliebt war der Wahlspruch »Patientia vincit omnia«. Nach Anfertigung der Tafel wurde diese vom Vorgeher beschaut, wofür 1 fl 30 kr. zu bezahlen waren. Fand die Tafel die Zustimmung des Vorgehers, dann wurde der Kandidat endgültig in die Reihe der Schreib- und Rechenmeister aufgenommen, indem er bei der Ratsdeputation angemeldet und von dieser auf die Schulordnung vereidigt wurde.[35]

Die Eröffnung der teutschen Schule

Wie grundsätzlich im Gewerbe, so mußten auch die Schreib- und Rechenmeister vor Eröffnung ihrer Schule das Bürgerrecht erwerben. Da mit der teutschen Schule in der Regel auch ein Internat verbunden war, mußte der Schulmeister auch eine Frau vorweisen. So verbot der Nürnberger Rat dem *Achatius Troschel* die Eröffnung einer Schreib- und Rechenschule »biß er sich verheiratet haben wird«.[36] Selbstverständlich erleichterte sich der Start, wie generell im Handwerk, wenn der junge Schreib- und Rechenmeister die Witwe eines teutschen Schulmeisters heiratete, für die er dann die Schule problemlos fortführen konnte. Die andere Möglichkeit war, daß sich ein Rechenmeister sein Geschäft erheiratete, indem er die Tochter eines verstorbenen Schulmeisters ehelichte.[37]

All die genannten Vorbedingungen zur Eröffnung einer Schreib- und Rechenschule, nämlich die Lehrzeit, das Examen, das Bürgerrecht und die Verheiratung wurden von der reichsstädtischen Obrigkeit und von den Vorgehern im »Schulmeister-Handwerk« streng überwacht. Auch kümmerte sich der Rat um den Leumund der angehenden Schulmeister. So verwehrte der Nürnberger Rat dem Schreib- und Rechenmeister *Gabriel Götsch* und seiner Verlobten *Eva Regina,* der Witwe des Schulhalters *Johann Georg Karl* die Weiterführung der Schule »wegen seines ergerlichen Lebens und Wandels«.[38]

Die Schule, die Schüler und die Lehrtätigkeit

Im 15. und 16. Jahrhundert eröffneten die Schreib- und Rechenmeister in bevorzugter Geschäftslage ihre Schule, meist an geräumigen Plätzen und in der Nähe von Wirtshäusern. Dies führte dazu, daß sich in manchen Vierteln die Schulen drängten, weshalb die Nürnberger Schulordnung von 1665 bestimmte, daß mindestens 2 Gassen zwischen den einzelnen Schulen liegen müßte.[39] Bei Verstößen griff die Obrigkeit ein und ließ die Schule verlegen. War aber einmal ein bestimmter Platz für die Schule angewiesen, so durfte sie nicht mehr verändert werden, selbst wenn in einem anderen Viertel günstig ein Haus erworben oder gemietet werden konnte.
Die Schüler wurden in der Regel mit 6 Jahren in der Schule aufgenommen, manchmal waren sie auch älter, weil sie zuvor die Lateinschule besucht oder schon eine Lehre absolviert hatten, ehe sie bei einem Rechenmeister ihre Kenntnisse zu vervollkommnen suchten. So nahm beispielsweise *Johann Sebastian Troschel* einen 14jährigen Kaufmannssohn aus Reichenbach »in Haus und Information«.[40] Mädchen waren bis ins 16. Jahrhundert bei den Schreib- und Rechenmeistern in der Minderzahl, doch danach wuchs ihre Zahl so sehr an, daß sie zeitweise sogar das Übergewicht über die Knaben erhielten.
Da das Einkommen und der Verdienst des Rechenmeisters in erster Linie von der Zahl seiner Schüler abhing, mußte er alles daran setzen, um möglichst viele zu gewinnen, was oftmals zu Lasten der Qualität des Unterrichts ging. 1681 sah sich der Nürnberger Rat sogar veranlaßt, eine fleißigere Visitation und »restriction der Lehrkinder auff eine gewisse anzahl« anzuordnen, weil es »in denen teutschen Schulen wegen Menge der Kinder und übler Unterrichtung derselben ziemlich unrichtig dahergehe«.[41]
Die Zahl der Kinder schwankte sehr stark, da die Eltern ihre Kinder problemlos aus der Schule nehmen und einem anderen Lehrer übergeben konnten. Doch das Minimum für eine Schule waren wohl 40 Schüler, um von dem Schulgeld einigermaßen leben zu können. Im Jahre 1701 unterrichteten in Nürnberg die 20 Rechenmeister und 8 gemeinen Schulhalter zusammen 824 Knaben und 987 Mädchen, was einem Durchschnitt von 65 Schülerinnen und Schülern pro Schule entspricht.[42] Die meisten Schüler stammten, wie die Schülerlisten zeigen, aus dem Handwerker- und Kaufmannsstand, wo die praktischen Kenntnisse der Schreib- und Rechenmeister unverzichtbar waren. Die Kinder der armen Schichten besuchten nun die neuen kostenlosen Armenschulen.
Die Schulen der berühmten Rechenmeister aber wurden im ausgehenden Mittelalter und selbst noch im 17. und 18. Jahrhundert von Schülern aus ganz Europa besucht, unter denen sogar junge Adelige waren. So zählte der Rechenmeister *Karl Michel,* der 1688 verstarb, zu seinen Schülern Adelige und Bürgersöhne aus Breslau, Erfurt, Frankfurt, Schaffhausen, Preßburg und sogar aus Genf und Grenoble, die bei ihm Deutsch, Rechnen und Buchhaltung lernten. Der berühmte Rechenmeister *Johann Baptista Fabritius* gar hatte Schüler aus England, Frankreich, Italien, den Niederlanden, der Schweiz und Savoyen.[43]

Was die Lehrtätigkeit oder Methoden anbelangt, so wurde im Laufe der Frühneuzeit die früher ängstlich gehütete Geheimhaltung bei den einzelnen Schreib- und Rechenmeistern aufgegeben. Das Lesen wurde mit einer Art Fibel gelernt, und gleichzeitig erfolgte auch die Unterweisung im Schreiben, wobei als Schreibvorlagen neben Bibelstellen auch kleine Erzählungen und vor allem Briefe aus dem täglichen Leben dienten.[44] Auch der Rechenunterricht war praxisbezogen, wie das erste gedruckte Rechenbuch des Nürnberger Schreib- und Rechenmeisters *Ulrich Wagner* von 1482[45] und das »Große Nürnbergische Rechenbuch« des Altdorfer Rechenmeisters *Johann Kleemann* von 1715 zeigen und belegen. Großer Wert wurde auf den Moral- und Religionsunterricht gelegt, worauf insbesondere die Herren Vorgeher und vor allem die Visitatoren oder Diakone ein strenges Auge hatten.[46]

Die soziale Stellung der Schreib- und Rechenmeister

Die Herkunft

Überwiegend stammten die Schreib- und Rechenmeister aus dem Handwerkerstand, dem sie auch zugezählt wurden. So war der Vater des berühmten Modisten *Johann Neudörfer* ein wohlhabender Kürschner[47], und der Rechenmeister *Peter Probst* war der Sohn eines Beutlers.[48] Viele Schreib- und Rechenmeister hatten zuvor lange Jahre ein Handwerk ausgeübt oder waren in einem Kaufmannskontor tätig gewesen, ehe sie dann im Alter eine eigene Schule eröffneten. Nach der Reformation entstammten viele Schreib- und Rechenmeister den Pfarrhäusern, wie etwa *Caspar Schleupner* oder *Johann Baptista Fabritius.*[49] Auch der Pfarrer *Erhard Bezzel* aus Feucht ließ seinen 7. Sohn als Schulmeister ausbilden, da er ihm ein Studium nicht mehr bezahlen konnte. Viele Lateinschüler oder Studenten brachen ihr Studium ab und wurden teutsche Schulmeister. »Weiln er seine Studien aus Armuth nit fortsetzen können, hab er dieselben verlassen und sich auf das Rechnen und Schreiben gelegt«, heißt es in vielen Schulmeister-Biographien.[50] Auch belegen die zahlreichen in lateinischer Sprache abgefaßten Gesuche um Eröffnung einer teutschen Schule diesen Weg. Oftmals diente in späterer Zeit die Tätigkeit als teutscher Schulmeister auch nur für fertige Theologen zur Überbrückung bis zur Erlangung einer Präzeptoren- oder Pfarrstelle. Immer häufiger aber übernahmen die eigenen Söhne vom Vater die teutsche Schule, so daß ganze Rechenmeistergeschlechter entstanden, wie z. B. die *Neudörfer* oder die *Düstau*, die nicht weniger als 6 Generationen von Schulmeistern stellten.

Der soziale Rang der Schreib- und Rechenmeister

In den Reichsstädten bestimmten vorrangig die Berufszugehörigkeit und die Vermögenslage den sozialen Status des einzelnen Bürgers. Neben Vermögenslage und Berufszugehörigkeit waren weitere »soziale Lagemerkmale« die Wohnlage oder Stadtteilzugehörigkeit, denn es gab zwischen den einzelnen Stadtteilen ein deutliches soziales Gefälle. Ein viertes wesentliches Element des sozialen Status war, zumindest in den kleineren Reichsstädten, die Bildung.[51] Während die Nürnberger Kleiderordnungen, in denen der einzelne Bürger je nach Herkunft, Vermögen, Beruf und Amt genau in seinen sozialen Rang eingewiesen wurde, auf die Bildung als Kriterium für den sozialen Status keine Rücksicht nahmen, schrieben in der Reichsstadt Rothenburg die sog. »Rangordnungen« von 1654 bzw. 1695 folgende soziale Hierarchie vor[52]:

1. Rang: die 5 Alten Bürgermeister, die Superintendenten, die Ratskonsulenten, die Doctores Medicinae, alle in der Stadt befindlichen Adeligen, Offiziere und alle graduierten Personen;
2. Rang: die 4 Außenamtsverwalter, die Stadtdiakone, der Rektor des Gymnasiums, die Mitglieder des Äußeren Rates »so von der Literatur sind«, die Landgeistlichen, der Konrektor und die übrigen Lehrer der Lateinschule und schließlich auch die Mitglieder des Äußeren Rates, »so nicht von der Literatur sind«;
3. Rang: die übrige Bürgerschaft, die Handwerker, Kaufleute und Bauern.

In Schweinfurt legte eine Rangordnung aus dem Jahre 1760 folgende soziale Hierarchie fest[53]:

1. Klasse: der Innere Rat, der Reichsvogt, der Syndicus, die Träger akademischer Titel, die Geistlichen sowie der Rektor und der Konrektor der Lateinschule;
2. Klasse: die Mitglieder des Äußeren Rates, die übrigen Lehrer der Lateinschule, die Handelsleute;
3. Klasse: einfache Handwerker, Künstler, Teutsche Schulmeister;
4. Klasse: Bauern und Häcker.

Neben politischer Macht und Vermögen war also in Schweinfurt und Rothenburg auch die Bildung zu einem wichtigen Kriterium für den Rang in der reichsstädtischen Gesellschaft geworden. Allerdings galt dies nur für die humanistische Bildung und für die Lateinschul-Lehrer, nicht aber für die teutschen Schreib- und Rechenmeister, deren sozialer Rang im allgemeinen dem eines Handwerkers entsprach. So gelang es in Schweinfurt zwar dem Lateinschul-Magister *Paulus Rosa* bis zum Bürgermeister aufzusteigen, doch erscheinen niemals teutsche Schulmeister in Ratspositionen.[54] Auch in Nürnberg wurden die teutschen Schulmeister in der Regel wie Handwerker behandelt und war vom »Schulmeister-Handwerk« die Rede, auch wenn sie seit 1614 unter einer eigenen Rats-Deputation standen und nicht dem für das Handwerk zuständigen Rugsamt unterstellt waren. Auch durften die Nürnberger Schreib- und Rechenmeister nach Art der freien Künstler seit 1715 ihre Vorgeher frei wählen[55], und

seit 1756 durften sie sich das Prädikat »ehrbahr, wohlgelehrt und kunstberühmt« zulegen[56], nachdem sie bisher nur »ehrbar und kunstberühmt« gewesen waren und im 15./16. Jahrhundert gar nur »achtbar« oder »ehrbar und fürnehm«.
Das Standesbewußtsein und die Selbsteinschätzung der Schreib- und Rechenmeister aber lag viel höher und entsprach nur in einigen Fällen ihrer wirtschaftlichen Stellung und dem sozialen Rang in der Reichsstadt. Aufgrund ihres Könnens und ihrer speziellen Fähigkeiten hielten sich viele für unersetzlich und den einfachen Bürgern und Handwerkern weit überlegen.[57] So lud der Modist *Philipp Stoß,* der sich als »Römischer Kayserlicher Majestät Commissarius und Diener« bezeichnete, zu seiner Hochzeit sogar den patrizischen Rat ein, was dieser aber vornehm ignorierte.
Der Nürnberger Rat verstand es aber sehr geschickt, immer wieder besonders herausragende Schreib- und Rechenmeister mit Ehrenämtern auszuzeichnen und gesellschaftlich herauszuheben. So wurden mehrere Rechenmeister und Modisten in das Genannten-Kollegium des Größeren Rates berufen, so daß sie auf der Herrentrinkstube verkehren und mit den Patriziern gesellschaftlichen Umgang pflegen durften, wie etwa die Familien *Neudörfer* und *Brechtel.* Mit dem Genannten-Status[58] waren noch weitere Vergünstigungen und Privilegien verbunden, womit gerne die verdienten »Vorgeher im Schulmeister-Handwerk« ausgezeichnet wurden, wie *Caspar Schmid* (1540), *Sebastian Kurtz* (1643), *Ulrich Hofmann* (1649) oder *Johann Tischberger* (1762).[59] Andere Schreib- und Rechenmeister wurden zu Gassenhauptleuten bestellt oder mit sonstigen kommunalen Aufgaben betraut. So waren viele Rechenmeister bis in das 17. Jahrhundert hinein noch als reichsstädtische Visierer oder Eichmeister tätig, andere waren Waagmeister, und in der Familie *Düstau* war das Organistenamt in der St. Jakobskirche erblich. Verschiedene Schreib- und Rechenmeister waren auch als Anwälte und Notare, als Testamentsvollstrecker und als Vormund tätig und gesucht, was ebenfalls ihre öffentliche Wertschätzung belegt.[60]
Doch mehrheitlich nahmen die teutschen Schreib- und Rechenmeister in den Reichsstädten den sozialen Rang von Handwerkern ein, wenn sie selbst auch als Ausübende eines freien Gewerbes sich über dem Handwerk stehend einschätzten. Nur einigen wenigen herausragenden Persönlichkeiten und Modisten-Familien wurde durch die Berufung in den Genannten-Status vom Nürnberger Rat ein höherer sozialer Rang verliehen, was an der allgemeinen Einschätzung aber nicht viel änderte.
Die herausragende soziale Stellung der beiden Modisten-Familien *Neudörfer* und *Brechtel* wurde endgültig festgelegt, als die Frau *Stephan Brechtels* beim Fünfergericht angezeigt wurde, da sie bei einer Hochzeit eine goldene Kette getragen hatte, was nach den reichstädtischen Kleiderordnungen den Frauen von Handwerken und »nur Schreibern« verboten war. Doch der Rat entschied, daß die beiden Modisten-Familien als Angehörige des Größeren Rates dem mittleren Stande zugeordnet seien, also über dem Handwerk stünden, dem ansonsten die teutschen Schulmeister zugeordnet wurden.[61]

Hervorragende Schreib- und Rechenmeister

Unter den Nürnberger Rechenmeistern, in der langen Reihe der »Nurenbergenses docti numerandi artifices«, ist *Ulrich Wagner*[62] von besonderer Bedeutung, denn von ihm stammt das erste gedruckte Deutsche Rechenbuch. Erstmals erscheint er 1486, als er in verschiedene Streitigkeiten mit seinen Kollegen und Konkurrenten *Jobst Jöppel* und *Ruprecht Kolberger* verwickelt war. Seine angesehene und gut besuchte Schreib- und Rechenschule ermöglichte ihm bald danach den Kauf eines Hauses in der Spitalgasse. Sein Sohn *Hans* übernahm nach dem Tod des Vaters (um 1490) die teutsche Schule, konnte sich aber bald gegen die Konkurrenz des *Johann Neudörfer* nicht behaupten und mußte das Haus in der Spitalgasse verkaufen. Von *Ulrich Wagner* stammt wahrscheinlich auch das 1483 in Bamberg gedruckte sog. »Bamberger Rechenbuch«, das einen sehr guten Einblick in die Themen und Methoden der damaligen Rechenkunst vermittelt.

Ein vielbeschäftigter Schulmann, tüchtiger Rechenmeister und erfahrener Techniker auf dem speziellen Gebiet des Baus von Waagen war *Ruprecht Kolberger*[63], der von 1470 bis 1505 in Nürnberg wirkte. Er hatte maßgeblichen Anteil an der Errichtung einer Schnellwaage bei der Nürnberger Stadtwaage und später am Bau einer eigenen Heuwaage. Bei dem Rechenmeister *Kolberger* erfuhr auch der junge Patrizier *Christoph Fürer* seine Ausbildung in der Mathematik, nachdem er zuvor die Lateinschule beim Heilig-Geist-Spital besucht hatte. Kurze Zeit bekleidete *Kolberger* auch das Amt des städtischen Visierers und besaß das Recht, jungen Leuten Unterricht im Visieren zu erteilen. Auch war er an der Fertigung des berühmten »Weltapfels« beteiligt, des ersten Globus, den *Martin Behaim* im Auftrag und auf Kosten der Stadt Nürnberg 1491/92 schuf.

Als Schreib- und Rechenmeister war in Nürnberg auch der berühmte Kartograph, Kompaß- und Uhrenmacher *Erhard Etzlaub* (ca. 1460–1532) tätig.[64] Er gilt als der Autor der ältesten Straßenkarte des christlichen Europa, einer Romweg-Karte. *Etzlaub*, der in Erfurt geboren wurde, zog früh nach Nürnberg, weil hier die Herstellung wissenschaftlicher Instrumente in hoher Blüte stand. Er fertigte in Nürnberg zunächst kleine Taschensonnenuhren, die mit einem Kompaß kombiniert waren, die sog. Horologiae. *Etzlaub*, der auch als Astronom und Arzt sich bezeichnete, bekleidete seit 1511 das wichtige Ehrenamt eines Hauptmanns im Viertel am Salzmarkt und war später als reichsstädtischer Kartograph in der Landpflegestube tätig. 1492 erschien sein erstes selbständiges kartographisches Werk, eine Karte der Umgebung Nürnbergs. Da zum Heiligen Jahr 1500 mit einem starken Pilgerverkehr zu rechnen war, erstellte *Etzlaub* eine Romweg-Karte, die ein bisher unbekanntes Kartenbild von Mitteleuropa zeigte, von Jütland bis Neapel und von Paris bis Krakau. Deutlich wurde darauf auch die zentrale Lage Nürnbergs im Fernstraßensystem Mitteleuropas herausgearbeitet.

Johann Neudörfer[65] wurde 1497 als Sohn eines angesehenen Kürschners geboren. Bei dem Schreib- und Rechenmeister *Caspar Schmid* und bei dem Kanzleischreiber *Paulus Vischer* wurde er zum »Modisten« und bei *Erhard Etzlaub* zum »Arithmeti-

cus« ausgebildet. Bereits mit 22 Jahren gab er das erste Schreibmusterbuch nördlich der Alpen heraus, das »Fundament ..., seinen schülern zu unterweysung gemacht«. Seine Muster und seine Methoden blieben bis in das 18. Jahrhundert vorbildlich. *Neudörfers* besondere Bedeutung aber lag in seiner kunstpädagogischen Wirksamkeit, denn sein Einfluß auf die Ausbildung und Festlegung der deutschen Gebrauchs-, Kanzlei- und Zierschrift, die durch seine zahlreichen Schüler im gesamten deutschen Sprachraum verbreitet wurde, ist ohne Vergleich. Er legte die Basis für die Frakturschrift, die bis in das 19. Jahrhundert vorherrschende Drucktype war, und er schuf die wichtigsten Vorgaben für die Entwicklung einer deutschen Kurrentschrift.
Neudörfer erwarb bereits 1524 in bester Wohnlage unter der Burg ein eigenes Haus. Er war der Schwager des großen Druckers und Verlegers *Petrejus.*[66] Ab 1531 war er Genannter des Größeren Rats, seit 1543 führte er den Titel eines kaiserlichen Pfalzgrafen und besaß ein eigenes Wappen, das wenige Jahre später sogar noch verbessert wurde. Die zahlreichen Bildnismedaillen und Portraits belegen das hohe Selbstbewußtsein des Schreib- und Rechenmeisters, der in regem freundschaftlichen Umgang mit den ersten Männern der Reichsstadt stand, mit dem Ratsschreiber *Christoph Scheurl,* mit *Hieronymus Baumgartner,* mit *Caspar Nützel* und *Albrecht Dürer.* Der Nürnberger Rat zog ihn mehrfach als sprachen- und schriftenkundigen Dolmetscher beim Briefwechsel mit dem Ausland hinzu, wie er ihn auch als Vermittler in der Reichsstadt und mit Auswärtigen in Anspruch nahm. Im Auftrag des Rates nahm der kundige Rechenmeister die Überprüfung der Rechnungen der Fränkischen Stände nach Beendigung des 2. Markgräflerkrieges vor, und er selbst scheint seine besonderen mathematischen Fähigkeiten als Häusermakler und Spekulant mit Bergwerksanteilen, mit Kuxen, gewinnbringend genutzt zu haben. Als er 1563 starb, ließ ihn der Rat von Kanzleiboten in roten Röcken feierlich zu Grabe tragen.

Mathematici et Malefici

Die Schreib- und Rechenmeister galten mehrheitlich aber, zumindest im 15. und 16. Jahrhundert, als ein unruhiger, anmaßender, scharfzüngiger und »mutwilliger« Berufsstand, dessen Mitglieder manche Turmhaft absitzen mußten.[67] So war der teutsche Schreiber *Martin Glaser* so »ungeschickt« und »rumorisch«, daß der Rat ihm riet, als Feldschreiber nach Ungarn zu gehen. »Rumor und ausgegossene böse Reden« brachten ihm schließlich einen »guten ruck«, also die Folter, ein.[68] Denn der »ungestüme« Mann war ein wüster Trunkenbold und ein leidenschaftlicher Büchsenschütze, der »in voller bezechter weiß« Weib und Kinder mißhandelte und nächtens zum Fenster hinausschoß.[69]
Peter Feuerstein und seine beiden Söhne, die ebenfalls Schulmeister waren, hatten »allerley böse schwürige Reden« gegen Bäcker, Metzger und Bierbrauer gebraucht, was sie in den Turm brachte.[70] Auffallend häufig aber blieb es nicht bei verbalen Injurien, sondern die Schulmeister wurden handgreiflich. Aber auch Unterschlagun-

gen und Diebstahl kamen vor, wie etwa bei *Ruprecht Kolberger*[71], und dem Rechenmeister und Kornschreiber *Adam Strobel* warf der Rat Urkundenfälschungen und Veruntreuungen vor.[72] Der Rechenmeister *Michel Pogner* stach sogar 1584 auf dem Heimweg von einem Zechgelage in Fürth den Buchhalter *Hiob Finkenkeller* nieder und hatte es sicher nur guter Fürsprache zu verdanken – er wohnte im Hause *Neudörfers* –, daß er nur aus der Stadt ausgewiesen wurde.[73] Zwei besonders verkommene Rechenmeister vergriffen sich sogar an ihren Schülerinnen und wurden deshalb hingerichtet.[74]
Nach dem 30jährigen Krieg wurden die Schreib- und Rechenmeister offensichtlich ruhiger und gesitteter, denn wir hören nur noch selten von Verfehlungen. Häufiger jedoch führen die Totenbücher des 18. Jahrhunderts verstorbene Schreib- und Rechenmeister und ihre Angehörigen als »unbesungene Leichen« auf, d. h. sie wurden als Armenleichen ohne Gesang bestattet. Viele Schulmeister und vor allem Witwen wurden auf Gemeindekosten ohne die üblichen Ehren zu Grabe getragen.[75] Hinter diesen dürftigen Mitteilungen verbergen sich viel menschliches Elend, harte Not und erbarmenswerte Schicksale. Nicht zuletzt diese Seite gehört zu den Schreib- und Rechenmeistern des ausgehenden Mittelalters und der Frühen Neuzeit in den fränkischen Reichsstädten.

Anmerkungen

[1] Siehe *Endres* (1982), (1983a), (1983b).
[2] *Endres* (1984).
[3] *Bauer* (1979), S. 13–23.
[4] *Mahr* (1978), S. 49–62.
[5] *Estermann* (1967), S. 55.
[6] *Mödl* (1977), S. 6–11.
[7] Abgedruckt in: *Heerwagen* (1860), Beilage I.
[8] Staatsarchiv Nürnberg (StAN) Rep. 90 S I L 205 Nr. 20; vgl. *Endres* (1984), S. 112.
[9] *Jäger* (1925), S. 190ff.; *Endres* (1983a), S. 190ff.; *Endres* (1983b), S. 148ff.
[10] *Bauer* (1979), S. 23f.
[11] StAN Rep. 52b Nr. 303 fol. 102.
[12] Vgl. *Endres* (1983a), S. 191.
[13] *Endres* (1970).
[14] StAN Ratsverlässe vom 11. Juni 1612 und vom 19. November 1613.
[15] *Mahr* (1978), S. 100.
[16] *Estermann* (1967), S. 55.
[17] *Frank* (1973), S. 25 (Literatur).
[18] Abgedruckt in: *W. K. Schultheiß* (1853): Geschichte der Schulen in Nürnberg, Heft 2. Nürnberg, S. 105–107.
[19] *Heisinger* (1927), S. 5.
[20] *Schultheiß* (1853), S. 53; S. 105–107; S. 113–126.
[21] StAN Ratsverlässe vom 1. November 1613.

[22] So wurde die Schulordnung von 1698 von dem Prediger *Tobias Winkler* überarbeitet und revidiert, wobei sich der Geistliche mehrmals auf *August Hermann Francke* berief, *Schultheiß* (1853), S. 113–120.
[23] *Endres* (1977).
[24] StAN Rep. 52b Nr. 334.
[25] *Jäger* (1925), S. 154f.
[26] Schulordnung von 1665, in: *Schultheiß* (1853), S. 105–107; *Heisinger* (1927), S. 9f.
[27] StAN Ratsverlaß vom 23. Oktober 1633.
[28] *Schultheiß* (1853), S. 95.
[29] Siehe »Fragen für diejenigen, so sich in das Schreib- und Rechen-Examen begeben wollen«, abgedruckt in: *Schultheiß* (1853), S. 107–112.
[30] *Heisinger* (1927), S. 11f.
[31] StAN Ratsverlaß vom 9. November 1644. Vergleichsweise beliefen sich beim Bauhandwerk die Gesamtkosten bei Meisterprüfungen nachweislich ebenfalls bis zu 200 fl., vgl. *Fleischmann* (1985), S. 207–215.
[32] StAN Ratsverlaß vom 26. April 1729.
[33] *Endres* (1983a), S. 194f.
[34] StAN Ratsverlaß vom 13. Juni 1648.
[35] *Schultheiß* (1853), S. 32f.; *Heisinger* (1927), S. 14.
[36] StAN Ratsverlaß vom 17. April 1662.
[37] Siehe die Beispiele bei *Heisinger* (1927), S. 15f.
[38] StAN Ratsverlaß vom 6. September 1665.
[39] *Schultheiß* (1853), S. 106.
[40] StAN Ratsverlaß vom 21. Oktober 1713.
[41] StAN Ratsverlaß vom 16. Dezember 1681.
[42] *Heisinger* (1927), S. 24.
[43] Ebenda, S. 25.
[44] Siehe die Beispiele, die bei *Schultheiß* (1853), S. 35–37 abgedruckt sind.
[45] *Brunner* (1937).
[46] Vgl. die Schulordnung von 1698, abgedruckt in: *Schultheiß* (1853), S. 113–120.
[47] *Neudörffer* (1828), S. 67f.
[48] Stadtarchiv Nürnberg Cons. 74 fol. 52.
[49] *Nopitsch* (1802), S. 90.
[50] StAN Rep. 52b Nr. 310 fol. 40.
[51] Vgl. *Endres* (1982), S. 37–72.
[52] *Endres* (1987).
[53] Ebenda.
[54] *Mahr* (1978), S. 193–196.
[55] Instruction für die Vorgehere bey denen Schreib- und Rechen-Meistern, abgedruckt in: *Schultheiß* (1853), S. 131–138.
[56] StAN Ratsverlaß vom 27. August 1756.
[57] *Heisinger* (1927), S. 65–68.
[58] Vgl. *Schall* (1971).
[59] *Roth* (1802); *Heisinger* (1927), S. 59.
[60] *Heisinger* (1927), S. 69–71.
[61] StAN Ratsverlaß vom 12. Januar 1571; siehe auch *Lehner* (1984), S. 62f.
[62] *Brunner* (1937); von Imhoff (1984), S. 67f.
[63] *Gümbel* (1926).

[64] *Krüger* (1942); *Krüger* (1958); *Schnelbögl* (1959); *Schnelbögl* (1966), S. 6f.; *von Imhoff* (1984), S. 76f.
[65] *Doede* (1957); *von Imhoff* (1984), S. 119f.
[66] *von Imhoff* (1984), S. 117f.
[67] Vgl. *Jäger* (1925), S. 170–175 und S. 92–96.
[68] StAN Ratsverlässe vom 15. und 18. Juli 1589.
[69] StAN Ratsverlaß vom 1. März 1576.
[70] StAN Rep. 52b Nr. 200 fol. 287a.
[71] *Gümbel* (1926), S. 285–290.
[72] StAN Ratsverlässe vom 17. und 18. Januar 1577.
[73] Stadtarchiv Nürnberg, Handschriften der Merkelschen Sammlung 568 2o: Chronica der Stadt Nürnberg von Anfanb biss 1647; StAN Ratsverlaß vom 24. März 1585.
[74] StAN Ratsverlässe vom 3. September 1515 und 3. April 1537; Rep. 52b Nr. 221 fol. 112a.
[75] Siehe *Heisinger* (1927), S. 82f.

Literaturverzeichnis

Bauer, W. (1979): Die Reichsstadt Rothenburg und ihre Lateinschule. Rothenburg

Brunner, H. (1937): Das erste deutsche Rechenbuch. In: Mitteilungen des Vereins für Geschichte der Stadt Nürnberg, Bd. 35, S. 1–16

Doede, W. (1957): Schön schreiben, eine Kunst. Johann Neudörfer und und seine Schule im 16. und 17. Jahrhundert (= Bibliothek des Germanischen National-Museums Nürnberg, Bd. 6). München

Endres, R. (1970): Zur Einwohnerzahl und Bevölkerungsstruktur Nürnbergs im 15./16. Jahrhundert. In: Mitteilungen des Vereins für Geschichte der Stadt Nürnberg, Bd. 57, S. 242–272

Endres, R. (1977): Zur Lage der Nürnberger Handwerkerschaft zur Zeit des Hans Sachs. In: Jahrbuch für fränkische Landesforschung, Bd. 37, S. 107–124

Endres, R. (1982): Sozial- und Bildungsstrukturen fränkischer Reichsstädte im Spätmittelalter und in der Frühen Neuzeit. In: Literatur in der Stadt, hrsg. von H. Brunner. Göppingen, S. 37–72

Endres, R. (1983a): Das Schulwesen in Franken im ausgehenden Mittelalter. In: Studien zum städtischen Bildungswesen des späten Mittelalters und der frühen Neuzeit, hrsg. von B. Moeller, H. Patze und K. Stackmann. Göttingen, S. 173–214

Endres, R. (1983b): Die Bedeutung des lateinischen und deutschen Schulwesens für die Entwicklung der fränkischen Reichsstädte des Spätmittelalters und der frühen Neuzeit. In: L. Kriss-Rettenbeck und M. Liedtke (Hrsg.) Bad Heilbrunn, Schulgeschichte im Zusammenhang der Kulturentwicklung (= Schriftenreihe zum Bayerischen Schulmuseum Ichenhausen, Bd. 1), S. 144–162

Endres, R. (1984): Nürnberger Bildungswesen zur Zeit der Reformation. In: Mitteilungen des Vereins für Geschichte der Stadt Nürnberg, Bd. 71, S. 109–129

Endres, R. (1985): Stadt und Umland im bildungspolitischen Bereich im Spätmittelalter und in der Frühneuzeit, in: Städtisches Um- und Hinterland in vorindustrieller Zeit, hrsg. von H. K. Schulze. Köln–Wien

Endres, R. (1987): Die soziale Problematik in den kleineren Reichsstädten. In: Reichsstädte in Franken, hrsg. von R. A. Müller. München, S. 70–83

Estermann, A. (1967): Bad Windsheim. Bad Windsheim
Fleischmann, P. (1985): Das Bauhandwerk in Nürnberg vom 14. bis zum 18. Jahrhundert (= Nürnberger Werkstücke 38). Nürnberg
Frank, H. J. (1973): Geschichte des Deutschunterrichts. Von den Anfängen bis 1945. München
Gümbel, A. (1926): Der Rechenmeister und Wagmacher Ruprecht Kolberger in Nürnberg 1470–1505. In: Mitteilungen des Vereins für Geschichte der Stadt Nürnberg, Bd. 26, S. 279–308
Heerwagen, H. W. (1860): Zur Geschichte der Nürnberger Gelehrtenschulen in dem Zeitraum von 1485 bis 1526. Nürnberg
Heisinger, H. (1927): Die Schreib- und Rechenmeister des 17. und 18. Jahrhunderts. Nürnberg
Imhoff, Chr. von (Hrsg.) (1984): Berühmte Nürnberger aus neun Jahrhunderten. Nürnberg
Jäger, A. (1925): Stellung und Tätigkeit der Schreib- und Rechenmeister (Modisten) in Nürnberg im ausgehenden Mittelalter und zur Zeit der Renaissance. Diss. Erlangen (mschr.)
Krüger, H. (1942): Die Romweg-Karte Erhard Etzlaubs in ihren verschiedenen Ausgaben seit 1492. In: Petermanns Geographische Mitteilungen. Bd. 11/12, S. 285–296
Krüger, H. (1958): Des Nürnberger Meisters Erhard Etzlaub älteste Straßenkarten von Deutschland 1500/1501. In: Jahrbuch für fränkische Landesforschung, Bd. 18, S. 1–393
Lehner, J. (1984): Die Mode im alten Nürnberg (= Nürnberger Werkstücke 36). Nürnberg
Mahr, M. (1978), Bildungs- und Sozialstruktur der Reichsstadt Schweinfurt. Würzburg
Mödl, G. (1977): schola nostra uuizzinburgi. Weißenburg
Neudörffer, J. (1828): Nachrichten von den vornehmsten Künstlern und Werkleuten so innerhalb hundert Jahren in Nürnberg gelebt haben 1546 nebst der Fortsetzung von Andreas Gulden 1660, Nürnberg
Nopitsch, Chr. C. (1802), Nürnbergisches Gelehrtenlexikon. Nürnberg
Roth, J. F. (1802): Verzeichniß aller Genannten des größeren Raths. Nürnberg
Schall, K. (1971): Die Genannten in Nürnberg (= Nürnberger Werkstücke 6). Nürnberg
Schnelbögl, F. (1959): Erhard Etzlaubs Karten des Nürnberger Landgebiets 1516/19. In: Mitteilung des Vereins für Geschichte der Stadt Nürnberg, Bd. 49, S. 170–177
Schnelbögl, F. (1966): Dokumente zur Nürnberger Kartographie. Nürnberg
Schultheiß, W. K. (1853–1857): Geschichte der Schulen in Nürnberg. 5 Hefte. Nürnberg.

Alfred Fickel

Die Entwicklung des städtischen Lehrerstandes von den Anfängen bis zum Beginn des 19. Jahrhunderts, illustriert an den Schulverhältnissen in Mühldorf am Inn

Wer die Entwicklung des städtischen Lehrerstandes an einer in Altbayern gelegenen Stadt aufzeigen will und dabei versucht, möglichst früh zu beginnen, den belehrt ein Blick in den bayerischen Geschichtsatlas[1], daß die Zahl der Städte zwar nach 1200 rasant ansteigt, vor 1200 die Auswahl aber nicht sehr groß ist.[2] Außer den altbayerischen Bischofsstädten, die durch ihre Domschulen ohnehin anderen bildungsgeschichtlichen Gesetzen unterworfen waren, finden sich nur sechs weitere Städte: Laufen und Burghausen a. d. Salzach, München a. d. Isar, Neuburg und Kelheim a. d. Donau, sowie Mühldorf a. Inn. München, Burghausen, Neuburg und Kelheim kommen für eine erste Untersuchung ebenfalls nicht in Frage, denn als dauernde, beziehungsweise vorübergehende Residenzstädte waren sie bildungsgeschichtlich bevorzugt.

So bleiben also nur noch Laufen und Mühldorf übrig. Da im Gegensatz zu Laufen das Archiv in Mühldorf problemlos zu benützen ist[3] und auch im Münchner Hauptstaatsarchiv ein reicher, Mühldorf betreffender Urkundenbestand lagert, fällt die Entscheidung nicht schwer.

Nach gründlicher Auswertung des Münchner und Mühldorfer Materials[4] konnten den 30 Heldbelegen für Mühldorf[5] noch weitere 283 hinzugefügt werden.[6] Mehrfach wird dieses Mühldorf schon vor 1200 genannt. Manche Belege sind falsch, andere umstritten, oder es handelt sich um einen Lesefehler, indem man Mildorf, statt Wildorf gelesen.[7] Auf jeden Fall findet sich im Traditionskodex von St. Emmeram für die Jahre 994–996 eine Stelle, wo von einem Grundstück »in loco episcopali Mulidorf«, also beim bischöflichen Ort Mühldorf die Rede ist.[8]

Da schon in den Synoden des 9. und 10. Jahrhunderts und in den Konzilien des 12. und 13. Jahrhunderts den Pfarrherrn neben der Seelsorgspflicht auch die Verbreitung der Schulbildung an allen Kirchen anempfohlen wurde, ist bei der Entwicklung des Schulwesens, besonders in den Anfängen, immer auch die Entwicklung der Pfarreien in die Untersuchungen mit einzubeziehen. Ferner darf auch Auf- und Ausbau der städtischen Verwaltung nicht übersehen werden.

Während der Amtszeit des ersten Mühldorfer Pflegers *Chŏnradus*[9] wird 1201 auch schon der Mühldorfer Pfarrer genannt.[10] »Chunradus plebanus de Muldorf«, nennt er sich in der Regel in den Urkunden bis 1224.[11] Dieser Mühldorfer Pfarrer *Konrad* steht 1214 auch als Zeuge am Sterbebett seines Pflegers, des *Herren von Schneittsee* und Werfen, als dieser im Angesicht des Todes für sich und seine Vorfahren ein Gehöft als Seelgerät[12] an die Kirche von Mühldorf verbriefen läßt.[13] Damit war für die Mühldorfer Kirche ein erstes solides Fundament gelegt.[14] Solche Stiftungen waren für die

Entwicklung einer Pfarrei und für das in den Anfängen immer eng mit der Kirche verbundene Schulwesen von enormer Bedeutung. Fehlte mangels Schenkung die finanzielle Grundlage, so konnten Pfarrei wie Schule sich nie richtig entwickeln. Das gilt nicht nur für die Städte, sondern ebenso auch für Märkte und Dörfer.[15]
Die Mühldorfer Pfarrei hat sich gut entwickelt. 1230 ist bereits ein Magister *Ulschalcus* Pfarrherr in Mühldorf.[16] *Ulschalcus* hatte damals schon wahrscheinlich auf einer der zahlreichen »Hohen Schulen« studiert und war auf Grund seines Magistertitels wohl auch Jurist. Ein solcher Pfarrherr hatte sicher nicht nur das Seelenheil seiner Gläubigen im Auge, sondern wird sich auch, wohl zusammen mit einem Gehilfen[17] um die Bildung der ihm anvertrauten Pfarrkinder gekümmert haben. Dies um so mehr, als *Gregor IX.* im Jahre 1234 die Empfehlungen der Synoden und Konzilsbeschlüsse des 9. bis 13. Jahrhunderts bezüglich der schulischen Unterweisung zum gemein kirchlichen Gesetz erhoben und damit zur Rechtsgültigkeit im ganzen Abendland erklärt hat.[18]
Die schulische Unterweisung war in Mühldorf offensichtlich erfolgreich, denn immer mehr Leute, auch aus einfachem Stande, finden sich jetzt in den Urkunden als Zeugen[18a], gelegentlich schon mit Berufsbezeichnung. 1242 *Henricus Hospes,* ein Wirt oder Gastgeber[19], 1251 *Hermann* Praxator, also ein Brauer[20], 1278 *Christian* Pelefix, ein Kürschner[21], 1292 *Rudolfus,* wieder ein Wirt[22].
Zeugen waren in der Regel angesehene Persönlichkeiten, die in dieser Zeit oft auch bei der Rechtsfindung mitgewirkt haben. Auch die Geldgeschäfte wurden nun von Bürgern abgewickelt. So transferierten 1297 die Mühldorfer Bürger *Liebhart* und *Samson* der Jud, 200 Pfund Regensburger Pfennige zwischen dem Erzbischof von Salzburg und *Herzog Otto von Bayern.*[23]
Auch die städtische Verwaltung wurde in der 2. Hälfte des 13. Jahrhunderts in Mühldorf weiter ausgebaut. 1278 ist ein Land- und Vogtrichter[24], sowie ein Stadtrichter[25] zu belegen. 1281 ist ein Kastner nachweisbar.[26] Doch zu den großen Rechts- und Verwaltungsangelegenheiten wurden immer auch noch die Pfarrherren herangezogen. So wurden z. B. 1275 lange, tiefgreifende Streitigkeiten zwischen *Herzog Heinrich von Niederbayern* und dem Erzbischof von Salzburg durch ein Schiedsgericht beigelegt. Der Pfarrer von Mühldorf, wiederum ein *Chunradus,* war als »Kenner der Umstände und Verhältnisse« hinzugezogen worden.[27]

Vom ersten Schulmeister Läutwein bis zur Reformation

Unter dem oben erwähnten Mühldorfer Pfarrer *Konrad* findet sich auch eine Seelgerätstiftung für das Kloster Raitenhaslach aus dem Jahre 1294, ausgestellt zu Mühldorf.[28] In der Zeugenliste heißt es: »Chunrat der Pfarrer von Mühldorf, sein Geselle Ullrich ... Läutwein der Schulmeister.« Für Mühldorf ist damit erstmals ein Schulmeister, sogar namentlich zu belegen.
Bei diesem *Läutwein* handelt es sich wohl auf Grund der fehlenden Ortsangabe um

einen im Dienste des Mühldorfer Pfarrherrn stehenden Schulmeister. Wäre *Läutwein* ein selbständiger Schulmeister gewesen oder einer im hohen kirchlichen Dienst, dann wäre die Ortsangabe[29] oder eine nähere Erklärung[30] beigefügt worden. Schulmeister sind übrigens in Altbayern auf den Dörfern (in den Klöstern ohnehin) schon wesentlich früher zu belegen. So findet sich z. B. in den Tegernseer Klostertraditionen für die Jahre 1206 bis 1217 in der Zeugenliste ein »Chvnradus Schvhelare de Riedern«.[30a]

Das Amt eines Schulmeisters war im 13. und auch noch im 14. Jahrhundert oft Anfang einer beruflichen Karriere. Bei unserem *Läutwein* war dies auch der Fall. 1305 ist er Kaplan des Erzbischofs von Salzburg[31], 1318 sein Kämmerer[32] und 1341 ist er Pfarrer zu Mettenheim[33], heute noch ein Dorf unweit von Mühldorf. Auch als Pfarrer dürfte sich Läutwein um die schulische Bildung seiner Pfarrkinder gekümmert haben.[34]

Außer *Läutwein,* 1294, ist bis zum Jahre 1510 kein weiterer Schulmeister in den einschlägigen Quellen für Mühldorf namentlich zu belegen, was aber nicht bedeutet, daß es keine Schule gegeben hat.[35] Zu dieser Feststellung berechtigt uns eine Stiftungsurkunde aus dem Jahre 1359. In ihr erhält »der Pfarrer oder sein Vikar 32 Pfennig, die Gesellen und der Schulmeister je 6 Pfennig, der Mesner und sein Knecht je 4 Pfennig«.[36] Später erhält der Schulmeister 8 Pfennig, manchmal auch mehr. Insgesamt sind von 1359 bis 1514 fünfzehn Verstiftungsurkunden erhalten, in denen der Schulmeister für kirchliche Leistungen mit einem Geldbetrag bedacht wird.[37] Wenn bereits 1359 der Schulmeister fest in eine Stiftung miteinbezogen war, so muß das Amt des Schulmeisters schon vorher Institution geworden sein, denn ein Bürger bedachte nur jene Institutionen mit Geld, von denen er überzeugt war, daß sie die Jahrhunderte überdauern würden. Tatsächlich haben sich auch fast alle diese Stiftungen bis zur Säkularisation gehalten. Das Stiftungsvermögen selbst wurde übrigens schon seit 1242 von einem[38], später von zwei Mühldorfer Bürgern[39] in der Funktion eines weltlichen Kirchpropstes verwaltet. Analphabeten hat man für solche Aufgaben sicher nicht genommen.[40]

Um 1400 muß sich die Mühldorfer Schule schon in eine lateinische und in eine nicht lateinische Schule geteilt haben, andernfalls hätte in der folgenden Belegstelle »ad scholam« genügt. »Cunradus Khra(e)mel, antea Cooperator in civitate anno 1395 aedes ad Scholam Latinam Ecclasiae pro celebrando anniversario dedit.«[41] Der ehemalige Kooperator *Kraemel* hat also ein Gebäude *bei* oder *für* die lateinische Schule gestiftet und verlangt dafür einen Jahrtag. Dieser Heldbeleg für das Jahr 1411 war im Original nicht zugänglich, wird aber durch ein Vidimus, also eine Urkundenbestätigung aus dem Jahre 1549 glaubhaft.[42] Daraus ist ersichtlich, daß *Kraemel* seit 1409 Pfarrer von Altmühldorf war und im Jahre 1411 noch eine weitere Stiftung getätigt hat.

An der *nicht* lateinischen Schule war wohl ein Mann aus dem städtischen Personal tätig. In diesem Zusammenhang ist ein weiterer Beleg von Held für das Jahr 1425 »Meister Jakob an der Schule Mühldorf tätig«, interessant.[43]

Um 1425 kommen auf Grund der Urkunden nur drei Männer mit dem Namen *Jakob* dafür infrage.

1. *Jakob der Zollner,* ein Mühldorfer Bürger und salzburgischer Beamter ohne

Meister- bzw. Magistertitel, wäre zwar aufgrund seiner Schreib- und Verwaltungserfahrung als Lehrer für die deutsche Schule geeignet, kommt jedoch aufgrund seiner Stellung dafür nicht infrage.[44]
2. *Jakob, der ehemalige Bruckmeister* von Mühldorf, hätte mit einer Tätigkeit an der deutschen Schule eine ideale Austragsbeschäftigung gehabt. Als Bruckmeister hatte er einst mit 23 Pfennig pro Tag das höchstbezahlte Amt in der Stadt.[45] Meister *Jakob* war nicht nur für die Brücke zuständig, sondern auch für die Uferverbauungen, den Hochwasserschutz und die Wasserversorgung. Ferner hatte er wasserrechtliche Verträge auszuhandeln, zu formulieren und zu protokollieren, außerdem Kalkulationen und statistische Berechnungen zu erstellen. Daher war er sowohl in der Schriftlichkeit, als auch im Rechnen ein Mann »mit Übung und Erfahrung«.[46]
3. Bleibt noch Kaplan *Jakob Arnstorffer*, ein Geistlicher ohne Meistertitel. Er hat eine Reihe von kirchlichen Werken auf Pergament geschrieben und wurde deshalb vielleicht von den Leuten in Mühldorf als Meister im Sinne von Schreibmeister angesehen. Bemerkenswert ist ferner, daß *Arnstorffer* 1423 ein Haus neben der Schule als Wohnung erhält.[47]
Vielleicht ist durch weitere Nachforschungen in den Archiven Klarheit zu gewinnen.
Auf jeden Fall haben sich die schulischen Verhältnisse in Mühldorf in den folgenden Jahrzehnten konsolidiert, denn 1480 hat die Stadt ein eigenes Schulhaus gebaut. Es muß ein stattlicher Bau gewesen sein, denn die Kosten beliefen sich auf »70 Pfund Pfennig minus 8«[48] und dieses Schulhaus hatte mindestens zwei Räume, eine obere und eine untere Stube und war mit »pankhen« ausgestattet.[49] Seit dem Bau des neuen Schulhauses spricht die Stadt von »unserm Schuelmeister«.[50] Personell war also eine Trennung zwischen städtischem und kirchlichem Schulmeister eingetreten. Durch diese Trennung standen nun die kirchlichen Einkünfte aus den Meßstiftungen etc. jetzt natürlich ausschließlich dem kirchlichen, dem lateinischen Schulmeister zu. Wie aber hat sich der städtische, der deutsche Schulmeister »unterhalten«? Sicher wurde für den städtischen Unterricht Schulgeld verlangt[51], was ab 1552 zu belegen ist.[52] Das Schulgeld allein aber reichte sicher nicht aus und daher mußten für den städtischen Schulmeister neue Nebenerwerbsquellen zur Verfügung gestellt werden. Nebenerwerb war zur damaligen Zeit und bis herauf ins 19. Jahrhundert absolut normal.[53] Da die städtischen oder deutschen Schulmeister Mühldorfs zumindest am Anfang ohnehin aus der Verwaltung kamen, war es naheliegend den Schulmeister nebenbei mit städtischen Angelegenheiten zu betreuen. Diese Schulmeister müssen hochgebildete Männer gewesen sein, wie wäre es sonst erklärlich, daß die Stadt Mühldorf in einem Rechtsstreit mit Kaiser und Kurie, Mühldorf war mit dem neuernannten Erzbischof nicht einverstanden[54], ihren Schulmeister zur Regelung der Angelegenheiten nach Graz und nach Rom geschickt hat. 1483 steht in den Stadtkammerrechnungen: »Unsrm Schuelmeister haben wir geben 5 rheinische Gulden als wir ihm viel genutzt haben nach Graz zu dem Legaten und daß er uns viel ystrament (Schriftsätze) geschrieben hat.«[55] Im folgenden Jahr, 1484, erhält der Schulmeister »für einen Ritt nach Rom ... 14 rheinische Gulden, wovon er einen dem Procurator geben mußte«.[56]

60 Jahre später spricht die Stadt immer noch von »unserm Schuelmeister«, denn 1548 lesen wir: »Beim lateinischen Schuelmeister und bei unserm werden die Rauchfänge gekehrt«[57], vier Jahre früher, 1544 heißt es im Stadtgerichtsbuch aber auch schon: »Hannsn Lanndauer Teutzn Schuelmeister hie als anwesen.«[58] Die Kirche jedoch spricht schon 1510 von einem deutschen Schulmeister. Im Gültbuch der Pfarrei St. Nikolaus steht: »Haus in der St. Petergasse 2 Pfund Pfennig Jetzt Wolf Muthauser, deutscher Schuelmaister, hat 1 Pfund um 20 Pfund abgelöst.«[59]
Unwillkürlich stellt sich die Frage, wer hat Schule gehalten, wenn der Schulmeister wochen-, oder wie im Falle Rom, sogar monatelang unterwegs war? So wie der Pfarrer von Mühldorf seit 1359 einen Vikar und drei Gesellen hatte[60], die ihn vertraten, wenn er z. B. auf Reisen, oder zu Studien auf einer »Hohen Schule« war[61], so hatte auch der Schulmeister Gesellen[62], die für ihn Schule hielten, wenn er selbst mit städtischen Angelegenheiten betraut war.
Reichten Schulgeld und Nebenerwerb nicht aus, so wurden Schulmeister und Gesellen aus dem Stadtsäckel unterstützt. 1524 werden »dem Schuelmeister und seinen Gesellen damit sie sich besser unterhalten mögen 1 Pfund 6 Schillinge« aus der Stadtkasse gegeben.[63] Das waren 520 Pfennige und soviel wie 65 Stiftungsmessen à 8 Pfennige. Auch lateinische Schulmeister wurden bei Krankheit oder aus anderen Gründen gelegentlich von der Stadt unterstützt.[64]
Die deutsche Schule zu Mühldorf hatte auf jeden Fall drei Lehrer, einen Meister und zwei Gesellen[65] und zwei Schulräume.[66] Die lateinische Schule hatte mindestens zwei Lehrer.[67] Zusätzlich hatte die deutsche, wie die lateinische Schule mindestens noch einen Practentarius, oder Adstanten.[68] Bei einer angenommenen 6jährigen Schulzeit, wahrscheinlich war sie wesentlich kürzer, dürften beide Schulen zusammen etwa 100 Kinder unterrichtet haben.[69]
In Summa kann festgehalten werden, daß die Mühldorfer Schullehrer von den Anfängen bis etwa zur Reformation Männer mit Bildung und Verwaltungserfahrung waren.[70] Ein Teil dieser Schullehrer hatte sicher eine Universität besucht und daher ist es nicht verwunderlich, daß die Zahl der Mühldorfer Studenten von 1377 bis 1520 an den neu gegründeten Universitäten, Wien 1365, Leipzig 1409 und Ingolstadt 1472 fast kontinuierlich zunahm.[71] Bis 1450 sind allein in Wien 87 Mühldorfer Studenten nachweisbar, der erste schon vor 1377. Nur 3% der Studenten hatten begüterte Eltern und knapp 30% waren sogar arm.[72] Eine Reihe von Mühldorfer Bürgerssöhnen hat Karriere gemacht. So war z. B. *Heinrich Spitz* schon 1412 Notar für den Bischof von Passau[73] und *Johann Angerer* ist 1417 Rektor der Wiener Universität.[74]
Ab 1450 lassen sich fast jedes Jahr 2 oder 3 Studenten belegen, in manchen Jahren sogar fünf, sechs, sieben und acht. Wenn man davon ausgeht, daß estwa 15 Kinder, Knaben und Mädchen, jährlich die Schule verlassen haben, so müssen etwa jährlich 20%, in manchen Jahren aber mindestens 40–50% auf eine Universität gegangen sein.
Etwa mit der Reformation hört der Besuch der Universitäten durch Mühldorfer Studenten fast schlagartig auf.[75] Ein bis zwei Studenten war dann das Maximum pro Jahr und über viele Jahre hinweg ist nicht ein einziger Student nachweisbar, und das herauf bis ins 19. Jahrhundert, obwohl Ingolstadt nicht weit und die Salzburger Universität, 1623 gegründet, sozusagen vor der Haustüre lag.

Von der Reformation bis in die Zeit des 30jährigen Krieges

Die Zeit von der Reformation bis etwa zum Ende des 30jährigen Krieges wird nun von einem Lehrerstand geprägt, der sein Handwerk vorwiegend in der Stadtschreiberei, in der Schule und im Kirchendienst erlernt hat. Derjenige, der auch noch in diesem Zeitraum eine Universität besucht und eventuell den Magistergrad erworben hatte, fand als Lehrer vor allem in der Lateinschule seine Anstellung und sein Auskommen. In diesen gut hundert Jahren war der Schulmeister noch angesehen und der Beruf erstrebenswert. Man konnte Bürger und Hausbesitzer werden, wie 1510 schon *Wolf Muthauser*. Man konnte es zu einem bescheidenen Vermögen bringen, dreißig oder fünfzig Gulden[76], bei manchen war es auch mehr. So versteuerte z. B. der deutsche Schulmeister *Erhard Paur*, 1608 286 Gulden, wobei er 86 Gulden allein in sieben Jahren auf die hohe Kante legen konnte.[77] Für etwa 100 Gulden konnte man in Mühldorf zur damaligen Zeit ein Haus erwerben.[78]

Je nach Begabung bot die Stadt eine Reihe von Nebenbeschäftigungen an. Die Listen über die Kredite der Bürger waren auf den neuesten Stand zu bringen, dafür gab es 1525 88 Pfennige[79], an der »Herren Fastnacht« konnte man beim Pfarrer singen und wurde mit 52 Pfennigen entlohnt.[80] Seit 1533 war der deutsche Schulmeister Schriftführer bei den Schützen und auch für die städtische Verteidigung mit verantwortlich. Dieses Amt brachte ihm jährlich zweimal 1 Schilling 22 Pfennige 1 Heller, also insgesamt 105 Pfennige.[81] Für 31½ Pfennige konnte man jährlich die städtischen Rechnungen und Protokolle binden.[82] Aber auch sonst hatte der Schulmeister allerhand Vergünstigungen. Er wohnte mietfrei oder bekam 2 Pfund Pfennig Mietzuschuß, dafür mußte ein Arbeiter in der Regel 20 Tage schwer arbeiten[83], zusätzlich war er heizungsfrei, außerdem wurden »die Rauchfänge gekehrt« und »Öfen und Fenster gebessert«.[84] Hatte ein Lehrer eine schriftstellerische Ader, so konnte sich der deutsche wie der lateinische Schulmeister durch das Verfassen von Tragödien jeweils 2 Pfund verdienen.[85] Bei Krankheit oder in Notfällen wurde er von der Stadt finanziell unterstützt[86], sogar für Witwen und Waisen war in bescheidenem Maße gesorgt.[87] War der Lehrer alt geworden, so konnte er sozusagen ins städtische Seniorenheim gehen. So bittet z. B. 1602 *Thoman Kreizer* um Aufnahme in die untere Pfründe des Spitals, was ihm laut Protokollzusatz gewährt wird.[88]

Vier gängige Möglichkeiten, Schulmeister zu werden, boten sich in dieser Zeit an:

1. Man erlernte das Schreiberhandwerk bei einem Stadtschreiber, Mühldorf hatte zwischen 1500 und 1600 hervorragende Chefs in der Stadtschreiberei. Von 1513–1529 war es der kaiserliche Notar *Medlinger*[89] und von 1555 bis 1575 ein gewisser *Pumpler*, öffentlicher Notar von kaiserlicher Gewalt.[90] Auch in einer herzoglichen, bischöflichen oder klösterlichen Verwaltung, in der Hofmarkskanzlei und in der Marktschreiberei konnte man eine solide Ausbildung erhalten. Juristisch präzise und stilistisch einwandfrei, schön und richtig mußte der Sachverhalt zu Papier gebracht werden, ferner waren Kalkulations- und Etatfragen zu bewältigen. Vielseitigkeit war gefragt und Geschick im Umgang mit Menschen und Problemen. Nebenbei erwarb sich der Schreiber die nötigen schulischen Kenntnisse als Practentarius oder Adstant an der

deutschen Schule.[91] War er »fleißig und geschickt« wurde er bald als Aushilfslehrer herangezogen, versah aber auch weiterhin seinen Dienst in der Stadtschreiberei, oft schon als Procurator, oder Gehilfe eines Procurators. War durch Abwanderung oder Tod eine ständige Schulmeisterstelle frei geworden, konnte der Schreiber um Aufnahme als Schulmeister bitten.[92] Umgekehrt bewarben sich deutsche Schulmeister mit einer Schreiberausbildung und Kanzleierfahrung im ausgehenden 16. und frühen 17. Jahrhundert immer öfters auch um das nebenberufliche Amt eines Procurators. So bittet z. B. 1629 der Schulmeister *Hans Hager* auch als Procurator zugelassen zu werden, was ihm laut Ratsprotokoll »einhellig bewilligt« wird.[93] 1630 wird *Hans Steub* von Tegernsee als deutscher Schulmeister und Procurator aufgenommen.[94] Im Gegensatz zum hauptberuflichen Stadtprokurat waren sie die Prozeß-Stellvertreter der einfachen Bürger und leisteten u. a. durch kanzleimäßige Schriftsätze und bei mündlichen Verhandlungen Rechtsbeistand.[95]

Bei der Aufnahme als Schulmeister war eine Empfehlung oft von Vorteil, wobei Kanzleiempfehlungen vor Schulmeisterempfehlungen rangierten. So wird z. B. 1622 *Hannß Reinprechtinger,* deutscher Schulmeister zu Ampfing, auf Empfehlung des Mühldorfer Gerichtsschreibers und des Ampfinger Mautners als Schulmeister aufgenommen.[96] Doch sind die Zeiten religiös schon sehr eng geworden und im Ratsprotokoll wird zusätzlich vermerkt: »Bei der geistlichen Obrigkeit hier soll er sich der Religion halber erzeigen.« Als *Reinprechtinger* nach 8jähriger Tätigkeit stirbt[97], bittet der Marktschreiber *Thoman Fischer* von Gars um die Stelle.[98] *Fischer* wird Mühldorfer Bürger, hat eine Frau und drei Kinder, erwirbt das bescheidene Vermögen von 50 Gulden und zahlt dafür 3/8% Vermögenssteuer.[99] Dieser *Fischer* ist u. a. ein Beleg, wie ernst die Stadt ihre Fürsorgepflicht gegenüber den Schulmeistern nahm. Als *Thoman Fischer*, 1639, nach neunjähriger Dienstzeit starb, erhielt die Witwe »weil sich ihr Mann im Schulehalten fleißig verhalten, vom Bruderhaus wöchentlich 15 Kreuzer, vom Spital einen Laib Brot«.[100] Die 15 Kreuzer entsprachen etwa einem Arbeitslohn von 2–3 Tagen.[101] Bei mietfreier Wohnung, einem Laib Brot und zusätzlichen milden Gaben, sowie etwas Nebenverdienst, z. B. Wäscherin, war diese Witwe nicht schlechter gestellt als eine heutige Lehrerswitwe mit drei Kindern, wenn der Mann bereits nach neun Dienstjahren stirbt.

Auch um Angehörige von längst verstorbenen Schulmeistern kümmerte sich die Stadt. Als z. B. *Helena* aus Neuötting, Tochter des *Jakob Hannsler,* der vor 45 Jahren lateinischer Schulmeister in Mühldorf war[102], laut Protokoll »das Gehör verloren und an Gesicht und Verstand großen Mangel hatte«, wurde sie in das Bruderhaus zu Mühldorf aufgenommen und erhielt wöchentlich 12 Kreuzer.[103]

2. Oft aber erschien jungen Männern der Weg zum Schulmeister über eine Schreiberkanzlei viel zu mühsam und daher wählten sie den vermeintlich bequemeren Weg und gingen sofort bei einem deutschen Schulmeister in die Lehre. Aber spätestens wenn sie in einer Stadt eine Lehrerstelle angetreten hatten und im Ratsprotokoll ausdrücklich vermerkt worden war: »will sich allein mit der deutschen Schuel unterhalten«[104], haben diese jungen Männer gemerkt, daß es an der Zeit war eine solide Schreiberausbildung nachzuholen. Das Schulgeld der Kinder allein war trotz mancher Vergünstigungen für den Lebensunterhalt zu wenig.

So sind diese Schullehrer von Stadt zu Stadt gezogen um ihre Kenntnisse zu vervollkommnen. Mit anderen Berufsgruppen haben sie auch der Stadt Mühldorf »ihre Aufwartung gemacht«[105] und die üblichen »2 Schilling Hilfsgeld« erhalten. Manchen Schulmeistern gefiel dieses Wanderleben so gut, daß sie ihr ganzes Leben lang umherzogen.[106] Andere wiederum wollten in einer Stadt bleiben und bewarben sich um eine gerade freigewordene Stelle. Nach Vorlage des Geburtsscheines, der Bestätigung ehelicher Geburt und frei von Leibeigenschaft zu sein, sowie eines zusätzlichen Nachweises der Rechtgläubigkeit, wurden sie gewöhnlich gegen Zahlung von 4 Pfund Pfennigen, wenn man mit ihnen zufrieden war, als Bürger aufgenommen.[107] In der Regel blieben sie einige Jahre in der Stadt, manche blieben länger, vierzehn, ja sogar achtzehn Jahre.[108] Bei je drei Lehrern für die deutsche und lateinische Schule, war somit eine gewisse Kontinuität gewährleistet.
Ein langer Aufenthalt bedeutete aber nicht immer, daß mit dem Schulmeister alles in Ordnung war; ausgenommen bei Faulheit und schulischen Zwistigkeiten, konnte ein Bürger nicht ohne weiteres, nur weil es gelegentlich Querelen gab, aufgefordert werden, sich »an andern Orts zu begeben«.[109] Ein gewisser *Wolf Martanner* war 18 Jahre, von 1553–1571 Schulmeister in Mühldorf. Bereits im Jahr seines Einstandes wird er wegen 20 Gulden 33 Kreuzer Schulden verklagt.[110] 15 Jahre später nimmt er sogar ohne Wissen der Obrigkeit eine ledige Dirn bei sich auf und wird dafür mit 1 Pfund Pfennigen Strafe belegt.[111] Als *Martanner* dann 1570 sein Bürgerrecht aufgeben will, wird ihm der Abschied nur bewilligt, wenn er zuvor seine Gläubiger bezahlt.[112] Ein Jahr später ist dies noch nicht geschehen und »beiden deutschen Schuelhaltern wird auf ihr supplicirn hin der Bescheid erteilt, daß man mit dem Marthaner bis auf Ostern, in Bedenkung seiner Armut Geduld haben soll«.[113] Letztlich erhält er zwei Gulden Reisegeld »um sich anderwärts zu bewerben«. Dieser *Wolf Martanner* hatte offensichtlich auch nur sein Schulhandwerk erlernt und war für das einträgliche Schreibergeschäft nicht zu gebrauchen. Trotzdem haben auch solche Schulmeister gelegentlich sich in der Schreiberei versucht und sie sind gemeint, wenn der Erzbischof von Salzburg *Wolf Dietrich* schon 1594 schreibt: »... besonders die deutschen Schulmeister schreiben weitschweifige und völlig unzutreffende Eingaben für die unerfahrenen Bürger und Bauersleute, machen ihnen überflüssige Kosten. Künftig dürfen nur solche Leute Schreiben verfassen, welche die ausdrückliche Erlaubnis dazu erhalten. Im übrigen soll man sich an die ordentlich angenommenen Advocaten und Procuratoren wenden. ...«[114]
Gelegentlich ist den deutschen Schulmeistern auch das Temperament durchgegangen und sie wurden wegen Beleidigung bestraft.[115] Dies wurde ihnen aber nicht nachgetragen, wenn sie in der Schule »fleißig gewesen und die Kinder ordentlich unterhalten haben«. Als *Georg Zerer* sich 1577 nach 2jähriger Tätigkeit andernorts bewerben will, wird ihm, trotz einer Bestrafung wegen Beleidigung sogar versprochen, das Bürgerrecht 1 Jahr lang aufzubehalten.[116]
Nicht immer war die Aufforderung an den Schulmeister, die Stadt zu verlassen, gleichbedeutend mit Unfähigkeit oder Faulheit. So wird 1574 ein *Bernhard Wagner* »gewesener Bürger und Schulhalter von Trotzberg« als Schulmeister zu Mühldorf aufgenommen.[117] Zwei Jahre später aber wird »dem Bernhard Wagner, deutschem

Schulmeister auferlegt, daß er sich samt Weib und Kind zu Quatember-Pfingsten aus der Stadt entferne und anderswo sein Unterkommen suche«.[118] *Wagner* hat sich nach Laufen begeben, denn mit Datum vom 20. April 1578 existiert ein Gesuch an den Herrn Pfleger und Stadtrichter von Laufen, worin *Wagner* sich u. a. beklagt, daß er »wenig Zucht und Mores unter seinen Schulkindlein spür und finde, ... daß sie gar zu Püffeln werden, und alsdann soll ein Schulmaister in acht Tagen aus einem Rabn ein Zeisl ziechen, ...«[119] Letztlich beschwert sich der Laufner Schulmeister auch noch über das zu geringe Schulgeld. Das Gesuch wurde noch im gleichen Jahr positiv beschieden, denn es erging für die Pfarrschule zu Laufen eine Besoldungsordnung.[120] Die wichtigsten Punkte darin sind wohl die Erhöhung des Quatembergeldes von 15 Kreuzer auf 2 Schilling 20 Pfennig, also von 60 auf 80 Pfennig, der Betrag für das Licht und Holz, ein Erholungsgeld für den Lehrer und zwar jährlich 5mal 4 Pfennig von jedem Kind. Außerdem müssen große Personen, welche Rechnen lernen, vierteljährlich 6 Schillinge oder wöchentlich 14 Pfennige bezahlen. Für das ABC-Büchl darf der Lehrer 4 Pfennig, für ein Silben-Büchl 8 Pfennig, für ein Namen-Büchl sogar 16 Pfennig verlangen. Der gewiß fähige *Bernhard Wagner* war wahrscheinlich 20 Jahre in Laufen als Schulmeister tätig. Auf jeden Fall ist erst 1599 ein neuer Schulhalter für Laufen zu belegen.[121] 1615 ist *Wagner* wieder in Trostberg, von wo aus er vor über 40 Jahren als junger Schulmeister nach Mühldorf gekommen war.[122]

3. Die lateinischen Schulmeister hatten in der Regel bis herauf in die zweite Hälfte des 17. Jahrhunderts eine Universität besucht[123] und oft den Magistergrad erworben.[124] Diese Magistri waren ohnehin in der Schriftlichkeit geübt, hatten oft neben der Theologie noch Jurisprudenz studiert und in einer Kanzlei gearbeitet. Sie konnten sofort die erste Stelle als lateinischer Schulmeister bzw. die zweite lateinische Schulmeisterstelle, das Kantorenamt, übernehmen. Eventuelle Verbindungen, bzw. Fürsprachen waren auch hier von Vorteil und Bürgerssöhne wurden bevorzugt.[125] Selbstverständlich mußte man als lateinischer Schulmeister ein guter Musikus sein. Der erste lateinische Schulmeister war als regens chori auch für die gesamte Kirchenmusik zuständig und der zweite lateinische Schulmeister als Kantor insbesondere für die Gesänge und den Chor verantwortlich.[126] Als ehemalige Lateinschüler waren sie ohnehin musikalisch bestens ausgebildet, hatten Chorerfahrung und waren mit allen kirchenmusikalischen Gepflogenheiten bestens vertraut. Im Gegensatz zu den deutschen Schulmeistern die in der Regel »einig und friedlich waren«, kam es in der Lateinschule zwischen Schulmeister und Kantor oft zu Streitigkeiten[127], dabei »ging die Schule oft sichtlich zurück«. Nur wenn es um Gebühren ging, war man sich einig. So verlangten sie z. B. 1623 für eine Beerdigung 9 Gulden, während der Herr Dechant für sich nur 5 Gulden forderte.[128] Auch den Wein liebten sie und wurden wegen »Weinzechens« und »weil sie voll und toll gewest« gelegentlich verwarnt.[129]

Konnte der deutsche Schulmeister nebenberuflich Procurator oder hauptberuflich Stadtprocurator werden, so hatte der lateinische Schulmeister die Möglichkeit, die Stadtschreiberei zu übernehmen. 1590 wird dem Magister *Gamaliel Sigmair,* als er von Mühldorf abzieht, vom Rat bestätigt: »... daß er bei vier Jahren Stadtschreiber und zuvor sieben Jahre lateinischer Schulmeister gewesen ist.«[130]

Gelegentlich hat man auch einen candidatus philologiae als lateinischen Schulmeister aufgenommen.[131] Solche candidati et studiosi waren oft Verlegenheitslösungen und für Rat und Kirche unbefriedigend. Bald haben solche Kandidaten gemerkt, daß man das Schulehalten nicht aus dem Ärmel schütteln kann. Vier Schilling Hilfgeld erhielt *Johann Winckler* 1587, auf daß er noch im gleichen Jahre weiterziehe.[132]

Wer glaubt, die lateinische Schule sei ausschließlich Angelegenheit der Kirche gewesen, irrt. Ein gewichtiges Wort hatten die Ratsherren immer in die Waagschale geworfen, wenn man mit dem lateinischen Schulmeister nicht zufrieden war. Die Ratsherren des 16. und 17. Jahrhunderts waren noch keine satten Spießer, sie waren gebildet, weltoffen und belesen und in ihren Truhen und Schränken befanden sich die großen und kleinen reformatorischen Schriften und zwar in einer Zahl die jedem evangelischen Pfarrhaus zur Ehre gereicht hätte.[133] Eine Universität besucht zu haben, oder gar Magister zu sein, das allein reichte nicht, um bei einem Ratsherren Eindruck zu erwecken.[134] Fleiß und Können war gefragt. So wird dem Magister *Peter Walther* 1578 erklärt: »man sei mit ihm unzufrieden, die Schule geht sichtbar zurück, er kümmert sich wenig um sie, sondern überlasse den Unterricht dem Kantor etc. Wenn das nicht besser werde, so müsse man sich um jemanden andern umsehen.«[135] 1567 wird dem *Mathias Edlinger* gekündigt und ein neuer lateinischer Schulmeister »wird aufgestellt«. Über die Kündigung und Neuaufnahme beschwert sich der Herr Pfarrer bei der Stadt. Die Ratsherren teilen ihm mit, »daß man sich zur Aufnahme eines Schulmeisters von einem Kirchherrn einen Rat einholen soll, dessen kann man sich nicht erinnern«.[136]

Lateinische Schulmeister blieben in der Regel einige Jahre in der Stadt, zwei Schulmeister taten acht Jahre in Mühldorf Dienst und der Magister *Oelhafen* war 28 Jahre von 1621–1649 erster lateinischer Schulmeister.[137]

4. Auch ein guter Musiker hatte selbst ohne Studium die Möglichkeit Schullehrer zu werden. Als Chorbuben begannen sie ihre Laufbahn, wurden mit etwa 17 Jahren Choralist, Mühldorf hatte in unserem Zeitraum jeweils vier, und erwarben sich nebenbei in der deutschen Schule als adstanti oder practendarii die notwendigen deutschen schulmeisterlichen Kenntnisse. Nach einigen Jahren konnten sie zum Organisten aufsteigen und waren damit gleichzeitig dritter, bzw. Aushilfsschulmeister an der deutschen Schule. Interessierten sich diese Organisten auch noch für den Unterricht an der lateinischen Schule, so sammelten sie auch dort noch Erfahrung und dann stand einem Aufstieg zum Kantor und damit zum zweiten lateinischen Schulmeister nichts mehr im Wege. Organisten wie Kantoren sind, wenn der kirchliche Dienst ihnen entsprach, oft sehr lange in einer Stadt geblieben. Der Organist und Aushilfsschulhalter an der deutschen Schule *Hanns Zellhofer* z. B., war 22 Jahre in Mühldorf tätig[138] und der Kantor *Markus Wendel* ist sogar 28 Jahre von 1590–1618 in Mühldorf nachweisbar.[138a] Organisten wie Kantoren war bis etwa 1650 ein Aufstieg zum ersten lateinischen Schulmeister und regens chori nicht möglich, das blieb in der Regel ehemaligen Universitätsstudenten vorbehalten. Doch war auch den Organisten und Kantoren der Weg für einen weiteren beruflichen Aufstieg nicht verbaut. Sie hatten die Möglichkeit in der deutschen Schule als erster, bzw. zweiter Schulmeister aufgenommen zu werden. In größeren Städten standen entsprechend mehr Schulhalterstellen zur Verfügung.[139] Von der Möglichkeit in einer Stadt deutscher Schulmeister

zu werden, haben Organisten wie Kantoren wenig Gebrauch gemacht, ihre musikalischen Fähigkeiten waren in dieser Funktion nicht besonders gefragt und entsprechend geschätzt. Daher zogen die Organisten lieber auf das Land, wo sie bei den Pfarrherren als Dorfschulmeister und Kirchenmusiker wegen ihrer Ausbildung gesucht und geachtet waren.[140] Die Kantoren hingegen bemühten sich mehr in größeren Orten und Märkten um eine Anstellung, denn dort wurde der Unterricht sowohl für die deutschen, wie auch für die lateinischen Schüler oft von einem einzigen Lehrer erteilt. Zusätzlich fanden sie dort oft auch noch als Organisten und regens chori im Kirchendienst Verwendung. Viele dieser ehemaligen Kantoren erwarben sich beim Marktschreiber zusätzliche Schreib- und Verwaltungskenntnisse und hatten dann in dieser dreifachen Funktion als deutscher und lateinischer Schulmeister, als Kirchenmusiker und als Schreiber ein gutes, oft sogar sehr gutes Einkommen.[141]

In der Zeit zwischen Reformation und Ende des 30jährigen Krieges nahmen auch die Bürger aktiv und interessiert am schulischen Geschehen Anteil. Der Mühldorfer Bürgerssohn *Leonhard Alber* hatte Medizin studiert und wollte in Mühldorf die Praxis seines Schwiegervaters, des Physikus *Georg Fest* übernehmen. Nachdem diesem Schwiegervater 1557 aber der fatale Irrtum unterlaufen war, die Schneidersfrau aus Erharting für »ausmärtlig«, also für aussätzig zu erklären[142], zog *Leonhard Alber* es vor, als Stadtphysikus nach Wasserburg zu ziehen. Dort verfaßte er 1562 eine lateinische Schulordnung »Brevis institutio et restauratio apud Wasserburgense«. Paulsen hat nachgewiesen, daß sie der Schulordnung *Melanchthons* von 1528 nachempfunden ist.[143]

Zwar haben sich in der Zeit von 1520–1650 die Mühldorfer Studentenzahlen drastisch verringert, dies bedeutete aber nicht, daß man an den geistigen Strömungen der Zeit keinen Anteil nahm. Im Gegenteil, man hat offensichtlich viel gelesen, was wiederum ein Beweis für die Leistungsfähigkeit der Mühldorfer Schule ist. Bereits 1538 wird *Gilg Khelner,* ein Buchführer, also ein Buchhändler, gegen Zahlung von 10 Pfund Pfennigen als Bürger in Mühldorf aufgenommen.[144] Aufgrund der hohen Aufnahmegebühr, die Regel waren 4 Pfund Pfennige, rechnete man offensichtlich mit einem sehr guten Einkommen des Buchhändlers und das nicht zu unrecht, denn das Interesse an Büchern war groß. Anläßlich einer Visitation im 100. Jahr der Reformation wurden allein bei 26 Mühldorfer Bürgern 63 verbotene Bücher gefunden.[145] Arme und Reiche waren unter den Besitzern, Ratsherren und Bürgermeister, Gastwirte und Händler, natürlich der Apotheker, der Bruckmeister und der Schulmeister. Die gefundenen Bücher bieten einen repräsentativen Querschnitt reformatorischer Literatur der damaligen Zeit. Luther-Bibeln, Schriften von Erasmus, theologische Bekenntnisse und Streitschriften, aber auch medizinische, geographische und historische Werke waren darunter. Eine ganze Reihe von Bürgern, auch Frauen, besaßen lateinische Bücher.

Beim deutschen Schulmeister *Onophoro Asam* wurden vier verbotene Bücher sicher gestellt: Enchyridion historicum, also ein historisches Handbüchl, Hochpreisung der unermeßlichen Barmherzigkeit Gottes, von Erasmus in Latein, die Vergleichung einer wahren Jungfrau und eines Märtyrers, ebenfalls von Erasmus, sowie ein

Büchlein, wie man kranke und sterbende Menschen ermahnen, trösten und Gott befehlen soll. Der Besitzer dieser Bücher, *Onophoro Asam,* verkörpert den typischen Schulmeister dieser Zeitepoche. Er war gescheit und belesen, in Schule und Verwaltung ein Meister, tapfer und äußerst selbstbewußt, aber auch hitzköpfig und manchmal »toll und voll«. 1609 kam er 19jährig aus Kraiburg zum Stadtschreiber *Wagenbauer*[146], wurde 1612 Schulmeister[147] und zwei Jahre später, gegen 4 Pfund Pfennige Aufnahmegebühr, Mühldorfer Bürger.[148]
1621 wurde er neben seiner Schulmeistertätigkeit zusammen mit dem Buchführer Sartori »Furier« und war damit für die Verpflegung der 500 bayerischen Reiter in der Stadt verantwortlich.[149] 1625 wechselte er in das Amt des städtischen Procurators[150], wurde 1629 wegen ungebührlichen Verhaltens vom Amt suspendiert[151], jedoch nach vier Wochen wieder aufgenommen, da die »Untergebenen« seinem Nachfolger den Dienst verweigerten. 1632 war Stadtprocurator *Asam* außerdem noch »Feldwaibl«[152], also für die städtische Verteidigung zuständig, und forderte die Bürger auf »die Trommel zu schlagen und scharf zu laden«.[153] Auseinandersetzungen mit dem Rat in Sachfragen waren an der Tagesordnung. *Asam* fühlte sich als fürstlicher Offizier, für Pfleger und Schloß verantwortlich, und anläßlich einer hitzigen Debatte weigerte er sich den Degen niederzulegen und verließ, nicht zum erstenmal, »mit großem Ungestüm« die Ratsstube.[154]

Vom Ende des 30jährigen Krieges bis zum Beginn des 19. Jahrhunderts

Seit man 1617 aufgrund der literarischen Zensur den Bürgern aus Schränken und Truhen die verbotenen Bücher genommen, haben Zeit und Menschen sich langsam aber sicher verändert. Der Horizont war enger, das geistige Gesichtsfeld schmaler geworden, Sprüche wurden geklopft von hoher Moral, von Disziplin und Fleiß und der Bürger merkte nicht, wie er langsam zum Spießer wurde. Alles wurde »geordnet und geregelt«. Die so beliebten Musikantengruppen waren verboten, das Sternsingen untersagt, der Fasching und das »Mascara« abgeschafft, ja sogar die Zahl der Hochzeitsgäste war vorgeschrieben und die Höhe des Mahlgeldes festgelegt. Die Kinder durften ihre Eltern nicht mehr »dusigen«, sie mußten jetzt »sie« sagen und der Schulmeister hatte auch außerhalb der Unterrichtszeit »obsorge zu tragen«, für die der »Schule noch nicht entlaufenen Kinder«.
Die Mühldorfer Pfarrherren, einst hatten sie Verträge für Herzöge und Erzbischöfe ausgehandelt, Regionalkonzilien, Bischofsweihen und Ritterturniere in Mühldorf vorbereitet, sind jetzt damit beschäftigt, ob, wann und in welcher Reihenfolge der deutsche und der lateinische Schulmeister die Kinder zur Messe und zur Predigt zu führen habe.[155]
Hatten die Schulmeister einst im Auftrag der Stadt mit herzoglicher, kaiserlicher oder päpstlicher Kanzlei verhandelt, so werden ihnen jetzt sogar procuratorische Hilfsleistungen untersagt; »höchstens als Beiständer bei Hochzeiten dürfen sie sich noch

gebrauchen lassen«[156], so verfügen die Ratsherren. Das Interesse der Schulmeister konzentriert sich immer mehr auf Holzgeld, Mietzins und Postenhascherei. Ihre Tätigkeit beschränkt sich zusehends ausschließlich auf die Vermittlung von Kenntnissen und Fertigkeiten in Religion, Lesen, Schreiben, Rechnen und Moralität. Für weitere anspruchsvolle Tätigkeiten in der Verwaltung sind sie nicht mehr zu gebrauchen. Die große Zeit der angesehenen Schulmeister ist endgültig vorbei. Die Schule geht rapide zurück und schon 1647 konstatiert der Rat der Stadt, daß »nicht alle Bräuer und Wirte mehr lesen und schreiben können«.[157] So mußten die Schulmeister die Posthalterei übernehmen und wurden zu Nachtzettelschreibern degradiert, ein trauriger Abgesang auf Schule und Lehrer.[157a]
In der lateinischen Schule wird 1654 schon das »Rechnen lernen« abgeschafft[158], ab 1670 dürfen keine Mädchen mehr unterrichtet werden und ebenso keine Knaben, »die nicht Latein können«[159] und der lateinische Schulmeister und regens chori kommt nur noch in die Kirche, wenn es Geld dafür gibt.[160]
Obwohl die Kinderzahl in etwa gleich bleibt, reduziert sich die Zahl der Schullehrer um 1700 auf je einen Schullehrer und einen Gehilfen und Ende des 18. Jahrhunderts ist dann an der deutschen wie an der lateinischen Schule nur noch ein Lehrer tätig.
Die Bürokratie aber nimmt zu. 1713 wird von der Stadtschreiberei eine neue Schulordnung verfaßt, die Geschlechter werden in den Sitzplätzen getrennt und Heiligenbilder und Weihwasser müssen vorhanden sein.[161]
Seit etwa 1530 hatte die Stadt den Schulmeistern die Rauchfänge gekehrt, Öfen und Fenster unterhalten, nun muß der Lehrer sich selbst um diese Dinge kümmern und die Versorgung der Witwen und Waisen darf er auch übernehmen; 10–15 Kreuzer pro Woche muß er dafür bei der Stadt abliefern.[162]
1777 wird in Mühldorf die »neue Lehrart« eingeführt. Doch die meisten Eltern haben aus »allzu großem Abscheu und schlechten Vorurteilen gegen die neue Normal-Methode die Kinder daheim behalten und selber unterrichtet«.[163]
Im Jahre 1785 schreibt der Hofrat von Salzburg an den Pfleger zu Mühldorf: »Eine der ersten Pflichten eines Regenten ist, die Jugend zu nützlichen Mitgliedern des Staates ausbilden zu lassen, wozu die Förderung der Erziehungsanstalten vorzüglich abzielt.«[164] Und die Praxis? Als 1798 der lateinische Schulmeister *Michael Haimerer* seinen Dienst quittiert, wird das lateinische Schulhaus verkauft und alle Mühldorfer Kinder, etwa 90, werden nun von einem Schullehrer und einem Gehilfen in zwei Klassen unterrichtet. In zwei kleinen finsteren Zimmern sind sie untergebracht und teilweise müssen bis zu 30 Kinder dem Unterricht stehend beiwohnen.
1801 wird dem Lehrer *Franz Gries* ein gewisser *Anton Reiter* mit einem Viertel seines Jahreslohnes, 6 Gulden 15 Kreuzer, zur Seite gestellt.[165] *Reiter* übernimmt 1802 den ganzen Schuldienst und ist fast 60 Jahre als Lehrer in Mühldorf tätig, ehe er 77jährig, 1858 von »all seinen Funktionen« zurücktritt. Jahrelang unterrichtete er die anfänglich 90 Kinder allein, erhielt 1807 bei 150 Kindern einen ersten, und 1815 bei 200 Kindern einen zweiten Adstanten. *Reiter* war, wie fast alle seiner Salzburger Kollegen, ein glänzender Lehrer und bald wurde die Mühldorfer Schule zur Musterschule. *Reiter* zog aber auch sonst alle Register seiner Begabung. Er verstand »manch philosophische Aufsätze«[166], er verstand es aber auch seine Bezüge von 395 Gulden

12 Kreuzer im Jahre 1803, auf 907 Gulden 25⅖ Kreuzer im Jahre 1852 zu erhöhen.[167] Zur gleichen Zeit verarmten *Reiters* Kollegen auf dem Lande, weil ihnen durch die Säkularisation alle Legate und Stiftungen genommen, was einer realen Gehaltskürzung von 50–75% gleichkam.

Im Jahre 1801, als der Adstant *Anton Reiter* an der Mühldorfer Schule seinen Dienst aufnahm, kam auch ein gewisser *Matthäus Fingerlos*, ehemaliger Regens des Priesterseminars in Salzburg, als Stadtpfarrer, Dechant und Oberinspektor des Schulwesens nach Mühldorf.[168] Fingerlos war ein Aufklärer der reinsten Form und fast ein krankhafter Eiferer für den Untertanengeist. Amtsadjunkt *Ruland* war von ihm begeistert. Unter Umgehung seines Vorgesetzten, des Mühldorfer Pflegers *Christoph von Hartmann*, schreibt er am 22. Dezember 1802 an den General-Commissaire Freiherrn *von Aretin* nach München: »... P. Raitmair (Kanonikus) ... stellte den widerspenstigen Thomas Morus[169] auf eine gar erbauliche Art als Muster dar etc. Ich gab Herrn Dechant mein Mißvergnügen zu erkennen – und das nächstemal suchte er [Fingerlos] seine Sache wieder gut zu machen – indem er aus Schrifttexten für den Untertangehorsam eiferte.«[170]

Am 4. März des folgenden Jahres berichtet *Ruland* über *Fingerlos*: »Herr Stadtdechant hielt nun selbst schon mehrere Kanzelreden, worin er auf eine ihm eigene Weise die reine Moral popularisierte. Mit jedem Tag bewundere ich diesen Mann mehr, auf den unsere Regierung stolz sein darf.«[171] Das erklärt auch die Äußerung *Rulands* vom 6. Februar 1803: »Ich bin nun mehr als je überzeugt: wenn Beamte und Ortspfarrer für die Regierung zusammenwirken (oder nur nicht widerstreben), kann die Regierung – *was sie will*.[172] So gesehen ist es mehr als verständlich, wenn *Ruland* bezüglich *Fingerlos* zwei Monate später gegenüber dem Freiherrn *von Aretin* den Wunsch ausspricht: »möchte ihm [Fingerlos] doch bald wieder die Bildung junger Priester, Geistlicher wollte ich sagen, anvertraut werden«.[173]

Schon ein Jahr später ging dieser Wunsch, leider könnte man sagen, in Erfüllung. *Fingerlos* wurde Direktor des Gregorianums[174] in Landshut. Zusätzlich war er zehn Jahre Professor für Pastorrallehre[175] und einer der erbittertsten Feinde des hochangesehenen *Johann Michael Sailer*. Die jungen Geistlichen aber, die unter *Fingerlos* in den zehn Jahren ausgebildet worden waren, kamen als Orts-, vor allem aber als Distriktsschulinspektoren, also als pädagogische Aufsichtsinstanz auf die Dörfer und in die Städte, angeblich um die Volksbildung, in Wahrheit aber »um Liebe und Gehorsam der Unterthanen gegen Fürsten und Unterthanen mehr zu befördern«.[176]

Das Zeitalter der pädagogischen Alphabetisierung war eingeläutet. Die Kulturstrategen, die Manager der Pädagogik und die Superstars der Didaktik beherrschten die Szene und überschwemmten den Markt mit Literatur. Ein Bauernpfarrer aus dem Landkreis Friedberg sah sich zu der Bemerkung veranlaßt: »Die Zeitschriften wollen meistens nur glänzen, nicht nützen und ihren Namen wie Herostrat verewigen; wenigstens ist es in unsern hochgelehrten Tagen gar oft der Fall, daß man weniger die gute Sache, als sich, und sein Interesse zu befördern suche.«[177]

Jetzt begann endlich auch die Zeit der »nur Schulmänner«. Schulmeister »aus altem Schrot und Korn«, die etwas mehr »auf dem Kasten hatten«, wie die alten Bauernpfarrer sich auszudrücken pflegten, waren den pädagogischen Aufsichtsinstanzen insge-

heim schon immer ein Ärgernis, denn ihnen konnte der »Unterthanen-Geist« schwer verständlich gemacht werden. Sie gaben nicht klein bei, nahmen lieber den »Gratifikationsverlust« in Kauf und lebten trotzdem besser wie viele ihrer Kollegen.[178]
Im Bildungsrausch des frühen 19. Jahrhunderts wurden die Worte des alten Friedberger Bauernpfarrers von 1810 als »Beleidigung Allerhöchster Stellen« betrachtet und auch geahndet und der schulische Erfolg des Mesnerlehrers *Völtl* wurde in ein Verdienst des »im Schulwesen erfahrenen Kooperator *Joseph Hazinger*« umgemünzt. Die Bewunderung der Eltern über das große Wissen und Können der 76 Schüler bei der Schulprüfung am 5. Mai 1805 nahm der im aufklärerischen Geist ausgebildete junge Geistliche natürlich für sich in Anspruch, denn er sei es schließlich gewesen, dem »diese Schule ihr Dasein, Leben und Geist zu verdanken habe«.
Die Aufsichtsinstanzen überdrehten die pädagogische Schraube und man verlor die Orientierung im Durcheinander von Plänen, Verbesserungen, Verfügungen und Erlassen. Die Auswirkungen dieses Paragraphengewirrs führte auch in den einfachen Volksschichten zu Unbehagen und zu allmählicher Ernüchterung. Man sprach von »siebengescheiten Schullehrern« und stellte fest, daß, je höher sie sich auf der beruflichen Leiter emporgedient hatten, um so mehr beanspruchten sie in der Gesellschaft die Rolle eines Beckmessers. Mit ihren kleinlichen Nörgeleien verärgerten sie die Leute und dies wurde sogar gelegentlich aktenkundig.[179]

Anmerkungen

[1] *Spindler,* M. (Hrsg.) (1969): Bayerischer Geschichtsatlas. München, S. 22. Vgl. dazu auch den Kommentar von S. Hiereth u. G. Diepolder »Städte und Märkte im Mittelalter«, S. 81.

[2] Um 1200 sind in ganz Deutschland etwa 250 Städte nachweisbar, bis etwa 1300 sind weitere 800 Städtegründungen zu belegen.

[3] An dieser Stelle sei dem Stadtarchiv Mühldorf für die ungehinderte und problemlose Benützung der entsprechenden Archivalien aufrichtig gedankt. Mein besonderer Dank gilt dem Mühldorfer Stadtarchivar *Rudolf Angermeier,* der mit unendlicher Geduld auch außerhalb der Dienstzeit schnell und mit großer Fachkenntnis behilflich war.

[4] Vgl. Literaturverzeichnis, Quellen.

[5] *Held,* H. (1926/28): Altbayerische Volkserziehung und Volksbildung, 3 Bde. München; für Mühldorf Bd. III, S. 126f.

[6] *Held* hat für sein Standardwerk zwar eine sehr große Zahl kirchlicher, jedoch verhältnismäßig wenig weltliche Quellen ausgewertet. Daher entspricht der bei Held dargebotene Quellenstand nicht den tatsächlichen historischen schul- und bildungsgeschichtlichen Gegebenheiten. Es wäre dringend geboten, *Held* völlig neu zu bearbeiten, gerade auch im Hinblick auf die Prüfungsordnung von 1978, wo die Bewerber um die Lehrämter in Pädagogik auch Kenntnisse aus der Geschichte der Pädagogik, insbesondere auch im Hinblick auf das bayerische Schulwesen, nachweisen müssen. In München befindet sich gegenüber der Universität eines der größten Urkundenarchive der Welt und daher sollten die mittelalterlichen und frühneuzeitlichen Quellen zur bayerischen Schul- und Bildungsgeschichte auch von den Pädagogen herangezogen werden. Soweit ersichtlich, ist dies jedoch in den letzten Jahren nicht mehr der Fall.

[7] Vgl. *Gollwitzer,* H. (1962–1964): Erste urkundliche Nachrichten. In: Das Mühlrad, Blätter zur Geschichte des Inn- und Isengaues, Bd. XI, Jg. 1962–1964, S. 10ff.

[8] Widemann, H. (1943): Die Traditionen des Hochstiftes Regensburg und des Klosters St. Emmeram. München, S. 213, Nr. 255.

[9] 1197 Januar 12 Hauthaler-Martin, Salzburger Urkundenbuch (SUB), Bd. II, U 523
1202 Hauthaler-Martin, SUB, Bd. III, U 551 ab

[10] 1201 Oktober 24 Friesach, *Hauthaler-Martin,* SUB III, U 542.

[11] 1203 Salzburg, SUB III, U 563
1208 Mai 27, SUB III, U 618
1208 November 15 Salzburg, SUB III, U 621
1212 Bayerisches Hauptstaatsarchiv München (BHStAM), Gerichtsurkunden Traunstein, U 119
1212 SUB III, U 651
1214? März 27, *Hauthaler-Martin,* SUB I, U 320 (Traditionen des Domkapitels 1196–1214)
1215 September 14, SUB III, U 687
1216 September 24, SUB III, U 694
1216 September 24, Salzburg, BHStAM, Klosterurkunden Formbach 18
1217 Salzburg, SUB III, U 699
1218 September 25, Salzburg, SUB III, U 729
1219 SUB III, U 739b
1220–1224 SUB III, U 750
1222 Salzburg, SUB III, U 771 (dominus Chunradus plebanus de Muldorf)
1222 November 13, Salzburg, SUB III, U 777
1223 Oktober 21, Schloß Dornberg, SUB III, U 783
1224 August 8, SUB III, U 793

[12] Das Seelgerät war eine Stiftung, in der Regel aus dem Nachlaß eines Verstorbenen, wobei die Erben, zumeist die Angehörigen, einen Teil dieses Nachlaßes, Geld oder Besitz, für das Seelenheil des Toten der Kirche übergaben. Auch zu Lebzeiten – oft erst auf dem Totenbett – konnte man schon für sein eigenes Seelenheil der Kirche Geld oder Besitz zur zeitlichen oder ewigen Nutzung überschreiben. Die lateinische Formulierung in den entsprechenden Urkunden lautet: »pro remedio animae suae«, die deutsche Formulierung heißt in der Regel »selgerate«. (Gerate war bei den germanischen Frauen eine Opfergabe).

[13] 1214 März 27, *Hauthaler-Martin,* SUB I, U 320. Traditionen des Domkapitels 1196–1214.

[14] Diese Stiftung war für die Mühldorfer Kirche die erste große, kleinere Stiftungen gingen schon voraus, die erste bereits um 1150, Monumenta Boica II, 1764, München, Typis Academicis, Monumenta Canonicae Chiemseensis, Codex traditionum U 224.

[15] Noch im ausgehenden 18. Jahrhundert war es oft nur durch Stiftungen, die jetzt Legate genannt werden, möglich einen Schullehrer anzustellen. Im Landkreis Friedberg z. B. läßt sich dies in einer Reihe von Fällen belegen.

[16] 1230 Januar 5, *Hauthaler-Martin,* SUB III, U 847. Sein Vorgänger *Hainreich der Visler,* 1323 März 3 (*Hör-Morenz,* St. Veit U 45) hatte schon um 1304 in Bolognia studiert. (1304? Acta nat. Germ., S. 55, Z. 43) Vgl. auch Acta Salzburgo-Aquilejensia, Bd. I, Graz 1903, Nr. 64 u. 163.

[17] Für 1294 Mai 1 ist erstmals zu belegen, daß der Pfarrherr von Mühldorf einen Gesellen hatte. *Krausen,* E. (1959): Die Urkunden des Klosters Raitenhaslach 1034–1350. München, U 455. Ab 1359 November 25 waren es drei Gesellen und dabei bleibt es das ganze Mittelalter und die frühe Neuzeit hindurch bis zur Erhebung der Pfarrkirche St. Nikola zum Stift im Oktober 1610. Von da ab sind dann andere Rechtsverhältnisse maßgebend.

[18] *Gregor IX.* c. 3, X, 3, I anno 1234: »... ut quisque presbyter, qui plebem regit, clericum habeat, qui secum cantet et epistolam et lectionem legat, et qui posit scolas tenere et admonere suos parochianos, ut filios suos ad fidem discendam mittant ad ecclesiam, quos ipse cum omni castitate erudiat.« (... daß jeder Priester, der einer Pfarrei vorsteht, einen Cleriker habe, der mit ihm singt, die Epistel und Lektionen liest, und der imstande ist, Schule zu halten und Parochianen zu ermuntern, daß sie ihre Kinder zur Katechese in die Kirche schicken, die er selbst [der Pfarrer] mit aller Sittsamkeit unterrichten soll.) Was die Katechese, bzw. den Religionsunterricht betrifft, so wird noch 1610, als die Pfarrkirche St. Nikolaus zu Mühldorf zum Stift erhoben wird, ausdrücklich vermerkt, daß der neue Pfarrherr, der seit vier Jahren in Mühldorf und Altmühldorf als Provisor tätig war, der 32jährige *Johannes Hueber* »in Mühldorf die Verrichtung der Kinderlehre« übernehmen muß. (HStAM, St. Nikolaus Mühldorf, KL 899/1) Pfarrer *Huber* war übrigens im Besitz eines neuen Testaments von Luther aus dem Jahre 1523. Vgl. *Fickel,* Mühldorfer Literaturleben. In: Literatur in Bayern, Nr. 1, S. 6 Michael Mößl, Ursula Thalhaimer. Kleriker, die mit dem Pfarrer sangen und Schule hielten, wurden Cantoren genannt. Diese Cantoren hatten aber auch Schreiber- und Verwaltungserfahrung und waren daher vielseitig zu verwenden. Im 50 km von Mühldorf entfernten Kloster Raitenhaslach, das sich schon vor 1161 für jährlich 80 Laufener Pfennige von der Reichung des Zehnten von seinen Besitzungen an den Pfarrer von Mühldorf loskaufte (*Krausen* U 14b), und seit 1242 ein von allen Abgaben und Steuern freies Haus samt Zubehör in Mühldorf besaß (*Krausen* U 138), ist für 1286 Oktober 13 ein Frater Bozanus als Cantor belegt (*Krausen* U 408). Schon ein Jahr früher, 1285, war dieser Bozanus nicht nur Zeuge in einem Rechtsgeschäft, er war auch der Schreiber der Urkunde »prvder Pozan von Mueldorf der den brif hat geschriben« (*Krausen* U 404). 1291 hat sich Bruder *Pozan* als Prediger in Ablaßsachen bewährt (*Krausen* U 4) und 1294 April 4 wird er als Begleiter des Abtes *Conrad von Raitenhaslach* genannt (*Krausen* U 454). Ein Mann wie dieser Bruder *Bozanus,* sogar in Mühldorf zu Hause, könnte durchaus Vorgänger eines Schulmeisters gewesen sein. Schreib- und wortgewandt, Cantor und in Verwaltungssachen erfahren, war er für einen Pfarrherrn der ideale Geselle für Kirche, Chor, Schule und Verwaltung.

[18a] Wir wissen noch nichts über das Maß der schulischen Unterweisung, aber die Zeugenschaft läßt erkennen, daß die Leute um die Macht der Schriftlichkeit und ihrer Verwendung im Alltag wußten. Der Urkundenbestand vervielfachte sich ab 1200 von Jahrzehnt zu Jahrzehnt.

[19] 1242 November 15 Mühldorf, *Krausen* U 133.

[20] 1251 Mühldorf St. Nikolaus, *Krausen* U 194.

[21] 1278 September 20, BHStAM, Mühldorfer Gerichtsurkunden U 578.

[22] 1292 *Krausen* U 447.

[23] 1297 April 18 Salzburg, Monumenta Boica, LIII. U 177. Vgl. auch Regensburger Urkundenbuch München 1912.

[24] 1278 September 19, *Martin,* Die Regesten der Erzbischöfe Nr. 881
1278 September 20, BHStAM, Hochstift Salzburg, Urk. 35.

[25] dito, Stadtrichter nur L genannt. 1279 Juli 1, *Martin,* Die Regesten der Erzbischöfe Nr. 915, Stadtrichter Liebhart.

[26] 1281 Januar 1, *Martin,* Die Regesten der Erzbischöfe Nr. 978, Cristan granator. *H. Stahleder* belegt den ersten Kastner für Mühldorf erst 1321 März 8 im Historischen Atlas von Bayern, Mühldorf a. Inn, München 1978, S. 169. Auch für andere Berufsgruppen sind die Angaben *Stahleders* überholt. Die Berichtigungen von *Gollwitzer* (30 Seiten, Oktober 1978) liegen dem Handexemplar in der Bavarica Abteilung der Bayerischen Staatsbibliothek München bei.

[27] 1275 Juli 20, Erharting, BHStAM Kaiser-Selekt Nr. 1101, inseriert; BHStAM Hochstift

Salzburg Nr. 30; *Martin,* Die Regesten der Erzbischöfe Nr. 735. Dieser rechtskundige Mühldorfer Pfarrer war keine Ausnahme. So vermachte z. B. schon im Jahre 1180 der Pfarrer von Moosburg a. d. Isar sein Exemplar des Gratian dem Kloster Schäftlarn und die Sentenzen des Petrus Lombardus dem Kloster Neustift bei Freising. Vgl. *Becker,* G. (1885): Catalogi bibliothecarum antiqui, co., Bonn. Pfarrbibliotheken waren gelegentlich schon zur Zeit *Ludwig des Frommen* (814–840) beachtlich ausgestattet. So besaß z. B. die Pfarrkirche von Tannkirchen in Oberbayern folgende Werke: missales III, lectionarios III, istoria in singulis codicibus II, collectarium I, plenarium I, expositio psalmorum, psalterium in tribus codicibus, antefonarium I, commentarium I super Matheum, missales II, lectionarios II, XL omelias, officialem I, penitentialem I, aliam omeliam, psalteria II, pastorale I, antefonarium I, compotum I, ipacta. Freising. Tradit. I S. 617; zitiert nach Hauck, A. ([8]1954): Kirchengeschichte Deutschlands, Bd. II, Berlin/Leipzig, S. 204.

[28] 1294 Mai 1, Mühldorf, *Krausen* U 455. An diesem Tag übergibt Adelheid von Tann ihre Mühle zu Schoßbach »ze rehtem selgraet« an das Kloster Raitenhaslach.

[29] Z. B. 1311 Januar 6, Leonberg, Zeuge: ... Hartlieb der schuelmaister von Dingolfing; in: *Hör-Morenz,* Die Urkunden des Klosters St. Veit Nr. 28. 1328 Juli 8, Zeugen: ... Chunrad schuelmaister ze Wasserburch ... 1339 Juni 3, ... geben wir disen brief versigelt mit Chunrad des schuelmaisters insigel ze Wasserburch ... in: *Krausen* U 673 und U 702. 1379 November 11, Zeugen: ... Nikla der Hueltz, den zeiten schuelmaister zue Laentzhuett ...; in: *Hör-Morenz,* Die Urkunden des Klosters St. Veit Nr. 130.

[30] In einer Urkunde aus dem Jahre 1300 März 8, ausgestellt zu Mühldorf, ist von einem »Heinrich dem Schulmeister an der Altenkapell zu Regensburg, des Erzbischofs Schreiber« die Rede. *Martin,* Die Regesten der Erzbischöfe Nr. 483.

[30a] *Acht,* Die Traditionen des Klosters Tegernsee, Nr. 383.

[31] 1305 Mai 24, *Martin,* Die Regesten der Erzbischöfe, Band II, Nr. 741. Kaplan *Läutwein* vertritt den Erzbischof von Salzburg in einem Rechtsgeschäft.

[32] 1318 Juni 26, *Martin,* Die Regesten der Erzbischöfe, Bd. III, Nr. 103.

[33] 1341 August 22, Pfarrarchiv St. Nikolaus, Regesta Geissiana, A 12/8, S. 17.

[34] Je nach den finanziellen Ausstattungen entwickelte sich in der Pfarrei eine Pfarr- oder Mesnerschule. War die Pfarrei mit Stiftungen gut dotiert, so konnte sich der Pfarrer einen Gesellen, bzw. einen Cooperator halten und die Schule wurde Pfarrschule. War die Pfarrei arm, so konnte nur ein Mesner eingestellt werden, der aus Kirchengut etwas Grund übereignet bekam, um wenigstens die Bedürfnisse des täglichen Lebens bestreiten zu können. Nebenbei half der Mesner dem Pfarrer in der Schule, oder umgekehrt. Wer sich die Mühe macht die Universitätsmatrikel der abendländischen Universitäten zu studieren, der stellt fest, daß besonders vor der Reformation hunderte von Studenten aus altbayerischen Dörfern und Märkten kamen. Die Anfangsgründe im Lesen und Schreiben, aber auch im Latein, haben sie sicher in der heimatlichen Pfarr- oder Mesnerschule erworben. Auch Söhne von Mesnerlehrern haben es gelegentlich zu Ehre und Ansehen gebracht. Der Sohn *Wolfgang* des Mesnerlehrers *Kolbinger* wurde Kanzler des *Herzog Georg des Reichen* von Niederbayern. Er wurde Reichsfreiherr und Reichsgraf, sowie Besitzer mehrerer Hofmarken und Herrschaften. Vgl. das weitere Schicksal bei Doeberl, M.: Entwicklungsgeschichte Bayerns, Bd. I, S. 329. Der Bruder von *Wolfgang, Georg Kolbinger,* wurde Pfarrer in Eggenfelden und später Bischof von Gurk.

[35] 1303 April 5, *Martin,* Die Regesten der Erzbischöfe, Bd. II, Nr. 642. In dieser Urkunde sind Mühldorfer Ratsmitglieder bereits namentlich erwähnt. 1312 Januar 25, *Martin,* Die Regesten der Erzbischöfe, Bd. II, Nr. 1050. Unter den Siegelzeugen ein *Konrad,* der Schreiber. 1317 Juli 8, *Martin,* Die Regesten der Erzbischöfe, Bd. III, Nr. 47. Unter den Zeugen ein

Heinrich, der Schreiber. (Bei *Stahleder,* Historischer Atlas von Mühldorf, erscheint der erste Stadtschreiber erst 1407.)

36 BHStAM, Kollegiatstift Mühldorf, Urk. 6.

37 BHStAM, Kollegiatstift Mühldorf, Urk. 6: 1359 November 25; Urk. 38: 1393 Dezember 6; Urk. 64: 1405 Mai 4; Urk. 78: 1412 Februar 5; Urk. 103: 1425 Januar 28; Urk. 106: 1426 November 11; Urk. 110: 1429 September 20; Urk. 114: 1430 Mai 22; Urk. 144: 1441 September 25
Stadtarchiv Mühldorf, Urk. 14: 1450 Oktober 20; Urk. 27: 1463 Dezember 4; Urk. 55: 1495 Dezember 22
BHStAM, Chorstift Mühldorf, 17. Fasc. 1510 November 4; 17. Fasc. 1512 April 1; 17. Fasc. 1514 April 26

38 1242 Juli 13, Salzburg, *Hauthaler-Martin,* SUB III, U 993.

39 BHStAM, Chorstift Mühldorf, Literalien 1, 1339 Oktober 21. Zechmeister: *Chunrat* der Neunmaister, *Hainrich* der junger *Grien.*

40 1360 Januar 6, bestätigen der Richter, der Rat und die Bürgerschaft zu Mühldorf den »Lotmeistern« (Lodenmeister-Tuchmacher) eine Handwerksordnung. Erste Mühldorfer Zunft-Ordnung; BHStAM, Gerichtsurkunde (GU) Mühldorf, Nr. 35.

41 Pfarrbeschreibung im Ordinariatsarchiv, Copie: de Parochis et vicariis in Altenmühldorf. Zitiert nach Held III, S. 126.

42 1549 Oktober 1, Burghausen, BHStAM, Chorstift Mühldorf, 19. Fasc. Vgl. auch Anm. 44 1409 April 22.

43 *Held,* H. (1926/28): Bd. III, S. 126f. *Held* beruft sich auf Zillner, Geschichte des Fürsterzbistums Salzburg, S. 169. Dort ist die Stelle aber nicht zu belegen. *Helds* Belege sind in der Regel immer zuverlässig, doch tauchen sie verschiedentlich an anderer Stelle auf als zitiert, oft auch mit einer anderen Jahreszahl. Aus diesem Grunde bin ich dem Namen Jakob und dem Titel Meister in den Urkunden nachgegangen.

44 *Jakob Zollner,* bzw. *Jakob der Zöllner,* ist 1409 April 22, erstmals zusammen mit Chunrat Chrämel, Pfarrer zu Altenmühldorf als Zeuge zu belegen. BHStAM, Kollegiatstift Mühldorf, Urk. 71
1410 Oktober 12, Jacob Zolner zu Muldorf, Siegelbittzeuge; *Hör-Morenz,* Die Urkunden des Klosters St. Veit, Nr. 173
1412 Dezember 6, Jacob der Zollner Bürger zu Mühldorf, Zeuge; BHStAM, Kollegiatstift Mühldorf, Urk. 81
1416 Dezember 14, Jacob der Zolner zu Mühldorf, Siegler der Urkunde; dito, Urk. 87
1418 Mai 21, Jacob der Zolner Probst zu Altenmühldorf, Siegler der Urkunde; dito, Urk. 92
1419 März 16, *Erzbischof Eberhard* von Salzburg verleiht *Jacob Zollner* und seinen Söhnen eine Reihe von Lehen; Mell, R. (1904): Abhandlungen zur Geschichte der Landstände im Erzbistum Salzburg, Anhang. In: Mitteilungen der Gesellschaft für Salzburger Landeskunde XLIV. Vereinsjahr 1904, S. 243.

45 Die Tageslöhne betrugen 1468 (frühester Beleg) zwischen 12 und 18 Pfennig. Gelegentlich bezahlte die Stadt auch 20 Pfennig, im Winter gab es weniger; Stadtkammerrechnungen Mühldorf, 1468 R 1/1.

46 1408 April 24, Der Mühldorfer Bürger *Meister Jacob* bekennt, daß ihm die Stadt Mühldorf alle Ansprüche, welche ihm wegen der von ihm dortselbst in ihrem Auftrage über den Inn geschlagenen Brücke erwachsen sind, ausgerichtet hat; BHStAM, Mühldorfer Gerichtsurkunden, U 76
1419 November 9, *Meister Hainreich,* Brückenmeister von Mühldorf, ist in einem Schiedsge-

richts-Verfahren unter den Schiedsleuten aufgeführt; Obb. Archiv, 55. Band (1910) S. 341, Regesten des Klosters Altenhohenau U 316
1421 November 6, *Meister Hainreich,* Bruckmeister zu Muldorf, ist Urteiler in einem Schiedsgerichtsverfahren; BHStAM, Kloster-Urkunden Attel, U 117
Eine Austragsbeschäftigung, die zur damaligen Zeit durchaus üblich war, hätte *Meister Jakob* an der deutschen Schule spätestens 1419 ausüben können.

47 1414 Dezember 6, in dieser Verkaufs-, bzw. Verstiftungsurkunde nennt er sich *Jacob der Arnstorffer,* Capellan der ewigen Messe, die Wolfhart der Öder gen unser Frauen zu Mühldorf gestiftet hat; BHStAM, Kollegiatstift Mühldorf, Urk. 84
1417 Juni 29, in dieser Erbrechtsangelegenheit nennt er sich Herr *Jacob Arnstorffer,* Chappelan der Ewigen Messe unserer Frauen zu Mühldorf; dito, Urk. 90
1423 Juli 12, *Jacob Arnstoffer,* der erste Cappelan des Altars der »Heilig drey Chining« in unserer Frauen Kirche zu Mühldorf und der ewigen Messe, die Wolfhart der Öder, gestiftet hat, erhält von den Zechleuten von St. Niclas ein Haus, gelegen zu Mühldorf zwischen der Schule und Urban des Tumpergers Stadel. Ferner wird erwähnt, daß Arnstorffer ein Tagezeitbuch und einen Psalter auf Pergament geschrieben hat; dito, Urk. 99
1426 November 11, *Jacob Awrstorffer,* Pfarrer zu Erharting, ist Zeuge in einer Verstiftung; dito, Urk. 106
1431 März 11, Aus dem Nachlaß des Herrn *Jacob Awrstorffer,* früher Pfarrer zu Erharting selig, erhält das Gotteshaus zu Erharting ein Meßbuch, ein weißes Tagzeitbuch, einen großen Psalter und das Gotteshaus St. Ulrich auf dem Dornberg, das zur Erhartinger Pfarrei gehört, auch ein Meßbuch und einen vergoldeten kupfernen Kelch. Ferner erhalten die zwei Gotteshäuser je zur Hälfte zwölf Gulden ungarische Tukaten; BHStAM, Kollegiatstift Mühldorf, U 119.

48 Stadtkammerrechnungen Mühldorf, 1480, R 1/5.

49 1535, Ausgaben für die Schule: In den vier Tagen vor »Vasten« wurden »pankhen« angefertigt 2 Schilling 10 Pfennig. In der Woche vor »viti« hat die Stadt in der untern Stube der Schule den Boden ausbessern lassen 3 Schilling 6 Pfennig; Stadtkammerrechnungen Mühldorf, 1535, R 1/53.

50 Vgl. Anm. 55.

51 An der lateinischen Schule mußte unentgeltlich unterrichtet werden nach dem Grundsatz: gratis accepistis, gratis date (decr. Greg. IX, V, 5, I, 2, 3.). Dabei darf nicht übersehen werden, daß der lateinischen Schule zahlreiche Stiftungen zur Verfügung standen, für die sie allerdings Leistungen erbringen mußte. 1416 Dezember 13 erfolgte eine Stiftung von 8 Pfund Pfennig Landeswährung an die Pfarrkirche St. Nikola zu Mühldorf. Dafür wurde u. a. die Verpflichtung eingegangen: Wenn ein Priester einen Versehgang macht, so sollen ihn vier Schüler mit Chorrock und Chorkappe begleiten und jeder soll eine Wandelkerze tragen, die 1½ Pfund Wachs hat. Sie sollen den Gesang singen, der zu Gottsleichnam gesungen wird. ...; BHStAM, Kollegiatstift Mühldorf, Urk. 86. Vgl. *Held* III, S. 127. Auf dem Hinweg mußte der Kopf unbedeckt bleiben aus Ehrfurcht vor dem Allerheiligsten, auch bei strengster Kälte. Viele Kinder haben sich bei solchen Versehgängen ein »lebenslanges Kopfreissen« zugezogen. Auch der berühmte Lehrer, Organist und Komponist Anton Bruckner führte seine immer wieder auftretenden neuralgischen Kopfschmerzen auf solche Versehgänge zurück.

52 1552 Mai 20, *Milhauser* bittet um Bezahlung des Schulgeldes von den Kindern; 1552 Juli 29, *Mülhauser* »von wegen des Schulgeldes«; Stadtgerichtsbuch Mühldorf, 1552, B 1/2, S. 22 u. S. 24.

53 Noch im 19. Jahrhundert wurde den Universitätsprofessoren empfohlen, sich um einen Nebenerwerb zu bemühen.

[54] Vgl. dazu *Widmann* H. (1909): Geschichte Salzburgs, Bd. II. Gotha, S. 328ff. und *Lichnowsky,* Geschichte Habsburgs, VIII. Teil.

[55] Stadtkammerrechnungen Mühldorf, 1483, R 1/7.

[56] Stadtkammerrechnungen Mühldorf, 1484, R 1/8. Ob »Maister Jürgen Kriechpawn« der 1487 von der Stadt wegen »Instrumentea und Appellacion gen Rom 2 rhein. Gulden« erhält mit dem Schulmeister von 1484 identisch ist, muß offen bleiben; Stadtkammerrechnungen Mühldorf, 1487, R 1/9.

[57] Stadtkammerrechnungen Mühldorf, 1548, R 1/65.

[58] Stadtgerichtsbuch Mühldorf, 1544, B 1/1.

[59] BHStAM, Chorstift Mühldorf, Literalien 4.

[60] BHStAM, Kollegiatstift Mühldorf, Urk. 6.

[61] So studierte z. B. 1357 ein Pfarrer *Johann von Altenmühldorf* in Bologna. (acta nat. Germ., S. 124, Z 45 Suppl. 38, fol. 71)

[62] Andernorts wurden sie oft auch »Knechte« genannt.

[63] Stadtkammerrechnungen Mühldorf, 1524, R 1/41.

[64] 1558 Item dem lateinischen Schuelmaister auf sein Anhalten für das Ausreiten am Tag Galli, aus Ursach seiner Schwachheit und daß er mit keinem Cantor versehen, aus gutem Willen und keiner Gerechtigkeit, werden durch den Rat bewilligt 2 Pfund; Stadtkammerrechnungen Mühldorf, 1558, R 1/75.

[65] 1571 wird erstmals von zwei Schulhaltern gesprochen; Stadtgerichtsbuch Mühldorf, 1571, B 1/3, S. 354. Vgl. *Held* III S. 128. Dazu kommt als dritter Schullehrer der Organist, welcher 1576 Oktober 5 erstmals zu belegen ist. An diesem Tag wird Johannes Maenwinckhler von Burghausen als Organist angenommen; Stadtgerichtsbuch B 1/4 S. 199.

[66] Bei der deutschen Schule blieb es bei zwei Schulräumen bis zum 19. Jahrhundert.

[67] Es gab einen lateinischen Schulmeister und einen Cantor. Beide sind erstmals 1558 Juni 3 namentlich zu belegen; Stadtgerichtsbuch Mühldorf, 1558, B 1/2 S. 253. Der Organist hat zwar unter dem lateinischen Schulmeister »die Orgel geschlagen«, war aber als Lehrer an der deutschen Schule tätig.

[68] Die deutschen und lateinischen Schulmeister wurden vom Rat der Stadt aufgenommen, die practentarii und adstanti vom jeweiligen Schulmeister. Letzterer hatte dies dem Rat persönlich oder schriftlich anzuzeigen und der Adstant mußte persönlich vor dem Rat erscheinen.

[69] Aufgrund einer Steuerbeschreibung aus dem Jahre 1637, (BHStAM, Gerichtsliteralien Mühldorf, 424) hatte Mühldorf im Jahre 1637 bei 1090 anwesenden Einwohnern höchstens 268 Kinder bis 14 Jahre. Das ergibt jährlich etwa 19 Kinder. Bei einer 6jährigen Schulpflicht, wahrscheinlich war sie um 1500 wesentlich kürzer, wären es also 114 Kinder für vier Klassen. Mühldorf hatte um 1500 sicher weniger Einwohner. Bei einem 100%igen Schulbesuch und vier Klassen kann also von einer durchschnittlichen Klassenstärke von höchstens 25 Kindern ausgegangen werden. Die tatsächlichen Klassenstärken haben aber sicher sehr geschwankt. Der alte, erfahrene Lehrer an der deutschen Schule hatte oft doppelt soviel Kinder als sein junger Kollege, dafür stand ihm aber auch der Organist und Adstant als Hilfe zur Verfügung. Aufgrund von Visitationsakten läßt sich dies jedoch erst für die Zeit um 1550 einwandfrei belegen, jedoch nicht für Mühldorf, da diese Stadt als Salzburger Enklave der bayerischen Visitation unter *Albrecht V.* »nicht unterworfen war«.

[70] Dies trifft nicht nur für Altbayern, sondern auch für Schwaben zu. So ist z. B. 1422 August 29 ein *Geori Pruggschlegel,* in den sieben freien Künsten Baccalaureus, Schulmeister zu Kaufbeuren. Vgl. *Dertsch,* R. (1955): Die Urkunden der Stadt Kaufbeuren. Augsburg. 1477 August 8 ist Ulrich Weinmann Notar und Schulmeister von Dillingen. Vgl. *Buchner,* K. (1953): Die Urkunden des Klosters Oberschönenfeld. Augsburg 1953.

[71] 1377–1400 14 Studenten in Wien
1401–1420 19 Studenten in Wien
1421–1440 31 Studenten in Wien
1441–1460 54 Studenten in Wien
1461–1480 49 Studenten 42 Wien, 3 Leipzig, 4 Ingolstadt
1481–1500 70 Studenten 48 Wien, 11 Leipzig, 11 Ingolstadt
1501–1520 71 Studenten 50 Wien, 1 Leipzig, 20 Ingolstadt
1521–1540 3 Studenten 3 Ingolstadt

[72] Vgl. *Gollwitzer* H., Mühldorfer Studenten an der Wiener Universität. In: Das Mühlrad, Bd. XI, S. 83ff.

[73] Adler, Zeitschrift für Genealogie und Heraldik, 10. (XXIV.) Band, Heft 11, 1976, S. 314ff., S. 318; S. 327 findet sich sein Notariatssignet.

[74] Matrikel der Universität Wien, Bd. I, S. 293, Spalte 2.

[75] 1515 7 Studenten 1518 1 Student
1516 8 Studenten 1519 1 Student
1517 5 Studenten

[76] 1637 März 30, Sylvester Eder, deutscher Schulhalter, 30 Gulden [Vermögen] 27 Pfennig [Steuer]
1637 März 30, Thoman Vischer, Schulhalter, 50 Gulden [Vermögen] 1 Schilling 15 Pfennig [Steuer] (BHStAM, Gerichtsliteralien Mühldorf, 424)
1608 Wolf Gasteiger, lateinischer Schulmeister, 100 Gulden Vermögen (BHStAM, Gerichtsliteralien Mühldorf, 250).

[77] 1601 Paur Erhard, deutscher Schulmeister, 200 Gulden
1608 Paur Erhard, deutscher Schulmeister, 286 Gulden
(BHStAM, Gerichtsliteralien Mühldorf, 249, 1601,
250, 1608).

[78] 1604 wurde ein neues Bruckmeisterhaus gebaut um den Preis von 98 Pfund 3 Schilling 28 Pfennig
1 Pfund Pfennig = 240 Pfennig = 8 Schilling
1 Gulden = 210 Pfennig = 7 Schilling
8 Gulden entsprechen 7 Pfund Pfenningen. Somit kostete das Bruckmeisterhaus etwa 112½ Gulden.

[79] Dem Teutschen Schuelmaister Trinkgeld von wegen der Schulden der Burger zuschreiben 88 Pfennig; Stadtkammerrechnungen Mühldorf, 1525, R 1/42.

[80] 1528 Dem Schulmaister, so an der Herrn Fastnacht im Pfarrhof gesungen Trinkgeld 42 Pfennig, ab 1532 1 Schilling 22½ Pfennig = 52½ Pfennig; Stadtkammerrechnungen Mühldorf, 1528, R 1/46; 1532, R 1/50.

[81] 1533 erhielt er den Betrag nur einmal, ab 1535 zweimal; Stadtkammerrechnungen Mühldorf, 1533, R 1/51; 1535, R 1/53
Noch 1777 November 11 erhält *Andreas Beer* »auf sein Ansuchen« die Schützenschreiberei; Ratsprotokolle Mühldorf, 1777, B 1/106.

[82] 1614 bindet *Onopherus Asam*, deutscher Schulmeister, die Rechnungen der Stadt;
1615 Oktober 2, erhält der lateinische Schulmeister für das Einbinden des Rapulars (mittellateinische Verserzählungen) 1 Schilling 1½ Pfennig;
1619 erhält *Onopherus Asam* für das Einbinden eines Rapulars und für das Pergament 1 Schilling; Stadtkammerrechnungen Mühldorf, 1614, R 1/131; 1615, R 1/138; 1619, R 1/138.
Da Schulmeister sehr viel mit der Schreiberei zu tun hatten, haben sie oft auch mit Papier und

Pergament gehandelt. Ausweislich der Ratsprotokolle hat die Stadt Mühldorf im Jahre 1481 beim Neumarkter Schulmeister (17 km von Mühldorf entfernt) Papier und Pergament gekauft.

83 Aufgrund der Stadtkammerrechnungen bezahlte die Stadt an Tageslöhnen:
1550 Zimmerer 22 Pfennig, im Winter 18 Pfennig
1550 Aufleger 16 Pfennig, im Winter 14 Pfennig
1539 Taglöhner 5 Kreuzer = 17½ Pfennig, im Winter 14 Pfennig
1620 Zimmerleute 8 Kreuzer = 28 Pfennig
1621 Zimmerleute 9 Kreuzer = 31½ Pfennige
1602 Aufleger 6 Kreuzer = 21 Pfennig
1601 Taglöhner 5–6 Kreuzer=17½ Pfennig–21 Pfennig
1621 kostete ein Pfund bestes Ochsenfleisch 13 Pfennig, ein Pfund Kalbfleisch 9 Pfennig, ein Pfund Schaffleisch 8 Pfennig, ¼ gemeines Bier (etwa 1½ Liter) 9 Pfennige

84 1496 ... 1 Fenster in dem Stübl in der Schule 50 Pfennig;
1548 Beim lateinischen Schulmeister und bei unserm werden die Rauchfänge gekehrt;
1543 ... für Glas bessern beim Schulmeister und Thurner 5 Schilling 17 Pfennig;
Stadtkammerrechnungen Mühldorf, 1496, R 1/16; 1548, R 1/65; 1543, R 1/62.

85 1563 Adam Obermayr, deutscher Schulmeister, erhält für sein Spiel das er am Sonntag Lätare auf dem Rathaus gehalten hat, 2 Pfund verehrt; Stadtkammerrechnungen 1563, R 1/80.
1577 Magister Peter hat gemeiner Stadt zu Ehren eine Tragedi agiert und erhielt verehrt 2 Pfund; Stadtkammerrechnungen Mühldorf, 1577, R 1/94.
Neben dem Aufführen der »Tragedi et Comedi« erhielten die Schulmeister auch noch für das Recordieren, also das Umhersingen, 2 Pfund. Z. B. 1563 Dem lateinischen Schulmeister wegen der Recordation Galli vom ehrsamen Rat 2 Pfund; Stadtkammerrechnungen Mühldorf, 1563, R 1/80.

86 1558 ... aus Ursach seiner Schwachheit und daß er mit keinem Cantor versehen, aus gutem Willen und keiner Gerechtigkeit ... 2 Pfund; Stadtkammerrechnungen Mühldorf, 1558, R 1/75.

87 Vgl. Text zu den Anm. 100–103.

88 Ratsprotokolle Mühldorf, 1602, B 1/7.

89 1513 Juni 26–1529 Oktober 4, Leonhard Medlinger; BHStAM, Chorstift Mühldorf, 17. Fasc. u. 18. Fasc.

90 1555 Dezember 30–1575 Mai 22, Clement Pumpler; Stadtarchiv Mühldorf, Ratsprotokolle 1555, B 1/2. BHStAM, Chorstift Mühldorf, 21. Fasc.

91 Vgl. Anm. 68.

92 Gelegentlich findet sich in den Ratsprotokollen, nicht nur in Mühldorf, die Aufnahme eines Schulmeister zweimal im Abstand von einigen Tagen, Wochen oder Monaten. In diesem Fall ist die erste Aufnahme zur Probe, die zweite Aufnahme ist erst die endgültige.

93 1629 Januar 12; Ratsprotokolle Mühldorf, 1629, B 1/18.

94 1630 November 22; Ratsprotokolle Mühldorf, 1630, B 1/19.

95 1612 hatte Mühldorf drei Procuratoren. Am 2. Juli wurde jeder von ihnen mit 1 Pfund Strafe belegt, weil sie sich nicht zur gebührlichen Stunde vor der Ratsstube eingefunden haben.

96 1622 März 4; Ratsprotokolle Mühldorf, 1622, B 1/12. Solche Empfehlungen waren früher auch schon andernorts üblich. So haben sich z. B. 1559 für den *Antonius Obernperger,* lateinischer Schulmeister in Eggenfelden, bei der Anstellung der Pfarrvikar, der Landrichter und der Kastner verwendet. *Haushofer,* J. (1976): Die Schulgeschichte von Eggenfelden bis zum Dreißigjährigen Krieg. In: Beiträge zur Heimatkunde von Niederbayern, Bd. III. Landshut, S. 263.

[97] 1630 Januar 29; Matrikel Mühldorf, B 94/18, Original im Pfarrarchiv, Kopie im Stadtarchiv Mühldorf.

[98] Ratsprotokolle Mühldorf, 1630, B 1/19.

[99] 1637 März 30, Thoman Vischer, Schulhalter, H(ausfrau), 3 K(inder) unter 14 J(ahren) 50 Gulden [Vermögen], 1 Schilling 15 Pfennig [Steuer].

[100] 1639 Juli 15; Ratsprotokolle Mühldorf, 1639, B 1/27.

[101] Zwar mag eine Lehrerswitwe im 19. Jahrhundert einige Kreuzer mehr erhalten haben, doch ist zu bedenken, daß ein Anspruch auf Versorgung erst durch Einzahlung in eine Witwen- oder Waisenkasse bestand, andererseits hat sich die Kaufkraft schon seit 1605 zusehends reduziert. Die Geschichtsforscher in ganz Europa stellen fest, daß im Vergleich zum 15. und 16. Jahrhundert, schon vor Beginn des 30jährigen Krieges ein Reallohn-Verfall eingesetzt hat, der erst im ausgehenden 19. Jahrhundert zu einem ersten Stillstand gebracht werden konnte.

[102] 1653 August 20, Jakob Hannsler ist vom Capitel zum lateinischen Schulmeister acceptiert worden und erbittet das gleiche von der Obrigkeit, sowie den freien Holzgenuß – Wird genehmigt, Eidesleistung vor dem Amtsbürgermeister; Ratsprotokolle Mühldorf, 1653, B 1/41.

[103] 1698 Februar 15; Ratsprotokolle Mühldorf, 1698, B 1/53.

[104] 1569 Juni 3, Zerer Georg, deutscher Schulmeister; Bürgerbuch Mühldorf, 1569, B 3, S. 362.

[105] *Gesandte* kamen von Neuenstadt in Sachsen und Geiersberg in Schlesien, sie kamen aus dem Land der Ungarn und der Türken, *Buchdrucker* aus Augsburg und Mainz zogen durch Mühldorf, *Studenten* aus Mainz und Bamberg, aus Coburg und Ulm, aus Goldberg in Schlesien und aus Luzern, aus Eßlingen und Eichstädt, von Rom kommend und nach Rom ziehend, baten sie in Mühldorf um ein »Viaticum«. *Schreiber* aus Salzburg und Ingolstadt, aus Eger und Bozen im Etschland, aus Kärnten, Kufstein, Laibach und Heidelberg, aus Steyr, Breslau, Erfurt, Prag und Braunschweig boten ihre Dienste an, *Organisten und Schulmeister* aus Graz, Landsberg und Weißenhorn, aus Bamberg, Weißenburg und Willentzheim bei Würzburg, aus Sterzing, Eichstädt, Erfurt und Abensberg, aus dem Kloster Dießen und der Markgrafschaft Baden, suchten in Mühldorf Arbeit. *»Ein Zwergl von Felgkhlprugkh«* reiste durch Mühldorf und *»Meister Michael Märckhl,* ein Luftspringer« zeigte seine Künste und erhielt wegen seiner vielen kleinen Kinder von der Stadt drei Äcker als Pachtgründe.
Dies ist nur eine Auswahl aus der 2. Hälfte des 16. Jahrhunderts. Die Angaben wurden den Stadtkammerrechnungen entnommen.

[106] Ein eindrucksvolles Beispiel ist hier der oft genannte *Kristofferus Hueber.* Er ist der Typ des unruhigen, weit gereisten Schulmeisters und Schreibers, der nicht nur in Bayern umherzog, sondern auch in Österreich und Ungarn, in der Schweiz und in Italien »sein Geschäft betrieb«. Sein Handbuch, (Staatsbibliothek München, Cgm 216) ein 163 Blatt starker Foliant, vermittelt uns interessante und aufschlußreiche Einblicke in den Tätigkeitsbereich eines deutschen Schulmeisters und Schreibers in der zweiten Hälfte des 15. Jahrhunderts. Manches erscheint abwegig, wie z. B. 23^{r}, die Verproviantierung der durch König *Mathias v. Ungarn* belagerten Wiener-Neustadt durch *Ruprecht v. Rechenberg* (5. Febr. 1487). Das Ganze gewinnt jedoch an Sinn angesichts der Tatsache, daß die deutschen Schulmeister im Amt des Furiers oft nebenbei für die Verpflegung der Stadt bei Belagerungen zuständig waren. In Mühldorf war dies z. B. der deutsche Schulmeister *Onopherus Asam.*

[107] Die Aufnahmegebühr richtete sich nach dem zu erwartenden Einkommen. 4 Pfund war die Regel. Gastgeber, Bräuer, Kaufleute und Buchführer zahlten 8–10 Pfund. Hatte der aufgenommene Schulmeister nur Schulerfahrung, oder waren z. Zt. keine Nebenbeschäftigungen frei, wurde dies ausdrücklich vermerkt, z. B. 1569 Juni 3, *Georg Zerer,* deutscher Schulmeister, will sich allein mit der Schule unterhalten; Bürgerbuch Mühldorf, 1569, B 3, S. 362.

[108] Lateinische Schulmeister, vor allem aber Kantoren und Organisten, blieben oft noch viel länger in der Stadt.

[109] 1562 Juni 8, der deutsche Schulmeister *Oderperger* soll sich des Metschenkens neben der Schulhaltung enthalten, oder die Schule aufgeben; Stadtgerichtsbuch Mühldorf, 1562, B 1/2, S. 475. Nebentätigkeiten die mit Schreiben, Papier, Singen oder Kirchendienst zu tun hatten, waren »erlaubt«, nicht aber die Tätigkeit als Wirt.

[110] Stadtgerichtsbuch Mühldorf, 1553, B 1/2, S. 60.

[111] Stadtkammerrechnungen Mühldorf, 1568, R 1/80.

[112] Stadtgerichtsbuch Mühldorf, 1570, B 1/3, S. 290.

[113] Stadtgerichtsbuch Mühldorf, 1571, B 1/3, S. 354. Vgl. *Held* (1926/28), III, S. 128.

[114] BHStAM, Erzstift Salzburg, 1037, Mandat vom 31. März 1594.

[115] 1576, BHStAM, Kollegiatstift Mühldorf, Literalien 5. Vgl. *Held* (1926/28), III, S. 129.

[116] 1577, »wenn er wiederkommt, soll er günstigen Bescheid erhalten«; Bürgerbuch Mühldorf, 1577, B 3b, S. 414.

[117] 1574 September 3; Stadtgerichtsbuch Mühldorf, 1574, B 1/4, S. 24. Aufgrund dieses Beleges war *Wagner* also schon vor dem 3. September 1574 in Trostberg als Schulmeister tätig. Bei *Held* (1926/28), Bd. II, S. 133 ist *Wagner* erst für 1615 als Schulmeister in Trostberg belegt.

[118] Stadtgerichtsbuch Mühldorf, 1576, B 1/4, S. 157f.

[119] Vorläufig zitiert nach *Heigenmooser-Bock,* Geschichte der Pädagogik I, S. 75.

[120] Zitiert nach Gentner (1883): Geschichte der Stadt Laufen. München, S. 78. Vgl. auch *Held* (1926/28), III, S. 398.

[121] Vorläufig zitiert nach Held (1926/28), III, S. 398.

[122] Held (1926/28), II, S. 133.

[123] Z. B. *Jörg Lackhners* Sohn, der ältere, ist heute zum Cantor auf Befürwortung und Fürbitte des *Sebastian Veichtner,* Schulmeister, aufgenommen worden. Er soll die Kinder in aller Zucht gebührlich unterweisen; Stadtgerichtsbuch Mühldorf, 1558, B 1/2, S. 253. *Jörg Lackhner* ist 1556 an der Universität Ingolstadt als Student nachweisbar. Sein Vater, ebenfalls *Jörg,* ist 1519 in Ingolstadt zu belegen.

[124] Z. B. 1577 Januar 28, Magister *Peter Walther* ist lateinischer Schulmeister; Stadtgerichtsbuch Mühldorf, 1577, B 1/4, S. 232; 1583 April 29, Magister *Gamaliel Sigmair,* lateinischer Schulmeister, soll der Schule und Kirche besser als bisher aufwarten; dito, 1583, B 1/5, S. 300; 1627 Januar 29, Magister *Wendelin Ölhafen* ist lateinischer Schulmeister; Ratsprotokolle Mühldorf, 1627, B 1/15.

[125] Die Begründung lautete dann in der Regel: »Der Bitte wird willfahren, weil er eines so alten Bürgers Kind ist.«

[126] Gelegentlich übernahm auch ein »Jungmeister«, also ein Geselle, aus einem anderen Berufsstand vorrübergehend die lateinische Schule. 1530 Dem Gregori Wienner, Schnitzer, für den Jungmeister als er Chor und Schule regiert, weil Schulmeister gefangen gewest Zehrung 1 Gulden 17 Pfennig; Stadtkammerrechnungen Mühldorf, 1530, R 1/48. Dies ist ein schöner Beleg für den hohen Bildungsstand der Handwerksgesellen.

[127] Das Ende einer Auseinandersetzung wurde dann im Gerichtsbuch so festgehalten: »Im übrigen sollen beide in Kirche und Schule fleissiger sein als bisher und künftig einig und friedlich sein. Visitation werde demnächst vorgenommen«; Stadtgerichtsbuch Mühldorf, 1583, B 1/5, S. 319f.

[128] 1623 September 20; Ratsprotokolle Mühldorf, 1623, B 1/13.

[129] Z. B. 1583 Juni 6; Stadtgerichtsbuch Mühldorf, 1583, B 1/5, S. 319f.; 1589 Oktober 6; Ratsprotokolle Mühldorf, 1589, B 1/6, S. 847.

[130] 1590 Juni 8; Ratsprotokolle Mühldorf, 1590, B 1/6, S. 1035.

[131] 1587 Mai 8, *Johann Winckler,* candidatus philologiae, des Herrn von Maxlrain und des Closters Praeseptor und Oeconoms, erhält die »Function« der lateinischen Schule übertragen. So oft er einen »Practendarien« oder »Astanten« aufnimmt, hat er dies dem Rat persönlich oder schriftlich anzuzeigen und der Astant muß jedesmal persönlich vor dem Rat erscheinen; Ratsprotokolle Mühldorf, 1587, B 1/6, S. 301.

[132] Stadtkammerrechnungen Mühldorf, 1587, R 1/104.

[133] Vgl. *Fickel* (1985), S. 12f.

[134] Nur dem *Gereth Daniel* aus Torn in Preußen gebürtig, ist dies gelungen. Stiftsdechant und Rat haben den ehrsamen *Daniel Gereth* zu einem »schuelhalter auf- und angenumen«, das Konsistorium hatte Bedenken, denn ohne die Stelle angetreten zu haben, beklagte *Gereth* schon die geringe Besoldung und bat um Addition. Das war am 6. Juni 1614. Am 9. Juni wollte dann der Dechant den Schulmeister beurlauben, da er u. a. mit Gesang und Stimme untauglich sei und präsentierte am 28. Juni den »fürnemen conradus fölkh von Pabenham aus dem Schwaben«. Mit Entschließung vom 18. Juli besteht nun das Konsistorium auf Gereth und der Dechant nimmt ihn auf; zitiert nach *Held* (1926/28), III, S. 129. *Gereth* war sicher nur kurz in Mühldorf, denn er ist in den Mühldorfer Büchern nicht zu belegen.

[135] 1578 September 26; Stadtgerichtsbuch Mühldorf, 1578, B 1/4, S. 382.

[136] 1567 Mai 5; Stadtgerichtsbuch Mühldorf, 1567, B 1/3, S. 125; *Held* (1926/28), III, S. 127/28.

[137] 1637 März 30, Visitationsprotokoll: Magister *Wendelin Oelhafen* aus Irschhausen im Bistum Constanz, hier seit 16 Jahren, unterrichtet die Jugend lateinisch und deutsch, hat drei »Rudimentisten«; zitiert nach *Held* (1926/28), III, S. 130;
1649 Dezember 3 ist Stiftsschulmeister Magister *Wendelin Oelhafen* letztmals belegt; Ratsprotokolle Mühldorf, 1649, B 1/37;
1653 ist der Nachfolger von *Oelhafen* zu belegen. *Johann Turnplaster,* lateinischer und deutscher Schulmeister, bei Laufen geboren, 32 Jahre alt, vom Dechant und dem Stadtrath vor 2½ Jahren aufgenommen, hat im ganzen 43 Schüler; die lateinischen unterrichtet er in principiis und in rudimentis; zitiert nach *Held* (1926/28), III, S. 131.

[138] Im Protokoll über die Erhebung der Pfarrkirche St. Nikolaus zum Stift, heißt es 1610: *Hans Zellhover,* Organist, geboren zu Burghausen, seit 14 Jahren hier im Dienst, verheiratet, keine Kinder, soll alle Sonn- und Feiertage wie auch alle Donnerstage und wenn sonst Feste sind oder wenn es der Dechant ihm befiehlt, die Orgel schlagen; BHStAM, Kollegiatstift St. Nikolaus Mühldorf, KL 899/1;
1618, aus dem Urbarium für das Bruderhaus ... *Hannß Kholnhover,* Organist, geboren zu Burghausen, verheiratet, hat Besoldung von der S. Peters-Capellen, darin ein Regal [= harmoniumartiges Tasteninstrument, der Ton wird durch kleine Zungen erzeugt, die von einem Blasbalg mit Wind gespeist werden] und bisweilen ein Gottesdienst gehalten wird, 12 Gulden ... Daneben hat er Teutsche Schuel; da es ohne die wär, möcht er sich nit erhalten; BHStAM, Erzstift Salzburg, 714. *Hannß Kholnhover* ist identisch mit *Hanns Zellhover.*

[138a] *Marcus Wendl,* Cantor, bei 20 Jahren hier im Amt, geboren zu Freising, verheiratet, 3 Kinder, ein schwacher Mann, soll dem Chor und Gesang täglich beiwohnen, auch sich, wie seit jeher, in der Schule gebrauchen lassen; Stiftserhebung 1610, BHStAM, Kollegiatstift St. Nikolaus Mühldorf, KL 899/1; 1618 ist *Marcus Wendl* immer noch Cantor; BHStAM, Erzstift Salzburg, 714.

[139] 1560, bei der altbayerischen Visitation, gab es z. B. in Landshut den lateinischen Schulmeister und seinen Cantor, sie hatten 50 Kinder; den Poet und den Poeten substitut, sie hatten bei 40 Knaben; sowie 10 deutsche Schulmeister mit zusammen 342 Kindern. Die meisten Schüler hatte Leonhart Khueschenckh und zwar 76 und *Hanns Ostermayr* hatte nur

14 Schüler; BHStAM, Kurbayern Äußeres Archiv, 4207, 711 r/719r. Im Unterschied zum lateinischen Schulmeister, der an der Pfarrkirche auch den Chordienst inne hatte – daraus hat sich ja sein Amt entwickelt – waren die Poetenschulmeister sozusagen selbständige lateinische Schulmeister ohne »den lästigen Kirchendienst«. Durch die Gründung von Jesuitenschulen (Ingolstadt 1556, München 1559/60, Regensburg 1590) waren die Poetenschulmeister einem erheblichen Konkurrenzdruck ausgesetzt, was letztlich zu ihrer Reduzierung, ja sogar zur Auflösung führte. Die lateinischen Schulmeister an den Kirchen waren davon kaum betroffen.

140 An den Dorfschulen vermittelten die ehemaligen Organisten aus Städten und größeren Märkten den Bauernkindern einen auf Landverhältnisse modifizierten Lernstoff aus der deutschen Stadt- oder Marktschule. Oft hatten solche Organisten auch schon Erfahrung im Umgang »mit dem Lateinischen« und brachten den »guten ingenia« auch die lateinischen Grundkenntnisse bei. Das weitere Wissen erwarben diese Bauernbuben dann beim Pfarrer, oder in einem nahegelegenen Kloster. So ist es nicht verwunderlich, daß auch Studenten aus Dörfern in den Universitätsmatrikeln auftauchen, besonders bis zur Reformation. Abgelegene Dörfer und schlecht dotierte Pfarreien waren auch oft mit einem Choralisten (Vorstufe zum Organisten) zufrieden. Sie hatten in der Regel eine schöne Stimme, etwas Orgelkenntnis und beherrschten mehr oder minder auch den Stoff der deutschen Schule.

141 Auch Marktschulen hatten mitunter ein beachtliches Niveau. Erich Stahleder bezeichnet das Eggenfeldener Marktrechtsbüchlein von 1519/20, verfaßt von einem »etwa sechzehnjährigen Eggenfeldener Lateinschulabsolventen, dem der Vater als Ratsherr, Bürgermeister und Spitalverwalter die Schreibarbeit übertragen hatte«, als ein »respektables Zeugnis von der Qualität der damaligen Lateinschule in Eggenfelden«. *Stahleder,* E. (1968): Das Eggenfeldener Marktrechtsbüchlein von 1519/20. In: Heimat an Rott und Inn, S. 127ff.
Der Weinwirtssohn *Johannes Turmair* (geb. 1477, *Aventinus* genannt), hat seinen ersten Schulunterricht vom Marktschreiber und Lehrer Bernhard Wallenhauser erhalten.
Der Erwerb von Schreib- und Kanzleierfahrung war noch bis herauf ins ausgehende 19. Jahrhundert erstrebenswert, denn aufgrund der sich immer weiter entwickelnden Bürokratie waren solche Leute gesucht und auch verhältnismäßig gut bezahlt. So wird auch dem *Anton Bruckner,* von 1845–1855 im Stift St. Florian Schulmeister und Organist mit schon beachtlichen Kompositionen, vom Bezirksgericht mit Datum vom 20. Juli 1853 ausdrücklich bestätigt, daß er »seit dem Jahre 1851 öfters aushilfsweise in der Bezirksgerichts-Kanzlei zu St. Florian gearbeitet und sich durch besonderen Fleiß und Geschicklichkeit den Kanzleidienst derart zu eigen gemacht hat, daß er in dieser Beziehung als sehr verwendbar empfohlen werden kann«. Vgl. *Auer,* M. (1947): Anton Bruckner. Wien, S. 81.

142 Stadtgerichtsbuch Mühldorf, 1557 März 5 und April 2, B 1/2, S. 191 u. 194.

143 *Paulsen* (1896): Geschichte des gelehrten Unterrichts. Leipzig, I, S. 391; *Lurz,* Dok. I, S. 311, bringt den lateinischen Text und weist auf die deutsche Überarbeitung hin.

144 1538 Februar 26, Stadtarchiv Mühldorf, Bürgerbuch B 3, S. 197. In unruhigen Zeiten wurde den Mühldorfer Buchführern verboten übers Land »ins Gey« zu ziehen. Buchführer haben offensichtlich auch auf dem Land verkauft, was sowohl für die Lesefähigkeit der Landbewohner spricht, als auch die Rasanz erklärt, mit der Luthers Schriften sich auch auf dem Land verbreitet hatten.

145 Vgl. *Fickel* (1985).

146 Steuerbuch des Stadtgerichts Mühldorf, 1608; BHStAM, GL Mühldorf, 250. Im *Nachtrag* dieses Steuerbuches steht »Onopherus Asam, Teutscher Schuelmeister und Inmann, 20 [Gulden Vermögen]«
1612 Juli 23 heißt es im Ratsprotokoll (B 1/7) »Der Stadtschreiber Wagenpauer hatte als

Gesellen den Onoferus Asam von Kraiburg«. Asam war somit von 1609–1612 sowohl Stadtschreibergeselle, als auch Schulmeister.

147 1612 August 27, *Onoferus Asam* von Kraiburg wird gleichfalls (?) als deutscher Schulmeister aufgenommen; Ratsprotokolle Mühldorf, 1612, B 1/9. Die endgültige Aufnahme Asams als Schulmeister hängt wohl mit dem Tod des Stadtschreibers *Wagenpauer* zusammen. 1612 Mai 8, war er schon verstorben.

148 Ratsprotokolle Mühldorf, 1614, B 1/10.

149 1621 Oktober 1; Ratsprotokolle Mühldorf, 1621, B 1/12.

150 Ratsprotokolle Mühldorf, 1625, B 1/13.

151 1629 Juli 30; Ratsprotokolle Mühldorf, 1629, B 1/18.

152 1632 Mai 12; Ratsprotokolle Mühldorf, 1632, B 1/20. In anderen Städten können Schulmeister als »Feldwaibel« schon wesentlich früher belegt werden, in Buchloe z. B. 1473: »Johans Schuelmeister und Waibel«. *Dertsch*, R.: Die Urkunden der Stadt Kaufbeuren Nr. 1121. Waren militärische und polizeiliche Funktionen im weitesten Sinn bis etwa 1650 Zusatzfunktionen für einen Schulmeister, so werden sie im letzten Drittel des 17. und verstärkt im 18. Jahrhundert oft Ausgangspunkt für eine Schulmeisterlaufbahn. Büchsenmacher, Fortifikationszeichner, Kartenilluminatoren und Militärs verschiedener Chargen hatten gute Chancen Schulmeister zu werden. Diese »Militärkübel« waren zwar nicht immer die besten Schulmeister, dafür aber Meister in punkto Ordnung, Gehorsam und Disziplin. In Mühldorf wird erstmals 1678 Juni 25 von Disziplin im Zusammenhang mit Schule und Kindern gesprochen. »Hans Unger, deutschem Schulhalter wird aufgetragen, auf die Kinder fleißiger Aufsicht und diese in guter Disciplin zu halten«; Ratsprotokolle Mühldorf, 1678, B 1/51
1705 »wird *Max Zeisenhofer*, gewester Churbayr. Kunststäbler [Konstabler] als deutscher Schulmeister und Nachtzettelschreiber aufgenommen«; Ratsprotokolle Mühldorf, 1705, B 1/55. Zeisenhofer war wohl Polizist, könnte aber auch Kanonier gewesen sein.

153 1632 Mai 22; dito.

154 1632 Mai 15; dito.

155 1654 November 13; Ratsprotokolle Mühldorf, 1654, B 1/42.
Die Kirche selbst aber wird immer intoleranter. Im gleichen Jahr, 1654, verfügt der Erzbischof von Salzburg am 16. Juni »Zigeuner dürfen im Lande nicht geduldet werden«; BHStAM, Erzstift Salzburg, 596.
1714 August 25, die Zigeuner werden für vogelfrei erklärt; BHStAM, Erzstift Salzburg, 398 a
1716 Februar 3, ist von der Ausrottung des landesschädlichen Gesindels der Zigeuner die Rede; BHStAM, Erzstift Salzburg, 398 a
Andererseits ergeht am 14. Oktober 1641 ein Mandat über Einführung und bessere Bestellung der Christenlehre; BHStAM, Erzstift Salzburg, 1037 II
Dieses Mandat wird in zahlreichen Erinnerungen bis zum Überdruß in den folgenden 150 Jahren den Gläubigen nahe gebracht.

156 Sogar der Schullehrer *Andre Beer*, der von 1777–1796 als Lehrer in Mühldorf tätig war, ehe er aufgrund seines nebenberuflichen Theologiestudiums in den »Geistlichen Stand« trat, wird ab 1790 mehrmals hingewiesen, daß er sich »außer bei Hochzeiten zu keinen anderen gerichtlichen Geschäften gebrauchen lasse«.

1790 Dezember 17;	Ratsprotokolle Mühldorf,	1790, B 1/117
1794	dito	1794, B 1/122
1795	dito	1795, B 1/122

157 1647 März 9; Ratsprotokolle Mühldorf, 1647, R 1/167.

157a In den altbayerischen Klöstern, vor allem in den Prälatenklöstern war das Gegenteil der Fall. *Haushofer* und *Stutzer*, die wohl besten Kenner nicht nur der altbayerischen Agrargeschichte, sondern auch der Bildungsgeschichte, weisen immer wieder darauf hin, betonen aber auch das große Forschungsdefizit. Haushofer hat nachgewiesen, daß in Oberbayern alle 14 km und in Niederbayern etwa alle 24 km eine kombinierte Grund- und weiterführende klösterliche Schule zur Verfügung stand. Auf diese Weise haben die Klöster in Bayern »ihr Bildungs-, Schul- und Wissenschaftsmonopol aufrichten, ausbauen und festigen« können. »Auf diese Art wurden Häuslersbuben und Tagelöhnerskinder Prälaten, Fürstäbte, Universitätsprofessoren und Mathematiker oder Schriftsteller«; *Stutzer* (1978), S. 230. Die Säkularisation hat die Klöster brutal zerschlagen und »mit großem Geschrey die Schulpflicht eingeführt«.

158 1654 November 13; Ratsprotokolle Mühldorf, 1654, B 1/42.

159 1670 Oktober 10; Ratsprotokolle Mühldorf, 1670, B 1/50.

160 1697; zitiert nach Held (1926/28), III, S. 131.

161 1713; Stadtkammerrechnungen Mühldorf, 1713, R 1/259.

162 1717 Mai 22, *Pichler Peter Ignatius* wird auf ein Jahr zur Probe eingestellt. Muß der alten Schulmeisterin das erste Jahr vierteljährlich 2 Gulden Beihilfe geben, Ratsprotokolle Mühldorf, 1717, B 1/56.

163 Vgl. Aussage des *Michael Haimerer,* Kollegiat-Stifts-Musicus und Schulhalter, Punkt 4 und 5, 1785; BHStAM, Amtsgericht Mühldorf 27.

164 1785 April 8, Einleitung zu einem angeforderten Bericht über das Mühldorfer Schulwesen; BHStAM, Amtsgericht Mühldorf 27.

165 Stadtkammerrechnungen Mühldorf, 1801, R 1/360.

166 1802 Dezember 22, »... Der Schullehrer ist ein junger tätiger Mann, wie ich noch beinahe keinen Schullehrer kenne. Er liest Herrn Dekan vor und versteht manch philosophische Aufsätze ...« Aus dem Schreiben des Amtsadjunkten Ruland an den General-Commissaire *Freiherrn von Aretin*; BHStAM, Gerichtsliteralien Mühldorf, 2572.

167 Die Angaben über die Schülerzahlen und die Lehrereinkünfte verdankt der Verfasser *Gabriele Peche,* die bei ihm 1983 eine Zulassungsarbeit über: die Werktagsschule in Mühldorf von 1802–1861 aufgrund der Quellen, erstellt hat. Die Arbeit ist im Stadtarchiv Mühldorf einzusehen.

168 Zu *Fingerlos* vgl. *Marquart,* H. (1977): Matthäus Fingerlos (1748–1817). Leben und Wirken eines Pastoraltheologen und Seminarregenten in der Aufklärungszeit. Göttingen (mit vollständigem Schrifttum). Was die Tätigkeit in Landshut betrifft, vgl. vor allem S. 123–192.

169 *Thomas Morus* hat auch später noch für Komplikationen gesorgt. Als 1935 in München–Giesing eine neue Pfarrei gegründet wurde, hat Pfarrkurat *Alfons Beer* den hl. *Thomas Morus* als Kirchenpatron vorgeschlagen. Erzbischof Kardinal *Michael Faulhaber* befürchtete jedoch, daß *Adolf Hitler* in der Namenswahl eine Anspielung auf seine Gewaltherrschaft sehe und bestimmte das Fest »Maria Königin des Friedens« zum Patrozinium.

170 BHStAM, Gerichtsliteralien 2572.

171 dito.

172 dito.; die Unterstreichung ist auch im Original.

173 Schreiben vom 4. März 1803; BHStAM, Gerichtsliteralien 2572.

174 Dem Gregorianum in Landshut war durch die Neuorganisation von 1804/05 von der Regierung die Funktion eines Generalseminars der altbayerischen Bistümer zugewiesen worden.

175 Seit dem Sommersemester 1805 hielt *Fingerlos* Pastoralvorlesungen im Seminar und wurde am 15. Juli 1806 durch die Regierung zum Professor der Pastoral und damit vollberechtigtes Mitglied der theologischen Fakultät.

176 Aus einem Schreiben des Friedberger Distriktsschulinspektors *Ignaz Lindl* vom 5. März

1810 an das Königliche Bairische General-Kommissariat des Lech-Kreises; BHStAM, Gerichtsliteralien Friedberg 1099.

177 Vgl. *Fickel,* A. (1988): Lesegesellschaften im Urteil Augsburgischer Landpfarrer um 1800. In: Jahrbuch für Volkskunde d. Görres-Gesellschaft.

178 Das begann schon im ausgehenden 18. Jahrhundert. Der Mesner und Schullehrer, *Johann Adam Völtl* aus Schwanenkirchen im bayerischen Wald, ist ein typisches Beispiel. *Völtl* war ein guter Schulmeister. Gelegentlich ließ er sich von seinem Adstanten vertreten, wenn er, ein Mann mit Kanzlei- und Procuratorenerfahrung, übers Land zog um den Leuten und »rechtsunerfahrenen Bauern« bei der Durchsetzung ihrer Rechte gegenüber Pfarrern und Grundherren behilflich zu sein. Obwohl sein Honorar wesentlich geringer war als das der Advokaten, konnte er sich ein schönes Haus bauen. In den Akten von 1788 liest sich das so: »... ferner hat er Valtl nicht ganz nach der Verfaßung der Überschläge, sondern ohne Anfragen nach seiner Willkühr gebaut. Aus einem vorher eingadigen und hinlänglich erkleklichen Hausstok ein zweygadiges Haus erbaut, welches wirklich viell prächtiger auffällt als der dortige Pfarrhof.... Überdies ist das Haus nicht aus Holz, sondern aus Steinen wie die Kirche.« Völtl aber hat »seine arrogance noch weiter getrieben ... er ließ sich in Kirche und Schul vertreten, fährt übers Land, hetzt die Leute sogar in kostspielige Prozesse ...«; BHStAM, GL 4532.

179 Selbst Genies waren gegen Nörgeleien nicht gefeit, bzw. blieben von ihnen nicht verschont. *Anton Bruckner,* schon Organist in Linz, fuhr gelegentlich am Abend aufs Land, um sich in einem der Landgasthäuser als Sänger und Geiger zu vergnügen. »Einmal nahm auch Adalbert Stifter, der die Schule inspiziert hatte, an einem solchen Abend teil. Er konnte den ›Schulmeister‹ auch an diesem Abend nicht unterdrücken und hatte an der Aussprache der jungen Leute immer herumzunörgeln. Auch Bruckner blieb dabei nicht verschont, als er vom Wein sagte, er sei noch nicht ›ausgegärt‹, belehrte ihn Stifter sogleich: ›Man sagt: Der Wein hat noch nicht ausgegoren!‹«; *Auer* (1947), S. 50.

Quellen- und Literaturverzeichnis

Ungedruckte Quellen

Bayerisches Hauptstaatsarchiv München (BHStAM)
- Chorstift Mühldorf
- Erzstift Salzburg Literalien, Urkunden
- Gerichtsliteralien Mühldorf, Trostberg, Neuötting, Kraiburg, Neumarkt, Mörmoosen, Traunstein
- Gerichtsurkunden Mühldorf, Trostberg, Neuötting, Kraiburg, Neumarkt, Mörmoosen, Traunstein
- Klosterurkunden Formbach
- Kollegiatstift Mühldorf, Literalien, Urkunden
- Kurbayern Äußeres Archiv 4207
- Regierungsakten Amtsgericht Mühldorf Signatur AR, KL, RFK

Bayerische Staatsbibliothek München Cgm 216

Stadtarchiv Mühldorf
- Urkunden
- Stadtgerichtsbücher 1496–1584 Band 1–5 Sign. B 1/

Ratsprotokolle 1485–1779 Band 6–107 Sign. B 1/
Stadtgerichtsprotokolle 1778–1780 Band 108 Sign. B 1/
Ratsprotokolle 1780–1809 Band 109–131 Sign. B 1/
Briefprotokolle 1657–1797 Band 1–85 Sign. B 2/
Bürgerbuch 1506–1622 Sign. B 3/
Stadtkammerrechnungen 1468–1527 Band 1–44 Sign. R 1/
Stadtkammerrechnungen 1528–1533 Band 46–51 Sign. R 1/
Stadtkammerrechnungen 1535 Band 53 Sign. R 1/
Stadtkammerrechnungen 1536–1803 Band 55–362 Sign. R 1/
Sterbe- und Heiratsmatrikel ab 1680 (Photokopie), Original im Pfarrarchiv Mühldorf

Gedruckte Quellen

Acht, P. (1952): Die Traditionen des Klosters Tegernsee 1003–1242. In: Quellen und Erörterungen zur bayerischen und deutschen Geschichte (= QE) N. F. 9, 1. München

Buchner, K. (1953): Die Urkunden des Klosters Oberschönenfeld. Augsburg

Dertsch, R. (1955): Die Urkunden der Stadt Kaufbeuren. Augsburg

Dumrath, K. (1938): Die Traditionsnotizen des Klosters Raitenhaslach. In: QE N. F. 7. München

Hauthaler, W. / Martin, F. (1898 ff.): Salzburger Urkundenbuch, 4 Bde. Salzburg

Herzog, T. (1956 ff.): Landshuter Urkundenbuch. Neustadt / Aisch

Hör, H. / Morenz, L. (1960): Die Urkunden des Klosters St. Veit 1121–1450. In: QE N. F. 15. München

Krausen, E. (1958): Stadtarchiv Mühldorf am Inn. In: Archivinventare, Bd. 13. München

Krausen, E. (1959/60): Die Urkunden des Klosters Raitenhaslach 1034–1350. In: QE N. F. 17, 1 und 2. München

Krenner, F. v. (1803/1805): Baierische Landtagshandlungen in den Jahren 1429 bis 1513, 18 Bde. München

Martin, F. (1926/43): Die Regesten der Erzbischöfe und des Domkapitels von Salzburg 1247–1343, 3 Bde. Salzburg

Meiller, A. v. (1866): Regesten der Salzburger Erzbischöfe 1106–1246. Wien

Monumenta Boica, hrsg. seit 1763 von der bayr. Akademie d. Wissenschaften

Widemann, J. (1942): Die Traditionen des Hochstifts Regensburg und des Klosters St. Emmeram. In: QE N. F. 8. München

Matrikel der Universität Ingolstadt, Leipzig, Salzburg und Wien

Literatur

Auer, M. (1947): Anton Bruckner. Wien

Cheney, C. R. (1972): Notaries Public in England in the 13th and 14th Century. London

Clanchy, M. T. (1979): From Memory to Written Record, England 1066–1307. Cambridge

Classen, P. (Hrsg.) (1977): Recht und Schrift im Mittelalter, Vorträge und Forschungen 23. Sigmaringen

Erben, E. (1911): Beiträge zur Geschichte der Ministerialität im Erzstift Salzburg. In: Mitt. der Ges. f. Salzburger Landeskunde 51. Jg.

Fastlinger, M. (1897): Die Kirchenpatrozinien in ihrer Bedeutung für Altbayerns ältestes Kirchenwesen. In: Oberbayerisches Archiv 50
Ferchl, G. (1908): Bayerische Behörden und Beamte 1550–1804. In: Oberbayerisches Archiv 53
Fickel, A. (1985): Mühldorfer Literaturleben im 100. Jahr nach der Reformation. In: Literatur in Bayern, hrsg. vom Institut für Bayerische Literaturgeschichte der Universität München, Nr. 1
Fraitzl, K. (1951): Das Kollegiatstift Mühldorf. In: Das Mühlrad Jg. 1951, Nr. 5
Fraitzl, K. (1952): Das alte Pfleg- und Stadtgericht Mühldorf. In: Das Mühlrad Jg. 1952, Nr. 3
Frauendorfer, S. v. / Haushofer, H. (²1963): Ideengeschichte der Agrarwirtschaft und Agrarpolitik im deutschen Sprachgebiet, Bd. I, II. München
Franz, G. (Hrsg.) (1963/68): Deutsche Agrargeschichte, Bd. I–V. Stuttgart
Gentner, H. (1883): Geschichte der Stadt Laufen. München
Göllerich, A. / Auer, M. (1922/36): Anton Bruckner, 4 Bd., in 9 Büchern. Regensburg
Gollwitzer, H. (1962/64): Ergänzungen und Berichtigungen zur Mühldorfer Heimatgeschichts-Forschung. In: Das Mühlrad, Bd. XI, S. 5–17
Gollwitzer, H. (1962/64): Mühldorfer Studenten an der Wiener Universität, 1377–1450. In: Das Mühlrad, Bd. XI, S. 83–96
Hartmann, M. (1930): Salzburger Pfarreien und Benefizien im südöstlichen Bayern um 1541. In: Der Inn-Isengau 28
Haushofer, J. (1976): Die Schulgeschichte von Eggenfelden bis zum Dreißigjährigen Krieg. In: Beiträge zur Heimatkunde von Niederbayern, Bd. III. Landshut
Heigenmooser, J. / Bock, A. (1909): Geschichte der Pädagogik. Quellenbuch und Überblick der Geschichte der Pädagogik, Teil I u. II. München
Held, H. (1926ff.): Altbayerische Volkserziehung und Volksschule, Bd. I, II, III. München
Hemmerle, J. (1951): Die Benediktinerklöster in Bayern. München (Bayerische Heimatforschung, Heft 4)
Hiereth, S. (1950): Die bayerische Gerichts- und Verwaltungsorganisation vom 13. bis 19. Jahrhundert. München
Illich, I. (1971/72): Deschooling society, 1971, dt. Die Entschulung der Gesellschaft
Illich, I. (1984): Schule ins Museum, Phaidros und die Folgen. Bad Heilbrunn (Schriftenreihe zum Bayerischen Schulmuseum Ichenhausen, Bd. 3,1)
Illmer, D. (1971): Formen der Erziehung und Wissensvermittlung im frühen Mittelalter. Quellenstudien zur Frage der Kontinuität des abendländischen Erziehungswesens. München (Müchner Beiträge zur Mediävistik und Renaissance-Forschung, Bd. 7)
Klebel, E. (1930): Studien zum historischen Atlas von Bayern: Das Inn-Salzachgebiet. In: Zeitschrift für bayerische Landesgeschichte (ZBLG), Bd. 3
Klebel, E. (1939/40): Die Städte und Märkte des baierischen Stammesgebietes in der Siedlungsgeschichte. In: ZBLG 12
Krausen, E. (1955): Ein Heiliger mit Grundbesitz. Aus der frühen Besitzgeschichte der Kirche von Aspertsham. In: Das Mühlrad, Jg. 1955
Krausen, E. (1961): Beiträge zur sozialen Schichtung altbayerischer Prälatenklöster des 17. und 18. Jahrhunderts. Die Zusammensetzung der Konvente von Metten, Raitenhaslach, Reichersberg und Windberg. München
Lurz, G. (1907/08): Mittelschulgeschichtliche Dokumente Altbayerns, einschließlich Regensburgs. Mon. Germ. Paed. XLI, 2 Bde. Berlin
Paulsen, P. (1919/21): Geschichte des gelehrten Unterrichts auf den deutschen Schulen und Universitäten vom Ausgang des Mittelalters bis zur Gegenwart, 3. Auflage, Bd. I, Leipzig 1919, Bd. II, Berlin–Leipzig 1921

Spindler, M. (Hrsg.) (1968): Bayerischer Geschichtsatlas. Red. Gertrud Diepolder. München
Stahleder, E. (1968): Das Eggenfeldener Marktrechtsbüchlein von 1519/20. In: Heimat an Rott und Inn
Stahleder, H. (1976): Mühldorf am Inn. Historischer Atlas von Bayern, Teil Altbayern, Heft 36, München
Störmer, W. (1973): Früher Adel. Studien zur politischen Führungsschicht vom 8. bis zum 11. Jahrhundert. Stuttgart (Monographien zur Geschichte des Mittelalters 6)
Stutzer, D. (1978): Die Säkularisation 1803. Der Sturm auf Bayerns Kirchen und Klöster. Rosenheim
Widemann, H. (1914): Geschichte Salzburgs, Bd. 1, 2, 3. Gotha

V. DER LEHRER DES NIEDEREN UND HÖHEREN SCHULWESENS IM DEUTSCHLAND DES 18. BIS 20. JAHRHUNDERTS

Rudolf W. Keck

Die Entwicklung der Lehrerbildung in Deutschland im 18. und 19. Jahrhundert

Man erlaube einem Bildungshistoriker, der zugleich Allgemeine Didaktik vertritt, zur thematischen Eröffnung und Motivation mit einigen historischen Zitaten zu spielen!
1819: Erlaß des preußischen Kultusministers (30. 10. 1819): »Alles unnötige Räsonnieren und Diskutieren mit der Jugend ist zu vermeiden, damit sie früh lerne, ohne Widerspruch den vorgeschriebenen Gesetzen zu folgen und sich willig der bestehenden Obrigkeit zu unterwerfen.«
1866: Ausspruch des preußischen Königs anläßlich der Schlacht von Königgrätz: die Schlacht habe im Grunde der deutsche Schulmeister gewonnen!
1890: *Wilhelm II.* hält auf der Reichsschulkonferenz eine harte Ansprache an die Pädagogen, daß, wenn die Schulmeister ihre Schuldigkeit getan hätten, es keine Sozialdemokratie in Deutschland geben würde.
1913: Eduard *Spranger* beschwört in einem Brief an Käthe *Hardlich* die Furcht vor einer politisierten Lehrerschaft; in deren Zugang zur Universität sieht er eine »nationale Gefahr«: »... eine Schule als politisches Instrument in den Händen einer halbgebildeten Lehrerschaft – das geht nicht ... wenn in den Kreisen der Lehrerschaft latente Sozialdemokratie herrscht« (zit. nach *Meyer-Willner* (1986), S. 101).
Wie wir sehen: Der Lehrer in einem Mosaik von Erwartungen auf der historischen Strecke, die uns beschäftigen wird. Die Position des Lehrers erhält offensichtlich im Zuge der modernen Staats- und Gesellschaftsentwicklung eine zunehmend zentrale Bedeutung. Aus allen Zitaten spricht ein Loyalitätsanspruch und eine Instrumentalisierungsabsicht der jeweils Herrschenden gegenüber der Position des Lehrers. In der nüchternen Sprache des Bildungshistorikers: Der moderne Kulturverwaltungsstaat, der im letzten Drittel des 18. Jahrhunderts die Schule für alle Schichten in seine Verwaltung übernimmt – das preußische Allgemeine Landschul-Reglement von 1763 kennzeichnet dies auf markante Weise –, muß auch den Lehrer in seine Verwaltungs- und Kulturverpflichtung einbeziehen. Der Staat »verstaatlicht« mit der Schule auch die Lehrerschaft. Der Lehrer wird zum »Kulturbeamten« des Staates – allerdings für die einzelnen Lehrergattungen in unterschiedlichen Schüben und mit unterschiedlicher ideologisch-politischer und bildungstheoretischer Befrachtung.
Wer den Stand der bildungsgeschichtlichen Forschung auch nur annähernd zu überblicken vermag, vor allem den sozialgeschichtlicher Provenienz, der wird feststellen, daß der Lehrer verstärkt in den Forschungsblick gerät. Der Lehrer und seine Organisation, die Rolle des Lehrers als wichtiger Faktor innerhalb der Entwicklung von Gesellschaft und Bildungssystem (vgl. u. a. M. *Heinemann* (1977); L. *Kunz* (1984)) – das sind neuentdeckte Fragestellungen des letzten Jahrzehnts. Insbesondere

findet Interesse das Verhalten der Lehrer und ihrer Standesorganisationen in der Weimarer Republik (vgl. u. a. G. *Geißler* (1973); F. *Hamburger* (1974); *Krause-Vilmar* (1978); R. *Bölling* (1978/1981); U. *Sandfuchs* (1978/1986) und im Dritten Reich (vgl. u. a. M. *Heinemann* (1980); O. *Ottweiler* (1979); H. *Scholz* (1978) u. (1983); U. *Sandfuchs* (1981); W. *Feiten* (1981)), vor allem die These *Breyvogels* (1978) und *Tenorths* (1981), Lehrer hätten dem Dritten Reich gegenüber eine besondere Affinität gezeigt – eine These, die inzwischen hinsichtlich ihres generellen Anspruchs durch die Arbeit von *Günther-Arndt* (1983) doch etwas differenzierter zu sehen ist. Von nicht geringem Interesse ist ferner die Erforschung der Überfüllungskrisen bei der Lehrerversorgung im 19. und 20. Jahrhundert, vor allem angesichts der derzeitigen Lage des Lehrerarbeitsmarktes (vgl. H. *Titze* (1981); A. *Nath* (1981); H.-G. *Herrlitz* / H. *Titze* (1977)). Rainer *Bölling* legt schließlich 1983 nach den Versuchen von K. *Trinks* (1933), K. *Fischer* (1892/1969) und K. *Bungardt* (1965) eine »Sozialgeschichte der deutschen Lehrer« von 1800 bis zur Gegenwart vor.
So nimmt es auch nicht wunder, wenn nach der Epoche stürmischer Schul- und Lehrerbildungsreform zwischen 1965 und 1975 *Anfragen an die Geschichte der Lehrerbildung* wieder verstärktes Interesse finden, wie ich an meinem Versuch, einen Forschungsstand zur Lehrerbildungsgeschichte zu ermitteln, selbst feststellen konnte (*Keck* (1984), S. 161–189). Dieses Interesse ist international und es hält an, wie das Thema des Ichenhausener Symposions von 1987 beweist.
Zu meinen folgenden Ausführungen zur »Entwicklung der Lehrerbildung in Deutschland«, die ja den Rahmen für das Thema »Der Lehrer des niederen und höheren Schulwesens im Deutschland des 16. bis 20. Jahrhunderts« abgeben sollen, ist es aus methodologischer und sachlicher Sicht notwendig, ein *Theoriebett* zu zimmern, um die Lehrerbildung als Teil des historischen Lehrerbildes und der Bildungsgeschichte insgesamt isolierbar und in ihrer Bedeutung für das Gesamtbild interpretierbar zu machen. Nachforschungen nach dem Lehrerbild in der Geschichte stellen wir nicht an aus archivalischem Selbstzweck mit der Nennung von Faktenketten, wir versuchen auch keine Standesgeschichte als »l'art pour l'art« aus nostalgischer Versonnenheit, sondern versuchen in der geschichtlichen Rückblende Sinn für die Gegenwart für die soziale Identität des Lehrers in dieser Gesellschaft erweisbar zu machen. Eine solche historische Rekonstruktion des Lehrerbildes fasse ich dabei auf als ein dominant *sozialgeschichtliches* Unternehmen; es geht davon aus, Hauptbedingungen der vielfältigen Verflochtenheit des Lehrerbildes und seiner sich organisierenden Ausbildung im 18., 19. und 20. Jahrhundert zu strukturieren.

I. Der notwendige Theorierahmen

Eine grundlegende Überlegung bei der Findung eines Theorierahmens ist, daß das Lehrerbild und die Lehrerausbildung nicht gezeichnet werden können ohne das *Berufsfeld* einzugrenzen; anders gesagt, eine *Sozialgeschichte des Lehrers* ist zunächst

eine abhängige Größe der *Sozialgeschichte der Schule*. Von hier aus, der gesellschaftlichen Position und Entwicklung der Schule, lassen sich Linien ziehen zur Position des Lehrers, seinem objektiven Sozialstatus, der Subsistenzstruktur seiner sozialen und personalen Existenz, was wiederum Aussagen zuläßt über seine Berufsmentalität und die Rekrutierung der Lehrerschaft, die sich auch in einer spezifischen Lehrerverbandsstruktur wiederspiegelt. Dies ist die eine Achse seiner Abhängigkeit.
Als *Hauptachse* aber begreife ich die Genese seiner *Professionalisierung*, und zwar einerseits aus der Disposition einer sich entwickelnden staatlichen *Kulturverwaltung*, die für ihn und für die Schulstruktur (Lehrerversorgung) vor dem Hintergrund von Überfüllungs- oder Mängelkrisen bestimmte Strukturen einer *professionellen Ausbildung* bereithält, sie kontrolliert, behindert oder fördert. Dies begreife ich als das Koordinatenkreuz für die Entwicklung des Lehrerbildes in der Geschichte.

Koordinaten einer Lehrerbildungsgeschichte
(als Teil einer Sozialgeschichte des Lehrers)

Die sozialgeschichtliche Vernetztheit der Lehrerbildungsfrage herauszustellen scheint mir notwendig, auch wenn im folgenden die Professionalisierungsfrage, noch enger: die Ausbildungsfrage zum Hauptbetrachtungspunkt gemacht wird.
Mit der Hauptachse kennzeichnen wir also die Professionsgeschichte des Lehrers im engeren Sinne. Verfolgt man die Professionalisierungsdiskussion, wie sie im Rahmen der Sozialwissenschaften sich abzeichnet, dann haben wir vor allem den Zuschnitt und die Genese des *Ausbildungsstandards* einzurechnen. »Eine professionalisierte Berufsposition ist dadurch bestimmt«, heißt es bei Hans Jürgen *Daheim* im »Handbuch der empirischen Sozialforschung« von 1969 (S. 365), »daß vom Inhaber dieser Position ein hochgradig spezialisiertes und systematisiertes Wissen verlangt wird«. Mit diesem korrespondiert ein »Grad der Definitheit von Anforderungen an die Berufsausbildung« und eine Reihe von Auswirkungen (R. W. *Mack* (1956)): »Die

Inhaber professionalisierter Berufspositionen sehen ihre Tätigkeit als Ziel an sich an und definieren ihre Lebensziele als Berufsziele« (nach *Daheim* (1969), S. 365). D. *Rüschemeyer* (1961) führt als Definitionsmerkmal die »Verantwortung gegenüber der Gesellschaft« ein, d. h. daß für die Gesellschaft die Anwendung einer »gelehrten Tradition« zur Pflege zentraler sozial-kultureller Werte von funktionaler Bedeutung werde. So wichtig eine solche Merkmalsdiskussion ist, so sehr verdient aus anderer Sicht das Moment des Professionalisierungs-*Prozesses* besondere Beachtung. Schon 1933 haben die Amerikaner A. M. *Carr-Saunders* und P. A. *Wilson* darauf aufmerksam gemacht, daß die »intellektuelle Technik« aufgrund einer sozial anerkannten Ausbildungsinstitution ihren Wert bekommt. Sie weisen dies nach an der professionellen Herausentwicklung der Juristen, Mediziner und Theologen aus der mittelalterlichen Universität; so läßt sich im Zuge der Säkularisierung von Schule und Universität um 1800 die *Professionalisierungsgenese des höheren Lehramtes* schlüssig erklären.

Von H. W. *Martin* (1958) wird ein Ablaufmuster für Professionalisierung entworfen, an dem ihr Prozeß und Grad ablesbar wird und das sich für die *Verberuflichung des Volksschullehrers* als besonders ergiebig erweist: Der 1. Schritt: Gründung bzw. Aktivierung einer Berufsorganisation, aus welcher die nicht-qualifizierten Berufsangehörigen ausgeschlossen werden, verweist auf das Schnittjahr 1848 und der damit verbundenen allgemeinen Durchsetzung des Lehrerseminars. Der 2. und 3. Schritt: Wechsel der Berufsbezeichnung und Einführung eines Titels verdeutlicht den Schritt vom Schulmeister und Küsterlehrer zum *Schullehrer*. Der 4. Schritt: Aufbau eines Ausbildungswesens versinnbildlicht die Verbreitung und nachfolgende Normierung des *Seminars*. Auch die folgenden Schritte: Formulierung eines beruflichen Ehrenkodex, informelle Zugangskontrollen (Eignungsprüfung und zunehmende Akademisierung) sind verfolgbare Topoi auf dem Weg der Lehrerbildung in die Pädagogische Hochschule bzw. ihre Integration in die Universität.

Der Weg der Findung eines fachlichen Wissensstandards in Form institutionalisierter Ausbildung und die zunehmende Sicherung sozial zuträglicher Subsistenz kennzeichnet den Weg des Volksschullehrers von 1800 bis 1900.

Ab 1800 lassen sich beide Lehrerbilder und Lehrerbildungsformen in ein *Strukturschema* bringen:

Für das *höhere Lehramt* in Form *universitärer Fachausbildung* (mit zwei Haupt- und zwei Nebenfächern), allerdings aufgrund der philologischen und fachwissenschaftlichen Formierung in der ersten Phase bei Verlust einer eigenständigen Berufswissenschaft, der Pädagogik. Im Rahmen einer um 1900 im ganzen Reich gegebenen zweiten Prüfung nach einer meist zweijährigen Vorbereitungszeit führt die berufsspezifische Pädagogik ein praktizistisch orientiertes Winkeldasein, ist gerade gut genug für die Methodisierung der Lehrproben – kurzum: zu sprechen ist von einer *Quasi-Professionalisierung*.

Für das *Volksschullehramt* besteht das Modell der *Allfach-Ausbildung im Seminar*, das mit der Präparandie ab 1872 zu einem sechsjährigen einheitlichen Studiengang sich formiert, wobei ab diesem Zeitpunkt im letzten Jahrhundertdrittel die Berufswissenschaft Pädagogik mit Psychologie sich zunehmend als Studienbasis herausbildet.

Dennoch ist (aus der Sicht der Professionalisierungstheorie) mehr von einer *Semi-Professionalisierung* zu sprechen (*La Vopa* (1980); *Skopp* (1980)), da erst die akademische Ausbildung notwendiges Maß an Unabhängigkeit, sozialer Einschätzung und Einheitlichkeit bietet.[1]

Die Elaboration eines Systemrahmens für die Genese der Lehrerbildung führt zu einer *dichotomen und segmentierten Epochalisierung.* Mit »Segmenten« meinen wir Einschnitte institutioneller, curricularer, qualitativ und quantitativ bedingter Art, die sich verzahnen. Die Segmentierung hilft, die Veränderungen etwa durch zunehmende Hierarchisierung des Schulsystems, der Berechtigungsstruktur und der sozialen Rekrutierung der Lehrer aus der Sicht der Veränderung des Schulsystems überhaupt besser zu verstehen. Ihr Vorteil liegt demnach in einer größeren Integration der Lehrer(bildungs-)geschichte in der Gesamtsystementwicklung der Bildung im 19. Jahrhundert (vgl. Detlev K. *Müller* (1977)). Damit kann die Modernisierungshypothese, die Konrad H. *Jarausch* in seinem Band »The Transformation of Higher Learning 1860–1930« 1982 für die Entwicklung des sekundären Bildungssystems – zu dem auch die Lehrerbildung gehört – (mit den Begriffen: Expansion, Diversification, Opening, Recruitment und Professionalization) gesetzt hat, auch schlüssig auf die Lehrerbildungsgeschichte übertragen werden.

II. Dichotomisierung und Segmentierung der Lehrerbildung

1. Dichotomisierung der Lehrerbildung

Zwei entscheidende Tatbestände kennzeichnen den Ausgangspunkt für die Entstehung eines Berufsbildes des Lehrers:
- die Genese des Ausbildungs- und Arbeitsmarktes des Klerikerstandes
- das Aufkommen eines Bildungsinteresses und seine Reichweite bzw. sein Obligationscharakter, wir meinen also den sozialen Verpflichtungscharakter von Bildung allgemeiner Art.

Für beide Aspekte ergibt sich mit der Reformation eine neue Ausgangslage: Bildung wird zu einem allgemeinen, wenn auch religiös fundierten Topos; die Intention der Reformation zielt auf Wissen um das Heil für jedermann durch die Fähigkeit, die Bibel selbst zu lesen und zu deuten – und entsprechend enthält sie Impulse für die individuelle Lebensgestaltung und für ein neues Kirchenverständnis, das anstelle der hierarchischen Gnadenvermittlung auf ein allgemeines Priestertum bzw. auf die besondere Gewichtung der Seelsorge statt kirchlicher Machtausübung setzt. Für den Arbeitsmarkt des Klerikers bzw. der Prädikanten ergibt sich ein neuer Bedarf: die *Klerikerfachausbildung* wird angekurbelt, und dabei kommt, vor allem im 18. Jahrhundert angestoßen durch den Pietismus und die nachfolgende Aufklärung, auch die *Bildung des Volkes* in den Blick.

Daß Bildung demnach auf *zwei Ebenen* organisiert ist,
- auf der *Ebene der Verwaltungs- und Kirchensprache Latein* für professionelle und

sozial höherstehende Belange in der *Lateinschule,* wahrgenommen vor allem durch *Theologen,* und
- auf der *Ebene der Seelsorge in der Volkssprache Deutsch* für sozial mittelständische Interessen und Unterschichtsbedürfnisse in Form der *Pfarrschulen* (z. T. vermischt sich in sog. »deutschen Schulen« das religiöse Elementarbildungsinteresse mit kaufmanns-bürgerlichen Bedürfnissen vor allem in den Techniken des Lesens, Schreibens und der Sonderkunst Rechnen), wahrgenommen von *Küster-Lehrern,* z. T. auch von *Schreib- und Rechenmeistern*:

diese bipolare Bildungsstruktur erzeugt also eine dichotome Professionsstruktur der Lehrer.

2. Segmentierung der Ausbildung für das höhere Lehramt

Der erste Schultypus (Lateinschule) wird zu einer spezifischen Durchgangsstation der Klerikerprofession. Bei dem Gießener Theologen und geistigen Vater des Jan Amos *Comenius* Johann Heinrich *Alstedt* (1588–1638) lesen wir in seiner philosophischen Enzyklopädie von 1620 erstmals von dem Heraustreten eines »Status scholasticus« aus dem »Status ecclesiasticus«, so, wie auch seine Wissenschaftseinteilung erstmals eine Didactica und eine Scholastica kennt, also Spezialdisziplinen für die pädagogische Profession. Nach wie vor besteht die Zuständigkeit der Kirche für diese Bildung, der *Lehrer ist Kirchenmann* und als solcher Scholaster oder Magister, Pädagogarch oder Kantor, wie er hauptsächlich an lateinischen Schulen bezeichnet wird, bis er eine feste Pfarrstelle antreten kann. Die Überfüllungskrise im geistlichen Beruf in der zweiten Hälfte des 18. Jahrhunderts, wobei sich das Theologenstudium – zu dem jeder Stand, eben auch einfache Bürgerliche, über ein Stipendienwesen Zugang zur Universität hatte – als Nadelöhr für ein breiter werdendes aufklärerisches Bildungsinteresse erweist, diese Überfüllungskrise schafft Voraussetzungen für eine zweite explizite Professionalisierungsphase in den höheren Schulformen, als der aufgeklärte Staat sich aufgrund breiter Bildungsnachfrage gezwungen sieht, die Stipendien zu ordnen und für den Zugang allgemeine Leistungsgesichtspunkte anzulegen. Das »Examen pro facultate docendi«, von Wilhelm v. *Humboldt* mit seiner neuen, ersten rein staatlichen, Universität Berlin als staatliche Eingangsprüfung für den höheren Schuldienst aus der Taufe gehoben, schafft die neuen Bedingungen für die eigenständige Profession des akademisch gebildeten »Oberlehrers« im 19. Jahrhundert, vornehmlich zunächst über das Studium der Philologie. Aus dem *Kirchenmann* wird der *Schulmann,* besser: der fachspezifische Quasi-Gelehrte an den sog. Gelehrtenschulen des 19. Jahrhunderts, der »Philologe«. Die pädagogischen oder katechetischen Seminare, die sich im Rahmen der Theologieausbildung in Aufklärungsuniversitäten wie Halle, Göttingen oder Jena im 18. Jahrhundert für eine spezifische Zurüstung des pädagogischen Durchgangsamtes von Theologen gebildet hatten, sie werden am Beginn des 19. Jahrhunderts aufgegeben zugunsten der sich etablierenden *Philologischen Seminare.* Für den Lehrer der höheren Schule des 19. und 20. Jahrhunderts ist damit allerdings nicht Pädagogik, sondern *Philologie* (ab dem

ersten Drittel des 19. Jahrhunderts auch andere Fächer wie Mathematik und die Realienwissenschaften) die *Professions-Leitdisziplin*. In struktureller Hinsicht entspricht die Kritik, die der Direktor des Berliner Friedrich-Wilhelm-Gymnasiums, *Spilleke*, 1837 äußerte, einer allgemeinen Tendenz: »Es ist eine sehr merkwürdige Erscheinung, daß ... die Gymnasien von den großen Veränderungen in der pädagogischen Welt gar keine oder doch nur sehr geringe Notiz genommen haben. Es fehlt nicht viel daran, daß sich ein Gymnasiallehrer vor seinen Kollegen scheuen und für einen armseligen Schulmeister gehalten zu werden fürchten muß, wenn er sich soweit herabläßt, ein pädagogisches Buch zu lesen oder überhaupt nur ein pädagogisches Interesse zu zeigen. Der herrschende Grundsatz bei nicht wenigen Gymnasiallehrern ist der: was man gelernt habe, darin könne man auch unterrichten« (zit. nach *Paulsen* I (1896), S. 275 f.). Und der Direktor des Erlanger Gymnasiums Ludwig *Döderlein* mahnt in seinem »Beitrag zur Gymnasialpädagogik und Philologie« von 1843: »die Lehrer sollen eingedenk sein, daß sie nicht Philologen zu erziehen« haben (*Döderlein* 1843, 83). Es ist erst ein Ergebnis der letzten zehn Jahre, nicht zuletzt ein Ergebnis der Integration der Pädagogischen Hochschule in die Universität, daß Pädagogik mit schulpädagogischen Praxisstudien – in Verbindung mit Psychologie, Philosophie und Soziologie – zur allgemeinen und verbindlichen Professionswissenschaft werden kann (vgl. *Schwenk* (1977/78), S. 103 ff.; *Pöggeler* (1975), S. 967 ff.; *Hettwer* (1974), S. 593 ff.). Dies ist unter struktureller Rücksicht kurz die Entwicklungslinie der Professionsgeschichte der Lehrer des höheren Schulwesens, auch wenn in den differenzierenden Blick genommen werden müßte, daß Pädagogik neben der fachwissenschaftlich-philologischen Dominanz immer eine gewisse Berücksichtigung erfuhr, allerdings entweder in »steriler und philosophischer« Manier (*Blättner* (1960), S. 115) oder in praktizistischer und reduktionistischer Form als Element der 2. Ausbildungsphase.[2]
Im einzelnen sehe ich folgende Segmentierungsmöglichkeit:

2.1. Eine erste Periode, die zu überschreiben ist: *»Vom Kirchenmann zum Schulmann«* – sie umgreift den Zeitraum von den protestantischen Kirchenordnungen der Reformationszeit oder der Ratio Studiorum der Jesuiten (1599) bis zum Jahre 1809/10. Vergleichbar dem *Humboldt*schen »Examen pro facultate docendi« (1810) wird in Bayern schon 1809 eine spezifische wissenschaftliche Prüfung »für das Lehramt an Studienanstalten« erstmals eingerichtet, nachdem Heinrich *Brauns* Plan für einen eigenen Gymnasiallehrstand von 1777 nicht umgesetzt werden konnte (vgl. *Neuerer* (1978)). Mit diesen Daten löste sich das Schulamt allmählich vom geistlichen Amt und der Staat »verstaatlicht« die Lehrerschaft. Zuerst vor allem gilt sein Zugriff der Abwehr vom Mißbrauch der Patronatsrechte bei der Stellenbesetzung und dem Fertigwerden mit der ersten Überfüllungskrise der Theologen und damit implizit der Pädagogen.
Mit der Trennung vom Kirchenamt vollzog sich auch eine Trennung der Theologie als der Berufswissenschaft des Kirchenamtes von der Philologie (vgl. *Keck* (1984), S. 172 ff.). Die entscheidende Prägung erhielt das neue Lehramt hierbei an den zwei herausragenden Aufklärungsuniversitäten *Halle* und *Göttingen*. Mit Friedrich Au-

gust *Wolf* (1759–1814) holt *Zedlitz,* der preußische Innenminister, einen der bedeutendsten Neuhumanisten nach Halle. 1787 gründet er dort in Ablösung des Pädagogischen das erste Philologische Seminar. In Göttingen wird die Philologie mit Christian Gottlieb *Heyne* (1729–1812), dem profilierten Nachfolger Joh. Matthias *Gesners,* der 1737 dort schon ein »seminarium philologicum« einrichten konnte, zur tragenden und einflußreichen Säule für die Universitätsentwicklung überhaupt. In Göttingen waren sowohl W. v. *Humboldt* wie F. A. *Wolf* als »studiosi philologiae« eingeschrieben. Über *Wolf* vor allem, der ab 1807 dann in *Berlin* wirkt (neben *Gedike*), führt der Weg des höheren Lehramtes geradewegs in das Fahrwasser der *Humboldt*schen Universitätsreform in Berlin. Der Weg, wie er sich im Rahmen der Katechetischen Seminare für die Theologenausbildung zunächst ebenfalls in Halle und Göttingen (auch in *Jena* und mit einer Kombination als philologisch-pädagogisches Institut an der Universität *Helmstedt* (1779–1810)) ausgebildet hatte, um in Verbindung mit Waisenhäusern die angehenden Pfarrer durch *Katechisation* zu schulen, kommt in Verfall. Im Rahmen dieses Ausbildungskonzepts hat Johann Peter *Miller* (1725–1789) in Göttingen sein erstes Systemwerk der Pädagogik: »Grundsätze einer weisen und christlichen Erziehungskunst« 1769 geschrieben, und sein Schüler Ernst Christian *Trapp* (1745–1818) hat in Halle (1779–1782) auf der Grundlage seiner Pädagogik-Antrittsvorlesung (1779) sein Systemwerk: »Versuch einer Pädagogik« im Jahre 1780 geschrieben. Doch dieser Weg war mit der Fundierung des neuen staatlichen Lehramtes auf der Philologie und auf der ihrer Sprachphilosophie immanenten Bildungstheorie für immer abgeschnitten – damit zugleich – wie gesagt, der Weg des höheren Lehramtes zu einer eigenen Berufswissenschaft Pädagogik (vgl. *Keck* (1983), S. 68–71; 77–81; 87–89).

2.2. Die zweite Periode fasse ich als die Zeit der *Etablierung und Stabilisierung* dieser philologischen Ausbildungsstruktur von 1810 bis 1870. Allerdings bezieht sich diese Charakterisierung auf den preußischen Weg (vgl. *Roeßler* (1960b), S. 705–720), dem sich Sachsen, Hessen und Baden sowie die mittel- und norddeutschen Kleinstaaten anschließen. *Bayern* und *Württemberg* gehen *Sonderwege:* in Württemberg gilt noch in der Ordnung von 1853 »die Verbindung des theologischen Studiums mit der Vorbildung fürs Lehramt« als »Norm und Regel« (*Romberg* (1979), S. 496f.), und in Bayern hat sich ein sog. »Theologenprivileg« für die Besetzung von Schulstellen bis 1854 de facto gehalten (*Romberg* (1979), S. 488f.). Insgesamt lebt vor allem der preußische Weg von dem quasi-professionellen Selbstverständnis *Wolfs,* daß, wer ein guter Wissenschaftler sei, per se ein guter Lehrer sei. Nach wie vor stellte auch in Preußen angesichts der Überfüllungskrise die Theologenschaft das Gros der Lehrer, die Durchsetzung des Philologen erfolgte auch hier erst in den 20er und 30er Jahren mit der Prüfung in den »wesentlichen Stücken des höheren Schulunterrichts« (vor allem in den Hauptfächern Sprachen, Naturwissenschaft und Mathematik, Geschichte und Geographie sowie Theologie), wie es in der Ordnung von 1831 für Preußen heißt (vgl. *Wiese* (1902), V, S. 749ff.; *Beier* (1909); *Paulsen* (1885), S. 347).

2.3. Die dritte Periode bezeichne ich als die der *Spezialisierung* (1870–1918). Mit der Spezialisierung hatte sich auch das Selbstverständnis des akademisch gebildeten Philologenstandes verschoben; nicht mehr der für die Breite der Fächer zuständige praktische Schulmann war das Ideal, sondern der *fachwissenschaftlich gebildete Gelehrte,* wie ihm Friedrich *Paulsen* in seinem Buch von 1902: »Der höhere Lehrerstand und seine Stellung in der gelehrten Welt« Ausdruck gab. Zum Beispiel wird in der bayerischen Ordnung von 1873 nicht mehr nach Schularten, d. h. den humanistischen bzw. realistischen, geprüft, sondern nach Fachgebieten: in historisch-philologischen Fächern, neuen Sprachen, Mathematik und Physik u. a.. Diese Spezialisierung wird kompensiert in *Preußen* in Form einer sog. »Allgemeinen Prüfung« in Deutsch, Philosophie und Pädagogik, in *Bayern* und *Württemberg* in Form einer getrennten, nach der einjährigen Vorbereitungszeit liegenden, zweiten Prüfung. Das Modell Bayern und Württemberg, die die Fachstudien-Spezialisierung auffangen mit einer *Trennung in eine erste wissenschaftliche und eine zweite praktische Prüfung,* wird schließlich auch von Preußen in der Ordnung vom 28. 7. 1917 übernommen, so daß man von einer einheitlichen Prüfung für das höhere Lehramt ab diesem Zeitpunkt in Deutschland sprechen kann (vgl. *Dolch* (1963), S. 20–24). Damit war allerdings zugleich der hohe Selbstbewußtseinsgrad, der in den Altertumswissenschaften und ihrer Bildungstheorie wurzelte und dem er seine wissenschaftliche Dignität verdankte, verspielt; insbesondere die Gleichsetzung der Reallehrerausbildung hatte diese Entwicklung forciert. Dagegen lag der Prestigegewinn, den sich die Lehrerverbände versprachen, vor allem in der Gleichstellung mit den übrigen akademischen Berufen; der »Oberlehrer« wollte als spezialisierter Fachmann gelten, vergleichbar, wie mit Vorliebe argumentiert wurde, dem Richter und seiner Stellung in der Gesellschaft.

3. Segmentierung und Ausbildung für das niedere Lehramt

3.1. Epoche der seminaren Profilfindung: 1750–1800

Von den hier für den historischen Weg der Lehrerbildung anzusetzenden drei Segmenten begrenze ich eine erste Epoche ab Mitte des 18. Jahrhunderts bis zur Wende 1800: es ist die *Epoche der seminaren Profilfindung.* Ich möchte diese in das System von *drei sich ausbildenden Profilen* bringen, die ich extensiver darstellen möchte, weil sie in dieser Form ein Produkt eigener Forschungsarbeit sind.

3.1.1. Ein erstes, wohl auch das paradigmatischste, Profil entwickelt sich dominant zunächst im *Interessenbereich des Stadtbürgers,* dem, wie wir wissen, ja auch der pietistische Reformimpetus gilt und der sodann auch dominant in den Emanzipationssog der Aufklärung gerät: es ist das *Lehrerseminar.* In dem für die Vorbereitung der pietistischen Bewegung wichtigen Fürstentum *Gotha* trifft Herzog *Ernst der Fromme* (1601–1675) Anstalten zur Errichtung eines Lehrerseminars – meines Wissens liegt hier die erste Stiftungsurkunde für eine spezielle Lehrerausbildungsinstitution vor: »... auf daß man künftig in allen Aembtern zuverlässige qualifizierte

Persohnen habe, deren man Versicherlich in des Landes nutz beständig gebrauchen könne. Und weil nicht zu zweiffeln ist, daß of solche gemachte anstalt sich viel expectanten im Schul – Und Kirchendiensten herbeyfinden ... so wäre auch erspriеslich, daß sie inmittelst an einem gewissen Ort unterhalten, und nur dasjenige practiciren lernten, wo zu sie inskünfftige gebraucht werden sollen. Dafern wir nun bei unserem Leben keine solche anstallt machen, und einen gewissen ort und Mittel dazu deputiren kondten, so werden unsere Erben und successores inskünfftige ... mit der Landschaffts-Beyhilfe dieses intent gebührlich zu werk richten.« (zit. nach *Gelbke* (1888), III, S. 61f.)

a) Das Lehrerseminar, das als grundständige Ausbildungsform vor diesem Hintergrund Gestalt annimmt, entsteht zuallererst *in Verbindung mit der Gründung von Waisenhäusern,* in musterhafter Ausprägung und als Wiege der gesamten seminaren Bewegung im Waisenhaus August Hermann *Franckes* in *Halle* (einem ehemaligen Schüler am Gothaer Gymnasium, dem auch der »Schulmethodus« bekannt war) und dem dort angegliederten »Seminarium praeceptorum« von 1696, schließlich dem »Seminarium selectum« von 1707 und dem »Institut der Praeparandi« von 1717. Darin übten sich die Kandidaten »fleißig in den Dingen, so zum Schulwesen gehören« – so *Francke* (zit. nach *Paulsen* (1885), S. 574): vgl. *Francke* (1957), S. 101ff. u. S. 107ff.). Dieses Konzept findet eine Verbreitung zunächst durch den *Francke*-Schüler J. C. *Schinmeier* in *Stettin* im Jahre 1732, sodann im Seminar am Kloster *Berge* bei Magdeburg unter dem pietistisch orientierten Abt *Steinmetz* im Jahre 1736, schließlich am bekanntesten in der Einrichtung des *Francke*-Schülers und Verfassers des General-Landschul-Reglements Julius *Hecker* am *Potsdamer Waisenhaus* im Jahre 1748, die 1753 in das staatliche »Kurmärkische Küster- und Schullehrerseminar für die königl. Amtskirchen« umgewandelt wurde (1–2jährig: außer Lesen, Schreiben, Rechnen, Singen und Religion, Maulbeerbaumzucht und Seidenbau, Katechisieren und Orgelspiel) (vgl. *Kehr* (1878), S. 5ff.; *Frick* (1893). An diesem orientierte sich auch die Einrichtung am Waisenhaus in *Braunschweig* vom Jahre 1751, in *Wolfenbüttel* und nachfolgend in *Helmstedt.* (Aber auch in *Stuttgart* entsteht am Ende des 18. Jahrhunderts am städtischen Waisenhaus unter dem Einfluß des Pfarrers *D'Autel* eine kurzzeitige Seminareinrichtung.) Dieses Konzept findet seine maßgebliche Fortführung einmal über die preußische Annexion des katholischen Schlesien, wobei der mit der Reform des katholischen Neu-Preußen beauftragte Abt von Sagan Ignaz *Felbiger* – in engem Einvernehmen mit Julius *Hecker* – in *Sagan* 1763 und in *Breslau* 1765 (das evangelische Seminar in Breslau folgt 1767) ein Lehrerseminar einrichtet. (Hier kamen neben den Kenntnissen, wie sie *Hecker* forderte, noch Realien, Meß- und Baukunde, Landwirtschaft sowie Latein hinzu; methodisch die Ausrichtung auf die Tabellarmethode.) Die andere Fortführung gelingt über Holland und die Harlemer Lehrerbildungseinrichtung, von wo sie, wenn auch verspätet, nach *Hamburg* ans Große Waisenhaus am Beginn des 19. Jahrhunderts gelangt. Ich habe an anderer Stelle ausgeführt, welche *Gründe* für diese Waisenhaus- und Armenschulanbindung der Lehrerausbildung sprachen (vgl. *Keck* (1983), S. 86f.).

b) Die andere Variante des Lehrerseminars entwickelt sich in *Verbindung mit der Gründung bzw. Stiftung von Armen- und Freischulen* relativ selbständig; als paradig-

matisch hierfür kann in solcher Stiftungskombination das erste städtische Lehrerseminar von *Hannover* im Jahre 1751 genannt werden (vgl. *Keck* (1985), S. 5–30). Aber auch *Basedows* Aufruf zur Gründung von Schulen »für den großen Haufen« in seiner »Vorstellung an die Menschenfreunde« (1768) liefert das Modell eines Lehrerseminars, eines »Elementar-Instituts«, wie er es nannte in seinem »Vorschlag und Nachricht von bevorstehender Verbesserung des Schulwesens« von 1770 und in seinem »Methodenbuch« von 1771, das, wie *Kämmel* (1882), S. 806) ausführt, eine breite Ausstrahlung zeitigte. Zwischen 1770 und 1780 entstehen – dominant dieser Profilierung nie verpflichtet – Lehrerseminare in *Detmold, Idstein* (Hessen-Nassau) *Klein-Dexen* (Preußisch-Eylau) bis 1772, zwischen 1780 und 1800 in *Kiel, Kassel, Wesel, Glaz, Dresden, Petershagen, Weißenfels, Freiberg, Ludwigslust, Greifswald* etc.
c) Schließlich verdient die Variante eine besondere, meist aber vernachlässigte Erwähnung, die eine seminaristische Einrichtung *in Verbindung mit bestehenden Gymnasien oder Realschulen* vornahm, meist in Form eines *Zusatzunterrichts* in Pädagogik, Katechetik und Musik für die mittleren Gymnasialklassen, und zwar für ärmere Schüler, für die Stipendien, Freiplätze bzw. Currende-Einkommen bestanden. Das Amt des Seminarlehrers war Nebenamt. Für *Herders* Verbindung des Seminars in *Weimar* (1786) war diese Konstruktion geradezu eine Grundsatzempfehlung wert: »Ein solches Institut so verschränkt und verbunden mit anderen Instituten zu machen, als nur möglich war, weil sonst das Institut in kurzer Zeit verfallen könnte ...« (*Schweitzer* (1838, S. 11f.). Neben Weimar wurde nachweislich dieser Weg verfolgt in *Karlsruhe* (1768), *Halberstadt* (1778), *Soest, Erfurt, Minden, Oldenburg, Magdeburg, Gera, Gotha, Schaumburg-Lippe* (1793) und *Altenburg,* in Süddeutschland in *Öhringen* und *Rastatt.*

3.1.2. Das zweite Profil, das der *Normalkurse,* wurde mit einer Wende der Aufklärungsansatzes zu einer verstärkten *landpädagogisch-aufklärerischen Reformbewegung* eingeleitet; gestützt durch den Physiokratismus entdeckt der aufklärerische Staat seine Verpflichtung für das flache Land, eine Tendenz, der das General-Landschul-Reglement Preußens von 1763 den Boden bereitet und das *Rochow* mit seiner *Reckan*schen Schuleinrichtung als mit wenig Mitteln umsetzbar vor Augen führt: »Es ist das einzig Nothwendige, daß ein zweckemäßiges Volksschullehrer-Seminarium angelegt werde, worin christlich gesinnte, geschickte junge Männer auf Kosten des Staats von einem musterhaft christlichen, das ist edel denkendem Manne (es ist wohl an seinen Musterlehrer *Bruns* als Vorbild zu denken) zu Volksschullehrern gebildet und somit die Millionen des Volks durch Aufklärung ... und durch bessere Erkenntnis für Erde und Himmel tüchtig gemacht werden« (*Rochow:* Vorrede. In: *Riemann* (1781)). Die Konstruktion ist, aus »deutschen« Musterschulen begabte Schüler herauszuziehen, sie als Hilfslehrer einzusetzen und sie in Fortbildungskursen, sogenannten *Normalkursen,* drei bis sechs Monate zusammenzuziehen und auszubilden.
Dieses Fortbildungskonzept findet vor allem seine entscheidende Ausprägung durch die Berufung des schlesisch-preußischen Abtes *Felbiger* nach Österreich im Rahmen der Theresianischen »Trivialschulordnung« von 1774 unter dem Begriff *»Normal-*

schule« (vgl. *Gönner* (1967)). Es verbreitet sich über den katholischen Einflußbereich Österreichs nach Böhmen und in die vorderösterreichischen und reichsunmittelbaren Gebiete Süddeutschlands (z. B. *Freiburg* (1773), *Neresheim* und Oberschwaben), schließlich über *Mainz, Trier, Würzburg, Koblenz, Köln, Essen* und *Bonn* (*Oberthür* 1777) nach *Münster* (*Overberg* 1783), *Büren* und *Hildesheim* (*Lüsken* 1790) in Norddeutschland (vgl. u. a. *Keck* (1982), S. 167–191; *Hanschmidt/Kuropka* (1980), S. 9–55).

3.1.3. Zwischen und neben diesen gezeichneten zwei Profillinien verbleiben *Rückzugsgebiete des traditionellen und zunftmäßigen Meister-Lehre-Profils.* Zwei größere Regionen will ich paradigmatisch anführen. Die eine ist im protestantischen Süddeutschland anzusiedeln: in *Württemberg und Franken.* So sagt der Seminartheologe Theodor *Eisenlohr* nach einer pädagogischen Reise durch Mittel- und Süddeutschland im Dienste des württembergischen Kultministeriums in seiner Bestandsaufnahme »unter besonderer Rücksicht auf Württemberg« von 1837: »Auffallend ist ..., wie sehr in Rücksicht auf rührige Thätigkeit auf diesem Boden Süddeutschland hinter Norddeutschland zurückblieb« (*Eisenlohr* (1840), S. 3).

In Norddeutschland stellt eine vergleichbare Rückzugsregion der Meister-Lehre *Ostfriesland* dar; die Konstituentien dieses Profils habe ich an anderer Stelle näher beleuchtet (vgl. *Keck* (1984), S. 177f.), nämlich die Bedeutung von Ausschreibung, Probeunterricht, Musterlehrer, dem sog. »Lehrerschriftwechsel« bzw. freien Schulmeisterkonferenzen und von »Schullehrervereinen zur genossenschaftlichen Belehrung«, wie es Rudolf *Vandré* (1973), S. 76ff.) zu entnehmen ist. Die ostfriesische Region fand erst mit dem Seminar *Aurich* ab 1852 Anschluß an den seminaristischen Ausbildungsweg. Eine zusammenfassende Übersicht über die drei seminaren Hauptprofile ermöglicht das folgende *Diagramm:*

A. *Das Lehrerseminar* im Interessenbereich des Stadtbürgers (meist 2-jährige grundständige Ausbildungsform)
   - in Verbindung mit der Gründung von Waisenhäusern nach dem Modell Halle
   - in Verbindung mit Armen- und Freischulen
   - in Verbindung mit Gymnasien/Realschulen

B. *Die Normalkurse* im Rahmen der landpädagogischen Aufklärungsbewegung (Aufbau und Kursform)
   - die Seminarschule *Rochows*
   - die Normalschule *Felbigers* nach der österr. Trivialschulordnung von 1774

C. *Das traditionelle Meister-Lehre-Profil* in Rückzugsgebieten (Württemberg, Franken, Ostfriesland)

3.2. Die zweite segmentierende Periode setze ich zwischen 1800 und 1870 an; ich nenne sie die *Periode des regionalen Ausbaus und der zunehmenden Absicherung. Preußen* kann für diese Zeit der staatlichen Reform im Zuge der Befreiungskriege als der *entscheidende Träger der Seminaridee* betrachtet werden. Zwei Maßnahmenstränge, die im wesentlichen pestalozzianisch bestimmt sind, leiten diese Trägerfunktion ein:

1. Die Berufung des württembergischen Pestalozzianers C. A. *Zeller* (1774–1846) im Jahre 1809 nach *Königsberg* zur Neuorganisation des Schulwesens und der Einrichtung bzw. Organisation von Lehrerseminaren in Ostpreußen, so z. B. am Waisenhaus in Königsberg.
2. Die Entsendung von sog. *Eleven* zu *Pestalozzi* nach Iferten im Staatsauftrag. Im selben Jahr der Berufung *Zellers* schrieb der preußische Staatsrat *Nicolovius,* dem Hauptantriebsmotor neben *Süvern,* an *von Türk* nach Iferten: »Die Section des öffentlichen Unterrichts bittet Ew. zu glauben und Herrn Pestalozzi zu versichern, daß die Sache Angelegenheit der Regierung und Sr. Majestät des Königs persönlich ist, welche sich überzeugt haben, daß Erlösung von außerordentlichen Drangsalen ohne innere Regenration fruchtlos und nur vermittelst einer durchgreifenden Verbeserung der Volkserziehung zu bewirken ist« (nach *Pestalozzi:* Wochenschrift für Menschenbildung (1809), II, S. 232). *Bayern, Sachsen* und *Württemberg* als die nächstgrößten Regionalstaaten folgten Preußen nach bzw. begannen miteinander in der Preußennachfolge zu konkurrieren. *Eisenlohr* führt aus der Sicht seiner Bestandsaufnahme von 1840 aus: »Gegenüber von diesen Bestrebungen des preußischen Staats darf keck gesagt werden, daß die Bestrebungen aller deutschen Staaten für eine umfassende und tüchtige Seminarbildung Nachwirkungen, häufig sogar unmittelbare Nachahmungen der preußischen Einrichtungen sind« (*Eisenlohr* (1840), S. 12).

Zwei bedeutsame Namen von Pestalozzianern sind in dieser Phase des Ausbaus mit großem inner- wie außerpreußischem Einfluß zu nennen: einmal Christian Wilhelm *Harnisch* (1787–1864). An *Harnisch* läßt sich exemplarisch verfolgen, wie die Männer der preußischen Reformbewegung unter »Demagogen-Verdacht« gerieten und die Reaktion nach 1819 sich negativ ausgewirkt hat. Dennoch wird *Harnisch* – nach Entlassung und Wiederberufung im Jahre 1822 zur Einrichtung des *Weißenfelser Seminars,* das bald das »2. Iferten« heißen wird und das Zentrum einer Pädagogen-Wallfahrt wird – zum Symbol des Durchhaltens der Seminaridee im Vormärz.

Der zweite Name ist Adolf *Diesterweg* (1790–1866), der Direktor des Seminars in *Mörs* und *Berlin,* Opfer der restaurativen Vormärz-Politik am Vorabend der Revolution (1847) und Kämpfer gegen die Regulativpolitik *Stiehls* von 1854.

Beide wirken für den verbandsmäßigen Zusammenschluß von Volksschullehrern durch die Etablierung von zwei pädagogischen Presseorganen: *Harnisch* in seinem »Schulrat an der Oder« und *Diesterweg* ab 1827 durch seine »Rheinischen Blätter für Erziehung und Unterricht«. Beide sind herausragende Gegner der Regulativpolitik, die von Preußen durch *Stiehls Regulative* von 1854 ausgehend von allen deutschen Staaten übernommen wird. Doch müssen die Regulative aus einer übergeordneten Entwicklungssicht nicht bloß als restaurationspolitische Maßnahme, sondern als umsetzungsfähiger *Kompromiß* nach der 48er Bewegung – als gesamtstaatliche Ratio gegenüber einem großen Gefälle in den regionalen Lehrerausbildungsstandards gesehen werden. Insofern bedarf die Kennzeichnung der Regulative durch *Spranger* als »dunklem Fleck in der Geschichte der preußischen Volksschule« ((1949), S. 44) durchaus einer distanzierten Betrachtung.

Man muß *Stiehls Intention* zur »Neugestaltung des Elementarschulwesens« ins Auge

fassen und damit in den Regulativen aus der Sicht der Lehrerbildung den Versuch sehen, eine *Vereinheitlichung gegen Wildwuchs* und auseinanderklaffende Entwicklungstempi zu erreichen; dafür brauchte er die stärkere Zusammenführung von Staat und Kirche. *Stiehl* in seiner Rechtfertigungsschrift: »Durch Revision der Seminare und vieler Schulen in allen Provinzen war es mir klar geworden, daß es auf dem Gebiete des Unterrichtswesens in großem Maße an einheitlichen Prinzipien in den Ausgangspunkten, in dem Verfahren und in dem Stecken der Ziele fehlte; weil aber vom Centrum, dem Ministerium, die energische und normierende Einwirkung nicht in dem erforderlichen Maße geübt worden war, war das subjektive Ermessen einzelner Schulräte und einzelner Seminardirektoren für die betreffenden Bezirke maßgebend geworden (*Stiehl* (1867), S. 12).
Worin kann nun die Vereinheitlichungstendenz gesehen werden? *Stiehl:* »Das Maß sei nicht ›diejenige Bildung, welche in einzelnen Fällen von einem Lehrer für eine gehobene Stadtschule gefordert werden mag‹, sondern ›die Bildung und das Können, welche das Schulehalten in der gewöhnlichen, aus Einer Klasse bestehenden Elementarschule von dem Lehrer erfordert‹« (*Stiehl* (1867), S. 6).
Die Regulative legen damit für die Lehrerbildung eine Basis, nämlich das zweijährige, grundständige Seminar als Norm, fest, alle Kurz- und Schnellkurse werden gestoppt, und dem traditionellen Wildwuchs der Meister-Lehre wird bis 1870 ein Ende gesetzt. Im Jahre 1864 haben nach den Berichten des »Statistischen Büros« von Preußen die seminaristisch gebildeten Lehrer inzwischen einen Anteil von zwei Dritteln (vgl. *Sauer* (1985), S. 76).

3.3. Die dritte segmentierende Epoche ist die der *Systembildung im Kaiserreich,* des qualitativen und quantitativen Ausbaus und der Subsistenzhebung des Lehrerstandes (1870–1918). Durch die *»Allgemeinen Bestimmungen«* Ministers A. *Falk* von 1872 werden im tonangebenden Land Preußen – verbunden mit dem Schulaufsichtsgesetz vom 11. 3. 1872, das allerdings nur formal die Schule von kirchlicher Aufsicht befreite – *neue Maßstäbe* für die Lehrerbildung gesetzt. Als Normalform gilt jetzt, 1. die Ausrichtung auf die mehrklassige Schule, 2. die Berücksichtigung der Realien sowie Raumlehre und Zeichnen und 3. die Ersetzung der »Schulkunde« durch Pädagogik, Psychologie und die Einführung einer Fremdsprache, 4. die curriculare und organisatorische Anbindung der Präparandien (auf drei Jahre) an eine nunmehr *dreijährige Seminarform.*
Ab 1872 kann von einer eigentlichen *Investitionspolitik des Staates* in Preußen in Sachen Lehrerbildung gesprochen werden. Nach *Sauers* Analyse des preußischen Schulwesens erhöhen sich z. B. die Ausgaben für Seminare von ca. 1,2 Mio. im Jahre 1872 auf 4,4 Mio. in 1882, für Aus- und Neubauten kommen nochmals über 17 Mio. Mark dazu. Zwischen 1846 bis 1872 waren insgesamt für Seminarbauten nur 3 Mio. Mark aufgewendet worden. Entsprechend wird auch die Personalausstattung an den Seminaren gesteigert. Durchschnittlich verdoppelt sich auch die Zahl der Seminaristen von ca. 5000 im Jahre 1870 auf 10 000 in 1881 (vgl. *Sauer* (1985), S. 80f. – nach der preußischen Statistik des Königlichen Statistischen Büros von 1891). Auch wenn zwischen 1872 und 1918 nennenswerte Subsistenzverbesserungen und Anreize für

den Lehrerberuf geschaffen werden, so in den 70er Jahren eine Mindestbesoldungsgarantie dadurch, daß die Gemeinden die Schulstellen finanziell genau auszuweisen hatten, 1873 durch die Einführung einer Dienstalterszulage, womit de facto eine Gleichsetzung mit Beamten erreicht wird, 1885 ein neues Lehrerpensionsgesetz und 1897 ein Lehrerbesoldungsgesetz in Preußen in Anwendung kam, so ist es doch zu einer Überfüllung, wie dies öfter im höheren Schulbereich der Fall war, nie gekommen. Man darf dabei nicht übersehen, daß mit der Möglichkeit der *Weiterqualifikation* über die *Mittelschullehrer- und Rektorenprüfung* vom 15. 10. 1872 die Lehrerlaufbahn durch Aufstiegsanreize flexibel wurde, desgleichen durch das Übersteigen zur Hilfsschule und zur Berufsschule.
Der *Lehrermangel,* der um die Jahrhundertwende (1906: 3% Minusquote) zu registrieren war, ist indes strukturell bedingt durch die starke Bevölkerungsexpansion nach 1890 einerseits und andererseits durch die Maßnahme, daß die Lehrer nach der Cabinetts-Ordre vom 27. 1. 1895 einen *einjährigen Militärdienst* abzuleisten hatten, die ab 1900 einen gesamten Seminarjahrgang vom Schuldienst fernhält.
Nicht zuletzt als Maßnahme gegen diesen erzeugten Lehrermangel wurden deshalb nach 1900 zunehmend *Lehrerinnen* in den Volksschuldienst aufgenommen. Im Jahre 1911 werden nach Auskunft des »Statistischen Jahrbuches für Preußen« (Berlin 1912, 379) schon über 20% Lehrerinnen beschäftigt. Bereits 1907 war die Zölibatsklausel für Lehrerinnen durch ihre Anstellungsmöglichkeit auf Widerruf gefallen. In Preußen stehen 1901 zwölf *staatlichen Lehrerinnenseminaren* 45 *private* gegenüber, die mit Lyzeen durch eine einjährige Kursfortführung verbunden waren (E. v. *Bremen* (1908), S. 10). Aufgrund dieser Anbindung konnte die Ausbildung selten den Stand der berufsspezifischen Lehrerseminare erreichen. Bis zur Neuordnung des Mädchenschulwesens im Jahre 1908 war ihr Einsatz sowohl für die Volksschule wie für die höheren Mädchenschulen möglich.

Im Vergleich zum Gymnasiallehrer war der Volksschullehrer in vieler Hinsicht schlechter gestellt. Ihm wurden bis 1918 de jure die Beamtenrechte verweigert, sein Gehalt war um die Hälfte geringer. Der Kontrolle durch Staat und Kirche, vor allem durch die lokale, nicht fachliche geistliche Schulaufsicht, war der Lehrer stärker ausgesetzt, seine Arbeitsbedingungen waren unvergleichlich schlechter. Die *Standesorganisationen,* in denen sich das professionelle Selbstverständnis darstellen konnte, waren nach 1849 zerschlagen worden. Dem 1871 neu gegründeten »Deutschen Lehrerverein«, der allen Lehrern offenstehen sollte, stellten die Lehrer für das höhere Lehramt 1872 den Philologenverband gegenüber, womit auch hier der ständischen Dichotomie Genüge getan war – eine Dichotomie, die schließlich in der Seminarstruktur für die Volksschullehrerbildung einerseits und der universitären Einbindung der höheren Lehrerbildung andererseits ihre Abbildung findet.
Diese Dichotomie zeigt sich auch in der *Frage der Professionswissenschaft Pädagogik.* Während sich das Gymnasiallehrerstudium quasi-professionell an den Philologien und in Erweiterung an den einzelnen Fachwissenschaften festmachte und Pädagogik ab dem letzten Jahrhundertdrittel der praktizistischen zweiten Phase überlassen wurde, richten sich die Emanzipationsbestrebungen der Volksschullehrerschaft ge-

rade auf die Pädagogik als argumentativer wissenschaftlich-professioneller Instanz. »Denn unser Beruf«, heißt es in den Reheinischen Blättern von 1864 (Bd. 14, 110), »ist so eigenartiger Natur, unsere Thätigkeit so wenig scharf in ihren Wirkungen zu ermessen und zu würdigen, ... die Erprießlichkeit unseres Thuns wird so oft theoretisch und praktisch in Frage gestellt, daß wir selten zu einiger Ruhe und Selbstgewißheit gelangen, und sehr geneigt sind, aufzuschrecken und zu erschrecken, ja uns selbst zu verurtheilen, wenn uns Vorwürfe ins Gesicht geschleudert werden, die ihren Ursprung entweder in der reactionären List oder der Unwissenheit und Kurzsichtigkeit in pädagogischen Dingen verdanken«. In der seminaren Lehrerbildung schlug sich dies nieder in einer starken Orientierung an *Pestalozzis Elementarmethode* und in den letzten Dezennien des 19. Jahrhunderts – als deren Ablösung – in einer Anhängung an die herbartianisch interpretierte Artikulationstheorie, wie Bernhard *Schwenks* Arbeit von 1963 zur *Herbart*-Rezeption ergeben hat. Mit der Berufung auf eine wissenschaftliche Pädagogik indes verband sich zugleich die seit 1848 genährte Hoffnung, die Ausbildung der Volksschullehrer an die Universität gemeinsam mit den Gymnasiallehrern zu verlagern (vgl. *Pretzel* (1921), S. 33), jedenfalls war die Berufung auf sie ein Argument gegenüber dem Vorwurf der sog. »After- und Halbbildung« der Volksschullehrer, d. h. ihrer Semi-Professionalität.

Anmerkungen

[1] In einer Auseinandersetzung mit H. L. *Smith* (1957) prägt H. *Daheim* (1969, S. 388) den Begriff *»Quasi-Professionalisierung«*, insofern ein hoch spezialisiertes Wissen zum Maßstab wird, das die praktische Berufsanforderung vereinseitigend übersteigert. Diesen Fall sehen wir in der tendentiellen Ausrichtung des Gymnasiallehrers auf die Philologie bzw. Fachwissenschaft gegeben, wobei Pädagogik und Didaktik bzw. Psychologie als das Berufsfeld reflektierende Berufsdisziplinen vernachlässigt werden.
Der Begriff *»Semi-Professionalisierung«* geht, soweit ich sehe, auf die Arbeit von *La Vopa* (1980) zurück. Er soll deutlich machen, daß neben dem Ausbildungswissen noch andere Faktoren wie z. B. die »Prisonisierung« in der seminaristischen Lebensform mit ihren eingeschränkten Sozialisationsmustern oder eine bestimmte Rekrutierung für die Berufsgenese entscheidend werden.

[2] Bei der gebotenen Kürze und in Abhebung auf eine vergleichende Strukturskizze der Lehrerbildungswege kann diese Entwicklung hier nur holzschnittartig verfolgt werden. Auf differenzierende Aspekte hinsichtlich der begleitenden Studienmöglichkeit von Pädagogik wird sowohl bei H. *Morsch* (1910), W. *Roeßler* (1960, S. 705–720), J. *Dolch* (1963, S. 20ff.), J. *Guthmann* (1964), H. *Scholtz* (1965, S. 128–181) als auch bei H.-J. *Apel* (u. a. 1983, S. 145–158; vgl. auch ders. in diesem Band!) nachzulesen sein.

Literaturverzeichnis

Apel, H.-J.: Der Gymnasiallehrer zwischen Universität und Pädagogikum. Die Diskussion um die Festlegung des Ausbildungsweges im Reheinland um 1820. In: IZEBF 1983 (Nr. 10/21), S. 145–158

Beier, A. (1909): Die höheren Schulen in Preußen und ihre Lehrer

Blättner, F. (1960): Das Gymnasium. Heidelberg

Bölling, R. (1978): Volksschullehrer und Politik. Der Deutsche Lehrerverein 1918–1933. Göttingen

Bölling, R.: Lehrerschaft, Schulpolitik und Arbeiterbewegung in der Weimarer Republik. In: Archiv für Sozialgeschichte 1981, S. 602–612

Bölling, R. (1983): Sozialgeschichte der deutschen Lehrer. Göttingen

Bremen, E. von (1908): Das höhere Mädchenschulwesen. Stuttgart/Berlin

Breyvogel, W. (1978): Die soziale Lage und und das politische Bewußtsein der Volksschullehrer 1927–1933. Königstein

Breyvogel, W./Tenorth, H.-E.: Lehrerschaft und Faschismus. In: ZfPäd 1981, S. 169–182

Bungardt, K. (1965): Die Odyssee der Lehrerschaft. Sozialgeschichte eines Standes. Hannover

Carr-Saunders, A. M./Wilson, P. A. (1933): The Professions. Oxford

Daheim, H.: Soziologie der Berufe. In: König, R. (Hrsg.) (1969): Handbuch der Empirischen Sozialforschung II. Stuttgart, S. 365–399

Döderlein, L. (1843): Reden und Aufsätze. Ein Beitrag zur Gymnasialpädagogik und Philologie. Erlangen

Dolch, J.: Zur Geschichte des Paedagogicums der Gymnasiallehrer im 19. Jh. In: ZfPäd 1963, S. 20–24

Eisenlohr, Th. (1840): Die Schullehrer-Bildungsanstalten in Deutschland. Stuttgart

Feiten, W. (1981): Der Nationalsozialistische Lehrerbund. Weinheim

Fischer, K. (1892): Geschichte des deutschen Volksschullehrerstandes. 2 Bde. Hannover. Nachdruck Leipzig 1969

Francke, A. H. (1957): Pädagogische Schriften, ed. H. Lorenzen. Paderborn

Frick, O. (1893): Das Seminarium praeceptorum

Geißler, G. (1973): Eingliederung der Lehrerbildung in die Universität. Das Hamburger Beispiel. Weinheim

Gönner, R. (1967): Die österreichische Lehrerbildung von der Normalschule zur Pädagogischen Akademie. Wien

Günther-Arndt, H. (1983): Volksschullehrer und Nationalsozialismus. Oldenburg

Guthmann, J.: Über die Entwicklung des Studiums der Pädagogik. In: MUND 111 (ADL). Bühl 1964

Hamburger, F. (1974): Lehrer zwischen Kaiser und Führer. Der Deutsche Philologenverband in der Weimarer Republik. Phil. Diss. Hanschmidt/Kuropka (Hrsg.) (1980): Von der Normalschule zur Universität. Bad Heilbrunn, S. 9–55

Heinemann, M. (Hrsg.) (1977): Der Lehrer und seine Organisation. Stuttgart

Heinemann, M. (Hrsg.) (1980): Erziehung und Schulung im Dritten Reich. 2 Bde. Stuttgart

Herrlitz, H. G./Titze, H.: Überfüllung als bildungspolitische Strategie. In: ZfPäd 1977, 348ff.

Hettwer, H.: Geplanter und geltender Stellenwert der Pädagogik in der Lehrer-Ausbildung. In: Päd. Rundschau 1974, S. 593–624

Jarausch, K. H. (1982): The Transformation of Higher Learning 1860–1930. Boston

Kämmel, H.: Philanthropismus. In: K. A. Schmid (Hrsg.) (1882): Encyclopädie des gesammten Erziehungs- und Unterrichtswesens, Bd. V. Gotha, S. 806ff.

Keck, R. W. (1982): Die Normalschule zu Hildesheim in ihrer Gründungsphase 1790–1820. In: Die Diözese Hildesheim. Hildesheim 1982, S. 167–191.
Keck, R. W. (1983): Die Aufklärungsuniversität Göttingen als Wiege entscheidender pädagogischer Reformideen zur Lehrerbildung im ausgehenden 18. Jh. In: Informationen zur Erziehungs- und Bildungshistorischen Forschung, 1983, Nr. 20/21, S. 65–99
Keck, R. W. (1984): Historische Konzepte der Lehrerausbildung und Desiderate ihrer Erforschung. Der Versuch eines Forschungsberichts zum Stande der Lehrerbildungsgeschichte. In: VfwP 1984 (H. 2), S. 161–189
Keck, R. W.: Das Lehrerseminar zu Hannover. In: Schmid (Hrsg.) (1985): Beiträge zur Geschichte der Lehrerbildung. Hannover
Kehr, C. (1878): Die Geschichte des Königl. Schullehrer-Seminars zu Halberstadt. Gotha
Krause-Vilmar, D. (Hrsg.) (1978): Lehrerschaft, Republik und Faschismus 1918–1933. Köln
Kunz, L. (1984): Höhere Schule und Philologenverband. Frankfurt
La Vopa, A. J. (1980): Prussian Schoolteachers. Profession and Office 1763–1848. Chapel Hill
Mack, R. W. (1956): Occupational Determinateness: A Problem and Hypothesis in Role Theory. In: Social Forces Bd. 35
Martin, H. W. (1958): The Behavioral Science and Nursing Education. In: Social Forces Bd. 37, 1958
Meyer-Willner, G. (1986): Eduard Spranger und die Lehrerbildung. Die notwendige Revision eines Mythos. Bad Heilbrunn
Morsch, H. ([2]1910): Das höhere Lehramt in Deutschland und Österreich. Leipzig/Berlin
Müller, D. K. (1977): Sozialstruktur und Schulsystem. Göttingen
Nath, A. (1958): Der Studienassessor im Dritten Reich. Eine sozialhistorische Studie zur Überfüllungskrise des höheren Lehramts in Preußen 1932–1942. In: ZfPäd 1981, S. 281–306
Neuerer, K. (1978): Das höhere Lehramt in Bayern im 19. Jh. Berlin
Ottweiler, O. (1979): Die Volksschule im Nationalsozialismus. Weinheim
Paulsen, F. (1920): Der höhere Lehrerstand und seine Stellung in der gelehrten Welt. Berlin
Paulsen, F. (1885, [2]1896/97, [3]1919/21): Geschichte des gelehrten Unterrichts. 2 Bde. Berlin
Pöggeler, F. (1975): Zur Entwicklung der Erziehungswissenschaft in der BRD von 1950–1975. In: Päd. Rundschau 1975, S. 967–990
Pretzel, C. L. (1921): Geschichte des deutschen Lehrervereins in den ersten 50 Jahren seines Bestehens. Leipzig
Riemann (1781): Beschreibung der Reckahn'schen Schuleinrichtung. Berlin/Stettin
Roeßler, W. (1960a): F. A. Wolf. Ein Beitrag zum Verhältnis von Wissenschaft und Pädagogik um die Wende zum 19. Jh. In: Bildung und Erziehung 1960, S. 143ff.
Roeßler, W. (1960b): Das Problem der Vor- und Ausbildung der Lehrer historisch gesehen. In: Bildung und Erziehung 1960, S. 705–720
Romberg, H. (1979): Staat und höhere Schule. Ein Beitrag zur deutschen Bildungsverfassung vom Anfang des 19. Jh. bis zum I. Weltkrieg. Weinheim
Rüschemeyer, D.: Rekrutierung, Ausbildung und Berufskultur. In: Glass/König (Hrsg.) (1961): Soziale Schichtung und soziale Mobilität. Sonderheft 5 der Kölner Zeitschrift für Soziologie und Sozialpsychologie. Köln
Sandfuchs, U. (1978): Universitäre Lehrerausbildung in der Weimarer Republik und im Dritten Reich. Bad Heilbrunn
Sandfuchs, U. (1981): Die Reminarisierung der Lehrerausbildung im Dritten Reich – aufgezeigt am Beispiel Braunschweig. In: Braunschweigisches Jahrbuch 62, 1981, S. 137ff.
Sandfuchs, U. (1986): Strukturwandel der Volksschullehrerausbildung 1927–1952. Das Beispiel Braunschweig. In: Braunschweigisches Jahrbuch 67, 1986, S. 141–169

Sauer, M. (1985): Die staatliche Steuerung der preußischen Volksschullehrerbildung im Kaiserreich. In: H.-D. Schmid (Hrsg.) (1985): Beiträge zur Geschichte der Lehrerbildung. Hannover

Scholtz, H. (1965): Friedrich Gedike (1754–1803). In: Jahrbuch für die Geschichte Mittel- und Ostdeutschlands. Berlin 1965, S. 128–181

Scholtz, H. (1978): Zum Stand der erziehungswissenschaftlichen Erforschung der Schule unter der NS-Herrschaft. In: ZfPäd 1978, 965ff.

Scholtz, H. (1983): Politische und gesellschaftliche Funktionen der Lehrerbildungsanstalten 1941–45. In: ZfPäd 1983

Scholtz, H. (1985): Erziehung und Unterricht unterm Hakenkreuz. Göttingen

Schweitzer (1838): Geschichtliche Nachrichten über das Schullehrerseminar in Weimar. Weimar

Schwenk, B. (1963): Das Herbart-Verständnis der Herbartianer. Weinheim

Schwenk, B. (1977/78): Pädagogik in den philosophischen Fakultäten. In: Jahrbuch für Erziehungswissenschaft 1977/78, S. 103–130

Skopp, D. R. (1980): Auf der untersten Sprosse: Der Volksschullehrer als »Semi-Professional« im Deutschland des 19. Jh. In: Geschichte und Gesellschaft 6, 1980, S. 388–402

Smith, H. L. (1957): Psychiatrie in Medicine: Intra- or Interprofessional Relationship. In: American Journal of Sociology Bd. 63, 1957

Spranger, E. (1949): Zur Geschichte der deutschen Volksschule. Berlin

Statistisches Jahrbuch für Preußen. Berlin 1912

Stiehl, F. (^{8}1867): Die drei preußischen Regulative. Berlin

Titze, H. (1977): Die soziale und geistige Umbildung des preußischen Oberlehrerstandes von 1870–1914. In: ZfPäd 1977. 14. Beiheft, hrsg. v. U. Herrmann. Weinheim/Basel

Titze, H. (1981): Überfüllungskrisen in akademischen Karrieren: eine Zyklustheorie. In: ZfPäd 1981, S. 187–224

Trinks, K. (1980): Die Sozialgestalt des Volksschullehrers. (1933), bearb. u. hrsg. v. R. Bölling. Stuttgart

Vandré, R. (1973): Schule, Lehrer und Unterricht im 19. Jh. (Regionalgeschichte für Ostfriesland) Göttingen

Wiese, L. (1902): Das höhere Schulwesen in Preußen. Bd. IV, I–III 1864–74, ed. Irmer. Berlin

Franz Hauzenberger

Kaspar Buchner

Ein niederbayerischer Lehrer des 19. Jahrhunderts

Vorbemerkung

Das vorliegende Fallbeispiel *Kaspar Buchner* beschreibt das Leben und Wirken des Schullehrers *Kaspar Buchner,* der insgesamt 50 Jahre in diesem Beruf tätig war. Aufgrund seiner über 40jährigen Dienstzeit sowie seiner schulischen wie außerschulischen Verdienste in dem kleinen Pfarrdorf Thurmansbang zeichnet sich *Kaspar Buchner* unter den nahezu 300 Lehrpersonen (wobei kurzzeitige Unterrichtsaushilfen in dieser Zahl nicht berücksichtigt sind), die an der Volksschule Thurmansbang in den 300 Jahren ihres Bestehens unterrichtet haben, in ganz besonderer Weise aus.
Da bereits vor der Ära *Kaspar Buchners* Schulmeister in Thurmansbang am Werke waren und vor allem nach dessen Ableben zahlreiche Lehrpersonen nachfolgten, lassen sich umfangreiche und vielfältige Vergleiche sowohl mit Lehrern derselben Schule wie auch mit Lehrkräften anderer Schulorte Niederbayerns herstellen (siehe z. B. unter 3. Buchners Leistungen im Schuldienst oder 4. Buchners wirtschaftliche und soziale Situation).
Die Fallstudie *Kaspar Buchner* steht somit nicht isoliert im Raum, sondern veranschaulicht exemplarisch Leben und Wirken eines Schullehrers des 19. Jahrhunderts aus einer ganz bestimmten Region, nämlich des Bezirkes Niederbayern, und trägt damit dem aktuellen Bemühen der gegenwärtigen bayerischen Schulgeschichtsforschung Rechnung, über historische Detailuntersuchungen, die sich vor allem auf zeitliche und räumliche Ausschnitte beziehen, eine Basis für eine bayerische Schulgeschichte zu schaffen.[1]

1. Zur Person Kaspar Buchner

Kaspar Buchner wurde am 17. Juli 1804 in Breitenweinzier, königliches Landgericht Mitterfels (im heutigen Landkreis Straubing–Bogen gelegen) geboren. Seine Eltern waren katholisch und bewirtschafteten an besagtem Ort einen Bauernhof.[2]

2. Buchners beruflicher Werdegang

Seinen ersten Dienstposten als Schulgehilfe bekleidete *Kaspar Buchner* vom Jahre 1824 bis Februar 1827 in Künzing, Landgericht Vilshofen. Anschließend wirkte er vom Februar 1827 bis zum Dezember 1828 in gleicher Funktion im Nachbarort Pleinting, ebenfalls Landgericht Vilshofen.[3]

Nachdem *Buchner* die erforderlichen drei Jahre als Schulgehilfe abgeleistet hatte, legte er im Jahre 1828 am königlichen Schullehrerseminar in Straubing die Beförderungsprüfung ab. Für seine erbrachten Leistungen erhielt er die Gesamtnote II zugesprochen und erreichte damit Platz 7 unter 36 Kandidaten.[4]

Noch im selben Jahre, nämlich am 15. Dezember 1828, wurde *Buchner* zum Lehrprovisor in Längthal, Landgericht Landau/Isar, befördert.[5] Dort versah *Kaspar Buchner* über viereinhalb Jahre als Provisor den Schul- und Mesnerdienst, bis er schließlich am 20. Juni 1833 zum Schulverweser von Schöllnach, Landgerichtsbezirk Deggendorf, bestellt wurde.[6]

Obwohl *Buchner* zur vollen Zufriedenheit seine Dienstaufgaben in Schöllnach erledigte, sollte er auf Weisung der Regierung bereits zum 1. Januar 1834 Schöllnach wieder verlassen und eine Verweserstelle in Oberried, Landgerichtsbezirk Cham, antreten.

Seinem Ansuchen auf Dispens von dieser Versetzung wurde zwar stattgegeben, dafür beorderte man *Buchner* aber Ende Januar 1834 als Schulverweser nach Thurmansbang im Landgerichtsbezirk Passau (später Landgerichtsbezirk Grafenau).

Am 4. Februar 1834 trat *Kaspar Buchner* seinen neuen Dienstposten in Thurmansbang an. Per Regierungsschreiben vom 27. Januar 1838 erhielt der Schulprovisor *Kaspar Buchner* den »... Schullehrer-, Meßner- u. Organistendienst zu Thurmansbang ... in definitiver Eigenschaft übertragen ...«[7], welchen er bis zu seiner Pensionierung am 1. August 1874 in stets vorbildlicher Weise ausübte.[8]

3. Buchners Leistungen im Schuldienst

Bereits in den Jahren, in denen *Buchner* in Längthal und Schöllnach als Lehrprovisor tätig war, zeichnete er sich als hervorragender Pädagoge und engagierter Schulmann aus. Zahlreiche Zeugnisse bzw. Testate vorgesetzter Schulbehörden belegen diese Aussage.

So hatte beispielsweise die Distriktschulinspektion Gottfrieding, zu der das Schulprovisorat Längthal gehörte, im Dezember 1829 von der Regierung den Auftrag erhalten »... dem Lehrprovisor *Buchner* zu Längthal wegen dessen im verflossenen Schuljahre mit dem besten Erfolg für die Schuljugend daselbst bewiesenen Fleiß u. Eifer im Unterrichte das höchste Wohlgefallen der k. Regierung erkennen zu geben.«[9]

Vier Jahre später bestätigte dieselbe Distriktschulinspektion, daß *Kaspar Buchner* als Lehrprovisor in Längthal »... bei sehr vielen pädagogischen Fähigkeiten und Kenntnißen ... (und) stets unermindeten [= unverminderten] Fleiß im Schulunterrichte, welcher auch für die ihm anvertraute Schule den besten Erfolg hatte[,] ... als ein sehr geschickter und fleißiger Schulmann vorzüglich empfohlen zu werden verdient ...«.[10]

An anderer Stelle heißt es: »Kaspar Buchner hat als Lehrprovisor der ... Filialschule zu Längthal nichts als Großes u. Vorzügliches geleistet ... Seine eigene musterhafte Sittlichkeit wandelte baldest, u. zwar zur allgemeinen Verwunderung[,] die vorige Rohheit der Zöglinge zu[r] reinsten Gesittung um. Vorzüglich befähigt im Orgel u. Violinspiele, wie im Gesang ...«[11]

Die Lokalschulinspektion Schöllnach vermerkte, daß *Buchner* die vorzüglichsten Zeugnisse von seinen früheren Vorgesetzten hierher gebracht hätte. »Allein sie blieben dennoch seinen ausgezeichneten Eigenschaften in der Wirklichkeit weit zurück; und Unterzeichneter findet sich für wahr verlegen, das ihm [Buchner] gebührende Lob mit den verdienten Ausdrücken ertheilen zu können.«[12] Von der Distriktschulinspektion Schwanenkirchen als vorgesetzter Dienststelle von Schöllnach ist folgendes zu erfahren: »Kaspar Buchner, seit den 25ten Juli 1833 gnädigst angestellten Verweser des Lehr-, Meßner- und Organisten-Dienstes in Schöllnach hat während seines Hierseyns vorzügliche Fähigkeiten in allen Lehrgegenständen, und forthin einen ausgezeichneten Fleiß in seinem Berufe an den Tag gelegt, und mit diesen seltenen Attributen eines Lehrers zugleich eine musterhafte, moralische Conduite verbunden, und sich stets so benommen, daß er die Achtung seiner Vorgesetzten, und Eltern, so wie die Liebe aller Schulkinder im vollkommensten Grade gewonnen.«[13]

Auch an seinem nächsten Dienstort, nämlich in Thurmansbang, einem Pfarrdorf des unteren Bayerischen Waldes »... mit 16 Häusern und 100 Einwohnern ...«[14], zeichnete sich *Buchner* erneut durch beispielhafte Hingabe an seine Erzieher- und Unterrichtstätigkeit sowie durch stets vorbildliches persönliches Verhalten sowohl in als auch außerhalb der Schule aus.

Wie die Schulvisitationsprotokolle aus der Amtszeit *Buchners* in Thurmansbang eindeutig belegen, erzielte dieser bereits nach wenigen Jahren überdurchschnittliche bis hervorragende Ergebnisse mit den ihm anvertrauten Schülern bei den jährlichen Schulvisitationen durch den vorgesetzten Distriktschulinspektor. Zwischen den Schuljahren 1836/37 und 1866/67 wurden die Leistungen der Schüler *Buchners* – bis auf drei Ausnahmen – in allen Fächern stets mit den Noten gut, sehr gut und vorzüglich bewertet.[15] Im einzelnen ging es dabei um die Fächer Religion und Biblische Geschichte, Gedächtnisübungen, Lesen, Rechtschreiben, Schönschreiben, schriftliche Aufsätze, Erdbeschreibung bzw. Weltkunde unter besonderer Berücksichtigung der Kunde des Vaterlandes sowie um das mündliche und schriftliche Rechnen. Die Resultate in den Fächern Gesang und Zeichnen wurden verbal umschrieben.

Daß die Gesamtleistungen der Thurmansbanger Schuljugend in der II. und III. Klasse über einen Zeitraum von 30 Jahren ein derart hohes Niveau erreicht hatten und – wie

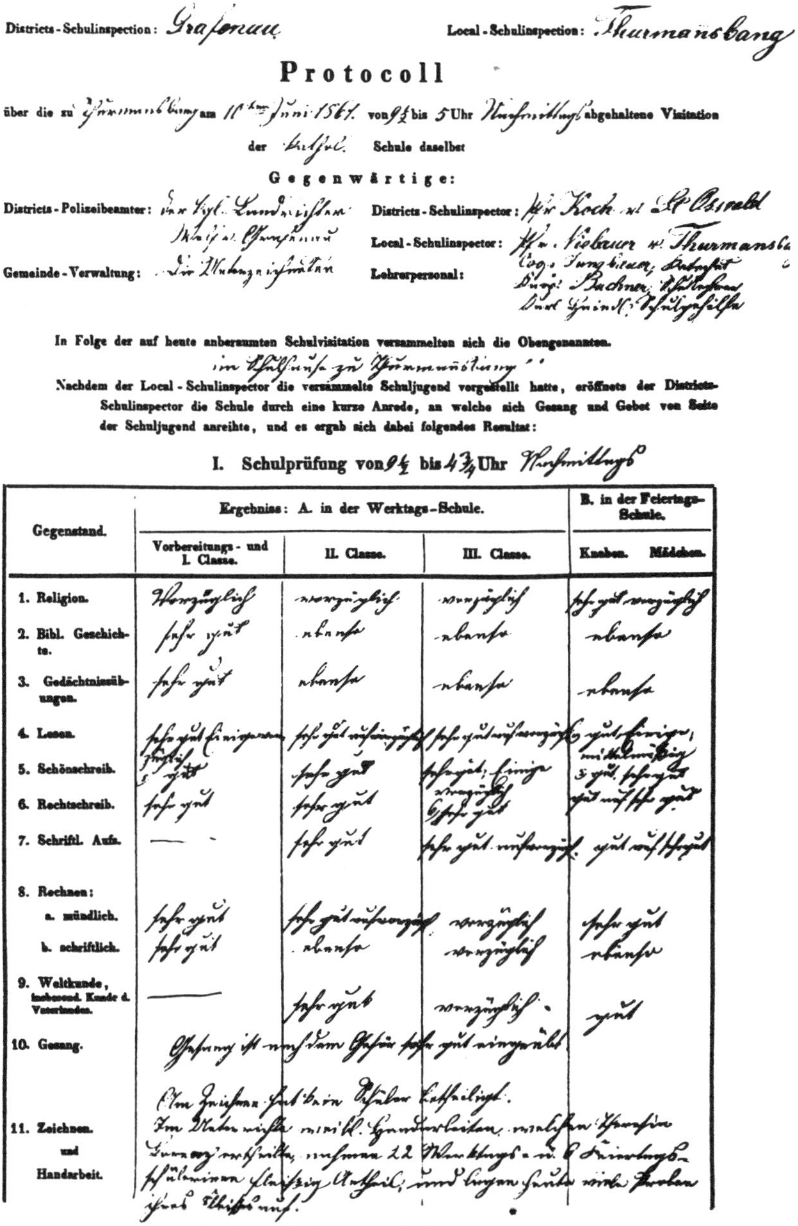

Districts-Schulinspection: Grafenau Local-Schulinspection: Thurmansbang

Protocoll

über die zu Thurmansbang am 10ten Juni 1861. von 9½ bis 5 Uhr Nachmittags abgehaltene Visitation der kathol. Schule daselbst

Gegenwärtige:

Districts-Polizeibeamter: der kgl. Landrichter Weiß v. Grafenau

Gemeinde-Verwaltung: Die Gemeindeverwaltung

Districts-Schulinspector: Hr. Koch v. St. Oswald

Local-Schulinspector: Hr. Niebauer v. Thurmansbang

Lehrerpersonal: Georg Jungbauer, Lehrer; Georg Buchner, Schulverweser; Carl Heindl, Schulgehilfe

In Folge der auf heute anberaumten Schulvisitation versammelten sich die Obengenannten im Schulhause zu Thurmansbang.

Nachdem der Local-Schulinspector die versammelte Schuljugend vorgestellt hatte, eröffnete der Districts-Schulinspector die Schule durch eine kurze Anrede, an welche sich Gesang und Gebet von Seite der Schuljugend anreihte, und es ergab sich dabei folgendes Resultat:

I. Schulprüfung von 9½ bis 4¾ Uhr Nachmittags

Gegenstand.	Ergebniss: A. in der Werktags-Schule. Vorbereitungs- und I. Classe.	II. Classe.	III. Classe.	B. in der Feiertags-Schule. Knaben. Mädchen.
1. Religion.	Vorzüglich	vorzüglich	vorzüglich	sehr gut, vorzüglich
2. Bibl. Geschichte.	sehr gut	ebenso	ebenso	ebenso
3. Gedächtnissübungen.	sehr gut	ebenso	ebenso	ebenso
4. Lesen.	sehr gut, Einige genügend	sehr gut, einige vorzügl.	sehr gut, einige vorzügl.	gut, Einige mittelmäßig
5. Schönschreib.	gut	sehr gut	sehr gut, Einige vorzüglich	gut, sehr gut
6. Rechtschreib.	sehr gut	sehr gut	sehr gut	gut auch sehr gut
7. Schriftl. Aufs.	—	sehr gut	sehr gut, einige vorzügl.	gut auch sehr gut
8. Rechnen: a. mündlich.	sehr gut	sehr gut, einige vorzügl.	vorzüglich	sehr gut
b. schriftlich.	sehr gut	ebenso	vorzüglich	ebenso
9. Weltkunde, insbesond. Kunde d. Vaterlandes.	—	sehr gut	vorzüglich	gut
10. Gesang.	Gesang ist nach dem Gehör sehr gut eingeübt.			
11. Zeichnen. und Handarbeit.	Am Zeichnen hat kein Schüler theilgenommen. Im Nähen, Stricken u. Handarbeiten, welchen Therese Jungbauer ertheilte, nehmen 22 Werktags- u. 8 Feiertagsschülerinnen fleißig Antheil, und liegen heute viele Proben ihres Fleißes vor.			

(PfATh, Visitationsprotokoll vom 10. Juni 1861)

bereits ausgeführt – nahezu ausnahmslos beibehalten werden konnten, war sicherlich das Hauptverdienst ihres Lehrers *Kaspar Buchner*.
Die königliche Lokalschulinspektion Thurmansbang bestätigt diese Annahme, indem sie *Buchner* wiederholt attestiert, daß er neben seiner ausgezeichneten Aufführung insbesondere einen musterhaften Fleiß und vorzügliche Geschicklichkeit im Unterricht und in der Bildung der Jugend zeige.[16] Im Gegensatz zu seinem Vorgänger *Jakob Lorenz*, dem es nicht nur an fachlichem Können, sondern sehr häufig auch an Pflichtbewußtsein und Diensteifer mangelte und deshalb das Leistungsniveau an der Werktagsschule Thurmansbang nicht allzu hoch war, brachte es *Kaspar Buchner* bereits sechs Jahre nach seinem Dienstantritt in Thurmansbang, nämlich schon im Jahre 1840 fertig, daß die Schule Thurmansbang zu den besten des Landgerichtsbezirkes zählte.[17] Sicherlich wurde *Buchners* Bemühen um schulische Erfolge zu dieser Zeit durch die Tatsache begünstigt, daß ihm mit dem für schulische Belange sehr aufgeschlossenen Ortsgeistlichen und Lokalschulinspektor von Thurmansbang, dem späteren Stadtpfarrer von Grafenau, *Joseph Stephaner*, sowie dem überdurchschnittlich qualifizierten und eifrigen Schulgehilfen *Martin Eckl*, der neben *Buchner* zu dieser Zeit die Vorbereitungs- und I. Klasse an der Schule Thurmansbang unterrichtete, zwei tatkräftige Mitstreiter zur Seite standen.
Neben der Unterweisung in den elementaren Unterrichtsgegenständen wie etwa im Lesen, Schreiben, Rechnen und in Religion lag *Kaspar Buchner* insbesondere die Ausbildung der Thurmansbanger Schuljugend auf dem musischen Sektor, d. h. in Zeichnen, Musik und Handarbeit, am Herzen. Vor allem in die musikalische Erziehung und Weiterbildung investierte Lehrer *Buchner* große Anstrengungen. Ein vielseitiges Angebot, bestehend aus der Einführung in die Notenlehre, praktischen Gesangsübungen nach Gehör sowie der Möglichkeit der Teilnahme am Instrumentalunterricht, wie etwa in Violine, ließ Buchner vor allem den Schülern der II. und III. Klasse über 40 Jahre hinweg unentwegt zuteil werden.[18] Besonders begabte Sängerinnen förderte *Buchner* zusätzlich, indem er mit ihnen Kirchenlieder einstudierte und sie auf diese Weise auf eine Mitwirkung am Kirchenchor vorbereitete.[19]
Zusätzlich zum Fach Zeichnen wurde ab dem Schuljahr 1849/50 auch Unterricht in den weiblichen Handarbeiten an der Schule Thurmansbang erteilt. *Theres Lorenz*, eine Stieftochter *Kaspar Buchners*, wirkte bis zu *Buchners* Pensionierung im Jahre 1874 – obwohl ihr unentwegter Einsatz zunächst nur mit 5 fl. und später mit 10 fl. entgolten worden war – mit großem Erfolg als Handarbeitslehrerin an der Volksschule Thurmansbang.[20]
Kaspar Buchner übte während seiner 40jährigen Dienstzeit in dem kleinen Pfarrdorf Thurmansbang im unteren Bayerischen Wald eine Vielzahl von Funktionen aus. In gleicher Weise, wie er seine Tätigkeit als Schulprovisor bzw. Schullehrer versah, versuchte er seinen vielfältigen Aufgaben als Mesner, Organist und Chorregent gerecht zu werden. Außerdem war *Kaspar Buchner* seit seiner Verehelichung mit der Lehrerswitwe *Anna Maria Lorenz* im Jahre 1836[21] Mitinhaber des der Pfarrkirchenstiftung Thurmansbang eigentümlichen Kramerrechtes, welches nachweislich seit 1776 dem jeweiligen Mesner und Schullehrer von Thurmansbang ›leibslebenlang‹ bzw. ›nutznießlich‹ für einen geringen jährlichen Pachtzins überlassen worden war.[22]

4 Abschrift.

VII. Besondere, für die öffentliche Verhandlung nicht geeignete Bemerkungen der Districts-Polizey- und Schul-behörde.

1. Im Allgemeinen: die Schule zu [illegible]

2. Insbesondere:	Fähigkeiten.	Fleiß.	Sittliches Betragen.	Bemerkungen.
a. hinsichtlich des Local-Schulinspectors . . .	I. 1.	I. 1.	I. 1.	
b. des Lehrpersonals:				Thätigkeit.
1. [illegible], Schullehrer.	I. 1.	I. 1.	I. 1.	I. 2.
2. [illegible] Martin Schulgehilfe.	I. 1	I. 1.	I. 1.	I. 2.

VIII. Anträge und sonstige Bemerkungen.

Schlüßlich vereinigte man sich, Nachstehendes der höchsten Stelle in Antrag und zur besondern Kenntnißnahme zu bringen:

Der k. Lokal- und derzeitige funktionirende Distrikts-Schulinspektor Pfarrer [illegible] hat auch in diesem Jahre seinen mühevollen Beruf mit solchem Eifer und Erfolg erfüllt, daß er sich gewiß einer gnädigsten Anerkennung der k. Regierung würdig gemacht hat, welche ihm allerdings zur Aufmunterung in seinem Eifer zu dienen gereichen dürfte. –

Grafenau am 4 Aug. 1841

Königl. Landgericht Grafenau.

[illegible] Strelin.

(PfATh, Auszug aus dem Visitationsprotokoll vom 4. August 1841)

Beim Betreiben des Kramerladens, der im Schul- und Mesnerhaus untergebracht war, unterstützte ihn zunächst seine Ehefrau *Anna Maria*. Nach deren Ableben kümmerte sich *Buchners* Stiefsohn *Franz Xaver Lorenz* um die Krämerei im Schulhaus, die er schließlich unter Mitwirkung seines Stiefvaters *Kaspar Buchner* im Januar 1863 käuflich von der Pfarrkirchenstiftung Thurmansbang erwerben konnte.[23] Daneben erledigte *Kaspar Buchner* noch die Aufgaben des Gemeindeschreibers – wobei er häufig als Aktuar zu fungieren hatte – sowie das jährliche Einsammeln der Läutgarben.
Daß *Kaspar Buchner* trotz seiner vielfältigen Verpflichtungen seine eigentliche Aufgabe als Lehrer und Erzieher nicht vernachlässigte, beweisen die jahrzehntelang hervorragenden Ergebnisse bei den jährlichen Schulvisitationen, die *Buchner* mit der ihm anvertrauten Schuljugend erzielte.[24] Ein weiteres Indiz, das für diese Annahme spricht, ist die Tatsache, daß *Kaspar Buchner* als Schullehrer stets überdurchschnittliche Qualifikationen zugesprochen erhielt. Neun verschiedene Pfarrherren waren es, die *Buchner* in ihrer Eigenschaft als Lokalschulinspektor während dessen 40 Dienstjahren in Thurmansbang zu beurteilen hatten. Allein 30 Jahre billigten sie dem engagierten Schulmann *Buchner* für Kenntnisse und Fähigkeiten sowie für Fleiß die Note I zu und selbst in seinen letzten 10 Berufsjahren – und das im Alter von 60 bis 70 Jahren – erhielt Buchner für seine persönlich erbrachten Leistungen noch die Note II in denselben Beurteilungskriterien. Eine zweifellos außergewöhnliche Erfolgsbilanz in einem Lehrerleben![25] Testate wie »... verdient dieselben Noten, wie im vorigen Jahr. Fähigkeiten u. Kentniße I.1 Fleiß I.1 Sittliches Betragen I.1 In Kirchenmusik leistet er Vorzügliches ...«[26] oder »... ein eifriger Anhänger an König u. Vaterland, welche Anhänglichkeit er auch in die Herzen der Kinder einzupflanzen versteht ...«[27] zeichneten *Buchner* wiederholt als tüchtigen Schulmeister und getreuen Anhänger der Monarchie aus.
Keineswegs aber erhielt *Buchner* diese herausragenden Qualifikationen – wie man möglicherweise vermuten könnte – nur deshalb von seinen Vorgesetzten zugesprochen, weil er ein unkritischer und stets gehorsamer Untergebener, ja vielleicht sogar ein vom Untertanengeist völlig beherrschter Zeitgenosse war. Ganz im Gegenteil! *Kaspar Buchner* war sehr wohl ein selbstbewußter Pädagoge und scheute auch nicht davor zurück, zu gegebener Zeit seine persönliche Meinung unmißverständlich zum Ausdruck zu bringen.
So teilte er beispielsweise der königlichen Bezirksregierung des Unterdonaukreises (dem heutigen Niederbayern) in seinem Ansuchen um die Verleihung des Schul- und Mesnerdienstes zu Thurmansbang im Juli 1834 u. a. mit: »Ich glaube daher mir schmeicheln zu dürfen, daß zumal die von mir errungene Beförderungs-Konkurs-Note sehr gut ist, ich auf gnädigste Verleihung eines definitiven Lehrpostens ohnehin gerechte Ansprüche haben dürfte ...«[28] In einem anderen Falle reagierte *Kaspar Buchner* äußerst vehement auf die Ungerechtigkeit, die seine Stieftochter *Theres Lorenz* erfahren mußte, indem man ihr jahrelang das ohnehin sehr geringe Entgelt für ihre Tätigkeit als Handarbeitslehrerin an der Volksschule Thurmansbang vorenthielt. Das Schreiben an den königlichen Lokalschulinspektor *Max Lanz* spiegelt *Buchners* Enttäuschung und Erbitterung wider: »Tröste mich mit dem Gedanken, daß Undank Weltlohn ist, daß dies nicht die einzige Verdrießlichkeit, die mir seit meinem

39jährigen Wirken in Thurmansbang widerfahren ist.«[29] »[Ich] erkläre [daher] die 24 Jahre bestehende Arbeitsschule für geschlossen, die Arbeitslehrerin legt ihre mühsame Stelle nieder – und ersuche ... dieses dem k(öniglichen) Bezirksamte anzuzeigen, ... daß eine andere Arbeitslehrerin für die Arbeitsschule aufgestellt wird.«[30]

Buchner bewies also schon Zivilcourage, wenn er sich ungerecht behandelt oder vernachlässigt fühlte. So auch im Jahre 1864, als mit der Neugründung des Schulsprengels Saldenburg dem Schullehrer *Kaspar Buchner* 75 bis 80 Kinder und mit ihnen ein nicht unerheblicher Betrag an Schulgeld zukünftig verlorengingen. *Buchners* Protest gegen diese Schulsprengelerrichtung[31] hatte letztendlich auch Erfolg in der Weise, daß ihm *(Buchner)* für den entstandenen Schulgeldausfall nunmehr eine Entschädigung in Höhe von 48 fl. gewährt wurde.[32]

Um über Jahre bzw. Jahrzehnte hinweg einen hohen Leistungsstandard als Lehrer zu erbringen, bedarf es sicherlich nicht nur einer einmalig zur Zufriedenheit absolvierten Ausbildung an einem Schullehrerseminar, sondern vor allem auch einer kontinuierlich praktizierten Fort- und Weiterbildung. *Kaspar Buchner* erfüllte diese Bedingungen weitestgehend. Schon als sehr junger Lehrer, nämlich im Jahre 1829, war er bemüht, mit Hilfe des Selbststudiums einschlägiger Literatur sich fortlaufend weiterzubilden, so beispielsweise durch das Abonnement der ›Pädagogischen Quartal-Schrift für Volksschullehrer und Schulfreunde‹, welche erstmals in diesem Jahr in Passau herausgegeben wurde.[33]

Konferenzaufgaben, die *Buchner* im Rahmen der regionalen Lehrerfortbildung, d. h. bei Fortbildungsveranstaltungen innerhalb der Distriktschulinspektion Grafenau, mit Bravour erledigte, lassen klar erkennen, daß der Thurmansbanger Schullehrer sein Sach- und Fachwissen stets auf den jeweils aktuellen Stand gebracht hatte.[34]

Fundiertes Wissen und schulpraktisches Können waren es schließlich auch, die wiederholt den Ausschlag für eine Berufung *Kaspar Buchners* als Präparandenlehrer gaben. So wurde *Kaspar Buchner* nicht nur im ›Verzeichnis der Vorbereitungslehrer für die Schullehrlinge‹ ausgewiesen, sondern auch in die ›Übersicht der für den Vorbereitungsunterricht der Schullehrlinge ernannten Kommissäre und Vorbereitungslehrer in Niederbayern‹ aufgenommen.[35]

Der erste Zögling, der bei *Buchner* eine Lehre als Vorbereitung auf das Schullehrerseminar ableistete, war dessen Stiefsohn *Karl Lorenz*, und zwar in der Zeit von 1835 bis 1838.[36] Zwischen 1858 und 1861 betreute *Buchner* die letzten Schullehrlinge aus dem Schulsprengel Thurmansbang.[37] Um den Anforderungen des Normativs von 1857 zu genügen, erklärte sich *Buchner* sogar bereit, diesen drei letzten Schullehrlingen zur Mittagszeit Unterkunft und Kost zu gewähren.[38]

21 Schulgehilfen waren es, die an der Seite *Buchners* während dessen 40jähriger Dienstzeit den Vorbereitungs- und I. Kurs an der Volksschule Thurmansbang unterrichteten. Gerade sie bestätigen in augenfälliger Weise *Buchners* menschliche und pädagogische Qualitäten. Nicht alle Lehrgehilfen brachten nämlich beste Resultate vom Schullehrerseminar her mit und bedurften deshalb einer zusätzlichen fachkundigen Unterweisung und kontinuierlichen Anleitung vor Ort, um den nicht gerade geringen Anforderungen des Lehrfaches gewachsen zu sein.

Andere Schulgehilfen wiederum wurden aufgrund von Disziplinarverstößen – sei es, daß sie zu sehr dem Alkohol zugesagt hatten oder daß wie in einem Falle eine Jungfrau von einem Schulgehilfen geschwängert worden war – nach Thurmansbang gewissermaßen ›straf‹-versetzt, um dort eine letzte Chance der Bewährung im Schuldienst zu erhalten.
Buchners Vorbild und Engagement in der Aus- und Weiterbildung dieser Schulgehilfen zeitigte bei den allermeisten Erfolg. Die Berufung mehrerer ehemaliger Thurmansbanger Schulgehilfen auf einen Schulverweserposten mag als Indiz dafür gewertet werden.[39]

4. Buchners wirtschaftliche und soziale Situation

Über *Buchners* wirtschaftliche und soziale Situation existieren vor allem für die Jahre in Thurmansbang größtenteils sehr differenzierte Aufzeichnungen. So belief sich beispielsweise das Einkommen des Schulprovisors *Kaspar Buchner* – gleich seinem unmittelbaren Vorgänger *Jakob Bachmeier* – zwischen 1834 und 1838 auf 200 fl., weshalb er sich schon sehr bald um die definitive Verleihung des Schul- und Mesnerdienstes in Thurmansbang bemühte. Allerdings dauerte dies dann noch bis zum Jahre 1838.[40]
Im Jahre 1840 stellte sich *Buchners* finanzielle Situation folgendermaßen dar:
»a) ... Einkommen: 423 fl. 2 kr.; rein: 213 fl. 43 kr.
b) Grundstücke: 1/10 Tgw. Garten, 1½ Tgw. Ackerland und 1/1 Tgw. Wiesengrund ...
Als Meßner bezieht der Schullehrer 4 Schäffel Roggen, 90 Laibe Brod, 400 Stück Eier und 12 Klafter Brennholz ...«[41] Bis zum Jahre 1855 blieb das Einkommen *Buchners* in dieser Höhe konstant. Die augenfälligste Änderung, die die neue Fassion im selben Jahre mit sich brachte, war die Erhöhung des Reineinkommens von 213 fl. 43 kr. auf 261 fl.. Im Bereich der Naturalien ergaben sich nur geringfügige Änderungen.[42]
Laut Statistik der Volksschulen vom 20. März 1874 belief sich *Buchners* Reineinkommen zu dieser Zeit auf 508 fl. 40 kr., wobei mehr als die Hälfte dieses Betrages aus der Entlohnung für den Chor- und Mesnerdienst in der Pfarrei stammte. Als Gemeindeschreiber verdiente *Kaspar Buchner* zusätzlich 60 fl. im Jahre 1874. Die Reinigung der Schullokalitäten brachte ihm weitere 3 fl. 30 kr. ein.[43]
Der Vergleich des Einkommens *Kaspar Buchners* mit dem von *Karl Heiß* aus Achdorf, Bezirksamt Landshut, dem Initiator des Bayerischen Lehrervereins von 1861, ermöglicht eine Relativierung der finanziellen Situation vom Jahre 1867: Obwohl *Buchner* um 23 Jahre älter und 13 Jahre länger definitiv angestellt war sowie ca. 50 Schüler mehr zu betreuen hatte als *Heiß*, verdiente er exakt um 76 fl. weniger im Jahr (*Buchner* 414 fl. – *Heiß* 490 fl.), hatte er 0,62 Tagwerk weniger Schulgründe zur Verfügung (*Buchner* 2,00 Tagwerk – *Heiß* 2,62 Tagwerk) und erhielt er qualitativ wie quantitativ geringere Naturalien als der Achdorfer Lehrer *Karl Heiß*.[44]

Die Einkommen von Kaspar Buchner und Karl Heiß im Jahre 1867 im Überblick:

Schulort	Thurmansbang Bezirksamt Grafenau	Achdorf Bezirksamt Landshut
Geburt	1804	1827
Schulgehilfe	1824	1846
Schulprovisor	1828	–
Anstellung als Lehrer	1838	1851
Konkursjahrgang	1828	1848
Werktagsschüler	214	165
Feiertagsschüler	63	50
Reinertrag an Geld	414 fl.	490 fl.
Schulgründe	2,00 Tgw.	2,62 Tgw.
Naturalien	3½ Schäffel Korn aus Läutgarben, 89 Laib Brot, 400 Eier	1 Klafter Holz, 18 Weizengarben, 59 Korngarben, 11 Gerstengarben

(vgl. StAL 168/1/310/772)

Dennoch schien der Thurmansbanger Schullehrer und Mesner *Kaspar Buchner* – abgesehen von einigen ganz wenigen Bittgesuchen um Ergänzung seines fassionsmäßigen Einkommens[45] – mit seinem Verdienst zufrieden gewesen zu sein. Er verfügte ja bis zum Jahre 1863 auch noch über regelmäßige Einkünfte aus der Krämerei, die jährlich mit 30 fl. veranschlagt worden war (und wofür er lediglich 45 kr. jährlich an die Thurmansbanger Pfarrkirchenstiftung zu entrichten hatte).[46]
Zur sozialen Absicherung *Buchners* ist zu sagen, daß dieser auf Betreiben der Gemeindeverwaltung und des Armenpflegschaftsrates von Thurmansbang anläßlich der Verehelichung mit der Lehrerswitwe *Anna Maria Lorenz* im Jahre 1836 gleichsam als conditio sine qua non dem ›Kreis-Verein für Unterstützung der Schullehrer-Wittwen und Waisen‹ beizutreten hatte und diesem dann auch fortwährend angehörte.[47] Mit dieser Mitgliedschaft sollten vor allem die Angehörigen *Buchners* bei dessen Ableben abgesichert sein und nicht wie im Falle *Jakob Lorenz,* dem Vorgänger *Buchners,* bei dessen plötzlichem Absterben völlig mittellos dastehen.[48]

5. Buchners außerschulische Verdienste

Kaspar Buchner war es, der durch seine Verehelichung mit der Lehrerswitwe *Anna Maria Lorenz* am 5. Oktober 1836 das Schicksal dieser Frau mit ihren sechs noch unversorgten Kindern wieder zum Besseren wendete und auch stets seinem Versprechen, für die Lorenzischen Kinder so lange aufzukommen, bis diese versorgt seien, treu blieb. Das Bemühen *Buchners* bei der käuflichen Übereignung der Krämerei im Schul- und Mesnerhaus zu Thurmansbang an seinen jüngsten Stiefsohn *Franz Xaver* kann als ein Beispiel für die Einlösung seines Versprechens betrachtet werden.
Neben seiner vorbildlichen Berufsauffassung und steten Pflichterfüllung war es auch das Engagement im sozialen Bereich, das Schullehrer *Buchner* nicht nur im Schulsprengel, in der Pfarrei und in der Gemeinde Thurmansbang, sondern sogar darüber hinaus vielfach Respekt und Anerkennung einbrachte.[49]

6. Buchners letzte Lebensjahre

Zum 1. August 1874 schließlich wurde der Schullehrer *Kaspar Buchner* offiziell von der Regierung von Niederbayern in den Ruhestand verabschiedet.[50] Aufgrund der dadurch eingetretenen personellen Notsituation versah *Buchner* aber noch seine bisherigen Dienstaufgaben bis zum 26. August 1874, also bis zum Beginn der Sommerferien, weiter. Die Dienste als Mesner und Chorregent übte er auf Wunsch sogar noch bis Ende September 1874 aus.[51]
Trotz dieser großzügigen Geste kam es nochmal zu einer heftigen Auseinandersetzung zwischen dem mittlerweile pensionierten Schullehrer *Kaspar Buchner* und dem jugendlichen Pfarrprovisor von Thurmansbang *Max Lanz*, weil dieser es ablehnte, *Buchner* für seine Dienstleistungen als Mesner im Jahre 1874 noch die üblichen 12 Klafter Brennholz zuzubilligen.[52]
In seiner Erwiderung des Anschreibens von Pfarrprovisor *Lanz* brachte *Buchner* seine große Enttäuschung über dessen Ansinnen unmißverständlich zum Ausdruck: »Schmerzt mich jedesmal innigst eine Zurücksetzung eine Geringschätzung, so kehrt es mein Innerstes ganz um, wenn ich mich gegen einen Vorgesetzten vertheitigen oder dagegen schreiben muß, denn von Kindesbeinen schon an wurde mir eingepflanzt, u. auf meiner ganzen Lebensbahn habe ich es mir zur Aufgabe gemacht, gehorsam, unterthänig, pünktlich u. rechtlich gegen meine Vorgesetzten zu sein, u. ich kann mir schmeicheln, daß ich mir bis auf Ihre Zeit von geistlichen u. weltlichen Vorständen, reichliche Liebe, Vertrauen und Achtung erworben habe, nur Sie finden an meinem 70jährigen Alter keinen Geschmack mehr. Darnach können Sie ermessen den Schmerz den ich jedesmal hatte, wenn ich von Ihnen seit längerer Zeit keinen freundlichen Blick, kein freundliches Wort sehen oder hören konnte, ja sogar Zurechtweisungen mußte ich erfahren, die mir in meiner Laufbahn nicht ein einziges-

mal zu Theil wurden, mein 50jähriges Wirken wird in den Schatten gestellt, werde überall zurückgesetzt, u. wie bisher, so verfahren Sie auch jetzt noch mit mir. Statt mich zu schützen in meinen rechtlichen Forderungen, verfolgen Sie mich und sprechen mir ab, was von rechtes wegen mir gehört.«[53]
Nach diesem für ihn sicherlich sehr bedauerlichen und auch völlig unverständlichen Vorgang verblieb *Kaspar Buchner* nur mehr wenig Zeit im Ruhestand gegönnt, denn bereits am 28. Oktober 1875, also gut ein Jahr nach seiner Pensionierung, verstarb er im Alter von 71 Jahren.
18 Lehrer und sechs geistliche Herren erwiesen dem langjährigen Schullehrer, Mesner und Chorregenten von Thurmansbang die letzte Ehre, was bei den geografischen Gegebenheiten des Bayerischen Waldes und den verkehrstechnischen Bedingungen dieser Region im 19. Jahrhundert keine Selbstverständlichkeit bedeutete und für Thurmansbanger Verhältnisse sicherlich einen nicht alltäglichen Vorgang darstellte.[54]

Abkürzungen

HStAM	=	Bayerisches Hauptstaatsarchiv München
StAL	=	Staatsarchiv Landshut
PfATh	=	Pfarrarchiv Thurmansbang
IBl	=	Koeniglich-Baierisches Intelligenz-Blatt des Unterdonaukreises

Anmerkungen

1 Vgl. *Liedtke* (1984), S. 9.
2 Vgl. StAL 168/1/1206/254.
3 Vgl. IBl 1827, S. 83.
4 Vgl. StAL 168/1/1206/254.
5 Vgl. ebenda; StAL 168/1/103/74.
6 Vgl. StAL 168/1/1206/254.
7 PfATh, 27. 1. 1838.
8 Vgl. PfATh, 6. 9. 1874.
9 StAL 168/1/1206/254.
10 Ebenda.
11 Ebenda.
12 Ebenda.
13 Ebenda.
14 *Engelbrecht* (1840), S. 194.
15 Vgl. PfATh, Visitationsprotokolle 1836–1867.
16 Vgl. PfATh, Nachweisung 1835/36 vom 18. 4. 1836; Nachweisung 1836/37 vom 8. 5. 1837; Nachweisung 1837/38 vom 17. 5. 1838.

[17] Vgl. PfATh, 11. 7. 1840; 3. 7. 1841.
[18] Vgl. PfATh, Visitationsprotokolle 1834–1874.
[19] Vgl. PfATh, 10. 6. 1850.
[20] Vgl. PfATh, 10. 6. 1850; Visitationsprotokolle 1853–1874.
[21] Vgl. PfATh, Heiratsmatrikel, IV, S. 27.
[22] Vgl. PfATh, Bittgesuch des Jakob Lorenz sen., o. J.; StAL 168/1/1206/254; HStAM M Inn 22693.
[23] Vgl. PfATh, 23. 1. 1863.
[24] Vgl. PfATh, Visitationsprotokoll 1836ff.
[25] Vgl. *Hauzenberger* (1986), S. 98.
[26] PfATh, 30. 4. 1840.
[27] PfATh, 6. 7. 1862.
[28] StAL 168/1/1206/254.
[29] PfATh, 17. 12. 1872.
[30] Ebenda. Würde sich ein heutiger Lehrer getrauen, seinem Schulrat oder gar der Regierung mit einem solchen Tonfall gegenüberzutreten?!
[31] Vgl. *Knauer* (1946), S. 4ff.
[32] Vgl. StAL 168/1/346/996.
[33] Vgl. Pädagogische Quartal-Schrift für Volksschullehrer und Schulfreunde I. Jg., IV. Quartal, Passau 1829, III.
[34] Vgl. PfATh, Konferenz-Aufgaben.
[35] Vgl. IBl 1843, S. 180ff.; IBl 1846, S. 276.
[36] Vgl. PfATh, 18. 4. 1836; 8. 6. 1837; 17. 5. 1838.
[37] Vgl. PfATh, 3. 1. 1858; 15. 9. 1861.
[38] Vgl. PfATh, 1. 12. 1857.
[39] Vgl. *Hauzenberger* (1986), S. 118ff.
[40] Vgl. StAL 168/1/1206/254.
[41] *Engelbrecht* (1840), S. 194.
[42] Vgl. PfATh, 17. 6. 1856.
[43] Vgl. StAL 168/1/346/996.
[44] Vgl. StAL 168/1/310/772.
[45] Vgl. PfATh, 8. 6. 1867.
[46] Vgl. PfATh, 12. 2. 1836.
[47] Vgl. ebenda.
[48] Aufgrund der fehlenden Absicherung der Angehörigen eines Schullehrers bei dessen Tod schlossen sich die Lehrer des Unterdonaukreises zusammen und gründeten am 1. Oktober 1823 den ›Kreis-Verein für Unterstützung der Schullehrer-Wittwen und Waisen‹. Ziel dieser Selbsthilfeeinrichtung war die Unterstützung hinterbliebener Witwen und Waisen verstorbener Schullehrer im damaligen Unterdonaukreis, dem späteren Niederbayern. Allerdings beruhte bis zum Jahre 1850 der Beitritt zu dieser Eigenhilfeorganisation auf Freiwilligkeit. Erst ab dem Jahre 1850 wurde diese Freiwilligkeit aufgehoben und eine Mitgliedschaft für alle seit dem 5. Februar 1850 angestellten bzw. beförderten Schullehrer und Schulprovisoren ohne Rücksicht auf den Familienstand sowie für die Schulgehilfen bei eintretender Verehelichung verpflichtend vorgeschrieben. Die zur Aufnahme anstehenden Schullehrer, Schulprovisoren und verheirateten Schulgehilfen konnten sich wahlweise für eine Mitgliedschaft in der I. bzw. II. Klasse entscheiden. Aufnahmegebühr, Jahresbeitrag und jährliche Unterstützung waren je nach Klassenzugehörigkeit unterschiedlich hoch. Vgl. Schematismus des Lehr-Personals an den deutschen Volksschulen im Regierungsbezirke Niederbayern 1876, S. 173ff.

[49] Vgl. *Hauzenberger* (1986), S. 75ff.
[50] Vgl. PfATh, 6. 9. 1874.
[51] Vgl. PfATh, 8. 9. 1874.
[52] Vgl. PfATh, 22. 11. 1874.
[53] Ebenda.
[54] Vgl. Hauzenberger (1986), S. 132ff.

Quellen- und Literaturverzeichnis

Bayerisches Hauptstaatsarchiv München
M Inn 22693 Mesner – Sölde zu Thurmansbang betr.
Staatsarchiv Landshut
168/1/103/74 Schule zu Lengthal 1817–1868
168/1/310/772 Schematismus des Lehrpersonals an den Volksschulen in Niederbayern. 1852/1904
168/1/346/996 Hauptübersichten über die lokalen Schulstatistiken in dem Bezirk Grafenau aufgestellt zw. 1873/76
168/1/1206/254 Die Schule zu Thurmansbang, Landgericht Grafenau 1809–1837
Pfarrarchiv Thurmansbang
Bittgesuch des Jakob Lorenz sen., o. Jahr
Heiratsmatrikel IV (1802–1840) des Kath. Pfarramtes Thurmansbang
Konferenz-Aufgaben, o. Jahr
Nachweisungen der Lokalschulinspektion über den Stand und die Verhältnisse der Schule Thurmansbang. 1833/34ff.
Protokolle über die zu Thurmansbang abgehaltenen Visitationen der Schule daselbst (Visitationsprotokolle). 1834ff.
Engelbrecht, Augustin E. (1840): Uebersicht der teutschen Schulen und des Lehrer-Personals von Niederbayern. Passau
Hauzenberger, Franz (1986): Die Geschichte der Schule und des Schulsprengels Thurmansbang (1700–1985). (Diss.) Passau
Knauer, Roland (1946): Schulchronik der Volksschule Saldenburg. Saldenburg
Koeniglich-Baierisches Intelligenz-Blatt des Unter-Donau-Kreises. Jahrgang 1827ff.
Liedtke, Max (1984): Regionale Schulgeschichte und ihr überregionaler Zusammenhang. In: Kriss-Rettenbeck, L. / Liedtke, M. (Hrsg.): Regionale Schulentwicklung im 19. und 20. Jahrhundert. Bad Heilbrunn / Obb. (Schriftenreihe zum Bayerischen Schulmuseum Ichenhausen, Bd. 2)
Pädagogische Quartalschrift für Volksschullehrer und Schulfreunde (1829). Passau
Schematismus des Lehr-Personals an den deutschen Volksschulen im Regierungsbezirke Niederbayern 1876. Landshut

Gerhard Silberer

Stellung und Ausbildung der Volksschullehrer im Baden des 18. und 19. Jahrhunderts

In memoriam Josef Spieler 1900–1987

In einem ersten Teil soll hier die Entwicklung einer Lehrerausbildung in jenem Territorium aufgezeigt werden, das wir heute mit dem Namen Baden zu bezeichnen gewohnt sind.
In einem zweiten knapperen Teil sollen sodann zusammenfassend jene pädagogischen Strömungen herausgestellt werden, die diese Entwicklung vorherrschend getragen haben.
Auf die Stellung des Volksschullehrers soll hier nur soweit eingegangen werden, als es zum Verständnis der die Ausbildung vorantreibenden Faktoren notwendig erscheint.

I. Die organisatorische Entwicklung der Volksschullehrerausbildung im Territorium des heutigen Landes Baden

Die Entwicklung vor 1803

Man muß sich bewußt halten, daß es im 18. Jahrhundert weder eine *Volksschule* noch ein *Baden* im heutigen Verständnis gab. Legen wir jedoch jene vier Eigenschaften zugrunde, die für *E. Spranger* den Begriff der Volksschule konstituieren, so war die Schule des 18. Jahrhunderts bereits Volksschule, als man sie noch mit anderen Namen, etwa »Landschule« oder »Trivialschule« benannte.[1] Sie war nämlich *allgemeinverbindlich,* bot eine allgemein *grundlegende* Bildung, war *öffentlich* errichtet und *muttersprachlich* orientiert.
In diesem Sinne gab es deshalb auch eine Volksschullehrerausbildung.
Ähnliche Schwierigkeiten macht der Begriff »Baden« für das 18. Jahrhundert. Streng genommen galt er nur für die beiden badischen Markgrafschaften Baden-Baden und Baden-Durlach, die im vornapoleonischen Deutschland nur ein Viertel des 1810 als Großherzogtum Baden existierenden Territoriums ausmachten.[2] Wenn nun hier von der Volksschullehrerausbildung in Baden gesprochen wird, so beziehen sich diese Aussagen auf das gesamte, durch die napoleonische »Flurbereinigung« entstandene Gebiet, dessen Geschlossenheit erst ein Jahrzehnte umfassender Integrationsprozeß erbringen sollte.

1. Die Schulmeisterlehre

Für dieses gesamte Gebiet und weit darüber hinaus bestand Lehrerausbildung mindestens seit Beginn der Neuzeit in dem, was wir heute gewöhnlich als Schulmeisterlehre bezeichnen. Im Gegensatz zu einer in den spätmittelalterlichen Städten auf genossenschaftlicher Basis entstandenen, d. h. in Zünften greifbaren, handwerklich organisierten, begegnet sie uns im 18. Jahrhundert als eine staatlich reglementierte, z. T. auch der Kirchenordnung verpflichtete Weitergabe von meist der Erfahrung entnommenen Kenntnissen und Fertigkeiten.[3]

Fast alle Schulordnungen, die am Ende des 18. Jahrhunderts in den verschiedensten Herrschaften auf dem Gebiet des heutigen Baden entstehen, versuchen deshalb, auch die Lehrerausbildung staatlicherseits zu vereinheitlichen.

Dabei kommt für die evangelischen Territorien der für die badische Markgrafschaft *Baden-Durlach* durch *Karl Friedrich* 1757 gegebenen Schulkandidatenordnung eine besondere Bedeutung zu. Die Ausbildung zerfiel in einen mehr theoretischen, in einem Gymnasium oder bei einem Landpfarrer vermittelten Teil, der durch ein Examen abgeschlossen wurde und einen zweiten, mehr praktischen, der bei einem tüchtigen Schulmeister zu absolvieren war.[3a]

Für die katholischen Territorien hat die für die Markgrafschaft *Baden-Baden* 1770 erscheinende »Allgemeine Landschulordnung etc.« eine vergleichbare Bedeutung.[4] Sie kennt noch vereinzelt ein Recht von Städten und Gemeinden, ihre Lehrer selbst zu bestimmen (§ 77) und grenzt dies durch nähere Bestimmungen über vorgängig abzulegende Examina aus (§§ 78–80). Als zu überprüfende Kenntnisse werden neben »Christentum« und »Katechismus«, »Deutsch- und Lateinisch Buchstabieren«, »Lesen und Schreiben«, »Orthographie« und »Rechenkunst« angegeben. Auch über »Choral«, »Orgelschlagen« und die »Stimm« soll eine »Prob« abgelegt werden (§ 80).

Wie dies konkret verlief, läßt sich einem Buch entnehmen, in dem ein J. Jakob *Ekert*[5] 1820 seinen Werdegang erzählt. Danach erhielt er seinen ersten Unterricht von seinem Vater, einem Schulmeister. Dieser schickte ihn mit 14 Jahren zu »andern braven Schulmännern«, bei denen er »etwas lernen konnte«. Ein Jahr lang war er auch in einem »Institut«, was immer man darunter verstehen mochte. Mit 17 Jahren wurde er als Unterlehrer angestellt »und von dieser Zeit an«, sagt er rückschauend, »war ich mir fast ganz selbst überlassen«. Förderung erhielt er durch andere »Schullehrer« und die Lektüre »pädagogischer Schriften«. Mit 21 Jahren bekam er sodann das »Anstellungs-Dekret« als Schullehrer, wie es scheint, völlig überraschend.

Auch wenn hier der Eindruck entsteht, dies sei ohne vorangehende Prüfung geschehen, so haben sich, ähnlich wie solche Anstellungsdekrete, auch Dokumente solcher Examina erhalten. Sie wurden in Übereinstimmung mit dem Amtmann und dem Pfarrer der anstellenden Gemeinde vom Dekan des Landkapitels abgenommen und erstreckten sich bereits 1741 auf fast alle in der späteren Land-Schulordnung genannten Kenntnisse.[6]

2. *Die seminaristische Ausbildung*

Es ist nicht eindeutig anzugeben, wie sich jener Übergang von der Schulmeisterlehre zur seminaristischen Ausbildung vollzogen hat.[7] Man wird wohl in dem von mir zu berücksichtigenden Territorium annehmen können, daß sich aus der eben aufgezeigten Form der Schulmeisterlehre zunächst gewisse private oder halböffentliche Formen einer zentralisierten Schulmeisterlehre herausgebildet haben, d. h. auf die Initiative eines Geistlichen oder einer Gemeinde hin entstanden bereits gegen Ende des 18. Jahrhunderts einzelne Verdichtungen der Schulmeisterlehre, die als Privatseminare im badischen Raum jedoch nicht jene Bedeutung erlangen wie im benachbarten Württemberg.[8] Hier im äußersten Südwesten nimmt sich schon verhältnismäßig früh die staatliche Seite dieser ersten Formen einer Seminarausbildung an.

Im evangelischen Bereich ist es wiederum *Karl Friedrich* v. Baden Durlach, der 1768 auf Anregung von Kirchenräten ein sog. Schul-Seminarium am Gymnasium seiner Residenzstadt *Karlsruhe* errichtet.[9] Typisch dafür ist, daß es keine eigenständige Institution darstellt, sondern zumeist zwei, später auch mehr Stipendiaten eine quasigymnasiale Ausbildung zu geben sucht. Die vorgesehenen Stipendiaten sind bereits im Dienst stehende Elementarschullehrer, also Leute, die die übliche Schulmeisterlehre bereits durchlaufen haben. Seminarbildung dieser frühsten Form ist also eine *Zusatzausbildung*, nicht Grundausstattung.

Eine andere Variante bildet sich in den katholischen Gebieten des späteren Landes Baden heraus. Diese für die gesamten habsburgischen Territorien und deshalb auch für Vorderösterreich geltende Neuordnung bewirkte die Gründung einer Normalschule in *Freiburg i. Breisgau*, die wir bereits für das Jahr 1773, also noch vor Erscheinen der »Allgemeinen Schulordnung etc.« ansetzen dürfen.[10] Diese uns aus *Gönners* Arbeiten gut bekannte Ausbildungsform[11] war als Kurssystem organisiert und bemühte sich zunächst auch nicht um eine Grundausbildung sondern um eine Zusatzqualifikation bereits im Dienst stehender Lehrpersonen.

Das Freiburger Dozentenkollegium, das in Wien vier Monate lang ausgebildet worden war, bestand aus zwei Professoren der Universität, bezeichnenderweise Juristen, einem Weltpriester, einem Schulmeister und einem Buchhalter.[12]

1796 ist das Kollegium neben einem Oberaufseher und vier territorial eingegrenzten Visitationskommissaren auf sieben Lehrer angewachsen.[13]

Zusammen mit den von *Moser* sehr gut beschriebenen *Musterschulen* bewirkte die Freiburger Normalschule eine vielleicht etwas rigide[14], aber doch echte Reform des bestehenden elementaren Schulwesens, deren Auswirkungen nur detaillierte örtliche Untersuchungen ergeben könnten.

Die »Tragik« der Freiburger Normalschule bestand darin, nach 1803 durch die dezentrale Lage der Stadt im neuen Staat so rasch an Bedeutung zu verlieren, daß sie bereits 1809 aufgelöst wurde.

Ähnlich wie in Karlsruhe und Freiburg dürfte es auch in anderen Teilen des späteren Landes Baden von staatlicher Seite betriebene Seminargründungen gegeben haben. Die Initiative müßte hierbei ähnlich wie in Freiburg von der Zentralverwaltung der jeweiligen Territorialherrschaft ausgegangen sein.[15]

Nachgewiesen sind solche Seminare, Normalschulen oder Präparandenanstalten meines Wissens für Baden-Baden seit 1788[16], Stockach, Konstanz, Donaueschingen, Mannheim, Heidelberg und Bruchsal.[17] Ähnlich wie in anderen Kleinstädten, für die kein Nachweis vorliegt, ist auch hier ein privater Charakter dieser Gründungen nicht auszuschließen. Dabei wird die Frage in Gebieten der theresianischen Schulreform noch durch die Unschärfe belastet, die dem Begriff *»Normalschule«* anhaftet. So wird die »Deutsche Hauptschule Konstanz« ähnlich wie die von Stockach seit 1787 als »Deutsche Normalschule« bezeichnet.[18] Diese Unschärfe findet sich heute auch in der Sekundärliteratur.[19]

Die organisatorische Entwicklung nach 1803

Die Umwälzungen der napoleonischen Zeit betrafen auf dem Territorium des heutigen Landes Baden auch die schulischen Verhältnisse.
Nach einer zunächst zurückhaltenden Phase der Harmonisierung, in der ein Vertrauter des Monarchen, *J. N. F. Brauer,* durch Organisationsedikte die bisherige Vielfalt der schulischen Verhältnisse zu vereinheitlichen suchte[20], erfolgte eine straffe Zentralisation des gesamten Bildungswesens.[21] Anstelle der bisherigen konfessionellen Schulaufsichtsbehörden wurde 1807 eine dem Departement des Inneren unterstellte *Generalstudienkommission* gebildet.[22] Diese von einem Vertrauten *Dalbergs*[23], Graf *Bentzel-Sternau,* geleitete Behörde entwickelte eine für die kriegerischen Zeiten erstaunliche Aktivität, deren eine Seite der Plan eines »allgemeinen«, d. h. überkonfessionellen »Schullehrerseminars« war.[24] Überraschend dabei könnte sein, daß er von einem staatskirchlich denkenden katholischen Theologen, *Ph. J. Brunner* (1758–1829), ausging und seine heftigsten Widerstände in den Reihen der evangelischen Kirchenräte gefunden hatte.
Als 1809 unter Sigismund *v. Reitzenstein* die Umorganisation des neuen Staatswesens zum Abschluß kam, hatte der im Wesentlichen seine Zentralisation durchsetzende Staatsmann die für ihn peripheren bildungspolitischen Streitpunkte und damit auch die überkonfessionelle Generalstudienkommission und ein »allgemeines Schullehrerseminar« geopfert.[25]
Ganz im Zuge der neu gestärkten Konfessionalität des elementaren Schulwesens[26] wurde nun anstelle eines zumindest ins Auge gefaßten überkonfessionellen Landesseminars am 29. 3. 1809 ein katholisches Präparandeninstitut in *Rastatt* gegründet[27], bzw. das bereits seit 1788 am Lyceum in Baden-Baden bestehende dorthin verlegt.
Als sein Direktor war schon seit 1807 der aus Augsburg stammende Ignaz *Demeter* (1773–1842) im Gespräch, ein Jugendfreund des für die badische Kirchengeschichte des Vormärz maßgebenden Konstanzer Generalvikars *I. v. Wessenberg* (1774–1860).
Als Pfarrer des kleinen Albdorfes Lautlingen hatte er sich in Wessensbergs »Geistlicher Monatsschrift« durch Veröffentlichungen über pädagogische Fragen bereits einen Namen gemacht[28] und wenigstens den Versuch unternommen, durch Gründung eines privaten Lehrerbildungsinstituts auch praktische Erfahrungen seiner schulischen Tätigkeit weiterzugeben.

In den neun Jahren seiner Rastatter Wirksamkeit entwickelte *Demeter* zusammen mit dem erfahrenen Oberlehrer Wilhelm *Wittmer* Grundlagen einer Lehrerbildung, die nach dem stillen Eingehen des Karlsruher Schul-Seminariums und der Freiburger Normalschule um 1809 für das gesamte Land wegweisend wurden. Sie fanden Eingang in sein Hauptwerk: Grundsätze für die Bildung der Schullehrer, das eine sich an *Vierthalers* Sokratik anlehnende, im übrigen eklektisch vorgehende Summe des pädagogischen Denkens seiner Zeit darstellt, die bis 1831 dem Pädagogikunterricht in Rastatt zugrundegelegt wurde und auch außerhalb des Landes geschätzt war.[29]
Das Rastatter Schullehrerseminar, wie das Präparandeninstitut von *Demeter* vorzugsweise genannt wurde, hat als erste staatliche Institution in einem didaktisch klar umschriebenen Zeitraum die grundlegende Lehrerausbildung in Baden vermittelt, es aber doch, trotz der ideellen Neuansätze[30] nicht geschafft, sich aus der personellen und organisatorischen Abhängigkeit vom dortigen Lyceum zu lösen. Auch *Demeters* Nachfolgern, *G. A. Holdermann* (1818–1828), *J. A. Schump* (1829–1830) und *J. Haberstroh* (1830–1833) gelang es nicht, diesen grundsätzlichen Hemmschuh einer Lehrerausbildung abzustreifen.
Es sollte dies erst einer Neugründung möglich sein, die das inzwischen entstandene Vakuum einer evangelischen Seminarbildung des Landes ausfüllen sollte: dem neuerrichteten evangelischen Schullehrerseminar in *Karlsruhe*.
Johann Peter *Hebel*, der durch seine »Alemannischen Gedichte« in ganz Deutschland bekannt gewordene Prälat brachte 1819 als Mitglied der 1. Kammer der Ständeversammlung eine Motion ein, in der ein protestantisches Schullehrer-Seminarium gefordert wurde.[31] Auch wenn im Blick auf das alte eine ähnliche Anbindung an eine bereits bestehende Institution gesucht wurde, so hat das schließlich 1823 in Karlsruhe eröffnete Seminar eine organisatorisch selbständige Form erhalten. Zwar lag die Direktion zunächst noch in der Hand des ersten evangelischen Stadtgeistlichen, der als erster Hauptlehrer berufene Theologe Wilhelm *Stern* war jedoch eine so starke Persönlichkeit, daß ihm nach Durchlaufen der Gründungsphase 1837 auch nominell die Direktion des Seminars übertragen wurde.[32]
Diese gestärkte Stellung ergab sich auch durch eine Regierungsverordnung v. 12. 10. 1829, in der für alle evangelischen Schulpräparanden der Seminarbesuch verpflichtend vorgeschrieben wurde.[33] Es bedeutete das Ende der bisherigen Schulmeisterlehre und ließ die Zahl der das Karlsruher Seminar besuchenden Präparanden von durchschnittlich 25 auf 45 Besucher ansteigen. Die eigentliche Expansion der Besucherzahlen gegen 85 erfolgte jedoch nach einem kurzen Rückgang erst nach 1835.[34]
Wie 1819 die Existenz eines katholischen Lehrerseminars Rastatt die Wiedererrichtung des evangelischen Seminars Karlsruhe vorangetrieben hatte, so war der ausgezeichnete Stand dieses Lehrerseminars 1833 der Anlaß, daß ein Abgeordneter der Bodenseegegend im Landtag ein katholisches Lehrerseminar für den sog. Seekreis forderte.[34a] Die ungünstige topographische Lage Rastatts hatte es nur wenigen Lehramtsbewerbern ermöglicht, eine Seminarbildung in Rastatt zu durchlaufen und viele hatten deshalb die für Katholiken noch immer mögliche Form der Schulmeisterlehre oder den Besuch eines halböffentlichen Seminars in Konstanz[35] der Rastatter Ausbildung vorgezogen.

Als nun die neue Volksschulgesetzgebung von 1834 für alle Lehramtskandidaten eine an einem staatlichen Lehrerseminar zu erbringende Prüfung vorschrieb[36], wurde auch für die Seegegend ein staatliches Lehrerseminar dringend. Zunächst aber wurde man der Mängel des bereits bestehenden Rastatter Seminars bewußt.[37] Kompetenzfragen zwischen Lyceums- und Seminardirektion hatten nach Berufung eines neuen Direktors dieses meist verächtlich Präparandeninstitut genannten Seminars die Atmosphäre so vergiftet, daß man am 6. 11. 1834 die Trennung beider Institutionen beschloß.

Der neue Direktor, der auch 1835 den Umzug nach dem als neuen Standort gewählten *Ettlingen* bei Karlsruhe durchführte, war der damals 52jährige Seminardirektor im schweizerischen Aarau, Philipp *Nabholz.* Er war ähnlich wie Demeter von Wessenberg gefördert worden und hatte schon früh das Vertrauen *Pestalozzis* und seiner Mitarbeiter gewonnen.[38] Nun versuchte er in Ettlingen seine Vorstellungen von Lehrerbildung zu verwirklichen, kritisch beobachtet von den Mitgliedern der Oberschulkonferenz in Karlsruhe, die schon seiner Berufung nicht ungeteilt zugestimmt hatte.[39]

Große Belastungen entstanden *Nabholz* aus dem baulichen Zustand des ehemaligen Jesuitenkollegs, dem man die Schuld für viele Erkrankungen der Seminaristen zuschreiben mußte.[40] Empfindlicher trafen ihn Vorwürfe, die von dem erstarkenden Katholizismus der vormärzlichen Zeit ausgingen und seine wessenbergianischen Auffassungen als unvereinbar mit dem Amt des Direktors eines katholischen Lehrerseminars bezeichneten.

So war es wohl der Wunsch, aus der Ettlinger Luft, die ihm in verschiedener Hinsicht nicht bekam, wegzukommen, der *Nabholz* bestimmte, nach der am 7. Dez. 1837 entschiedenen Neugründung eines Lehrerseminars in *Meersburg* sich für dessen Direktion zu bewerben.[41] Mit drei Lehrkräften des Ettlinger Seminars bildete er Ende Mai 1839 die Grundzelle jener dritten Seminargründung, die Baden in der ersten Hälfte des 19. Jahrhunderts erhalten sollte.

Nach seinem bereits 1842 erfolgten Tod übernahm 1844 ein von ihm geförderter Geistlicher, der damals 34jährige K. L. *Nesselhauf* die Leitung.

In seine Amtszeit fiel die Revolution von 1848/49, die unabhängig davon, wie man sie beurteilen mag[42], die Lehrerschaft und damit auch die Lehrerbildung in vielfacher Weise berührte.

Während *Nesselhauf* selbst in den Verdacht geriet, die revolutionären demokratischen Organe der Stadt Meersburg in den kritischen Tagen unterstützt zu haben, beschuldigten Theologen wie *Döllinger* und *Hirscher* die Lehrerbildner in den Seminaren ganz allgemein, eine jahrelange »geistige Brunnenvergiftung« betrieben zu haben.[43]

Ohne der These *Thiens* widersprechen zu wollen, daß die Volksschullehrer in ihrer überwiegenden Zahl gegen eine kämpferische Lösung der 48er Probleme waren[44], wäre es doch eine Untersuchung wert, wieviel Lehrer in jener badischen Revolution, die mit den Namen *Hecker*s und *Struve*s unlösbar verbunden ist, mitgewirkt und nach deren blutigem Zusammenbruch ihr Leben oder ihre bürgerliche Existenz verloren haben. Dabei wäre auch interessant, aus welchen der drei Lehrerseminare die einzelnen kamen.

Schulrechtliche Folgen im Sinne der Stiehl'schen Regulative hatte der Ausgang der badischen Revolution für die Seminarbildung nur insoweit, als nun durch Verordnungen von 1850 und 1851 die ältere Form der Schulmeisterlehre wieder geduldet wurde[45], trotz des Widerstandes von Seminardirektoren wie *Stern,* der den Tendenzen einer Reorganisation des Seminarbildungswesens in diesem Sinne, bei aller konservativen Gesinnung, die man ihm damals vorwarf, bereits 1844 entgegengetreten war.

Im übrigen kann man Th. *Schieder* zustimmen, wenn er im Blick auf die gesamte deutsche Szene nach 1849 sagt, daß man »am wenigsten« in Baden »von einem ausgeprägten System der Reaktion sprechen« könne.[46] Das mag verwundern, wenn man bedenkt, daß zunächst mit den preußischen Kanonen regiert werden mußte. Doch der seit 1852 amtierende Großherzog *Friedrich I.* war ein Mann echter Liberalität, dem man eine Aussage, wie die so oft zitierte König *Friedrich Wilhelms IV.* von Preußen nicht zumuten könnte.[47] In dem nach 1862 einsetzenden sog. Badischen Kulturkampf bzw. Schulstreit sollte sich diese Liberalität erst noch bewähren. Während es hier jedoch vorwiegend um die Frage der geistlichen Schulaufsicht ging, standen in der Lehrerbildung weniger dramatische Aufgaben an.

So berief man als Nachfolger des als Gegner einer staatlichen Schulaufsicht sich exponierenden *Stern* 1865 Ferdinand *Leutz,* einen jener Kreisschulräte, die die Affekte der kirchlichen Parteien erregt hatten, zum Direktor des *Lehrerseminars Karlsruhe.* Er war von Haus aus auch Theologe und hat vor und nach dem Abtreten des agierenden liberalen Ministers K. *Knies,* der den zerstrittenen Parteien geopfert wurde, aus seiner Einstellung kein Geheimnis gemacht.[48]

Die katholischen Seminardirektoren in Ettlingen und Meersburg, meistens auch Theologen, hatten es noch schwerer, zwischen dem kämpferischen Freiburger Erzbischof *Hermann v. Vicari* (1773–1868) und den staatlichen bzw. staatskirchlichen Aufsichtsorganen eine kontinuierliche Ausbildung zu vermitteln.

1868/69 wurde die Seminarausbildungszeit von zwei auf drei Jahre verlängert, was auch eine räumliche Ausweitung der bisherigen Ausbildungsstätten mit sich bringen mußte.[49] In Karlsruhe bezog man 1870 ein neu errichtetes stattliches Gebäude. Die Zahlen wuchsen an, in Karlsruhe 1871/72 auf 124, in Ettlingen auf 114 und in Meersburg auf 121 Seminaristen.[50] Dabei wurden z. B. in Karlsruhe von 64, die sich Ostern 1873 zur Aufnahmeprüfung gemeldet hatten, 45 aufgenommen. Zur Erleichterung der erwarteten Vorbildung gründete man 1876 in *Gengenbach* und 1892 in *Meersburg* eine Präparandenschule, die im Sinne der 1868 durch einen Lehrplan für Schullehrerseminare vereinheitlichten Ausbildung vorarbeiten sollte.

Mit der Gründung eines simultanen, d. h. konfessionell gemischten Lehrerseminars in *Karlsruhe* versuchte man 1875 auf den Kompromiß des eben zuende gegangenen Schulstreites zu antworten. Hier war bei grundsätzlichem Festhalten am konfessionellen Charakter der Schule die Errichtung von konfessionell gemischten, d. h. Simultanschulen ermöglicht worden. Der erste Rektor dieses sog. *Lehrerseminars II,* W. *Berger* (1832–1883)[51], aber auch seine Nachfolger F. X. *Lehmann* (1823–1889) und W. *Zengerle* konnten durch ihre Amtsführung die neue, auf Versöhnung der

Konfessionen angelegte Ausbildung zwischen dem evangelischen Seminar I in Karlsruhe und dem katholischen in Ettlingen vorbildhaft entwickeln.
Eine auch qualitativ neue Form von Lehrerbildung bedeutete das 1878 als *Prinzessin-Wilhelm-Stift* gegründete Lehrerinnenseminar in Karlsruhe.[52] Es führte die bisher nur vereinzelt und meist auf privater Basis erfolgende Ausbildung von Lehrerinnen in feste Formen, auch wenn die im Prinzessin-Wilhelm-Stift versuchte im gesamten Land Baden die einzige bleiben sollte. Die noch vor der Jahrhundertwende einzelnen Höheren Mädchenschulen des Landes angegliederten »Seminarklassen« müssen wohl als Rückschritt bezeichnet werden, da sie Lehrerbildung in Abhängigkeit von einer Institution des sekundären Schulwesens betreiben wollten.[53]
Wir haben somit gegen Ende des 19. Jahrhunderts ein in der Seminarform organisiertes Lehrerausbildungssystem vor uns, das laufbahnmäßig überschaubar und rechtlich abgesichert war. Um nicht nur dem Buchstaben nach mit 1900 abzuschließen, müßte man darauf hinweisen, daß durch Verordnung und einen Lehrplan von 1904 die Ausbildung insofern neu geregelt wurde, als nun bestimmt wurde, daß sich im Regelfall an die Volksschulentlassung ein dreijähriger Vorseminarbesuch und daran der dreijährige Seminarbesuch anzuschließen hatte.[54]
Eine mehr quantitative Erweiterung der Lehrerausbildung zeigte sich im gleichen Jahr 1904 durch die Neugründung eines Lehrerseminars in *Heidelberg* und einer zunächst als Vorseminar, seit 1907 als Seminar geführten Anstalt in *Freiburg i. Br.* Gleichzeitig wurden auch im Hinterland der Seminare die als Aufbauzüge geltenden Vorseminare vermehrt.[55]
Als Grundbestand der Seminarform dieser letzten Ausbaustufe kann ein *selbständiges Lehrerkollegium,* ein *Internat* und eine in einem engeren Verhältnis zum Seminar stehende *Übungsschule* gelten.
Jedes dieser Essentiale müßte nun eigentlich im Detail erörtert werden, auch weniger wichtige Daten, wie z. B. die örtliche und soziale Herkunft der Seminaristen u. a. m.[56]
Die Stärken und Schwächen dieser Seminarform sind bekannt und in den Auseinandersetzungen der 20er Jahre unseres Jahrhunderts bei der Neuregelung einer akademischen Lehrerbildung von verschiedener Seite genügend herausgestellt worden.

II. Pädagogische Strömungen in der badischen Lehrerausbildung des 18. und 19. Jahrhunderts

Auch wenn hier bereits Gesagtes teilweise rekapituliert werden muß, soll doch in Kürze versucht werden, die innere Ausgestaltung der bisher mehr organisatorisch und personell aufgewiesenen Entwicklung aufzuhellen und zu periodisieren. Wir sehen dabei von der Form der Schulmeisterlehre ab, weil hier so viele individuelle und aufs Ganze gesehen verschiedene Wirkungen angenommen werden können, daß sie sich einer Generalisierung entziehen.
Anders bei der ersten Gründung eines Schul-Seminariums in *Karlsruhe.* Sie ist, wie schon angedeutet, an dem bei der *Hecker*'schen Realschule in Berlin befindlichen

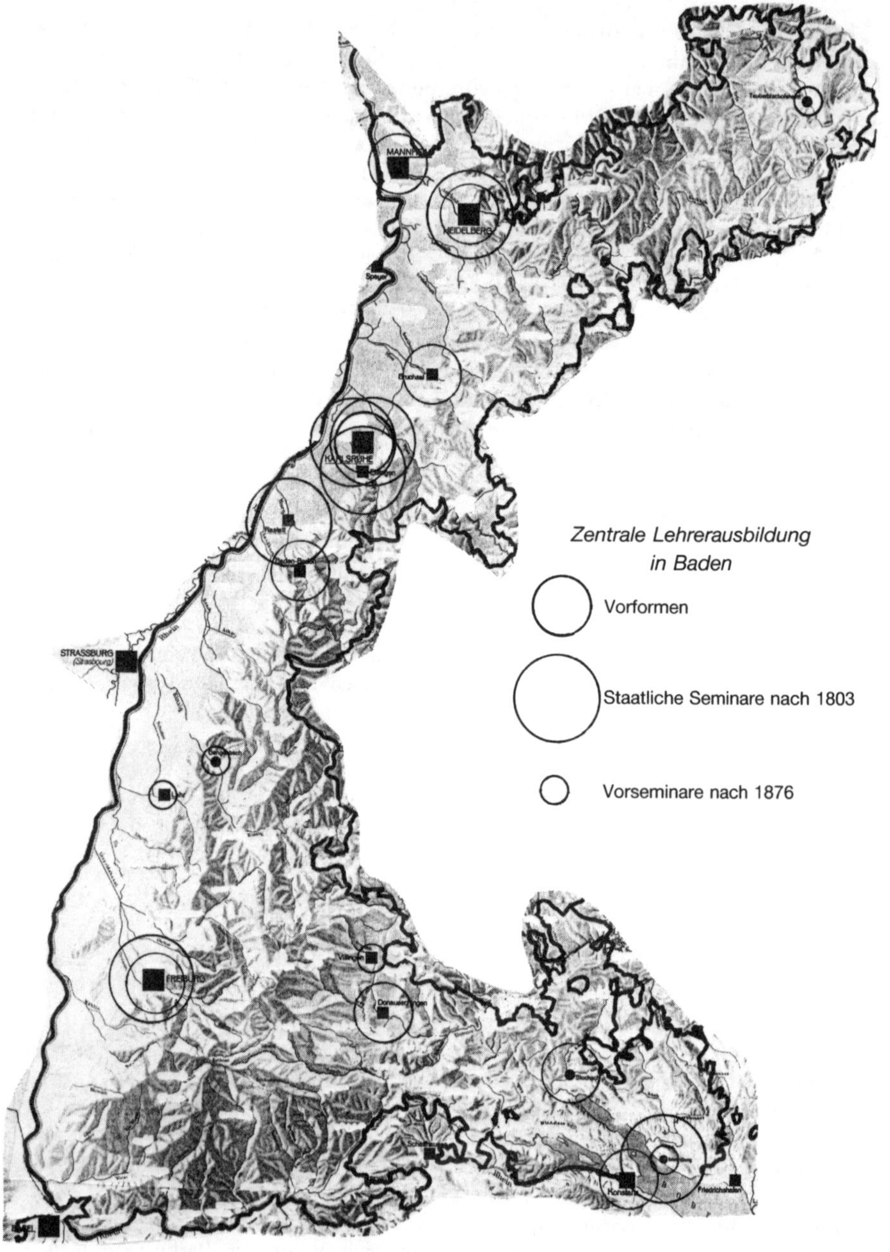

Zeichnung G. Silberer nach Bl. IV,5 des Historischen Atlas v. Baden-Württemberg (1973)

Schullehrerseminar orientiert und wird von den planenden Kirchenräten *Waltz* und *Mauritii* und Professoren des Karlsruher Lyceums wie *Boeckmann* auch in diesem Sinne geleitet. Ideen der pietistischen Pädagogik H. A. *Francke*s verbinden sich hier mit physiokratischer Staatsauffassung Karl Friedrichs und Gedankengut der *Philanthropen*. Gegen Ende des Jahrhunderts werden bei Prof. *Wucherer* pädagogische Gedanken F. M. *Vierthaler*s wirksam.

Was die *Freiburg*er Normalschule von 1773 angeht, so erübrigt sich ein Hinweis auf ihre geistige Ausrichtung. Nicht unwichtig ist aber vielleicht die Erinnerung, daß auch *Felbiger* Anregungen von einem Besuch des *Hecker*'schen Schulseminars in Berlin empfangen hatte.[57]

Soweit die Gedankenwelt I. *Demeters*, der 1809 in Rastatt das erste katholische Lehrerseminar des neugebildeten Großherzogtums leitet, erkennbar von außen bestimmt ist, sind Einflüsse F. M. *Vierthaler*s und seines Lehrers J. M. *Sailer*s, auch zeitgenössische Literatur wie die *Pestalozzi*s, in zuweilen falschem Verständnis, nachzuweisen.[58]

Der persönlichen Begegnung mit diesem großen Schweizer Pädagogen verdanken erst W. *Stern* und Ph. *Nabholz* ihre pädagogischen Auffassungen. In *Karlsruhe* hat Stern über 40 Jahre die Entwicklung der Lehrerausbildung in diesem Sinne beeinflußt, wobei gegen Ende seiner Tätigkeit aufgrund seiner neupietistischen Einstellung das von C. H. *Zeller* (1779–1860) in Beuggen vertretene Armenschullehrerideal die aufgeklärt-christlichen Vorstellungen *Pestalozzis* verdrängte.[59]

Nabholz, der *Pestalozzi* bis zu seinem Tod nahestand, hat in *Ettlingen* und *Meersburg* Ideale des pestalozzischen Denkens vor allem in der Internatsführung durchzusetzen[60] und auch seine elementarmethodischen Anstöße im Sprachunterricht weiterzuführen gesucht.[61]

Ein Vorschlag, der zumindest für einen Seminardirektor überraschend scheint, war der, die Lehrerbildung an die Universität zu verlegen, wo sie im Rahmen einer neuanzugliedernden »Kulturfakultät« Lehrer aller Schulstufen auf den Beruf vorbereiten sollte.[62]

Mit Beginn der 60er Jahre wird in der Lehrerbildung Badens der pädagogische Einfluß *Herbart*s erkennbar.

Als sein undogmatischer Vertreter kann F. *Leutz* gelten, der sich in seinem dreibändigen »Lehrbuch der Erziehung und des Unterrichts« klar zu ihm bekennt.[63]

In abgeschwächter Form gilt dies auch für H. *Oeser* und andere, die in leitenden Positionen die Lehrerbildung jener Jahre bis zur Jahrhundertwende tragen.[64] Kennzeichnend für diese gemäßigten Herbartianer ist wohl, daß sie in keinem persönlichen Lehrverhältnis zu *Herbart* oder einem der bekannteren Herbartianer gestanden haben. Ihre theoretischen und praktischen Auffassungen verdanken sie Büchern oder jenen Studienreisen an norddeutsche und mitteldeutsche Seminare, denen man damals auch behördlicherseits große Bedeutung zugeschrieben zu haben scheint.

Gegen Ende des Jahrhunderts dürfte in Baden auch ein gewisser Antagonismus zu den bekannteren Herbartianern wie *Ziller* u. a. modisch geworden sein, wie er sich etwa bei dem die badische Schulverwaltung jahrelang prägenden Pädagogen E. v. *Sallwürk* nachweisen läßt.[65]

Eine eigenständige pädagogische Richtung läßt sich in der Seminarbildung Badens vielleicht nur bei *einem* Pädagogen nachweisen, dem über Jahrzehnte hinweg im simultanen Lehrerseminar II in Karlsruhe wirkenden W. A. *Lay* (1862–1926).[66] Er hat, zum Teil gegen Widerstände im eigenen Haus, dann aber auch in Konkurrenz zu dem an der Universität lehrenden E. *Meumann* (1862–1915) eine empirische Pädagogik entwickelt, die das Karlsruher Seminar auch für die internationale pädagogische Welt interessant werden ließ. Wenn wir die Entwicklung bis heute verfolgen, so werden seine seit 1890 nachweisbaren Forschungen auf dem Gebiet des Rechtschreib- und Rechenunterrichts in ihrer bahnbrecherischen Bedeutung sichtbar.[67] Weniger originär dürften die gegen Ende seiner Tätigkeit gemachten Anstrengungen, eine »Tat-« oder »Lebensgemeinschaftsschule« zu begründen, angesehen werden.
Interessant und vielleicht bezeichnend ist auch die Tatsache, daß der spätere Kronzeuge der nationalsozialistischen Pädagogik, E. *Krieck,* von 1898–1900 im Karlsruher Seminar seine Ausbildung erhalten hatte, ehe er über die Pädagogischen Akademien in Frankfurt/M. und Dortmund auf den Heidelberger Lehrstuhl berufen wurde.[68]
Damit aber stehen wir schon in unserem Jahrhundert. Es lebt, wie gerade das Beispiel *Krieck* zeigt, aus der Tradition des vorangegangenen und es liegt auf der Hand, daß alle Phasen seiner organisatorischen und ideellen Genese in unsere Gegenwart hineinwirken.

Anmerkungen

[1] *Spranger* (1949), S. 12.

[2] *Gönner* (1975), S. 35.

[3] Vgl. die Graphik »Wie man um 1800 Schulmeister wurde«. In: »Pestalozzis Einfluß auf Württemberg und die Gründung des ersten Lehrerseminars in Eßlingen 1811.« In: 450 Jahre usw. 1985, S. 170, auch die Beiträge der Kollegen R. *Endres* und R. W. *Keck.*

[3a] *Gerstlacher* (1773), S. 164–169; *Leutz* (1889), S. 250; *Fischer* (1892), S. 236 ff.; *Stiefel* (1977), S. 1997.

[4] *Brunner* (1902), S. 210–246.

[5] J. Jakob *Ekert* (1820): Der badische Schulmeister ohne Stecken. Rastatt, S. 17f.

[6] So eine Urkunde vom 4. 11. 1741, ausgestellt von J. A. Eckstein, Dekan und Pfarrer in Au a. Rhein. In: Silberer (1988).

[7] Vgl. hierzu *Hüttner* (1982), S. 85 ff.

[8] Vgl. die Stellung des Stuttgarter Waisenhauses unter M. Riecke, des Eßlinger Alumneums und des Tübinger Pauperats in *d'Autels* Darstellung: Freimütige Jahrbücher der allgemeinen deutschen Volksschulen etc. hrsg. v. F. H. C. *Schwarz* u. a. (1819) Darmstadt, S. 131 ff., 164.

[9] Vorbild dieser Institution war das 1753 von J. Julius Hecker (1707–1768) an der Berliner Realschule errichtete Schulmeisterseminarium: *Gerstlacher* (1773), S. 172; Generallandesarchiv Karlsruhe Abt. 206, Fasz. 2889 Gutachten Waltz v. 2. 11. 1768, S. 3; *Silberer* (1968), S. 40f.

[10] Generallandesarchiv Karlsruhe (GLA) 235/21337: 11. 7. 1816: Bericht über die Entstehung der Freiburger Normalschule; 234/1036: 18. 6. 1807; *Moser* (1908) 76; *Quarthal* (1977),

S. 124f., 126; *Rühm-Constantin:* Freiburger Lehrerbildung mit Pausen. Das politische Schicksal der Stadt spiegelt sich im Schicksal ihrer Schulen und ihrer Lehrerbildung. In: Badische Zeitung vom 23. 6. 1970. Der Zeitpunkt der Errichtung der Normalschule wird hier mit dem 29. 4. 1773 angegeben. Sie soll in der Pfaffengasse 334, der heutigen Herrenstraße, untergebracht gewesen sein, in einem Haus, das 1944 bei der Bombardierung Freiburgs zerstört worden sein soll.

[11] *Gönner* (1966), S. 26ff., S. 40f.; *Gönner* (1984), S. 17–30.

[12] *Rühm-Constantin* a.a.O.; *Quarthal* (1977), S. 304ff.

[13] Landesstellen-Schematismus 1796, S. 58; *Quarthal* (1977), S. 304ff.

[14] *Moser* (1908), S. 108, 157, 173, 175f.; *Müller* (1959), S. 227.

[15] Auf Seminargründungen, die außerhalb des später badischen Gebietes entstanden, aber für später badische Gebiete Lehrer ausbildeten, soll hier nicht eingegangen werden, z. B. Würzburg. Hierfür vgl. Hüttner (1982), S. 93ff., S. 102–117.

[16] *Silberer* (1968), S. 59; *Brunner* (1902), S. 460f.

[17] *Silberer* (1968), S. 29f.; *Jehle* (1923), S. 31f.; nach *Volksschulwesen* (1861), S. VII soll Felbiger auf Ersuchen des Markgrafen v. Baden-Baden und des Fürstbischofs v. Speyer nach Bruchsal gekommen sein und dort einige Geistliche in seiner neuen Lehrweise unterrichtet haben.

[18] *Quarthal* (1977), S. 449, S. 397; vgl. auch S. 454 eine »Normalschuldirektion« in der Reichsgrafschaft Falkenstein mit nur zwei Geistlichen als Personal.

[19] *Revellio* spricht davon, daß im Oktober 1773 in Villingen eine Normalschule eröffnet worden sei; *Vorderösterreich* (1967), S. 476. Ähnlich bezeichnet J. B. *Hornung* (1964) in seiner »Geschichte der Stadt Bräunlingen«. Bräunlingen, S. 202 die dortige Hauptschule, wenn er eine Anordnung der k. u. k. Regierung von 1773 anführt, in der vom Vorstand der dortigen Normalschule gesprochen werde.

[20] *Silberer* (1968), S. 97.

[21] Ebenda S. 98ff.

[22] Ebenda S. 65.

[23] Braubach (1974), S. 56.

[24] *Silberer* (1968), S. 107; *Baden* etc. (1987), S. 172.

[25] *Silberer* (1968), S. 109ff.

[26] Ebenda S. 112f.

[27] Ebenda S. 73.

[28] Ebenda S. 77f.; *Graf* (1980), S. 451–459.

[29] *Silberer* (1968), S. 94.

[30] Ebenda S. 150ff. das sog. »Rastatter Experiment«, eine »Gesandtschaft« von 1810 an *Pestalozzi,* an der zwar nicht *Demeter,* doch *W. Wittmer,* sein Oberlehrer, teilnahm.

[31] Auch in Baden gab es wie in Bayern seit 1818 eine Verfassung und Volksvertretung: *Maier* (1984), S. 121; *Schieder* (1975), S. 14f.; *Silberer* (1968), S. 242.

[32] *Silberer* (1968), S. 279.

[33] Ebenda S. 273f.

[34] Ebenda Skizze VIIb.

[34a] Ebenda S. 296.

[35] Ebenda S. 32ff., 297; auch *Silberer* (1974), S. 141–143.

[36] Regierungsblatt 1834, S. 183; *Silberer* (1968), S. 280, S. 328f., Anm. 1361a.

[37] *Silberer* (1968), S. 232, S. 297.

[38] Ebenda S. 301–326.

[39] Ebenda S. 321, 328.

[40] Ebenda S. 327.

[41] Ebenda S. 363.
[42] *Schieder* (1975), S. 104.
[43] *Silberer* (1968), S. 368, Anm. 1946; *Döllinger* (1890), S. 78; *Verhandlungen* (1850 u. 1851), Protokollheft S. 69f., zweites Beilagenheft S. 35.
[44] *Thien* (1984), S. 192ff. Auch *Valentins* (1970), S. 537 Angaben sprechen gegen eine unverhältnismäßig starke Teilnahme von Lehrern an der revolutionär-kriegerischen Phase der Revolution, da er nur für die Standgerichte in Freiburg und Mannheim eine Hinrichtung von Lehrern anführt. Eine andere Sprache scheinen jedoch Flugblätter bzw. jene »plakativen Bekanntmachungen« zu führen, in denen der Bevölkerung die Todesurteile und deren Vollstreckung mitgeteilt wurden; vgl. *Real* (1983), S. 173.
[45] Vgl. die Verordnungen v. 14. 12. 1850 und 3. 10. 1851. In: *Volksschulwesen* (1861), S. XIII, S. 61, S. 20; *Silberer* (1968), S. 292, Anm. 1419.
[46] *Schieder* (1975), S. 114.
[47] *Thien* (1984), S. 197: »All das Elend, das im verflossenen Jahre über Preußen hereingebrochen ist, ist Ihre, einzig Ihre Schuld, die Schuld der Afterbildung, der irreligiösen Menschenweisheit, die Sie als echte Weisheit verbreiten, mit der Sie den Glauben und die Treue in dem Gemüte meiner Untertanen ausgerottet und deren Herzen von mir abgewandt haben.«
[48] *Armbruster* (1935), S. 350.
[49] *Holtzmann* (1876), S. 375; Großherzoglich Badisches Regierungsblatt 66 (1868), S. 259: Gesetz den Elementarunterricht betr. v. 8. 3. 1868.
[50] *Holtzmann* (1876), S. 375.
[51] *Badische Biographien* (1891), S. 22–24.
[52] *Silberer* (1984), S. 156.
[53] Bereits 1892 gibt es in Heidelberg an der städtischen Höheren Mädchenschule drei Seminarklassen: Statistisches *Jahr*buch etc. 1892/93, 2. Abt. Nr. 507; 1909/10, 2. Abt. Nr. 626, 627.
[54] *Stiefel* (1977), S. 1998.
[55] Statistisches Jahrbuch 1909/10, 2. Teil, Nr. 609, 611, 620ff.: Vorseminar Tauberbischofsheim 1904, Lahr 1908, Villingen 1908. Vgl. Skizze: Zentrale Lehrerausbildung. Trotz dieses Ausbaus der Vorseminare wird man sagen können, daß sich bereits damals die Mehrzahl der Seminarbesucher aus ehemaligen Mittelschülern, d. h. Gymnasiasten, zusammensetzte, die entsprechend ihrer Vorbildung in die entsprechenden Kurse des Seminars eintraten: Jahresbericht, 1908/09, S. 5: »Statistik zum gegenwärtigen Stand der Klassen«; Manuskript ohne Verfasserangabe von ca. 1955 in den Akten des Rektorats der Pädagogischen Hochschule Karlsruhe mit dem Titel: »Äußerer Rahmen der Lehrerbildung bis in unsere Zeit«, S. 16. Aus welcher Klasse diese »Gymnasiasten« ins Seminar eintraten, ließe sich wohl nur durch Auswertung der evtl. noch vorhandenen Bewerbungsakten ermitteln.
[56] Angaben hierfür finden sich für den Zeitraum bis 1850 in der von mir oft benutzten Dissertation von 1968.
[57] *Gönner* (1966), S. 35.
[58] *Silberer* (1968), S. 88ff., S. 93f.
[59] Ebenda S. 290f., S. 21f.
[60] Ebenda S. 344f.
[61] Ebenda S. 335ff.
[62] Ebenda S. 333f.
[63] Lehrbuch der Erziehung und des Unterrichts mit besonderer Berücksichtigung der psychologischen Grundlagen für Lehrer und Lehrerinnen, I. Teil, Tauberbischofsheim 1882, S. V; Karlsruhe [4]1899, S. III f.
[64] *Silberer* (1984), S. 154.

[65] *Saupe* (1929), S. 28; *Die Pädagogik* etc. (1926/27), S. 226ff.
[66] *Saupe* (1929), S. 46–58.
[67] *Weigl* (1932), S. 163.
[68] *Saupe* (1929), S. 384–397; *Hehlmann* (1942), S. 237f.

Literaturverzeichnis

Armbruster, K. (1935): Ferdinand Leutz. In: A. Krieger/K. Obser (Hrsg.): Badische Biographien, Bd. 6, Heidelberg

Baden und Württemberg im Zeitalter Napoleons (1987), hrsg. v. Württembergischen Landesmuseum Stuttgart, Bd. 1.1. Stuttgart

Badische Biographien (1891): hrsg. v. F. v. Weech, 4. Bd. Karlsruhe

Braubach, M. (1974): Von der Französischen Revolution bis zum Wiener Kongreß. München (Handbuch der deutschen Geschichte. 9. Aufl. hrsg. v. H. Grundmann, 14. Bd.)

Brunner, K. (1902): Die badischen Schulordnungen, I. Bd. Die Schulordnungen der badischen Markgrafschaften. Berlin

Döllinger, I. (1890): Die Freiheit der Kirche. In: J. Döllinger: Kleinere Schriften, hrsg. v. F. H. Reusch. Stuttgart

Fischer, K. (1892): Geschichte des deutschen Volksschullehrerstandes. Hannover (ND: Leipzig 1969)

Gerstlacher, C. F. (1773): Sammlung aller Baden-Durlachischen etc. Anstalten und Verordnungen, 1. Bd. Carlsruhe. In: Schulgeschichtliche Urkunden Badens 1773, zum 200. Gründungstag des Markgräflich Baden-Durlachischen Schul-Seminarii am 4. Nov. 1968, hrsg. v. Pädagogische Hochschule Karlsruhe. Stuttgart 1968

Gönner, E. u. G. Haselier (1975): Baden-Württemberg. Geschichte seiner Länder und Territorien. Würzburg

Gönner, R. (1966): Die österreichische Lehrerbildung von der Normalschule bis zur Pädagogischen Akademie. Wien

Gönner, R. (1984): Felbigers Schulreform und die Auswirkungen über Österreich hinaus. In: L. Kriss-Rettenbeck/M. Liedtke (Hrsg.): Regionale Schulentwicklung im 19. und 20. Jahrhundert. Bad Heilbrunn (Schriftenreihe zum Bayerischen Schulmuseum Ichenhausen, Bd. 2), S. 17–30

Graf, F. (1980): Ignaz Demeter als Verfasser pädagogischer Beiträge im »Archiv« und als Herausgeber der Zeitschrift zur Bildung katholischer Schullehrer. In: Freiburger Diözesanarchiv, 100. Jg., S. 451–459

Hehlmann, W. (1942): Pädagogisches Wörterbuch. 3. Aufl. Stuttgart

Holtzmann, H. (1876): Baden. In: Enzyklopädie des gesamten Erziehungs- und Unterrichtswesens, hrsg. v. K. A. Schmid, 1. Bd. Gotha

Hüttner, D. (1982): Von der Normalschule zum Lehrerseminar. München

Statistisches Jahrbuch der höheren Schulen (1892), 13. Jg. 1892/93; 30. Jg. 1909/1910. Leipzig

Jahresbericht, 63. des Seminars I Karlsruhe (1908/09). Karlsruhe

Jehle, E. (1923): Das niedere Schulwesen unter August Graf v. Limburg-Stirum, Fürstbischof v. Speyer (1770–1797). Freiburg

Kaiserlich-königlicher Hof- dann Vorderösterreichischer Landesstellen Schematismus samt einem Kalender für das Jahr 1796. Konstanz

Leutz, F. (1889): Lehrbuch der Erziehung und des Unterrichts, 3. Teil. Tauberbischofsheim

Maier, K. E. (1984): Schulpolitische Auswirkungen der Reaktion vor und nach 1848 in Bayern. In: L. Kriss-Rettenbeck/M. Liedtke (Hrsg.): Regionale Schulentwicklung im 19. und 20. Jahrhundert. Bad Heilbrunn (Schriftenreihe zum Bayerischen Schulmuseum Ichenhausen, Bd. 2), S. 121–129

Moser, M. (1908): Der Lehrerstand des 18. Jahrhunderts im vorderösterreichischen Breisgau. Berlin/Leipzig

Müller, Wolfgang (1959): Vorderösterreich. Eine geschichtliche Landeskunde, Bd. 1. Freiburg i. B.

Die Pädagogik der Gegenwart in Selbstdarstellungen (1926/27), 2. Bd. Leipzig

Quarthal, F./G. Wieland (1977): Die Behördenorganisation Vorderösterreichs von 1753 bis 1805 und die Beamten in Verwaltung, Justiz und Unterrichtswesen. Bühl

Real, W. (1983): Die Revolution in Baden 1848/49. Stuttgart

Großherzoglich Badisches Staats- und Regierungsblatt (1834), 32. Jg. Karlsruhe

Saupe, E. (1929): Deutsche Pädagogen der Neuzeit. 8. Aufl. Osterwieck

Schieder, Th. (1975): Vom deutschen Bund zum Deutschen Reich, 1815–1871. München (Handbuch der deutschen Geschichte. 9. Auflage, Bd. 15)

Silberer, G. (1968): Pestalozzi und die Anfänge einer zentralen staatlichen Lehrerbildung im deutschen Südwesten. Diss. Heidelberg

Silberer, G. (1974): Von der Normalschule zum Schullehrer-Seminar. Die Bräunlinger Musterschule des Oberlehrers Mathäus Blanche (1825–1845). In: Schriften des Vereins für Geschichte und Naturgeschichte der Baar, 30. Jg. Donaueschingen

Silberer, G. (1984): Die Anfänge einer Lehrerinnenbildung in Baden. In: L. Kriss-Rettenbeck/M. Liedtke (Hrsg.): Regionale Schulentwicklung im 19. und 20. Jahrhundert. Bad Heilbrunn (Schriftenreihe zum Bayerischen Schulmuseum Ichenhausen, Bd. 2), S. 152–161

Silberer, G. (1988): Geplagte Schulmeister von anno dazumal. Das Verhältnis von Lehrer und Gemeinde in Karlsruhe-Bulach von 1741–1810. In: Badische Heimat, 68. Jg. Karlsruhe

Spranger, E. (1949): Zur Geschichte der deutschen Volksschule. Heidelberg

Stiefel, K. (1977): Baden (1648–1952), Bd. 1. Karlsruhe

Thien, H. G. (1984): Schule, Staat und Lehrerschaft. Frankfurt/M.

Valentin, V. (1970): Geschichte der deutschen Revolution 1848–1849, 2. Bd. Köln/Berlin

Verhandlungen der Ständeversammlung des Großherzogtums Baden, I. Kammer. 1850 u. 1851. Karlsruhe

450 Jahre Kirche und Schule in Württemberg (1985), hrsg. v. Pädagogisch-Theologischen Zentrum Stuttgart, 2. Aufl. Stuttgart.

Das badische Volksschulwesen (1861), 2. Aufl. Karlsruhe

Vorderösterreich. Eine geschichtliche Landeskunde (1967), 2. Aufl. Freiburg

Weigl, F. X. (1932): Lay, W. A. In: Lexikon der Pädagogik der Gegenwart, 2. Bd. Freiburg, Sp. 162–164

Hubert Buchinger

Die Realschullehrerbildung in Bayern von ihren Anfängen bis zum Ende des 19. Jahrhunderts

1. Die Anfänge der Realschullehrerbildung im Zeitalter der Aufklärung

Als Papst *Clemens XIV.* am 21. 7. 1773 den Jesuitenorden aufhob, ging das bisher von den Jesuiten beherrschte höhere Schulwesen auf den Staat über und zwang diesen zu einer umfassenden Schulreform. »Gleich nach der Publication der Aufhebung stürmte es gewaltige Schulsysteme. Man konnte sich in der Eile nicht hinausfinden, und man beschloß es auf ein Jahr beym Alten zu lassen ...«.[1] Insbesondere die von *Johann Adam von Ickstatt* (1702–1776) mit soziologischer und nationalökonomischer Begründung vor der Akademie der Wissenschaften am 18. 3. 1770 erstmals »als Teil eines Schulprogramms in Bayern«[2] geforderte Realschule schuf eine Reihe schulorganisatorischer Probleme. Doch schon am 8. 10. 1774 erfolgte die Gründung der Realschule, die damals »ein hier zu Land ganz neuer, und bisher vielen unbekannter Gegenstand«[3] war. An diesem Tag ratifizierte *Max III. Josef* (1745–1777) nämlich die erste bayerische Realschulordnung nachdem er mit Kurfürstlicher Verordnung vom 12. 8. 1774 bereits befohlen hatte, daß »mit den Realschulen gleich künftiges Jahr zu München, Landshut, Straubing, Burghausen, Amberg, und Ingolstadt, und zwar mit der ersten Classe, in München aber mit zwo Classen nach der im Plan entworfenen Lehrart angefangen werden«[4] sollte. Bayern schuf sich damit vor allen anderen deutschen Staaten »ein öffentliches, durch staatlichen Hoheitsakt errichtetes Realschulwesen«.[5]

Obwohl *Heinrich Braun* (1732–1792) und *von Ickstatt* mit ihren großen Schulreformentwürfen vom 1. bzw. 28. 3. 1774 das Werden der Realschule maßgeblich befördert hatten, enthielt die neue Realschulordnung kaum etwas von ihren Intentionen. *Ickstatts* Idee einer stufenmäßigen Einheitsschule mit ihrer zwischen Trivial- und Lateinschule sich schiebenden vierklassigen ›Bürgerlichen Realschule‹ war bereits von der Schulplankommission verworfen worden. Dieses von *Max III. Josef* berufene Gremium begründete seine Ablehnung mit dem Hinweis auf die schulsystemverändernde Wirkung dieser Konzeption und insbesondere mit der von Ickstatt geforderten, vom Staat aber nicht zu finanzierenden Zahl von »in Summa 70 Professores für Realschulen«.[6] Wie wenig *Ickstatt* dabei aber an einen die weitere Existenz der Realschulen sichernden Realschullehrerstand mit eigenständiger Lehrerbildung gedacht hatte, belegen seine Einlassungen vom 28. 3. 1774: »Die Lehrer und Professoren, welche ausser dem Schreib- und Zeichnungsmeister, Priester seyn müssen, werden theils aus dem hiesigen albertinischen Kollegium, theils aus abteylichen Klöstern genommen«.[7]

Im Gegensatz zu *Ickstatts* Vorschlägen wurde *Brauns* allgemeinbildende und vom Gymnasium völlig getrennte Realschule mit ihren drei einander nicht subordinierten, sondern koordinierten Klassen[8] von den sowohl das lateinische wie auch das bürgerliche Schulwesen leitenden und schließlich auch die Realschulordnung ausarbeitenden Schuldirektoren *Johann Baptist von Steeb* und *Jakob Anton Kollmann* zur Seite geschoben. Sie »fuhren ihm durch den Sinn, und subordinirten die Realclassen unter einander nicht nur, sondern knüpften sie an die lateinische Classen stuffenweise hinan«[9] und brachten so »das Braun'sche Projekt überhaupt zu Fall«.[10] Damit aber war die Realschule unbeschadet der ihr in § LVI der Schulordnung vom 8. 10. 1774 »zugewiesenen Aufgabe, nämlich eine bürgerliche Bildung zu vermitteln, in die Stellung der bislang auf das Gymnasium vorbereitenden und mit Verordnung vom 3. 10. 1774 aufgehobenen Prinzipienschulen eingerückt. Die Kompromißrealschule von 1774 blieb bis 1777 nichts anderes als eine gymnasiale Unterstufe«.[11]

Aufbau des bayerischen Bildungswesens gemäß der Schulordnung vom 8. 10. 1774

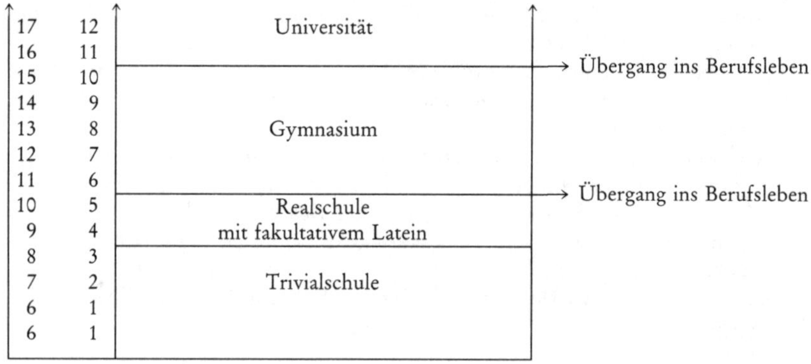

Quelle: Skizziert nach Lurz 2, 1908, 224f.

Neben der Ausrichtung der zwei nun aufeinanderfolgenden Realschulklassen auf das Gymnasium hin und dem fakultativen Latein erwies sich vor allem das Fehlen einer Verfügung zur Realschullehrerbildung als folgenschwerster Mangel der Schulordnung. Während *Braun* in seinen ›Gedanken über die Erziehung und den öffentlichen Unterricht‹ noch drei »ordentliche öffentlich lehrende Professoren«[12] sowie »Künstler, Handwerker, Rechen- und Schreibmeister, Sprachlehrer im französischen, italiänischen u. s. f.«[13] für die jeweilige Realschule gefordert und für die Einführung des Fachlehrersystems plädiert hatte, schenkten weder die beiden Schuldirektoren noch die Planungskommission der Realschullehrerbildung die nötige Beachtung. Das Fachlehrersystem verfiel der Ablehnung, nachdem *Wiguleus Freiherr von Kreittmayr* ein Gegengutachten abgegeben hatte, und bezüglich der Realschullehrer und ihrer Ausbildung beließen es die Mitglieder der Planungskommission bei der Feststellung:

»Wenn die bisherigen Professores Principiorum fähig sind, so können sie Professores in der Realschule bleiben. Die übrigen nimmt man daher, wo man diejenigen hernimmt, die man für Gymnasien nöthig hat«.[14]
Angesichts der beabsichtigten Verwendung von Gymnasiallehrern an den Realschulen war es nur billig, wenn *Max III. Josef* verfügte, daß »die Professores der Realschulen Rang und Salarium im gleichen Maaße mit dem Gymnastischen zu genießen haben«[15] sollten. Daneben wurde den im »Range nach den wirklichen, und Titularräthen«[16] kommenden Realschullehrern das nur herausgehobenen Personen zustehende Recht der Siegelmäßigkeit verliehen.
Erst als die Anstellung von Gymnasiallehrern, vornehmlich Exjesuiten, an den Realschulen in der Öffentlichkeit auf Kritik stieß und zeitgenössische Stimmen sich aus Staatsgründen für die Berufung »von Weltgeistlichen oder noch besser von weltlichen Lehrern«[17] aussprachen, kam die Schulkommission diesem Ansinnen zum Teil entgegen:

Lehrpersonal an den Realschulen im Schuljahr 1775/76

Schule	Exjesuit	Weltpriester	weltl. Lehrer
Amberg	1	1	2
Burghausen	1	1	2
Ingolstadt	–	2	–
Landsberg	1	–	–
Landshut	–	2[1]	–
Mindelheim	–	–	1
München	–	2	4
Straubing	–	1	2
Summe	3	9	11

[1] Davon ein Ordensgeistlicher aus dem Kloster Metten

Quelle: Hof- und Staats-Kalender für das Schaltjahr 1776, S. 107ff.

Obwohl die Schulordnung vom 8. 10. 1774 bezüglich einer Prüfung für das Lehramt an Realschulen nur die Weisung enthielt, daß bei der Anstellung neuer Professoren »Sr. kurfürstl. Durchlaucht der mündliche Vortrag durch das Schuldirektorium hierüber gemacht, und Ihre höchste Entschlüßung erbethen werden«[18], wurden die Kandidaten schon bald einer eigenen Prüfung unterworfen. Ein Prüfungsprotokoll mit 18 Fragen sowie die von Rektor *Anton Bucher* und den Professoren *Florian Pichelmayer* und *Lorenz Westenrieder* am 22. 9. 1776 ausgestellten Zeugnisse machen deutlich, daß neben Religion, Deutsch, Mathematik, Geographie, Geschichte, Naturgeschichte und methodisch-didaktischen auch pädagogische Probleme Gegenstand der Realschullehrerprüfungen waren. Themenbereich 12 im genannten Protokoll ist hierfür ein Beleg: »Der Lehrer hat in seiner Schule einen lügenhaften, halßstörigen Schüler, was weiß er für Mittel ihn zu bessern, wie verhüttet er das Ärgernuß, welches darüber bey andern entstehen konnte? Sind die Schläge bey der Schulzucht zu verwerfen, oder können sie auch ein heilsames und dauerhafftes Besserungsmittel seyn? Wie?«[19] Während das Schuldirektorium mit der Abnahme dieser Prüfungen von Fall zu Fall Münchner Gymnasialprofessoren betraute, war hinsichtlich der Sprach- und Zeichenmeister bereits am 2. 11. 1774 vom Kurfürsten verfügt worden, »daß die erstere einer ordentlichen Prüfung unterworfen, und von den anderen auch in Gegenwarth der Commißion sowohl über die Mathematisch- und Architectonische Zeichnung, als über die Ornamenten und Figuren, hinreichende verfertiget; sohin von beeden die besten ausgesuchet werden sollen«.[20]

Dieser Zustand einer im Auftrag des Schuldirektoriums zwar durchgeführten, aber von keiner Schul- bzw. Prüfungsordnung normierten Realschullehrerprüfung endete am 1. 9. 1777. An diesem Tag erschien die von *Braun* verfaßte ›Schulverordnung für die churbaierischen Lyceen und Gymnsaien‹. Zusammen mit der ebenfalls von *Braun* stammenden ›Churfürstlichen Schulordnung für die bürgerliche Erziehung der Stadt- und Landschulen in Baiern‹ vom 8. 8. 1778 bildete sie die Grundlage für das staatliche Realschulwesen der nächsten Jahre. Verhängnisvoll für die infolge der großen Finanznot nur mehr aus zwei Klassen bestehenden Realschule war dabei »die neuerliche Einführung der als Vorstufe für das auf vier Klassen reduzierte Gymnasium gedachten Prinzipien- oder Vorbereitungsklasse, die *Braun* mit der Realschule verband«.[21] Obschon *Braun* die Prinzipienklasse als »Gränzscheidung zwischen der bürgerlichen und der gelehrten Erziehung«[22] verstand, verschwamm diese in der Praxis mit der Realschule und machte dadurch »die prinzipielle Scheidung des Gymnasial- und Realschulwesens illusorisch«.[23]

Auch wenn zuletzt »von den Realschulen blos der Name geblieben«[24] war, so kommt *Braun* doch das Verdienst zu, mittels einer in die Schulverordnung vom 1. 9. 1777 integrierten Prüfungsordnung die Gründung eines Realschullehrerstandes versucht zu haben. Gemäß § 8 dieser Ordnung hatten sich die Lehramtskandidaten bei Braun zu melden und »demselben glaubwürdige Attestaten ihres Wohlverhaltens, guter Aufführung, und des ehemal in Studiis gehabten Fortganges vor(zu)weisen«.[25] Hierauf war vom einzelnen Prüfling »mit Beyziehung derjenigen Professoren aus dem Corpore in München, in deren Fach das Lehramt ein(schlug), eine Probrelation ab(zu)legen«.[26] Darüber hinaus wurde er um seiner »Fähigkeit wegen nicht nur 1) in der theoretisch- und praktischen Erziehungskunst überhaupt, sondern auch 2) in den zu jedem Fache gehörigen besten Lehrmethoden, und dann auch 3) in schriftlichen Aufsätzen der zum Lehramte nöthigen Sprachen geprüft«.[27] Erstrebte einer der dann angestellten und rangmäßig wie 1774 eingestuften Realschulprofessoren eine Beförderung, so bestimmte § 24: »Fordern seine Verdienste, wie seine Lust eine Beförderung zu einer höhern Classe in einem andern Fache; so ist er zwar einer fernern Prüfung überhoben, muß aber doch seine Fähigkeit entweder durch gelehrte Arbeiten, oder auf eine andere Art neuerdings an den Tag gelegt haben«.[28]

Doch nicht nur Prüfung und Beförderung, sondern auch die Vorbildung – insbesondere der nicht aus den Reihen der Geistlichen kommenden Lehramtsanwärter – war *Braun* ein Anliegen. Nachdem die von ihm erwogene Einrichtung eines auch der Realschullehrerbildung dienenden »Professor-Seminarium(s)«[29] an der Kostenfrage gescheitert war, stellte er allenthalben die besten Realschulabsolventen als Repetitoren an und versah sie mit einem geringen Gehalt. Aus diesem Kreis schulpraktisch geschulter und durch Eigenstudium fachlich gebildeter Repetitoren gewann *Braun* seinen Realschullehrernachwuchs. Diese Form der Ausbildung blieb jedoch nur wenige Jahre in Kraft.

Da nach dem Tode *Max III. Josef* dessen Nachfolger *Karl Theodor* (1777–1799) den bisher für Schulzwecke bestimmten Jesuitenfonds für die Errichtung einer bayerischen Malteserzunge benötigte, zwang er am 29. 7. 1781 den heftig widerstrebenden Prälatenstand zur Übernahme der Real- und Personalexigenz für die höheren Schulen. Dieser wiederum stellte die Realschulen insofern in Frage, als er nur das von Jesuiten innegehabte Schulwesen übernehmen wollte und »die dermal ebenmäßig zu bestreiten habende Realschule von sich abzuleinen, und auf den deutschen Schulfond hinüber zu wälzen«[30] suchte. Sieht man von den Benediktinern und ihren schulnah ausgebildeten Lehrkräften ab, so machte in der Folgezeit nicht nur die Realschule, sondern auch die Realschullehrerbildung »in den Händen der Klostergeistlichen beklagenswerthe Rückschritte«.[31]

Damit bleibt als Fazit: »Aufgrund lascher Handhabung der Lehramtsprüfungen, sofern solche überhaupt stattfanden, verfiel der von *Braun* im § 8 der Schulordnung von 1777 begründete und durch strenge Examen ausgewiesene Mittelschullehrerstand, noch ehe er sich richtig bilden konnte«.[32]

2. Die Realschullehrerbildung in der Zeit des Neuhumanismus

Der betrübliche Zustand der Realschule, die laut Protokoll vom 13. 8. 1784 nur mehr als »Höhere Bürgerschule«[33] bezeichnet worden war, änderte sich erst, als mit Kurfürst *Max IV. Josef* (1799–1806) und nachmaligen König *Max I. Josef* (1806–1825) sowie *Maximilian Josef Freiherr von Montgelas* (1759–1838) zwei vom Geist der Aufklärung durchdrungene Männer die Regierungsgeschäfte übernahmen. Beide sahen es »als vordringliche Aufgabe an, das unter *Karl Theodor* in Rückstand geratene Schulwesen«[34] nicht nur »nach rationalistischen und utilitaristischen Gesichtspunkten zu reformieren«[35], sondern auch für dessen völlige Neuorganisation auf realistischer Grundlage zu sorgen.

Schon die Verordnung vom 24. 9. 1799 stellte fest »daß man bisher die sogenannten lateinischen oder gelehrten Schulen zum Nachtheile der Real- und Bürgerschulen zu sehr begünstigte«[36] und ordnete die Umwandlung der in den Prälatenklöstern befindlichen Studenten-, Seminar- und Lateinschulen in Realschulen an. Gleichzeitig entzog die Regierung dem Prälatenstand das Besetzungsrecht und verfügte, daß die Schulen »von nun an wieder ohne Unterschied des Standes mit Professoren von allgemein anerkannter Fähigkeit besetzet werden soll(t)en«.[37] Die Ernennung derselben behielt sich der Kurfürst selbst vor. Die neue Wertschätzung der Realschule seitens der Regierung fand neben dieser den Realschullehrerstand wiederbegründenden Anordnung auch in einer verbesserten Lehrerbesoldung ihren Ausdruck.

So wurde beispielsweise mit Mandat vom 3. 12. 1799 das Jahresgehalt der Münchner Realschullehrer um 125 fl. erhöht. *Anton Winkler* bezog daraufhin 718 fl., *Johann Baptist Fischer* 593 fl. und *Xaver Fuchs* 568 fl. 45 kr. Hinzukamen jeweils etwa 60 fl. Oster- und Gregorigeld und ein jährliches Schulgeld von 80 fl. für *Winkler,* 152 fl. für *Fischer* und 50 fl. für *Fuchs.*[38] Obschon dies in Anbetracht der 400 fl. eines Gerichtsdieners[39] und des zwischen den Realschullehrern in München und im übrigen Bayern bestehenden Lohngefälles nicht viel war, empfand man die regierungsamtlichen Maßnahmen als Fortschritt. Ferner wurde auf Ansuchen von *Winkler, Fischer* und *Fuchs* sämtlichen Realschullehrern mit Verordnung vom 17. 9. 1801 Titel, Rang und Uniform der Professoren verliehen.[40] »Das war freilich nur eine Rückkehr zur früheren Rangordnung und die notwendige Erneuerung zeugt davon, wie sehr das Ansehen der Realschulen während der Regierung *Karl Theodors* durch die Auslieferung an den Prälatenstand gesunken war«.[41] Doch alle das staatliche Realschulwesen vorantreibenden Verfügungen blieben zunächst unbefriedigend, da sie keine die Realschullehrerbildung regelnden Bestimmungen enthielten.

Wie schon einmal im Jahr 1773 so stellten auch dieses Mal die Übernahme der höheren Lehranstalten, die Säkularisation der Klöster und eine durch Gebietszuwächse uneinheitlich gewordene Schullandschaft die Regierung vor das Erfordernis einer Schulreform. *Josef Wismayr* (1767–1858), der durch seine Tätigkeit am Lodronisch-Rupertinischen Institut zu Salzburg ausgewiesene Pädagoge, wurde mit der kaum lösbaren Aufgabe betraut, die »gelehrte Bildung zu reformieren und gleichzeitig in die schon bestehende Schulstruktur ein den vorgegebenen Grundsätzen der Brauchbarkeit und Nützlichkeit genügendes realistisches Schulwesen zu integrieren«.[42] Wie wenig *Wismayr* dieses Ansinnen erfreute, sagt er selbst: »Diesem Ministerial-Auftrage, so wenig er auch meiner Neigung und meinen Wünschen entsprach, konnte und durfte ich aus Pflicht- und Ehr-Gefühl nicht widersprechen«.[43]

Der Wismayrsche ›Lehr-Plan für alle kurpfalzbayerischen Mittel-Schulen, oder für die sogenannten Real-Klassen (Principien), Gymnasien, und Lyceen‹ vom 27. 8. 1804 entwarf eine ausgeklügelte, dem enzyklopädischen Ideal des Philanthropismus verbundene Einheitsschule mit Realschule, Gymnasium und Lyzeum von jeweils dreijähriger Dauer. Obwohl *Wismayr* die ihm zur Auflage gemachte Verschmelzung realistischer und humanistischer Ziele durch eine »Art Realgymnasium zu lösen versucht hatte«[44], konnte »dieses Konzept auf die Dauer nicht befriedigen«.[45]

Bezüglich der Realschullehrer und ihrer Bildung enthielt der als Fundgrube pädagogischen Gedankenguts anzusehende Mittelschullehrplan samt Anhang und Nachtrag vom 12. 11. 1805 Feststellungen hinsichtlich der anzustellenden Lehrer und der »Lehr-Art nach Fächern«[46] sowie erstmals Angaben zur Lehrmethode. »Was die eigentliche Lehr-Methode betrifft, welche von allen Lehrern, in allen Klassen und in allen Fächern zu beobachten ist, so darf es ohnehin von jedem an den kurpfalzbayrischen Mittel-Schulen angestellten, oder noch anzustellenden Lehrer, wie billig, vorausgesetzt werden, daß ihm die allgemeinen und besonderen Gesetze der zwäckmäßigsten Unterrichts-Art, so wie sie von den erfahrensten Pädagogen entwickelt und aufgestellt sind ... bekannt seyen«.[47] Um sich die Elemente dieser Methode wie Motivation, Lebensbezug, Anschauung, Selbsttätigkeit etc. anzueignen, wurden die

Kandidaten auf ein intensives Eigenstudium und die schulpraktische Tätigkeit als Adstant verwiesen. Da es aber nach wie vor an tüchtigen Lehrern fehlte, an Lehrern also, die die Kunst beherrschten, »Lernen zur süßen Pflicht, zur angenehmen, sich selbst lohnenden Arbeit ... zu erheben«[48], erlaubte es die Verordnung vom 12. 11. 1805 solchen Realschulprofessoren das eingeführte Fachlehrersystem im »ersten Triennium«[49], also in der Realschule, durch das Klassenlehrersystem zu ersetzen.

Im Zuge »der 1805 einsetzenden Abkehr der bayerischen Regierung von der bisher im Geist der Aufklärung und des Realismus betriebenen Schulpolitik und der Hinwendung zum Neuhumanismus«[50] schlug der Präsident des ›Geheimen Schul- und Studien-Bureaus‹, *Georg Friedrich Freiherr von Zentner* (1752–1835), die Errichtung spezieller, insbesondere Handel und Gewerbe genügender Bürgerschulen vor. Gleichzeitig beantragte er die Gründung eines Lehrerinstituts, worin »sehr zum Nutzen der Schule, deren Ansehen durch akademisch gebildete Lehrer steige, und der Nationalbildung die künftigen Bürgerschullehrer ausgebildet werden sollten«.[51] Die Regierung beauftragte jedoch den vom neuhumanistischen Geist durchdrungenen *Friedrich Immanuel Niethammer* (1767–1858) mit der Neuordnung des bayerischen Schulwesens. Zentners bahnbrechender Gedanke hingegen »auf Schaffung eines akademisch gebildeten Bürger- und Realschullehrerstandes«[52] fiel dem Vergessen anheim.

Am 3. 11. 1808 erhielt das Niethammersche ›Allgemeine Normativ der Einrichtung der öffentlichen Unterrichts-Anstalten in dem Königreiche‹ die landesherrliche Genehmigung.

Aufbau des bayerischen Bildungswesens gemäß dem Niethammerschen Normativ vom 3. 11. 1808

Das Niethammersche Normativ vom 3. 11. 1808

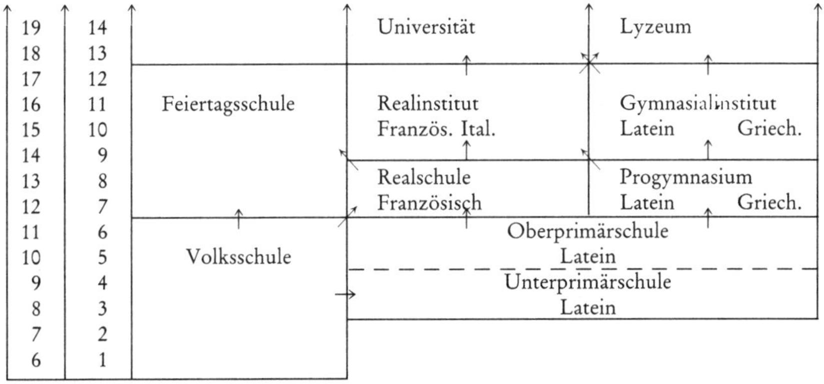

Quellen: Skizziert nach Regierungsblatt 1803, 757ff. und Lurz 2, 1908, 561ff.

Niethammers revolutionäre Neuerung bestand in der Trennung der realistischen Bildung von der humanistischen. Die von ihm als besondere Bildungseinrichtungen konzipierten Studienanstalten bauten auf einer sechsjährigen Volks- bzw. vierjährigen Primärschule auf. Ihnen folgte die zweijährige Sekundärschule, die mit Progymnasium und Realschule »zwei verschiedene, nebeneinander parallel laufende Anstalten«[53] in sich vereinte. »Die in der Sekundärschule beginnende Zweiteilung in einen realistischen und einen humanistischen Zweig fand in den vierjährigen, auf Progymnasium und Realschule fußenden und zur Universitätsreife führenden Gymnasial- und Realinstituten ihre schulorganisatorische Fortsetzung«.[54] Mit diesen schließlich 18 Realschulen und 2 Realinstitute umfassenden Bildungseinrichtungen waren die realistischen Unterrichtsanstalten »Staatlich anerkannt und praktisch durchgeführt und das Realschulwesen Bayerns ... vorbildlich für ganz Deutschland geworden«.[55]

Zur endgültigen Absicherung seiner Reformen setzte *Niethammer* drei Maßnahmen. Einmal berief er »auf Grund persönlicher Bekanntschaft und Beurteilung«[56] für die Realinstitute Nürnberg und Augsburg mit den nachmaligen Universitätsprofessoren *Gotthilf Heinrich von Schubert, Simon Erhardt, Johann Baptist Hermann, Johann Arnold Kanne, Johann Wilhelm Pfaff, Johann Salomon Schweigger* bzw. *Johann Karl Friedrich Hauff, Karl Wilhelm Juch, Georg Heinrich Keyser* und *August Stark* Lehrerkollegien, die damals in Deutschland kaum ihresgleichen hatten. Zum andern wurden mit Bekanntmachung vom 9. 7. 1809, die ›Prüfungen der Kandidaten zum Lehramte an den Studienanstalten betreffend‹, in München und Nürnberg ständige Prüfungskommissionen eingesetzt, vor denen die Kandidaten der humanistischen und realistischen Lehrämter alljährlich an Michaelis die nämliche Prüfung abzulegen hatten.[57] (Regierungsblatt 1809, 1131 ff.). Und drittens erschien mit der ›Instruktion zur Prüfung der zum Lehramte an den Studien-Schulen oder Studien-Instituten sich anmeldenden Kandidaten betreffend‹ vom 30. 9. 1809 die erste, für Real- und Gymnasiallehrer gleichermaßen geltende Prüfungsordnung Bayerns.

Die Instruktion stellte dabei bezüglich der schriftlich und mündlich zu prüfenden Gegenstände Philologie (§ 1), Philosophie, Geschichte, Altertumskunde, deutsche klassische Literatur, Mathematik und den Naturwissenschaften (§ 2) ausdrücklich fest, daß »dieser Kreis von Kenntnissen ... von Allen ohne Ausnahme zu fordern«[58] sei. Innerhalb des Fächerkanons konnten jedoch insofern Akzente gesetzt werden, als angehende Reallehrer vor allem in den mathematisch-naturwissenschaftlichen Disziplinen und die Gymnasiallehrer in den klassischen Sprachen geprüft wurden. Aus diesem Grund waren anläßlich der ersten Lehramtsprüfung, die am 26. 10. 1809 stattfand, von den 28 schriftlich zu beantwortenden Fragen auch 14 den Fächern Mathematik, Naturlehre und Naturgeschichte gewidmet.[59] Von diesen 28 Fragen mußte übrigens die Hälfte »in lateinischer Sprache«[60] beantwortet werden. Gemäß den ›Nachträglichen Bestimmungen zur Prüfungsinstruktion der Studienlehramts-Kandidaten‹ vom 31. 8. 1811 wurden deren Leistungen wie folgt klassifiziert: »Vorzüglich, Sehr gut, Gut, Hinlänglich, Nothdürftig«.[61] Während das erste Prädikat zum Unterricht an einem Gymnasial- bzw. Realinstitut berechtigte, befähigten die beiden nächstfolgenden Qualifikationen für die Lehrämter am Progymnasium bzw. an der

Real- und Primärschule. Ein Bewährungsaufstieg war jedoch möglich. Die schon erwähnten ›Nachträglichen Bestimmungen‹ erweiterten die Fächerpalette um »die französische ... (und) die orientalischen Sprachen«.[62] Gleichzeitig führten sie eine praktische Prüfung ein, indem sie jeden Kandidaten verpflichteten, »unmittelbar in einer Schülerclasse selbst einen ihm aufzugebenden Gegenstand mit den Schülern zu behandeln«.[63]

Da Preußen das »Examen pro facultate docendi«[64] erst am 12. 7. 1810 zur Einführung brachte, war Bayern mit der einen wissenschaftlich ausgebildeten Lehrerstand begründenden Prüfungsordnung vom 30. 9. 1809 auch hier zum Vorreiter geworden.

Obschon die Regierung den Lehrern an den Realinstituten mit Entschließung vom 14. 8. 1810 noch die pragmatischen Rechte verliehen und gleichzeitig »auch das Schicksal der übrigen öffentlichen Lehrer seiner Zeit nach Möglichkeit zu verbessern«[65] versprochen hatte, wurden die Realinstitute am 24. 8. 1816 aufgehoben. »Anlaß hierzu bot neben der Finanznot des Staates vor allem der permanente Widerstand, den die altbayerischen Aufklärer um *Weiller* und *Wismayr,* die Patriotenpartei um *Johann Christoph Freiherr von Aretin* und katholische Kreise sowohl den zur Neugestaltung Bayerns ins Land geholten Ausländern und Protestanten als auch dem Niethammerschen Normativ entgegenbrachten«.[66] Da die Realschulen nach »erfolgter Auflösung der Real-Institute ihren ersten und vorzüglichen Zweck, die Schüler zum Eintritt in diese Institute vorzubereiten«[67] verloren hatten, wurden sie am 28. 9. 1816 in zweikursige ›Höhere Bürgerschulen‹ umgewandelt, die als Gemeindeanstalten das bisherige staatliche Realschulwesen ersetzten.

Das Prüfungsrecht an den nunmehrigen Bürgerschullehrern ging mit Verordnung vom 26. 3. 1818, die ›Prüfung der Kandidaten des Lehramtes an den Studien-Anstalten und Bürgerschulen betreffend‹, auf die Kreisregierungen über. Bezüglich des Verfahrens wurde dabei bestimmt, nur »im Fall der Erledigung einer solchen Lehrstelle einen Prüfungsconcurs für diejenigen (auszuschreiben), die sich darum bewerben woll(t)en ... Zu diesen Concursen (konnten) auch aus der Classe der Volks-Schullehrer solche zugelassen werden, die sich in ihren Schulen durch Gründlichkeit und Gewandtheit ihrer Lehrart, und durch genaue und wohlgeordnete Kenntnisse in den Realgegenständen vorzüglich auszeichne(te)n«.[68] Gegenstände dieser Prüfung waren Deutsch, Mathematik, Geschichte, Geographie, Naturlehre, Naturbeschreibung, Französisch, Kalligraphie, Zeichnen und zur Feststellung der »Lehrgeschicklichkeit«[69] eine Lehrprobe.

Mit den Ereignissen von 1816 endete abermals ein Abschnitt in der bayerischen Realschulgeschichte. Erneut war einer der seit 1774 zur Errichtung eines allgemeinbildenden und zur Hochschulreife führenden Realschulwesens unternommenen Versuche gescheitert. Gleichzeitig wurde der eben erst sich entwickelnde Stand akademisch gebildeter staatlicher Realschullehrer dem Zerfall preisgegeben.

3. Die Realschullehrerbildung in der Phase des Übergangs von der technischen Fachschule zur allgemeinbildenden Realschule

Nachdem der Staat mit der Errichtung der ›Polytechnischen Zentralschule‹ in München am 27. 9. 1827 in die Verantwortung für das Realschulwesen zurückgekehrt war, übernahm er am 29. 12. 1827 die Oberaufsicht über die Nürnberger polytechnische Schule und schuf so ein höheres realistisch-technisches Schulwesen. Die Basis hierfür sollten Fachschulcharakter tragende Gewerbeschulen abgeben, deren Errichtung König *Ludwig I.* (1825–1848) am 7. 2. 1829 »in allen größern Städten des Reichs«[70] befohlen hatte. Dies geschah bemerkenswerterweise einen Tag vor Unterzeichnung des von *Friedrich Wilhelm Thiersch* (1784–1860) verfaßten Schulplans, den nicht nur die von ihm als »Philanthropen, Pseudoliberale, Materialisten und Industrielle«[71] befehdeten Realisten als »Ausgeburt des Ultrahumanismus«[72] bekämpften, sondern über den auch »die öffentliche unparteiische Stimme der Nation ... eine scharfe Kritik ergehen (ließ)«.[72] Offensichtlich hielt selbst der Philhellene *Ludwig I.* angesichts der nach staatlicher Hilfe verlangenden Volkswirtschaft den Thierschen Schulplan mit seinem vereinseitigenden Intellektualismus und der Verabsolutierung der alten Sprachen für wenig geeignet, die notwendige Verbesserung eines über die Volksschule hinausgehenden und den Bedürfnissen von Industrie und Gewerbe genügenden Unterrichts auch tatsächlich leisten zu können.

Mit der Allerhöchsten Verordnung vom 16. 2. 1833, die ›Gewerbs- und polytechnischen Schulen betreffend‹, wurde die Ankündigung vom 7. 2. 1829 realisiert. Es entstand ein aus den dreiklassigen Landwirtschafts- und Gewerbeschulen, den dreiklassigen polytechnischen Schulen in Augsburg, München und Nürnberg sowie der ›Technischen Hochschule‹ bestehender Zug technischer Schulen, der gleichberechtigt neben das allgemeinbildende Schulwesen trat.

»Ein finanzielles wie ausbildungsmäßiges Problem stellte die Versorgung der neuen Anstalten mit tüchtigen Lehrern dar«.[74] Deshalb erschien auch bereits am 28. 3. 1833 mit der Ministerialentschließung, die ›Gesuche und Präsentationen zu Lehrstellen an den Gewerbs- und polytechnischen Schulen betreffend‹, eine vorläufige Prüfungsordnung. Sie machte die Anstellung an einer »Gewerbs- oder polytechnischen Schule ... (von einer) mit Erfolg bestandenen Prüfung«[75] abhängig, wovon nur der dispensiert war, der »durch wissenschaftliche Leistungen in dem betreffenden Fache sich bereits öffentlich legitimirt, und eine wissenschaftliche Celebrität sich erworben hat(te)«.[76] Der Bewerber konnte sich in einem oder auch in mehreren der Fächer Zeichnen, Enzyklopädie der Gewerbe, Mathematik, Physik, Naturgeschichte, Chemie, Produkten- und Warenkunde sowie Mechanik oder Maschinenlehre, Landwirtschaft, Ökonomie der Landwirtschaft und landwirtschaftliche Technologie prüfen lassen. Die Prüfung erstreckte sich »a) auf das gründliche Innhaben des Gegenstandes, als auch b) auf die Lehrgabe«.[77] Das Mittel aus beiden Leistungen ergab die Gesamtnote. Laut Prüfungsprotokoll der polytechnischen Schule München vom 5. 8. 1843 mußten pro Fach jeweils zehn Fragen schriftlich und mündlich beantwortet werden.[78] Abgesehen von einer gewissen Übergangszeit, in der sich neben ehemaligen

Aufbau des bayerischen Bildungswesens gemäß dem Schulreformplan vom 16. 2. bzw. 28. 3. 1833

Der bayerische Schulreformplan vom 16. 2. bzw. 28. 3. 1833

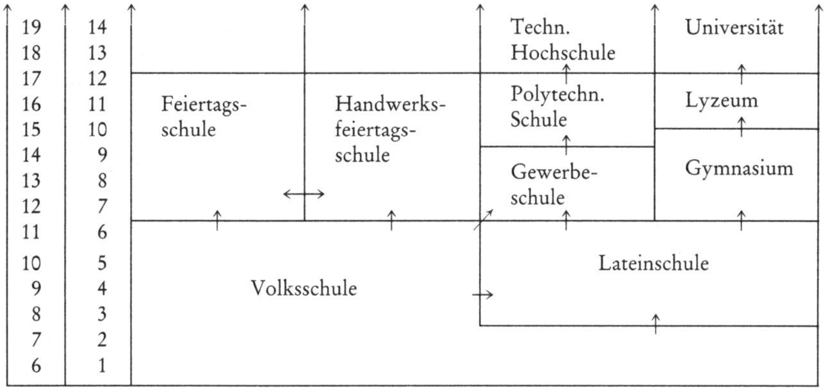

Quelle: Döllinger 9, 1838, 1509ff.
Regierungsblatt 1830, 877ff. und 1833, 1378ff.

Bürgerschullehrern auch Volksschullehrer zur Prüfung melden konnten, bildeten hervorragende Abschlüsse an Gewerbe- und polytechnischen Schulen die Zulassungsvoraussetzungen zur Staatsprüfung.

Die vorläufige Prüfungsordnung bekam durch die »von nun an allein giltige Vollzugs-Instruction«[79] vom 4. 4. 1836 ihre abschließende Fassung. Ihr zufolge mußte der Bewerber für das Lehramt am »technischen Gymnasium«[80] – so wurden die Landwirtschafts- und Gewerbeschulen fortan auch genannt – ab dem Jahr 1840 einen geregelten Studiengang nachweisen. Waren für den Gewerbeschullehrer Abschlüsse von Gewerbe- und polytechnischer Schule sowie ein einjähriges Studium an der ›Technischen Hochschule‹ erforderlich, so benötigte der angehende Landwirtschaftsschullehrer nebst einem Gewerbeschulabschluß und einem einjährigen Studium an der ›Technischen Hochschule‹ auch ein dreijähriges landwirtschaftliches Praktikum. Während ersterer sein Examen an einer polytechnischen Schule ablegte, wurde letzterer an der Staatswirtschaftlichen Fakultät der Universität München geprüft.

Die Anwärter des neu geschaffenen Realienlehramts mit den Fächern Deutsch, Geschichte und Geographie hatten sich der »von 2 zu 2 Jahren regelmäßig abgehalten werdenden Gymnasiallehramts-Prüfung zu stellen, und daselbst die specielle Prüfung über den von ihm vorzutragenden Realien-Gegenstand zu bestehen«.[81] Erstrebte jemand das Lehramt an den nunmehr als ›technische Lyzeen‹ bezeichneten polytechnischen Schulen, so mußte er ab 1842 »neben einer der drei polytechnischen Schulen auch die technische Hochschule mit Auszeichnung bestanden, und in der an der technischen Hochschule zu bestehenden Lehramtsprüfung die Note der sehr guten Befähigung zum Lehramte erhalten«[82] haben.

So trefflich diese Verordnungen auch waren, dem Realschullehrermangel vermochten sie kaum abzuhelfen. Obschon die Regierung den 24 Unterrichtsstunden erteilenden Lehrern »an Geld und sonstigen Emolumenten in Minimo 500 fl.«[83] zugestanden hatte, war deren Remuneration »so gering, daß ihr ganzes Leben ein beständiges Ringen mit Noth und Entbehrungen aller Art«[84] war. Die willkürliche und zumeist in das Belieben der Gemeinden gestellte Art der Besoldung wurde erst am 9. 5. 1851 beendet, als *König Max II.* (1848–1864) einen Landtagsbeschluß vollzog und den Realschullehrern eine gesicherte und von 600 fl. auf 1000 fl. ansteigende Besoldung gewährte. Welche Bedeutung dieser Maßnahme zukam, zeigt die Anzahl der in München und Nürnberg abgenommenen Prüfungen für das Lehramt an Landwirtschafts- und Gewerbeschulen: Während sich von 1833–1850 nur 74 Kandidaten anmeldeten und davon 57 bestanden, waren es von 1851–1868 immerhin 217 Anmeldungen und 185 mit Erfolg abgelegte Prüfungen.[85]
Im Zuge der seit 1849 offiziell laufenden Bemühungen um eine Reform der Gewerbeschulen verloren diese gemäß Allerhöchster Verordnung vom 14. 5. 1864, die ›Reorganisation der technischen Lehranstalten betreffend‹, das Übertrittsrecht an die polytechnische Schule an das neu geschaffene Realgymnasium.[86] Gleichzeitig wurden die bisher Fachschulcharakter tragenden Gewerbeschulen zu Anstalten umgeformt, die nunmehr »eine angemessene allgemeine Bildung«[87] vermittelten. »Ein wesentlicher Anteil an der Rückgewinnung von Berechtigungen und Ansehen für die Gewerbeschulen kam in der Folgezeit dem nachmaligen ‹Verein von Lehrern an technischen Unterrichtsanstalten Bayerns‹ zu, der ... (seit 1866) als Standesorganisation die Interessen der Gewerbeschule wahrte«.[88] (Buchinger 1983 a, 156). Bereits am 1. 10. 1870 erfolgte mit den ›Organischen Bestimmungen für die Gewerbeschulen in Bayern‹ die Rückkehr der Gewerbeschule in ein geschlossenes Schulsystem, das von der Volksschule über die Gewerbeschule und die am 3. 9. 1868 gegründete Industrieschule bis hin zur neuen ›Polytechnischen Schule‹ in München führte. Letztere war am 12. 4. 1868 an die Stelle der bisherigen polytechnischen Schule getreten und trug ab dem 6. 8. 1877 den Namen ›Technische Hochschule‹. Am 29. 4. 1877 erging mit Allerhöchster Verordnung, die ›Umbildung der Gewerbeschulen in Realschulen betreffend‹, die so lange ersehnte »Schulordnung für die Realschulen im Königreiche Bayern«.[89] Mit dieser allgemeinbildenden sechsklassigen Realschule hatte das realistische Unterrichtsprinzip »mehr als hundert Jahre nach seiner Einführung ... die schmerzlich entbehrte offizielle Anerkennung erfahren«.[90]
»Hand in Hand mit den schuladministrativen und -organisatorischen Veränderungen im realistischen Bildungswesen vollzog sich der Angleichungsprozeß an das gymnasiale Lehramt im Bereich der Gewerbeschullehrerbildung und die soziale Besserstellung des gesamten, an realistischen Schulen tätigen Lehrpersonals«.[91] Mit Allerhöchster Verordnung vom 24. 8. 1869, die ›Prüfungen für das Lehramt an technischen Unterrichtsanstalten betreffend‹, schuf die Regierung eine eigenständige Prüfungsordnung für den Unterricht an Gewerbe- und Industrieschulen bzw. Realgymnasien.
Bei den alljährlich in München stattfindenden Prüfungen konnten diese für die Lehrämter Mathematik, Naturwissenschaften, Realien (Deutsch, Geschichte, Ge-

ographie), Zeichnen und Modellieren sowie Handelswissenschaften abgelegt werden. Zulassungsvoraussetzungen für die ersten drei Lehrämter waren ein Gymnasialabschluß und ein Unversitäts- bzw. Hochschulstudium. Zur Realienlehramtsprüfung konnten »auch Lehramts-Candidaten, welche ihre Vorbildung an höhern Lehrerbildungsanstalten erhalten«[92] hatten, zugelassen werden. Während für das Lehramt im Zeichnen der Abschluß eines Gymnasiums, einer Latein- oder Gewerbeschule sowie der Besuch einer Kunstgewerbeschule und einer Kunstakademie Vorbedingung waren, benötigte der Kandidat der Handelswissenschaften noch den Nachweis einer »praktischen kaufmännischen Ausbildung«.[93] Neben einer schriftlichen Prüfung hatte jeder Lehramtsbewerber »über ein mindestens 24 Stunden vorher gegebenes Thema einen mündlichen Vortrag«[94] nebst Kolloquium zu halten und seine praktischen Fähigkeiten zu erweisen. Die hieraus für das jeweilige »Lehramt (mathematisches, naturwissenschaftliches, Realien-, Handels-Lehramt, für Ertheilung des Zeichnungs-Unterrichts«[95] anteilig zu bildenden und zur Anstellung führenden Befähigungsnoten lauteten:
I vorzüglich befähigt, II sehr gut befähigt und III gut befähigt. »Nach bestandener Prüfung hat(te) der Candidat seine praktische Befähigung entweder als Assistent an einer Unterrichtsanstalt oder durch Ertheilung von Privatunterricht, Verwendung in Laboratorien oder durch sonstige, durch glaubwürdige Zeugnisse nachweisbare Fortbildung zu vervollkommnen«.[96]
Das für die Realschullehrerbildung historische Datum ist jedoch der 26. 5. 1873. An diesem Tag erschien mit Königlich Allerhöchster Verordnung die ›Prüfungsordnung für das Lehramt an humanistischen und technischen Unterrichtsanstalten‹. Hatte es bisher für die Lehrämter gesonderte Prüfungsordnungen gegeben, so setzte die neue Prüfungsordnung nun in § 1 einheitliche Prüfungsbestimmungen fest: »Wer an einem humanistischen Gymnasium, einer Lateinschule oder einer technischen Unterrichtsanstalt (Realgymnasium, Industrieschule, Gewerbeschule, Handelsschule) als Lehrer verwendet werden will, hat sich den vorschriftsmäßigen Prüfungen zu unterziehen«.[97] Diese bestanden aus einem schriftlichen, einem mündlichen und einem an Münchner Studienanstalten zu erbringenden praktisch-didaktischen Teil. Während für die philologisch-historischen Fächer, die neueren Sprachen und die Realien eine Haupt- und eine Spezialprüfung gefordert waren, wobei letztere »eine freie, auf selbständiger Forschung beruhende Abhandlung«[98] umfaßte, begnügte man sich bei den übrigen Lehrämtern mit der Hauptprüfung. Obwohl für die einzelnen Lehrämter in der Regel der Gymnasialabschluß und ein drei- bis vierjähriges Universitätsstudium vorausgesetzt wurden, war für die Lehrämter der Mathematik und der Physik an den Gewerbeschulen nun auch der Abschluß einer Industrieschule als Zulassungsvoraussetzung anerkannt«.[99] Für das Realienlehramt genügte nach wie vor »statt des Gymnasialabsolutoriums das Schlußzeugnis eines Lehrerseminars mit der ersten Note«.[100] (Regierungsblatt 1873, 1023).
Die überragende Bedeutung der Prüfungsordnung von 1873 liegt in der weitgehenden Angleichung aller Lehrer hinsichtlich der Vor- und Ausbildung sowie der Examina. Aufgrund der Gleichstellung von Gymnasial- und Reallehrern verlieh König *Ludwig II.* »den wirklichen Lehrern der bestehenden Gewerbschulen«[101] mit Verordnung

vom 7. 1. 1875 »dieselben Rechte ..., welche in der neunten Beilage zur Verfassungs-Urkunde und in der Dienstespragmatik vom 1. Januar 1805 den Staatsdienern zugestanden«[102] worden waren. Die Verleihung des Titels ›Professor an der Realschule‹ für ältere und verdiente Reallehrer seitens der Staatsregierung war dafür ein weiterer Beleg. Die ›Prüfungsordnung für das Lehramt an humanistischen und technischen Unterrichtsanstalten‹ vom 21. 1. 1895 brachte nur noch einige inhaltliche und prozedurale Modifikationen und hob vor allem die Anforderungen in der pädagogischen Theorie und Praxis an. Letzteres geschah, soweit dies für das jeweilige Lehramt vorgeschrieben war, durch den Besuch eines pädagogisch-didaktischen Seminars.[103] Nach zwei vergeblichen Anläufen 1774 und 1808 und einem nahezu hundertjährigen Ringen hat die Realschullehrerbildung mit der Verordnung von 1873 schließlich ihre Form und der Realschullehrerstand die lang ersehnte Anerkennung und Gleichstellung mit dem Gymnasiallehrerstand gefunden.

Anmerkungen

1 Beyträge (1778), S. 163.
2 *Ebner* (1924), S. 1.
3 *Lurz* (1908), 2, S. 214.
4 Intelligenzblätter (1774), S. 256.
5 *Buchinger* (1983 a), S. 41.
6 *Zwerger* (1914), S. 41.
7 *Ickstatt* (1774), S. 24.
8 Vgl. *Braun* (1774), S. 124 ff.
9 Pragmatische Geschichte (1783), S. 84.
10 *Küffner* (1908), S. 8.
11 *Buchinger* (1983 a), S. 42.
12 *Braun* (1774), S. 306.
13 Ebenda, S. 304.
14 *Zwerger* (1914), S. 50 f.
15 Intelligenzblätter (1774), S. 281.
16 *Lurz* (1908), 2, S. 206.
17 *Zwerger* (1914), S. 38.
18 *Lurz* (1908), 2, S. 206.
19 *Zwerger* (1914), S. 77.
20 Ebenda, S. 78.
21 *Buchinger* (1983 a), S. 48.
22 *Lurz* (1908), 2, S. 250.
23 *Wolfram* (1892), Anm. 7, S. 90 f.
24 Beyträge (1778), S. 217.
25 *Lurz* (1908), 2, S. 238.
26 Ebenda.
27 Ebenda.
28 Ebenda.
29 Pragmatische Geschichte (1783), S. 273.
30 *Mayr* (1784), 2, S. 999.
31 *Kluckhohn* (1878), S. 54.
32 *Buchinger* (1983 a), S. 57.
33 *Zwerger* (1914), S. 159.
34 *Buchinger* (1983 a), S. 64.
35 Ebenda.
36 *Lurz* (1908), 2, S. 285.
37 Ebenda.
38 Vgl. *Gebele* (1896), S. 94 ff.
39 Regierungsblatt 1803, S. 416.
40 Vgl. *Mayr* (1802), 2, S. 268.
41 *Ebner* (1924), S. 22.
42 *Buchinger* (1983 a), S. 70.
43 *Wismayr* (1857), S. 18.
44 *Buchinger* (1983 a), S. 74.
45 Ebenda.
46 *Lurz* (1908), 2, S. 527.
47 Ebenda, S. 549.
48 Ebenda, S. 550.
49 Ebenda, S. 558.
50 *Buchinger* (1983 b), S. 16.
51 *Küffner* (1908), S. 27.
52 *Buchinger* (1983 a), S. 77.
53 Regierungsblatt 1809, S. 267.
54 *Buchinger* (1983 b), S. 16.

[55] *Widenbauer* (1927), S. 13.
[56] *Küffner* (1908), S. 74.
[57] Vgl. Regierungsblatt 1809, S. 1131 ff.
[58] Ebenda, S. 1642.
[59] Vgl. HStAM M Inn 19604.
[60] Regierungsblatt 1809, S. 1643.
[61] *Döllinger* (1838), S. 753.
[62] Ebenda, S. 751.
[63] Ebenda.
[64] *Giese* (1961), S. 84.
[65] Ebenda, S. 789.
[66] *Buchinger* (1983 a), S. 95.
[67] *Döllinger* (1938), S. 1685.
[68] Intelligenzblatt (1818), S. 371.
[69] Ebenda.
[70] *Döllinger* (1838), S. 1691.
[71] *Thiersch* (1829), S. 200.
[72] *Widenbauer* (1927), S. 21.
[73] *Thiersch* (1831), S. 32.
[74] *Buchinger* (1983 a), S. 140.
[75] *Döllinger* (1838), S. 1552.
[76] Ebenda.
[77] Ebenda, S. 1653.
[78] Vgl. HStAM MK 20946.
[79] *Döllinger* (1838), S. 1570.
[80] Ebenda, S. 1575.
[81] Ebenda, S. 1594.
[82] Ebenda, S. 1606.
[83] Ebenda, S. 1594.
[84] *Widenbauer* (1927), S. 58.
[85] Vgl. HStAM MK 20946, 20947, 20948.
[86] Vgl. Regierungsblatt 1864, S. 537 St.
[87] Ebenda, S. 546.
[88] *Buchinger* (1983 a), S. 156.
[89] Ministerialblatt 1877, S. 197.
[90] *Buchinger* (1983 a), S. 168.
[91] Ebenda, S. 162.
[92] Regierungsblatt 1869, S. 1659.
[93] Ebenda, S. 1662.
[94] Ebenda, S. 1656.
[95] Ebenda, S. 1669.
[96] Ebenda, S. 1672.
[97] Regierungsblatt 1873, S. 1007.
[98] Ebenda, S. 1011.
[99] *Buchinger* (1983 a), S. 164.
[100] Regierungsblatt 1873, S. 1023.
[101] Ministerialblatt 1875, S. 2.
[102] Ebenda.
[103] Vgl. Ministerialblatt 1895, S. 41.

Quellen- und Literaturverzeichnis

Quellen

Bayerisches Hauptstaatsarchiv München (HStAM):
1. Akten des Ministeriums des Innern: HStA MInn 19604
2. Akten des Kultusministeriums: HStA MK 20946, 20947, 20948
Churbaierische Intelligenzblätter für das Jahr 1774
Königlich-Baierisches Regierungsblatt 1803, 1809
Allgemeines Intelligenz-Blatt für das Königreich Baiern 1818
Regierungs-Blatt für das Königreich Bayern 1864, 1869, 1873
Ministerialblatt für Kirchen- und Schul-Angelegenheiten im Königreiche Bayern 1875, 1877, 1895
Döllinger, G. (1838): Sammlung der im Gebiete der inneren Staats-Verwaltung des Königreichs Bayern bestehenden Verordnungen, Bd. 9. München
Mayr, G. K. (Hrsg.) (1784/1799): Sammlung der Kurpfalz-Baierischen allgemeinen und besonderen Landes-Verordnungen, 6 Bde. München

Literatur

Beyträge zu einer Schul- und Erziehungsgeschichte in Baiern (1778): o. O.

Braun, H. (1774): Gedanken über die Erziehung und den öffentlichen Unterricht in Trivial-, Real- und lateinischen Schulen nach den katholischen Schulverfassungen Oberdeutschlands. Ulm

Buchinger, H. (1983a): Die Geschichte der bayerischen Realschule. Erster Teil. Die Entwicklung der bayerischen Realschule von ihren Anfängen bis zur Errichtung der Oberrealschule im Jahre 1907. Passau (Schriften der Universität Passau. Reihe Geisteswissenschaften. Bd. 4)

Buchinger, H. (1983b): Für den Bildungswert der Realien: Das Normativ von 1808. In: Schulreport. Tatsachen und Meinungen zur aktuellen Bildungspolitik in Bayern, 1983, H. 6. München

Ebner, E. (1924): Geschichte des Realschulwesens in Bayern. I. Teil: Von 1774 bis 1833. Festschrift. Hrsg. v. Bayerischen Realschulmännerverein anläßlich seines 50jährigen Bestehens. München und Berlin

Gebele, J. (1896): Das Schulwesen der königl. bayer. Haupt- und Residenzstadt München in seiner geschichtlichen Entwicklung und unter Berücksichtigung der älteren bayerischen Schulzustände aus archivalischen Quellen dargestellt. München

Giese, G. (1961): Quellen zur deutschen Schulgeschichte seit 1800. Göttingen

Ickstatt, J. A. Freiherr von (1774): Akademische Rede von der stufenmäßigen Einrichtung der niederen und höheren Landschulen in Rücksicht auf die churbaierischen Lande. In: Bock, Alfons (Hrsg.) (1916): Des Freiherrn von Ickstatt akademische Schulrede v. J. 1774. München (Päd. Quellenschriften, Heft 2)

Kluckhohn, A. (1878): Über das technische Unterrichtswesen in Bayern bis zur Gründung der polytechnischen Centralschule in München (1827). München

Küffner, K. (1908): Die bayerische Oberrealschule vor 100 Jahren. Ein Beitrag zur Geschichte des Allgemeinen Normativs von 1808 und des Realschulwesens. Nürnberg

Lurz, G. (1908): Mittelschulgeschichtliche Dokumente Altbayerns, einschließlich Regensburgs. Monumenta Germaniae Paedagogica, Bd. XLII. Berlin

Pragmatische Geschichte der Schulreformation in Baiern aus ächten Quellen. Frankfurt 1783

Thiersch, F. (1826/1829): Ueber gelehrte Schulen, mit besonderer Rücksicht auf Bayern, 3 Bde. Stuttgart und Tübingen

Thiersch, F. (1831): Geschichte des bayerischen Schulplans von 1829 und seiner Revision im Jahre 1830. Stuttgart und Tübingen

Widenbauer, G. (1927): Geschichte des bayerischen Realschulwesens von 1816 bis heute. München und Berlin

Wismayr, J. (1857): Meine Selbst-Biographie für Freunde und Freundlichgesinnte. Freysing

Wolfram, L. (1892): Heinrich Braun. Geboren 1732, gestorben 1792. Ein Beitrag zur Geschichte der Aufklärungsepoche in Bayern. München (Historische Abhandlungen aus dem Münchener Seminar. Hrsg. von Heigel, Th. und Grauert, H., Heft III)

Zwerger, F. (1914): Geschichte der realistischen Lehranstalten in Bayern. Monumenta Germaniae Paedagogica, Bd. LIII. Berlin

Albert Reble

Volksschullehrerbildung in der Weimarer Zeit

Für Elisabeth Neuhaus-Siemon zum 60. Geburtstag

Vorbemerkungen

Bei diesem Thema sind von vornherein zwei besondere Schwierigkeiten zu bedenken.

Erstens muß gesehen werden, daß es in den 14 Jahren der Weimarer Republik (Ende 1918 bis Anfang 1933) bei der Volksschullehrerbildung eigentlich mehr Abbau als Aufbau gegeben hat; jedenfalls ist bei dem, was als Volksschullehrerbildung von dieser Republik intendiert war und realisiert werden sollte, manches kaum über Anfänge hinausgekommen.

Zum Beispiel begann der Aufbau der Pädagogischen Akademien in Preußen erst 1926. Sie konnten sich also insgesamt nur sieben Jahre entwickeln, haben zum größten Teil aber wesentlich kürzere Zeit existiert, nämlich bloß drei, ja in manchen Fällen sogar nur ganze zwei Jahre. Denn 1926 nahmen erst drei Pädagogische Akademien (in Elbing, Kiel und Bonn) ihre Arbeit auf; und nachdem die Gesamtzahl bis 1930 auf fünfzehn gestiegen war, wurden im Zuge der Finanz- und Wirtschaftsmisere bereits 1932 nicht weniger als acht von ihnen wieder geschlossen, und von diesen acht hatten fünf nur von 1930–1932 bestanden.

Aber auch in Fällen kontinuierlicherer institutioneller Existenz – wie etwa in Hamburg, Braunschweig und Mecklenburg-Schwerin, wo die neue Volksschullehrerbildung 1927 begann – hat sie nur sechs Jahre gedauert, hat also in ihrer Arbeit nicht einmal die sieben Jahre der ersten preußischen Pädagogischen Akademien erreicht. Und selbst in denjenigen Ländern, die relativ früh zu gesetzlichen Neuregelungen gelangten – so Thüringen 1922 und Sachsen 1923 –, konnte der Aufbau frühestens 1923 (so in Jena und Dresden) oder 1924 (so in Leipzig) beginnen. Auch in diesen Fällen existierte die neue Lehrerbildung somit bis zum Ende der Weimarer Republik nicht einmal zehn Jahre. Und auch hier lief die alte seminaristische Volksschullehrerausbildung noch eine Reihe von Jahren – zwar ohne Neuaufnahmen – daneben weiter. Zum Beispiel wurden die Lehrerseminare in Sachsen erst 1928 geschlossen. Die neue Ausbildung der Volksschullehrer war somit auch in denjenigen Ländern des Reiches, in denen sie während der Weimarer Zeit neu geordnet wurde, nur relativ kurze Zeit in der Lage, das Feld ganz zu bestimmen, und konnte sich selbst hier kaum ausreichend entfalten.

Zweitens – und von der kurzen Dauer ganz abgesehen – bietet die Volksschullehrerbildung in der Weimarer Zeit ein *buntscheckiges und fast unübersichtliches Bild* unterschiedlicher Institutionen, Typenabwandlungen und Studiengänge. Es wäre also zu einfach, wenn man nur eine Form als maßgeblich bzw. als repräsentativ hinstellen würde. Dieses Faktum erschwert es, ein überschaubares Bild zu zeichnen, erst recht bei dem hier vorgegebenen engen zeitlichen Rahmen.

Andererseits und zugleich ist festzustellen: bei der Volksschullehrerausbildung hat sich *nie in so kurzer Zeit soviel ereignet* wie in der kurzen Zeitspanne der Weimarer Republik; und dabei handelt es sich um *einschneidende* Veränderungen. Ohne Übertreibung kann man sogar sagen: kaum ein anderer Beruf hat damals einen so tiefgreifenden Wandel seines Ausbildungsfeldes erfahren. Das hat ebenso komplexe wie gewichtige Gründe und Hintergründe; diese müssen deshalb genauer betrachtet werden. Und es ist selbst wiederum Ansatz für zahlreiche Probleme, die bis in die Gegenwart hineinreichen. Zugleich muß jedoch betont werden, daß das Geflecht von Fakten und Problemen, das hier zu skizzieren ist, selber *historischen Charakter* hat und in die *damalige* Zeit hineingestellt werden muß. Manche Fakten, Probleme und Argumente haben sich seit jener Zeit erheblich verschoben. Dem heutigen Betrachter ist damit die Aufgabe gestellt, jene Weimarer Zeit mit bewußt historischer Einstellung ins Auge zu fassen.
Ins Blickfeld zu rücken sind dabei zunächst die *Grundlagen und Hintergründe* für die damaligen Diskussionen, Entscheidungen und Wege. Dann muß kurz die *institutionelle Vielfalt* mit ihrer tatsächlichen Entwicklung beleuchtet werden. Und schließlich soll von *den Grundstrukturen und den Haupttypen* mit ihren (damaligen) Problemen die Rede sein.

I. Grundlagen und Hintergründe

Hierzug seien in aller Kürze folgende fünf Punkte genannt:
1. Die *rechtlich-politische Grundlage* dafür, daß sich bei der Volksschullehrerbildung in der Weimarer Zeit soviel getan hat, war bekanntlich der Artikel 143 Absatz 2 der Reichsverfassung vom 11. August 1919 mit seiner Formulierung:

»Die Lehrerbildung ist nach den Grundsätzen, die für die höhere Bildung allgemein gelten, für das Reich einheitlich zu regeln.«

Diese Fassung geht zurück auf *Richard Seyfert,* den nachmaligen sächsischen Kultusminister (1919-20) und späteren Direktor des Pädagogischen Instituts an der Dresdener TH., einen alten Kämpfer für die akademische Volksschullehrerausbildung. Auf seinen Antrag wurde die Formulierung von der Weimarer Nationalversammlung mit großer Mehrheit angenommen. Jede Gruppe oder Partei hätte sich damals mit einem Eintreten für das überkommene Lehrerseminar wohl auch starker Kritik ausgesetzt und wäre in allgemeinen Mißkredit geraten. Andererseits korreliert mit dieser Breite der Zustimmung der Umstand, daß die Formulierung sehr allgemein gehalten war, sich als eine Art Kompromiß präsentieren konnte und manche Fragen offen ließ.

Zum Beispiel wurde nur durch mündliche Erklärung des Berichterstatters vor der Abstimmung auf Anfrage festgestellt bzw. festgesetzt, daß dabei die Ausbildung der Lehrer an Volksschulen, mittleren und höheren Schulen gemeint war, also nicht etwa auch die der Lehrer an Fortbildungsschulen oder an anderen speziellen Bildungsgängen. Immerhin waren damit trotz der vagen Formulierung »Lehrer« und angesichts der zusätzlichen mündlichen Fixierung die Lehrerausbildungsgänge für die grundlegenden, allgemeinbildenden Schulen in allen drei Sparten gemeinsam angezielt, und zwar wurden sie hier in bezug auf die Ausbildungsgrundsätze klar zusammengeordnet – was doch nur heißen konnte, daß die allgemeine Vorbildung für die Berufsausbildung bei allen drei Gruppen gleich sein sollte, also höhere Schule und Abitur erforderte. Die institutionelle Regelung ihrer Berufsbildung selbst wurde allerdings nicht ausdrücklich genannt, war aber mindestens für die Gymnasiallehrer ja eindeutig und traditionell die Universität. Da das jedoch nicht für alle drei Lehrersparten expressis verbis festgelegt wurde, und da es in der damaligen Diskussion für die Volksschullehrer in diesem Punkte bereits längere Zeit konkurrierende Vorstellungen gab, schien es beinahe offen zu bleiben.[1]

An der Verfassungsformulierung hängt ferner das Faktum, daß die akademische Volksschullehrerbildung, an deren Niveau und Vorbildungsanspruch eigentlich kein Zweifel mehr bestehen konnte, durch die Verfassung noch nicht unmittelbar geltendes Recht wurde, sondern nur zur *Richtschnur* und zum *Prinzip der künftigen Reichsgesetzgebung* gemacht war (wie dies durch das Reichsgericht dann 1926 auch in aller Form bestätigt wurde). Das war zwar viel: nämlich bindende Richtlinie; es war aber auch wenig: nämlich eben bloße Richtlinie für ein künftiges Reichsgesetz. Was bis zum Erlaß einer solchen Reichsregelung bei den einzelnen Ländern geschah, hatte rechtlich sozusagen vorläufigen Charakter und konnte, wenn es diesem Prinzip nicht entsprach, durch Reichsgesetz annulliert werden – jedoch eben nur und erst durch solche reichsgesetzliche Regelung. Bis dahin hatten die Länder freie Hand – immerhin konnte man doch wohl meinen, daß dieser ihrer Freiheit durch jene Richtlinie bereits der Rahmen abgesteckt war. Rein rechtlich war es jedoch laut Reichsgerichtsurteil vom 19. 5. 1926 sogar zulässig, wenn bis zur reichsgesetzlichen Regelung auf den Anspruch der allgemeinen Hochschulreife als Grundlage der Berufsausbildung der Volksschullehrer verzichtet wurde, und so schien es rechtlich auch zulässig, wenn man sich mit einer Fortführung der alten seminaristischen Lehrerbildung »vorerst« begnügte.

Während in der *Reichsschulkonferenz* von 1920 dann zwar noch Einigkeit über den notwendigen Abbau der überkommenen Lehrerseminare und über die allgemeine Hochschulreife als erforderliche Berufsbildungsbasis zu bestehen schien, wurde in diesem Gremium um die Frage »Universitätslösung« oder »PH-Lösung« für die berufliche Ausbildung heftig gestritten, und eine Einigung oder auch nur eine Annäherung der Standpunkte kam nicht in Sicht, zumal die Universitäten sich damals zum großen Teil auch nicht bereit zeigten, die Ausbildung der Volksschullehrer mit zu übernehmen. Eduard Sprangers literarische Initiative (*Spranger* (1919/20)) mit ihrer entschiedenen, bildungstheoretisch unterbauten wie auch überhöhten Abwehr gegen das Eindringen dieses Ausbildungsganges in die Universität hat die Auseinandersetzung ebenfalls verschärft, sie aber keinesfalls erst geschaffen.

Dagegen wurde die von der Verfassung geforderte Regelung »für das Reich einheitlich« *auf der politischen Ebene* zunächst ernsthaft angestrebt und auch in die Wege geleitet: das Reichsministerium des Innern verhandelte in den ersten Jahren der Republik mit den Vertretern der Länder über gangbare Wege und über einen – sehr allgemein gehaltenen – Entwurf des entsprechenden Reichsgesetzes. Dabei schoben sich nun als *weiterer Problemkomplex* die *finanziellen* Schwierigkeiten in den Weg (vgl. hierzu *Sandfuchs* (1978), S. 77ff., auch *Weber* (1982)). Der Neuaufbau der akademischen Volksschullehrerbildung ließ ja in mehrfacher Hinsicht Mehrkosten gegenüber der alten Lehrerbildung erwarten (Personal- und Sachausstattung für Aufbau und für Fortführung; Beihilfen und Stipendien für sozial Schwache, denen gleichwohl der Weg zum Volksschullehramt nicht versperrt werden sollte; Besoldungsanhebung bei den akademisch ausgebildeten zukünftigen Volksschullehrern und -lehrerinnen); und die allgemeine Rechtslage verlangte, daß bei Zuweisung neuer Aufgaben an die Länder und die Kommunen die Beteiligung des Reiches an den Kosten gesetzlich geregelt werden mußte. Damit war die finanzielle Regelung eigentlich sachliche Voraussetzung für ein reichseinheitliches Lehrerbildungsgesetz, wie es von der Verfassung gefordert war. *Dadurch war ein Teufelskreis geschaffen.* Denn die Kosten ließen sich nicht nur nicht einmal annähernd abschätzen, sie ließen sich auch nicht einvernehmlich regeln, da einerseits die Länder (verständlicherweise) dabei das Reich möglichst weitgehend beteiligen wollten und da andererseits das Reich sich bei seiner damaligen desolaten finanziellen Situation (bedingt durch wirtschaftliche Misere, Inflation und Alliiertenforderungen) gar nicht imstande sehen konnte, sich finanziell (über allenfalls in Aussicht zu stellende Beihilfen und Stipendien hinaus) zu beteiligen – ganz abgesehen davon, daß eine Verständigung über die Kostenprobleme wiederum Einvernehmen über Strukturfragen der Lehrerbildung voraussetzte. So war trotz des ernsthaften und respektgebietenden Engagements mancher Beteiligten das dann Anfang 1923 eingetretene Scheitern der Bemühungen um eine reichseinheitliche Regelung schon von vornherein eigentlich programmiert und kaum abzuwenden.[2]

Dieser Prozeß mit dem traurigen Ende kann hier nicht im Detail nachgezeichnet werden, aber folgender Punkt muß klargestellt werden: es wäre viel zu einfach, wenn man es so sehen würde, als sei die von der Reichsverfassung postulierte einheitliche Gesetzesregelung über die strukturellen Grundsatzfragen der Lehrerbildung – die eigentlich sogar die Lehrer aller drei Schularten grundlegender Bildung betreffen sollte – an den *finanziellen* Problemen gescheitert. Man muß vielmehr umgekehrt sagen: die damalige finanzielle Elendssituation war geradezu der Prüfstein für die Frage, ob die Länder zu einer Reform der Volksschullehrerbildung, genauer und schärfer formuliert: zum Handeln in Konformität mit der Reichsverfassung in diesem Punkte, wirklich fähig und bereit waren. Der Verlauf der Verhandlungen im Jahre 1922 zeigt eindeutig, daß diese Bereitschaft der Länder sehr verschieden groß, ja in manchen Fällen sehr gering bzw. kaum vorhanden war. Im Februar 1922 wollten manche Länder (Bayern, Preußen und ein paar kleinere) die Neuordnung absolut von der Kostenübernahme durch das Reich abhängig machen, andere hingegen (vor allem Sachsen, Thüringen, Hessen) drängten auf jeden Fall zur Neuordnung, auch wenn das Reich zur Übernahme von Kosten nicht in der Lage war. Vom Februar 1922 über Dezember 1922 bis zum Februar 1923 verschoben und verhärteten sich die Fronten dann dahin, daß jetzt Sachsen, Thüringen, Hessen, Hamburg, Bremen, Braunschweig und Lippe doch zu einem bestimmten Minimalkonsens – wenn auch noch ohne feste rechtliche Bindung – für die Volksschullehrerbildung im akademischen Sinne bereit waren (allgemeine Hochschulreife, Berufsstudium mit zwei Jahren Mindestdauer auf

einer Hochschule und einem mit der Hochschule verbundenen pädagogischen Institut), während an der auf diese Vereinbarung zielenden Besprechung die Vertreter von Oldenburg, Mecklenburg, Baden nur noch als Gäste und andere Länder (u. a. Bayern und Preußen) überhaupt nicht mehr teilnahmen (vgl. *Sandfuchs* (1978), S. 81 u. 88). Die Vermutung von *Sandfuchs,* daß Preußen seine Vorstellungen und Absichten in diesem Kreise wohl nicht offenlegen und preisgeben wollte, ist sicher nicht abwegig, sie muß nach den gründlichen Untersuchungen *Rita Webers* zur Entwicklung in Preußen (*Weber* (1982)) aber ergänzt und relativiert werden durch einen Hinweis auf das Faktum, daß in Preußen damals noch alles in der Schwebe und nicht einmal das Abitur als Ausbildungsgrundlage gesichert war, weil der Finanzminister sich noch vehement dagegen zur Wehr setzte (vgl. *Weber* (1982), S. 350f. u. S. 352ff.). Im Falle Bayerns ist jedoch zu sagen, daß in seiner durchweg ablehnenden Haltung bei den Verhandlungen eine entschiedene Reformunwilligkeit ihren Ausdruck fand, die sich mehrfach belegen läßt (vgl. *Renner* (1979) und s. u.) und für die ein deutliches Signal schon dadurch gesetzt wurde, daß Bayern den Abbau seiner alten Lehrerseminare 1922 wieder einstellte (*Führ* (1970), S. 77; *Sandfuchs* (1978), S. 84).
Hinter diesen Frontbildungen bei den Ländern standen zweifellos auch, aber eben keinesfalls nur und wohl nicht einmal in erster Linie finanzielle Fragen und Sorgen. In hohem Maße wirkten dabei, wie mir scheint, *konfessionelle* Gesichtspunkte sowie – vielfach damit verquickt – *allgemeine konservativ-restaurative* Tendenzen mit. Diese enge Verflechtung war anscheinend besonders dominant in Bayern und wurde hier noch angereichert durch einen kräftigen Schuß Besonderheitsstreben mit dem Aushängeschild »Eigenrecht und Eigenständigkeit« des »gewachsenen Bildungswesens dieses Landes« gegenüber einer befürchteten zentralistischen Bevormundung aus Berlin. Daß angesichts so unterschiedlicher Reformbereitschaft der Länder die Finanzprobleme auch noch als taktisches Moment benutzt und entsprechend variabel eingesetzt werden konnten – zumal sie eine sehr schwammige Größe waren –, liegt auf der Hand und darf im Gesamtfeld der damaligen Verhandlungen und Entscheidungen nicht übersehen werden. Daß es außerdem in den zwanziger Jahren, ganz besonders in deren erster Zeit, fast überall einen großen Überschuß an Lehramtsanwärtern gab[3], konnte die Reformlust und den Aufbaueifer für die Lehrerbildung ebenfalls nicht gerade beflügeln und gab erst recht den Reformunwilligen mit ihrer Verzögerungstaktik die willkommene Gelegenheit, das Aufschieben der Reform sachlich begründet erscheinen zu lassen. Und im Hinblick auf die schon länger existierenden Diskussionen und Differenzen ist der Artikel 143 Abs. 2 selbst wohl schon als eine taktisch geschickte Formulierung zu werten, die freilich den Streit um die Form der akademischen Volksschullehrerbildung nicht beseitigen konnte und die zudem rechtlich und politisch eben nur den Ansatz für die Realisierung schuf.
2. Als ein ganz wesentlicher Hintergrund für die Akademisierungsbemühungen bei der Volksschullehrerausbildung ist ferner die *Volksschullehrerbewegung* anzusehen, die schon in der ersten Hälfte des 19. Jahrhunderts entstanden, im Laufe des 19. Jahrhunderts dann zu einer beachtlichen gesellschaftlichen Macht mit Profil und Dynamik geworden war. Während sich im gymnasialen Bereich zwar auch Lehrervereine

und -verbände bildeten, sich aber niemals eine Lehrerbewegung entwickelt hat, kann, ja muß bei der Volksschullehrerschaft wirklich von einer Bewegung gesprochen werden. Dabei bildeten sich regional (Norddeutschland–Süddeutschland) und weltanschaulich (z. B. Diesterweg – Dörpfeld – Bayerischer Lehrerverein u. ä.) wohl unterschiedliche Tönungen heraus, aber es formierte sich eine große einheitliche Stoßrichtung. Zu dieser Bewegung der Volksschullehrerschaft gehört ein ganzer Komplex von unterschiedlichen Motivationen, beruflichen und persönlichen Problemen und Nöten. In ihr verflochten sich aufs engste miteinander zum Beispiel das Bedürfnis nach Geselligkeit, ernstes Fortbildungsstreben, persönlicher Bildungshunger und Berufseifer mit defizitärer Grundbefindlichkeit, ferner massives Standesbewußtsein und sozialer Aufstiegswille, aber auch ein Gefühl von der Verantwortung und der Würde des Amtes, das Bewußtsein vom Eigenrecht und von der Bedeutung der Erziehungsaufgabe und nicht zuletzt das Bedürfnis nach voller geistiger Mündigkeit der Lehrerschaft und nach Befreiung von dem Druck teils obrigkeitsstaatlich-bürokratischer und feudalistisch-hierarchischer, teils frömmelnd-patriarchalischer Gängelung. Aus diesem Komplex heraus entstanden in der Volksschullehrerschaft die lauten Rufe in die Öffentlichkeit hinein, zum Beispiel mit der Forderung nach einer allgemeinen Staatsschule, nach Abschaffung der Patronatsrechte und der geistlichen Schulaufsicht, nach einer einheitlichen Schulorganisation, nach wirtschaftlicher und geistiger Hebung des Lehrerstandes und nicht zuletzt nach Verbesserung der Lehrerausbildung.

Es wäre eine ebenso arrogante wie sachunkundige Versimpelung, wenn man das alles einfach auf maßlosen Standesehrgeiz zurückführen wollte. Daß dabei eine gehörige Portion von sozialem Druckgefühl und Standesehrgeiz mitspielte, kann zwar nicht bestritten werden; doch muß man dazu mitbedenken, daß beim Volksschullehrer noch Ende des 19. Jahrhunderts ein geradezu schreiendes Mißverhältnis bestand zwischen der ihm in seinem Amt und Tun abgeforderten geistigen Leistung und persönlichen Verantwortung auf der einen Seite und der ihm zuteil werdenden Berufseinschätzung und Bezahlung auf der anderen Seite. *Friedrich Wilhelm Dörpfeld* (1824–93), einer der führenden Geister in der damaligen Lehrerbewegung, hat die soziale und finanzielle Stellung der Volksschullehrer um 1890 so geortet: sie gehörten damals noch mitten hinein in die Masse der *unteren* Beamten und ordneten sich dabei zwischen folgenden großen Gruppen ein: »etwas *unter* ihnen standen im Gehalt die Amtsdiener, die Gewichtsetzer, die Bootsführer, Matrosen und Heizer, aus der Eisenbahnverwaltung die Portiers, Billetschaffner und Weichensteller, ebenso die Schuldiener bei höheren Lehranstalten und Lehrerseminaren, die Büro- und Hausdiener. Etwas *über* ihnen standen dann u. a. die Wiesenmeister, die Schleusenmeister, die unteren Schiffahrts- und Hafenbeamten, die Kastellane und Hilfspedelle (wohl der Hochschulen), die Gerichtsdiener und Gefangenenaufseher und die Kreis- und Polizeiboten« (*Reble* (1958), S. 63). Die Volksschullehrer wurden also wirtschaftlich und gesellschaftlich in absoluter Subalternität gehalten und rangierten zum Beispiel ganz weit unterhalb der Gruppe der Gymnasiallehrer; und wenn diese damals schon mit Vehemenz darum kämpften, den Richtern und entsprechenden juristischen Beamten gleichgestellt zu werden, die ebenfalls ein Universitätsstudium absolviert hatten, dann kann man erst recht den ungeheueren wirtschaftlichen und sozialen Druck verstehen, dem sich die Volksschullehrer ausgesetzt fühlten, wobei ihre untergeordnete Dienststellung gegenüber den sie oft amtlich beaufsichtigenden Geistlichen und ihre vielfach zu leistenden subalternen Kirchen- und Gemeindedienste als noch verschärfende Momente zu bedenken sind.

In dieses Bild gehört als angemessener Verengungs- und Einpassungsfaktor auch das Lehrerseminar, inhaltlich wie strukturell und auch atmosphärisch. Was das Lehrerseminar nicht nur zur Disziplinierung und »Einpassung« der jungen Geister, sondern auch zur Weckung ihres pädagogischen Ethos, zur Ausbildung und Stabilisierung der Berufsgesinnung und zur Einführung in die Unterrichtspraxis im Sinne und Stile einer handwerklichen Meisterlehre geleistet hat, auch daß es oft eine Aufstiegschance für begabte Söhne kleiner Leute bot, darf hier keineswegs gering geschätzt werden. Aber das alles war erkauft bzw. korrelierte mit einer frühen Berufsentscheidung, mit einer Verflechtung von Allgemeinbildung und Berufsbildung ohne wirkliche Gründlichkeit, mit geistiger Enge und mit Abgesperrtsein, nicht zuletzt durch den Internatsbetrieb und seine Gefahr des Festhaltens in unfreier Haltung, mit der Überbetonung des methodisch-handwerklichen Elements im pädagogischen Bereich usw.
So mußte die alte seminaristische Lehrerausbildung in der Volksschullehrerbewegung zu einem besonderen Stein des Anstoßes werden.[4] Das Verlangen nach Verbesserung der allgemeinen Grundbildung und der beruflichen Ausbildung war in der Lehrerschaft daher allgemein und machte sich besonders lautstark bemerkbar, wie schon die zahlreichen einschlägigen Publikationen aus den Kreisen der Lehrerschaft vor 1918 und die vielen Diskussionen und Beschlüsse auf Lehrerversammlungen bereits seit 1848 eindrucksvoll zeigen. Man forderte dabei einhellig eine stufenmäßige und institutionelle Abtrennung von Allgemeinbildung und Berufsbildung, mit einem höheren Niveau der Allgemeinbildung, auf der die berufliche Ausbildung anzusetzen habe.
Es gab aber unterschiedliche Vorstellungen von der anzustrebenden Lösung, wobei besonders das Verhältnis von Theorie und Praxis, die Rolle des musischen Feldes, soziale Rekrutierungsfragen, vorzugsweise auch konfessionelle Gesichtspunkte eine Rolle spielten. Schon seit der Mitte des 19. Jahrhunderts profilierten sich dadurch verschiedene Gruppen innerhalb der Lehrerschaft. Die einen zielten darauf, daß der angehende Volksschullehrer eine höhere Bürger- oder Realschule absolvieren und von dieser mittleren allgemeinen Bildungsstufe aus dann ein erheblich verbessertes Lehrerseminar im Sinne und auf der Stufe einer höheren Fachschule durchlaufen sollte. Andere plädierten für den Abschluß einer höheren Schule als allgemeinbildender Basis und forderten als darauf aufbauende berufsbildende Stufe eine Fachhochschule, eine »Pädagogische Akademie«. Die dritte Gruppe verlangte in stärkerer institutioneller Angleichung an den Bildungsgang der anderen akademischen Berufe den Weg durch die höhere Schule und die Universität, wobei in Abwehr einseitiger Vertheoretisierung vielfach gleichzeitig an eine Reform der Universität gedacht wurde (zur genaueren Analyse dieser Hintergründe vgl. *Reble* (1958)).
In den großen Lehrerorganisationen, besonders im Deutschen Lehrerverein, verstärkte sich allmählich die Tendenz zur Universitätsausbildung. Sie wurde dann fest und programmatisch verankert in seinem Königsberger Beschluß von 1904 (was aus manchen Zusammenhängen heraus plausibel erscheinen kann, vgl. *Reble* (1958), S. 61 ff.). In dem Beschluß von 1904 hieß es: »Die Universität als Zentralstelle wissenschaftlicher Arbeit ist die geeignetste, durch keine andere Einrichtung vollwertig zu ersetzende Stätte für die Volksschullehrerbildung« (*Pretzel* (1921), S. 258; vgl.

auch *Sandfuchs* (1978), S. 28ff.). Mit Vehemenz wurde nun also von der Lehrerschaft – jedenfalls von ihrer organisierten Repräsentanz in der Öffentlichkeit – die traditionelle wissenschaftliche Hochschule als Ort der beruflichen Ausbildung angestrebt. Sie erschien ihr als Ausweg aus dem »geistigen Ghetto« *(E. Weniger)* und als Befreiung aus den »Hinterhäusern der Wissenschaft« *(Joh. Tews)*, in die sie sich beim Lehrerseminar eingesperrt fühlte. Die Nähe der Gymnasiallehrerausbildung und der Glanz der Wissenschaft ließen bei vielen die beiden großen Problem- und Aufgabenfelder »musisch-manueller Bereich« und »schulpraktische Ausbildung« eher in den Hintergrund treten; bei anderen verband sich mit dem Postulat der Universitätslösung zugleich die Forderung nach Universitätsreform, um den genannten beiden Problembereichen auch in der Universität eine Heimstatt zu schaffen. Jedenfalls trug die Stoßkraft der Lehrerbewegung wesentlich dazu bei, nach 1918 den tiefgreifenden Wandel in der Volksschullehrerbildung herbeizuführen.

3. Als weitere Kraft, die den alten Seminarausbildungsstil unhaltbar werden ließ, ist die *reformpädagogische Bewegung* zu nennen. Sie veränderte die pädagogische Situation in einschneidender Weise, und aus ihren zahlreichen Ansätzen und Impulsen, Auseinandersetzungen und Widersprüchen heraus entstanden für den Lehrer gravierende pädagogische, didaktisch-methodische und geistige Probleme, Orientierungs-, Haltungs- und Handlungsschwierigkeiten und -aufgaben, denen die seminaristische Ausbildung kaum gewachsen sein konnte und jedenfalls nicht angemessen war. Zu ihr gehörte ja das handwerklich strukturierte Darstellen und Vermitteln, Anlernen und Tradieren, eine Art Rezeptpädagogik des herbartianischen oder eines anderen praktikablen pädagogischen Systems, das fest übernommen und »gehandhabt« werden konnte. Die reformpädagogische Bewegung stellte dies jedoch gerade in Frage und brachte mit ihren Herausforderungen, ihren heterogenen Reformthesen und Theoriebildungen für den Lehrer eine entsprechend große Verunsicherung und einen hohen Reflexions- und Sichtungs-, Beurteilungs- und Entscheidungsbedarf, der ihn bedrängen mußte und der nur mit entsprechender geistiger Flexibilität und Souveränität bewältigt werden konnte; und die mußte kritisch-wissenschaftlich mitfundiert und abgestützt sein. Das Lehrerseminar hatte die Volksschullehrerschaft mit dem Herbartianismus wohl an die untere Grenze der pädagogisch-wissenschaftlichen Orientierung heran – aber noch nicht in sie hineingeführt und hatte dem hohen Reflexionsanspruch der Erziehungswissenschaft aus zahlreichen Gründen noch nicht gerecht werden können. Doch es ging da nicht etwa nur um das Reflektieren und um sein theoretisches Niveau, sondern ebenso sehr um pädagogische Sensibilität und Beweglichkeit, um didaktische Phantasie und um methodischen Wagemut, um persönliches Sicheinlassen, um Freudigkeit und offene Haltung im erziehlichen Tun und um Erprobungskraft. Die reformpädagogischen Impulse waren ja weitgehend gerade aus pädagogisch sensiblen und pädagogisch wagemutigen Volksschullehrern und aus ihrem Unbehagen an der »alten Schule« erwachsen. Und es ist wohl zugleich kein Zufall, daß das alte Lehrerseminar, von wenigen Ausnahmen abgesehen, eigentlich nicht an ihnen beteiligt war. Diese Impulse mußten jedoch nun nicht nur auf der wissenschaftlich-theoretischen Ebene mit wahrgenommen und abgeklärt werden; sie konnten auch nur mit wissenschaftlich-kritisch abgestützter praktisch-pädagogischer

Haltung in die Schularbeit selbst breiter hineingeführt, umsichtig verarbeitet und produktiv weiterentwickelt werden. Die Volksschullehrerbildung, ja alle Lehrerbildung stand dank der reformpädagogischen Bewegung somit unweigerlich unter der Aufgabe und dem Zwang, die angehenden Lehrer zu größerer pädagogisch-didaktischer Aufgeschlossenheit und Urteilsfähigkeit zu führen und zugleich mit ihr eine besonnen-tatkräftige pädagogische Handlungs- und Verantwortungsbereitschaft in ihnen zu wecken. In dieser Richtung waren neue, ebenso anspruchsvolle wie problembeladene Wege für die Lehrerbildung zu suchen und zu erproben. Und sie mußte deshalb selbst mit dem Öl der reformpädagogischen Bewegung gesalbt sein.

4. Als weiterer Punkt ist bei dem Hintergrund für die neue Volksschullehrerbildung in Korrespondenz zur reformpädagogischen Bewegung und zu ihren Anforderungen an den Lehrer die *Entwicklung der pädagogischen Theorie* zu beachten. Im Zuge der allgemeinen Wissenschaftsentwicklung, aber gerade auch im Zusammenhang mit der Entwicklung der praktischen pädagogischen Fragen, des pädagogischen Reformbemühens und der Schulprobleme bildete sich allmählich seit Ende des 19. Jahrhunderts eine relativ selbständige Erziehungswissenschaft heraus, mit einer Vielfalt von Ansätzen, Perspektiven und Richtungen (mehr empirisch-psychologisch oder mehr philosophisch akzentuiert, etwa neukantianisch oder geisteswissenschaftlich-historisch oder mehr religiös orientiert), für die hier eine ganze Reihe von Namen zu nennen wäre (vgl. *Reble* (¹⁴1987), S. 336ff.). Wenn man den weiteren, rasanter verlaufenen Entwicklungsprozeß bedenkt, handelte es sich dabei gewiß noch um relativ bescheidene Ansprüche, um Anfänge, Versuche und Erprobungen; doch immerhin war bis etwa 1920 schon eine beachtliche Dynamik und Entfaltungspotenz in diesem Bereich sichtbar geworden. Besonders fällt dabei ins Gewicht, daß diese Erziehungswissenschaft – zumal bei der damals entstehenden Dominanz der geisteswissenschaftlichen Pädagogik – sich selbst prononciert als Theorie für eine pädagogische Praxis verstand und also von der wissenschaftlichen Reflexion und Forschung her die pädagogische Orientierung und Verantwortung des angehenden Lehrers für Schule und Unterricht mit zu stützen und zu steuern im Sinne hatte und sich dazu auch vom Ansatz her in der Lage sah. Damit konnte sich das traditionelle Defizit an pädagogischer Theorie und an Lebensbezug bei den deutschen Universitäten spürbar weiter vermindern, und das Wechselspiel von Ämterbedarf und Wissenschaftsentwicklung konnte sich für einen Neuaufbau der Volksschullehrerbildung positiv auswirken. Was von der reformpädagogischen Bewegung her als notwendige Konsequenz erscheinen mußte, legte sich auch von der Wissenschaftsentwicklung her nahe: daß die Volksschullehrerausbildung den unmittelbaren Anschluß an das Leben der pädagogischen Wissenschaft gewann, wie umgekehrt diese Wissenschaft wiederum für ihre Lebendigkeit und Fortentwicklung eine engere Beziehung zur pädagogischen Praxis, zum Bildungswesen und zum Schulunterricht dringend brauchte.

5. Schließlich – aber keineswegs bloß am Rande – gehört zum Hintergrundkomplex für die Volksschullehrerbildung in der Weimarer Republik die Frage, welche Bezüge zwischen der nach 1918 aufzubauenden *demokratischen Grundordnung* und dem breiten Bereich Volksbildung, Volksschule, Volksschullehramt bestehen. Wenn die Reste einer halbfeudalen Gesellschaftsordnung beseitigt oder wenigstens zurückge-

drängt werden sollten, wurde dadurch das genannte Aufgabenfeld ganz erheblich berührt. Eine politische Ordnung, die in aller Form das Volk zum Souverän erhob, konnte wirkliches Leben und innere Stabilität nur dann gewinnen, wenn das Volk in seiner Gesamtheit von Jugend auf durch eine entsprechende Orientierung und Führung, Erziehung und Schulbildung diese große Aufgabe und Verantwortung richtig sehen und erfahren, sie in sich hineinnehmen und üben lernte. Das verlangte aber gebieterisch auch in der Volksschule eine Weckung voller politischer und menschlich-persönlicher Mündigkeit, eine Anbahnung selbständigen Denkens und Urteilens. Damit der Lehrer diese Aufgabe vernünftig angehen und lösen konnte, mußte er selbst entsprechend mündig und persönlich wie geistig souverän sein. Damit war den Lehrern aller Schularten, aber gerade auch dem Volksschullehrer eine höhere Verantwortung als bisher auferlegt und eine dafür ausreichende Zurüstung abgefordert – wodurch sich übrigens auch das Verbindende und Gemeinsame bei den pädagogischen Aufgaben *aller* Schularten und Schulstufen im Kindes- und Jugendalter verstärken mußte, also alle Lehrersparten der Nation von ihrer Aufgabe her mehr innere Tuchfühlung miteinander erhielten und somit auch die traditionell so großen gesellschaftlichen Unterschiede samt wechselseitigen sozialen Vorurteilen abzubauen hatten. Subaltern-unfreie Haltung konnte dafür keinesfalls in Frage kommen, und auch der Ausbildungsgang der Volksschullehrer hatte dem Rechnung zu tragen.
Alle diese Hintergründe und größeren Zusammenhänge ließen die Akademisierung der Volksschullehrerausbildung nach 1918 nicht nur sinnvoll und wünschenswert erscheinen, sie machten diesen tiefgreifenden Wandel direkt notwendig.

II. Institutionelle Vielfalt

Da schon bald abzusehen war, daß das in der Reichsverfassung postulierte einheitliche Reichsrahmengesetz nicht zustande kommen würde, und da die konkrete Gesetzgebungskompetenz im Bildungswesen ohnehin bei den Ländern lag, drohten die Bemühungen um die Neuordnung relativ früh entsprechend den in den einzelnen Ländern jeweils maßgeblichen, eventuell ja auch wechselnden politischen Kräften auseinanderzudriften.[5] Die Entwicklung vollzog sich dann sowohl in verschiedener Richtung wie auch in unterschiedlichem Tempo. Das bunte Bild, das dabei entstand, soll hier wenigstens an einigen Beispielen verdeutlicht werden.
Thüringen, das als Land mit einheitlicher Verwaltung aus dem vielfarbigen Strauß von sieben (früher acht) thüringischen Teilstaaten erst 1920 gebildet worden war, am 11. 2. 1921 seine Verfassung und im Oktober 1921 überhaupt erst ein selbständiges Ministerium für Volksbildung erhalten hatte, erließ – wie schon erwähnt – sein Lehrerbildungsgesetz bereits im Sommer 1922 (vgl. *Kittel* (1957), *Möller* (1976)), und zwar unter einer Regierungskoalition von SPD und USPD. Es bestimmte als Grundlage der Berufsausbildung auch für die Volksschullehrer und -lehrerinnen das Abitur der regulären höheren Schule und legte für sie als Berufsweg den »Besuch einer

Hochschule« fest, wobei die »Art und Dauer des Bildungsweges« formell noch offen blieb für spätere fachministerielle Regelung, obwohl über die Ausrichtung auf die Universität Jena kaum ein Zweifel bestehen konnte – zumal an der Hochschule das Fach Pädagogik seit langem vertreten war und sich auch schon einige Zeit in der Lehrerfortbildung einen Namen gemacht hatte. Das Volksbildungsministerium ordnete diese Ausbildungsaufgabe dann erst im Dezember 1924 der Universität Jena ausdrücklich zu, forderte aber schon durch die Lehrerprüfungsordnung vom 23. 1. 1923 ein Studium an der Universität Jena. Bei dieser *»Universitätslösung«* blieb es in Thüringen auch für die weitere Zeit der Weimarer Republik, während es bei der Studiendauer und bei der Zuordnung der didaktischen und der schulpraktischen Ausbildung gewisse Probleme und Schwankungen gegeben hat, die zum großen Teil politisch bedingt waren.

Was die *Studiendauer* betrifft, so sollte sich eine vierjährige Gesamtausbildung zunächst in ein zweijähriges mehr theoretisches Studium an der Universität und eine ebenfalls zweijährige mehr praktisch-pädagogische Ausbildung gliedern, wobei zwischen beiden Gliedern eine besonders enge Verzahnung vorgesehen war. Bereits Ende 1923 wurden im Interesse eines gründlicheren, vollakademischen Studiums dem ersten Ausbildungsabschnitt sechs Semester zugeteilt und der folgenden pädagogisch-schulpraktischen Vorbereitungszeit nur noch zwei Semester. Soweit ich mich erinnere, wurde dann um 1930 die Studiendauer an der Universität (aus »Ersparnisgründen und/oder im Zusammenhang mit neuerlichem Regierungswechsel?) von drei Jahren auf zwei Jahre zurückgenommen.[7]

Was die *Studienstruktur* angeht, so wurde das sechssemestrige Hochschulstudium insgesamt, also einschließlich der didaktischen und der schulpraktischen Ausbildung, zuerst im universitären Raum selbst unter maßgeblichem Einfluß *Peter Petersens* und seiner »Erziehungswissenschaftlichen Anstalt« gehalten, zu Beginn sogar ca. ein Jahr lang für die erziehungswissenschaftlichen Studien eine fakultätsartige eigene erziehungswissenschaftliche Abteilung in der Universität aufgebaut (jedoch ohne Beachtung des entsprechenden Selbstbestimmungsrechts der Universität, weshalb sie wieder abgebaut werden mußte). Nach erneutem Regierungswechsel wurden der didaktische, der musisch-technische, der schulpraktische Ausbildungsteil 1927 an ein »Pädagogisches Institut« verlagert, »das nur noch locker der Universität angeschlossen war« (*Möller* (1976), S. 303), das von *Georg Weiß*, dem Schwiegersohn des alten Herbartianers und Petersen-Vorgängers *Wilhelm Rein*, geleitet und »in dem die neuherbartianische Didaktik und Methodik wieder bestimmend wurde« (*W. Flitner* (1976), S. 173). Auch bei dieser Unstrukturierung waren offenbar politische Gesichtspunkte mit im Spiel, wie überhaupt das Bildungswesen in Thüringen durch wechselnde politische Mehrheiten und Regierungsumbildungen stark beeinträchtigt und verändert worden ist.

Hinsichtlich der *erziehungswissenschaftlichen* Ausbildung ist hervorzuheben, daß das erziehungswissenschaftliche Grundstudium einen breiten Raum einnahm und das wirkliche Zentrum der theoretischen Orientierung bildet und daß das entsprechende Lehrangebot an der Universität Jena personell durch Schaffung von Lehrstühlen und Dozenturen erstaunlich schnell sowie geistig weiträumig und wissenschaftlich differenziert aufgebaut wurde. Es waren auf diesem Gebiet für die Studierenden auch unterschiedliche Kombinationen mit individuellen Akzenten nach der psychologischen oder nach der philosophischen Seite sowie in Richtung des »Wahlfaches« möglich, wobei sie einen relativ großen Freiraum für persönliche Wahl hatten. Charakteristisch und bemerkenswert ist ferner die Einschätzung und Einordnung des sogenannten *Wahlfaches*. Es war nicht etwa unmittelbar auf die spätere Schularbeit bezogen, war also nicht als Qualifikation für einen persönlichen Unterrichtsschwerpunkt im Sinne eines Fachlehrers gemeint, sondern es sollte primär, ja grundsätzlich der eigenen Weiträumigkeit und geistigen Souveränität, der Vertiefung des wissenschaftlichen Denkens und der Verfeinerung des inneren Gespürs, kurz: der persönlichen Bildung des angehenden Volksschullehrers dienen. Zunächst auf das Spektrum der Volksschulfächer begrenzt, wurden die Auswahlmöglichkeiten in der Zeit von 1924 bis 1926 sogar noch stark erweitert, wovon die Ausdehnung auf den musisch-technischen Bereich auch nach 1926 erhalten blieb. Bei dem Wahlfachstudium war seit 1924 also eigentlich nicht mehr bloß von wissenschaftlicher Vertiefung zu sprechen, sondern von einer persönlichen Erweiterung und Bereicherung nach der wissenschaftlichen oder nach der musisch-technischen Seite. Wenn die Ausbildung auch auf den All-round-Lehrer im Volksschulbereich gerichtet blieb, so bot ihm das Wahlfach im Studium doch die Möglichkeit, neben dem Feld der pädagogischen Fragen und Aufgaben, das für ihn allerdings unbedingt das Zentrum der Orientierung und des Engagements sein mußte, eine spezielle persönliche Neigung und ein fachliches Interesse zur Geltung zu bringen und darin dann zusätzliche Erfüllung und besondere Befriedigung zu erfahren, auch später hier in hohem Maße »zu Hause« zu sein. So hatte das Wahlfach eine wichtige Bildungsaufgabe, rein quantitativ aber mit seinen ca. 18 Wochenstunden in Thüringen nur eine Randstellung im Gesamtstudium.[8]

In *Sachsen* wurde die akademische Volksschullehrerbildung, wie schon erwähnt, ebenfalls relativ früh und gleichfalls an den bestehenden Hochschulen (Universität Leipzig und Technische Hochschule Dresden) aufgebaut. Es scheint mir erwähnenswert, daß das grundlegende Gesetz vom 4. 4. 1923 im sächsischen Landtag einstimmig angenommen wurde. Das Studium konnte in der Allgemeinen Abteilung der TH Dresden bereits 1923, in der Philosophischen Fakultät der Universität Leipzig dann 1924 anlaufen, und zwar waren diese Hochschulinstitutionen jeweils für die grundwissenschaftlichen Studienbereiche allgemeine Pädagogik und Geschichte der Pädagogik, Philosophie, Psychologie, Anthropologie und Hygiene zuständig. Für die didaktisch-schulkundliche, die fachdidaktische und die schulpraktische sowie die musisch-werkliche Ausbildung wurden von vornherein besondere Pädagogische Institute geschaffen. Sie wurden organisatorisch in den beiden Fällen jedoch etwas unterschiedlich zugeordnet: während das Pädagogische Institut in Dresden voll in die Technische Hochschule eingegliedert, von deren stärker pragmatischer Gesamtausrichtung also offenbar ohne Vorbehalt akzeptiert wurde, hatte das Pädagogische Institut in Leipzig nur eine lockere Verbindung mit der Universität und war organisatorisch selbständig (für diese Trennung hatte z. B. *Theodor Litt* plädiert).
Wenn man die *Studienstruktur* in Sachsen mit der in Thüringen vergleicht, so zeigen sich zwar relativ geringe, dennoch bemerkenswerte Unterschiede. So war z. B. das erziehungswissenschaftliche Grundstudium in Jena thematisch breiter ausgelegt und differenzierter fixiert, es

umfaßte etwa auch die allgemeine Unterrichtslehre und die Schulkunde, während es an den sächsischen Hochschulen mehr philosophisch-historisch konzentriert und insgesamt weniger festgelegt schien. Daß dabei die speziellen Lehrstuhlverhältnisse in Leipzig und Dresden mit ihren spezifischen Auffassungen und Perspektiven gewissen Einfluß hatten und entsprechende Akzente gesetzt haben, scheint mir nicht ausgeschlossen; diese Frage mag aber hier dahingestellt bleiben. Tatsache ist jedenfalls, daß die Studienstruktur an der Universität Jena zunächst maßgeblich durch *Petersen* und seine pädagogische Auffassung mitbestimmt worden ist. Während so die sächsischen Pädagogischen Institute bei ihrer Vertretung der »praktischen Pädagogik« breiter und weiter auch nach der allgemeinen didaktischen und schulkundlichen Theorie auszugreifen hatten, waren sie andererseits besonders nahe bei der Schulpraxis angesiedelt. Sie hatten nämlich jeweils eine eigene Institutsschule, und die Dozenten der Fachdidaktiken hatten parallel zu ihren Lehrveranstaltungen im Pädagogischen Institut auch noch Unterricht an der Institutsschule zu halten. Hier blieb also in der akademischen Volksschullehrerbildung ein Stück fachdidaktisch-unterrichtspraktischer »Meisterlehre« aus der Struktur der alten Lehrerseminare erhalten, den Lehrenden ein besonderes Maß von fachlich-persönlicher Glaubwürdigkeit abgefordert und für die Lehrenden wie für die Lernenden die besonders enge Verbindung von pädagogischer Theorie und pädagogischer Praxis gewahrt. Infolgedessen hatte die Institutsschule eine zentrale Funktion und Position im Pädagogischen Institut, und der Gesamtstudienbereich der angehenden Lehrer schien hier von der stark philosophisch-historisch zentrierten pädagogischen Theorie in der Philosophischen Fakultät bzw. der Allgemeinen Abteilung bis hin zur Unterrichtspraxis mit der unmittelbaren Verantwortung und Gestaltung durch die Dozenten in der Institutsschule besonders weitgespannt. Dazu kam auch in Sachsen ein Wahlfachstudium, das die gleiche Funktion und Einordnung aufwies wie in Thüringen, d. h. wissenschaftlichen oder künstlerisch-technisch-werklichen Charakter im Rahmen aller Volksschulfächer haben konnte, auf Antrag und mit spezieller Genehmigung im Ausnahmefall dieses Gesamtfeld sogar überschreiten konnte, also in betonter Weise auf die persönliche Bildung des angehenden Lehrers und nicht auf seine spätere unterrichtsfachliche Lehrqualifikation ausgerichtet war. Das Studium dauerte in Sachsen sechs Semester.

Auch *Hessen,* das seine akademische Volksschullehrerbildung 1925 aufbaute, band sie an seine bestehende Hochschule: die Technische Hochschule in Darmstadt, entwickelte dabei aber wiederum eigene Nuancen dieses Lösungstyps, wobei es innerhalb des Landes sogar zwei Varianten schuf. Die hessischen Spezifika beruhten zum Teil auf einer besonderen Vorgeschichte, zum Teil darauf, daß man verschiedene Wege erproben und Erfahrungen für eine spätere Entscheidung sammeln wollte (wie überhaupt zum Aufbau der Volksschullehrerbildung in der Weimarer Zeit manche Versuche und Erprobungen sowohl bei den Planungen wie auch bei der Praxis gehörten).

Was die Vorgeschichte in Hessen angeht, so ist auf folgende Besonderheit hinzuweisen. Hessen hatte schon seit Anfang des 20. Jahrhunderts neben dem normalen Weg durch das Lehrerseminar eine zweite Ausbildungsbahn für den Volksschullehrerberuf entwickelt, die auf dem Abitur aufsetzte und durch »Pädagogische Kurse« an der TH Darmstadt hindurchführte (zunächst Kurzkurse, ab 1908 einjährig, ab 1909 sogar zweijährig). Dieser Seitenweg ist in gewisser Weise mit der oben anmerkungsweise (Anm. 4) kurz erwähnten Nebenlinie vergleichbar, die bei der Lehrerinnenausbildung dadurch entstand, daß mancherorts auf höheren Mädchenschulen pädagogische Ausbildungsklassen aufgebaut wurden, wobei sich die Proportion von Allgemeinbildung und beruflicher Ausbildung gegenüber den normalen Lehrerinnenseminaren ja erheblich verschob. Im Falle Hessens war beim Weg über die »Pädagogischen Kurse« diese Verschiebung noch radikaler dadurch, daß die allgemeine Vorbildung zum Abitur hinaufgetrieben und die Kurse selbst in der TH angesiedelt wurden. Damit hatte Hessen bereits einen wesentlichen

Ansatz für die akademische Volksschullehrerbildung geschaffen und erprobt. Er wurde 1925 nun dadurch weiterentwickelt, daß das Studium der Grundwissenschaften (einschließlich der allgemeinen Unterrichtslehre) an bzw. von der TH Darmstadt abgewickelt und für die fachdidaktisch-schulpraktischen Ausbildungsbereiche zwei Pädagogische Institute gegründet wurden, das eine in Darmstadt, das andere in Mainz. Beide waren der TH Darmstadt angegliedert; es gab also für das Aufgabenfeld des Pädagogischen Instituts zwei verschiedene Institutionen mit je eigenem Lehrkörper, für das grundwissenschaftliche Studium dagegen nur einen: den in Darmstadt. Dessen Dozenten kamen zu ihren Lehrveranstaltungen auch nach Mainz, so daß die Studierenden ihr Gesamtstudium an einem Ort durchführen konnten.
Zu der Kuriosität des von den Darmstädter Dozenten der Grundwissenschaften »mitbespielten« zweiten Ortes gesellte sich noch die – das »Probieren« betreffende – besondere Tatsache, daß die beiden Pädagogischen Institute unterschiedlich strukturiert waren. Dahinter stand allerdings als Gemeinsamkeit die für Hessen spezifische Aufgabe, daß sich die beiden Pädagogischen Institute nicht nur der didaktisch-methodischen und der schulpraktischen Aufgaben anzunehmen hatten, sondern daß sie für die Studierenden auch noch eine inhaltliche Vertiefung der Volksschulunterrichtsbereiche bringen sollten (dafür scheint Hessen auf ein Wahlfachstudium verzichtet zu haben). Diese inhaltliche Befestigung und Vertiefung – also eine Art von Fortsetzung der Allgemeinbildung über das Abitur hinaus – vollzogen die beiden Institute nun unterschiedlich. Sie war in Darmstadt mit der fachdidaktisch-methodischen Ausbildung personell gekoppelt, wurde von den »Methodikern« mitgeleistet und erschien für die angehenden Lehrer somit in engem Konnex mit dem Aufgaben- und Bildungsfeld der Volksschule, während sie in Mainz Studienräten der höheren Schule anvertraut war, die mit der didaktisch-methodischen und schulpraktischen Ausbildung am Pädagogischen Institut nichts zu tun hatten. Dieser Bereich lag in Mainz wie in Darmstadt in den Händen besonders bewährter Volksschulpraktiker und wurde zum Teil auch in engster Verbindung mit deren eigenem Schulunterricht gehalten, der ihnen also wie in Sachsen mit und neben der Dozententätigkeit abverlangt wurde. Offensichtlich zielte diese Einordnung des fachdidaktisch-methodischen Lehr- und Studiengebietes weniger auf Ansätze zum Aufbau einer theoretischen Unterrichtslehre als auf unmittelbare pädagogische Anschauung und praktische Unterrichtseinübung, obzwar die Pädagogischen Institute in Hessen keine eigenen Institutsschulen hatten. Anders als in Sachsen war die Studiendauer in Hessen nur auf vier Semester angesetzt; die Prüfungen fanden aber erst im fünften Semester statt (so die Angaben bei *Kittel* (1957), S. 291; *Zierold/Rothkugel* ([2]1931) nennen als Studiendauer 2½ Jahre).

Während in Thüringen (abgesehen von der allerersten Zeit), in Sachsen und auch in Hessen bei der Einbindung der akademischen Volksschullehrerbildung in die bestehenden Hochschulen jedesmal für die didaktischen, die musisch-technischen und die schulpraktischen Ausbildungsanteile spezielle Pädagogische Institute aufgebaut wurden, die in unterschiedlicher Weise mit der Hochschule selbst verbunden waren, hat es auch Fälle gegeben, in denen auf die Schaffung besonderer Pädagogischer Institute verzichtet und einfach die Institution (Pädagogisches Seminar) in der Hochschule entsprechend ausgebaut wurde: Hamburg und Braunschweig.

In *Hamburg*, wo eine sechssemestrige Ausbildung der Volksschullehrer an der Universität durch Gesetz vom 20. 12. 1926 geregelt wurde und im Frühjahr 1927 offiziell anlief, bestanden für den pädagogischen Studiengang insofern besonders günstige Rahmenbedingungen, als die Lehrerschaft dort so breit und so intensiv von der reformpädagogischen Bewegung erfaßt und erfüllt war wie kaum an einem anderen Ort Deutschlands und als ferner die Universität erst 1919 gegründet, somit nicht in alten Strukturen verkrustet, noch dazu in hervorragender Entfaltung begriffen und für die Fragen und Aufgaben der Volksbildung sehr aufgeschlossen war. Es dürfte auch ein besonderer Glücksfall gewesen sein, daß sie mit *Gustav Deuchler* (bereits ab 1923) und *Wilhelm Flitner* (zusätzlich ab 1929) Erziehungswissenschaftler hatte, die für die akademische Volksschullehrerbildung persönlich stark engagiert waren, wobei im Falle Flitners seine mehrjährige Pionierarbeit und Erfahrung an der Pädagogischen Akademie in Kiel (seit deren Gründung 1926) zusätzlich zu Buche schlug.

Was die Studienstruktur angeht, so kann man wohl von einer hervorstechenden geistigen Weiträumigkeit der Ausbildung und von einer herausragenden individuellen Studienfreiheit der angehenden Lehrer sprechen. Dazu gehört, daß deren Blick in betonter Weise auf das Ganze der Kultur gerichtet wurde, daß man auch das Wahlfach (mit breiter Palette im wissenschaftlichen oder im künstlerisch-technischen Felde) als Eindringen in ein konkretes Kulturgebiet verstand, es auf seine Struktur und Funktion im kulturellen Gesamtleben bezog und ihm entsprechend große Bedeutung im Studiengang zumaß. Der Gesamttendenz entsprach auch, daß bei der schulpraktischen Ausbildung die persönliche Einbindung in die Schule und längere Praktika mit wechselnden unterrichtsfachlichen Akzenten eine besondere Rolle spielten und daß über den Schulbereich hinaus die sozialpädagogische Arbeit, Aufgabe und Verantwortung breit berücksichtigt wurde. So zielte man in Hamburg auf einen Lehrer mit betont selbständiger und in sich gegründeter geistiger Orientierung und Flexibilität, dem eine enzyklopädisch-didaktische handwerkliche Einpassung fremd war, der sich aber in neue Aufgaben und Stoffe gut einzuarbeiten und einzuleben verstand.

Auch in *Braunschweig* bestanden besonders günstige, geschichtlich gewachsene Voraussetzungen für eine Eingliederung der Volksschullehrerbildung in die dortige Technische Hochschule. Manche von ihnen hatte Braunschweig mit Hamburg gemeinsam, z. B. die Überschaubarkeit der schulischen und der Hochschulverhältnisse in dem kleinen Lande, den Wegfall der Konfessionsproblematik in der traditionell protestantischen Region, die relativ hohe Aufgeschlossenheit und Übernahmebereitschaft der Hochschule, wobei im Falle Braunschweigs die pragmatischere Einstellung der Technischen Hochschule, ihr Offensein für Fragen der Volksbildung und der geschichtliche Hintergrund ihres Gleichberechtigungskampfes gegenüber der Universität zusätzlich der Lehrerbildungsaufgabe entgegenkamen. Auch daß dieses kleine Land in krassem Gegensatz zur Großlage im übrigen Reich nach dem ersten Weltkrieg keine Junglehrerarbeitslosigkeit kannte, aus der sich Gegner einer Lehrerbildungsreform hätten Aufschubargumente holen können, begünstigte die Chancen des Neuaufbaus. Vor allem war die Volksschullehrerschaft im Lande Braunschweig nicht nur reformpädagogisch interessiert und engagiert, sie hatte auch eine besonders weitsichtige und rührige, tatkräftige und taktisch geschickte Führung, so daß sie eine nachhaltige bildungspolitische Aktivität und Wirksamkeit entfalten konnte (vgl. hierzu und zum folgenden besonders *Sandfuchs* (1978) und *Sandfuchs* (1986)). Andererseits erlebte das Land Braunschweig während der Weimarer Zeit nacheinander nicht weniger als 14 Regierungen unterschiedlicher Parteicouleur und -koalitionen, seit 1930 sogar unter nationalsozialistischer Beteiligung.

Um so bemerkenswerter ist der konsequente und in seinem Ansatz einmalige Weg, den Braunschweig beim Aufbau seiner akademischen Volksschullehrerausbildung ging und durchgehalten hat. Zwar baute es seine alten Lehrerseminare erst ab 1923 ab und ließ sie endgültig erst 1928 auslaufen. Aber bereits 1921 wurde eine Entwicklung eingeleitet, die die Technische Hochschule in den Ausbildungsprozeß, genauer: in die *Fortbildung* der (seminaristisch ausgebildeten) *Junglehrer,* also in die *Zweite Phase* der Lehrerausbildung, einbezog, und zwar durch folgende Regelung, die dann für die jeweiligen Seminarabsolventen bis 1928 praktiziert wurde: diese jungen Lehrer wurden nach zweijähriger Tätigkeit an den Schulen des Landes für ein Jahr in die Stadt Braunschweig versetzt, hatten dort bei voller Vergütung erheblichen Stundenerlaß (von 32 auf 20, ab 1924 sogar auf 18 Wochenstunden) in der Schularbeit, erhielten eine verstärkte schulpraktische Ausbildung durch besondere Könner im Schulehalten und absolvierten in dieser Zeit zusätzlich als Gasthörer an der Technischen Hochschule ein theoretisches Vertiefungsstudium auf pädagogisch-philosophischem und psychologischem Gebiet, so daß einerseits ihre erziehungswissenschaftlichen Grundorientierungen entschieden verbessert, zum andern von der Schulpraxis her intensivere reformpädagogische Impulse ins Spiel gebracht wurden. Daß auf diese Weise nicht zuletzt pädagogische Theorie und pädagogische Praxis besonders eng und wirksam aufeinander bezogen werden konnten, dürfte für jeden klar sein, der mal mit jungen, bereits in der Praxis stehenden und von ihren pädagogischen und didaktischen, psychologischen und persönlichen Problemen existentiell angerührten Lehrern erziehungswissenschaftlich zu arbeiten und sich ihren Fragen auszusetzen hatte. Von Bedeutung war auch, daß beim Abschlußexamen des ganzen Vorbereitungsdienstes, das nach einem weiteren Jahr des Schuldienstes (außerhalb Braunschweigs) abzulegen war, die theoretischen Fächer von den an der braunschweigischen akademischen Fortbildung beteiligten Hochschullehrern geprüft wurden.

Konsequenz dieser Regelung war zum einen, daß der spätere Aufbau der akademischen Volksschullehrerbildung in diesem kleinen Lande wie damals wohl in keinem anderen sowohl strukturell und erfahrungsmäßig wie auch öffentlich-psychologisch und politisch gut vorbereitet wurde, zum andern, daß an der Technischen Hochschule der dafür notwendige personelle und institutionelle Ausbau frühzeitig erfolgte (bereits ab 1922 durch *Oswald Kroh*, ab 1924 durch dessen Nachfolger *Willy Moog*, ferner durch *August Riekel* u. a.).

So war der Boden bestens bereitet, als dann – nach nochmaligen kraftvollen Initiativen der Lehrerschaft – mit Verordnung vom 1. 4. 1927 die neue Volksschullehrerausbildung an der Technischen Hochschule mit einer Studiendauer von sechs Semestern eingeführt und dazu durch Beschluß des TH-Senats vom 13. 7. 1927 aus der alten, bereits stark ausgebauten Abteilung für allgemeinbildende Wissenschaften, Mathematik und Naturwissenschaften eine neue »Abteilung für Kulturwissenschaften« ausgegliedert wurde.

Was die Struktur des Studiums betrifft, so ist bemerkenswert, daß die grundwissenschaftliche Ausbildung neben Erziehungswissenschaft, Philosophie, Psychologie auch Nationalökonomie (ab 1929 dazu alternativ wählbar auch Soziologie!) und Staatsbürgerkunde umfaßte und daß ab 1930 auch die Promotion (zum Doktor der Kulturwissenschaften) möglich war.[9] Die grundwissenschaftliche theoretische Ausbildung scheint in Braunschweig einen relativ hohen, ja sehr hohen Studienanteil gehabt zu haben. Als Zusatzfächer fungierten noch Schulhygiene, Schulrecht und Jugendwohlfahrt. Ein besonderes Pädagogisches Institut für den schulpraktischen und den musisch-technischen Bereich wurde nicht aufgebaut, weil die sächsischen Erfahrungen mit der Gefahr der Zweigleisigkeit den Braunschweigern nicht gerade positiv erschienen. Zum »Braunschweiger Modell« gehört ferner, daß die musisch-technische Ausbildung verhältnismäßig randständig gehalten wurde (nur zwei ihrer Fächer waren überhaupt verbindlich) und daß die »praktische Pädagogik« betont auf reformpädagogische Tendenzen ausgerichtet war, wozu auch besonders profilierte und engagierte Reformpädagogen wie etwa Adolf Jensen und Wilhelm Paulsen herangezogen wurden. Die schulpraktische Ausbildung wurde während des Gesamtstudiums in ebenso kontinuierlicher wie systematisch-konsequenter Weise geführt und scheint sich großenteils an Versuchsschulen mit ausgeprägt reformpädagogischer Prägung vollzogen zu haben, während das fachdidaktische Feld mindestens in der Lehre offenbar sehr wenig differenziert und zu wenig akzentuiert war und kaum zur Entfaltung gekommen ist. Trotz des Verzichts auf ein besonderes Pädagogisches Institut hat es auch den Anschein, daß in Braunschweig eine gute Koordinierung oder gar eine Integration von pädagogischer Theorie und pädagogischer Praxis nicht gelungen ist. Auch muß die Arbeitsbelastung der Studierenden im Gesamtstudium enorm hoch gewesen sein[10] und ihre individuelle Wahlfreiheit recht gering (vgl. *Sandfuchs* (1986), S. 149).

Auch in Braunschweig gehörte zum Volksschullehramtsstudium ein *Wahlfach* (dort vielfach »Sonderfach« genannt), dem in der Gesamtgewichtung »Hauptfachcharakter« zukam, das aber etwas anders angesiedelt und ausgerichtet war als in den bisher besprochenen Ländern. Seine Auswahlliste umfaßt auch hier die Volksschulfächer, jedoch im musisch-technischen Bereich konnte nicht nur Zeichnen, Musik, Turnen oder Werken gewählt werden, sondern auch Kurzschrift oder Gartenbau, von den Frauen auch Nadelarbeiten, Hauswirtschaft oder Säuglingspflege (während für sie Gartenbau nicht in Frage kam).[11] Läßt schon diese große Erweiterung und Aufsplitterung im »technischen« Felde die Vermutung aufkommen, daß damit weniger auf breite, rein persönliche Bildungsschwerpunkte der angehenden Lehrer und Lehrerinnen als auf wahlfachmäßige Erweiterungsmöglichkeiten des Volksschulkanons oder mindestens mit auf sie gezielt wurde, so lag, wie *Uwe Sandfuchs* (1978 und 1986) mehrfach betont hat, in der ganzen Braunschweiger Wahlfachkonzeption insofern eine Widersprüchlichkeit vor, als es zum einen auch hier der persönlichen, schulzweckfreien Bildungsbereicherung dienen und dem Studierenden entsprechendes Eindringen in seine Struktur, seinen Ort im menschlich-geistigen Kosmos und in seine Methode ermöglichen sollte, er zum andern und zugleich aber auch seine »pädagogische Verwertbarkeit« erfahren und beurteilen sollte. Dabei standen nicht nur diese beiden Grundausrichtungen eventuell schon in Spannung zueinander, an ihnen hing vor allem noch das Problem, daß für die zusätzlichen pädagogischen Implikationen und »schulpädagogischen Einbindungen« die reinen Fachvertreter der Hochschule durchweg weder interessiert noch sachkompetent waren. Daß dies mit der ohnehin zu geringen fachdidaktischen Komponente im Gesamtstudium zu negativem Effekt kumulieren mußte, liegt auf der Hand und gehört zu den Schwächen der damaligen Braunschweiger Lösung.

Es bleibt noch zu erwähnen, daß die Braunschweiger Lehrerausbildung durch den nationalsozialistischen administrativ-politischen Einfluß in der Regierung ab 1931 schweren und brutalen »personellen Säuberungen« ausgesetzt wurde, daß der nationalsozialistische Minister Dietrich Klagges aber an der 1927 etablierten »TH-Lösung« persönlich festhielt, vor den höheren Instanzen seiner Partei dann freilich ins Abseits geriet.

Während in Braunschweig der institutionelle und substantielle Neuaufbau der akademischen Lehrerbildung bei allem politischen Wechsel im Grundkonzept durchgehalten werden konnte, ist *Mecklenburg-Schwerin* ein – hier nur kurz erwähntes – Beispiel für die damalige Anfälligkeit dieses Aufgabenfeldes gegenüber wechselnden politischen Machtverhältnissen (vgl. hierzu *Kittel* (1957), S. 293). Dieses Land schuf nämlich zunächst durch Gesetz von 1925 eine Form der Volksschullehrerbildung, die zwar die alte, auf der Volksschule aufbauende Seminarausbildungsform etwas verbesserte, aber die Grundbedingung jedes akademischen Bildungsweges: das Aufsetzen der Berufsbildung auf der allgemeinen Hochschulreife, ausdrücklich verfehlte, indem sie auf einer besonderen fünfjährigen Lehrerbildungsanstalt noch ein »Pädagogisches Institut« mit zweijährigem Kurs aufbaute und hierfür als Vorbildung auch eine dem Abschluß der Lehrerbildungsanstalt »gleichartige« Vorbildung in der höheren Schule gelten ließ. Es muß uns heute fast grotesk anmuten (steht aber auf einer Linie mit manchen anderen politisch merkwürdigen Gerichtsentscheidungen der Weimarer Zeit[12]), daß das Reichsgericht den Antrag, die Reichsverfassungswidrigkeit dieser neuen Lehrerbildungsregelung festzustellen, ausdrücklich abwies. Jedenfalls führte erst ein Wechsel in der politischen Regierungskoalition dazu, daß mit Gesetz vom 19. 1. 1927 auch in Mecklenburg-Schwerin die allgemeine Hochschulreife als Grundlage der Volksschullehrer-Berufsausbildung und für diese selbst ein viersemestriges Studium an der Universität Rostock und dem ihr angegliederten Pädagogischen Institut festgelegt wurde.

Auch in *Bayern* beeinflußte ein Regierungswechsel die Volksschullehrerausbildung in tiefgreifender Weise, aber diesmal in negativer Richtung (vgl. zum folgenden vor allem *Renner* (1979)). Während die ersten Regierungen nach 1918 einer Reform der Volksschullehrerbildung noch aufgeschlossen gegenübergestanden hatten und speziell das Ministerium Hoffmann sie ins Auge gefaßt hatte (*Renner* (1979), S. 286), erhielten ab dem Regierungswechsel im Jahre 1921 in der bayerischen Kulturpolitik diejenigen Kräfte bestimmenden Einfluß, die in der Lehrerbildung mit aller Kraft am status quo festzuhalten versuchten. Um das bayerische Beharrungsvermögen und Nachhinken in Fragen der Volksschullehrerausbildung richtig einzuschätzen, muß man zusätzlich bedenken, daß in Bayern bis 1912 ein nur fünfjähriger Ausbildungskurs (drei Jahre Präparande und zwei Jahre Seminar) existiert hatte und daß erst mit der Neuordnung von 1912 die Gemeindeschreiberei als eigenes Unterrichtsfach für die angehenden Volksschullehrer beseitigt worden war.

Renner (1979) hat aus den Quellen heraus im einzelnen aufgezeigt, daß bereits bei den frühen Verhandlungen der Reichsregierung mit den Ländern (s. o.) von der bayerischen Seite eine *konsequente Verzögerungstaktik* verfolgt wurde (vgl. *Renner* (1979), S. 286ff.). Das zeigte sich bereits bei der Stellungnahme zum Reichsreferentenentwurf vom Herbst 1921, als Bayern im Unterschied von allen anderen Ländern auf der radikalen Ablehnung beharrte.[13] Diese seine Reformunwilligkeit schien sich noch zu verhärten nach Abschluß des bayerischen Konkordats mit dem Heiligen Stuhl von 1924/25, »da nach der Interpretation des Vatikans wie der bayerischen Regierung hierin eine konfessionelle Lehrerbildung verankert war« (*Renner* (1979), S. 291). Als der bayerische Landtag im Januar 1925 (auf SPD-Antrag) das Ministerium beauftragte, eine Denkschrift zur Frage der Lehrerbildung auszuarbeiten, dauerte es volle drei Jahre, bis das Ministerium diesen Auftrag endlich erfüllte. Diese im Januar 1928 dem Landtag vorgelegte Denkschrift hat jedoch praktisch nichts bewegt und bewirkt. Als Weg für den angehenden Volksschullehrer sah sie im Sinne der allgemeinbildenden Basis nach einem siebenjährigen Volksschulbesuch das Durchlaufen einer sechsjährigen »Deutschen Oberschule in Aufbauform« vor – das heißt einen Schultyp, den zwar andere Länder des Reiches seit Anfang der zwanziger Jahre aufgebaut hatten, den aber Bayern strikt abgelehnt hatte, *den es hier also überhaupt nicht gab,* der somit erst hätte in Bayern geschaffen werden müssen! Darauf aufbauend sollte die Berufsbildung dann in einem zweijährigen Studium an einer »Pädagogischen Akademie« erfolgen – offenbar in Anlehnung an das preußische Modell, das ja in fast allen Fällen konfessionellen Charakter hatte. Entscheidender als dieser institutionelle Aufriß fällt für seine Würdigung die Tatsache ins Gewicht, daß erstens die in Aussicht gestellten Pädagogischen Akademien ihre Arbeit frühestens im Jahre 1934 hätten beginnen können, und daß zweitens – und vor allem – das Ministerium keinerlei Schritte unternahm, ja sie nicht einmal plante, um auch nur ansatzweise an eine Realisierung zu gehen.[14]
Vermutlich hat das Faktum, daß die Denkschrift von 1928 mit der »Deutschen Oberschule« und mit der »Pädagogischen Akademie« zwei von den drei bayerischen Universitäten (München, Würzburg, Erlangen) scharf abgelehnte Institutionen ins Spiel brachte, diese Hochschulen auf den Plan gerufen; jedenfalls erklärten sie sich 1929 im Gegensatz zu ihrer früheren Einstellung zur Übernahme der Volksschullehrerausbildung bereit! Doch änderte auch dies nicht das Geringste an der seminaristischen Ausbildung der Volksschullehrer und -lehrerinnen in Bayern. Bis 1931 hielt Bayern es nicht einmal für nötig, die alte Seminarlehrordnung von 1912 und die dazugehörige Prüfungsordnung von 1914 zu verbessern. Auf dem Felde der Volksschullehrerbildung hatte für Bayern also die Weimarer Republik zehn Jahre nach ihrer Geburt sozusagen noch gar nicht begonnen – wahrlich ein dunkler Fleck in der Geschichte der bayerischen

Kulturpolitik. Und als 1931 endlich wenigstens eine neue Lehrordnung für die bayerischen Lehrerseminare erlassen wurde, richtete sie zwar das sechste Seminarjahr straffer auf die Berufsaufgabe aus, strukturell brachte sie jedoch keine Veränderung. »Die wichtigsten inhaltlichen Änderungen bestanden in der Einführung von Englisch als Pflicht- und Prüfungsfach und in der Ausweitung des Stoffes in der Mathematik und den Naturwissenschaften« (*Renner* (1979), S. 294), also in winzigen Zugaben im Bereich der seminaristischen Allgemeinbildung, die jedoch weiter auf dem Volksschulniveau aufbaute. Den Bemühungen der bayerischen Lehrerverbände, besonders des Bayerischen Lehrer-Vereins, der sich auch mit mehreren Denkschriften für die Akademisierung der Volksschullehrerbildung eingesetzt hatte, war jeder Erfolg versagt geblieben; und daß die Lehrerorganisationen damals eine um so größere Aktivität bei der Lehrerweiterbildung entwickelten, konnte den katastrophalen Mangelzustand der Lehrerausbildung in Bayern nur in sehr geringem Maße mindern.

Daß auch *Württemberg* die seminaristische Volksschullehrerausbildung während der ganzen Weimarer Zeit beibehielt, sei hier nur am Rande erwähnt, aber nicht weiter dargestellt, obwohl dieses Faktum natürlich ebenso schwer wiegt wie die traurige Bilanz in Bayern.
In *Preußen* vollzogen sich, wie schon kurz angemerkt wurde, mindestens in den ersten Jahren die einschlägigen kulturpolitischen Diskussionen und Planungen durchaus nicht so geradlinig, wie das von weitem erscheinen könnte, und der Klärungsprozeß nahm auch längere Zeit in Anspruch, obwohl der Kultusminister Carl Heinrich Becker eine relativ klare und geschickte Strategie entwickelte und obwohl ja in der Programmschrift des seit 1920 am zentralen Ort Berlin wirkenden Hochschullehrers Eduard Spranger eine durchgefeilte Konzeption und Option für eine eigenständige Pädagogische Hochschule vorlag (*Spranger* (1919/20)). Nachdem *Becker* selbst ursprünglich eine Sonderhochschule abgelehnt und eine Universitätsreform mit umfassenderer Rückbeziehung auf die Aufgabe der Menschenbildung angestrebt hatte, führten die realen Machtverhältnisse, nicht zuletzt wohl das Insistieren der katholischen Kirche und der Zentrumspartei auf Konfessionalisierung der Volksschullehrerbildung – trotz des dadurch heraufbeschworenen Konflikts mit der Lehrerschaft, insbesondere mit dem Preußischen Lehrerverein – zur »PH-Lösung«. Daß auch *Sprangers* Konzeption bei der Gesamtentwicklung in Preußen eine wesentliche Rolle gespielt hat, kann nicht bestritten werden, wenngleich spätestens seit *Paffraths* Spranger-Untersuchung (*Paffrath* (1971)) bekannt und klar genug dargelegt ist (vgl. dazu auch *Sandfuchs* (1978)), daß der tatsächliche Ansatz bei der preußischen »Pädagogischen Akademie« nur teilweise dem Entwurf und Plan *Sprangers* gefolgt ist. Inzwischen haben umfangreiche und gründliche weitere Forschungen (vor allem *Weber* (1982), *Meyer-Willner* (1986)) das Bild von der Entstehung dieser preußischen Fachhochschule noch erheblich präziser gefaßt, mit zahlreichen Details angereichert, wesentlich erweitert und vertieft, worauf hier aber aus Zeitgründen nicht eingegangen werden kann. Erwähnt werden muß allerdings, daß *Meyer-Willner* zu der spektakulären These gelangt ist, *Sprangers* »Bildnerhochschule« sei nur eine taktische Hilfs- und Ablenkungskonstruktion des Verfassers gewesen, die die Universität von den Volksschullehramtsaspiranten freihalten sollte, und *Spranger* selbst habe gar nicht hinter ihr gestanden, sondern habe im Grunde auf eine verbesserte seminaristische

Ausbildung der Volksschullehrer gezielt. *Meyer-Willners* These ist von ihm nicht ohne Überspitzungen entwickelt, aber in ihrem Kern bei der heutigen Quellenlage m. E. nicht einfach aus den Angeln zu heben, und es kann auch kaum in Abrede gestellt werden, daß dadurch ein Schatten auf *Sprangers* Person und auf sein Agieren fällt. Mindestens muß wohl gesagt werden, daß *Sprangers* Konzeption der »Bildnerhochschule« für ihn selbst einen hohen taktischen Funktionswert hatte. *Meyer-Willner* scheint mir aber viel zu wenig die Dimension der *Wirkungsgeschichte* beachtet und nach der tatsächlichen Ausstrahlungskraft der von *Spranger* in so leuchtenden Farben hingeworfenen Idee gefragt zu haben, und zwar weniger im realpolitischen Felde als vielmehr im atmosphärischen Bereich, und auch weniger in den Details als vielmehr in bezug auf den Grundriß. Und da ist bei aller Abwandlung, die *Sprangers* Entwurf in der Realisierung von Details erfahren hat, doch zu sagen, daß seine *Grundstruktur* in der Diskussion der Öffentlichkeit und gerade auch bei den an der Arbeit der Pädagogischen Akademien unmittelbar Beteiligten – sei es die Dozentenschaft oder die Studentenschaft – eine besondere Leuchtkraft entfaltet hat und daß *Sprangers* Grundgedanken zum Bild und zum Verständnis bzw. zum Selbstverständnis der Betroffenen und Interessierten ganz wesentlich beigetragen, ja daß sie es entscheidend profiliert haben.

Diese Konzeption muß deshalb hier wenigstens umrißhaft vor Augen gestellt werden, wobei ich sie auf folgende fünf Hauptpunkte zusammenziehe (unter Einschluß sich einordnender Diskussionsaspekte):

1. *Spranger* stellt die Idee und Aufgabe der *»Bildung«* als eigenständiges und gleichrangiges Hochschulkonstitutivum neben und gegen die beiden anderen »Ideen« und Aufgabenbereiche »Wissenschaft« und »Technik«. Immer wieder wird von ihm die grundsätzliche Gleichwertigkeit und Eigenstruktur aller drei Verantwortungsfelder und der aus ihnen abzuleitenden Institutionen betont, wobei hervorsticht, daß der Ort der dritten Institution und somit der pädagogischen akademischen Berufsausbildung nicht etwa auf alle pädagogischen Berufe bezogen wird, sondern nur auf das Volksschullehramt (als den »eigentlichen«, gleichsam den genuinen, den vollbluthaften pädagogischen Beruf).

2. Die Aufgabe der Menschenbildung wird besonders scharf abgehoben von der Aufgabe und Struktur der Wissenschaft mit der Grundthese: während es in der Wissenschaft nur um Prozeß, Erfahrung und Ethos des Denkens und Erkennens geht, sind an der Bildung alle Kulturbereiche und menschlichen Kräfte beteiligt. Als Konsequenz wird hervorgekehrt:

a) die Universität kann das nicht leisten,

b) einseitige Vertheoretisierung muß entschieden abgewehrt werden, sie ist für den angehenden Volksschullehrer eine große Gefahr.

3. Das Ziel, auf das die Pädagogische, die »Bildner-Hochschule« klar und entschieden auszurichten ist, läßt sich im Kern umschreiben mit pädagogischem Ethos, pädagogischer Haltung und pädagogischem Können vom menschlich-persönlichen Geleiten und Führen bis zum unterrichtlichen Geschick, für das mindestens der Grund gelegt und der Ansatz entwickelt werden muß.

4. Es handelt sich um eine strukturell mehrschichtige, komplexe Aufgabe. Dazu gehört *wissenschaftliches* Orientieren und Arbeiten (Erziehungswissenschaft mit ihren Bezugswissenschaften, vor allem mit philosophischer Fundierung, ferner didaktische Theorie) ebenso wie *pädagogisch-praktische* Anleitung und Ausbildung (Schulpraxis, persönliche erziehliche Betreuung), aber auch *musisch-technische* Betätigung und *geselliger* Umgang (»Gemeinschaftsle-

ben«) in einer *überschaubaren* Gemeinschaft. Als Konsequenz daraus ergeben sich folgende sechs Aspekte als Konstitutiva der »Bildnerhochschule«:
a) voller wissenschaftlicher Anspruch im erziehungswissenschaftlichen Bereich;
b) ein relativ hohes Maß von unterrichtspraktischer Ausbildung (bei *Sprangers*, auf drei Studienjahre ausgelegtem Modell vor allem im dritten Studienjahr);
c) eine musisch-gesellige Atmosphäre als ein bestimmendes Strukturelement;
d) kleine Hochschulen (maximal 300 Studierende) und enger Kontakt zwischen den Lernenden untereinander sowie zwischen Lehrenden und Lernenden;
e) eine enge Koppelung von unterrichtsfachlicher Sachorientierung mit fachlicher Didaktik und Methodenlehre, wobei die fachliche Sachorientierung nicht auf Fachstudium zielt, sondern sich am »Bildungswert« des Faches orientiert, auf eine bildende Begegnung mit den Sachverhalten, geistigen Kräften und Bildungsmächten gerichtet ist, die hinter den Fächern und Bildungsfeldern der Volksschule stehen;
f) nach eigener Wahl und als Gegengewicht gegen die Gefahr des Enzyklopädismus persönliche Vertiefung in ein »Wahlfach«, wobei wieder die »bildende Begegnung« (und nicht ein ausgewachsenes Fachstudium) die zentrale Aufgabe und Zielsetzung darstellt.
5. Es geht in der Pädagogischen Hochschule nicht nur um eine Anleitung des angehenden Volksschullehrers zu dem Amt und Geschäft, Kinder in der Schule zu erziehen und unterrichtlich zu bilden, sondern es geht darüber hinaus um Menschenbildung in der Hochschule selbst. Die Bildner-Hochschule ist in dieser Sicht also auch eine Stätte der Bildung für die Studierenden selbst, vor dem Hintergrund der *Spranger*-These: andere bilden kann nur, wer selbst gebildet ist und weiterhin stets bildend an sich selbst arbeitet. Auch – und gerade auch – in diesem Sinne soll die »Bildner-Hochschule« von einer pädagogischen Atmosphäre geprägt sein und durch alle ihre Maßnahmen, Veranstaltungen und Einrichtungen auf die angehenden Lehrer einwirken.

Bei der Realisierung von 1926, hinter der ein ganzes Geflecht von Wirkfaktoren im Spiele war, blieb *Sprangers* Konzeption freilich eben nur in der Grundrichtung und Gesamtstruktur maßgebend (vgl. dazu *Kittel* (1957), *Weber* (1982)). Variierende Einflüsse kamen z. B. von *Carl Heinrich Becker,* der den Geist und Stil der Jugendbewegung stark in die neue Lehrerbildung hineinwirken lassen wollte, weiterhin von *Johannes von den Driesch,* der die ministerielle Denkschrift von 1925 ausarbeitete, von den parteipolitischen Kräften des Zentrums und von der katholischen Kirche, die nur konfessionell ausgerichtete Lösungen anerkennen wollten, ferner von der finanziellen Notlage, die die Studiendauer auf vier Semester reduzierte, was fast einer Amputation des ursprünglichen Konzeptes gleichkam und den Studienplan erheblich vollstopfte (wenn auch nicht in der Braunschweiger Dimension), damit zugleich den individuellen Bewegungsspielraum der Studierenden sehr einengte.[15] Auch der Praxisbezug erhielt nicht den von *Spranger* ursprünglich intendierten Stellenwert, obwohl institutionell eine enge Bindung zur Schule dadurch geschaffen wurde, daß die Pädagogische Akademie eine eigene »Akademieschule« erhielt und der Akademiedozent für Didaktik jeweils gleichzeitig deren Schulrat war.
Der äußere Aufbau in Preußen ging, wie schon erwähnt, so vor sich, daß 1926 die ersten drei Pädagogischen Akademien mit der Arbeit begannen (evangelisch in Kiel und Elbing, katholisch in Bonn), daß 1927 die simultane in Frankfurt/Main hinzukam (sie blieb die einzige mit diesem Charakter), daß dann 1929 als dritter Schub die vier weiteren evangelischen Hochschulen in Hannover, Dortmund, Breslau und Erfurt und dann 1930 sogar noch sieben Neugründungen folgten: sechs evangelische

(Altona, Cottbus, Kassel, Stettin, Halle/Saale, Frankfurt/Oder) und eine katholische (Beuthen), so daß 1930 bereits 15 Pädagogische Akademien arbeiteten.[16] Die wachsende finanzielle Misere verhinderte nicht nur den weiteren Ausbau (z. B. war für 1931 die Gründung von drei Pädagogischen Akademien in Berlin – eine evangelische, eine katholische und eine »weltliche« – vorgesehen, und die bis 1930 gegründeten 15 stellten etwa die Hälfte der vom preußischen Staat für notwendig erachteten Gesamtzahl dar). Sie führte sogar bereits 1932 zur Schließung von sieben Hochschulen (Altona, Beuthen, Erfurt, Frankfurt/Oder, Halle/Saale, Kassel, Stettin).

Zu den Fragen der Detailentwicklung, der Abweichungen der einzelnen Institutionen im Arbeitsstil, in ihren besonderen Akzenten und in ihrem Image sowie zu zahlreichen anderen Komplexen in ihrem Binnenbereich und in ihren Umfeldern muß hier auf die ebenso umfassende wie differenzierende Darstellung von *Helmuth Kittel* (1957) verwiesen werden. Nur drei Punkte seien noch kurz angesprochen:
a) *Kittel* sagt wohl richtig: »Die Lehrkörper stellten eine gesunde Mischung von bisherigen oder gleichzeitigen Universitätsdozenten und früheren Seminar- oder Volksschullehrern dar. Dazu kamen in Einzelfällen Männer und Frauen aus nichtstaatlicher erzieherischer Tätigkeit und aus anderen freien Berufen« (*Kittel* (1957), S. 95). Es ist allerdings die Frage, ob die Vielfalt der Erfahrungs- und Wirkungskreise, die sich da zusammenfand, dennoch in eine einigermaßen stimmige reformpädagogische Grundausrichtung einmündete und ob ferner der stark jugendbewegte Stil, der einem Teil der Dozentenschaft, dazu auch einem relativ großen Teil der Studentenschaft eigen war, zu einem tragfähigen Konsens oder gar einem guten Zusammenspiel mit dem übrigen, dem »bürgerlich« angerichteten Teil gelangte. Aus meiner eigenen Erfahrung heraus (Studierender an der Päd. Akademie Erfurt 1930–32), aber auch auf Grund der Äußerungen *Wilhelm Flitners* aus seinem Erfahrungsbereich (Lehrender an der Päd. Akademie Kiel 1926–29) muß jedoch bezweifelt werden, daß das Ministerium für die genannten beiden Punkte personalpolitisch stets eine glückliche Hand gehabt hat. Auf Grund von Initiativen *Wilhelm Flitners* und *Herman Nohls* scheint das bei anderen, erst 1930 gegründeten Akademien dann besser gelaufen zu sein.
b) Trotz der gemeinsamen Festlegung auf die oben gekennzeichnete Struktur der Pädagogischen Hochschule hatte jede einzelne Pädagogische Akademie in Preußen ihr eigenes Gesicht, ihre besonderen Schwerpunkte und ihre speziellen Leistungen und Ansprüche, woran die Zusammensetzung und das Zusammenspiel des jeweiligen Lehrkörpers erheblichen Anteil hatten. Z. B. hat Kiel den Akzent stärker nach der Seite der Erziehungswissenschaft gesetzt, während Frankfurt/Oder in besonders hohem Maße den musischen Bereich gewichtet und kultiviert hat.
c) Obwohl die Volksschulen im Gebiet von Hessen-Nassau seit ca. 1875 eine kontinuierliche und also längst eingebürgerte Simultantradition hatten, somit über fünfzig Jahre lang nicht mehr konfessionell geprägt waren, rief die Gründung der simultanen Pädagogischen Akademie in Frankfurt/Main 1927 einen ungeheueren Wirbel in der Öffentlichkeit und bei den leitenden Stellen der katholischen Kirche sogar helle Empörung hervor. Der Streit ging so weit, daß den dort ausgebildeten jungen katholischen Lehrern und Lehrerinnen von seiten ihrer Kirchenleitung die Missio canonica, also die Befugnis zur Erteilung der Religionsunterrichts, verweigert wurde. Man kann daran beispielhaft sehen, welches Problemfeld die Konfessionsfrage in der Volksschule und in der Volksschullehrerbildung damals darstellte.[17]

Als weiteres Beispiel für die institutionelle Vielfalt der Volksschullehrerbildung in der Weimarer Zeit sei hier noch *Baden* erwähnt, dessen Regelung (ab 1. 4. 1926) schon

Helmuth Kittel ((1957), S. 294) mit Recht als »Zwischenlösung zwischen dem alten Seminar und einer Hochschulform alter oder neuer Art« gekennzeichnet hat. Sie schuf zweijährige Kurse an »Lehrerbildungsanstalten« simultaner (so Karlsruhe ab 1926) oder konfessioneller (so Heidelberg evangelisch und Freiburg katholisch ab 1928) Art, die Abiturienten aufnahmen, aber auch einen einjährigen Vorkurs hatten, der auf der Primareife aufsetzte. Auch der Studienplan der Lehrerbildungsanstalt hielt sich strukturell eher in der Nähe des alten Lehrerseminars.
Die ganz kleinen Länder – Anhalt, Lippe-Detmold, Lübeck usw. – bauten, wie hier noch abschließend erwähnt sei, keine eigene Volksschullehrerbildung auf, sondern schlossen Verträge mit größeren Ländern, die für sie die Ausbildungsaufgaben mit übernahmen, oder überließen ihren Lehramtsaspiranten die persönliche Wahl eines Landes für ihr Studium.

III. Zu den Grundstrukturen und Haupttypen

Bei aller Vielfalt im Detail lassen sich in der Weimarer Zeit drei Typen von Ausbildungsformen beim Lehramt für die Volksschule unterscheiden. Im ersten Falle (Bayern, Württemberg) wurde das Postulat der Reichsverfassung von 1919 nicht eingelöst, also die alte Seminarausbildung beibehalten. Im zweiten Falle (Thüringen, Sachsen, Hamburg, Braunschweig, auch Hessen und Mecklenburg-Schwerin) wurde die Ausbildung in die bestehenden wissenschaftlichen Hochschulen hineingenommen, und im dritten Falle (Preußen) wurde für sie eine neue Fachhochschule aufgebaut. Es schiene mir relativ unfruchtbar, hier abschließend die von *Kittel* (1957) einerseits und von *Sandfuchs* (1978) und *Weber* (1982) andererseits so kontrovers diskutierte Frage aufzunehmen, ob die preußischen Pädagogischen Akademien wirkliche Hochschulen gewesen seien.[18] Überhaupt hat es heute den Anschein, daß die »Universitätslösung« und die »PH-Lösung« in den zwanziger Jahren, aber vielfach auch später gar zu kraß, zu leidenschaftlich-engagiert und zu einfach bewertend gegenübergestellt worden sind (wie das in zeitlich distanzierter Rückschau auch etwa von der damals so heftig geführten und so stark polarisierenden Auseinandersetzung um *Fröbel* und *Montessori* in bezug auf die vorschulische Erziehung zu sagen ist).
Sinnvoller erscheint es mir, von bestimmten Aufgabenkomplexen auszugehen und von ihnen aus abschließend hier danach zu fragen, welche Chancen oder Probleme für deren Bewältigung bei den beiden Grundtypen damals vielleicht bestanden. Es seien dazu in aller Kürze sechs Punkte anvisiert.

1. Was zunächst die komplexe *Gesamtaufgabe* betrifft, so läßt sich m. E. nicht bestreiten, daß die preußische Pädagogische Akademie dem angehenden Volksschullehrer einen geraden und direkten Weg, sozusagen die Lösung aus einem Guß anbot. Sie war ja zu diesem Zweck konstruiert und mit diesem Ziel geschaffen worden. Es war daher gewiß ihre Stärke, daß alles personell und institutionell relativ gut zusammenzustimmen schien und daß erst recht bei der kleinen Zahl ihrer Dozenten und ihrer Studierenden (die einzelnen Akademien wurden damals

ja nicht einmal voll ausgebaut und »ausgelastet«!) sich leicht eine sehr dichte kommunikative Atmosphäre und ein hohes *pädagogisches Ethos* entwickeln konnte. Das mag gelegentlich sogar etwas forcierten, »hochtourigen« Charakter gehabt haben, kam aber gewiß der pädagogischen Aufgabe und Haltung der angehenden Lehrer und Lehrerinnen zugute. Freilich war das erkauft mit einer gewissen Art von *Ghetto-Erfahrung*, nämlich dem Abgesperrtsein von allen übrigen akademischen Ausbildungsgängen, insbesondere auch mit dem Abgesperrtsein von allen Gymnasiallehrer-Studienwegen. Der überscharfe Trennungsstrich, den *Spranger* zwischen Gymnasiallehramt und Volksschullehramt gezogen hatte, und seine verkürzende Charakterisierung der Philosophischen Fakultät (der er den Berufsbezug ja weitgehend absprach) hatten die gemeinsame pädagogische Aufgabe und Verantwortung in den Hintergrund treten lassen. Daß das Bewußtsein für sie durch die institutionelle Abtrennung der Ausbildungswege schwerwiegend geschwächt wurde, konnte weder dem Verhältnis und der Selbsteinschätzung der beiden Lehrergruppen noch ihrem Arbeitsfeld in den Schulen gut tun.
Demgegenüber bot die »Universitätslösung« den Volksschullehramtsanwärtern zweifellos mehr geistige Weite und gegenüber den anderen Aspiranten pädagogischer Berufe auch mehr Nähe und besseren Austausch. Allerdings waren die dort eng beieinander lebenden und miteinander wirkenden geistigen Kräfte und Bereiche auch heterogener, und es fragt sich, ob sich ein pädagogisches Ethos für die der Volksschularbeit Zustrebenden so leicht und so gut herausbilden konnte. Mindestens dürfte das schwerer gewesen sein – wie natürlich auch die weltanschaulich-religiöse Geschlossenheit fehlte, andererseits die Toleranz und die Auseinandersetzung eher angeregt und belebt wurde.
2. Daß dem *musischen Leben* in der preußischen Pädagogischen Akademie von deren Konzept her ein breiter Raum und eine bestimmende Kraft zukam und daß dies auch eine positive Funktion für die Volksschule haben konnte, läßt sich m. E. nicht in Frage stellen. In diesem Punkte hat sich die »Universitätslösung« zweifellos schwerer getan. Wie der Aufgabe Rechnung getragen wurde, war von Land zu Land unterschiedlich; aufs Ganze gesehen, bedurfte es dabei aber angesichts der deutschen Tradition der wissenschaftlichen Hochschulen einer besonders klaren und aktiven Beachtung, und hier scheint ein schwacher Punkt der damaligen »Universitätslösung« zu liegen.
3. Man muß andererseits die Ambivalenz des Prinzips der *»Überschaubarkeit«* bedenken, das ein Strukturmerkmal der damaligen Pädagogischen Akademie war. Die Folge war nämlich, daß – zumal bei ihrem zeitbedingten Teilausbau – fast alle Studienbereiche mit einer Ein-Mann-Besetzung auszukommen hatten. Das hatte (über jene oben angesprochene Ghetto-Erfahrung hinaus) eine Auswirkung, die als gravierende Gefahr eingeschätzt werden muß: es erzeugte leicht eine stark personbezogene »Jüngerschaft« oder eine andere zu persongebundene und personeingeengte Sachorientierung, konnte jedenfalls das selbständig-kritische Denken, die Weite des Blickes und die gründlichere sachlich-fachliche Auseinandersetzung erschweren, stand somit in Spannung zu einer wichtigen Aufgabe akademischer Bildung, die an größeren Hochschulen mit ihren Mehrfach-Besetzungen eher zu erreichen oder wenigstens leichter anzubahnen war.
4. Es ist ferner nach der Rolle der *Erziehungswissenschaft* bei den beiden Grundtypen zu fragen, die hier zu vergleichen sind. Dazu muß daran erinnert werden, daß der Erziehungswissenschaft zwar auch in der Konzeption der Pädagogischen Hochschule eine wesentliche Aufgabe zugesprochen und ihr volle wissenschaftliche Dignität abverlangt wurde, daß sie aber wie alles andere letztlich in die Persönlichkeitsbildung eingeordnet wurde und daß Spranger selbst die Kraft der pädagogischen Theorie, erziehliche Haltung mit zu fördern und kritisch abzustützen, nicht gerade hoch einschätzte. Es fragt sich, ob die Einordnung der Erziehungswissenschaft in die »Persönlichkeitsbildung« ihren Beitrag in der Lehrerausbildung nicht beeinträchtigen und ihre

Entfaltung an der Pädagogischen Akademie nicht hemmen konnte. Tatsächlich ist jedoch an einer ganzen Reihe von preußischen Akademien auf diesem Gebiet Hervorragendes geleistet worden. Anderseits darf nicht verkannt werden, daß die »Universitätslösung« dem erziehungswissenschaftlichen Studienanteil oft mehr Raum und mehr Gewicht gegeben hat, ohne die Ausbildung etwa zu vertheoretisieren und die schulpraktischen Studienerfordernisse gering zu achten.

5. Auch bei dem Bezugsfeld *Unterrichtsfächer-Fachdidaktiken* bestanden bei den beiden Ausbildungsmodellen strukturbedingte Akzentunterschiede, die aber wiederum nicht in der Manier einer Schwarz-Weiß-Malerei zugespitzt und gar polar gewichtet werden können. In der Pädagogischen Akademie lagen, wie schon erwähnt, die fachlichen und die fachdidaktischen bzw. fachmethodischen Gesichtspunkte für die Studierenden besonders eng beieinander, was den Blick stärker und direkter auf die spätere Schularbeit richten konnte. Andererseits konnte das die Gefahr heraufbeschwören, daß die fachlichen Sachverhalte und Eigenstrukturen nur beiläufig oder ungenügend zur Geltung gebracht wurden und einer Tendenz zu übermäßiger oder vorschneller Pädagogisierung Vorschub geleistet wurde.[19] Bei der »Universitätslösung« schien dem Eigengewicht und der strukturellen Eigenart der Sachverhalte und der Fachgebiete von vornherein mehr Beachtung geschenkt zu werden, wobei jedoch unter Umständen die fachdidaktischen und fachmethodischen Gesichtspunkte ins Hintertreffen geraten und die Volksschullehrerbildung in die Defizitzone der Philologenausbildung hineingezogen werden konnte. Mindestens bestand die Gefahr, daß die Wechselbezüge zwischen fachlichem und didaktischem Bereich sich verdunkelten oder von den Studierenden erst nachträglich geknüpft werden mußten.

6. Zur akademischen Volksschullehrerbildung der Weimarer Zeit gehörte, wie sich zeigte, fast durchweg ein besonderes *Wahlfach* ohne unmittelbaren Schul- und Unterrichtsbezug. Es sollte also direkt der Persönlichkeitsbildung der angehenden Lehrer dienen. Es liegt auf der Hand, daß diese Bestimmung sich in die Struktur der Pädagogischen Akademie besonders gut und glatt einfügte, weil sie deren Gesamtgefüge entsprach. Natürlich hatte hier das Wahlfach, rein als Fach genommen, auch eine Randstellung und konnte nicht etwa zum Rang eines vollen Fachstudiums »aufsteigen« bzw. »entarten«. Deshalb haftete an ihm, zumal bei dem bloß viersemestrigen Studiengang in Preußen, ein Zug des Dilettantismus – obzwar im guten Sinne; doch tieferes Eindringen war eben im Grunde gar nicht möglich. Bei der »Universitätslösung« bestanden andere fachliche Möglichkeiten, aber auch entsprechende Auswucherungs-, Aufblähungs- und Pervertierungsgefahren.

Vom sogenannten Wahlfach her gerät auch das übergeordnete, allgemeine Prinzip der *»Persönlichkeitsbildung«* in kritische Beleuchtung. Während sich dem Wahlfach mit seiner damaligen Bestimmung als einem persönlichkeitsbezogenen und persönlichkeitsbildenden Studienelement angesichts der Enzyklopädismusgefahr für den Volksschullehrer in der damaligen Situation der Volksschule wohl noch ein begrenzter Sinn abgewinnen läßt, scheint es mir anders zu stehen bei dem so hochgeschätzten Prinzip der »Persönlichkeitsbildung« als dem zentralen Gestaltungspunkt der ganzen Volksschullehrerbildung und damit auch der umfassenden Sinngebung und Ausrichtung der »Bildner-Hochschule«. Erziehung und Persönlichkeitsbildung im unmittelbaren Sinne sind die zentralen Aufgaben aller allgemeinbildenden Schulen für das Kindes- und Jugendalter; sie können m. E. aber nicht die eigentlichen Aufgaben einer Hochschule sein, die auf erwachsene Menschen einzuwirken und sie für einen Beruf auszubilden hat – auch dann nicht, wenn es sich dabei um die Vorbildung für einen pädagogischen Beruf handelt. Auch die Tatsache, daß diese Aufgabe als umfassende Zielsetzung der Berufsausbildung nur für einen bestimmten pädagogischen Beruf, nämlich das Volksschullehramt, reklamiert und fixiert wurde, demgegenüber für die angehenden Gymnasiallehrer aber die Bildung durch die Wissenschaft des

Unterrichtsfaches im wesentlichen als ausreichend erachtet wurde, mußte diesen Gesichtspunkt ins Zwielicht bringen und seinen Problemcharakter offenbaren. Belud er die preußischen Pädagogischen Akademien einerseits mit einer Aufgabe, die sie bei solcher Überhöhung ihrer legitimen Kompetenzen im strengen Sinne auch nicht erfüllen konnten, kann doch andererseits nicht in Abrede gestellt werden, daß sie ihrer Struktur nach die Studierenden wiederum menschlich tiefer und umfassender ansprechen konnten als die traditionellen deutschen wissenschaftlichen Hochschulen, bei denen der Gesichtspunkt einer über das rein Fachliche hinausgehenden Menschenbildung im Laufe ihrer Entwicklung – aber eben erst im Zuge dieser Entwicklung – fast ganz auf der Strecke geblieben war. In etwas zugespitzter Formulierung läßt sich also sagen: während die Pädagogische Akademie sich mit der auf den angehenden Volksschullehrer bezogenen und eingeengten »Persönlichkeitsbildung« eigentlich übernahm, war die »Universitätslösung« in der Gefahr, den Studierenden für jedes Lehramt (nicht nur, aber gerade auch denen für das Volksschullehramt) gar zu wenig für ihre menschlich-persönliche Bereicherung mitzugeben.

Schließlich ist auch noch die damalige Schulsituation als Hintergrund und Zielfeld für die Volksschullehrerbildung der Weimarer Zeit ins Auge zu fassen. Es ist z. B. zu bedenken, daß es – abgesehen von wenigen Ausnahmen, zu denen vor allem Hessen-Nassau und Baden gehörten, also fast durchweg im Reich – ein konfessionell bzw. weltanschaulich geprägtes Volksschulwesen gab, und daß um seine weitere Gestaltung (konfessionell-simultan-»weltlich«) trotz bzw. gerade wegen der einschlägigen Schulartikel der Reichsverfassung ständig gestritten wurde, wovon die Volksschullehrerbildung nicht ganz unberührt bleiben konnte.
Es ist ferner z. B. daran zu erinnern, daß – ganz abgesehen von den politischen Kräften, die da hineinwirkten – der Anteil und die Rolle der weniggegliederten Volksschulen gegenüber den vollausgebauten und durchgegliederten sich ganz anders ausnahm als heute. Abgesehen von den Stadtstaaten, also in allen Flächenstaaten des Reiches, erst recht in den großen, überwog trotz der dazugehörigen Großstädte die Zahl der weniggegliederten Volksschulen den Anteil der vollausgebauten erheblich, und auch darauf hatte sich die akademische Volksschullehrerbildung einzustellen. Die Rahmenbedingungen waren somit bei den Stadtstaaten wesentlich anders als bei den Flächenstaaten, und wiederum in den Städten wesentlich anders als auf dem Lande. Und last but not least ist an die ländermäßig ganz unterschiedlichen Bestände und Kapazitäten der damaligen wissenschaftlichen Hochschulen zu denken. So konnte z. B. die Hamburger Universität ohne besondere strukturellen Probleme und organisatorischen Schwierigkeiten so ausgebaut werden, daß sie zusätzlich zu den in Hamburg benötigten Gymnasiallehrern auch die erforderliche Zahl der Volksschullehrer für den Stadtstaat (und sogar auch noch die Berufsschullehrer) ausbildete, diese Studierenden also nicht nur theoretisch, sondern auch schulpraktisch betreute und verteilte. Es wäre aber schon wegen der Erfordernisse der schulpraktischen Ausbildungsteile und der dafür notwendigen Zahl von Volksschulen in der Weimarer Zeit ganz unmöglich gewesen, in Bayern die gesamte Volksschullehrerausbildung an den damals bestehenden, insgesamt drei Landesuniversitäten mit ihren Universitätsorten München, Würzburg und Erlangen zu konzentrieren, also alle für das Land Bayern erforderlichen Volksschullehrer und -lehrerinnen in diesen drei Städten studien- und schulpraxismäßig zu versorgen und zu betreuen.

Daraus erhellt einmal mehr, wie wichtig es ist, bei der Betrachtung der damaligen Aufgaben und Probleme der Volksschullehrerbildung nach Möglichkeit die *Gesamtsituation* der Weimarer Zeit ins Blickfeld mit einzubeziehen – was im vorgegebenen Rahmen hier freilich nur ansatzweise geschehen konnte.

Anmerkungen

[1] Dazu kam, daß zwei Abgeordnete der Nationalversammlung bei ihrer Zustimmung zu Art. 143 Abs. 2 ausdrücklich erklärten, sie dächten sich die künftige akademische Lehrerbildung konfessionell gestaltet – was jedenfalls nicht der traditionellen Struktur der deutschen Universitäten entsprach.

[2] Das Reichskabinett beschloß auf Grund der Finanzierungskomplikationen (und sicher nicht ohne Zusammenhang mit den negativen Verhandlungsergebnissen) endgültig am 12. 1. 1923, kein Lehrerbildungsgesetz im Reichstag einzubringen, und das Reichsministerium des Innern teilte den Ländern am 20. 1. 1923 mit, »aus finanziellen Gründen bis auf weiteres von der Ausführung des Art. 143 Abs. 2 der Reichsverfassung absehen zu müssen«. Es stellte dazu noch fest: soweit einzelne Länder selbständig handeln würden, sei es Sache des Reichsministeriums des Innern, auf eine möglichst gleichmäßige Regelung hinzuwirken (vgl. *Kittel* (1957), S. 41; *Sandfuchs* (1978), S. 80; *Weber* (1982), S. 164). Dieser der Reichsinstanz zugesprochene Amtsauftrag konnte wohl nur noch »akademischen« Charakter, der für sie damit reklamierte Anspruch eigentlich nur noch deklamatorischen Wert haben.

[3] Dazu als Beispiel: in Preußen gab es im Jahre 1922 nach den Berechnungen der Unterrichtsverwaltung ca. 37000 (stellungslose) Lehramtsbewerber (*Weber* (1982), S. 550).

[4] Zu erwähnen ist allerdings, daß der Ausbau des höheren Mädchenschulwesens gegen Ende des 19. Jahrhunderts für die angehenden Volksschullehrerinnen eine zweigleisige Ausbildung geschaffen hatte: neben dem normalen Lehrerinnenseminar, das wie das Lehrerseminar auf dem Volksschulabschluß aufbaute, gab es nun an manchen höheren Mädchenschulen eine besonders aufgesetzte pädagogische Ausbildungsklasse (»Selekta«), die mit dem Lehrerinnenexamen abschloß und den Absolventinnen die Befähigung zur Lehrerin an der Volksschule und auch an der höheren Mädchenschule erteilte. Bei der Neuregelung des höheren Mädchenschulwesens um 1910 wurde dieser Weg noch weiter aufgestockt und ausgebaut.

[5] Daß die Gestaltung der Volksschullehrerbildung in der Weimarer Republik auch von wechselnden politischen Mehrheiten in den einzelnen Ländern stark beeinflußt werden konnte, hat sich eklatant in Bayern, in Thüringen und in Mecklenburg-Schwerin gezeigt.

[6] Für die angehenden Lehrer und Lehrerinnen der technisch-künstlerischen Fächer (Turnen, Zeichnen, Gesang, Werkunterricht, weibliche Handarbeit) wurde zunächst noch Mittelschulabschluß als Basis der Berufsbildung zugelassen.

[7] Bei *Möller* (1976), der sonst recht präzise Angaben bringt, ist diese einschneidende Studienamputation allerdings nicht erwähnt. *Zierold/Rothkugel* ([2]1931), S. 202ff.), die den Stand vom 1. 4. 1931 wiedergeben, nennen jedoch bei Thüringen als Studiendauer ausdrücklich »zwei Jahre«. Ihre Aufstellungen sind bei *Rita Weber* (1982) in Tabellenform zusammengefaßt.

[8] Bei dem Studienplan von 1926, der zwar nur empfehlenden Charakter hatte, aber eben als Richtlinie einzuschätzen ist, entfielen von insgesamt 155 Wochenstunden in den sechs Semestern auf die Erziehungswissenschaft 60 Wochenstunden. Daneben waren z. B. der

künstlerisch-technischen Ausbildung 36 Wochenstunden, der Psychologie 15 Wochenstunden, der Philosophie 12 Wochenstunden, dem Wahlfach 18 Wochenstunden zugesprochen (vgl. *Möller* (1976), S. 303 ff.).

[9] 1930 wurde auch ein besonderes »Forschungsinstitut für Erziehungswissenschaften« gegründet, das aber nicht zur TH gehörte, sondern Stiftungscharakter hatte.

[10] Aus leider nur beiläufigen Angaben dazu von *Sandfuchs* (1978), S. 314 und S. 316 ist zu ersehen, daß die (vermutlich nur als Richtlinie anzusehende, dennoch sicher maßgebliche) Gesamtwochenstundenzahl im sechssemestrigen Studium sich auf 206 belief, also eine fast schwindelerregende Höhe hatte (durchschnittlich ca. 34 Wochenstunden im Semester) und daß die erziehungswissenschaftlichen Fächer daran den überaus hohen Anteil von 84 Wochenstunden (= fast 41%) hatten.

[11] So die genaue Aufstellung bei *Kittel* (1957), S. 293, während *Sandfuchs* (1986), S. 149 bei der Liste der »Wahlfächer« den musisch-technischen Bereich nicht erwähnt.

[12] Es sei hierzu an manche damaligen Gerichtsentscheidungen über grobe Kränkungen und persönliche Beleidigungen erinnert, die dem Reichspräsidenten *Friedrich Ebert* zugefügt worden waren (vgl. *Maser* (1987), S. 307–313).

[13] Zur Serie charakteristischer damaliger Ablehnungsargumente aus Bayern gehörten z. B. die Warnung vor einer zu starken Zentralisierung und vor der »Zudrosselung« der klösterlichen Lehrerinnenbildungsanstalten (F. Eggersdorfer), das Hochspielen der Kostenfrage, die Sorge um geringere berufliche Tüchtigkeit und um mangelnde Bereitschaft akademisch gebildeter Lehrer, auf dem Lande oder in der Kleinstadt zu arbeiten *(O. Vogelhuber)*, die Betonung, daß Bayern »auf Selbständigkeit« seines »Unterrichtswesens Wert lege« (Kultusmin. *Matt*), die These, daß die Konfessionsschulen ein Recht auf entsprechend ausgebildete Lehrer hätten *(O. Vogelhuber)*, der nachdrückliche Hinweis, daß Bayern auf eine Reform der Lehrerbildung keineswegs angewiesen sei, weil es Lehrer und Lehrerinnen im Überfluß habe (Kultusmin. *Matt*), andererseits die Sorge, daß Lehrermangel speziell im Religionsunterricht eintreten würde (Erklärung Bayerns auf der Konferenz am 18. 2. 1922) und vieles andere mehr, was bei *Renner* (1979) nachzulesen ist.

[14] »Daß dies auch kaum beabsichtigt war, zeigt sich in der Antwort, die *O. Vogelhuber* auf die Anfrage eines Studenten gab. Er teilte nämlich mit, es sei schlichtweg falsch zu behaupten, das Kultusministerium plane eine Abschaffung der derzeitigen Lehrerseminare (Hauptstaatsarchiv München, Akten des Min. f. Unterr. u. Kultus, MK 22214)«; *Renner* (1979), S. 293. *Renner* gibt den genauen Zeitpunkt dieses ministeriellen Bescheides nicht an, es dürfte sich aber um das Jahr 1928 gehandelt haben.

[15] Die »Stundentafel für die Pflichtfächer«, die das Ministerium Anfang 1927 als Richtlinie herausgab, sah für die ersten drei Semester je 30 Wochenstunden, für das vierte Semester 24 Wochenstunden vor (*Kittel* (1957), S. 98). Von diesen insgesamt 114 Pflichtstunden entfielen auf die erziehungs- und sonstigen grundwissenschaftlichen Orientierungen ca. 35 Wochenstunden.

[16] Alle Pädagogischen Akademien nahmen Studierende beider Geschlechter auf – außer der Päd. Akademie in Bonn, die nur für männliche Bewerber offen war.

[17] Es sei auch daran erinnert, daß in der Weimarer Zeit dreimal Reichsschulgesetzentwürfe für die Gestaltung der Volksschule an diesem Problemkomplex gescheitert sind.

[18] Tatsächlich fehlte ihnen damals eine Reihe von rechtlichen Attributen echter Hochschulen. Aber mindestens waren die preußischen Päd. Akademien auf dem Wege, Hochschulen im vollen rechtlichen Sinne zu werden. Die spätere Entwicklung der Pädagogischen Hochschulen in den fünfziger und sechziger Jahren kann geradezu als Erläuterung für diese These genommen werden (vgl. hierzu *Reble* (1982) und *Reble* (1986)). Vergleichsweise zu beachten

ist auch die Entwicklung der Technischen Hochschulen, z. B. die Tatsache, daß ihnen nach ihrer stürmischen Entwicklung im 19. Jahrhundert erst 1899 das Promotionsrecht verliehen wurde.

[19] *Helmuth Kittel* (1957) ist der Auffassung, daß *Johannes von den Driesch* das *Spranger*-Konzept in dieser Richtung verwässert hat.

Literaturverzeichnis

Antz, J. (1930): Die seminaristische Lehrerbildung des 19. und 20. Jahrhunderts in historischer und kritischer Beleuchtung. In: Vierteljahrsschrift für wissenschaftliche Pädagogik 6 (1930), S. 9ff.

Bär, A., Böhm, A. u. a. (1920): Gutachten über Pädagogische Akademien. Langensalza

Becker, C. H. (1926): Die Pädagogische Akademie im Aufbau unseres Bildungswesens. Leipzig

Beckmann, H.-K. (1968): Lehrerseminar – Akademie – Hochschule. Das Verhältnis von Theorie und Praxis in 3 Epochen der Volksschullehrerausbildung. Weinheim

Boehm, E. (o. J.–1926): Der Streit um die Lehrerbildung. Kritisches zum akademischen Studium der sächsischen Volksschullehrer. Radebeul

Bungardt, K. (1964): Der Weg der Lehrerbildung vom Seminar zur Universität. Widerstand und Bereitschaft der Universitäten in Dokumenten. Material- und Nachrichtendienst (MUND) der Arbeitsgemeinschaft Deutscher Lehrerverbände, 15. Jhrg. Nr. 110. Bühl/Baden

Deuchler, G. (1925): Die neue Lehrerbildung. Braunschweig u. Hamburg

Eckardt, A. (²1927): Der gegenwärtige Stand der neuen Lehrerbildung in den einzelnen Ländern Deutschlands und in außerdeutschen Staaten. Weimar (3., vollständig neu bearb. Aufl. u. d. T. Die akademische Lehrerbildung. Eine zusammenfassende Darstellung ihrer Probleme wie ihres gegenwärtigen Standes im In- und Ausland. Weimar 1934)

Fadrus, V. (1926): Die Neugestaltung der Lehrerbildung in Deutschland und Österreich. Sonderdruck aus der pädagogischen Monatsschrift »Schulreform«, 5. Jhrg. Wien

Feldmann, E. u. Hoffmann, H. (Hrsg.) (1925): Denkschrift zur Neugestaltung der Lehrerbildung in Hessen. Karlsruhe

Fischer, A. (1922): Die Berufsbildung der Lehrer. In: Bayerische Lehrerzeitung, Jhrg. 1922, S. 89–96. Nürnberg

Fischer, A. (1924): Zur Frage eines einführenden pädagogischen Anschauungsunterrichts in der akademischen Lehrerbildung. In: A. Fischer, Leben und Werk, hrsg. v. K. Kreitmair, Bd. 5/6, München 1957, S. 383–407

Flitner, W. (1929): Das Pädagogikstudium an der Pädagogischen Akademie. In: Die Erziehung 4 (1929), S. 228–237. Abgedr. in: W. Fl., Ausgewählte pädagogische Abhandlungen, hrsg. v. H. Kanz, 1967, S. 79–94

Flitner, W. (1933): Die Entwicklung der Pädagogischen Akademien. In: Die Erziehung 8 (1933), S. 447–453

Flitner, W. (1976): Selbstdarstellung. In: L. J. Pongratz (Hrsg.): Pädagogik in Selbstdarstellungen, Bd. II, S. 146–197. Hamburg

Föhr, E. (1927): Die Neuregelung der Lehrerbildung in Baden. Düsseldorf

Führ, Chr. (1970, ²1972): Zur Schulpolitik der Weimarer Republik. Die Zusammenarbeit von Reich und Ländern in Reichsschulausschuß (1919–1923) und im Ausschuß für das Unterrichtswesen (1924–1933). Darstellung und Quellen. Weinheim

Gaudig, H. (1920): Schulreform? Gedanken zur Reform des Reformierens. Leipzig

Gebhard, J. (1948): Die Lehrerbildung im Pädagogischen Institut der Universität Hamburg. Hamburg
Geißler, G. (1973): Eingliederung der Lehrerbildung in die Universität. Das Hamburger Beispiel. Weinheim
Gönner, R. (1967): Die österreichische Lehrerbildung von der Normalschule bis zur Pädagogischen Akademie. Wien
Guachten der bayerischen Universitäten von 1929 zur Lehrerbildungsfrage. In: Die Bayerische Schule, Jg. 1953, 19, S. 329–333
Haaß, U. (1967): Die Kulturpolitik des Bayerischen Landtages in der Zeit der Weimarer Republik 1918–1933. Diss. München
Heinemann, M. (Hrsg.) (1976): Sozialisation und Bildungswesen in der Weimarer Republik. Stuttgart
Kästner, P. (1929): Vom Wesen der neuen Lehrerbildung. Langensalza
Kerschensteiner, G. (1921): Die Seele des Erziehers und das Problem der Lehrerbildung. Leipzig ('1965 München)
Kittel, H. (1932): Der Weg zum Volkslehrer. Über die Entwicklung der Pädagogischen Akademien. Jena
Kittel, H. (1957): Die Entwicklung der Pädagogischen Hochschulen 1926–1932. Eine zeitgeschichtliche Studie über das Verhältnis von Staat und Kultur. Berlin/Hannover/Darmstadt
Kittel, H. (1965): Die Pädagogischen Hochschulen. Dokumente ihrer Entwicklung (I) 1920–32. Weinheim
Kroh, O. (1929/30): Probleme der Lehrerbildung. In: Württembergische Schulwarte, Jg. 1929, S. 312–334, 385–395; Jg. 1930, S. 1–15
Kühnel, J. (1920): Gedanken über Lehrerbildung. Eine Gegenschrift. Leipzig.
Kühnel, J. (1923): Die Lehrerbildung auf der Hochschule. Dresden
Kummer, E. (1907): Die eigene Hochschule der deutschen Volksschullehrer. Frankfurt
Kutzner, O. (1920): Die pädagogische Fakultät. Ein Beitrag zur Reform der Lehrerbildung. Schulpädagogik und Volksbildung, Heft 1. Osterwieck
Lehrerbildungsausschuß des Sächsischen Lehrervereins (Hrsg.) (1923): Die Hochschullehrerbildung der Lehrer in Sachsen. Dresden
Lehrkörper der Päd. Akademie Kiel (Hrsg.) (1929): Aufbau und Arbeitsweise einer Päd. Akademie. Frankfurt/Main
Lehrkörper des Päd. Instituts zu Dresden (Hrsg.) (1925): Das Hochschulstudium der Volks- und Berufsschullehrer im Freistaat Sachsen. Leipzig
Maaß, N. (1930): Arbeitsgemeinschaft, Schulaufsicht und Pädagogische Akademie; ihr Anteil an der neuen Lehrerfortbildung. Langensalza
Maser, W. (1987): Friedrich Ebert, Der erste deutsche Reichspräsident. München
Meyer-Willner, G. (1986): Eduard Spranger und die Lehrerbildung. Die notwendige Revision eines Mythos. Bad Heilbrunn
Mitteilungen der Erziehungswissenschaftlichen Anstalt der Thüringer Universität, Heft 1 (1925): Die akademische Lehrerbildung an der Universität Jena
Möller, H. (1967): Der erste Aufbau einer vollakademischen Lehrerbildung in Deutschland. – Thüringen 1920–1926. In: Mitteldeutsche Beiträge 1967: Beiträge Mitteldeutschlands zur Universitätsgeschichte u. Lehrerbildung, hrsg. v. Mitteldeutschen Kulturrat, Bonn 1967, S. 41–62. Bonn
Möller, H. (1976): Aufbau einer vollakademischen Lehrerbildung in Thüringen. In: Heinemann, M. (1976, s. o.), S. 291–311
Muthesius, K. (1913): Die Berufsbildung des Lehrers. München

Muthesius, K. (1919): Die Zukunft der Volksschullehrerbildung. Berlin

Oestreich, P., u. Tacke, O. (Hrsg.) (1926): Der neue Lehrer. Die notwendige Lehrerbildung. Beiträge zur entschiedenen Schulreform. Osterwieck

Pädagogische Akademie Kiel (Hrsg.) (1929): Aufbau und Arbeitsweise einer Päd. Akademie. Heft 1 der Beiträge zur Lehrerbildung und Lehrerfortbildung. Frankfurt/Main

Pädagogische Akademien zu Bonn, Elbing u. Kiel (1926–28): Mitteilungen der Päd. Akademien in Preußen. 3 Hefte. Berlin

Paffrath, F. H. (1971): Eduard Spranger und die Volksschule. Eine historisch-systematische Untersuchung. Bad Heilbrunn

Paul, G. (1985): Lehrerbildung und Politik. Eine Analyse der Auseinandersetzungen in der Weimarer Republik. Hamburg

Peter, R. (1930): Die Durchführung der Lehrerbildung an der Hamburger Universität. In: Hamburger Lehrerzeitung, Jg. 1930, Nr. 4

Petersen, P. (Hrsg.) (1925): Die akademische Lehrerbildung in Thüringen. Verordnungen, Einrichtungen, Ratschläge. Weimar

Petersen, P. (1929): Akten zur Rückbildung der Lehrerbildung in Thüringen. Weimar

Pretzel, C. L. A. (1920): Die Neuordnung der Lehrerbildung. Schriftenreihe des Deutschen Lehrervereins, Heft 2. Berlin

Pretzel, C. L. A. (1921): Geschichte des Deutschen Lehrervereins in den ersten 50 Jahren seines Bestehens. Leipzig

Preußischer Lehrerverein (1924): Die Neugestaltung der Lehrerbildung. Denkschrift des Geschäftsführenden Ausschusses des Preußischen Lehrervereins. Magdeburg

Preußischer Lehrerverein (1930): Die Zukunft der Pädagogischen Akademien. Denkschrift des Geschäftsführenden Ausschusses des Preußischen Lehrervereins. Magdeburg

Preußisches Ministerium für Wissenschaft, Kunst und Volksbildung (1925): Die Neuordnung der Volksschullehrerbildung in Preußen. Denkschrift. Berlin

Reble, A. (1958): Lehrerbildung in Deutschland. Ratingen (mit umfassender Bibliographie)

Reble, A. (1982): Die philosophische Idee der Lehrerbildung. In de Rudder, H. (Hrsg.) (1982): Die Lehrerbildung zwischen Päd. Hochschule u. Universität. Bad Heilbrunn

Reble, A. (1986): Was fordert die Schule von der Erziehungswissenschaft in der Lehrerausbildung? In: Heim, H./Ipfling, H. J. (Hrsg.) (1986): Pädagogik in geschichtlicher Erfahrung und gegenwärtiger Verantwortung. Frankfurt/Main.

Reble, A. ([14]1987): Geschichte der Pädagogik. Stuttgart

Reichsministerium des Innern (1921): Die Reichsschulkonferenz 1920. Ihre Vorgeschichte und Vorbereitung und ihre Verhandlungen. Amtlicher Bericht. Leipzig

Rein, W. (1924): Zur gegenwärtigen Lage der Lehrerbildung, Langensalza

Rempele, A. (1926): Lehrerbildung und Sozialdemokratie. Pforzheim

Renner, K. (1979): Ernst Weber und die reformpädagogische Diskussion in Bayern. Bad Heilbrunn

Richter, J. (1932): Lehrerbildung als deutsche Kulturfrage. Leipzig

Riekel, A. (1925): Die Probleme der Lehrerbildung. Gedanken und Vorschläge. Braunschweig

Riekel, A. (1931): Die akademische Lehrerbildung. Idee und Geschichte. Langensalza

Rüttgers, S. (1920): Die pädagogische Fakultät. Notwendigkeit, Einrichtung, Aufgaben. Leipzig

Sacher, W. (1974): Die Zweite Phase in der Lehrerbildung. Ihre Entwicklung seit 1800, aufgezeigt am Beispiel Bayern. Bad Heilbrunn

Sächsisches Ministerium für Volksbildung (1929): Denkschrift zur Neuordnung der Lehrerbildung im Freistaat Sachsen. Dresden

Sandfuchs, U. (1978): Universitäre Lehrerausbildung in der Weimarer Republik und im Dritten Reich. Eine historisch-systematische Untersuchung am Beispiel der Lehrerausbildung an der TH Braunschweig (1918–1940). Bad Heilbrunn
Sandfuchs, U. (1986): Strukturwandel der Volksschullehrerausbildung 1927–52. Das Beispiel Braunschweig. In: Braunschweigisches Jahrbuch, Bd. 67, S. 141–169. Braunschweig
Sauer, M. (1987): Volksschullehrerbildung in Preußen. Die Seminare und Präparandenanstalten vom 18. Jh. bis zur Weimarer Republik. Köln/Wien
Schmidt, R. (1970): Die Lehrerfrage in der Reichsschulkonferenz von 1920. Diss. Gießen
Schoeps, H.-J. (Hrsg.) (1968): Zeitgeist im Wandel, Bd. II: Zeitgeist der Weimarer Republik. Stuttgart
Schriftennachweise der Comeniusbücherei, Bd. 2 (1929): Die akademische Lehrerbildung. Leipzig
Schulpolitische Schriftenreihe des Landeslehrervereins, Heft 4 (1928): Die gegenwärtige mecklenburgische Lehrerbildung im Pädagogischen Institut zu Rostock. Wismar
Schuwerack, W. C. (1929): Der Kampf um die simultane Pädagogische Akademie in Frankfurt (Main). Düsseldorf
Schwartz, H. (1925): Aufgabe und Einrichtung der Pädagogischen Akademien. Berlin
Schwartz, H. (1926): Die Lehrerbildungsfrage und ihre Lösung. Leipzig
Seyfert, R. (1905): Vorschläge zur Reform der Lehrerbildung. Leipzig
Seyfert, R./Richter, J. (Hrsg.) (1925): Gesetzliche Grundlagen der akademischen Lehrerbildung im Freistaat Sachsen. Leipzig
Spranger, E. (1919/20): Gedanken über Lehrerbildung. Leipzig
Stölzle, R. (1920): Universität und Lehrerbildung. Langensalza
Stückrath, F. (1933): Die Hamburger Lehrerbildung. Grundgedanken, Aufbau, Durchführung. Langensalza
Thormann, W. (1924): Die Lehrerbildung. Grundlagen, Weg, Aufbau. Leipzig
Treue, G. (1920): Die Doktorpromotion der Volksschullehrer und -innen an den Universitäten und Hochschulen Deutschlands. Dresden
Vogelhuber, O. (1927): Zum Stand der Lehrerbildungsfrage. In: Nichtamtliches Beiblatt zum Amtsblatt des Bayerischen Staatsministeriums für Unterricht und Kultus, Jg. 1927. München, S. 18–27, 89–101
Weber, R. (1982): Die Neuordnung der Volksschullehrerausbildung im Preußen der Weimarer Republik. Diss. F. U. Berlin
Weidel, K. (1928): Die neue Lehrerbildung in Preußen. Erfurt
Wende, E. (o. J., 1931): Die Pädagogische Akademie als Hochschule. Langensalza
Wende, E. (1959): C. H. Becker – Mensch und Politiker. Ein biographischer Beitrag zur Kulturgeschichte der Weimarer Republik. Stuttgart
Weniger, E. (1952): Die Eigenständigkeit der Erziehung in Theorie und Praxis. Weinheim
Zierold, K./Rothkugel (Hrsg.) (1930, ²1931): Die Pädagogischen Akademien. Amtliche Bestimmungen. Berlin
Zwei Jahre Lehrerbildung. Dokumente aus der Arbeit der Pädagogischen Akademie Frankfurt/Oder 1930–32. Langensalza

Hans-Jürgen Apel

Die Ausbildung zum Gymnasiallehrer im 19. Jahrhundert

Ein Vergleich zwischen Bayern und Preußen

1. Einleitung

Als der Gymnasialprofessor *Dr. Hans Morsch,* Oberlehrer am Königlichen *Kaiser-Wilhelms-Realgymnasium* zu Berlin, 1910 seine vergleichende Darstellung über »Das höhere Lehramt in Deutschland und Österreich« in zweiter Auflage herausgab, war er sich der spezifischen Differenzen, welche die Gymnasiallehrerbildung in den verschiedenen deutschsprachigen Staaten bestimmten, genau bewußt. *Morschs* Schrift informiert noch heute vorzüglich über Verschiedenheiten und Ähnlichkeiten in den Ausbildungsordnungen zum Universitätsstudium und in den Verfügungen zum Vorbereitungsdienst, wie sie um 1910 in den Staaten des Deutschen Kaiserreiches bestanden. Bei der Lektüre seiner Schrift wird klar, daß die fast nur auf Preußen bezogene Schulgeschichtsschreibung die traditionelle Vielfalt der deutschen Verhältnisse unterschlägt. Mit dem folgenden Vergleich bayerischer und preußischer Ausbildungsvorschriften wird an Morschs Intention wieder angeknüpft. Dadurch können zwei Entwicklungslinien vorgestellt werden, die bei nur teilweise übereinstimmenden, zeitweise auch unterschiedlichen politischen Rahmenbedingungen zu durchaus vergleichbaren, wenn auch nicht gleichartigen Ausbildungsvorschriften und -praktiken gelangten. Zugleich kann deutlich werden, daß die auch gegenwärtig in den Bundesländern vorhandenen Ausbildungsunterschiede sowie differierende Ansichten zu zentralen Bildungsfragen Ausdruck einer deutschen Tradition sind.

2. Methodische Überlegungen

Im Mittelpunkt des folgenden Beitrags steht die vergleichende Betrachtung der Ausbildung, die für Gymnasiallehrer in Bayern und Preußen seit dem Beginn des 19. Jahrhunderts vorgeschrieben war. Der Zeitraum der Untersuchung endet um 1900. Ausgangspunkt des Vergleichs werden Ausbildungs- und Prüfungsordnungen sein, wie sie in beiden Monarchien zur Regelung der universitären und der später eingeführten praktischen Ausbildung erlassen wurden. Die Verordnungen sind zunächst inhaltlich zu analysieren, dann aber insbesondere darauf zu betrachten, inwieweit sie den *Prozeß der Professionalisierung im Spannungsfeld von Allgemein-*

bildung und fachlicher Spezialisierung regelten. Mit Allgemeinbildung ist hier die Qualifikation gemeint, die auf ein breites fachliches Verständnis in Verbindung mit philosophisch-pädagogischen Kenntnissen abzielte, jene »Gesammtbildung«, die in preußischen Examina z. T. als grundlegend-philosophische und allgemeine Kenntnis über die Schulwissenschaften geprüft wurde. Gegenüber der zunehmenden fachlichen Spezialisierung der Gymnasiallehrer trat die Bedeutung der Allgemeinbildung im Verlauf des 19. Jahrhunderts allmählich in den Hintergrund, eine Entwicklung, welche die Revisionen der Prüfungsordnungen beeinflußte.

Weiter wird die Regelung des Verhältnisses von *Theorie* und *Praxis* in der Ausbildung zu beachten sein. Für den Lehrerberuf ist seit seiner Institutionalisierung die Praxisorientierung der wissenschaftlichen Ausbildung ein Hauptproblem geblieben. Umstritten war allerdings immer, was unter Praxisorientierung verstanden und inwieweit die Praxis des Schulunterrichts überhaupt in universitäre Lehrgänge einbezogen werden kann. Das Verhältnis von Theorie und Praxis in den Ausbildungs- und Prüfungsordnungen wird daher den zweiten Aspekt des Vergleichs bilden.

Ein *Vergleich* erfolgt durch prüfendes und wertendes Nebeneinanderstellen von Sachverhalten. Als wissenschaftliche Methode dient er vorzugsweise dazu, Ähnlichkeit oder Verschiedenheit im Hinblick auf ein Drittes festzustellen. Vergleicht man die Ausbildungs- und Prüfungsordnungen des 19. Jahrhunderts für Gymnasiallehrer in Bayern und Preußen, um die Entwicklung der Gymnasiallehrerbildung zu verfolgen und das Verhältnis von Allgemeinbildung und fachlicher Spezialisierung sowie die Beziehung zwischen Theorie und Praxis in der Ausbildung zu betrachten, dann bietet sich an, folgende *Schwerpunkte* zu setzen:

(1) die *Institutionalisierung der Prüfungsordnungen* am Beginn des 19. Jahrhunderts,
(2) die *Entwicklung der Ausbildung* während des 19. Jahrhunderts und
(3) die *Regelung der Ausbildung* um 1900.

Abschließend wird zu fragen sein, ob innerhalb der beiden Monarchien des Kaiserreichs ein Austausch der Gymnasiallehrer möglich war.

Über die Ausbildung zum höheren Lehramt in verschiedenen deutschen Ländern des 19. Jahrhunderts liegen nur wenige vergleichende Untersuchungen vor. An zeitgenössischen Arbeiten sind neben der Studie von *Hans Morsch* noch die Abhandlung von *Wilhelm Fries,* »Die Vorbildung der Lehrer für das Lehramt« (1895) und die Zusammenstellung *Otto Schröders* »Die Ordnung des Studiums für das höhere Lehramt in Deutschland ...« (1906) zu berücksichtigen. Die großen Sammlungen von *Wiese/Irmer* (1904) und *Adolf Beier* (1909) betreffen vorzugsweise preußische Verordnungen. In der Gegenwart hat *Christoph Führ* in Teil I seines Beitrags »Gelehrter Schulmann – Oberlehrer – Studienrat. Zum sozialen Aufstieg der Philologen« (1985) einen vergleichenden Überblick über die verschiedenen Prüfungsregelungen der deutschen Staaten für das 19. Jahrhundert zusammengestellt. *Helga Romberg* erörtert in ihrer Untersuchung »Staat und Schule« (1979) diese Zusammenhänge nur kurz. Einen orientierenden Überblick bietet auch *Rainer Bölling* in seiner »Sozialgeschichte der deutschen Lehrer« (1983), in der der preußischen Position jedoch ein Übergewicht zugeordnet wird.

Über die Professionalisierung der Gymnasiallehrer in Bayern während des 19. Jahr-

hunderts liegen verschiedene Arbeiten vor. Von Bedeutung für die hier abzuhandelnde Thematik sind vor allem zwei Beiträge: Zum einen die Untersuchung, die *Eugen Brand* 1904 über »Die Entwicklung des Gymnasiallehrerstandes in Bayern von 1773 bis 1904« vorgelegt hat. Neben einer Fülle akribisch recherchierter Aussagen zum Sozialstatus, zur Lebenslage und zum Kampf der Gymnasiallehrer um soziale Anerkennung findet man hier auch wichtige Hinweise auf die Frage der Ausbildung zum Gymnasiallehrer. Zum anderen ist die instruktive Arbeit von *Karl Neuerer*, »Das höhere Lehramt in Bayern im 19. Jahrhundert« (1978) zu berücksichtigen. *Neuerer* thematisiert in seiner Untersuchung sowohl die theoretische als auch die praktische Seite der Ausbildung und gelangt von der Analyse der Verordnungen bis hin zu einer genaueren Beschreibung der Ausbildungspraxis. Auf seine Untersuchung ist häufiger Bezug zu nehmen.
Die preußische Ausbildung wird öfter beschrieben und analysiert. Aus verschiedenen Arbeiten neueren Datums muß man *Hartmut Titzes* Untersuchung »Die soziale und geistige Umbildung des preußischen Oberlehrerstandes von 1870 bis 1914« (1977) vor allem deshalb nennen, weil *Titze* unter anderem pointierte Thesen über den gesellschaftlichen Zusammenhang der preußischen Oberlehrerausbildung vertritt, die zu weiteren Untersuchungen herausfordern. Einen anderen Weg ist *Gert Schubring* mit seiner Abhandlung »Die Entstehung des Mathematiklehrerberufs im 19. Jahrhundert« (1983) gegangen. Er thematisiert die Professionalisierung des Mathematikus, der als Gymnasiallehrer neben dem Philologen zunehmend an Bedeutung gewann, und zeigt damit an der Entwicklung eines Fachlehrerstandes, wie ungenau die verallgemeinernde Rede vom Philologen oder Gymnasiallehrer des 19. Jahrhunderts ist. Derartige Studien werden durch wirkungsgeschichtliche Analysen ergänzt, die *Hans-Jürgen Apel* unter Berücksichtigung bislang nicht benutzter Quellen zur Gymnasiallehrerbildung im Vormärz (1983–1986) und zur nachuniversitären Seminarbildung in Preußen um 1900 (1987) vorgelegt hat.
Betrachtet man die genannte Literatur, dann fehlt es an Studien zur Lehrerbildungsgeschichte, in denen die regionalen Sonderformen *vergleichend* betrachtet werden. Was bislang vorliegt, sind nur knappe Gegenüberstellungen. Bezogen auf die Aspekte »Allgemeinbildung und fachspezifische Ausbildung« sowie »Theorie und Praxis der Ausbildung« werden Grundzüge eines solchen Vergleichs nun für Bayern und Preußen entwickelt.

3. Ausbildungs- und Prüfungsordnungen für das höhere Lehramt in Bayern und Preußen zwischen 1809 und 1900

3.1 *Die Institutionalisierung einer höheren Lehrerbildung am Anfang des 19. Jahrhunderts*

In Bayern wie in Preußen wurde am Ende des 1. Jahrzehnts im 19. Jahrhundert eine Prüfungsverordnung für zukünftige Gymnasiallehrer erlassen, in Bayern 1809 die »Instruction zur Prüfung der zum Lehramte an den Studienschulen oder Studieninstituten sich anmeldenden Candidaten«, in Preußen 1810 das »Edikt wegen einzuführender allgemeiner Prüfung der Schulamts-Kandidaten«.[1] In Bayern war der Instruction eine Verordnung zur Einführung von Prüfungskommissionen in München und Nürnberg vorausgegangen, in der die Einführung einer Prüfung für die Bewerber um ein Gymnasiallehramt so begründet wurde: Es sei weder zweckmäßig, noch der Würde der Anstalten und ihrer Lehrer angemessen, wenn erledigte Lehrerstellen nur durch »einzelne Concursprüfungen« wiederbesetzt würden. Da »so bedeutende Stellen jederzeit nur dem Würdigsten zu ertheilen« (G. *Döllinger* (1838), Bd. IX, S. 746) seien, müsse sichergestellt sein, daß der Regierung die fähigsten Männer bekannt würden, damit sie zur Übernahme derartiger Stellen berufen werden könnten. Dies setze die Einführung einer »Prüfung nach einem gleichförmigen Maßstabe« (ebd., S. 746) voraus. An dieser Stelle wird das Interesse des Staates deutlich, im Bereich des von ihm verwalteten Bildungswesens zukünftige Bewerber um ein Schulamt nach der erbrachten Leistung auswählen zu können. In Preußen sprach man von der Notwendigkeit, das »Eindringen untüchtiger Subjekte in das Erziehungs- und Unterrichtswesen des Staats« zu verhindern. In der bayerischen Instruktion wurde betont, daß an den höheren Schulen »nur Gelehrte eine Stelle finden« sollten und daß vor allem von einem solchen Lehramtskandidaten »die Kenntnis der alten Sprachen als erste Bedingung gefordert« (ebd., S. 747) werden müsse. Deshalb werde »die Philologie zum ersten Gegenstande der Prüfung erhoben, welchem jeder Kandidat sich unterziehen muß, wenn er zu den übrigen Gegenständen der Prüfung zugelassen zu werden hoffen will« (ebd.). Neben den philologischen Kenntnissen wurden solche in Philosophie, Geschichte, Altertumsgeschichte, deutscher klassischer Literatur, Mathematik und Naturwissenschaften verlangt, doch war dem Kandidaten freigestellt, hier Schwerpunkte entsprechend der anvisierten Schulform (Gymnasial- oder Realinstitut) zu setzen.

Im preußischen Edikt wurde die Überprüfung philologischer, historischer und mathematischer Kenntnisse vorgeschrieben, um »die Tauglichkeit der Subjekte für die verschiedenen Arten und Grade des Unterrichts im Allgemeinen auszumitteln« (Amtsblatt Reg. Köln 1817, Beilage No. 7, 1). Daneben waren weitere Prüfungsgebiete nach Wahl der Kandidaten erlaubt. Eine schulformbezogene Schwerpunktbildung war nicht vorgesehen.

In Bayern stand die Instruktion in einem direkten Bezug zu dem 1808 von *Friedrich Niethammer* vorgelegten »Normativ der Einrichtung der öffentlichen Lehranstalten«.[2] In diesem Schulplan hatte *Niethammer* empfohlen, nach einem Elementarkurs vom 8. bis 12. Lebensjahr und 2 Real- bzw. Progymnasialklassen je 4 Klassen eines Gymnasial- und eines Realkurses einzurichten. Kandidaten, die in den Gymnasialklassen unterrichten wollten, mußten die Kenntnis der alten Sprachen und alle weiteren, zum Kreis der humanistischen wissenschaftlichen Bildung gehörigen Kenntnisse nachweisen. Kandidaten, die an den Realklassen unterrichten wollten, konnten Schwerpunkte in verschiedenen Fächern belegen. Die beste Prüfungsnote qualifizierte für ein Lehramt in den Gymnasial- oder Realklassen, die beiden schlechteren Noten für den Unterricht an Progymnasien bzw. Realschulen. Auch das preußische Edikt sah eine abgestufte Qualifikationsvergabe vor: Der Kandidat sollte ein Zeugnis erhalten, das seine fachlichen Stärken und Schwächen sowie seine Lehrgeschicklichkeit, also die »gesammte Tüchtigkeit« (ebd., 2) des Geprüften dokumentierte. Dadurch sollte festgestellt werden, für welche Schulstufe einer Gelehrtenschule der Geprüfte sich eignete.

Die Verordnungen müssen als Bestandteile einer größeren Gesellschafts- und Bildungsreform gesehen werden, die am Beginn des 19. Jahrhunderts in beiden Monarchien erfolgte. Die bisher herausgearbeitete Ähnlichkeit wichtiger Ziele, Inhalte und Bedingungen, welche die Einführung einer offiziellen Prüfung für Gymnasiallehrer bestimmten, darf über die prinzipielle *Verschiedenheit der politischen Voraussetzungen,* unter denen die Reform in jedem der Länder stattfand, nicht hinwegtäuschen. Anders als Preußen, das im Frieden zu Tilsit (1807) erhebliche Gebietsverluste nach einer entscheidenden Niederlage hatte hinnehmen müssen, hatte Bayern durch den 1803 erfolgten Reichsdeputationshauptschluß seine Fläche erheblich vergrößert und 1806 die monarchische Staatsform erlangt. In dem vergrößerten Bayern sah man sich vor der Aufgabe, die bereits begonnenen Maßnahmen einer grundlegenden Verwaltungs- und Staatsreform mit dem Ziel fortzusetzen, die notwendige Integration aller Teile zu einem geschlossenen Staatsgebilde zu fördern. Zu diesem Zweck konzentrierte sich Montgelas bei seinen Reformmaßnahmen darauf, eine zentralistisch-bürokratische Staatsform zu realisieren. Einen Schwerpunkt seiner Reformen bildete die Neuordnung des öffentlichen Dienstrechts: Der Aufbau der Verwaltung sollte nach dem Modell einer zentralen Leitung erfolgen, qualifizierter ausgebildete Beamte sollten zu einer höheren Leistung der Verwaltung beitragen. Im Kontext einer derartigen Modernisierung des Staates, die durch die Aufhebung ständischer Privilegien und Korporationen im Jahre 1807 und durch die Einführung eines einheitlichen Staatsrechtes im Jahre 1808 in das gesellschaftliche Leben eingriff, konnte auf eine Reform des Bildungswesens nicht verzichtet werden.[3]

In Preußen stand die Reform unter anderen gesellschaftspolitischen Vorzeichen.[4] Unter dem Eindruck der Niederlage von 1806 traten einflußreiche Mitglieder der Verwaltungsbürokratie entschieden für soziale Reformen ein, da sie in der veralteten absolutistischen Herrschaftsstruktur Preußens eine wesentliche Ursache des allgemeinen Niedergangs sahen. Das absolutistische Herrschaftsverhältnis zwischen Untertanen und Obrigkeit spiegelte sich vor allem in dem agrarischen Gewaltverhältnis, in der gewerblichen Bindung durch das Zunftwesen und in einer »Staatsapparatur«, die durch die praktizierte Bevormundung bei den Untertanen eine »dumpfe Bewußt-

losigkeit« und »Schicksalsergebenheit« (*C. Menze* (1975), S. 67) produzierte. Eine Modernisierung der Gesellschaftsstruktur sollte bei der Änderung dieser Verhältnisse ansetzen. Bauernbefreiung, Gewerbefreiheit und eine Selbstverwaltung der Städte sah der zur Durchführung der Reformen berufene *Freiherr vom Stein* als zentrale Aufgaben des politischen Handelns an, um aus Untertanen Bürger eines neuen preußischen Staates zu machen. Die Verbesserung der öffentlichen Erziehung muß in diesem Kontext als Aufgabe einer Nationalerziehung begriffen werden, als eine Maßnahme zur Förderung des »Patriotismus«, wie der spätere Kultusminister *von Altenstein* 1807 in einer Denkschrift zur Reform des Staates sagte.
Vergleicht man diese Voraussetzungen des politischen Handelns, dann ist festzustellen: Die schon ausgangs des 18. Jahrhunderts begonnenen Reformen des Bildungswesens und der Lehrerbildung wurden in Bayern wie in Preußen am Anfang des 19. Jahrhunderts konsequent fortgeführt. Mit der Einführung von Abschluß- und Zulassungsprüfungen verfolgte die Unterrichtsverwaltung in beiden Monarchien langfristig die Durchsetzung eines am Leistungsprinzip orientierten höheren Schulsystems. Die politischen Bedingungen und die gesellschaftspolitischen Zielsetzungen, welche diese Intention bestimmten, waren in beiden Staaten durchaus unterschiedlich, wenn auch die Maßnahmen sich ähnelten. In Bayern war der Instruktion das *Niethammer*sche Normativ vorausgegangen, zur gleichen Zeit wurde eine allgemeine Verordnung zur Durchführung der Absolutorialprüfung (Abitur) erlassen. Damit waren die wesentlichen Rahmenbedingungen für einen Neuaufbau des höheren Bildungssektors geschaffen. In Preußen stand dagegen das Lehrerprüfungsedikt am Anfang. Ihm folgten 1812 eine ausführliche Ordnung zur Abiturprüfung und 1815/16 die Verordnung zur Unterrichtsverfassung der Gymnasien und Stadtschulen in Preußen. Die den Gymnasialklassen gleichrangigen Realinstitute bestanden in Bayern nur bis 1816. Danach setzte sich im Bereich der Gymnasialbildung unter dem Einfluß von *Friedrich Wilhelm Thiersch* der Neuhumanismus sogar noch stärker als in Preußen durch.
In der bayerischen Prüfungsinstruktion waren zunächst keine pädagogischen Anforderungen enthalten.[5] Dies entsprach der verbreiteten Ansicht, daß derjenige eine Sache auch lehren könne, der sie beherrsche. In dem preußischen Edikt war immerhin vorgesehen, die Lehrgeschicklichkeit der Kandidaten durch eine Probelektion zu überprüfen. 1811 wurden auch in Bayern Ergänzungen zur Prüfungsinstruktion erlassen, in denen die Überprüfung unterrichtstheoretischer Kenntnisse und die Abhaltung einer Lehrprobe angeordnet wurden. *Neuerer* betont, daß *Friedrich Thiersch* in seinem 1812 gegründeten philologischen Seminar Musterlektionen anbot und Unterrichtsversuche durchführen ließ, die durch rhetorische Übungen ergänzt wurden. Im Jahre 1824 wurde zunächst in Bayern eine Probezeit für examinierte Kandidaten, 1826 dann in Preußen ein Probejahr für die Kandidaten des höheren Lehramts eingerichtet. Während in Preußen dieses Jahr mit einem gutachtlichen Zeugnis des zuständigen Gymnasialdirektors schloß, hatte der bayerische Schulamtskandidat sich ab 1834 nach einer zweijährigen Probezeit der »sog. praktischen Prüfung« (*K. Neuerer* (1978), S. 172) zu unterziehen, in der er seine fachdidaktischen Kenntnisse nachweisen mußte. erst nach dieser Prüfung erhielt er die Qualifikation,

die über seinen Einsatz in der Unter- oder Oberstufe eines Gymnasiums entschied. Damit war in Bayern, anders als in Preußen, der didaktische Bezug schon früh schwerpunktmäßig in eine zweite Phase der Ausbildung ausgegliedert worden, auch wenn die Organisation dieser Ausbildungsphase noch unzulänglich war. Diese Anordnung hatte aber nur bis zur Prüfungsordnung von 1854 Gültigkeit, in der eine Probelektion anstelle der praktischen Prüfung vorgeschrieben wurde.

3.2 Die Entwicklung der Ausbildung während des 19. Jahrhunderts

Oberflächlich betrachtet, fällt auf, daß in Bayern wie in Preußen zwischen 1830 und 1900 insgesamt je 4 Revisionen der 1809/10 begründeten Prüfungsordnung vorgenommen wurden, wobei deutliche Unterschiede in den Ansichten über Lehrerbildung zu erkennen sind. In Bayern erfolgten 1854 und 1873 erhebliche Eingriffe. 1854 wurde ein vierjähriges Universitätsstudium eingeführt. Die fachlichen Anforderungen wurden gesteigert, die pädagogischen Erwartungen gemindert. Die Entwicklung hin zum Fachlehrertypus wurde durch die Verminderung der Anforderungen in Mathematik für Altphilologen berücksichtigt, für die Ausbildung von Mathematiklehrern wurden wichtige Voraussetzungen institutionalisiert. Eine strenge Selektion der Kandidaten durch die Examensnote wurde beibehalten: Nur die beiden oberen Prüfungsnoten berechtigten zur Übernahme eines gymnasialen Lehramts, Note drei verwies an die Lateinschule. 1873 wurde die vierjährige Ausbildung dann in zwei Abschnitte unterteilt, in ein 6semestriges Studium, an dessen Ende die sog. Hauptprüfung stattfand, und in ein weiteres Studienjahr, zu dem nur zugelassen wurde, wer den ersten Abschnitt mit Note eins oder zwei bestanden hatte. Am Ende des vierten Studienjahres stand ein sog. Spezialexamen, nachdem der Kandidat eine wissenschaftliche Arbeit eingereicht hatte. Nur auf diesem Wege konnte die Lehrbefähigung für alle Klassen erreicht werden, die Voraussetzung für die Ernennung zum Gymnasialprofessor war. Die so geschaffene Zweiteilung des Gymnasiallehramts führte zu erheblichen Protesten seitens der Lehrer.[6]

1854 wurde die Überprüfung der Allgemeinbildung durch eine schriftliche Prüfung in der deutschen Literaturgeschichte eingeführt. Diese Absicht wurde 1873 durch eine Klausur über ein philosophisches, literaturgeschichtliches oder pädagogisches Thema fortgesetzt. Der sog. »›deutsche Aufsatz‹ hatte die Funktion, die Allgemeinbildung des Prüflings abzufragen« (*K. Neuerer* (1978), S. 50).

In der bayerischen Prüfungsordnung von 1873 war die Qualifizierung der Kandidaten zu drei verschiedenen Lehrämtern vorgesehen. Die Lehramtsstudenten konnten zwischen dem altphilologischen, dem mathematisch-physikalischen und dem neuphilologischen Lehramt wählen. Mit der Institutionalisierung der drei Lehrämter hatte die Unterrichtsverwaltung der eingetretenen Ausdifferenzierung der Wissenschaften, der Entwicklung des Schulwesens und den Anforderungen, die an die Qualifikation eines Gymnasiallehrers zu stellen waren, entsprochen.

In Preußen verliefen die Veränderungen der Prüfungsordnung ähnlich. In der Ordnung von 1831 wurde von dem Kandidaten noch die Kenntnis der Schulwissenschaften erwartet. Seine wissenschaftliche »Gesammtbildung« mußte er durch wenigstens zwei schriftliche Arbeiten, davon eine in lateinischer Sprache, unter Beweis stellen. Seiner Leistung entsprechend erhielt er die bedingte oder die unbedingte Fakultas. Nur die letztere erlaubte ihm den Unterricht in allen Klassen des Gymnasiums. Die noch 1831 geforderte Gesamtbildung wurde in der Ordnung von 1866 etwas reduziert.[7] Das gymnasiale Lehramt wurde nun in vier fachliche Schwerpunkte – philologisch-historisches, mathematisch-naturwissenschaftliches, neusprachliches Lehramt sowie Lehramt für Religion und Hebräisch (*C. Führ* (1985), S. 478) – unterteilt. Neben der Prüfung in dem gewählten Lehramt hatte der Kandidat seine Allgemeinbildung in anderen Schulfächern nachzuweisen und einen Aufsatz über ein philosophisches oder pädagogisches Thema zu liefern. Die Prüfungsleistungen wurden in drei Klassen beurteilt, womit eine Lehrbefähigung für die Unter-, Mittel- oder Oberstufe verbunden wurde. *Rainer Bölling* betont zu Recht, daß diese Prüfungsordnung mit ihren Erleichterungen in einer Zeit des Bedarfs an gymnasialen Lehrkräften erlassen wurde und deshalb eine großzügige, dreistufige Leistungsbewertung vorsah.[8]

Die Unterscheidung zwischen einer Allgemeinbildung der Kandidaten und speziellem Fachwissen wurde in der Prüfungsordnung von 1887 beibehalten, auch wenn die Allgemeinbildung der Kandidaten nicht mehr in dem Umfang wie früher überprüft wurde. Ausdrücklich wurde in § 7 der Prüfungsordnung verlangt, erstens die an das Wissen von Lehramtskandidaten allgemein zu stellenden Forderungen und zweitens die fachliche Lehrbefähigung in den gewählten Studienfächern zu überprüfen. Die fortgeschrittene Spezialisierung der Wissenschaften wurde in der Festlegung der zu studierenden Haupt- und Nebenfächer berücksichtigt. Beide Hauptfächer und eines der Nebenfächer mußten aus demselben Gebiet stammen, eine Vorgabe, die das sprachlich-philosophische ebenso wie das mathematisch-naturwissenschaftliche Lehramt prägte. Verschärft wurden in der gerade vorherrschenden Überfüllungskrise des Lehramts die Beurteilungsmaßstäbe: Die Kandidaten konnten nur noch das Oberlehrer- oder das Lehrerzeugnis erwerben. Damit fiel die einfachste Qualifikation für die gymnasiale Unterstufe weg.

Diese Entwicklung läßt in Bayern wie in Preußen Ähnlichkeiten, aber auch deutliche Unterschiede erkennen. Ähnlich verläuft die Entwicklung hinsichtlich der Unterscheidung von Allgemeinbildung und fachlicher Spezialisierung. Am Ausgang des 19. Jahrhunderts wählten die Kandidaten eindeutig Studienschwerpunkte im sprachlich-philologisch-historischen oder im mathematisch-naturwissenschaftlichen Gebiet, wie sich bereits seit den Prüfungen der 20er Jahre andeutete. Auch die Vergabe abgestufter Lehramtsqualifikationen war in ähnlicher Weise geregelt. Bayern beschritt allerdings 1854 und 1873 einen eigenen Weg mit der Institutionalisierung eines vierjährigen Studiengangs und der Einführung von zwei Lehramtsexamina. In dieser 4jährigen Anlage des Studiums unterschied sich Bayern schon früh von Preußen, für das noch in den 70er Jahren das Triennium galt, auch wenn schon längere Studienzeiten nachweisbar sind.

Abschließend bleibt noch die Entwicklung der praktischen Vorbereitung auf das höhere Lehramt zu betrachten. In Bayern wurde 1834 eine zweijährige Probezeit mit anschließender praktischer Prüfung eingeführt. In Preußen blieb es bis 1890 bei einer einjährigen Probezeit. Über die unzulängliche Ausbildung während dieser Zeit gibt es viele Klagen. Zwar wurde bereits in den Eingaben, welche die Gymnasiallehrer 1848 einreichten, die praxisnahe Ausbildung in Verbindung mit dem oder im Anschluß an das Universitätsstudium gefordert, zu öffentlichen Einrichtungen dieser Art kam es aber nicht. Nur wenige Seminare konnten einem kleinen Teil der Kandidaten eine didaktisch-methodische Ausbildung anbieten. Erst in den 80er Jahren wurde die Aufgabe der pädagogisch-praktischen Ausbildung als besonders dringlich erkannt, wesentlich angeregt durch die Diskussion über die Überbürdung der Jugend durch die Leistungsanforderungen der Schulen. Als einen Grund für die Überforderungssituation an den Gymnasien sah man die unzulängliche didaktisch-methodische Ausbildung der Gymnasiallehrer an, die u. a. durch eine veränderte pädagogisch-praktische Ausbildung verbessert werden sollte.

3.3 Die Festlegung der Ausbildung in zwei Phasen um 1900[9]

(a) Die pädagogisch-praktische Ausbildung

Die endgültige Festlegung des Ausbildungsgangs zum Gymnasiallehrer in der noch heute gültigen zweiphasigen Form erfolgte in Bayern wie in Preußen im letzten Jahrzehnt des 19. Jahrhunderts. Zunächst wurde die dringliche pädagogische Ausbildung durch die Einrichtung eines Seminarjahres geregelt. Die preußische Unterrichtsverwaltung führte 1890 eine zweijährige nachuniversitäre Ausbildung, unterteilt in Seminar- und Probejahr, ein. Man entschloß sich zu dieser Maßnahme zu der Zeit eines Überangebots an Lehramtskandidaten und ordnete die Seminare als kleine Ausbildungsstätten ausgewählten Gymnasien zu. Alle Kandidaten des höheren Lehramts mußten nun nach dem Studium die zweijährige Ausbildung ableisten, am Ende des ersten Jahres eine fachdidaktische Seminararbeit und am Ende des Probejahres einen Tätigkeitsbericht vorlegen. Die Direktoren der Gymnasien waren zur Beurteilung der Kandidaten verpflichtet. Nach erfolgreicher Ableistung dieser Zeit wurde dem Kandidaten die »Anstellungsfähigkeit« zuerkannt. Damit hatte Preußen eine zweiphasige Ausbildungsform institutionalisiert, in der ein fachwissenschaftliches Studium und eine pädagogisch-didaktische Professionalisierung nacheinander erfolgten.[10]
In Bayern wurde das Bedürfnis nach einer seminaristischen Ausbildung zu derselben Zeit offenkundig. Als der bayerische Philologen-Verband Ende der 80er Jahre eine stärkere Berücksichtigung von pädagogischer Theorie und Praxis des Unterrichts noch während der Studienzeit forderte, war die Vorentscheidung für die Einrichtung pädagogischer Gymnasialseminare in der Unterrichtsverwaltung bereits gefallen. Eindeutig wurde unterschieden: Theoretische Pädagogik sollte an der Universität gelehrt, pädagogisch-didaktische Übung an gymnasialen Seminaren erworben werden. 1893 erfolgte die Gründung der ersten 5 Seminare; eine Ausbildungsordnung wurde jedoch erst 1897 erlassen. Im Gegensatz zu Preußen war die Ausbildungszeit auf ein Jahr begrenzt und zunächst für Altphilologen verpflichtend, was mit der

Tatsache eines gewissen Lehrermangels zusammenhängen dürfte.[11] Erst nach 1900 wurden auch Seminare für die Kandidaten anderer Lehrämter eingerichtet.
Ein wichtiger Unterschied bestand in der Beurteilung der Kandidaten. In Bayern wurde am Ende des Seminarjahres ein Befähigungszeugnis mit vierfacher Abstufung ausgegeben. In Preußen wurde nach erfolgreicher Ableistung die Anstellungsfähigkeit ohne weitere Beurteilung zuerkannt. Die Durchführung der Seminare erfolgte nach z. T. übereinstimmenden Richtlinien. Sie wurden als pädagogisch-didaktische Kurse abgehalten, in deren Zentrum die Unterweisung in praktischer Pädagogik und der vorbildliche Unterricht neben dem Unterrichtsversuch der Kandidaten standen. Die Kandidaten beider Länder mußten am Ende des Kurses einen pädagogisch-fachdidaktischen Bericht vorlegen.

(b) Die wissenschaftliche Ausbildung
In Bayern nahm die Diskussion um eine Änderung der 1873 durch die Einführung des Spezialexamens geschaffenen Teilung des höheren Lehramts Anfang der 90er Jahre zu.[12] Im Zusammenhang mit Überlegungen zu einer stärkeren Gewichtung pädagogischer und fachdidaktischer Aspekte in der Ausbildung entschloß sich die Unterrichtsverwaltung zu einer Neuordnung, in der zwar die 4jährige Ausbildung mit zwei Prüfungen erhalten blieb, die zwei Kategorien von Gymnasiallehrern jedoch abgeschafft wurden. Der bayerische Kandidat für ein philologisch-historisches Lehramt mußte nach der Prüfungsordnung von 1895 in den ersten 3 Jahren 4 Semester klassische und deutsche Philologie studieren. Verpflichtend waren Studien in Latein, Griechisch, Deutsch und Geschichte. Nach dem sechsten Semester mußte er sich einem ersten Examen unterziehen. Nach einem weiteren Jahr reichte er eine Staatsarbeit, deren wissenschaftliche Anforderungen gegenüber den Ansprüchen der Prüfungsordnung von 1873 deutlich reduziert worden waren, ein und legte danach eine zweite wissenschaftliche Prüfung ab. In ihr wurden die wissenschaftlichen Fächer und Philosophie, Archäologie sowie Pädagogik geprüft. Das Wichtigste dieser Prüfungsordnung ist wohl darin zu sehen, daß »Studiendauer und Studienabfolge ... für alle (Gymnasiallehrer) wieder einheitlich« (*K. Neuerer* (1978), S. 51) waren. Die unterschiedlichen Kategorien von Gymnasiallehrern waren damit abgeschafft.
In Preußen erschien 1898 eine neue Prüfungsordnung, durch die ebenfalls ein einheitliches Lehramt eingeführt wurde. In § 34 hieß es: »Bestanden hat der Kandidat, wenn er in der Allgemeinen Prüfung genügt und die Lehrbefähigung mindestens in einem der ... genannten Fächer für die erste Stufe und noch in zwei Fächern für die zweite Stufe nachgewiesen hat.« Die Unterscheidung zwischen Oberlehrern und Lehrern war damit hinfällig. *Bölling* sieht diese Entwicklung im standespolitischen Interesse der Philologen, die dadurch eine Angleichung ihrer Ausbildung an die Standards der Juristenausbildung und eine bessere Ausgangsposition im Kampf um die besoldungsmäßige Gleichstellung erreichten.[13] Diese Neubestimmung des höheren Lehramts hatte für die Kandidaten unangenehme Folgen: Die Durchfallquote stieg in den folgenden Jahren, in denen zumindest in Preußen ein großer Andrang zum höheren Lehramt bestand, drastisch an.
Vergleicht man die Ausbildungsordnungen und -praktiken für das höhere Lehramt in

Bayern und Preußen am Beginn des 20. Jahrhunderts, dann ist festzuhalten: Die Lehrämter hatten sich in beiden Monarchien zu ähnlichen Grundtypen eines philologisch-historischen und eines mathematisch-naturwissenschaftlichen Lehramts entwickelt. In Bayern waren die Typen eindeutiger als in Preußen definiert, wo die Kombination der Fächer ein wenig mehr Spielraum ließ. Die Prüfungsdurchführung unterschied sich deutlich: In Bayern mußten die Kandidaten zwei Prüfungen in einem 8semestrigen Studium absolvieren; in Preußen erfolgten die Allgemeine und die Fachprüfung gebündelt am Ende des Studiums. In beiden Fällen wurde eine »Allgemeine Grundbildung« der Kandidaten mit Schwerpunkten in Philosophie und Pädagogik überprüft, in Preußen ergänzt durch das Gebiet »Deutsche Literatur«. Die allgemeine Prüfung war das Relikt des ursprünglichen Anspruchs, Gymnasiallehrern neben einer fachlichen auch eine anspruchsvolle Allgemeinbildung abzuverlangen. Die eingetretene fachliche Spezialisierung hatte jedoch zu einer Revision dieser Forderung geführt. Ihren rechtlich eindeutigen Abschluß erfuhr die Entwicklung der Gymnasiallehrerbildung zu einem zweiphasigen Ausbildungsgang 1912 in Bayern und 1917 in Preußen mit entsprechenden Prüfungsordnungen.
Einen Überblick über die Entwicklung der Ausbildungsordnungen für Gymnasiallehrer vermittelt die Darstellung der wichtigsten Fakten auf Abbildung (1).
Insgesamt ist in beiden Monarchien eine Verlängerung der Ausbildungszeit festzustellen. Bayern ging mit der frühen Einführung einer 4jährigen Studienzeit ebenso wie mit der kurzfristigen Verfügung einer 2jährigen Probezeit nach dem Studium voraus. Die Gesamtausbildungszeit hatte sich am Ende des Jahrhunderts um mindestens ein Jahr, in Preußen faktisch wohl um zwei Jahre verlängert. Die zwei Phasen der Ausbildung konnten nun schnellstens in 5 Jahren absolviert werden, was unter Einrechnung der Militärdienstzeit für die Kandidaten mindestens 6, meistens aber 7 Jahre mit erheblichen Kosten, aber ohne Einkommen bedeutete.

4. Abschlußbemerkung

Wenn auch die Prüfungsordnungen Unterschiede enthielten, so waren die wählbaren Lehrämter und die erreichbaren Qualifikationen doch durchaus vergleichbar. Zwar konnte man in Bayern behaupten, die höchsten Ansprüche an das altphilologisch-historische Lehramt zu stellen, doch erscheint der Unterschied aus historischer Distanz vernachlässigbar. Ein Austausch der Oberlehrer zwischen Bayern und Preußen dürfte also durchaus möglich gewesen sein. Auch wenn die Ausbildung nicht identisch ablief, stimmte die erreichte Qualifikation der Gymnasiallehrer doch weitgehend überein.

	BAYERN	PREUSSEN		
1800	1808 Niethammer: Normativ ... 1809 Instruction ...	1810 Edikt ...	1800	
1810	1811 Erste Ergänzung der Instruction 1818 (Ergänzende) Prüfungsordnung		1810	Mangel
1820	1824 Probezeit für Lehramtskandidaten	1826 Probejahrregelung	1820	
1830	1834 Die Vorbildung ... (allgemeine Grundbildung u. praktische Prüfung) in zwei Abschnitten	1831 Reglement ... (»Gesamt- und Fachbildung«)	1830	
1840			1840	Überfüllung
1850	1854 Prüfungsordnung (4jähriges Studium; Allgemein- u. Fachbildung, Probelektion)		1850	
1860		1866 Prüfungsreglement (3jähriges Studium; fachwissenschaftliche Ausrichtung; 3 Beurteilungsstufen)	1860	
1870	1873 Prüfungsordnung (4jähriges Studium; 2 Abschnitte, unterteilte Qualifikation; fachwissenschaftliche Orientierung)		1870	Mangel
1880		1887 Prüfungsreglement (3jähriges Studium; Fachorientierung: Haupt- u. Nebenfächer, nur 2 Qualifikationsstufen)	1880	Überfüllung
1890			1890	

		BAYERN	PREUSSEN		
Mangel	1890	1893 Gründung von Gymnasialseminaren 1895 Prüfungsordnung (Unterteilung des Lehramts abgeschafft) 1897 Seminarordnung	1890 Seminar- und Probejahr 1898 Prüfungsreglement (einheitl. Lehramt	1890	Überfüllung
	1900			1900	Mangel
	1910	1912 Prüfungsordnung (1. u. 2. Phase der Ausbildung)	1917 Prüfungsreglement (wiss. u. päd.-did. Phase)	1910	Mangel
	1920			1920	

Abb. 1 Entwicklung der Vorschriften zur Prüfung und Ausbildung der Gymnasiallehrer in Bayern und Preußen

Erläuterung: Die Gegenüberstellung wird durch eine angenäherte Darstellung der Phasen, in denen eine Überfüllung des Lehramts oder ein Mangel an Bewerbern oder ein Übergang zwischen beiden Zuständen festzustellen ist, ergänzt. Für Preußen ist dies dank der Vorarbeiten der QUAKRI-Gruppe (vgl. z. B. H. Titze 1981) möglich. Die angedeuteten Überschneidungen der Phasen sollen zeigen, daß es Übergangszeiten mit Mangel oder Überfüllung in bestimmten Fächern gab.
Für Bayern stehen derartige Untersuchungen noch aus. Daher ist auf der Seite der bayerischen Entwicklung nur der annäherungsweise Hinweis auf eine Mangelphase möglich.
Es zeigt sich, daß Prüfungsordnungen in Preußen an Nahtstellen, zwischen Mangel- und Überfüllungsphase, stehen, also zugleich die Aufgabe der Krisenbewältigung erfüllen sollen. In Bayern ist die Situation um 1890 Neuerer zufolge anders. Hier fällt die Ausweitung der Ausbildung in eine Mangelphase. Wegen fehlender Daten ist aber Vorsicht vor einer vorschnellen Interpretation geboten (vgl. Anm. 11).

Anmerkungen

[1] Zur bayerischen Instruktion vgl. *K. Neuerer* (1978), S. 20f.; *Buchinger* (1983).
[2] Vgl. *F. Paulsen* (1921), S. 422f.; *Buchinger* (1983), S. 76ff.
[3] Zu den Montgelas'schen Reformen in Bayern vgl. *Buchinger* (1983), S. 63f.; *Volkert* (1983), S. 503ff.

[4] Zur Reformorientierung in Preußen vgl. *F. Paulsen* (1921), S. 278ff.; *E. Müsebeck* (1918); *C. Menze* (1975).

[5] Zur pädagogischen Ausbildung der Gymnasiallehrer in Bayern vgl. *K. Neuerer* (1978), S. 170ff.; für Preußen vgl. *H.-J. Apel* (1984), (1985), (1987).

[6] Vgl. hierzu *E. Brand* (1904), S. 533ff.

[7] Zu den preußischen Prüfungsordnungen von 1866, 1887 und 1898 vgl. die Interpretation von *F. Paulsen* (1921); zusätzlich auch: *R. Bölling* (1983), S. 22f. und *C. Führ* (1985), S. 428f.

[8] *R. Bölling* (1983), S. 22.

[9] Daß an dieser Stelle zunächst die pädagogisch-didaktische Ausbildung dargestellt wird, hat seinen Grund im Ablauf der Entwicklung am Ausgang des 19. Jahrhunderts. Für die Unterrichtsverwaltung war die Frage einer pädagogisch-didaktischen Qualifizierung der Gymnasiallehrer in den 90er Jahren sicher vorrangig.

[10] Vgl. *H.-J. Apel* (1987).

[11] Zur Frage einer Mangelphase vgl. *K. Neuerer* (1987), S. 187f., der von einem Gymnasiallehrermangel um und nach 1890 an den bayerischen Gymnasien spricht. Wegen dieses Mangels habe die Einführung der Seminare nur allmählich erfolgen können. *E. Brands* Darstellung, daß zwar ab 1888 bis zu Beginn des 20. Jahrhunderts durch den bayerischen Landtag kontinuierlich ein – wenn auch zahlenmäßig bescheidener – Ausbau der Gymnasiallehrerstellen erfolgte, durch den aber nicht alle notwendigen Stellen geschaffen wurden, ist ohne genaueres Zahlenmaterial über sich bewerbende Lehramtskandidaten nicht sicher zu interpretieren (*E. Brand* (1904), S. 525f.). Einem Briefwechsel mit Prof. Dr. Hartmut Titze, Göttingen, verdanke ich wertvolle Hinweise zu dieser Frage:

- Der bayerische Staatsminister Freih. v. Lutz verneinte im Mai 1889 »die Notwendigkeit von Gegenmaßnahmen in Sachen akademisches Proletariat mit Hinsicht auf die bayerischen Verhältnisse« *(H. Titze)*.
- Er war der Ansicht, »daß in Bayern die beklagte Überfüllung des philologischen Berufs nicht besteht, im Gegenteil sogar ein gewisser Mangel an philologisch gebildeten Lehrkräften sich allmählich fühlbar zu machen droht« (Brief an Bismarck, 18. Mai 1889; Hinweis: *H. Titze*).
- 10 Jahre später sah die Situation anders aus: In einer Abhandlung »Die drohende Überfüllung im Lehrfach der klassischen Philologie, neueren Philologie und Mathematik« (in: Blätter für das Gymnasialschulwesen 1898, 1–10) wird von verschlechterten Anstellungschancen gesprochen und vom Studium der Philologie abgeraten, vor dem der Mathematik gewarnt.

H. Titze folgert aus der Analyse dieser und anderer Unterlagen, daß es in Bayern »ähnliche Wechsellagen« wie in Preußen gegeben habe, »vermutlich aber zeitversetzt«. Genaue Untersuchungen dieser Vorgänge stehen noch aus.

[12] Zur sog. »Dreierfrage« vgl. *E. Brand* (1904), S. 533ff.

[13] Vgl. hierzu *R. Bölling* (1983), S. 25.

Literaturverzeichnis

Apel, H.-J. (1983): Der Gymnasiallehrer zwischen Universität und Pädagogikum. In: Informationen zur erziehungs- und bildungshistorischen Forschung 20/21 (1983), S. 145–158

Apel, H.-J. (1984): Die Auslese des Gymnasiallehrernachwuchses in Preußen (1815–1830). In: Zeitschrift für Pädagogik 30 (1984), S. 297–322

Apel, H.-J. (1985): Preußische Gymnasiallehrer 1820–1850. Soziale Herkunft, Studienverhalten, Studienerfolg nach Prüfungszeugnissen insbesondere der Bonner Schulamtskandidaten. In: Vierteljahrsschrift für Sozial- und Wirtschaftsgeschichte, H. 3, 1985, S. 353–368

Apel, H.-J. (1986): Gymnasiallehrerbildung zwischen Wissenschaft und fachdidaktischer Orientierung. In: Vierteljahrsschrift für Wiss. Pädagogik, 62. Jg., H. 3, 1986, S. 289–319

Apel, H.-J. (1987): Durch Seminar und Probejahr zur »Anstellungsfähigkeit«. Die nachuniversitäre Ausbildung der Gymnasiallehrer in Preußen (1890–1918). In: Bildung und Erziehung, 40. Jg., H. 2, 1987, S. 151–166

Beier, A. (Hrsg.) (³1909): Die höheren Schulen in Preußen und ihre Lehrer. Halle

Bölling, R. (1983): Sozialgeschichte der deutschen Lehrer. Ein Überblick von 1800 bis zur Gegenwart. Göttingen

Buchinger, H., Die Geschichte der bayerischen Realschule. Erster Teil: Die Entwicklung der bayer. Realschule von ihren Anfängen bis zur Errichtung der Oberrealschule im Jahre 1907. Passau 1983

Denkschrift, betreffend die praktische Ausbildung der Kandidaten für das Lehramt an höheren Schulen. Hrsg. Ministerium der geistl. Unterrichts- und Medizinalangelegenheiten. 1890 (für: Haus der Abgeordneten, 17. Legislaturperiode, II. Session 1890; Aktenstück N° 22)

Döllinger, G. (1838): Sammlung der im Gebiete der inneren Staatsverwaltung des Königreichs Bayern bestehenden Verordnungen. Bd. IX, S. 2

Fries, W. (1895): Die Vorbildung der Lehrer für das Lehramt. Handbuch der Erziehungs- und Unterrichtslehre für höhere Schulen, hrsg. v. A. Baumeister. Bd. II.1. München

Führ, Ch. (1985): Gelehrter Schulmann – Oberlehrer – Studienrat. Zum sozialen Aufstieg der Philologen. In: (Conze, W./Kocka, J. (Hrsg.), Bildungsbürgertum im 19. Jahrhundert, I. Stuttgart, S. 417–457

Grosse, R. (1910): 1810–1910. Beiträge zur Geschichte des Oberlehrerstandes. Leipzig

Menze, C. (1975): Die Bildungsreform Wilhelm von Humboldts. Hannover

Morsch, H. (²1910): Das höhere Lehramt in Deutschland und Österreich. Ein Beitrag zur vergleichenden Schulgeschichte und Schulreform. Leipzig/Berlin

Müller, S. F./Tenorth, H.-E. (1984): Professionalisierung der Lehrtätigkeit. In: Enzyklopädie Erziehungswissenschaft, Bd. 5. Organisation, Recht und Ökonomie des Bildungswesens. Hrsg. von M. Baethge/K. Nevermann. Stuttgart

Münch, W. (1903): Geist des Lehramts. Eine Hodegetik für Lehrer höherer Schulen. Berlin

Müsebeck, E. (1918): Das Preußische Kultusministerium vor hundert Jahren. Stuttgart/Berlin

Neuerer, K. (1978): Das höhere Lehramt in Bayern im 19. Jahrhundert. Ausbildungsaspekte und ihre Realisationsformen dargestellt unter besonderer Berücksichtigung der Lehrämter des humanistischen Gymnasiums und der Ausbildungsverhältnisse an der Ludwig-Maximilians-Universität München. Berlin

Paulsen, F. (1904): Die höheren Schulen Deutschlands und ihr Lehrerstand in ihrem Verhältnis zum Staat und zur geistigen Kultur. Braunschweig

Paulsen, F. (1912a): Der höhere Lehrerstand und seine Stellung in der gelehrten Welt. In: Ders., Gesammelte pädagogische Abhandlungen (hrsg. u. eingel. von E. Spranger). Stuttgart/Berlin, S. 281–296

Paulsen, F. (1912b): Die Überbürdung der Gymnasiallehrer. In: Ders., Gesammelte pädagogische Abhandlungen (hrsg. und eingel. von E. Spranger). Stuttgart/Berlin, S. 218–223

Paulsen, F. (1921): Geschichte des gelehrten Unterrichts, Bd. II, 3. Aufl., Berlin/Leipzig

Schröder, O. (Hrsg.) (1906): Die Ordnung des Studiums für das höhere Lehramt in Deutschland und die gesetzlichen Prüfungsbestimmungen in den einzelnen deutschen Bundesstaaten. Leipzig, o. J.

Schubring, G. (1983): Die Entstehung des Mathematiklehrerberufs im 19. Jahrhundert. Studien und Materialien zum Prozeß der Professionalisierung in Preußen (1810–1870), Weinheim
Titze, H. (1977): Die soziale und geistige Umbildung des preußischen Oberlehrerstandes von 1870 bis 1914. In: Herrmann, U. (Hrsg.), Historische Pädagogik. Beiheft 14 der ZfPäd. Weinheim, S. 107–128
Titze, H. (1981): Überfüllungskrisen in akademischen Karrieren: eine Zyklustheorie. In: Zeitschrift für Pädagogik 27 (1981), S. 187–224
Titze, H./Nath, A./Müller-Benedict, V. (1985): Der Lehrerzyklus. Zur Wiederkehr von Überfüllung und Mangel im höheren Lehramt in Preußen. In: ZfPäd., 31. Jg., 1985, Nr. 1, S. 97–126
Voss, P. (1889): Die pädagogische Vorbildung zum höheren Lehramt in Preußen und Sachsen. Halle
Wiese, L. (Hrsg.) (1864): Das höhere Schulwesen in Preußen. Historisch-statistische Darstellung. Berlin
Wiese, L. (Hrsg.) (1868): Verordnungen u. Gesetze für die höheren Schulen in Preußen, Berlin, Bd. I.1 u. I.2
Wiese, L. (1902): Das höhere Schulwesen in Preußen. Bd. 4 hgg. von B. Irmer. Berlin
Zentralblatt für die gesammte Unterrichtsverwaltung in Preußen. Hrsg. in dem Ministerium der geistlichen, Unterrichts- und Medizinal-Angelegenheiten. Berlin 1872
Volkert, W. (1983): Bayern. In: Jeserich, K./Pohl, H./v. Unruh, G.-C. (Hrsg.): Deutsche Verwaltungsgeschichte, Bd. 2. Stuttgart

Heinrich Kanz

Die Politisierung der Lehrerbildung im Nationalsozialismus

Vorbemerkung

Das Thema: *Die Politisierung der Lehrerbildung im Nationalsozialismus* kann historisch und standesorganisatorisch aufgefaßt werden. Der geschichtliche Aspekt stellt sich u. a. sowohl global-kulturgeschichtlich als auch landesgeschichtlich dar. In erster Hinsicht soll im Bayerischen Schulmuseum Ichenhausen »die Geschichte der Schule in ihrer Bedeutung für die gesamte kulturgeschichtliche Entwicklung dargestellt werden«.[1] In zweiter Hinsicht will das Museum tragende Aspekte der Entwicklung der allgemeinen Probleme des Lernens und Lehrens in ganz Bayern über die gesamte Geschichte hin illustrieren.[2] In diesem Rahmen bietet sich die Strukturierung unserer Gedanken dar. Auf das Berufsfeld des Lehrers bezogen, stellen sich also die Fragen

- ob 1933–45 global-kulturgeschichtlich ein anderes Verständnis und eine andere Verwirklichung von Lehrertum als in bis dahin gezeigter Form (Schreiber, Magister, Lehrer) anzutreffen ist, und
- ob sich landesgeschichtlich eigene Ausprägungen von Lehrerprofil und Lehrerwirklichkeit zeigt.

Die letztgenannte Problematik läßt sich etwa unter anderem daran festmachen, daß München die Hauptstadt der NS[1]-Bewegung war, daß die Zentrale des NS-Lehrerbundes in Bayreuth lag und daß Nürnberg für die ideologische Dimension eine große Rolle spielte.

Wer sich die Jahre 1933–45 vornimmt, muß sich darüber im klaren sein, daß die dazu benutzten Worte jeweils aus ihrem Kontext heraus zu verstehen sind. Dies vermag man schon an dem Wort »Politisierung« aufzuzeigen. Wortgeschichtlich steht es in unauflösbarem Zusammenhang mit den Bedeutungen von »Politik« und »politisch«. Welche Grundauffassung von »politisch« in welchem Jahrzehnt gängiger war, zeigen entsprechende Wortfelduntersuchungen. Der NS-Politikbegriff artikuliert sich auch in Nachbarschaft mit Erziehung.

1936 erläuterte ein einflußreicher NS-Pädagoge in den Schriften der deutschen Hochschule für Politik, was nationalpolitische Erziehung sei. Er bestimmte sie als »Politik, Erziehung zu politischer Haltung im Sinne des Nationalsozialismus.«

»Haltung umschließt die aus einer bestimmten Weltanschauung fließende Gesinnung und zugleich ihre Betätigung. Politisch ist eine Haltung, wenn sie auf eine Gemeinschaft und ihre Förderung gerichtet ist.«[3]

Der NS-Wortgebrauch von »Politik« konnotiert die Verbindung von Weltanschauung und politischer Tätigkeit im andere Weltanschauungen ausschließenden Sinn. Politisch tätig sein heißt danach stets, nationalsozialistisch tätig sein. So ist auch die

Vorschrift für das amtliche Gutachten des Ausbildungsleiters in der Ordnung der Prüfung für das Lehramt an höheren Schulen 7. Juni 1937 (Reichsverordnung der Päd. Prüfung) zu verstehen:

»In einem zweiten Teil soll das Gutachten zusammenfassend die weltanschauliche und politische Haltung des Studienreferendars sowie seine Einsatz- und Opferbereitschaft für den nationalsozialistischen Staat kennzeichnen. Zur weltanschaulichen und politischen Haltung ist außerdem rechtzeitig vor der Vorlage der Meldung des Studienreferendars durch die zuständige Schulaufsichtsbehörde eine Äußerung der Partei einzuholen.«[4]

Wie es zu einer solchen »bürokratischen« Verfestigung eines einparteipolitischen Politikbegriff kommen konnte, hat jetzt in autobiographischer Rückschau *Wilhelm Flitner*, der große alte Mann der geisteswissenschaftlichen Pädagogik, zu schildern versucht. Das Kapitel 11 »Die Epoche der Diktatur« aus seinen »Erinnerungen 1889–1945« erörtert, wie sich die Gewaltübernahme der Nationalsozialisten in den Augen der Zeitgenossen 1933 ausnahm und wie sich dabei eine völlig neue Erfahrung von staatlicher Macht und diktatorischer Gewalt artikulierte. *Flitner* reflektierte zum 30. 1. 1933: Unter anderem auch deshalb, weil demokratie-überzeugte politische Kräfte vor einer gewaltsamen Verhinderung eines Bürgerkrieges mit Hilfe der Reichswehr, derer sie sich zudem nicht sicher waren, zurückschreckten, geschah

»das Unglaubliche: *Hindenburg* ließ sich von seiner Umgebung dazu drängen, einen gescheiterten Künstler und Abenteurer zum Kanzler zu ernennen, den Führer einer ideell konfusen ›nationalsozialistischen Arbeiterpartei‹, der schon einen Putsch versucht hatte.«[5]

Die damals kulturell Führenden hätten das Programm des Nationalsozialismus nicht ernst genommen.

»Über die wirkliche Gefahr, in der sich der Staat befand, täuschte man sich und wollte nicht glauben, daß sich in Deutschland eine unbeschränkte Diktatur auf Dauer halten könne. Es war bezeichnend für die gebildete Schicht, daß sie das Programm der Nationalsozialisten gar nicht recht zur Kenntnis genommen hatte. Weder meine Freunde noch wir selber waren imstande, den ›Mythos des 20. Jahrhunderts‹ oder das schreckliche, 1925 erschienene Buch ›Mein Kampf‹ überhaupt zu lesen.«[6]

Indes mußten die Träger der damaligen Kultur erleben, mit welchen Methoden eine entschlossene Minderheit durch Propaganda und Terror die Staatsmacht eroberte. Hitler verstand es,

»nach und nach alle neben ihm stehenden Gewalten zu brechen und sich zu einem absoluten Herrscher zu machen, wie es auf deutschem Boden keinen jemals gegeben hatte.«[7]

Ohne hier auf die geschichtliche Ursachenforschung einzugehen, erscheint für uns also wichtig, mit welchem Politikbegriff die Deutschen im 20. Jahrhundert konfrontiert wurden und welche Formen politischer Gewalt sie kennenlernten.

Man muß wohl daran erinnern, daß die Behandlung unserer Epoche allgemein besonderen Erkenntnisbedingungen unterliegt. Handelt es sich um einen Zeitgenossen, so führt eine Diskussion der damaligen geschichtlichen Sachverhalte »an tiefste ethische Probleme«[8]:

»Wer in der deutschen Epoche zwischen 1932 und dem Mai 1945 weder emigriert ist noch in einem Konzentrationslager eingesperrt war, weder öffentlich vor ein Gericht gestellt wurde noch sein Amt verloren hat, der wurde von den Späteren auf die Anklagebank verwiesen und verhört. Wieso hat er existiert, ohne sichtbaren Widerstand zu leisten? Warum ist er nicht als Held oder Märtyrer gestorben? War er Kollaborateur und irgendwo an den Verbrechen mitschuldig, die von Deutschen in ganz Europa verübt worden sind?«

Dieser Tatbestand gilt natürlich auch für Pädagogen im weitesten Sinn des Wortes. Gleichwohl bleibt die Besprechung der Entwicklung der Lehrerbildung 1933–1945 eine kognitive Aufgabe, die je nach Zusammenhang zu lösen ist. Aus Zeitgründen und in Angesicht der Forschungslage ist es sinnvoll, sich auf einen Aspekt und zwar hier auf den Aspekt der Politisierung zu beschränken. Politisierung war zwar auch schon in früheren Epochen anhängig. Z. B. könnte man die Stiehlschen Regulative so deuten, daß die Lehrerbildung bewußt in den zugehörigen Rahmen der damaligen politischen Macht- und Gewaltträger gestellt werden sollte. Politisierung jedoch als Nazifizierung wurde eine durchaus singuläre Erfahrung der Betroffenen. In den letzten Jahren geschah eine intensive Aufarbeitung der Deutschen Geschichte 1933–1945. Auf den verschiedensten Gebieten und in unterscheidbaren Dimensionen kristallisierte sich heraus, daß die NS-Bewegung, ihre Aktivisten und Opfer im strengen Sinn des Wortes keine Vorbilder oder Vergleiche erlauben. Die *Hitler-Bewegung* ist eine einmalige geschichtliche Erscheinung gewesen. Dies ist die Interpretationsthese bekannter bundesrepublikanischer Historiker. Sie ermöglicht die beste Grundlage zur Erforschung dessen, was gewesen ist.
Wie die Lehrerbildung nach 1933 gestaltet und formiert wurde, ist schon in vielen Untersuchungen durchaus deutlich dargestellt worden. Je nach dem Forschungsgesichtspunkt standen dabei u. a. Rechtfertigungsansätze der beteiligten Gruppen oder Maßstäbe im Vordergrund, die nach heutigen Erziehungs- und Bildungskonzeptionen angelegt waren. Zu wenig allerdings wurde gesehen, daß Lehrerbildung nicht nur von der inneren und äußeren Geschichte eines Berufsstandes her, sondern vielmehr auch von den Motivationen und Realisierungen des politischen Gesamtsystems aus interpretierbar wird. Wenn man z. B. die Volksschullehrerbildung ab 1933 verfolgt, die Umwandlung von den Hochschulen für Lehrerbildung in die späteren Lehrerbildungsanstalten, so mag man darin einerseits den Vorgang einer Reseminarisierung erblicken. Andererseits muß jedoch immer stärker betont werden, daß der Nationalsozialismus nach anfänglichem Werben um alle Schichten[9] »nicht nur die Traditionen gründlich in Frage stellte, aus denen die institutionalisierte Erziehung lebte, sondern auch, was meist übersehen wird, das Funktionieren des ›Führerstaates‹[10] neue Bedingungen für die Lehrerbildung schuf. Daher kann *Scholtz* verbalisieren, daß bei der Einrichtung der Lehrerbildungsanstalten der politische Wille des NS zum Zuge kam, der natürlich nicht aus der Traditionslinie der Geschichte der bisherigen Lehrerbildung heraus verständlich gemacht werden kann. Es handelte sich bei dieser Umstellung der Lehrerbildung um die bewußte Änderung der früher eher kognitiv gesehenen Aufgaben des Lehrers, d. h. um »den Wandel von der Lehrerbildung zur politischen Führerschulung«[11] im Sinn des Nationalsozialismus.
Es mag daher heute besonders interessieren, welche Politisierungsmomente am

Berufsbild des Lehrers nach 1933 feststellbar sind. Unsere These soll lauten: Das NS-Berufsbild des Lehrers und der Lehrerin enthält Politisierungsdimensionen, wie sie in der früheren deutschen Bildungsgeschichte nicht auftreten.
Um diese These idealtypisch und möglichst an authentischen Quellen zu verifizieren, ist im Hinblick auf die vorliegende Literatur aber keine empirische Geschichte der NS-Lehrerbildung bezüglich ihrer Wirkung und wirklichen Durchsetzung zu erwarten. Autobiographische, narrative und Spezialuntersuchungen haben viele Zweifel aufkommen lassen, bis zu welchem Grad die allmähliche Gleichschaltung beim Vorgang der Nazifizierung aller Lebensverhältnisse zum Erfolg gekommen ist.[12] Es gibt Sinn, einmal anhand von Verlautbarungen zur NS-Lehrerbildungspolitik in dem entscheidenden Amtsblatt des Reichsministeriums für Wissenschaft, Erziehung und Volksbildung, Grundzüge der NS-Lehrerbildungspolitik im Hinblick darauf zu artikulieren, welches Lehrerprofil die NAZI-Aktivisten anstrebten, und dabei besonders auf die Kategorie der Politisierung in einem Einparteienstaat totalitärer Prägung zu achten. Unsere Gliederung befaßt sich zur Ausarbeitung dieses Vorhabens zunächst mit äußeren Markierungspunkten der Lehrerbildung 1933–1945 (1.), dann mit kurzen Hinweisen auf den gesellschaftlich-politisch-rechtlichen Rahmen (2.) um die Doppelgesichtigkeit der NS-Lehrerbildung (3.) ins Blickfeld zu rücken und schließlich die Nazifizierung (Politisierung) der Lehrerbildung, soweit sie von außen angegangen werden kann, anzureißen.

1. Äußere (formale) Markierungspunkte der Lehrerbildung 1933–1945

Herausgegriffen werden Daten und Fakten aus der Lehrerbildung im Bereich der damaligen Volksschule und Höheren Schule, um an ihnen exemplarisch Grundzüge der Entwicklung der Lehrerbildung innerhalb der NS-Zeit aufzuweisen.

07. 03. 1933 Erlaß in Preußen: Aufnahme in den »ordnungsgemäßen Vorbereitungsdienst« für das Lehramt an der Höheren Schule nur für 50% der Bewerber[13]

06. 05. 1933 *Die Preußischen Akademien für Lehrerbildung* werden in Hochschulen für Lehrerbildung (= HfL) umbenannt

19. 12. 1933 Beginn der Umstrukturierung der preußischen Lehrerbildung durch Favorisierung ländlicher Regionen und Grenzräume (z. B. von Frankfurt/M. nach Weilburg, von Halle nach Hirschberg)

19. 12. 1933 Aufnahmebedingungen für das Studium an den preußischen HfL

30. 04. 1935 Lehr- und Unterrichtspläne für die Deutschen Aufbauschulen (Deutsche Oberschule in Aufbauform in Bayern, die anstelle der aufgelösten Lehrerbildungsanstalten nun zur »Vorschule« für das pädagogische Fachstudium *(Schemm)* werden sollen.)

18. 03. 1936 Richtlinien für die Lehrtätigkeit und das Studium an den *Hochschulen für Lehrerbildung*

22. 04. 1936 Zulassungsbestimmungen für die 2. Lehrerprüfung
07. 06. 1937 Reichsordnung der Pädagogischen Prüfung (Höhere Schulen)
16. 07. 1937 Richtlinien für die Ausbildung für das Lehramt an höheren Schulen
12. 10. 1937 Ordnung der ersten Prüfung für das Lehramt an Volksschulen
29. 01. 1938 Zulassungsbestimmungen zum Studium an den Hochschulen für Lehrer- und Lehrerinnenbildung werden im gesamten Reich einheitlich geregelt. Sie beinhalten auch die in Preußen schon 1936 ausgesprochene Verpflichtung der Studenten für das Lehramt an höhere Schulen, zwei ihrer insgesamt acht Fachsemester an den HfL zu studieren.
26. 10. 1938 Studienordnung für das Lehramt an Volksschulen
Ostern 1939 Einrichtung von Aufbaulehrgängen für das Lehramt an Volksschulen für Schüler mit abgeschlossener Volksschulbildung, Schüler nach mit besonderem Erfolg absolviertem Landjahr, Schüler mit abgeschlossener Mittelschulbildung, um diese zu einer »Sonderreifeprüfung« als Eingangsvoraussetzung zum Studium für das Lehramt an Volksschulen zu berechtigen.
29. 01. 1940 Reichseinheitliche »Ordnung der Zweiten Prüfung für das Lehramt an Volksschulen«
30. 01. 1940 Reichs-Prüfungsordnung für das höhere Lehramt geht von 6 Semestern mit drei Fächern und ohne Stufenbeschränkung aus
Ostern 1940 Lehrgänge für Schulhelfer zunächst in Preußen. Sie dauern 3 Monate für Bewerber zwischen 19 und 30 Jahren mit dem Abschluß der Mittelschule oder vergleichbarem Abschluß nach einer Aufnahmeprüfung. Schulhelfer werden an mehrklassigen Volksschulen mit Besoldung eines Junglehrers im ersten Dienstjahr eingesetzt, um nach Bewährung die Gelegenheit zu erhalten, ein einjähriges Studium einer HfL mit Abschlußprüfung zu absolvieren.
Ende 1940 Führerbefehl: Auflösung der HfL und Einrichtung von *Lehrerbildungsanstalten (= LBA)*
27. 12. 1940 Ordnung des Vorbereitungsdienstes für das Lehramt an Höheren Schulen im Deutschen Reich
08. 02. 1941 Verfügung zur Einrichtung von LBA
16. 02. 1941 Umbenennung der HfL und der staatlichen Aufbaulehrgänge in LBA
Jan./März 1942 »Vorläufige Bestimmungen für den Unterricht an Lehrerbildungsanstalten«
01. 10. 1944 »Ausbildungs- und Prüfungsordnung der Militäranwärter und der Anwärter des Reichsarbeitsdienstes für den Volksschullehrerberuf«

2. Politische Rahmenbedingungen für die geschichtlichen Möglichkeiten von Lehrerbildung

Um beurteilen zu können, ob und wie amtierende Lehrerinnen und Lehrer auf die Gestaltung von Lehrerbildung Einfluß nehmen konnten, sollte der betreffende politische Rahmen bedacht werden. Als geschichtliches Beispiel mag der Einsatz der staatlichen Gewalt etwa bei den *Stiehlschen* Regulativen in Preußen gelten. Wenn Schule ein Politikum ist, dann erst recht die Lehrerbildung.

Die Konsequenzen aus dieser These besagen für die NS-Zeit, daß sich hier die Bedingungen von Staatlichkeit und gesellschaftlicher Gewalt wie nie zuvor in der deutschen Geschichte verändern.

Die Regierung von Mittelfranken weist die neuen Schulräte folgendermaßen an: »Sie werden hierdurch zum Bezirks-Schulrat für den Bezirk ... ernannt ... Ihre Aufgabe besteht darin, die Schulen Ihres Bezirks in kurzer Zeit zu politisieren, d. h. nationalsozialistisch zu machen. Fürchten Sie nicht, daß Sie zu weit gehen. Eher das Gegenteil ist der Fall.«[14]

Der Politisierung der Schulen korrespondiert die Politisierung der Lehrerbildung und der Gestalt des Lehrers und der Lehrerin.

Der Prozeß der Politisierung, d. h. hier der Nationalsozialisierung von Gesellschaft und Staat ist aufgrund vieler Einzelstudien bekannt. Hier seien nur einige markante Punkte herausgegriffen.

- Die allmähliche Umpolung bzw. Auflösung bisheriger Lehrerverbände in einem Gleichschaltungsvorgang, der nach anfänglichen Unklarheiten dann doch zu einem total geführten NS-Lehrerverband führte. (2.1)
- die Politisierung bei der Verbeamtung und Anstellung als Lehrer (2.2)
- die Ausschaltung nichtnationalsozialistisch Denkender in dem Erziehungssektor, zuvorderst bei den Beförderungsstellen (2.3)
- die allgemeinen Auswirkungen der Durchsetzung der *Hitler-Diktatur:* wonach z. B. im Verlauf des 2. Weltkriegs eine Einzelanweisung *Hitlers* genügte, um den Stand der Lehrerbildung vollständig zu ändern. (2.4)

2.1 Die Einzelschritte des Gleichschaltungsvorgangs auf dem Sektor der Lehrerverbände verlaufen von heute aus gesehen komplizierter, als es manch simple Interpretation vorzeichnen möchte.

Man muß sich schon in den geschichtlichen Augenblick versetzen, der ja nicht das Wissen der Zukunft enthält. So ist auch etwa die Erklärung des *Badischen Lehrervereins* 15. März 1933 von der Situation der Wahl vom 5. März 1933 gezeichnet:

»An unsere Mitglieder!

Die am 30. Januar 1933 vom Herrn Reichspräsidenten berufene Regierung des nationalen Aufbaus ist durch die Wahl vom 5. März bestätigt worden. Die Reichsregierung kann nunmehr an ihre Aufbauarbeit herangehen.

Die Ziele der neuen Bewegung, soweit sie bis jetzt erkennbar wurden, sind großenteils schon seit Jahren die des Badischen und des Deutschen Lehrervereins ... Der Badische Lehrerverein ist zur tatkräftigen Mitarbeit beim Neuaufbau bereit und fordert die gesamte Mitgliedschaft auf, sich entschlossen einzusetzen für das Werden eines einigen, freien Volkes, für eine Bildung und Erziehung im Geiste des deutschen Volkstums ...«[15]

2.2 Das Anstellungs- und Verbeamtungsproblem lösten die Nationalsozialisten in ihrem Sinn.

Am 07. 04. 1933 besagte das Gesetz zur Wiederherstellung des Berufsbeamtentums, daß die Nichtarier mit Ausnahmen für Frontkämpfer ausgeschaltet werden sollten, daß Betroffene keinen Rechtsweg zur Verfügung hätten, daß geheime Prüfungsausschüsse die Entlassung von Beamten verursachen sollten, die »nicht die Gewähr dafür bieten, daß sie rückhaltlos für den nationalen Staat eintreten« (§ 4).

Die Interpretation des neuen Beamtengesetzes vom 26. Januar 1937 durch *Hans Seel* (Schriften der deutschen Hochschule für Politik I. Idee und Gestalt des NS H. 25) formulierte:

»Nunmehr liegt das von der ganzen deutschen Beamtenschaft und weit darüber hinaus mit Spannung erwartete neue Beamtengesetz = DBG sowie die Reichsdienststrafordnung, die beide für alle deutschen Beamten gelten, vor uns. Zum ersten Mal wird in einem Beamtengesetz ›der deutsche Beamte‹ überhaupt genannt. Das ist ein neuer Begriff ...«[16]

Seel bringt zum Ausdruck, daß der künftige deutsche Beamte immer Reichsbeamter sei, »der zum Führer des Deutschen Reiches und Volkes und zum Reich in einem öffentlich-rechtlichen Dienst- und Treueverhältnis steht«. Nunmehr stünden neben der einheitlichen Partei und der einheitlichen Wehrmacht auch das einheitliche deutsche Beamtentum. Dieses bilde somit einen »Grundpfeiler des neuen Staates«. Dieses »so zusammengeschweißte Instrument, das zum Führer des Deutschen Reichs und Volkes in einem unmittelbaren, persönlichen Treueverhältnis steht und ihm zum Gehorsam verpflichtet ist, bedeutet für den nationalsozialistischen Staat ein ganz anderes Machtmittel« als bisher.

Im folgenden nennen wir einige Beamtenmerkmale aus *Seel*[17] unter unserem Gesichtspunkt:

- Treue als Fundament aller Beamtenpflichten

  Dazu stellt *Seel* die Frage, ob es wohl vielen Beamten zum Bewußtsein gekommen sei, daß sie eigentlich einen Treueschwur brachen, als sie sich zum NS bekannten und sich damit in schroffen Gegensatz zu der von ihnen beschworenen Weimarer Verfassung stellten.

- Treue zum Führer endet nicht mit dem Ausscheiden aus dem Dienst.

  Der Beamte habe keinen Freibrief nach dem Verlassen des Dienstes; er müsse sich immer bewußt sein, daß er dem Führer Treue schulde.

- Die Gehorsamspflicht in dienstlichen Angelegenheiten geht jeder anderen Gehorsamsbindung vor.
- Echte Vaterlandsliebe (kein Hurra-Patriotismus) und Opferbereitschaft

  Der Beamte hat dies durch freudige Aufgeschlossenheit für das Winterhilfswerk der Partei, Halten des Eintopfsonntags, vor allem durch Zugehörigkeit zur NSV zu beweisen.

- Positive Einstellung zu seinem Staat und Bejahung der Ziele der Staatsführung aus innerer Überzeugung

Gewähr dafür biete die Zugehörigkeit des Beamten zur Partei und ihren Gliederungen, der Eintritt des Kindes des Beamten in HJ und BDM.

- Um die »Gleichschaltung des Beamtentums mit dem nationalsozialistischen Staat dauernd sicherzustellen, ist dem Stellvertreter des Führers eine Mitwirkung bei der Ernennung von Beamten eingeräumt«.
- Enge Verbundenheit zwischen Staat und Partei bewirkt, daß ein Beamter, der bei seiner Ernennung aus der Partei ausgestoßen oder ausgeschlossen war, nicht Beamter bleiben kann, sondern daß seine Ernennung für nichtig zu erklären ist.
- Der Beamte muß unparteiisch (nicht zu verwechseln mit unpolitisch) seines Amtes walten.

Diese Beamtenauffassungen müßten nun in der konkreten Ernennungspraxis daraufhin überprüft werden, was sie für die Lehrerschaft aller Berufsfelder bedeutete. Man kann wohl davon ausgehen, daß die politisierte Gleichschaltung, – nicht die innere Übereinstimmung der Betroffenen mit der NS-Ideologie – rabiat und brutal allmählich erfolgreich durchgeführt wurde. Lehrer waren seit 1939 rechtlich Reichsbeamte, der Staat übernahm erst Ende 1944 voll ihre Besoldung.[18]

2.3 In der heutigen Deutungslage sollten Wertungen dieser Art, daß die den Lehrern abverlangte Beamtentreue »deutliches Anzeichen für die der Diktatur gemäße Entpolitisierung«[19], daß nach der Parteistatistik 1935 jeder 3. Lehrer das Mitgliedsbuch der NS-Partei besessen habe, daß diese »eilfertige Politisierung eines beachtlichen Teiles der Lehrerschaft« bei den Philologen durch ihre unpolitische, gegenwartsabgewandte, wertneutrale Indifferenz bzw. deutsch-nationale Ablehnung der Demokratie, bei den Volksschullehrern eher aufgrund ihrer erzieherischen und sozialen Wunschvorstellungen ermöglicht worden sei[20], mit folgenden Vorgängen in Zusammenhang gebracht werden (Einzelbeispiele):

- Am 30. März entzog der Hessische Minister für Kultus und Bildungswesen die Unterrichtserteilung in Geschichte, Deutsch, Heimatkunde, Geographie und Staatsbürgerkunde vom Beginn des neuen Schuljahres

  »allen jüdischen Lehrpersonen, ebenso auch allen übrigen international(en), pazifistisch und atheistisch eingestellten Lehrern und Lehrerinnen für immer«.[21]

- In Preußen mußten von in der Ausbildung der Referendare tätigen 36 Seminardirektoren 1933 15 sofort ausscheiden – darunter die beiden einzigen Frauen –, 3 weitere bis 1934.
- Im gesamten höheren Schulwesen Preußens wurden 16% der Schulleiterstellen 1933 neu besetzt.[22]

2.4 Schließlich ist daran zu erinnern, daß in der NS-Diktatur, die in atemberaubendem Tempo alle demokratischen Machtträger bis 1934 ausschaltete, auch die Lehrerbildung dem Führerwillen ebenso wie alle anderen Bereiche unterlag.

3. Formale NS-Übereinstimmungen mit Entwicklungstrends in der Gestaltung von Lehrerbildung vor 1933

Was für den allgemeinen Bildungssektor gilt, daß in formaler Hinsicht Tendenzen von vor 1933 zentralen Lösungen zugeführt wurden (vgl. die Durchsetzung der Schulpflicht im Reichsschulpflichtgesetz vom 6. 7. 1938)[23], gewinnt auch für die Lehrerbildung zumindest in der ersten Phase der NS-Herrschaft Bedeutung. Je nach Ausgangsposition erfolgt eine heutige entsprechende Wertung. Die damalige Volksschullehrerschaft mußte es als Fortschritt[24] empfinden, wenn zunächst die Hochschulen für Lehrerbildung für das ganze Reichsgebiet durchgesetzt wurden, wenn dafür das Abitur reichseinheitlich Voraussetzung wurde, und wenn 1936 die Studenten des Höheren Lehramts 2 Semester an den Hochschulen für Lehrerbildung studieren mußten. So enthält die Reichsordnung der Pädagogischen Prüfung für das Lehramt an höheren Schulen vom 7. 6. 1937 im Teil II die Vorschrift:

»Der Meldung ist ferner beizufügen der Eignungsbericht der Hochschule für Lehrerbildung, an der der Studienreferendar die beiden ersten Halbjahre seines Studiums zugebracht hat.«[25]

Mit der formalen Strukturierung gingen jedoch von Anfang an ideologische Festlegungen zusammen, von denen nun einige unter dem Stichwort »Nazifizierung« aufgeführt werden.

4. Zum Prozeß der Nazifizierung in der Lehrerbildung

Aus Zeitgründen können hier nur einige Perspektiven und Markierungspunkte für die Veränderungen in der Lehrerbildung 1933–45 angesprochen werden. Dabei sollten zwei Gliederungspunkte ordnen helfen.

- Ereignisse und Strukturierungen, bei denen bisherige Gestaltungen von Lehrerbildung »gleichgeschaltet« werden, deren formale Elemente im herkömmlichen Sinn ansprechbar waren, diese »inhaltlich« jedoch einer weltanschaulichen »Umdrehung« unterlagen (1)
- Totaländerungen der Lehrerbildung im Verständnis einer direkten Nazifizierung, d. h. einer staatlich-gesellschaftlichen Gesamtprofilierung vom Boden der NS-Weltanschauung und ihrer politisierenden Gewaltstruktur her (2)

Die heute vorhandene Literatur zur NS-Lehrerbildung läßt sich nach diesen Einteilungsmomenten vornehmen, wobei der 2. Gesichtspunkt sich nicht überall und erst aufgrund späterer empirischer Untersuchungen verdeutlicht, etwa bei *Scholtz*[26], wenn die LBAn als Bestandteil einer neuen erziehungspolitischen Konzeption interpretiert werden, d. h. der »Wandel der Lehrerbildung zur politischen Führerschulung« offen zutage tritt. Die Aufgaben des Lehrers (die Lehrerin in abgestufter Weise) sind hier zu einem Berufsfeld umstilisiert, in das gleichermaßen die frühere kognitive Funktion wenn auch aufgrund einer nun fünfjährigen Seminarausbildung[27], wie auch die Kompetenz für mittlere Führungspositionen in Partei und Hitlerjugend eingehen.[28] Danach erscheinen die LBA-Absolventen nun z. B. im Ausland als Repräsentanten des NS-Regimes[29] und ihre politische Zuverlässigkeit wird höher als ihre fachliche Eignung bewertet.[30]

Ohne im folgenden diese beiden Gesichtspunkte getrennt aufzuführen, seien nun einschlägige Beispiele für den Vorgang der Nazifizierung genannt:

4.1 In den ersten Jahren wurde die Umwandlung der preußischen Pädagogischen Akademien in Hochschulen für Lehrerbildung einmal ausdrücklich durch Übereinstimmung mit alten Forderungen der Lehrerschaft begründet, die man jetzt reichseinheitlich durchgesetzt habe, zum anderen aber ebenso deutlich durch ideologische Hinweise darauf, daß die Verlegung der Hochschulstandorte in ländliche Gegenden dem Auftrag des Nationalsozialismus hinsichtlich der Verbindung mit »Blut und Boden« entspräche.[31]

4.2 Die reichseinheitliche Durchsetzung der Hochschulen für Lehrerbildung vollzog sich als Akt der bewußten Nazifizierung. Die jetzt zur Verfügung stehenden Studien im Bereich der Archivauswertung ergaben dies klar. Die neuen Hochschulen hätten einen »ursprünglich politischen Charakter«, in dem Sinn, daß dort der »Nachwuchs eines politischen Standes im Geist der Staatsführung erzogen« werde. So formulierte *Rust* in den Richtlinien für die Lehrtätigkeit und das Studium an den Hochschulen für Lehrerbildung am 18. 3. 1936.[32]

4.3 Die bayerischen Vorschulen für das pädagogische Fachstudium (Aufbauschulen) erhielten am 30. 04. 1935 Lehr- und Unterrichtspläne, die den Deutschunterricht als Zentrum der Bildungsarbeit mit ausdrücklich politisierender Zielsetzung ansetzten. Er solle »im besonderen der Stärkung des politischen Selbstbewußtseins« dienen. Die deutschen Aufbauschulen bezweckten die Erziehung »charakterlich gefestigter und nationalpolitisch gründlich geschulter junger Menschen« und dies »nach den Erziehungs- und Unterrichtszielen des Nationalsozialismus«.[33]

4.4 Die Schaffung eines neuen Lehrerbildes in den *Adolf-Hitler-Schulen* (= AHS) trägt eindeutig den Charakter der Politisierung. Dort sollte in revolutionärer Umkehrung herkömmlicher Lehrerkennzeichnungen ein neuer Berufstyp entstehen, der Kamerad und Führer in einem sein müsse. Ihn zeichneten »Jugendfrische« und zielbewußte Erziehungskompetenz aus. Die Verschmelzung der Aufgaben der Wissensübermittlung und der vorbildhaften Erziehung im Geist des NS wurde den Lehrern der AHS, die aus der HJ hervorgegangen waren und parteiliche Identifikation gezeigt hatten, nahegelegt. Die Lehrer der AHSn waren HJ-Führer und mußten jährlich den Führer-Zehnkampf absolvieren, zudem sollten sie alle Sportunterricht geben können. Ihre Ausbildung wurde insofern umstrukturiert, als sie neben dem Hochschulstudium eine ›vierjährige politische, wissenschaftliche und körperliche Ausbildung‹[34] in einer »Erzieherakademie« an der Ordensburg Sonthofen erhielten. Empirische Aussagen über die Qualität der Erzieher an AHSn lassen sich noch nicht auf einen Nenner bringen. Einerseits seien sie zumindest bis 1939 nicht professionell, andererseits wird gesagt, daß sie Vollakademiker gewesen seien.[35]

Die Figur des Lehrers an AHSn steht in Zusammenhang mit der Typisierung der

Gestalt des NS-Jugendführers. Anläßlich der Grundsteinlegung der *Akademie für Jugendführung der HJ* in Braunschweig sagte Reichsjugendführer *Baldur von Schirach* am 24. 1. 1936:

»Hier entsteht ein Institut, das erste in seiner Art, das den Begriff des Jugendführers als Beruf und Berufung in sich trägt. Nicht mehr wird der Jugendführer in den kommenden Jahren und Jahrzehnten eine Zufälligkeit sein, was gleichsam als Nebenberuf ausgeübt wird, sondern hier schaffen wir uns in der Akademie für Jugendführung in Braunschweig die Stätte, in der ein neuer Erzieherstand ausgebildet und für seine Aufgaben erzogen wird.
Zugleich verankern wir damit im Leben des Staates den großen revolutionären Gedanken der Selbstführung der Jugend, den wir als die uns alle verbindende Idee in unserer Jugendarbeit empfinden.«[36]

4.5 In der am 7. Juni 1937 erlassenen Reichsordnung der Pädagogischen Prüfung für das Lehramt an höheren Schulen behält sich der *Reichs- und Preußische Minister für Wissenschaft, Erziehung und Volksbildung* die Ernennung des Vorsitzenden, seines Stellvertreters und der Mitglieder des Prüfungsamtes in den Ländern vor. Die jeweilige Kandidatenvorschlagsliste »muß folgende Angaben enthalten«:

»Laufende Nummer, Name Vorname, Amtsbezeichnung, Schule, Lehrerbefähigung, Prüfungsfach, Bemerkungen (Stellung in der Partei und ihren Organisationen).«[37]

Folgende politisch relevante Prüfungsvoraussetzungen, Prüfungsbestandteile und Prüfungserfordernisse werden dem Kandidaten (Studienreferendar) und seinen Prüfern abverlangt (Auswahl):

- Nachweis, daß sich der Studienreferendar »in die Aufgaben und Grundsätze der Jugenderziehung und -bildung in der höheren Schule im Geist nationalsozialistischer Weltanschauung eingelebt hat und in der praktischen Berufsübung so weit ausgebildet ist, daß ihm die Fähigkeit der Anstellung an höheren Schulen zuerkannt werden kann«.
- Bei der Meldung zur Prüfung hat der Studienreferendar beizufügen:

  »d) amtlich beglaubigte Abschriften von Bescheinigungen über Tätigkeit in der NSDAP, ihren Gliederungen und den ihr angeschlossenen Verbänden, im Landjahr, Teilnahme am Arbeitsdienst sowie an Schulungslagern, über sportliche Ausbildung, Wehrdienst u. a.«[38]

- Der zweite Teil des Gutachtens des Leiters der Ausbildung

  »soll die weltanschauliche und politische Haltung des Studienreferendars sowie seine Einsatz- und Opferbereitschaft für den nationalsozialistischen Staat kennzeichnen ...«[39]

- Stellungnahme der NSDAP

  »Zur weltanschaulichen und politischen Haltung ist außerdem vor der Vorlage der Meldung des Studienreferendars durch die zuständige Schulaufsichtsbehörde eine Äußerung der Partei einzuholen.«[40]

- Der Eignungsbericht der Hochschule für Lehrerbildung, an der der Studienreferendar die beiden ersten Halbjahre seines Studiums zugebracht hat, ist beizufügen.
- Die Zulassung zur Prüfung ist zu versagen, wenn

»a) politische Unzuverlässigkeit nachgewiesen ist,
b) wenn begründete Zweifel bestehen, daß der Studienreferendar nach seiner sittlichen Haltung zum Jugenderzieher geeignet ist ...«.[41]

- Da die betreffenden Gutachten die Entscheidung über die Eignung vorbereiten, »muß die menschlich begreifliche Rücksicht auf den Studienreferendar hinter der Verantwortung gegenüber Volk und Staat zurücktreten«.[42]
- In der Hausarbeit »müssen die aus den nationalsozialistischen Erziehungsformen sich ergebenden Fragen der Bildung und Erziehung gebührend zur Geltung kommen«.[43]
- Bei der mündlichen Prüfung ist »namentlich in den grundsätzlichen Fragen der Erziehung und des Unterrichts im Geiste nationalsozialistischer Weltanschauung« genügend Zeit zur Verfügung zu stellen. »Auf allen Gebieten wird Vertrautheit mit dem entsprechenden nationalsozialistischen Schrifttum vorausgesetzt«.[44]
- Die Notenskala der Prüfung bezieht sich insgesamt auf die Eignung als »Erzieher und Lehrer«.[45]

4.6 Die Richtlinien für die Ausbildung für das Lehramt an höheren Schulen vom 16. Juli 1937 – E IIIc 1275 –[46], schreiben vor, daß der Philologe vor Eintritt in die Ausbildung den halbjährigen Arbeitsdienst und in der Regel auch den Wehrdienst abzuleisten habe. Die Ausbildung enthält folgende Bestandteile:
A. Ein einjähriges Studium an einer Hochschule für Lehrerbildung, B. Ein mindestens dreijähriges Studium an einer wissenschaftlichen Hochschule, bzw. Kunsthochschule, C. Die Wissenschaftliche bzw. Künstlerische Prüfung für das Lehramt an höheren Schulen, D. Die besondere berufspraktische Ausbildung, E. Die Pädagogische Prüfung für das Lehramt an höheren Schulen.
Das Studium an einer Hochschule für Lehrerbildung wird ideologisch und zugleich berufspraktisch begründet:

»Die einjährige gemeinsame Ausbildung der Philologen mit den Volksschullehrern verfolgt in erster Linie den Zweck der Ausrichtung der gesamten Erzieherschaft auf ein einheitlich politisch-weltanschauliches Ziel. Zugleich ermöglicht sie durch Einführung in die Berufspraxis an der Volksschule eine erste Auslese der nach Charakter und Anlagen für den Erzieherberuf überhaupt Geeigneten.
Der ersten Aufgabe dient das gemeinsame Leben im Kameradschaftshaus und im Lager, Leibeserziehung, die Einführung in die politisch-weltanschaulichen Grundwissenschaften: Erziehungswissenschaft, Charakter- und Jugendkunde, Vererbungslehre und Rassenkunde, Volkskunde ...«.[47]

Für die damalige Lage bezeichnend ist die Vorbemerkung für das wissenschaftliche Studium.
»Die grundlegende politisch-weltanschauliche Ausrichtung hat die Hochschule für Lehrerbildung zu geben«.[48]
4.7 Die »Bestimmungen über die Zulassung zum Studium an den *Hochschulen für Lehrer- und Lehrerinnenbildung*« vom 29. Januar 1938 schreiben u. a. folgende Unterlagen zum Zulassungsantrag vor:

»c) Nachweis deutschblütiger Abstammung.
Dieser ist durch den vorgeschriebenen Ahnennachweis zu erbringen, der durch Beifügung der eigenen Geburtsurkunde, der Heirats- und Geburtsurkunden der Eltern und der Geburtsurkunde der Großeltern zu belegen ist. An Stelle der Urkunden kann auch der Ahnenpaß vorgelegt werden,
h) gegebenenfalls Nachweise über die Mitarbeit in der Partei, ihren Gliederungen oder angeschlossenen Verbänden,

i) der Nachweis der Erfüllung der Arbeitsdienstpflicht und der Dienstpflicht in der Wehrmacht durch Beifügung des Arbeitsdienst- bzw. Wehrpasses.«[49]

Zum Erfolg des Zulassungsantrages heißt es:

»Zum Studium werden in erster Linie diejenigen Abiturienten und Abiturientinnen zugelassen, die in der Partei und in ihren Gliederungen – insbesondere in der Hitler-Jugend einschließlich des Bundes Deutscher Mädel – mitgearbeitet haben.«[50]

Weiterhin werden neben der Festschreibung der Gebührenfreiheit –, »so daß sich die Kosten im wesentlichen auf die Bestreitung des Lebensunterhalts beschränken«[51] – eine genügende Vorausbildung in Leibesübungen für jeden Bewerber und eine hinreichende musikalische Vorbildung erwartet.
Was die Frage des Zusammenstudiums männlicher und weiblicher Studierender betrifft, so sind drei Möglichkeiten zu unterscheiden:

1. »Männliche und weibliche Studierende« können sich einschreiben in Bayreuth, Braunschweig, Darmstadt, Dresden, Elbing, Eßlingen a. Neckar, Frankfurt a./O., Hamburg, Karlsruhe, Leipzig, Pasing vor München, Seestadt Rostock, Würzburg und an dem Päd. Institut Jena,
2. Studenten in Beuthen OS., Bonn, Cottbus, Dortmund, Hirschberg (Rsgb.) Kiel, Lauenburg i. O., Saarbrücken, Trier und Weilburg a./Lahn
3. Studentinnen nur in Hannover, Koblenz und Schneidemühl.[52]

4.8 Der Rundlaß des Reichsministers für Wissenschaft, Erziehung und Volksbildung vom 26. Oktober 1938 faßt die »Studienordnung für das Lehramt an Volksschulen« zusammen. Er fügt einen einheitlichen Studienplan für Lehrer und einen für Lehrerinnen an Volksschulen bei.
Die Studiendauer ist auf »in der Regel vier Semester« festgelegt.[53] Die Studienordnung kennt drei Bereiche der Ausbildung: 1. die politische und leibliche Erziehung, 2. das wissenschaftliche Studium, und 3. die berufspraktische Ausbildung. Die Einheit dieser Bereiche wird am Bezug auf die »nationalsozialistische Weltanschauung« festgemacht. So stellten Erziehung, Wissenschaft und Berufsausbildung an den Hochschulen für Lehrer- und Lehrerinnenbildung »in besonderem Maße eine Einheit dar«.
Die Studenten sollten nicht nur studieren. »Für ihren späteren Beruf ist die Mitarbeit an den sonstigen Aufgaben, welche sich die Hochschulen im Dienst für Volk, Bewegung und Staat gestellt haben, ebenso von Bedeutung wie der Besuch von Vorlesungen und Übungen und die Arbeit in der Schule.«[54] Der künftige Lehrer solle das Hochschulleben mitgestalten.
4.9 Als letztes Dokument sei auf seinen Politisierungsgrad befragt die »Ordnung des Vorbereitungsdienstes für das Lehramt an Höheren Schulen im Deutschen Reich«, RdErl. d. RMfWEV v. 27. 12. 1940.[55]
Sie ist in Verlängerung der betreffenden Richtlinien vom 16. 7. 1937 und der Richtlinien für die Päd. Arbeitsgemeinschaft vom 16. 8. 1938 *(s. 4.6)* zu interpretieren. Dabei fallen sofort Intensivierungen des Politisierungsvorgangs auf. Zum Beispiel ist danach für alle zum 1. Oktober 1940 eingetretenen Studienreferendare (-referendarinnen) das Gutachten des Stellvertreters des Führers sofort nachträglich einzuholen;

die Einsetzung von Seminarleitern erfordert ein »politisches Gutachten« zum 15. 2. 1941.[56]

Über diese Einzelmaßnahmen hinaus verbalisiert sich unsere Problematik besonders markant an folgenden Stellen (exemplarische Auswahl):

– zu A. Dauer und Gesamtziel des Vorbereitungsdienstes

»Im Vorbereitungsdienst sollen die Studienreferendare in die Verantwortung des nationalsozialistischen Erziehers hineinwachsen und die Aufgaben und Arbeitsweisen der Höheren Schule soweit kennen und beherrschen lernen, daß sie gegen Ende des Vorbereitungsdienstes zu selbständiger, erfolgreicher Arbeit in Erziehung und Unterricht fähig sind.«[57]

– zu B. Meldung, Zulassung, Ernennung und dienstliche Verhältnisse der Studienreferendare

»§ 1 (1) ... Der Meldung sind beizufügen ...
f) der ausgefüllte Fragebogen und der urkundliche Nachweis der deutschblütigen Abstammung ...,
h) eine parteiamtliche Bescheinigung über Zugehörigkeit zur NSDAP oder zu einer ihrer Gliederungen;
(2) über jeden Kandidaten ist sofort nach Eingang der Meldung ein politisches Gutachten beim Stellvertreter des Führers anzufordern. Außerdem ist über jeden Kandidaten ein Auszug aus dem Strafregister anzufordern.
§ 2 (1) Aufgrund der vorschriftsmäßig belegten Meldung und des politischen Gutachtens entscheidet die Schulaufsichtsbehörde, bei der sich der Kandidat gemeldet hat, über die Zulassung.[58] § 8 (3) Studienreferendare, die sich im Vorbereitungsdienst nach ihren Leistungen oder ihrem Verhalten für den Beruf eines Erziehers an Höheren Schulen als nicht geeignet erweisen, sind aus dem Vorbereitungsdienst zu entlassen.«[59]

– zu C. Das Staatliche Studienseminar für das Lehramt an Höheren Schulen

Die Dienstpflicht des Studienreferendars bezieht sich auch auf Maßnahmen zur Erlernung besonderer Fähigkeiten sowie auf die Teilnahme an den Leibesübungen, ferner auf Besuche wichtiger Bildungs- und Erziehungseinrichtungen, auf Veranstaltungen, die der Gemeinschaftserziehung dienen und auf andere vom Seminarleiter angeordnete Dienste.
»Jeder im höheren Schuldienst tätige Lehrer ist nach Aufforderung zur vorübergehenden Mitarbeit im Studienseminar verpflichtet«.[60] Der Seminarleiter »unterrichtet sich ständig über die außerschulische Betätigung der Studienreferendare in der NSDAP, ihren Gliederungen und angeschlossenen Verbänden und veranlaßt und fördert ihre Mitarbeit in der nationalsozialistischen Erzieherorganisation des NS-Lehrerbundes.«[61]

– zu D. Die Ausbildung

Ausdrücklich wird alles favorisiert, was Erziehung genannt ist. Die Studienreferendare sind zur Erkenntnis zu führen, daß der wirksamste Weg zur charakterlichen Beeinflussung die eigene von Hingabe und Selbstzucht bestimmte Haltung ist.« (ebenda S. 17) Sie sollen sich namentlich mit den Beziehungen zwischen Schule, Hitler-Jugend und Elternhaus vertraut machen.[62]
Durch die Sitzungen der Pädagogischen Arbeitsgemeinschaft ist »das Gefühl für die erzieherische Verantwortung zu fördern und zu festigen. Ihr Arbeitsgebiet ist die nationalsozialistische Erziehungsordnung. Da diese aber nur innerhalb der nationalsozialistischen Weltanschauung erfaßt werden kann, erwächst dem Seminarleiter die besondere Aufgabe, den Studienreferendaren das Verständnis für diese inneren Zusammenhänge zu erschließen.«[63]

Die Behandlung erziehungsgeschichtlicher Bezüge hat ihren Ausgang »von den heute gültigen Erziehungsgrundsätzen zu nehmen und sich auf die entscheidenden Wendepunkte des pädagogischen Denkens und Handelns zu beschränken.«[64]
Der Seminarleiter weist der häuslichen Lektüre die Erarbeitung u. a. der »weltanschaulichen Grundlagen der nationaalsozialistischen Pädagogik« zu:
»Wesensbestimmung der nationalsozialistischen Pädagogik (im Anschluß an das Schrifttum bedeutender Pädagogen der Gegenwart) und die allmähliche Verwirklichung ihrer Ideen. Der Durchbruch des Rassegedankens und seine umwälzende pädagogische Bedeutung. Der totale Erziehungsanspruch des nationalsozialistischen Staates, zu veranschaulichen an Gegenbildern vergangener Epochen, besonders des Liberalismus. Der neue Begriff von der wissenschaftlichen Bildung.«[65]
Die Studienreferendare sind angehalten, sich den Aufbau des Schulwesens klarzumachen und die einzelnen Schularten als »Glieder der nationalsozialistischen Erziehungsordnung« anzusehen. Sie absolvieren die »gemeinsame Besprechung der einschlägigen Abschnitte aus Hitlers »Mein Kampf«, der »Wege zur charakterlichen Erziehung auf der Höheren Schule« – des Verhältnisses zwischen Lehrer und Schüler »auf der Grundlage der vom Lehrer geführten Kameradschaft«, und u. a. der »besonderen Bedeutung der deutschkundlichen Fächer und der Biologie, u. a. ihrer politischen Sonderaufgabe in der Frühgeschichte, Volkstumsgeschichte-, Erbgesundheitslehre und Bevölkerungspolitik«.[66]
Wenigstens einmal sollen die Studienreferendare zu einem kurzfristigen Lager von etwa einwöchiger Dauer zusammenkommen. Zudem sind sie zur Teilnahme an den wöchentlich einmal stattfindenden Leibesübungen verpflichtet.[67]

Anmerkungen

1 *Muhri* (1983). In: IZEBF, S. 462f.
2 *Maier* (1983). In: IZEBF, S. 463.
3 *Benze* (1936). In: Kanz (Hrsg.) (1984), S. 152.
4 DWEuV (²1937), S. 290.
5 *Flitner* (1986), S. 358.
6 Ebenda, S. 359.
7 Ebenda, S. 360.
8 Ebenda, S. 356.
9 Vgl. *Kater* (1983).
10 *Scholtz* (1985), S. 9.
11 *Scholtz* (1985), S. 371.
12 Vgl. u. a. *Reich-Ranicki* (1982), *Hochhuth* (1985), *Schnorbach* (1983), *Seibert* (1985), *Weichert – von Hassel* (1980).
13 *Bölling* (1983), S. 177.
14 *Ottweiler* (1979).
15 *Kanz* (1984), S. 71.
16 Ebenda, S. 159.
17 *Seel* (1937). In: *Kanz* (1984), S. 159–161.
18 *Scholtz* (1983). In IZEBF (1983), S. 365.
19 *Scholtz / Stranz* (1980). In: *Heinemann* (1980), Teil 2, S. 114.

[20] *Scholtz* (1985), S. 41.
[21] *Kanz* (1984), S. 73.
[22] *Bölling* (1983). In: IZEBF (1983), S. 178.
[23] *Kanz* (1984), S. 227–231.
[24] Vgl. *Scholtz* (1983). In: IZEBF (1983), S. 358.
[25] DWEuV (1937), S. 291.
[26] *Scholtz* (1983). In: IZEBF (1983), S. 371.
[27] Vgl. *Sandfuchs* (1983). In: IZEBF (1983), S. 351.
[28] *Scholtz* (1983). In: IZEBF (1983), S. 371.
[29] Ebenda, S. 369.
[30] Ebenda, S. 370.
[31] Vgl. *Ottweiler* (1983). In: IZEBF (1983), S. 293.
[32] Interpretation ebenda, S. 297–299.
[33] Ebenda, S. 296f.
[34] *Hellmann* (1942).
[35] Zu 4.4 *Bernett* (1981), S. 42, S. 43f.
[36] In: *Schultz* (1978), S. 231.
[37] DWEuV 3 (1937), S. 289f.
[38] Ebenda, S. 290.
[39] Ebenda.
[40] Ebenda.
[41] Ebenda, S. 291.
[42] Ebenda.
[43] Ebenda.
[44] Ebenda, S. 292.
[45] Ebenda, S. 293.
[46] DWEuV 3 (1937), S. 363–365.
[47] Ebenda, S. 364.
[48] Ebenda.
[49] DWEuV 4 (1938), S. 62.
[50] Ebenda.
[51] Ebenda, S. 63.
[52] Ebenda, S. 62f.
[53] Ebenda, S. 492–495.
[54] Ebenda, S. 492.
[55] DWEuV 7 (1941), S. 13–19.
[56] Ebenda, S. 13.
[57] Ebenda, S. 14.
[58] Ebenda, S. 13.
[59] Ebenda, S. 15.
[60] Ebenda, S. 16.
[61] Ebenda.
[62] Ebenda, S. 18.
[63] Ebenda.
[64] Ebenda.
[65] Ebenda.
[66] Ebenda, S. 19.
[67] Ebenda.

Quellen- und Literaturverzeichnis

Quellen

Deutsche Wissenschaft, Erziehung und Volksbildung: Amtsblatt des Reichsministeriums für Wissenschaft, Erziehung und Volksbildung und der Unterrichtsverwaltungen der Länder. – 5. Bd. (1939), Berlin, 6. Bd. (1940) und weitere Bände, abgekürzt DWEuV

Kanz, H. (Hrsg.) (1984): Der Nationalsozialismus als pädagogisches Problem. Deutsche Erziehungsgeschichte 1933–1945. Frankfurt/M./Bern/New York, abgekürzt Kanz. Die vorgesehene 2. Auflage wird weitere Veröffentlichungen aufarbeiten.

Literatur

Folgende zum jeweiligen Zeitpunkt gut zusammenfassende Veröffentlichungen mit umfangreichen Literaturzusammenstellungen sind erwähnenswert: Heinemann, M. (Hrsg.) (1977): Der Lehrer und seine Organisation. Stuttgart

Heinemann, M. (Hrsg.) (1980): Erziehung und Schulung im Dritten Reich. Teil I: Kindergarten, Schule, Jugend, Berufserziehung. Einleitung Roessler, Wilhelm. Teil II: Hochschule, Erwachsenenbildung. Stuttgart (Veröffentlichungen der Historischen Kommission der Deutschen Gesellschaft für Erziehungswissenschaft Band 4.1 und 4. 2).

IZEBF = Informationen zur erziehungs- und bildungshistorischen Forschung, hrsg. vom Vorstand der historischen Kommission der Deutschen Gesellschaft für Erziehungswissenschaft, Hannover, IZEBF 14 (1980), IZEBF 20/21 (1983)

Außerdem sind neben anderen folgende Einzeluntersuchungen und Informationen namentlich zu Rate gezogen:

Bernett, H. (1981/2): Die Funktion des Sports im Erziehungssystem der Adolf-Hitler-Schulen. In: Kölner Beiträge zur Sportwissenschaft 10/11, S. 33–66

Eilers, R. (Hrsg.) (1985): Löscht den Geist nicht aus. Der Bund Neu-Deutschland im Dritten Reich. Mainz

Flitner, W. (1986): Erinnerungen 1889–1945. In: Gesammelte Schriften, Band 11. Paderborn

Herrmann, U. (Hrsg.) (1985): »Die Formung des Volksgenossen«. Der »Erziehungsstaat« des Dritten Reiches. Weinheim (Geschichte des Erziehungs- und Bildungswesens in Deutschland, Bd. 6)

Hochhuth, M. (1985): Schulzeit auf dem Lande 1933–1945. Gespräche und Untersuchungen in Wattenbeck. Mit einem Vorwort von Ariane Garlichs. Kassel

Kater, M. (1983): Analyse der NSDAP-Mitgliedschaft

Kuropka, J. u. a. (1986): Wanderausstellung »Zur Sache – Das Kreuz«. Museumsdorf Cloppenburg

Müller, M. (1985): Lehrerbildung in Rheinland-Pfalz. In: Jahrbuch für Westdeutsche Landesgeschichte 11, S. 285–298 (mit Literaturhinweisen für 1933–1945)

Rautenberg, W. (1982): Ilfeld. Die Evangelische Klosterschule und Nationalpolitische Erziehungsanstalt 1932–1935. Würdigung und Kritik. In: IZEBF 19, S. 63–126

Reich-Ranicki, M. (Hrsg.) (1982): »Meine Schulzeit im Dritten Reich«. Erinnerungen deutscher Schriftsteller. Köln

Reichwein, A.: siehe Schulz, U.

Schlau, W. – Schadwill, G. (1984): Lehrer in Rheinland-Pfalz. Gesellschaftlich-sozialer Wandel einer Berufsgruppe in den Jahren 1927–1976. Karlstein/Main

Schnorbach, H. (Hrsg.) (1983): Lehrer und Schule unterm Hakenkreuz. Dokumente des Widerstands von 1933–1945. Königstein/Ts.

Scholtz, H. (1985): Erziehung und Unterricht unterm Hakenkreuz. Göttingen

Derselbe (1985): Erziehung. In: Das Große Lexikon des Dritten Reiches

Schultz, Jürgen (1978): Die Akademie für Jugendführung der Hitlerjugend in Braunschweig. Braunschweig (Braunschweiger Werkstücke Reihe A Bd. 15)

Schulz, U. (Hrsg.) (1982): Adolf Reichwein. Ein Lebensbild aus Briefen und Dokumenten. Ausgewählt von Rosemarie Reichwein unter Mitwirkung von Hans Bohnenkamp. München

Seibert, H. (1985): Die Auseinandersetzungen der katholischen Kirche mit dem Nationalsozialismus im Rhein-Lahn-Gebiet. In: Archiv für mittelrheinische Kirchengeschichte 37, S. 157–193

Steinbruck, Eugen (1982): Erinnerungen an die frühere Lehrerbildung in Weilburg und Gießen. Gießen (Institut für Didaktik der Mathematik an der Universität Gießen)

Tenorth, H.-E. (1985): Zur deutschen Bildungsgeschichte 1918–1945. Probleme, Analysen und politisch-pädagogische Perspektiven. Köln/Wien

Weichert-von Hassel, M. (1980): Gymnasium und Politik 1864–1944. Einführung Jürgensen, K. Flensburg

VI. DER INTERNATIONALE VERGLEICH

Jürgen Zwernemann

Lehrer in traditionellen Kulturen Westafrikas

Westafrika gilt in der Ethnologie seit langem als klassisches Gebiet des Geheimbundwesens. Neben sozialen Institutionen, die auf Verwandtschaft beruhen, und neben der traditionellen politischen Struktur mit Häuptlings- oder Fürstentümern unterschiedlicher Größe oder auch mit Ältestenräten in sogenannten akephalen Gesellschaften haben Bünde unterschiedlichster Art eine beachtliche Rolle im kultischen und politischen Leben. Es gibt Männer-, Frauen-, Medizin-, Kult- und Kriegerbünde, um nur einige der wichtigsten Typen zu nennen. Allerdings haben nicht alle ethnischen Gruppen Westafrikas Bünde.

Fast jeder Bund ist bestrebt, bestimmte Glaubensvorstellungen, Praktiken, Riten und Objekte gegenüber Außenstehenden geheimzuhalten. Die Bünde sind oft nach Altersklassen gegliedert. Der Eintritt erfolgt durch eine Initiation, in deren Rahmen das geheime Wissen des Bundes den Novizen ganz oder teilweise vermittelt wird. Daneben werden aber auch praktische Dinge gelehrt, die der Mann oder die Frau im Leben benötigt. Tänze und Lieder des Bundes sowie manchmal auch eine Geheimsprache werden vermittelt. Außerdem hat die Initiation durch mit ihr verbundene Riten eine kultische Komponente. Die Geheimhaltung des Wissens wird mit zumeist drastischen Mitteln erzwungen. Wer die Geheimhaltungspflicht bricht, muß mit dem Tod rechnen. Der Bund sorgt im allgemeinen auch dafür, daß diejenigen, die durch Bruch der Geheimhaltung oder auf andere Weise gewollt oder ungewollt in den geheimen Wissensschatz eindringen, den Tod erleiden[1].

Geheimbünde haben naturgemäß in der ethnologischen Fachliteratur wie auch in Reiseberichten und in Veröffentlichungen von europäischen Beamten, Missionaren, Ärzten usw. Beachtung gefunden. Im Hinblick auf die Geheimhaltungspflicht der Bundmitglieder sind die von den Quellen gebotenen Informationen unterschiedlich. Immerhin gibt es aus einigen Gebieten eine Fülle wertvoller Angaben. Manche Autoren sind erstaunlich tief in das Bundwissen eingedrungen. Der äußere Ablauf der Initiation ist im allgemeinen bekannt. Unterschiedlich sind dagegen die Angaben über das Wissen des Bundes, d. h. über den während der Initiation vermittelten Lehrstoff. Im Vergleich dazu sind die Angaben über diejenigen, die dieses Wissen vermitteln, also über die Lehrer, fast immer geradezu kümmerlich. Dies ist ein Punkt, dem bisher noch kaum Aufmerksamkeit gewidmet worden ist. So bleibt es normalerweise bei dem Hinweis, daß der Unterricht im Initiationslager durch ältere Bundmitglieder erfolgt. Was diese dazu befähigt, ob jeder Altinitiierte die Novizen unterrichten kann und darf, ob es Spezialisten gibt, ob diese eine besondere Schulung haben, ob vielleicht nur wenige Älteste des Bundes das Wissen vermitteln dürfen und wie etwa eine Geheimsprache vermittelt wird, darüber schweigen die meisten Quellen. Es gibt allerdings rühmliche Ausnahmen.

Im folgenden möchte ich Beispiele aus zwei Gebieten vorstellen, nämlich aus dem Hinterland Liberias sowie aus Mali.

1. Der Poro-Bund in Liberia

Küste und Hinterland des Gebiets zwischen Guinea Bissau und der Elfenbeinküste können als ein Zentrum von Geheimbünden betrachtet werden, die allesamt in enger Verbindung zum Ahnenkult stehen und religiös-magische Riten pflegen. Ein wichtiger Bund ist in Sierra Leone und Liberia als *»Poro«, »Polo«* o. ä. bekannt.[2] Der Poro ist ein Männerbund. Ihm steht im allgemeinen ein Frauenbund gegenüber *(Zande)*. Der Poro kann unterschiedliche Gestalt haben. Das hier vorgestellte Beispiel kommt aus Nordost-Liberia, und zwar aus dem Dreiländereck Liberia – Republik Guinea – Elfenbeinküste. Es stützt sich auf Untersuchungen von *Westermann* bei den Kpelle sowie von *Harley* und *Schwab* bei den Mano und benachbarten Völkern wie den Gio (= Dan) und Ge. Leider ist nicht bekannt, was von den alten Riten heute noch so funktioniert, wie es von den Verfassern geschildert wird, denn die liberianische Regierung verbot den Poro zeitweilig. Schon *Harley* (1950, S. VI) spricht von einer stark abgemilderten Form. So gibt es vermutlich keine Menschenopfer mehr und manche Strafe ist wohl im Vergleich zu früheren Gegebenheiten milde. Die Schilderung erfolgt dennoch im »ethnographischen Präsens«.

Bei den genannten Völkern sind alle Männer Mitglieder des Poro (*Schwab* (1947), S. 283). Die vom Bundmeister getragene Maske verkörpert den »Big Devil«[3], den großen Bundgeist. Sie ist wichtigster Kultgegenstand. Unter dieser Maske erläßt der Bundmeister Gesetze und fungiert als Richter. Die Maske wird daher auch als »Richtermaske« bezeichnet. Sie ist ferner als »Große Maske« bekannt und gilt als Verkörperung der Ahnenseelen.[4]

Außer der zentralen Bundmaske gibt es weitere Masken, die besondere Aufgaben haben. Jede hat einen bestimmten Träger. Das Amt des Maskenträgers ist erblich. In jeder Familie, die eine Maske besitzt, stehen mehrere ausgebildete Träger zur Verfügung, damit eine Vertretung gewährleistet ist, wenn der eigentliche Inhaber der Maske erkrankt oder abwesend ist.

Früher dauerte die Initiationszeit theoretisch vier Jahre und wechselte mit der drei Jahre dauernden Initiation des Zande, des Frauenbundes, ab. Poro und Zande fanden und finden nie zur gleichen Zeit statt. Auch waren die angegebenen Zeiten nicht absolut. Sie konnten länger oder kürzer sein. Heute dauern sie allenfalls wenige Monate oder gar Wochen. Allerdings war es früher auch möglich, später in das Buschlager einzutreten, so daß die Initiationszeit bis auf ein Jahr schrumpfen konnte. Durch Geschenke konnten Wohlhabende die Initiationszeit ihrer Kinder abkürzen lassen. Sogar Privatunterricht war und ist möglich. In der Gegenwart ist der Poro nicht mehr die große Erziehungsinstitution, die er einst war (*Westermann* (1921), S. 241, S. 244 f.; *Schwab* (1947), S. 281 f.; *Harley* (1950), S. VI).

Die Initiation findet im Geheimen statt, in einem abgesonderten Teil des Waldes, dem Poro-Busch, bei einem Hauptort oder bei einem alten, besonders angesehenen Ort. Von Mitgliedern des Bundes werden dort Häuser für die Novizen und ihre Erzieher errichtet. Der Bundmeister und seine Gehilfen haben jeder ein eigenes Haus, das von den Knaben nicht betreten werden darf. Im Poro-Busch ist ferner ein Versammlungshaus (*Harley* (1941), S. 3; *Westermann,* (1921), S. 241).
Die Initiation beginnt mit der Trockenzeit, also im November. Der Eintritt im Alter von 7–15 Jahren ist nominell freiwillig, tatsächlich werden Widerstrebende aber gezwungen. Bei der Initiation wird der Novize vom Bundgeist, dem »Big Devil«, »gefressen« und am Ende der Buschzeit »wiedergeboren« oder »ausgespuckt«. Die inzwischen angebrachten Bundnarben gelten für Außenstehende als Spuren der Zähne des Bundgeistes. Die Operation, die zur Narbenbildung führt, ist nicht ungefährlich. Infektionen und Todesfälle sind als Folge dieser Operation wie auch der Beschneidung nicht selten. Die Beschneidung erfolgt vor oder zu Beginn der Initiation.[5] Man glaubt, daß die Initianden in der Buschzeit besonderen Kontakt zu übernatürlichen Mächten haben und sogar selbst als Geister anzusehen sind. Von Außenstehenden, insbesondere von Frauen, dürfen sie nicht gesehen werden (Vgl. hierzu *Harley* (1941), S. 3, S. 15f.; *Schwab* (1947), S. 281ff.; *Westermann* (1921), S. 244f.).
Ziel der gesamten Initiation ist, daß die Knaben eine Erziehung und Ausbildung im Sinne des Stammesideals erhalten. Gelehrt wird das gesamte Wissen und Können der betreffenden Gruppe auf religiösem, allgemein geistigem, gesellschaftlichem und technologischem Gebiet. Das sind z. B. mündliche Überlieferungen und Religion des Volkes, Tänze und Gesänge, Jagd und Krieg, Feldbau, handwerkliche Fertigkeiten, Belehrung über den Umgang mit dem anderen Geschlecht. Ein wichtiger Punkt ist der absolute Gehorsam gegenüber den Lehrern und den Funktionären des Bundes. Auch Schweigeübungen finden statt. Der Unterricht dauert den ganzen Tag über (*Westermann* (1921), S. 244, S. 247f.; *Harley* (1941), S. 15f.; *Schwab* (1947), S. 274).
In den ersten Monaten erhalten alle den gleichen Unterricht. Danach werden die Initianden entsprechend ihren Fähigkeiten und ihrer Herkunft in Klassen eingeteilt, nämlich in eine allgemeine Klasse, eine Klasse der Heilkundigen und Spezialisten unterschiedlicher Art auf religiösem Gebiet und eine Klasse der künftigen Häuptlinge und deren Berater. In der letztgenannten Klasse werden Verfassung der ethnischen Gruppe, Erbfolge, Häuptlingswahl, Zeremoniell, Verhältnis zu benachbarten Gruppen und früher auch Kriegsführung gelehrt. In der Klasse der Heilkundigen und Priester werden Kenntnisse von Medizinen, magischen Praktiken, Opferritualen, Ordalen und Orakelmethoden vermittelt. Ferner lernen die Novizen dort alles über Geister, Wasser- und Bergmenschen, heilige Tiere und Pflanzen und deren Behandlung. Was der einzelne Novize lernen soll, entscheiden die hohen Bundmitglieder (*Westermann* (1921), S. 240, S. 246ff.).[6]
Schon während der Initiationszeit können die Novizen sich auf vielen Gebieten tiefergehende Kenntnisse aneignen. Während der ersten Monate stellen die Lehrer fest, ob bei dem einzelnen Novizen besondere Stärken oder Schwächen vorhanden

sind. Entsprechend entscheiden sie bzw. der Bundmeister, wie die weitere Ausbildung verlaufen soll, d. h. ob ein Novize einer der besonderen Klassen zugeteilt werden soll. Die Masse der Novizen bleibt in der allgemeinen Klasse.
Es gibt im Poro-Busch für die Kinder bestimmte Strafen. Bei Prügeleien muß jeder Beteiligte ein Schaf, zwei Stück Tuch, eine Last Reis sowie ein gewisses Quantum Palmöl und Salz zahlen. Außerdem werden sie verwarnt und darauf hingewiesen, daß die Strafe bei Wiederholung höher ausfällt. Wenn ein Knabe einen anderen beschimpft, muß er auf einem Haufen zerbrochener Nußschalen knien, und zwar bis Sonnenuntergang, sofern seine von der Strafe informierten Verwandten ihn nicht mit vier Beinringen auslösen (*Harley* (1941), S. 17).
Lehrer der Novizen sind die *zo*, die eine Spezialausbildung – vor allem in magischen Praktiken – haben. Jeder *zo* hat eine eigene Maske. Die *zo* sind zugleich Funktionäre des Bundes und Ratgeber des Bundmeisters. Da sie ihr Wissen weitergeben sollen, gehören Heilkundige, Handwerksmeister, Priester und Häuptlinge zu den *zo*. Manchmal überschneiden sich die Ämter. So kann jemand gleichzeitig der führende Schmied sowie Häuptling und Priester sein. Die *zo* erhalten ihr besonderes Wissen von anderen *zo*, und zwar ohne Initiation, wenn das Wissen vom Vater an den Sohn weitergegeben wird. Auch der Wahrsager kann herausfinden, ob jemand dazu bestimmt ist, *zo* zu werden. Wer nicht in direkter Linie Nachfolger eines *zo* ist, muß für die Kenntnisse extra zahlen. (Vgl. *Harley* (1941), S. 8ff.; (1950), S. VIII, S. 27ff.; *Schwab* (1947), S. 273f., S. 278; *Westermann* (1921), S. 238.)
Wegen ihrer Masken werden die Poro-Funktionäre ›devil‹, ›country devil‹ oder ›bush devil‹ genannt. Wenn auch jeder *zo* seine Maske hat, so ist doch nicht jeder Maskenträger ein *zo*. Unklar ist, ob die *zo* bei ihrem Unterricht immer die Maske tragen. Ich halte dies für unwahrscheinlich, denn das Blickfeld ist unter der Maske sehr begrenzt, und dies ist etwa beim Suchen von Heilkräutern oder bei der Vermittlung handwerklicher Fertigkeiten sicher nicht förderlich. Offenbar werden die Masken aber aufgesetzt, wenn es darum geht, die Kinder zu disziplinieren, denn die Masken verkörpern auch die Ahnengeister. Während die *zo* die Kinder unterrichten, haben andere Masken bestimmte andere Aufgaben zu erfüllen wie Beschaffung der Nahrung, Bewachung des Busches vor Fremden und Uneingeweihten oder Sicherung des magischen Schutzes der Initianden. Für die Initianden sind die Masken lebende Geister. Im Laufe der Initiation wandelt sich die Furcht in kultische Verehrung (*Harley* (1950), S. 27, S. 29ff.; *Schwab* (1947), S. 268).
Die Buschzeit endet mit einer feierlichen Entlassung. In Prozession ziehen die Gäste durch alle Straßen des Ortes. Danach wird mitgeteilt, welche Kinder nicht wiederkehren, d. h. verstorben sind. Erst dann erscheinen die frisch Initiierten, angeführt von ihren Lehrern. Die Kinder haben in der Buschzeit vieles gelernt, aber der Lernprozeß ist damit nicht abgeschlossen, er dauert vielmehr das ganze Leben an. Auch enden Funktion und Einfluß des Poro nicht mit der Initiation. Er ist nämlich eine mächtige und einflußreiche Gesellschaft, die alle Mitglieder kontrolliert, d. h. alle Männer der betreffenden Gruppe. Diese Kontrolle erfolgt mit Hilfe von Gesetzen und der Furcht vor den übernatürlichen Mächten, die hinter diesen Gesetzen stehen (*Westermann* (1921), S. 250ff.; *Harley* (1941), S. 3, S. 32).

Im Bund gibt es verschiedene Grade. Insgesamt sollen es bis zu 99 sein.[7] Der Aufstieg in einen höheren Grad erfordert eine besondere Unterweisung und ist kostspielig. Die höchsten Grade sind bestimmten Familien vorbehalten (*Harley* (1941), S. 32). Mächtigster Mann ist der Bundmeister, der sogar den Häuptling oder den König – zumindest in Poro-Zeiten – in politischen Fragen mehr oder weniger ausschalten kann. Ihm stehen einige Bundmitglieder höheren Grades zur Seite. Sie bilden die Führungsspitze des Poro. Vorsitzender dieses Ältestenrates ist der Bundmeister als Besitzer der Großen Maske und »Inhaber« des Landes (*Schwab* (1947), S. 273f.; *Harley* (1941), S. 6, S. 9, S. 11, S. 31f.; (1950), S. 11ff.).

2. Drei Bünde der Bambara in Mali

Die Bambara, eine der wichtigsten ethnischen Gruppen in Mali, haben ein ganzes System unterschiedlicher Bünde. Es gibt einen Bund der unbeschnittenen Knaben sowie fünf bis sieben Männerbünde und drei Frauenbünde. Über den Bund der unbeschnittenen Knaben sowie über zwei Männerbünde liegen recht gute Information vor, über einen weiteren Männerbund gibt es eine Anzahl brauchbarer Informationen. Über alle anderen Bünde ist wenig bis nichts bekannt (vgl. *Dieterlen* (1951), S. 142; *Pâques* (1954), S. 84ff.). Alle Bünde haben ein System permanenten Lernens. Der Erziehungs- und Ausbildungsgang endet erst mit dem Tod, der die letzte Erkenntnis bringt. Ein Jüngerer kann einen Älteren niemals an Wissen und damit an Macht erreichen, ihm etwa gleichberechtigt sein (*Beuchelt* (1961), S. 155).
Auch für die Bambara stütze ich mich auf die vorhandene Literatur, vor allem auf die Arbeiten von *Beuchelt, Dieterlen* und *Cissé* sowie von *Zahan*. *Beuchelt* ist ethnologisch geschulter Psychologe, alle anderen sind Ethnologen.

a) N'domo, der Bund der unbeschnittenen Knaben

Der Bund der unbeschnittenen Knaben heißt bei den Bambara *N'domo* oder *N'tomo*. Mit dem Eintritt in diesen Bund beginnt die erste Stufe der formalen Erziehung der Knaben in intellektueller, religiöser und sozialer Hinsicht. Früher hatte jedes Dorf seinen *N'domo*. Obwohl der Bund heute in vielen Dörfern nicht mehr existiert, ist er nach dem *Komo* am weitesten verbreitet (*Zahan* (1960), S. 30).
Der Bund bemächtigt sich der Knaben im Alter von etwa sechs Jahren. Wenn einige Proben das normale Entwicklungsniveau erwiesen haben, werden die Kinder initiiert. In fünf Initiationsgraden erreichen sie das Beschneidungsalter. Wie bei den Erwachsenen gibt es eine strenge Altershierarchie: Innerhalb jeder Stufe ist ein Knabe der höchsten Altersklasse Anführer. Früher waren die Bundmitglieder Jugendliche oder gar Erwachsene, weil die Beschneidung viel später erfolgte. (Vgl. hierzu *Beuchelt* (1961), S. 151; *Dieterlen* (1951), S. 170f.; *Zahan* (1960), S. 47).

Der fähigste Junge des letzten Jahrgangs vor der Beschneidung ist Bundmeister. Er soll der Schnellste und Beste bei der Feldarbeit sein. Wichtiger sind aber wohl seine intellektuellen Fähigkeiten. Die Wahl des Bundmeisters erfolgt nach Rücksprache mit den Alten des Dorfes. Dem Bundmeister steht ein Vertreter zur Seite, der »Zeuge des Bundmeisters«. Ferner gibt es einen Opferer, den »Herrn des Messergriffs«, der alle Opferformeln kennt und die Opfer vollzieht. Nach Möglichkeit stammt er aus einer Schmiedefamilie. Als dritter Funktionär ist der »Herr der Kette« zu nennen. Er befaßt sich mit den Emblemen der fünf Altersklassen und sorgt dafür, daß sie in Ordnung sind. Er ist der Anführer der Löwenklasse. Dies ist die erste Initiationsklasse. Die Kette ist das Symbol der Lehrer und der Lehre. Sie symbolisiert die Beziehung zwischen Lehrer und Schüler. Was jemand von seinem Lehrer erfahren hat, das gibt er seinem eigenen Schüler weiter, der es wiederum an den nächsten vermittelt. So ist jeder Glied einer Kette. Auch der Opferer und der Herr der Kette haben ihre Vertreter, ihre »Zeugen«. Sie alle bilden den Rat des N'domo. Der Bundmeister wird vom scheidenden Rat bestimmt. Die anderen Funktionäre werden von den Mitgliedern des Bundes aus der höchsten Altersklasse gewählt. Die Aufgaben des Rates sind die Beilegung von Differenzen zwischen Bundmitgliedern, die Vorbereitung der Feste, die Verteilung der Arbeit, die Kontaktpflege zu den Erwachsenen und die Auswahl der Maskenträger für die Feste (*Zahan* (1960), S. 43, S. 52f.).
Die Anführer, die, wie erwähnt, der höchsten Altersklasse angehören, haben absolute Befehlsgewalt und disziplinieren die Gruppe durch Übungen wie gemeinsames Schweigen oder das Verbot zu niesen oder zu husten. Vergehen werden durch harte Strafen geahndet. Die intellektuelle Schulung der Kinder ist sehr praxisorientiert und arbeitet nicht mit abstrakten Vorstellungen, sondern bildhaft mit konkreten Realitäten. Vor allem geht es um die peinlich genaue Ausführung von Ahnenriten, deren Bedeutung die Kinder allerdings nicht genau verstehen. Letztlich interpretieren sie ein Stück heiliges Theater, dessen Sinn nur die Erwachsenen kennen. Durch Geheimhaltungszwang lernen die Mitglieder während der sukzessiven Initiationen in verschiedene Grade Schweigen, Beherrschung der Zunge und Selbstkontrolle. Durch ernste und feierliche Riten erwerben sie geistige Reife und Verantwortungsbewußtsein (*Zahan* (1960), S. 43, S. 47).
Das soziale Empfinden wird nicht nur durch die Einordnung in das Gruppenverhalten geschult, sondern auch dadurch, daß jeder vor der Initiation in die erste Klasse eine Freundin wählen muß, der er bei schwerer Arbeit hilft, die er vor anderen beschützt und die er beim jährlichen Fest der Initiation des nächsten Jahrgangs und des eigenen Aufstiegs in die nächsthöhere Klasse beschenkt. Die Mädchen wählen ihrerseits eine Anführerin, unter deren Leitung sie bei gemeinsamer Feldarbeit der Knaben sowie bei deren Festen die Speisen bereiten und Wasser herbeischaffen (*Beuchelt* (1961), S. 152; *Zahan* (1960), S. 48).
Der Bund hat fünf Grade oder Klassen. Theoretisch dauert die Mitgliedschaft fünf Jahre, da alljährlich die Initiation in die nächste Klasse erfolgt. Zum Initiationsfest werden von den Mitgliedern der einzelnen Klassen außerhalb des Dorfes in der Nähe des Baumheiligtums des Bundes umzäunte Plätze errichtet. Eigentlich hat jede Klasse ihren Platz, oft gibt es aber nur zwei oder drei Plätze für alle fünf Klassen. Die Mittel

zur Bestreitung des Festes, d. h. für die Speisen und die Opfertiere, werden durch den Ertrag eines eigenen Feldes, durch Mitgliedsbeiträge, durch Übernahme verschiedener Lohnarbeiten und durch Sammlung erworben. Neben Mutproben ist der wichtigste Teil der Initiation die Erklärung der Embleme der fünf Klassen: Schwirrholz, Reibetrommel, Mirliton, Hackenblatt und Schlüssel sowie Kalebassentrompete (*Zahan* (1960), S. 54ff., S. 93ff., S. 111ff.). Da die Initiation in dieser Form heute kaum noch durchgeführt werden kann, erfolgt sie oft in alle fünf Grade gleichzeitig. Der Bund wird dann nach einem Jahr verlassen (*Zahan* (1960), S. 124). Wer die letzte Klasse verläßt, geht ins Beschneidungslager (vgl. hierzu *Pâques* (1954), S. 91f.; *Zahan* (1960), S. 47; *Beuchelt* (1961), S. 152f.).
Von besonderem Interesse ist hier die Art der Weitergabe der Kenntnisse. Lehrer der Kinder sind Kinder. Sie geben ihr Wissen eigentlich nur einmal im Jahr weiter, nämlich bei der Initiation der nächsten Gruppe, die durch die Vorgänger erfolgt. Im übrigen lernen alle soziales Verhalten bei den gemeinsamen Aktivitäten und kultisches Verhalten sowie den Ablauf der Riten durch Präsenz bei den entsprechenden Anlässen in fünf Jahren. Bezeichnend ist hierbei, daß die Funktionäre, die diese wichtigen Handlungen vornehmen, ebenso wie die Anführer der Klassen immer der höchsten Initiationsklasse angehören.

b) Komo, Wächter der Tradition

Der *Komo* umfaßt alle beschnittenen männlichen Bewohner eines Dorfes mit Ausnahme der Musikanten.[8] Die Mitgliedschaft ist obligatorisch. Der Bund wacht über die traditionellen Kultpraktiken und Moralbegriffe, die allen Mitgliedern ebenso vermittelt werden wie die Regeln der Solidarität, die Rechte und Pflichten der Mitglieder, die Tabuvorschriften sowie die Strafen, die bei Tabubruch zu erwarten sind. Die Kenntnis religiöser und magischer Praktiken gehört genauso zum Wissen der Bundmitglieder wie die Herstellung und Weihe von Schutzzaubern und die Kenntnis von Giften und Gegengiften. Der Bund hat große Macht. In der traditionellen Gesellschaft wirkte er auf Justiz und öffentliche Angelegenheiten ein. Er garantiert das materielle und spirituelle Leben der Menschen sowie die Kontinuität der Kultur der Ahnen. In den Altären des Komo konzentrieren sich nach dem Glauben der Bambara die Seelen der Toten und die Lebenskraft des Getreides. Der Bund hat daher eine beachtliche Rolle im Feldbau. Durch besondere Riten sorgt er für Regen und das Gedeihen der Feldfrüchte. Das Saatgut der Mitglieder wird in einem Speicher aufbewahrt, für den der Bundmeister verantwortlich ist. Jeder Komo hat seinen besonderen Namen. Je älter der Bund ist, desto mächtiger ist er. (Vgl. hierzu *Dieterlen* (1951), S. 143f., S. 159f., S. 165; *Pâques* (1954), S. 84f.; *Dieterlen* u. *Cissé* (1972), S. 9f., S. 16ff.)
Der Komo ist hierarchisch organisiert. Er hat 33 Initiationsgrade, die sich auf vier Altersklassen verteilen. An der Spitze steht der Bundmeister, der im allgemeinen ein Schmied ist.[9] Ihm stehen zwei Älteste beratend zur Seite. Alle sieben Jahre findet ein großes Fest statt, das 15 Tage dauert und in dessen Verlauf in manchen Dörfern ein

neuer Bundmeister gewählt wird, während der alte sterben muß[10] (*Dieterlen* (1951), S. 143f.; *Pâques* (1954), S. 85; *Tauxier* (1927), S. 272ff.).
Die Initiation der Novizen erfolgt direkt nach der Beschneidung. Der Unterricht der Initianden beginnt schon am 6. Tag nach dieser Operation. Lehrer sind Schmiede oder Haussklaven. Unterrichtet werden Ethik und Moral, Benehmen, körperliche Ertüchtigung (Märsche durch den Busch, Jagd, Fischfang, Schwimmen, Spiele), sexuelle Erziehung sowie Gesänge und Riten des Komo. Gerade in dieser Phase der Initiation lernt der Novize vieles, dessen wirklichen Sinn er noch nicht versteht. Anderes wird genau erläutert. So präsentiert der Älteste der Schmiede den Initianden das Werkzeug der Ahnen. Er erklärt Ursprung, Geschichte, Rolle und geistigen Wert und erinnert an den Respekt, den jedermann den Ahnen für deren Mut, Arbeit und technische Erfindungen schuldet. Auch tritt die Bundmaske auf, deren Träger Stück für Stück seiner Ausrüstung ablegt und den symbolischen Sinn jedes Teils erläutert. Selbstverständlich werden den Novizen, die absolute Verschwiegenheit gegenüber Außenstehenden schwören müssen, die Altäre und heiligen Geräte des Bundes gezeigt. Sie lernen auch, wie der Bund organisiert ist (*Dieterlen* (1951), S. 155; *Dieterlen* u. *Cissé* (1972), S. 58f.).
Nach der Aufnahme in den Bund kann jedes Mitglied entscheiden, ob es durch weitere Initiation stufenweise zusätzliche Kenntnisse erwerben möchte. Jedes Jahr rückt das Mitglied weiter vor, bis der höchste Kenntnisgrad schließlich erreicht ist. Alle sieben Jahre kommt ferner die gesamte Altersklasse eine Stufe weiter. Die vierte und letzte Altersklasse wird spätestens mit etwa 48 Jahren erreicht. Ein Teil der Mitglieder tritt allerdings nach einigen Jahren in andere Bünde ein und erwirbt dann keine weiteren Kenntnisse im Komo. Niemand verliert jedoch seine Mitgliedschaft (*Dieterlen* u. *Cissé* (1972), S. 31f., S. 59, S. 215f.).
Zum geheimen Wissen des Bundes gehören 266 graphische Zeichen. Sie bilden die Grundlage des gesamten esoterischen Wissens und werden von den Alten weitergegeben, die den höchsten Grad erreicht haben. Diese Zeichen symbolisieren den Ursprung und die Entstehung des Alls sowie aller Lebewesen und Seelen. Sie entsprechen ferner den 266 Namen des Schöpfers, der sie parallel zur Schöpfung erdacht hat. Die heiligen Zeichen sind auf Tafeln notiert, die im Heiligtum des Bundes aufbewahrt werden. Jedes dieser Zeichen bedeutet ein Wort, einen Ausdruck, ein Glied einer Phrase und gilt als Ausgangspunkt einer neuen Serie von Graphemen (*Dieterlen* u. *Cissé* (1972), S. 10, S. 20f., S. 63f., S. 78ff.).
Mit Hilfe dieser Grapheme werden die Mitglieder immer weiter in die religiösen und philosophischen Vorstellungen des Bundes eingeführt. In der Trockenzeit organisiert der Bund Abende, an denen die heiligen Zeichen in den Sand gemalt, zerlegt und erläutert werden, und zwar entsprechend den Kenntnissen, die jede der vier Altersklassen hat. Für jede Altersklasse gibt es ein anderes Niveau der Erklärung. Jede Gruppe wird nach Hause geschickt, wenn die Erklärung der Grapheme für die nächsthöhere Altersklasse beginnen soll.
Die Gruppe der Ältesten und Ranghöchsten stellt die Lehrer für alle Altersklassen. Die Novizen werden freilich auch von besonders geschulten jüngeren Lehrern unterrichtet. Ausgewählte junge Leute erhalten nämlich schon früh zusätzlich einen

intensiven und vertieften Unterricht. Ihre Lehrer sind die Würdenträger des Bundes, die sie darauf vorbereiten, eines Tages im Bund eine führende Rolle zu übernehmen, sei es im Kult, sei es als Bewahrer des Wissens (*Dieterlen* u. *Cissé* (1972), S. 33f., S. 59ff.). Wer freiwillig tiefer in die Geheimnisse des Bundes eindringen will, der wird vom Bundmeister und den Ältesten nach seinen Absichten befragt, ehe ihm dies erlaubt wird (*Dieterlen* (1951), S. 156ff.).
Die Pädagogik der Bambara steht auf einem beachtlichen Niveau. Die Fähigkeiten der Kinder und jungen Männer werden sorgsam bewertet. Der Unterricht zeichnet sich durch eine kluge Progression und eine sorgsame Methodik bei der Vermittlung des Lehrstoffes aus, der physische, intellektuelle und moralische Bildung zum Inhalt hat (*Dieterlen* u. *Cissé* (1972), S. 60).

c) Kore, der Bund zur Erlangung höchster Weisheit

Als drittes Beispiel von den Bambara soll der *Kore* oder *Kwore* vorgestellt werden. Der Kore vollendet die moralische und intellektuelle Bildung des Mannes. Er gibt ihm seine ursprüngliche Harmonie wieder, die durch die Beschneidung zerbrochen worden ist und erlaubt ihm die mystische Vereinigung mit Gott und den Triumph über den Tod. Das Zeremoniell des Kore richtet sich auf die Vergeistigung des Menschen, auf die Erlangung der höchsten Weisheit und Unsterblichkeit. Der Kore führt ferner Riten aus, die den Himmel, die Himmelsrichtungen und alle atmosphärischen Erscheinungen betreffen, besonders den Regen (*Zahan* (1960), S. 132; *Dieterlen* (1951), S. 166; *Pâques*, (1954), S. 86).
Auch der Kore ist hierarchisch gegliedert. Er hat acht Initiationsgrade und ebensoviele Stufen des Wissens. Der Bundmeister ist – zumindest theoretisch – der älteste Mann des höchsten Initiationsgrades (*Zahan* (1960), S. 134, S. 142).[11]
Die großen Feste des Bundes, einschließlich der Initiation, finden alle sieben Jahre statt und werden in zwei Abschnitten in aufeinander folgenden Jahren gefeiert. Im ersten Teil erfahren die Novizen Leiden, Askese sowie symbolischen Tod und symbolische Wiederauferstehung. Dies ist der härteste Teil der Initiation. Manchmal laufen die erschöpften Novizen davon. Sie werden aber eingefangen und müssen noch härtere Leiden erdulden (*Zahan* (1960), S. 132; S. 280f.).
Dieser Teil der Initiation dauert 15 Tage und umfaßt drei Phasen, nämlich den symbolischen Tod, den Unterricht und die symbolische Wiederauferstehung. Gleich beim Eintritt in den heiligen Hain des Bundes werden die Novizen gegeißelt, mit Dornen gepiekt, mit Fackeln gebrannt und dreimal um den heiligen Hain und das Dorf gejagt, wobei sie immer wieder geprügelt, gepiekt und gebrannt werden. Ähnlich schmerzhafte Prüfungen erfolgen am zweiten und dritten Tag. U. a. muß ein 20–30 m langes Tal durchlaufen werden, dessen Sohle mit Glut bedeckt ist, die unter einer Sandschicht verborgen liegt. All dies dient der Purifikation und der Persönlichkeitsbildung (*Zahan* (1960), S. 283ff., S. 295, S. 297).
Danach erfolgt eine begrenzte Unterweisung durch die Alten des Bundes und durch Altinitiierte. Die Novizen lernen das, was ihre Klasse betrifft, aber nicht alles wird

ihnen erklärt. Der Unterricht zielt nicht so sehr darauf ab, eine Fülle von Kenntnissen zu vermitteln, sondern die qualitative Substanz des Stoffes auszuschöpfen. Die Novizen lernen, wie jedes Ding nach den Gesetzen eines besonderen Symbolismus entdeckt, betrachtet und interpretiert werden kann: Pflanzen, Tiere, Mineralien, Sterne, Gebrauchsgegenstände haben alle einen symbolischen Gehalt (*Zahan* (1960), S. 237). Dieser Unterricht kommt allerdings vor allem in der zweiten Initiationsphase zum Tragen, die der Theomorphose des Menschen gewidmet ist und ebenfalls 15 Tage dauert. In der Gegenwart werden beide Phasen der Initiation oft schon zu einem einzigen Block von 15 Tagen zusammengefaßt. Dennoch verliert der Bund an Bedeutung, da sich nur noch wenige junge Leute initiieren lassen (*Zahan* (1960), S. 132f., S. 280f.).
Eines der Embleme des 5. Initiationsgrades *(kore dugwa)* ist das *kala ni,* eine 3–4 m lange Bambusstange, an der zahlreiche Objekte befestigt sind, die Mann und Frau, Techniken und Waffen, Hausgerät, Mobiliar und Nahrung, die wichtigsten Sterne, Himmel und Erde, Tiere und Pflanzen repräsentieren. Im Prinzip ist es die Gesamtheit der Dinge und Wesen, die das Universum der Bambara umfaßt. An der Stange hängen Teilchen oder Zeichen der Objekte, denn selbstverständlich kann man dort nicht einfach ein Boot, Keramiken oder ein Fischnetz aufreihen. Theoretisch sollen 240 Objekte am *kala ni* hängen. Tatsächlich ist bei vielen Objektkategorien nur ein Objekt als Beispiel vorhanden, das die anderen mitverkörpert.
Bei der Initiation wird das *kala ni* auf zwei Gabelhölzer gelegt. Zwei Mitglieder des 5. Initiationsgrades stellen sich in die Nähe der Stange, der eigentliche Lehrer mit dem Rücken zu ihr. Der andere berührt beim Unterricht ein Objekt nach dem anderen und fragt: »Lehrer, was ist das?« Der Lehrer – immer mit dem Rücken zur Stange – nennt zunächst die Bezeichnung des Gegenstandes und erklärt dann alles, womit das Objekt zusammenhängt und woran es erinnert.[12] Der Unterricht wird mehrfach wiederholt (Zahan 1960: 161, 238). Der Initiand lernt, »sich von einer Bedeutung zur nächsten zu bewegen, vom Materiellen zum Geistigen zu gehen, vom Konkreten zum Abstrakten«. Abgesehen von den pädagogischen Fähigkeiten, die Dinge und ihre Verknüpfungen den Lernenden nahezubringen und zu erklären, benötigt der Lehrer ein ausgezeichnetes Gedächtnis für die Reihenfolge der 240 Gegenstände, die in 8 Serien zu 30 Objekten unterteilt sind, deren jede wieder 5 Gruppen zu 6 Gegenständen zusammenfaßt. Sicher ist damit ein mnemotechnisches Hilfsmittel gegeben (*Zahan* (1960), S. 255).
Die höchste Kategorie der Lehrer wird durch die Mitglieder des 8. Initiationsgrades repräsentiert. Sie müssen über eine hohe Intelligenz und ein hervorragendes Gedächtnis verfügen. Sie geben Unterricht und müssen in der Lage sein, das gesamte esoterische Wissen der Bambara darzulegen und zu erläutern. Ferner müssen sie eine Sammlung heiliger Sentenzen bei bestimmten Riten rezitieren können, ohne auch nur eine einzige Silbe falsch auszusprechen. Nur sie können die geheime Bedeutung dieser Sentenzen erläutern. Sie sind gewissermaßen gelehrte Priester (*Zahan* (1960), S. 143, S. 255, S. 276f.).

3. Schlußbemerkung

In westafrikanischen Geheimbünden gibt es Funktionäre, die als Lehrer bezeichnet werden können. Die vorgestellten Beispiele zweier Pflanzerkulturen aus dem Waldland und der Savanne belegen dies. Beim N'domo-Bund der Bambara kann man allerdings nicht von Lehrern sprechen, denn dort geben Kinder ihre Kenntnisse weiter. Anders ist es bei den Männerbünden. Dort gibt es Lehrer, die eine besondere Schulung erhalten haben. Daneben vermitteln zweifellos auch alte Männer ihr im Laufe eines langen Lebens erworbenes Wissen. Die Annahme, daß einfach Altinitiierte als Lehrer im Initiationslager fungieren, trifft nicht überall zu.
Die *zo* des Poro der Mano und ihrer Nachbarn haben eine besondere Schulung erhalten. Beim Komo der Bambara stellen zwar die Ältesten und Ranghöchsten die Lehrer, aber befähigten jungen Leuten werden relativ früh zusätzlich Kenntnisse vermittelt, so daß auch sie schon bald als Lehrer eingesetzt werden können. Beim Kore nehmen Mitglieder des 5. Initiationsgrades die Aufgabe als Lehrer wahr. Sie haben freilich noch nicht das letzte Wissen erlangt, das den Inhabern des 8. Initiationsgrades vorbehalten ist, aber fraglos müssen die Lehrer aus dem 5. Initiationsgrad besondere Fähigkeiten und Kenntnisse haben, um ihre Aufgabe erfüllen zu können. Soweit davon die Rede ist, daß die Ältesten und Ranghöchsten als Lehrer fungieren, müssen wir wohl davon ausgehen, daß auch bei ihnen die pädagogische Begabung unterschiedlich ist. So wird denn wohl auch nicht jeder Älteste als Lehrer tätig werden.
Sowohl bei den Mano in Liberia als auch bei den Bambara in Mali sind pädagogische Fähigkeiten und Kenntnisse vorhanden. Bei beiden Ethnien finden Lehrer und Älteste wohl schnell heraus, wer besondere Fähigkeiten besitzt. Bei den Mano erfolgt schon nach einem Aufenthalt von wenigen Wochen im Initiationslager eine Aufteilung in Klassen mit unterschiedlichem Lehrstoff. An die zukünftigen Lehrer werden besondere intellektuelle Anforderungen gestellt. Bei den Bambara dauert die Beobachtungsphase offenbar etwas länger, ehe die jungen Leute ausgewählt und dadurch zusätzliche intensive Ausbildung auf ihre künftige Rolle als Lehrer vorbereitet werden. In beiden ethnischen Gruppen werden die Fähigkeiten der Kinder und jungen Männer jedenfalls sorgsam bewertet.
Wichtig erscheint ferner, daß in beiden Gruppen lebenslanges Lernen bewußt praktiziert wird. Zwar wird der entscheidende Grundstock des Wissens wohl in Kindheit und Jugend gelegt, die höchste Erkenntnis des philosophischen und esoterischen Wissens ist jedoch dem reifen Alter vorbehalten. Nicht umsonst zollt man in den traditionellen Kulturen Afrikas dem Alter höchsten Respekt. Lebenserfahrung und Weisheit sind Werte, die jeder eines Tages zu erlangen hofft.

Anmerkungen

[1] Vgl. hierzu z. B. *Hirschberg* (1965), S. 62 f. (Bundwesen), S. 262 f. (Männerbund).

[2] Der Bund ist z. B. bei den Susu, Temne, Mende, Loko, Sherbro, Kono, Vai (unter dem Namen Bele), Gola, Kpelle, Gbunde, Bandi (Gbande), Loma und Mano belegt. Einige Autoren beziehen auch die Dan/Gio ein (*Harley* (1941) u. (1950) sowie Schwab (1947)), andere bestreiten, daß dieses Volk den Poro hat (H. u. U. *Himmelheber* (1958), S. 86, S. 203 ff.) und vermeiden den Begriff daher.

[3] Diese Bezeichnung geht vermutlich auf Missionare zurück, für die alles Teufelswerk war, was mit dem Heidentum zusammenhing. Möglicherweise war die Kultmaske als Verkörperung einer unheimlichen und grausamen Macht für die Missionare greifbarster Ausdruck böser Mächte. Dies umso mehr, als manche Poro-Maske ihre Kraft durch ein Menschenopfer erhielt.

[4] Vgl. *Harley* (1950), S. 11 ff., S. 17 ff.; *Schwab* (1947), S. 268 ff., S. 277. Die von der Maske geleiteten Gerichtssitzungen sind bei den Mano geheim, bei den Gio, Kran und Kono öffentlich (*Harley* (1950), S. 17).

[5] Vor der Initiation: Gbunde, Loma. Zu Beginn der Buschzeit: Ge. offenbar alternativ: Mano und Kpelle. Vgl. *Harley* (1941), S. 7; *Schwab* (1947), S. 278; *Westermann* (1921), S. 244.

[6] *Schwab* und *Harley* berufen sich in vielem auf *Westermann,* dessen Ausführungen sie in so gut wie allen Punkten bestätigen.

[7] *Harley* (1941), S. 5 f.; *Schwab* (1947), S. 272 f. B. *Holas* konnte 1948 die 99 Initiationsgrade bei den Mano allerdings nicht feststellen (*Holas* (1952), S. 33). Die Zahl 99 kann einfach für »eine große Anzahl« stehen.

[8] Die Musikanten bilden bei den Bambara eine Gruppe, die manchen besonderen Vorschriften unter worfen ist.

[9] In Mythen der Bambara ist der Schmied der erste Priester des Universums (*Dieterlen* u. *Cissé* (1972), S. 30).

[10] Der Grund hierfür ist unbekannt. Vielleicht glaubt man, daß dem Bundmeister die für sein Amt erforderliche magische Kraft nach einiger Zeit nachläßt.

[11] Zu den Initiationsgraden vgl. *Zahan* (1960), S. 161.

[12] Hier einige Beispiele (*Zahan* (1960), S. 240, S. 243, S. 244): Nr. 3 Kalebassenlöffel. Devise: »Helfer«. Analoge Bedeutungen: Nahrung, Leben, Tod, Vermittler, Regenzeit, Eifersucht, Frau, Kenntnisse, die man vermittelt. Nr. 31 Weberschiffchen. Devise: »vorbeigehen«. Analogien: Weg, Reise, Reisender, Schneiderarbeit, Entfernung, Quartiergeber (Wirt), Einbaum, Welt, Leitung, Kommen und Gehen, die Zahl 8. Nr. 44 Hundeknochen. Devise: »Guter Verwandter«. Analogien: Schutz, Wachsamkeit, Erde [der Hund ist das Symbol der Erde, S. 258], Feldarbeit, Pflanzenwachstum, Treue.

Literaturverzeichnis

Beuchelt, E. (1961): Traditionelle und moderne Jugenderziehung im West-Sudan. In: Sociologus, Bd. 11, S. 147–160.

Dieterlen, G. (1951): Essai sur la religion bambara. Paris

Dieterlen, G. et Y. Cissé (1972): Les fondements de la société d'initiation du komo. [Cahiers de l'Homme, n. s. X.] Paris – La Haye
Harley, G. W. (1941): Notes on the Poro in Liberia. Papers of the Peabody Museum of American Archaeology and Ethnology, Harvard University, Vol. XIX, No. 2. Cambridge (Mass.)
Harley, G. W. (1950): Masks as Agents of Social Control in Northeast Liberia. Papers of the Peabody Museum etc., Vol. XXXII, No. 2
Himmelheber, H. u. U. (1958): Die Dan – ein Bauernvolk im westafrikanischen Urwald. Stuttgart
Hirschberg, W. (1965). Wörterbuch der Völkerkunde. Stuttgart
Holas, B. (1952): Les masques kono – leur rôle dans la vie religieuse et politique. Paris
Pâques, V. (1954): Les Bambara. Paris
Schwab, G. (1947): Tribes of the Liberian Hinterland. Papers of the Peabody Museum etc., Vol. XXXI.
Tauxier L. (1927): La religion bambara. Paris
Westermann, D. (1921): Die Kpelle. Ein Negerstamm in Liberia. Göttingen und Leipzig
Zahan, D. (1960): Sociétés d'initiation bambara. Le n'domo, le korè. Paris – La Haye

Tomiji Nagao

Die Entwicklung der Lehrerbildung in Japan im 19. und 20. Jahrhundert[1]

Obgleich es auch in der frühen Erziehungs- und Schulgeschichte Japans Bemühungen gegeben hat, die erforderliche Zahl an Lehrern zu sichern, hat die Frage nach der Sicherung und Erhöhung der Lehrerqualität erst in neuerer Zeit erheblich an Gewicht gewonnen. Es gibt zwei Grundprinzipien der Lehrerbildung in Japan. Das eine ist das Prinzip, daß die Lehrerbildung an einer Hochschule stattzufinden hat. Das zweite Prinzip beinhaltet, daß ein freier Zugang zum Lehrberuf gewährleistet sein muß.[2] Beide Prinzipien beruhen auf Überlegungen, die nach 1945 aufkamen, als man die japanische Lehrerbildung der Kriegs- und Vorkriegszeit kritisch beleuchtete.
Die Lehrerbildung an einer Hochschule zielt nicht nur auf die Verbesserung der wissenschaftlichen Vorbereitung der Lehrer ab, sondern auch auf die Durchdringung des Lehramts mit wissenschaftlichem, kritischem Geist. Um dieses Ziel zu erreichen, sollen die künftigen Lehrer an in diesem Sinne geeigneten, anspruchsvollen Hochschulen studieren. Als zweites Prinzip war der freie Zugang zum Lehrerberuf genannt. Dieser Grundsatz beinhaltet, daß nicht nur die Studenten der pädagogischen Fakultäten an allgemeinen Hochschulen Lehrer werden dürfen, sondern auch jeder, der an einer anderen Fakultät studiert, vorausgesetzt er durchläuft die vorgeschriebene pädagogische Ausbildung.
Es ist keine Übertreibung, wenn man sagt, daß der Kampf um dieses Prinzip des freien Zugangs zum Lehrerberuf im Mittelpunkt der Reformbewegung des Lehrerbildungswesens in Japan steht. Die Ursache dieses Kampfes sollen und können wir nur in der Geschichte der Lehrerbildung in Japan finden.
Die Entwicklung der Lehrerbildung in Japan kann man in fünf Stufen einteilen:

1. von 1872 bis 1886
2. von 1886 bis 1908
3. von 1908 bis 1945
4. von 1945 bis 1965
5. von 1965 bis heute.

Die »Amtliche Bekanntmachung vom Schulwesen« (»Gakusei Hanpu«) von 1872 war der Ausgangspunkt des modernen Schulwesens und deshalb auch des modernen Lehrerbildungswesens in Japan. Bis zum Ende der Edo-Zeit (1603–1867), also bis zur Öffnung des Landes in der neuen, modernen Zeit, war das soziale Wesen Japans zwar feudalistisch, aber die Fähigkeit des Lesens, Schreibens und Rechnens war ziemlich weit verbreitet. Niedere Schulen für die Kinder aus dem Volk (Terakoya, d. i. Tempelschulen, oder Tenaraisho, d. h. Schreibschulen oder Kalligraphieschulen) konnte man sogar in den kleinen Dörfern leicht finden. Die Schulmeister (Shishou) dieser Schulen stammten zwar aus verschiedenen, aber nicht so niedrigen Ständen.

Die meisten lehrten die Kinder in Nebenbeschäftigung, manchmal aus Spontaneität. Sie waren finanziell nicht so günstig gestellt, aber sie waren bei ihren Nachbarn angesehen. Es gab auch einige wenige Schulmeisterinnen für die Mädchen. Schulen oder Anstalten für die Lehrerbildung gab es jedoch in Japan während der Edo-Zeit nicht.[3]

Die erste Lehrerbildungsanstalt in Japan wurde 1872 in Tokio gegründet. Man nannte diese Anstalt »Shihan Gakkou« (»Gakusei«, § 39). Das war das Übersetzungswort für »Normal School«. Das Wort »Shihan« bedeutet die »Norm« oder das »Muster«, und das Wort »Gakkou« bedeutet die »Schule«. »Shihan Gakkou« bedeutet deshalb die »Normalschule« oder die »Musterschule«.

Bekanntlich hat sich die Lehrerbildungsanstalt aus der Musterschule entwickelt. In der ersten Hälfte des 19. Jahrhunderts hatte man in Deutschland schon die selbständigen Lehrerbildungsanstalten mit den Übungschulen: das ist das Lehrerseminar. Aber in Frankreich oder in den U.S.A., wo man nach dem Muster Deutschlands solche Lehrerbildungsanstalten gegründet hat, nannte man diese selbständigen Lehrerbildungsanstalten »l'école normale« oder »Normal School«. In Japan ist man diesem Muster gefolgt. Diese Namensgebung in Japan rief bald ein merkwürdiges Durcheinander hervor, wie weiter unten noch zu berichten sein wird.

Die Regierung berief 1873 den Amerikaner *Marion M. Scott* (1843–1922) als einzigen ordentlichen Lehrer an die Tokio Shihan Gakkou. Er unterrichtete 54 Schüler, die 17 bis etwa 35 Jahre alt waren, ein Jahr lang mit einem Lehrbuch von *Norman A. Calkins* (1832–95), einem Pestalozzianer in den U.S.A.: »New Primary Object Lesson« (1870). Der Schuldirektor war *Morokuzu Nobuzumi* (1849–80), damals 24 Jahre alt. Er bezog die Lehrmittel und Lehrstoffe sämtlich aus den U.S.A.[4]

Die Regierung hat ähnliche Schulen hier und da gegründet: Zum Beispiel in Osaka, Sendai, Nagoya, Hiroshima, Nagasaki und Niigata.

1878 kehrten zwei wichtige Personen, *Izawa Shuji* (1851–1917) und *Takamine Hideo* (1854–1910), von einem Studienaufenthalt in den U.S.A. zurück, und sie wurden sofort zum Direktor und Vizedirektor der Tokio Shihan Gakkou ernannt. *Izawa* studierte von 1875 bis 78 an der Bridgewater State Normal School in Massachusetts. *Takamine* studierte auch von 1875 bis 78 an der Oswego State Normal School, New York. Somit kann man sagen, daß die japanische Lehrerbildung in ihrem Anfangsstadium starken Einfluß von den amerikanischen Pestalozzianern erfahren hat. Die Richtung war im allgemeinen liberal und demokratisch. Die Atmosphäre der Lehrerwelt war damals ziemlich lebhaft: nicht zuletzt, weil die lebhaften jungen Männer aus dem alten Kriegerstand hier und da an den Elementarschulen als Lehrer tätig waren.[5]

Aber die Situation hat sich etwa um 1880 geändert. Die rückläufige, anti-demokratische Tendenz wurde stärker. Das liberale Gesetz über die Erziehung von 1879 wurde ein Jahr darauf verbindlich geändert. Die »Dienstvorschriften für den Elementarschullehrer« wurden im Juni 1881 in Kraft gesetzt.

1885 wurde *Mori Arinori* (1847–89) zum Kultusminister im Kabinett von *Ito Hirobumi* (1841–1909) ernannt. Fürst *Ito* hatte besonderes Interesse am deutschen Verfassungsrecht, besuchte Deutschland und wollte *Lorenz von Stein* (1815–90), der damals schon in Österreich war, zum obersten Erziehungsberater in Tokio machen, was dieser aber ablehnte. *Mori* war eigentlich ein tüchtiger Diplomat und Aufklärer, und in den abendländischen Verhältnissen bewandert. Er schätzte zwar die Gewissensfreiheit hoch, doch glaubte er andererseits fanatisch an den Nationalismus: er wollte im Zeitalter des Imperialismus Japan im internationalen Wettbewerb voranbringen. Nach seiner Meinung ist der Lehrer »der Mönch des Staates« oder »der Sklave des Staates«. Er äußerte einmal, daß die Schüler des Lehrerseminars nicht für sich selbst, sondern nur für den Staat lernen sollen.[6]

Die Verordnung über das Lehrerseminar von 1886 wurde nach diesen seinen Vorstellungen über den Lehrerberuf proklamiert. Der 1. Artikel dieser Verordnung fordert von den Schülern drei Elemente des Charakters: *Gehorsam, Vertrauen* und *Würde.* Diese drei Elemente des Charakters konnte man nach seiner Meinung durch das militärische Turnen bilden. Mit dieser Verordnung begann die Kasernierung des Internats des Lehrerseminars. Es ist darauf hinzuweisen, daß man seither den Gedanken und das System der deutschen Erziehung zum Objekt der Aufmerksamkeit und Nachahmung gemacht hat. Die Heeresdienstpflicht wurde 1889 geändert und den Absolventen des Lehrerseminars eine Verkürzung der Wehrdienstzeit zuerkannt, soweit sie im Lehrerberuf tätig waren. Kultusminister *Mori* wurde 1889 wegen seines aufgeklärten Rationalismus ermordet, aber seine Verordnung hat einen großen Einfluß auf die japanische Schulerziehung, besonders auf die Lehrerbildung, ausgeübt.

Es wurde bereits erwähnt, daß man am Anfang der Meiji-Zeit die Lehrerbildungsanstalt »Shihan Gakkou« nannte, und daß »Shihan Gakkou« dabei das Übersetzungswort für »Normal School« war. Das Wort bezeichnete also eine Schule, welche ein Muster oder ein Norm für andere Schulen darstellte. Das japanische Wort »Shihan« bedeutet gleichzeitig aber auch »Meister« einer bestimmten Kunst. Dadurch entstand seit der *Verordnung von 1886* ein merkwürdiges Mißverständnis über das Wort »Shihan Gakkou«. Man verstand nunmehr unter dem Wort »Shihan Gakkou« auch eine Schule, die den »Meister«, das Muster eines guten Menschen, bildet. Dieses Mißverständnis verkehrte die Bildungsbemühungen des Lehrerseminars. Die Kritik am Lehrerseminar verstärkte sich.

Ende des 19. Jahrhunderts gab es schon scharfe Kritik an der Bildungspolitik von *Mori. Schon die Verordnung über die Lehrerbildung von 1897* milderte die Prinzipien, die *Mori* in der *Verordnung von 1886* ausdrückte, um einiges. Man erklärte nun die drei erwünschten Charaktereigenschaften zu drei Elementen der Moralität. Diese Forderung an die Schüler des Lehrerseminars ist noch bis 1943 bestehen geblieben.

Anfang des 20. Jahrhunderts erreichte der Einfluß der internationalen neuen Erziehung auch das ferne Japan, und zwar schon frühzeitig. Zum Beispiel wurde das Buch von *Edmond Demolins* (1852–1907), einem französischen Soziologen mit extrem imperialistischer Gesinnung, »A quoi tient la supériorité des Anglo-Saxons« (1897) 1902 ins Japanische übersetzt.[7]

Noguchi Entaro (1886–1941), ein hervorragender Leiter der japanischen, liberalen, neuen Erziehung, übernahm unter dem Einfluß von *E. Demolins* Formen der englischen Schulerziehung. Als Direktor des Lehrerseminars von *Himeji,* heute die Pädagogische Fakultät der Universität *Kobe,* hat er eine familiäre Atmosphäre in das militärische Internat hineingetragen und es reformiert (1901–19). Er hat auch »L'école active« (1922) von *Adolphe Ferrière* (1879–1960) ins Japanische übersetzt (1933).

1908 wurde die allgemeine Schulpflicht auf sechs Jahre verlängert, und der Prozentsatz der Elementarschüler lag schon über 97 von Hundert. Jede Präfektur hatte ein Lehrerseminar oder mehrere. Es gab 27 Lehrerseminarien, 19 Lehrerinnenseminarien und 23 Lehrer- und Lehrerinnenseminarien in Japan, insgesamt 69.

Die Verordnung über das Lehrerseminar von 1908 hat die japanische Lehrerbildung umorganisiert und ihr die Möglichkeit zur Erhebung zur Hochschule gegeben. Einer der Schwerpunkte der *Verordnung von 1908* war die Errichtung des »Zweiten Kurses« im Lehrerseminar. Der »Erste Kurs« war vierjährig und folgte auf 9 Jahre Elementar- und Fortbildungsschulerziehung. Der »Zweite Kurs« war ein- oder zweijährig und schloß sich an 11 Jahre Elementar- und Sekundarschulerziehung an. Dieser war damals nur ein Unterstützungskurs, aber mit der Zeit wurde der »Zweite Kurs« der Grund für die Erhebung des Lehrerseminars in den Rang der Hochschule.

Der Bericht der »Sondersitzung über die Erziehung« (»Rinji Kyouiku Kaigi«), 1918, gab noch wie früher dem »Ersten Kurs« die Hauptstellung im Lehrerseminar, weil der Erziehungsgeist, der für Elementarschullehrer unentbehrlich sei, nur nach längerer Übung gewonnen werden könne. *Kano Jigoro*, im Westen mehr bekannt als Begründer des modernen Judo, war der Vertreter dieser Meinung.[8]

In der »Beratenden Kommission für die Bildungspolitik« (»Bunsei Shingi Kai«), 1925, hat sich die Tendenz der Diskussion etwas geändert. Die Kritik gegen den »Ersten Kurs« wurde immer stärker. *Sawayanagi Seitaro* (1878–1927), Präsident der Kaiserlichen Universität von Tohoku, dann der Kaiserlichen Universität von Kyoto und ab 1917 Gründer und Leiter der Seijo-Schule, einer berühmten Schule der neuen liberalen Erziehung, behauptete, daß die Schüler des »Ersten Kurses« überfordert seien, weil sie ihren Weg zu früh wählen müßten. Er behauptete unter Hinweis auf die ausländische Situation, daß der künftige Lehrer unbedingt eine Hochschulbildung bräuchte.[9]

Aber man darf nicht übersehen, daß die Angriffe gegen den »Ersten Kurs« auch von einem Mißtrauen gegen die armen Schüler des »Ersten Kurses« herrührten, die mit dem Sozialismus sympathisierten.[10]

Der japanische Lehrerverein wurde erst 1920 gegründet. Dieser Verein ist jedoch nach einigen Jahren zusammengebrochen, weil die japanische Regierung die sozialistische Bewegung streng unterdrückte, und weil Anarchismus und Bolschewismus sich in diesem Verein feindlich gegenüberstanden. Es ist unleugbar, daß einige wenige Schüler des Lehrerseminars auch unter dem Einfluß des Sozialismus standen. Der Widerstand dieser Schüler gegen die Schulleitung ist von 1928 bis 1931 hier und da ausgebrochen.[11] Ein Teil dieser Schüler hat der Meinung widergesprochen, daß der »Zweite Kurs« der Hauptweg des Lehrerseminars werden sollte: sie glaubten, daß die Schüler des »Zweiten Kurses« aus der Bourgeoisie kämen. Dies war ein unglückliches Mißverständnis.[12]

In Dezember 1930 befragte die Regierung die »Beratende Kommission für die

Bildungspolitik« bezüglich der Verbesserung der Lehrerbildung. Man schlug vor, den »Zweiten Kurs« um zwei Jahre zu verlängern. So würde der »Zweite Kurs« mit dem »Ersten Kurs« gleichrangig. Die »Beratende Kommission« hat diesem Vorschlag der Regierung zugestimmt. *Die Verordnung über das Lehrerseminar von 1908* wurde im Januar 1931 geändert. Der erste Schritt des Lehrerseminars zum Rang einer Hochschule war so getan. Dabei gab es zwei Wege.
Entweder: man müßte besondere Hochschulen für die Lehrerbildung gründen. Oder: man müßte den künftigen Lehrern auf der Grundlage des höheren allgemeinen und speziellen Studiums[5] an den Hochschulen (oder parallel dazu) die professionelle Bildung für den Lehrerberuf geben.
Schließlich hat man in der *Verordnung über die Lehrerbildung von 1943* den ersten Weg gewählt. Durch diese Verordnung wurde der »Erste Kurs« und der »Zweite Kurs« abgeschafft und das Lehrerseminar mit dreijährigem Lehrkurs in den Rang einer Hochschule erhoben. Diese Einrichtung heißt »Shihan Gakkou« und entspricht einer »Pädagogischen Hochschule«.
Nach dem Zweiten Weltkrieg hat man durch *das Gesetz über die Erteilung der Lehrerlaubnis von 1949 und von 1953* die Koexistenz der zwei Wege ermöglicht. Die zwei Wege sind die folgenden: erstens über die Pädagogischen Hochschulen oder Pädagogischen Fakultäten, zweitens über jene Universitäten oder Fakultäten, die eine Genehmigung zur Einrichtung eines Lehrerbildungslehrgangs erhalten haben. Das ist das Prinzip des »Freien Zugangs zum Lehrerberuf« oder das Prinzip der »Offenheit der Lehrerausbildung«.
Dieses Prinzip hat zwar eine erhebliche Zunahme an Lehramtskandidaten zur Folge gehabt, aber diese Kandidaten haben zumeist nur das Befähigungszeugnis für die Sekundarstufe I erhalten, weil die meisten Hochschulen nur die Genehmigung für diesen Lehrgang besitzen. Überdies nahm die Zahl der Lehramtskandidaten durch das 1974 erlassene »Gesetz zur Gewinnung tüchtiger Lehrer« (»Jinzai Kakuho Hou«) schnell zu. Besonders hat die Zahl der weiblichen Bewerber sprunghaft zugenommen.
Früher gab es in Japan eine Redensart, die besagte: Wenn ein Mädchen Lehrerin wird, wird eine Verheiratung für sie schwierig; oder aber: Ein Mädchen sei Lehrerin gerade deshalb geworden, weil sie nur geringe Heiratschancen gehabt habe. Neuerdings aber heißt es: Wenn ein Mädchen ihre Heiratsaussichten steigern und das Fundament zu einer glücklichen Ehe legen will, so sollte sie vor allem einen Lehrerlaubnisschein erwerben. Sei ihr Mann strebsam, so könne sie ihn durch ihre eigene Berufstätigkeit noch unterstützen; sei ihr Mann aber ein Versager, so habe sie die Unabhängigkeit, ihn zu verlassen.
Dieser Meinungswandel spiegelt den Sachverhalt wider, daß der Lehrerberuf für weibliche Studenten sehr attraktiv geworden ist.
Aus diesem quantitativen Wachstum hat sich ergeben, daß die Frage nach der Qualität des Lehrers zum vieldiskutierten und vordringlichen Problem geworden ist. Darüber habe ich schon vor sieben Jahren unter dem Thema »Probleme der Lehrerbildung in Japan« in einigen Universitäten (Duisburg, Gießen und Münster) vorgetragen. Deswegen soll diese Frage hier nicht weiterverfolgt werden.[13]

Die Lehrerbildung an der Hochschule war von alters her ein Traum der japanischen Lehrerwelt. Dieser Traum ist jetzt im Begriff, in Erfüllung zu gehen.
Es gibt acht staatliche Hochschulen mit vierjährigem Normalstudiengang, die in erster Linie die Aufgabe der Lehrerbildung übernehmen. Diese Hochschulen hießen bis 1965 »Gakugei Daigaku«. Das bedeutet ungefähr »Hochschule für allgemeine Bildung« und entspricht im Englischen dem »Liberal Arts College«.
Unterdessen wurden diese Anstalten einfach in »Kyoiku Daigaku« umbenannt. Das bedeutet »Pädagogische Hochschule« oder »Erziehungshochschule« und läßt im Vergleich zu der Bezeichnung »Gakugei Daigaku« an ein auf die Lehrerbildung beschränktes engeres Ausbildungskonzept denken. Mit anderen Worten »Kyoiku Daigaku« (Pädagogische Hochschule) erinnert in gewisser Weise an das alte Lehrerseminar.
Der Anlaß dieses Namenswechsels war die Trennung der *Miyagi Kyoiku Daigaku* von der *Tohoku Universität*. Die *Tohoku Universität*, eine der alten, kaiserlichen Universitäten, hat die *Pädagogische Hochschule* Miyagi nach dem Krieg (1949) als einen Teil der Universität aufgenommen. Das war die einzige Ausnahme unter sieben alten, kaiserlichen Universitäten. Aber die Flitterjahre währten nicht lang. Es kam wieder zur Trennung. Der Unterschied zwischen der akademischen Universität und der praktischen Pädagogischen Hochschule war von Anfang an deutlich.[14]
Man wollte nach der endgültigen Trennung eine *Miyagi Gakugei Daigaku* errichten, womit man anderen Beispielen gefolgt wäre. Aber die Regierung hat die Bezeichnung »Gakugei Daigaku« nicht begrüßt, weil diese Bezeichnung unter dem Prinzip der Offenheit der Lehrerausbildung den Zweck der Lehrerbildung mehrdeutig gemacht hätte. So wurde die *Miyagi »Kyouiku« (nicht »Gakugei«) Daigaku* ins Leben gerufen, die anderen »Gakugei Daigaku« wurden allgemein in »Kyouiku Daigaku« umbenannt. Nur die Gakugei Daigaku in Tokio konnte diesen Namenswechsel nicht mitmachen, weil es schon eine *Tokio Kyouiku Daigaku* gab.
Diese *Tokio Kyouiku Daigaku,* Pädagogische Hochschule Tokio, die fünf Fakultäten besaß und nicht allein der Lehrerbildung diente, hatte sich aus der *Tokio Shihan Gakkou,* dem ältesten Lehrerseminar in Japan, entwickelt. Inzwischen ist diese alte Pädagogische Hochschule Tokio in die Präfektur *Ibaraki* verlagert worden und Bestandteil der neuen staatlichen Reformuniversität *Tsukuba* geworden (1973). Hätte man das Bedürfnis nach einer Namensänderung, könnte die *Tokio Gakugei Daigaku* (Hochschule für allgemeine Bildung in Tokio) nunmehr auch *Tokio Kyouiku Daigaku* (Pädagogische Hochschule Tokio) heißen, genauso wie ihre Schwesteranstalten in anderen Landesteilen. Aber bemerkenswerterweise will niemand einen solchen Namenswechsel.

Abgekürzte Zeittafel zur Lehrerbildung in Japan

1603–1867	Edo-Zeit	
1868–1912	Meiji-Zeit	
1872		»Amtliche Bekanntmachung vom Schulwesen« (»Gakusei Hanpu«): Shihan Gakkou« gegründet in Tokio
1873		M. M. Scott ans »Shihan Gakkou« berufen
1873–77		mehrere »Shihan Gakkou« (Lehrerseminar)-Gründungen
1875		Lehrerinnenseminar gegründet in Tokio
1876		Errichtung eines Sekundarschullehrerkurses im Lehrerseminar (Tokio)
1878		Izawa und Takamine aus den U.S.A zurück
1879		Erziehungsgesetz
1880		geändertes Erziehungsgesetz
1881		Dienstvorschriften für den Elementarschullehrer: Grundriß des Lehrplans des Lehrerseminars
1883		Generalreglement für Präfektur-Lehrerseminar
1885		Kabinett von Ito gegründet (Kultusminister: Mori)
1886		Verordnung über das Lehrerseminar (Drei Elemente des Charakters): Höheres Lehrerseminar in Tokio gegründet
1889		Verordnung über die Heeresdienstpflicht geändert
1890		Erziehungserlaß des Kaisers Meiji
1893		Politische Äußerungen des Lehrers verboten
1897		Verordnung über die Lehrerbildung: Höheres Lehrerinnenseminar in Tokio gegründet
1901		Himeji-Lehrerseminar gegründet
1908		Verordnung für das Lehrerseminar (der »Zweite Kurs« errichtet)
1911		Richtlinien für den Lehrgang des Lehrerseminars
1912–1026	Taisho-Zeit	
1917		Seijou-Schule von Sawayanagi gegründet: »Sondersitzung von der Erziehung« (»Rinji Kyoiku Kaigi«) gegründet
1918–19		Die Berichte der Sondersitzung
1920		Erster japanischer Lehrerverein gegründet (Keimei Kai)
1925		»Beratende Kommission für die Bildungspolitik« (Bunsei Shingi Kai) gegründet
1926	Shouwa-Zeit	
1926		Ausbildungszeit des Ersten Kurses verlängert (5 Jahre)
1931		Ausbildungszeit des Zweiten Kurses verlängert (2 Jahre)
1937		»Beratende Erziehungskommission« (Kyoiku Shingi Kai) gegründet
1941		Verordnung über die Nationalschule (Kokumin Gakkou Rei)
1943		Verordnung über die Lehrerbildung geändert
1945		Niederlage, Kriegszeit (1931–45) geendet
1946		Erste Erziehungsdelegation aus den U.S.A.
1947		Grundgesetz über Erziehung (Kyoiku Kihon Hou)
1949		Gesetz über die Erteilung der Lehrerlaubnis
1950		Zweite Erziehungsdelegation aus den U.S.A.

1953	Gesetz über die Erteilung der Lehrerlaubnis geändert
1965	Pädagogische Hochschule Miyagi gegründet (getrennt von der Tohoku Universtität)
1974	Gesetz zur Gewinnung tüchtiger Lehrer
1982	Reformentwurf des Gesetzes über die Erteilung der Lehrerlaubnis
1984	»Beratende Zentralkommission von der Erziehung« (Chuo Kyoiku Shingi Kai) gegründet (bis August 1987)
1987	Letzter Bericht der Beratenden Zentralkommission von der Erziehung

Anmerkungen

[1] Es ist mir ein Bedürfnis, der Deutschen Forschungsgemeinschaft und Herrn Professor Max Liedtke dafür besonders herzlich zu danken, daß ich nach Ichenhausen eingeladen worden bin, und daß ich auf diese Weise mit vielen Kollegen Kontakte aufnehmen konnte.

[2] Gesetz über die Erteilung der Lehrerlaubnis, § 5, Ausführungsbestimmungen, Kap. 2.

[3] Ototake, I. (1929): Die Geschichte der Volkserziehung in Japan. 3 Bde., Tokio.

[4] Tokio Bunrika Universität und Tokio Höheres Lehrerseminar (1931): Sechzig Jahre seit der Begründung, Kap. 1. Tokio.

[5] Ishitoya, T. (1958): Eine Forschung über die Geschichte des japanischen Lehrerstandes, Kap. 3. Tokio.

[6] Kusakabe, S. (1888): Die Ansichten von Visconte Mori über die Erziehung. Tokio.

[7] Keio Gijuku, übersetzt von (1902): Dokuritsu Jiei Daikokumin, d. i.: Die selbständige, große Nation. Tokio.

[8] Kaigo, T. (1960): Studien über die Sondersitzung von der Erziehung. Tokio.

[9] Sawayanagi, S. (1925): Der Reformplan für die Lehrerbildungsanstalt. In: Sämtliche Werke von Sawayanagi, Bd. 6. Tokio.

[10] Das Protokoll der »Beratenden Kommission für die Bildungspolitik«.

[11] Nakauchi, T. & Kawai, A., Hrsg. (1974): Lehrer in Japan, Bd. 6, S. 196ff.

[12] Ebenda.

[13] Nagao, T. (1985): Probleme der Lehrerbildung in Japan (in deutscher Sprache). In: Hundertjährige Gedächtnisnummer der Literarischen Fakultät der Chuo Universität.

[14] Miyagi Päd. Hochschule (1976–77): Quellen für die Zehnjahregeschichte der Miyagi Päd. Hochschule, 2 Bde., Sendai.

Literaturverzeichnis

Himeji Shihan Gakkou (1931): Dreißigjahre Lehrerseminar Himeji. Himeji

Ishitoya, T., Hrsg. (1970): Die Geschichte des Lehrerstandes. Tokio

Kaigo, T., Hrsg. (1974): Die Lehrerbildung (Die Erziehungsreform nach dem Zweiten Weltkrieg in Japan, Bd. 8). Tokio

Karasawa, T. (1955): Geschichte des Lehrerstandes. Tokio
Mori, A. (1953): Sämtliche Werke, Bd. 1 und 2. Tokio
Nihon Kyouiku Gakkai (Japanische Gesellschaft für Erziehungswissenschaft):
(1970): Quellen für das Lehrerbildungswesen
(1974): Die Reform der Pädagogischen Hochschule Miyagi
(1979–82): Quellen für die Probleme der Lehrerbildung, 4 Bde. Tokio
Nagao, T., Hrsg. (1983): Die Aufgaben der Lehrerbildung. Tokio
Okubo, T. (1944): Sawayanagi Seitaro
Yokohama Kokuritsu Daigaku (Staatliche Universität Yokohama):
(1980): Quellen zu Gedanken über den Lehrberuf. Tokio

VII. GEGENWART UND ZUKUNFT DER LEHRERBILDUNG

Max Liedtke

Zeitunabhängige und zeitgebundene Qualifikationen des Lehrers[1]

Herrn Ministerialrat a. D. Dr. Franz Otto Schmaderer,
der durch drei Jahrzehnte die bayerische Lehrerbildung wesentlich mitgestaltet hat

1. Das Lehrerbild in Geschichte und Gegenwart und die Kritik an der Lehrerbildung

Schulgeschichtsforschung muß nicht zugleich eine systematische Funktion haben. Sie ist auch Wissenschaft, wenn sie sich mit der akribischen Aufnahme historischer Fakten begnügt. Aber sie kann und sollte auch Anlaß systematischer Fragen sein. Dies schon deshalb, weil die in der Geschichte abgelagerte Menge an Informationen wesentlich größer ist, als sie durch irgendwelche aktuellen empirischen Untersuchungen bereitgestellt werden können. In der Geschichte liegt die Summe der Informationen aller bisherigen Gegenwarten und zugleich die Summe der Informationen, die sich durch die Kombination aller dieser Querschnittsinformationen ergeben. Zwar ist darunter eine Fülle Daten, die im Vergleich zum aktuellen Fachwissen naturwissenschaftlicher, anthropologischer und sozialwissenschaftlicher Art nur vorläufiges und überholtes Wissen darstellen. Aber sie markieren Stationen einer Entwicklung, lassen Zusammenhänge erkennen, und nur auf ihrer Basis sind Extrapolationen in die Zukunft möglich.
Die Markierung einiger Stationen der Geschichte des Lehrerberufes, wie sie auf diesem Symposion in der Spanne zwischen den frühen mesopotamischen Hochkulturen bis in die jüngste Vergangenheit vorgenommen worden ist, sollte nicht nur der geschichtlichen Rekonstruktion einer Standesgeschichte dienen, sondern sollte am Rande auch Auskunft geben, was der Lehrer geschichtlich bewirkt hat, wie er gesellschaftlich eingeschätzt wurde, was seine Qualifikation ausmacht, wie seine Ausbildung beschaffen sein muß.
Die Referate haben deutlich gemacht, daß die Geschichte des Lehrerstandes außerordentlich wechselvoll war und daß sie wie bei kaum einem anderen Berufsstand extreme Höhen und extreme Tiefen hatte. Aber wie immer der Lehrer gesellschaftlich eingeschätzt wurde, ob er – wie in der Lutherischen Übersetzung des 84. Psalms – als »mit viel Segen geschmücket« galt oder ob er sich – wie ein Bayerischer Lehrer 1820 deprimiert schrieb – als »Auskehricht der Welt« fühlen mußte (*Der Wittwen- und Waisenfreund*, 1823, I, S. 135), niemals stand in Frage, daß sein Tun wirkungslos oder unbedeutend geblieben ist. Lehren ist in biologischer Sicht die effektivste Anpas-

sungsleistung. Sie bleibt nicht leicht wirkungslos. So lange es Lehrer gibt, haben sie im positiven wie im negativen Sinn das Leben der ihnen anvertrauten Kinder mitbestimmt und sind wie die leiblichen Eltern zum Schicksal ihrer Kinder geworden. Der berufliche Lehrer und sein Ausbildungsgrad sind zuverlässige Parameter zur Berechnung der künftigen wirtschaftlichen, machtpolitischen und kulturellen Position eines Volkes.

Schon wegen der außerordentlich hohen gesellschaftlichen Bedeutung und wegen des öffentlichen Charakters des Lehrerberufs ist es nicht verwunderlich, wenn der Lehrer immer auch der kritischen Beobachtung ausgesetzt war und ist. Wenn dem Lehrerberuf eine so zentrale gesellschaftliche Bedeutung zukommt, hat die Gesellschaft auch das Recht und die Pflicht, die Arbeit des Lehrers beständig zu überprüfen, nach besseren Rahmenbedingungen für die Tätigkeit des Lehrers zu suchen und auch die Voraussetzungen für eine angemessene Lehrerbildung zu verbessern.

Im Anschluß an die Umstrukturierung der Bayerischen Lehrerbildung von 1977 (Lehrerbildungsgesetz: u. a. »Fach zu Fach-Integration« der Erziehungswissenschaftlichen Fakultäten in die Universitäten) und 1979 (Lehrerprüfungsordnung: u. a. stärkere Betonung der Unterrichtswissenschaften für Grund- und Hauptschulen) haben sich insbesondere *Werner Nicklis* (1982) und *Wolfgang Brezinka* (1984) kritisch zu Wort gemeldet.

Beide Autoren sind sich sicher, daß die seit 1979 in Bayern praktizierte Form der Lehrerbildung eine bildungspolitische Fehlentscheidung ist.

Nicklis sieht den Lehrer von dessen eigentlichen Berufsaufgaben als Erzieher entfremdet (1982, zu These 1.1), weil u. a. die Universität »als Fachhochschulriesenverband« keine Bildungsidee mehr habe, ein »Imperialismus der Fachwissenschaften« *(R. Curtius)* herrsche, die Pädagogischen Hochschulen zwar »verbandsrechtlich«, aber nicht »inhaltlich-substantiell« in die Universitäten, die sich im übrigen in einem Verfallsstadium befänden, integriert worden seien, der Lehrer ein überspezialisierter Fachlehrer geworden sei, der zwar Unterrichtsfächer studiert, aber nicht seine Berufswissenschaft, nämlich eine »viel weiter gespannte ›basale Anthropologie‹« (*W. Nicklis* 1982, 1. Generalthesen, 2. Thesenkommentar).

Brezinka bezieht seine Analyse stärker auf die Frage nach dem Berufsethos des Lehrers, der Berufsgesinnung, die er neben dem Berufswissen und dem Berufskönnen zu den zentralen Merkmalen der Berufstüchtigkeit des Lehrers zählt. Er glaubt Hinweise zu haben, daß sich das Berufsethos der Lehrer in den letzten Jahren negativ entwickelt habe. Diese negative Entwicklung stünde in Zusammenhang mit der »Krise der verwissenschaftlichten Lehrerbildung«, durch die »derzeit die Verwirklichung des Erziehungsauftrages der Schulen zutiefst gefährdet« sei (*W. Brezinka* 1984, 24). Bezogen auf die Ausbildung der Grund- und Hauptschullehrer stellt er fest: »Ganz besonders hat aber die Eingliederung der Pädagogischen Hochschulen in die Universitäten ... neben vielen anderen Nachteilen auch die Wirkung gehabt, die Möglichkeiten zur Förderung des Berufsethos auf einen Tiefstand zu bringen, den es in der Geschichte der Lehrerbildung noch nie gegeben hat« (*W. Brezinka* 1984, 25).

Ohne Zweifel kann bereits die Anlage des Lehrerbildungsgesetzes von 1977 und der Lehrerprüfungsordnung von 1979 etwa bezüglich der unterschiedlichen Gewichtung

der auch in der Bayerischen Verfassung geforderten unterrichtlichen und erzieherischen Aufgaben der Schule Anlaß zu Kritik und zu ernster Sorge sein, erst recht die zahlreichen Komplikationen und negativen Nebenwirkungen bei dem Vollzug des Gesetzes in den Massenuniversitäten, das ungünstige Fächerwahl-Verhalten der Studierenden, die häufig zu beobachtende Isolation der Dozenten wie der Studenten, das Nebeneinander der Fächer, Addition statt Integration.
Gleichwohl erscheinen mir die Ausführungen von *W. Nicklis* und *W. Brezinka* sowohl hinsichtlich der Situationsanalyse wie hinsichtlich der bildungspolitischen Forderungen im wesentlichen nicht akzeptabel.
Fehlentwicklungen zeigen sich häufig zwar zunächst in kleinen negativen Abweichungen an. Deswegen ist es notwendig, Entwicklungsverläufe sorgsam zu beobachten, auch kleinere Abweichungen zu prüfen, um schließlich frühzeitig zu warnen, wenn sich negative Entwicklungen abzeichnen.
Die Aussagen von *W. Nicklis* und *W. Brezinka* beruhen aber auf unzureichender Situationsanalyse, werden zudem meist in einer die Glaubwürdigkeit einschränkenden Weise dramatisiert, die bildungspolitischen Forderungen sind vielfach überzogen, einige der Forderungen sowohl in sachlicher Hinsicht wie insbesondere in historischer und politischer Hinsicht kaum zu rechtfertigen.
Die Situationsanalyse ist unzureichend, weil – wie auch eingestanden wird (*W. Brezinka* 1984, 13) – schon wegen des knappen Beobachtungszeitraumes noch keine qualifizierte Erhebung über die mittel- oder gar langfristigen Auswirkungen der veränderten Lehrerbildung vorliegen, insbesondere aber weil im gesamten Problemfeld der Zeitfaktor nur sehr unzureichend berücksichtigt ist. Berücksichtigung des Zeitfaktors heißt einmal, nach den relativ konstanten, aber eben auch nach den veränderlichen Anforderungen im Qualifikationsprofil des Lehrers zu fragen. Soweit auch der Lehrerberuf unter den Bedingungen eines unumkehrbaren Zeitfaktors steht, wird sich erwartungsweise auch das Qualifikationsprofil des Lehrers – positiv oder negativ – ändern, aber auch die rechtliche und gesellschaftliche Stellung und das Selbstverständnis des Lehrers.
Berücksichtigung des Zeitfaktors heißt sodann, den historischen Vergleich zu suchen, um dadurch die empirische Basis für die angemessene Beurteilung der Gegenwart zu verbreitern. Das Berufsethos der Lehrer mag sich in den letzten Jahren negativ verändert haben. Dies ist – nachdem die Zahl der Lehrer im Gefolge der Bildungsreformen explosionsartig angewachsen ist – vielleicht nicht einmal unwahrscheinlich. Andererseits muß es stutzig machen, daß sich vergleichbare Meinungsäußerungen, wie *Brezinka* sie für seine »Vermutung«, dem Lehrer mangele es gegenwärtig an angemessenem Berufsethos, heranzieht (*W. Brezinka* 1984, 13 ff.), gehäuft aus nahezu allen Epochen der Schulgeschichte einbringen ließen, wie die Klage über den moralischen Niedergang des Volkes (vgl. *W. Brezinka* 1984, 32) und der Jugend wohl in den meisten Jahrhunderten der schriftlich bezeugten Menschheitsgeschichte zu hören war. Diese Klage gehört zu den Stereotypien nahezu aller Generationen.[2]
Dieses Zeugnis der Geschichte schließt nicht aus, daß neuartige Entwicklungen sich abzeichnen, aber es muß Anlaß sein, vorsichtiger zu urteilen. Dies gilt umso mehr, als die Schule auch nur der letzten 200 Jahre, während welcher nach Brezinkas Formulie-

rung ja wenigstens die Möglichkeiten zur Förderung des Berufsethos der Lehrer günstiger waren als heute (vgl. *W. Brezinka* 1984, 25), keineswegs nur passiv in große geschichtliche Katastrophen unseres Volkes verwickelt war.[3]
Die von *W. Nicklis* und *W. Brezinka* gegebene Situationsanalyse mag der Anlaß sein, die Entwicklung der Lehrerbildung mit großer Wachsamkeit zu verfolgen und mögliche Fehlentwicklungen zu korrigieren. Ob sie allerdings ausreicht, auch die Grundsätze dieser Form der Lehrerbildung in Frage zu stellen und Gegenvorschläge – wie etwa *W. Brezinka* sie macht – zu rechtfertigen, erscheint mir fraglich. Zuvor wäre erneut zu fragen, durch welche Merkmale das Qualifikationsprofil eines Lehrers gekennzeichnet ist und wie diese Merkmale im Studium zu fördern oder zu vermitteln sind.

2. Zeitunabhängige und zeitabhängige Inhalte des Qualifikationsprofils eines Lehrers

2.1 Zeitunabhängige Inhalte des Qualifikationsprofils

Alltagserfahrung und Geschichte belegen, daß es offensichtlich eine große Streuung im Qualifikationsniveau der Lehrer gibt.
Worin bestehen die spezifischen Fähigkeiten, die den guten Lehrer kennzeichnen, dem schlechten Lehrer fehlen? Es liegt auf der Hand, daß dazu die sich unablässig mit der Wissenskumulation verändernden Kenntnisse zählen, die sich der Lehrer in seinen Unterrichtsfächern erwerben muß, die sprachlichen und methodischen Fähigkeiten, diese Kenntnisse weiterzugeben, ebenso die Bereitschaft und das Bemühen, die Wertvorstellungen, die er vermitteln soll, auch in seinem eigenen Leben umzusetzen (vgl. *Brezinka* 1984, 12).
Aber es gibt darüberhinaus einen Kanon an Einstellungen und Persönlichkeitsmerkmalen, die unabhängig von der geschichtlichen Situation grundlegende Qualifikationsmerkmale des Lehrers sind. Dabei handelt es sich zwar um allgemeinmenschliche Merkmale, die aber in ihrer besonderen Ausprägung grundlegende Qualifikationsmerkmale des Lehrers sind. Zu diesem Kanon zählt an erster Stelle ohne Zweifel ein hohes Maß an Bereitschaft, sich zum Wohle der nachfolgenden Generation einzusetzen, d. h. mindestens das Maß an Altruismus, ohne das sich im Laufe der Menschheitsgeschichte niemals die Fähigkeit, Traditionen zu bilden, hätte entwikkeln können und ohne welche menschliche Kultur auch künftig nicht erhalten oder gar fortentwickelt werden könnte (vgl. *M. Liedtke* 1984, 22 ff.).
Aus dieser Bereitschaft ergibt sich die Regel für alle weiteren Einstellungen und Haltungen. So zählt desweiteren dazu eine optimistische, zukunftsorientierte Grundhaltung, ohne welche kaum Hoffnung, von der wiederum Lebensfreude und Lebenswille der nachwachsenden Generation abhängen, zu vermitteln ist (vgl. *M. Liedtke* 1984, 22 ff.). Es zählen dazu ein hohes Maß der Fähigkeit, Kontakte zu Kindern, auch

zu den verschlosseneren, aufzunehmen und zu halten, ein großes Maß an Geduld, kindliche Fehlerhaftigkeit zu ertragen, Humor, über Unzulänglichkeiten hinwegzuhelfen, Güte, die zwar keine Ansprüche nivelliert, die aber verzeihen kann und neue Anfänge erleichtert usw. (vgl. *O. Fr. Bollnow* 1964).[4]

2.2 *Zeitabhängige Inhalte des Qualifikationsprofils*

a) Fachwissen
Als zeitabhängige Inhalte des Qualifikationsprofils des Lehrers können solche verstanden werden, die im Zeitablauf stark variieren. Dazu zählt zunächst das Fachwissen, das unterrichtlich vermittelt werden soll. Da der Mensch in großem Umfang in der Lage ist, nicht nur eigene Erfahrungen zu machen, sondern auch das Wissen anderer zu übernehmen, konnte er sein Wissen von Generation zu Generation steigern. Das Wissen ist in exponentieller Weise gewachsen. *Georg Christoph Lichtenberg* notierte bereits in seinen Sudelbüchern Ende des 18. Jahrhunderts: »Wo damals die Grenzen der Wissenschaft waren, da ist jetzt die Mitte.« (1972, H. 23). Diese Wissenskumulation schlägt sich unmittelbar in der Schule nieder.
Dabei geht es aber für den Lehrer keineswegs nur um die bloße Übernahme der neuesten wissenschaftlichen Informationen, sondern auch um die Abschätzung möglicher anthropologischer, gesellschaftlicher und weltanschaulicher Konsequenzen dieser Informationen. Die Einführung des heliozentrischen Weltbildes durch *Kopernikus* bedeutete für den Menschen ja nicht nur einfach die kognitive Umstellung auf ein neues Bezugssystem, sondern bedeutete ein Abgedrängtwerden aus der Mitte des Kosmos. Von keineswegs geringerer anthropologischer Bedeutung war die Entwicklung der Quantenphysik durch *M. Planck,* mit der die Auflösung des mechanistischen Weltbildes verbunden war. Die Astrophysik der jüngsten Vergangenheit überhäuft uns mit Beobachtungen und Hypothesen, die ebenfalls von kopernikanischem Rang sind (vgl. *C. Sagan* 1982).
Ein Lehrer, der an dieser Wissensentwicklung nicht teilhat und der nicht immer wieder angesprochen ist von den möglichen anthropologischen und gesellschaftlichen Konsequenzen seines Wissens, kann nicht qualifiziert sein.

b) Erziehungs- und unterrichtsmethodisches Wissen
Ganz ohne Zweifel ist auch das pädagogische und didaktische Wissen in den letzten Jahren außerordentlich angewachsen. Das bezieht sich nicht nur auf die Pädagogik des frühen Kindesalters u. ä., sondern ebenso auf breite Bereiche der Allgemeinen und Speziellen Didaktik.[5]
Insbesondere aber sind die unterrichtlichen und erzieherischen Anforderungen gewachsen. Die bloße Wissenskumulation hat für den Unterricht die Folge, daß in weitgehend gleichbleibender Zeit – die Kindheits- und Jugendphase ist nicht beliebig verlängerbar – mehr Informationen zu vermitteln sind. Eben deswegen werden diese Informationen abstrakter, und der Raum für das Sammeln eigener Erfahrungen, die wesentlich anschaulicher sind und subjektiv einen viel höheren Grad der Verläßlich-

keit und des Erlebniswertes besitzen, wird enger. Außerdem gerät der schulische Unterricht in immer stärkere Konkurrenzsituation zu dem wachsenden, inhaltlich und methodisch attraktiven, außerschulischen Informationsangebot.
Aber ganz ohne Zweifel unterscheidet sich das gegenwärtige durchschnittliche Tempo der gesellschaftlichen Veränderungen, aus dem erzieherische Probleme erwachsen können, deutlich von dem früherer Perioden. Die erzieherischen Probleme sind schon deswegen größer, weil mit größerem Tempo neuartige Einstellungen und Anpassungsleistungen erforderlich werden (vgl. Verstädterung, zunehmende Spezialisierung, berufliche Umstellung auf neue Techniken, Probleme der Akzeptanz von Technik, Medienvielfalt und Wertepluralismus, luxurierendes Konsumverhalten). Aber es tauchen auch Probleme auf, die es in dieser Eindringlichkeit in der Menschheitsgeschichte noch nicht gegeben hat und ohne deren Lösung das Überleben der Menschheit unwahrscheinlich ist. Es ist – wenigstens bezogen auf die jeweils folgende Generation – immer auch ein erzieherisches Problem, ob die Menschheit lernt, in humaner, d. h. Natur und Mitmensch schonender Weise, mit ihrer gewachsenen technischen Macht umzugehen und weltweit Frieden und Gerechtigkeit zu sichern.
Insoweit verändert sich das Qualifikationsprofil des Lehrers mit den wechselnden Bedingungen der jeweiligen Zeit.

3. Durch welche Bedingungen läßt sich sichern, daß der Lehrer die erforderliche Qualifikation erreicht?

3.1 Zeitunabhängige Qualifikationen

Von den zeitunabhängigen Qualifikationen des Lehrers sollen nur die skizzierten grundlegenden Einstellungen, von denen das schließliche Berufsethos abhängt, angesprochen werden (z. B. altruistische Motivation, optimistische, zukunftsoffene Grundhaltung, Kontaktfähigkeit usw.).
Betrachtet man diese Eigenschaften unter stammesgeschichtlichem Aspekt, so steht außer Frage, daß die genannten Merkmale zunächst keine spezifischen Berufsmerkmale des Lehrers sind. Sie zählen vielmehr zu der grundlegenden Verhaltensausstattung jedes Menschen. Anderenfalls wäre die Entwicklung und das Überleben einer traditionsabhängigen menschlichen Gesellschaft, deren Mitglieder während einer langen Kindheitsphase auf die Hilfe der jeweils älteren Generation angewiesen sind, nicht möglich gewesen (vgl. *M. Liedtke* 1976², 160). Die Menschheit erzog und unterrichtete schon mehr als 3 Millionen Jahre, bevor mit der Erfindung der Schrift zu Beginn der sumerischen und ägyptischen Hochkulturen vor etwa 5000 Jahren die ersten beruflichen Lehrer auftraten (vgl. *H. Brunner* 1983, 62ff.). Schon weil es sich bei diesen Eigenschaften um Bedingungen der Möglichkeit von lernabhängiger Traditionsbildung handelt, kann als sicher gelten, daß diese Eigenschaften auf

genetischen Dispositionen beruhen, wie vergleichbar die Lernfähigkeit zunächst einmal von der Entwicklung eines entsprechenden Nervensystems abhängt. Am deutlichsten wird dies am Beispiel der Bereitschaft, sich zum Wohle der nachfolgenden Generation einzusetzen. Diese – natürlich unterschiedlich ausgeprägte – Disposition ist ein altes genetisches Erbe, das uns mindestens mit allen Säugetieren verbindet. Kein Säugetier wäre ohne die Hilfe der älteren Generation überlebensfähig (vgl. *M. Liedtke* 1976[2], 160).

Die adäquate Entwicklung dieser Dispositionen beruht primär sicher nicht auf spezifischen Lernprozessen oder Belehrungen, wie *G. Kerschensteiner* – zwar von einem anderen wissenschaftlichen Ansatz herkommend, aber gleichwohl treffend – formulierte: »Wäre die pädagogische Begabung an Gelehrsamkeit oder auch nur an pädagogische Wissenschaft unauflösbar gebunden, das Menschentum hätte längst seinen Bankrott erklären müssen« (*G. Kerschensteiner* 1949, 24). Zwar hängt die Entwicklung von ›Lernerfahrungen‹ ab. Diese ›Lernerfahrungen‹ bestehen aber nur sekundär in Belehrungen, Ermahnungen usw. Sie beruhen vielmehr auf dem Angebot der für die Entwicklung dieser Dispositionen notwendigen Umweltbedingungen und auslösenden Reize. Die Grundlagen für die Entfaltung dieser Dispositionen werden sicher schon in der frühen Kindheit durch die Befriedigung der elementaren physiologischen und sozialen Bedürfnisse des Kindes, durch die Erfahrung elterlicher Hilfsbereitschaft, durch das Vorbild der nächsten Angehörigen usw. gelegt (vgl. *B. Hassenstein* 1973).

Das Repertoire an Einstellungen läßt sich schließlich stabilisieren, sensibilisieren und differenzieren durch Appelle und rationale Belehrung, insbesondere aber durch die Erfahrung von Ernstsituationen, in denen diese Einstellungen oder Eigenschaften gefordert sind, z. B. durch die selbstverantwortliche Betreuung von Kindern, von Hilfsbedürftigen, wenngleich man wegen der Komplexität des menschlichen Verhaltensrepertoires und der menschlichen Freiheit niemals sicher sein kann, ob tatsächlich die erzieherischen Bemühungen zum gewünschten Erfolg führen.

Weil bestimmte Einstellungen sich vielfach erst in einer Ernstsituation, wenn sie gefordert sind, einstellen und sich dann in der Regel auch verstärken – der Einstellungswandel junger Eheleute nach der Geburt des ersten Kindes mag dafür Beleg sein –, ist es auch keine grundsätzliche Beeinträchtigung des schließlichen Berufsethos, wenn selbst von einer größeren Anzahl Studenten das Lehrerstudium zunächst als »Auffangberuf« aufgenommen wird (vgl. *W. Brezinka* 1984, 19). Es besteht keine geringe Wahrscheinlichkeit, daß sich spätestens mit der Übernahme von Lehrerfunktionen auch die Einstellung zu den beruflichen Aufgaben in positiver Form ändert. Es gehört zur Alltagserfahrung in allen Berufen, daß man mit neuen verantwortlichen Aufgaben nicht nur wachsen kann, sondern in der Regel auch wächst.

Diese Regel im Prozeß der Einstellungsentwicklung und -veränderung kann nicht heißen, die Bemühungen um eine Verbesserung des Berufsethos des Lehrers geringzuschätzen. Sie kann zunächst nur Anlaß sein, eine dramatische Verschlechterung des Berufsethos der Lehrer, etwa auf Grund der sekundären oder tertiären Wahl des Lehrerberufs, in Zweifel zu ziehen.

3.2 Zeitabhängige Qualifikationsmerkmale

Da sich der fachwissenschaftliche, der erziehungs- und unterrichtsmethodische Informationsstand durch die Wissenskumulation unablässig ändert, müssen sich auch die Qualifikationsanforderungen an den Lehrer in diesen Bereichen ändern. Dieser Qualifikationsteil unterliegt keinen physiologischen Entwicklungsprozessen, sondern hängt fast ausschließlich von der Übernahme der kumulierenden Informationen ab und unterliegt daher einer starken Dynamik.

Eben deshalb kann kein Lehrer hinreichend qualifiziert sein, wenn er nicht wenigstens näherungsweise den jeweiligen Wissensstand seiner Unterrichtsfächer, der zugehörigen Didaktiken und der Pädagogik überblickt. Diesen Überblick, der selbstverständlich unter den konkreten geschichtlichen Gegebenheiten immer nur einen Kompromiß darstellen kann, nicht zu haben bzw. sich nicht unablässig darum zu mühen, verstößt zugleich gegen das Berufsethos des Lehrers.

Das Gewicht der einzelnen Fächer bleibt dabei aber keineswegs gleich. So wird in allen kumulierenden Systemen die Quantität schließlich zu einem eigenständigen Problem. Im Bereich der sogenannten Fachwissenschaften wird u. a. die Frage der Weitergabe dieses Wissens bei nicht beliebig zu verlängernden Lernzeiten zu einem solchen Problem. Das bedeutet, daß das Gewicht der Didaktiken, die sich mit der Frage der Tradierung des kumulierenden Wissens befassen, in Forschung und Lehre zunehmen muß. Das Wissenswachstum erfordert u. a. immer erneut die Suche nach exemplarischen Ausschnitten, die möglichst weiterführende, dem jeweiligen Entwicklungsstand entsprechende inhaltliche und methodische Zugänge zum Fachwissen erschließen, außerdem die Entwicklung von Modellen, die einen umfassenden Überblick über das Fach oder über Teilgebiete des Faches ermöglichen. In den didaktischen Überlegungen geht es zudem aber nicht nur um die anschauliche und in gewisser Weise nachentdeckende Tradierung von Wissen, es geht überdies zugleich um die Frage, wie die fachwissenschaftlichen Inhalte in einer Weise angeboten werden können, daß sie den jungen Menschen in allen seinen emotionalen, kognitiven und motorischen Kräften ansprechen. Das sind keine beiläufig zu erledigenden Fragen, sondern Fragen, die intensiver Forschung und Übung bedürfen.

Vergleichbares gilt sicher auch für die Pädagogik. Wenn es zutrifft, daß die aufgrund der Kumulationsprozesse komplizierter werdende Welt auch schwierigere und neuartige erzieherische Aufgaben stellt (vgl. 2.2b), ist nicht nur der Lehrer stärker auch als Erzieher gefordert, vielmehr bedarf es zugleich intensivierter Forschung und Lehre in diesem Bereich.

4. Systematische und historische Vorbemerkungen zu einer Lehrerbildungspolitik

Es ist Ausfluß eines angemessenen pädagogischen Berufsethos, unablässig auf Verbesserungen der Bedingungen zu drängen, unter welchen der junge Mensch lebt, heranwächst und lernt. Aber es gehört auch zum pädagogischen Berufsethos, unter welchen Bedingungen auch immer, sich darum zu bemühen, das jeweils Beste für die nachwachsende Generation zu erreichen. Insofern dürfen auch mißliche Bedingungen kein Anlaß sein, die pädagogischen Bemühungen einzuschränken.

Bei der Frage, ob und in welchem Umfang man seine Kräfte für konkrete gesetzliche oder organisatorische Veränderungen einsetzt, wird man unter Berücksichtigung des Prinzips der Verhältnismäßigkeit die jeweiligen Vor- und Nachteile einer Maßnahme abzuwägen haben.

Die Lehrerbildung ist – nicht nur in Bayern – in ihrer gesetzlichen Anlage wie auch in ihrer organisatorischen Durchführung verbesserungsbedürftig. Auch zwischen den von mir genannten Erfordernissen einer angemessenen Lehrerbildung, insbesondere hinsichtlich der sich unablässig verschiebenden Gewichte in den lehrerbildenden Fächern und der gegenwärtigen Form der Lehrerbildung in den einzelnen Ländern der Bundesrepublik Deutschland bestehen erhebliche Diskrepanzen.

Andererseits sehe ich nicht, daß – wie die Analysen von *W. Nicklis* (1982) und *W. Brezinka* (1984) es vorgeben – die Gesamtsituation der Lehrerbildung zu irgendeinem historischen Zeitpunkt günstiger gewesen ist. Damit ist nicht bestritten, daß es einzelne Bereiche gibt, die gelegentlich historisch vielleicht günstiger gelöst waren (z. B. die größere Übersichtlichkeit der Lehrerseminare, der Bezug zur Unterrichtspraxis). Aber berücksichtigt man die durchschnittliche Vorbildung der Lehramtsstudenten, den persönlichen Freiraum, die Informations- und Wahlmöglichkeiten, das Fächerangebot, die Möglichkeit wissenschaftlichen Studiums, die Dauer des Studiums, das durchschnittliche Alter der Studenten usw., kann man schon bezogen auf die Formen der Lehrerbildung in der frühen Nachkriegszeit oder in der Weimarer Zeit, erst recht bezogen auf die Lehrerbildung im 19. Jahrhundert oder gar im 18. Jahrhundert – und zwar sowohl im Volksschulbereich als auch im Gymnasialbereich – nur schwerlich der Meinung sein, die Bedingungen für die Lehrerbildung seien insgesamt günstiger gewesen.

Was die möglichen negativen Auswirkungen der Lehrerbildung auf die Schule betrifft, sind dabei auch die rechtlichen Instrumente der gesellschaftlichen Selbstregulation zu nennen (Klagemöglichkeiten von Eltern und Schülern, parlamentarische Mängelschelten, staatliche Rechtsaufsicht usw.).

Ohne Zweifel gibt es bei allen geschichtlichen Verläufen nicht nur positive Entwicklungen, es gibt auch katastrophale Rückschritte. Gleichwohl ist nicht zu sehen, daß es im Vergleich zur heutigen Situation jemals ein vergangenes Goldenes oder auch nur Silbernes Zeitalter von Lehrerbildung oder Schule gegeben hätte.

Hierin liegt ein weiterer Grund zu bezweifeln, ob man auf Grund der gegenwärtigen pädagogischen Ausbildungsbedingungen einen noch nie dagewesenen Rückgang des Berufsethos der Lehrer behaupten oder erwarten darf (vgl. *Brezinka* 1984, 25).

Obwohl auf Grund der historischen und systematischen Analyse Korrekturen in der Struktur der Lehrerbildung erforderlich sind, ein alarmierender Anlaß zu hastigen Reaktionen ist nicht gegeben, auf keinen Fall zur restaurativen Rückkehr zu Formen der Lehrerbildung des 19. und beginnenden 20. Jahrhunderts.
Man wird sich zwar auch unablässig darum bemühen müssen, die Bedingungen für die Entwicklung eines angemessenen Berufsethos der Lehrer zu verbessern, man wird immer wieder die Bedeutung dieser beruflichen Einstellung betonen müssen, man wird sich darum bemühen müssen, das Studium praxisnäher zu gestalten. Aber es bedarf zugleich mit Blick auf das erforderliche Berufsethos, das Selbstverständnis und das Selbstbewußtsein der Lehrer aller Schularten keiner Frage, daß der grundsätzliche Anspruch der Wissenschaftlichkeit der Lehrerbildung nicht beeinträchtigt werden darf.

Anmerkungen

1 In umfassenderer Weise ist dieser Fragenkreis in *M. Liedtke* 1986 abgehandelt.

2 Es wäre wohl ein Leichtes, binnen einer Woche mindestens 100 Belege aus der schriftlich fixierten 5000jährigen Kulturgeschichte zu erbringen, daß fast jede Generation von der Klage über den Niedergang des Ethos begleitet war.
Ähnliches meinte *W. Hornstein* 1966:
»So wäre es leicht, Geschichte der Jugend als »chronique scandaleuse« zu schreiben; an Berichten über jugendliches Rabaukentum, über Exzesse, Respektlosigkeiten, Ausschreitungen – und über die entsprechenden Klagen der Erwachsenen ist kein Mangel.
›Das Sittenverderben unserer heutigen Jugend ist so groß, daß ich unmöglich länger bey derselben aushalten kann‹, so drückte ein Schulmeister des 18. Jahrhunderts seine Enttäuschung über die Jugend aus.
Aber solche und ähnliche Äußerungen gibt es aus allen Epochen; sie beweisen nicht nur, daß die Jugend zu allen Zeiten Anlaß zu Klagen bot, sondern auch, daß die Historie stets geneigt ist, das Abweichende, nicht den Erwartungen Entsprechende mit besonderer Sorgfalt zu registrieren und der Nachwelt zu überliefern.«
Aber bereits *Erasmus von Rotterdam* hatte gewarnt, den »wunderlichen Klagen der Leute, wie sehr die Natur der Knaben zum Bösen neige« und »wie schwer sie dahin zu bringen seien, das Edle zu lieben« zu leichtgläubig zu trauen (nach *Fr. Maerz* 1980, 134).

3 Vgl. *M. Heinemann* (Hrsg.), Erziehung und Schulung im Dritten Reich, Stuttgart 1980.

4 In der von *A. Schnitzer* 1980 herausgegebenen Arbeit »Schwerpunkt: Lehrerpersönlichkeit« finden sich ebenfalls zahlreiche Informationen zu diesem Fragenkreis. *H. Hierdeis* (1980, S. 16–50) hat dabei mit *W. Dilthey*, *G. Kerschensteiner* und *E. Spranger* wichtige historische Ansätze zur Umschreibung der »Lehrerpersönlichkeit« referiert.

5 Wie in jedem Fach gibt es auch in der Pädagogik eine merkliche qualitative Streuung unter den Publikationen. Aber es fällt keineswegs schwer, hervorragende pädagogische und didaktische Arbeiten zu nennen: z. B. *H. Roth* (1966), *B. Hassenstein* (1973), *K. H. Beckmann* (1981), *E. E. Geißler* (1981), *K. Prange* (1983).

Literaturverzeichnis

Beckmann, H. K., Hrsg. (1981): Schulpädagogik und Fachdidaktik. Stuttgart

Bollnow, O. Fr. (1964): Die pädagogische Atmosphäre. Heidelberg

Brezinka, W. (1984): Das Berufsethos der Lehrer als erziehungspolitisches Problem. In: Th. Goppel (Hrsg.): Veröffentlichungen des Aktionskreises Wirtschaft, Politik, Wissenschaft e.V., München

Brunner, H. (1983): Schreibunterricht und Schule als Fundament ägyptischer Hochkultur. In: Kriss-Rettenbeck, L. / Liedtke, M. (Hrsg.), Schulgeschichte im Zusammenhang der Kulturentwicklung. Bad Heilbrunn (Schriftenreihe zum Bayerischen Schulmuseum Ichenhausen, Bd. 1), S. 62–75

Der Wittwen- und Waisenfreund (1823). – Zeitschrift des Lehrervereins des Isarkreises. München

Geißler, E. E. (1981): Allgemeine Didaktik. Stuttgart

Hassenstein, B. (1973): Verhaltensbiologie des Kindes. München (4. Auflage 1987)

Heinemann, M., Hrsg. (1980): Erziehung und Schulung im Dritten Reich. 2 Bde. Stuttgart

Hornstein, W. (1966): Jugend in ihrer Zeit. Geschichte und Lebensformen des jungen Menschen in der europäischen Welt. Hamburg

Kerschensteiner, G. (1949): Die Seele des Erziehers. München

Lichtenberg, G. Chr. (1975): Schriften und Briefe, 2. Bd., Sudelbücher II. München

Liedtke, M. (1976^2): Evolution und Erziehung. Göttingen

Liedtke, M. (1984): Warum Schule Schule gemacht hat. – Zum Zusammenhang von Schule, Kultur und Gesellschaft. Erlanger Universitätsreden 16

Liedtke, M. (1986): Was Lehrer bildet. – Von der Zeitgebundenheit eines Qualifikationsprofils. In: Th. Goppel (Hrsg.): Publikationen des Aktionskreises Wirtschaft, Politik, Wissenschaft. München

März, F. (1980): Problemgeschichte der Pädagogik. Bad Heilbrunn

Nicklis, W. (1982): Wege und Holzwege der Lehrerbildung. In: Th. Goppel (Hrsg.): Veröffentlichungen des Aktionskreises Wirtschaft, Politik, Wissenschaft e.V. München

Prange, K. (1983): Bauformen des Unterrichts. Eine Didaktik für Lehrer. Bad Heilbrunn

Roth, H. (1966): Pädagogische Anthropologie. Hannover

Sagan, C. (1982): Unser Kosmos. München

Schnitzer, A. (Hrsg.) (1980): Schwerpunkt: Lehrerpersönlichkeit. Pädagogische, psychologische und soziologische Aspekte einer Theorie des Lehrers. München

Autorenspiegel

Prof. Dr. Apel, Hans-Jürgen, Vor den Feldern 7, 5000 Köln 90

Prof. Dr. Buchinger, Hubert, Universität Passau, Lehrstuhl für Grundschuldidaktik, Innstraße 25, 8390 Passau

Prof. Dr. Endres, Rudolf, An den Hornwiesen 10, 8520 Erlangen

Dr. Fickel, Alfred, Siegerstetten 14, 8300 Kumhausen / Landshut

Dr. Fischer-Elfert, Hans-Werner, Sartoriusstraße 35, 2000 Hamburg 20

Dr. Hauzenberger, Franz, Universität Passau, Innstraße 25, 8390 Passau

Prof. Dr. Kanz, Heinrich, Universität Bonn, Römerstraße 164, 5300 Bonn

Prof. Dr. Keck, Rudolf, Institut für Pädagogik, Marienburger Platz 22, 3200 Hildesheim

Prof. Koenig, Otto, Glasergasse 20/4, A-1090 Wien

Prof. Dr. Liedtke, Max, Erziehungswissenschaftliche Fakultät der Universität Erlangen–Nürnberg, Lehrstuhl für Pädagogik I, Regensburger Straße 160, 8500 Nürnberg 30

Prof. Dr. Nagao, Tomiji, Mihara 3-12-20, 351 Asaka-shi, Saitamaken, Japan

Prof. Dr. Pöhlmann, Egert, Institut für alte Sprachen, Universität Erlangen–Nürnberg, Spardorferstr. 59, 8520 Erlangen

Prof. Dr. Reble, Albert, Anne-Frank-Str. 23, 8700 Würzburg

Dr. Rösger, Alfons, Universität Bonn, Seminar für Alte Geschichte, Am Hof 1e, 5300 Bonn 1

Dr. Rump, Hans-Uwe, Bayerisches Nationalmuseum, Prinzregentenstr. 3, 8000 München 22

Prof. Dr. Silberer, Gerhard, Pädagogische Hochschule Karlsruhe, Bismarckstraße 10, 7500 Karlsruhe

Prof. Dr. Waetzoldt, Hartmut, Universität Heidelberg, Seminar für Sprachen und Kulturen des Vorderen Orients, Lehreinheit Assyrologie, Sandgasse 7, 6900 Heidelberg

Prof. Dr. Wanke, Gunter, Am Röthelheim 58, 8520 Erlangen

Prof. Dr. Wirth, Gerhard, Universität Bonn, Seminar für Alte Geschichte, Am Hof 1e, 5300 Bonn 1

Prof. Dr. Zwernemann, Jürgen, Dieselweg 85, 2105 Seevetal 3

SCHRIFTENREIHE ZUM BAYERISCHEN SCHULMUSEUM ICHENHAUSEN

Bisher sind folgende Bände erschienen:

Band 1
Lenz Kriss-Rettenbeck / Max Liedtke (Hrsg.)
Schulgeschichte im Zusammenhang der Kulturentwicklung
1983. 283 Seiten, 2 Grafiken

Band 2
Lenz Kriss-Rettenbeck / Max Liedtke (Hrsg.)
Regionale Schulentwicklung im 19. und 20. Jahrhundert
Vergleichende Studien zur Schulgeschichte, Jugendbewegung und Reformpädagogik im süddeutschen Sprachraum
1984. 309 Seiten

Band 3, 1
Ivan Illich
Schule ins Museum – Phaidros und die Folgen
1984. 72 Seiten

Band 4
Lenz Kriss-Rettenbeck / Max Liedtke (Hrsg.)
Erziehungs- und Unterrichtsmethoden im historischen Wandel
1986. 302 Seiten, 16 Grafiken, 32 Abbildungen und Fotos

Band 5
Jozo Džambo
Erziehung, Bildung, Schule im Wandel der Geschichte
Eine Auswahlbibliographie
1987. 453 Seiten, 76 Abbildungen

Band 6
Johann Georg Prinz von Hohenzollern / Max Liedtke (Hrsg.)
Vom Kritzeln zur Kunst
Stammes- und individualgeschichtliche Komponenten der künstlerischen Fähigkeiten
1987. 312 Seiten, 132 Abbildungen und Fotos, 12 Grafiken

Band 7
Johann Georg Prinz von Hohenzollern / Max Liedtke (Hrsg.)
Naturwissenschaftlicher Unterricht und Wissenskumulation
Geschichtliche Entwicklung und gesellschaftliche Auswirkungen
1988. 363 Seiten, 63 Abbildungen

VERLAG JULIUS KLINKHARDT · BAD HEILBRUNN / OBB.